LEARNING SUCCESS
BEING YOUR BEST
AT COLLEGE & LIFE

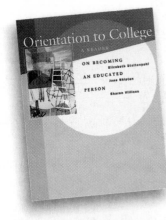

■ The Wadsworth College Success℠ Series

The Adult Learner's Guide to College Success, Revised Edition,
by Laurence N. Smith and Timothy L. Walter (1995), ISBN: 0-534-23298-1

Orientation to College Learning, by Dianna L. Van Blerkom (1995), ISBN: 0-534-24528-5

Learning Your Way Through College, by Robert N. Leamnson (1995), ISBN: 0-534-24504-8

Your Transfer Planner: Strategic Tools and Guerrilla Tactics, by Carey E. Harbin (1995),
ISBN: 0534-24372-X

I Know What It Says . . . What Does It Mean? Critical Skills for Critical Reading,
by Daniel J. Kurland (1995), ISBN: 0-534-24486-6

College Study Skills: Becoming a Strategic Learner, by Dianna L. Van Blerkom
(1994), ISBN: 0-534-21288-3

Mastering Mathematics: How to Be a Great Math Student, Second Edition,
by Richard Manning Smith (1994), ISBN: 0-534-20838-X

Toolkit for College Success, by Daniel R. Walther (1994), ISBN: 0-534-23052-0
with *The Pocket Toolkit: Study Skills Software* (1994), ISBN: 0-534-23054-7

Integrating College Study Skills: Reasoning in Reading, Listening, and Writing, Third Edition,
by Peter Elias Sotiriou (1993), ISBN: 0-534-17892-8

Right from the Start: Managing Your College Career, Second Edition,
by Robert Holkeboer (1996), ISBN: 0-534-21570-X

Turning Point, by Joyce D. Weinsheimer (1993), ISBN: 0-534-19422-2

Merlin: The Sorcerer's Guide to College Success, by Christopher F. Monte (1990),
ISBN: 0-534-13482-3

Your College Experience: Strategies for Success, Second Edition, by John N. Gardner
and A. Jerome Jewler (1995), ISBN: 0-534-30960-7

The 'Net, the Web and You: All You Really Need to Know About the Internet . . . and a Little Bit More,
by Daniel J. Kurland (1996), ISBN: 0-534-51281-X

Foundations: A Reader for New College Students, by Virginia Gordon and Thomas Minnick
(1996), ISBN: 0-534-25422-5

Orientation to College: A Reader on Becoming an Educated Person, by Elizabeth Steltenpohl,
Jane Shipton, and Sharon Villines (1996), ISBN: 0-534-26484-0

■ The Freshman Year Experience℠ Series

Success, Your Style! Left and Right Brain Techniques for Learners,
by Nancy L. Matte and Susan Green Henderson (1995), ISBN: 0-534-24468-8

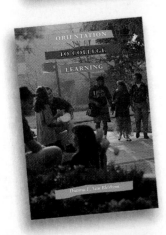

The Power to Learn: Helping Yourself to College Success, by William E. Campbell (1993),
ISBN: 0-534-19404-4

Your College Experience: Strategies for Success, Concise Second Edition,
by A. Jerome Jewler and John N. Gardner (1996), ISBN: 0-534-26520-0

■ The Senior Year Experience℠ Series

Ready for the Real World, by William C. Hartel, Stephen W. Schwartz, Steven D. Blume,
and John N. Gardner (1994), ISBN: 0-534-17712-3

For more information or to purchase any of these Wadsworth texts, please contact your local bookseller.

Learning Success

Being Your Best at College & Life

Carl Wahlstrom
GENESEE COMMUNITY COLLEGE

Brian K. Williams

STUDENT PHOTOGRAPHS BY MICHAEL GARRETT / GENESEE COMMUNITY COLLEGE

 Wadsworth Publishing Company

I(T)P® An International Thomson Publishing Company

Belmont · Albany · Bonn · Boston · Cincinnati · Detroit · London · Madrid · Melbourne
Mexico City · New York · Paris · San Francisco · Singapore · Tokyo · Toronto · Washington

TO NANCY, MY PARENTS,
AND ALL THE STUDENTS IN MY LIFE.
—C.W.

TO KIRK,
WHO KNOWS HOW TO LEARN SUCCESS.
—B.K.W.

The Wadsworth College Success_SM Series and the
Freshman Year Experience_SM Editor: *Angela Gantner Wrahtz*

Assistant Editor: *Rebecca Deans Rowe*

Editorial Assistant: *Royden Tonomura*

Production Services Manager: *Jerry Holloway*

Project Editor & Production Management: *Stacey C. Sawyer,
Sawyer & Williams, Incline Village, NV*

Interior Design & Illustration: *Seventeenth Street Studios*

Print Buyer: *Barbara Britton*

Permissions Editor: *Robert Kauser*

Copy Editor: *Stacey C. Sawyer*

Cover Design & Illustration: *Seventeenth Street Studios*

Compositor: *Seventeenth Street Studios*

Printer: *Von Hoffmann Press, Inc.*

Printed in the United States of America
1 2 3 4 5 6 7 8 9 10—

Library of Congress Cataloging-in-Publication Data
Wahlstrom, Carl
    Learning success : being your best at college & life / Carl
Wahlstrom & Brian K. Williams ; photography by Michael Garrett.
        p.   cm.
    Includes bibliographical references and index.
    ISBN 0-534-51346-8
    1. College student orientation—United States. 2. Study skills
    —United States.   I. Williams, Brian K.   II. Title.
LB2343.32.W35   1996
378.1'98—dc20   95–49458
                                                      CIP

For more information, contact Wadsworth Publishing Company:

Wadsworth Publishing Company
10 Davis Drive
Belmont, California 94002, USA

International Thomson Publishing Europe
Berkshire House 168-173
High Holborn
London, WC1V 7AA, England

Thomas Nelson Australia
102 Dodds Street
South Melbourne 3205
Victoria, Australia

Nelson Canada
1120 Birchmount Road
Scarborough, Ontario
Canada M1K 5G4

International Thomson Editores
Campos Eliseos 385, Piso 7
Col. Polanco
11560 México D.F. México

International Thomson Publishing GmbH
Königswinterer Strasse 418
53227 Bonn, Germany

International Thomson Publishing Asia
221 Henderson Road
#05-10 Henderson Building
Singapore O315

International Thomson Publishing Japan
Hirakawacho Kyowa Building 3F
2-2-1 Hirakawacho
Chiyoda-ku, Tokyo 102, Japan

brief contents

about the authors

CARL WAHLSTROM is Professor of Intermediate Studies and Sociology at Genesee Community College, Batavia, New York. He has been the recipient of the State University of New York Chancellor's Award for Excellence in Teaching, the National Freshman Advocate Award, and several other teaching honors. He is past president of the New York College Learning Skills Association and a member of the State University of New York College Transition Course Development Council.

Besides developing and teaching First-Year Experience courses, he has taught courses in human development, learning strategy, sociology, psychology, and human relations. He has a B.S. in Sociology and an M.S. Ed. in Counselor Education from SUNY Brockport and an M.A. in Sociology from the University of Bridgeport.

He lives with his wife, Nancy, an employee benefits consultant, in the Finger Lakes area of New York. He enjoys running, skiing, tennis, boating, mountain biking, karate, motorcycling, music, travel, and getting together with family, friends, and students.

BRIAN K. WILLIAMS has a B.A. in English and M.A. in Communication from Stanford University. He has been Managing Editor for college textbook publisher Harper & Row/Canfield Press in San Francisco; Editor-in-Chief for trade book publisher J. P. Tarcher in Los Angeles; Publications & Communications Manager for the University of California, Systemwide Administration, in Berkeley; and an independent writer and book producer based in San Francisco and in Incline Village (Lake Tahoe), Nevada.

He has co-authored several best-selling college textbooks, including *Invitation to Health* with Dianne Hales, *Computers and Data Processing* with H. L. Capron, and *Microcomputing: Annual Edition* and *Computing Essentials: Annual Edition* with Tim and Linda O'Leary. More recently he has co-written with Sharon Knight *Healthy for Life: Wellness and the Art of Living* in both comprehensive and brief versions. In 1995 he published the best-selling *Using Information Technology: A Practical Introduction to Computers & Communications* in both comprehensive and brief editions, co-authored with Stacey Sawyer and Sarah Hutchinson.

He is married to author/editor and book producer Stacey Sawyer, and the two have a passion for travel and for experimenting with various cuisines. He enjoys reading four daily newspapers and numerous magazines and books, hiking in the Sierra, playing blues on the guitar, and getting together with friends and family, including his children, Sylvia and Kirk.

detailed contents

3 resources

4 time

5 memory

6 lectures

reading

tests

9 communication

Making Powerful Written & Oral Presentations 177

Think & express yourself creatively & critically—successfully

10 money

How to Get It, How to Use It 215

You can master your finances, not let them master you

11

health

Taking Care of Yourself Mentally & Physically   239

Manage stress, look good, & feel good

12

relationships

The Important Other Side of Life   275

Can you deal successfully with other people?

13

the future

Finding a Major & a Career 307

When will you decide what to do with the rest of your life? Now is the time!

preface to the instructor

Q: "What's the story on this book? What's it about?"

A: "This book is about how _the keys to success in higher education_ are also _the keys to success in life_. It shows students how to BE THE BEST—for now, and for life."

—The Authors

LEARNING SUCCESS: Being Your Best at College & Life is intended for use in a one-term student-success or first-year experience course. Offered in community colleges, vocational-technical schools, four-year colleges, and universities, this course is designed to help students master the academic and personal skills needed to succeed in higher education.

THE PROMISES OF THIS BOOK

The _key features_ of *LEARNING SUCCESS* are as follows. We offer:

1. *A reality-based philosophy of effectiveness that really motivates students.*

2. *An accessible, engaging approach without loss of depth.*

3. *All the essential topics—plus some bonuses.*

4. *The personal voice of experience—from instructor and students.*

5. *A highly interactive approach to teaching and learning.*

Extra feature: We offer a special section at the end of the book, **"Productivity Tools for Your Future."**
We elaborate on these features next.

KEY FEATURE #1: WE OFFER A REALITY-BASED PHILOSOPHY OF EFFECTIVENESS THAT REALLY MOTIVATES STUDENTS. Philosophies of motivation come and go—est, Twelve-Step, "personal empowerment." In the end, though, what matters is not what students *think* but what they *do*. This book provides a ***practical philosophy based on action***.

This book is designed to help students *be the best*—that is, achieve mastery—in two areas:

- ***Be the best in college:*** We show readers how to master the academic and personal skills needed to succeed in college—how to manage their time, improve their memory, handle money, deal with relationships, and so on.

- ***Be the best in life:*** We point out how the skills one needs for success in college are the same skills one needs for success in life—in work, in relationships, in health, in finances, and so on. We pay great attention to the connection between higher education and the rest of one's life.

KEY FEATURE #2: WE PRESENT AN ACCESSIBLE, ENGAGING APPROACH WITHOUT LOSS OF DEPTH. Students won't find education by slogans and soundbites here. What they will find is ***visual excitement and lively style*** combined with ***depth of scholarship*** that stimulates their curiosity and challenges their beliefs.

- ***Visual excitement:*** *LEARNING SUCCESS* fully exploits the full-color printing process, typographical design, and a range of artwork and photos to present an attractive format that will appeal to all kinds of readers.

- ***Lively style:*** Written with journalistic flair in the warm, first-person "I" voice of Prof. Carl Wahlstrom, *LEARNING SUCCESS* personalizes the material in a way that readily engages student readers, whether of traditional or nontraditional college age.

- ***Depth of scholarship:*** As a glance at the "Notes" section in the back of the book indicates, *LEARNING SUCCESS* is unusual among books in this field for its depth of scholarship. Citations range from scholarly journals to *The New York Times*. However, the research is not intrusive and does not interfere with the readability of the book.

Throughout, students are shown ***a realistic view of the world of work and how to get ready for it***. Adult learners will find special connections here.

KEY FEATURE #3: WE PRESENT THOROUGH COVERAGE OF ESSENTIAL MATERIAL—AND SOME BONUSES. *LEARNING SUCCESS* provides exceptional coverage of ***academic success strategies*** and ***personal success strategies***, all in just 13 chapters. Special-interest, bonus material is covered within regular chapters.

- ***Academic success strategies—covered in nine chapters:*** We cover making the transition to college, goal-setting, campus resources, time and memory management, learning from lectures and readings, test taking, and researching and presenting written and oral reports.

- ***Personal success strategies—covered in four chapters:*** We cover money, health, relationships, and majors/careers. (Instructors of abbreviated courses may wish to skip these topics.)

- ***Bonus material—covered within regular chapters:*** Instead of having a full chapter for each special-interest topic, we discuss all such "bonus material" within the confines of regular material.
  Values clarification, for instance, is discussed in Chapter 1. ***Multicultural diversity*** is covered in Chapter 3, "Resources." ***Learning styles*** are considered in "Memory." ***Math confidence*** is discussed in "Reading." ***Critical thinking*** and ***creative thinking*** are considered in "Communication." ***Stress*** and ***substance abuse*** are described in "Health."

KEY FEATURE #4: WE OFFER THE PERSONAL VOICES OF EXPERIENCE—FROM INSTRUCTOR AND STUDENTS.

Experience is an important quality for students in this course. This book presents the experience of a much-liked, long-time instructor and the experiences of students in their first year in college. Here's how:

■ *The voice of an experienced instructor:* The warm, first-person "I" in this book is that of _Prof. Carl Wahlstrom, an instructor and counselor of over 20 years' experience_ and the recipient of _awards for teaching excellence._ By "bottling the spirit of Carl Wahlstrom," we hope to present student readers with the sense that they are being addressed by someone who is familiar with the difficulties and riches of higher education, who has a wealth of personal experience to relate, and who has an abiding interest in and empathy for students.

■ *The voices of student experience:* Prof. Wahlstrom's experience is reinforced by the voices of student experience. Students often think they are the only ones with problems, a trait that tends to foster isolation and prevent them from seeking assistance. *LEARNING SUCCESS* presents _brief interviews with 20 students_ of different majors, ages, and ethnic backgrounds. These interviews, we hope, will help the student reader, regardless of age, make a meaningful personal connection with the book.

KEY FEATURE #5: WE OFFER A HIGHLY INTERACTIVE AND SYSTEMATIC PEDAGOGICAL APPROACH TO TEACHING AND LEARNING.

LEARNING SUCCESS takes a very focused approach in presenting material—*heavy use of interactive features, techniques to reinforce learning,* and *flexible organization for instructors.* Here's how:

■ *Heavy use of interactive features:* Recognizing that most first-year classes are interactive ones, we provide a number of features that ask the student to become actively engaged with the material:

(1) _Personal Explorations,_ or learning exercises for individuals, are activities that ask students to examine their feelings and behaviors with regard to particular matters. There are _40 such Personal Explorations_ in the book.

(2) _Group Activities_ are collaborative exercises that instructors may elect to assign, in or outside of the classroom. There are _nearly 80 Group Activities_ in the book.

(3) _Making This Chapter Work for You/Skimming for Payoffs_ at the beginning of each chapter invites students to think about matters that are truly important to them and to skim the chapter for possible applications.

(4) _The Examined Life: Your Journal_ is a regular feature that asks students to explore their own thoughts with regard to something that is meaningful to them in the chapter they have just read.

(5) _Essentials for Time & Life Management_ is a six-step strategy that shows students how to set daily tasks from life goals.

■ *Techniques to reinforce student learning:* To help students in acquiring knowledge and developing critical thinking, we offer the following to provide learning reinforcement:

(1) _Interesting writing,_ studies show, significantly improves students' ability to retain information. Thus, we have employed a number of journalistic devices—such as the personal anecdote, the colorful fact, the apt direct quote—to make the material as interesting as possible.

(2) _Key terms are marked by a color underscore and definitions are printed in boldface_ in order to help readers avoid any confusion about what terms are important and what they actually mean.

(3) _Chapter overviews and section "previews"_ offer additional reinforcement.

(4) _Material is presented in "bite-size" portions._ Major ideas are presented in bite-size form, with generous use of advance organizers, bulleted lists, and new paragraphing when a new idea is introduced.

(5) *Sentences are kept short*—the majority not exceeding 22 – 25 words in length.

■ *Flexible organization:* After the first two chapters, the remaining 11 chapters may be taught in any sequence, or omitted, at the instructor's discretion. To make this possible, the authors have *repeated the definitions of key terms* throughout the text (also a part of the book's deliberate strategy of reinforcement).

BONUS FEATURE: WE OFFER A SPECIAL SECTION, "PRODUCTIVITY TOOLS FOR YOUR FUTURE." The special section in the back of the book presents tools of the Information Age that students will find useful—indeed, probably essential—in college and in their careers. These include word processors, personal computers (including notebooks and subnotebooks), computer software (including spreadsheets and database managers), communications tools (such as fax machines and e-mail), electronic bulletin board systems, online services, and the Internet.

SUPPLEMENTS & SUPPORT

Several useful supplements accompany this text. They include the following:

INSTRUCTOR'S RESOURCE MANUAL. This supplement for *LEARNING SUCCESS* helps instructors teach the chapters of this text by making available additional activities and exercises, advice, teaching suggestions, and answers to questions students commonly ask.

THE WADSWORTH COLLEGE SUCCESS INSTRUCTOR'S COURSE GUIDE. Suitable for instructors of all types—in community colleges, vocational-technical schools, four-year colleges, and universities—*The Wadsworth College Success Course Guide* is a general resource designed to offer general assistance in teaching the first-year experience course. Examples of subjects covered are how to build support

for such a course, how to administer it, and how to shape it for the future. Regarded as the most useful resource of its kind available in the market, it is available free to adopters of this text.

TEST PACKAGE. This collection of test and quiz items supports the main chapters of *LEARNING SUCCESS*.

FILMS & VIDEOS. Wadsworth's film and video policy is designed to help instructors enhance their course presentations. Ask your sales representative for more details.

NEWSLETTER. *The Keystone Newsletter* of the Wadsworth College Success Series enables instructors to share ideas with colleagues around the country.

CUSTOM PUBLISHING & BUNDLING OPTIONS. Wadsworth makes available several ways of customizing this text to specifically suit instructors' preferences. In addition, instructors may have local materials shrinkwrapped with *LEARNING SUCCESS*. For further information about content, binding options, quantities, and price, contact your local sales representative or Wadsworth's Customer Service Department at 1-800-245-6724.

ACKNOWLEDGMENTS

Two names are on the front of this book, but there are a great many other talented people whose efforts helped to strengthen our own.

Foremost among the staff of Wadsworth Publishing Company was our editor, Managing Editor Angela Gantner Wrahtz, who did a terrific job of supporting us and who backed the book under difficult circumstances. Angie, we really appreciate your belief in us and feel extremely lucky to have found someone of your talents and experience. We are also grateful for the cheerfulness and efficiency of others in the editorial department. Editorial assistant Royden Tonomura went out of his way to give us a helping hand, and we appreciate having had him in our corner. Assistant editor Rebecca Deans Rowe gave us great support on the supplements. Vice President and Editorial Director Gary Carlson actively supported the entire project. CEO Wayne Oler, a friend of Brian's from early publishing days, was kind enough to take time from his busy schedule to personally look at the project. This resulted in some terrific ideas regarding titles, themes, and marketing that truly help differentiate this book. Wayne, many thanks.

On the production side, we were fortunate to have as our contact Jerry Holloway, an old friend of Brian's for over 30 years. Jerry was backed and supported by other colleagues and friends of Brian's—Pat Brewer, Kathy Head, Bob Kauser, Peggy Meehan, Bill Ralph, and Stephen Rapley. Thank you, everyone!

The Wadsworth marketing staff has done everything we could expect a publisher to do. We're especially grateful for the fine marketing talents of David Leach, Assistant Director of Marketing. David was ably backed by Marketing Director Debbie Dennis and supported by Elaine Cline, Joy Westberg, and Marcia Skelton.

In addition, we would like to acknowledge the help of a number of people in New York City who contributed to the book's early development—you know who you are.

Outside of Wadsworth, we were ably assisted by a community of top-drawer publishing professionals. Directing the production of the entire enterprise, as well as doing the copyediting, was Stacey Sawyer—Brian's wife and an author herself and thus fully equipped to understand authors' travails. Stacey, once again you've pulled a book out under intolerable deadlines, and once again we're in your debt. Thanks for everything!

We also were extremely fortunate to be able to get the services of Seventeenth Street Studios and designer Randall Goodall, who came up with the highly colorful and inviting interior design and cover, and Lily Alnev, who created the illustrations. Seventeenth Street Studios also handled the composition and art preparation; we greatly appreciate the efforts of Lisa Chase and others in this effort. We're also happy that we can acknowledge the assistance of Tom Dorsaneo, a long-time publishing colleague of Brian's.

Both authors are grateful to proofreaders Anita Wagner and Linda McPhee, among the very best in spotting typos and inconsistencies. We'd also like to thank indexer and glossary builder Francine Cronshaw for her heroic efforts.

Carl Wahlstrom would like to acknowledge the encouragement of many friends and associates, including: Don Green for helping him become a "warrior," Bruce Hilyard for believing in the first place, Glenn DuBois for his insight, Phillip Venditti for his guidance, and finally Stuart Steiner for his enthusiastic support. Special thanks are due to Michael Garrett, without whose photographic help we would not have such a "student-centered" book. Acknowledgments are also due to librarians Patricia Jones and Nina Warren. Carl would also like to thank his colleagues at Genesee Community College, including Meredith Altman, Charley Boyd, Tom Clark, Mark Eckstein, Pat Fisher-Rodriguez, Shawn Gardner, Debbie Greene, Kathryn Knight, Katherina Kovach-Allen, John

Murray, Cliff Scutella, and Peg Sisson. In addition, he would like to thank his many colleagues in the New York College Learning Skills Association. Thanks also go to Gary Wakefield, friend, colleague, and student advocate.

Brian Williams would like to thank Tibby Storey of the San Francisco Public Library, who did a favor as an old friend in tracking down a very elusive citation. He would also like to thank Susan Antipa and Theresa Martin of the MacLean Library at Sierra Nevada College for their help. Finally, he would like to acknowledge the contributions of Kirk Williams, who read the manuscript from a student's point of view and provided a number of important insights.

Besides the students whose names and pictures appear in this book, we would like to acknowledge the contributions of Steven Baize, Linda Donofino, Gaye Drock, Brooke Glover, Michele Gray, Cornelius Johnson, Susan McFarland, Nancy O'Neill, Patricia Sackett, Jennie Tranquill, Sherrie Lynn Tyson, and Christina Waldmiller.

ACKNOWLEDGMENT OF REVIEWERS

We are grateful to the following people for their reviews on recent drafts of the book:

David M. DeFrain,
    Central Missouri State University

Mary Annette Edwards,
    Trident Technical College

Margaret Ann Maricle,
    Cuesta College

Donna S. Sharpe,
    Bellevue Community College

Lester Tanaka,
    Community College
    of Southern Nevada

Pat Zeller,
    Defiance College

We would also like to recognize the contributions and helpful feedback of instructors at the following institutions as well:

Appalachian State University

Cedarville College

Cerritos College

College of the Sequoias

Eastern Montana College

Florida Community College
    at Jacksonville

Grand Valley State University

Nassau Community College

New York Institute of Technology

Saint Cloud State University

Suffolk Community College

United States Military Academy

WE WANT TO HEAR FROM YOU!

We welcome your response to this book, for we are truly trying to make it as useful as possible. Write to us in care of

Angela Gantner Wrahtz,
Managing Editor, College Success Series,
Wadsworth Publishing Company,
10 Davis Drive, Belmont, CA 94002
(fax: 415-637-7544).

Or contact us directly at the following:

Carl Wahlstrom
    Genesee Community College
    One College Road
    Batavia, NY 14020
    Phone: 716-343-0055 ext. 6305
    or 607-522-4418 (Eastern Time)
    Fax: 716-343-0433
    E-mail: Wahlstrom@SGCCVA.SUNY
    GENESEE.CC.NY.US
    Wadsworth/ITP voice mail:
    1-800-876-2350 ext. 339

Brian K. Williams
    POB 10006, 771 Randall Avenue
    Incline Village, NV 89450
    Phone: 702-832-7336 (Pacific Time)
    Fax: 702-832-3026
    E-mail: c/o Stacey Sawyer,
    76570.1533@COMPUSERVE.COM
    Wadsworth/ITP voice mail:
    1-800-876-2350 ext. 858

to the student: directions to start you up

What if you knew that if you skipped this section your grade might go down?

Of course we can't *guarantee* you a high grade. But we can show you tricks to using a textbook successfully—tricks you'll want to know because they could affect your course grade.

Here's the first one: By taking time up front to get an OVERVIEW of a book, you can more easily master the details later.

WHAT THIS BOOK IS ABOUT. You will learn how the keys to success in higher education are also the keys to success in life. This book will help you BE YOUR BEST—for now, and for life.

We offer a reality-based philosophy of effectiveness so that you can master the academic and personal skills needed to succeed in college—*the same skills needed to succeed in the rest of your life.*

Chapters 1–3 cover motivation, goal-setting, and campus resources.

Chapters 4–9 discuss *academic strategies* for success.

Chapters 10–13 describe *personal strategies* for success.

In addition, throughout this book you will find brief interviews with students of different majors, interests, ages, and backgrounds. Reading these "voices of student experience" will remind you of an important fact: You are not alone. Others have the same concerns you do.

NOW LET'S LEARN TO SUCCEED. We hope you'll take a few minutes to read the next five pages. They will show you how valuable *LEARNING SUCCESS* will be to your college career—and to the rest of your life!

Carl Wahlstrom

Brian K. Williams

W Wadsworth Publishing Company

an International Thomson Publishing Company I⟨T⟩P

transition

becoming
the best—
for now &
for life

*learning how
to learn is
the key to college
& life success*

IN THIS CHAPTER Life is full of transitions and turning points, requiring us to take on new behaviors and responsibilities. Higher education is only one such experience. This chapter considers some of the changes you will face. We consider the following:

■ *How college is different:* Higher education is one of life's important turning points. It differs in many ways from high school.

■ *How college can better your life:* Compared to high-school graduates, college graduates usually make more money. They also experience gratifying personal growth during college. Finally, they probably have a better chance to discover what makes them happy.

■ *How college improves your career skills:* The skills that make you successful in college can make you successful in your career.

■ *Why some people have trouble with college:* We consider six reasons why students drop out of c...

■ *How your valu...* We define *valu...* acteristics, an... determine you...

FEATURES TO HELP YOU MAKE A SUCCESS OF THIS BOOK.
The following examples, which appear throughout the book, are designed to help you learn key concepts.

■ **In This Chapter** This section appears throughout the book at the start of each chapter, highlighting important topics to be described in the chapter.

■ MAKING THIS CHAPTER WORK FOR YOU

1. What is the *single most important thing* you think college could give you? Write it down here. (You can use personal shorthand to make it a private note to yourself. Example: "btr jb" for "better job.")

_____

_____

_____

_____

_____

_____

_____

_____

2. What is *one of the most important things* in the world to you? (Examples: family, religion, material success. Use personal shorthand, if you like.)

_____

_____

_____

_____

_____

_____

_____

■ SKIMMING FOR PAYOFFS

Skim through this chapter. Pick out *one single idea* that arouses your interest or that you know you can use. Put a big star (*) next to it in the margin.

2

I wish I had the opportunity to talk with you personally.

I wish that you and I could sit down together and discuss what you think about higher education—your hopes, concerns, and expectations.

However, a book is pretty much a one-way street, of course. I get to communicate with you, but you can't immediately communicate back, as we would in conversation.

Fortunately, there are two ways around this:

■ *This is an "interactive" book that you can use to gain important information about yourself:* By "interactive" I mean that the book is not meant to be read passively, like a novel. Rather, it is designed so that you can participate in it and get feedback—as if you were talking with another person.

■ *You have someone else to help you:* This book is meant to be used in a class on how to get the most out of college or other forms of higher education. That class, of course, is taught by an instructor. He or she can give you the assistance that this book cannot.

Without your involvement, however, this book is about as useful as a paperweight or a doorstop. The secrets of college survival can't simply be injected into you, like a shot of penicillin. Your participation is crucial. *The more you participate, in both the book and the class, the greater your chances for college success.* If you don't become actively engaged with the book, my efforts will have no more impact than a 30-second television commercial.

So, maybe we can't sit down and talk face to face. But we can try for the next best thing—a dialogue that you control through these pages.

■ **Making This Chapter Work for You & Skimming for Payoffs** Also appearing at the start of each chapter, Making This Chapter Work for You encourages you to think about what is important to you and what the chapter can help you with. Skimming for Payoffs invites you to skim the chapter for possible applications.

in terms of fulfilling your own potential. These goals should express *your* most important desires and values—not necessarily what your family wants you to do or what you think society expects of you. *(See ■ Panel 2.3.)*

As I've mentioned, college is not an easy experience. To pull yourself through some difficult times, you will need to know *why* you are doing all this. Now, then, is the time to set down your long-range goals. See Personal Exploration #2.4 below.

PERSONAL EXPLORATION #2.4

WHAT ARE YOUR LONG-RANGE GOALS?

Look back over your lists of reasons for attending college. Do they include what might be considered *life goals*—things you hope college will help you achieve, say, 10 years from now? If not, add some life goals to the list below.

The top five goals I hope college will help me reach are . . .

1. _____
2. _____
3. _____
4. _____
5. _____

GROUP ACTIVITY OPTION

In a small group, take turns describing your life goals. How do your goals compare to, or differ from, those of others? How will going to college help you reach these goals? How do the goals in your group compare with those of other small groups in your class?

PANEL 2.3 ■ Examples of life goals.

Heroes: To follow in the footsteps of . . . (name a hero or heroine). *(Example:* an entertainer, political figure, someone you know—a teacher, a successful relative or family friend.

Sacrifice: What is worth sacrificing for and what the sacrifice is. *(Examples:* giving up making a lot of money in order to help people; giving up close family life in order to travel the world.)

Values: What you hold to be most important and dear to you.

Love: How you would express it and to whom.

Family: What its importance is to you at present and in the future.

Security: What the least security is you would settle for financially, emotionally.

Principles: What you would stand up for and base your life on.

Creativity: What things you would like to create.

Curiosity: What questions you want to satisfy.

Personal challenges abilities you need to p yourself.

Death: What you ho accomplish in the fac own mortality.

■ **Onward: Applying This Chapter to Your Life** This end-of-chapter feature suggests that you write down something you've learned in the chapter that you can put into practice.

Onward: Applying This Chapter to Your Life

PREVIEW You are constantly changing.

Going to college is "like moving to a foreign country," says Karen Leven Coburn, an associate dean of students at Washington University in St. Louis. "There's a new landscape, a new culture, and a new language. . . . Even the food is different."[15] For many first-year students, college means making many decisions they have not had to think about much: what to study, who to hang out with, when to eat and sleep. There are anxieties about money, about succeeding in school, about finding new friends, about relations with their family. No wonder it has been said that the first college year "is punctuated by feelings of panic and incompetence."

The important thing to keep in mind is that, regardless of your present self-image, you are *constantly changing.* If you have negative beliefs about yourself, the way you see yourself today need not be the way you see yourself tomorrow or in future years. By keeping yourself open to new information and experiences, you can change your self-image so that most of the traits by which you identify yourself will be positive.

Now, before you wrap up the reading of this chapter, try to take something away from it so that you feel as though you "own" it—have made it yours. That is, if you were allowed to keep *only one idea,* what would it be and why would you want to keep it? Write it down here:

_____
_____
_____
_____
_____
_____

THE EXAMINED LIFE: YOUR JOURNAL

Why are you here? What is your fear? These are two of the most important questions you can consider in college. Write in your journal at least 25 words about each of these matters. Then write down what you consider to be the personal strengths that will help see you through.

INTERACTIVE FEATURES TO REINFORCE LEARNING. The best way to learn is to become actively engaged with the material. The following features are examples of ways you can use the book's exercises and activities to reinforce learning.

■ **Personal Exploration Exercises & Group Activities** Personal Exploration exercises are self-discovery questionnaires that enable you to focus on your feelings, beliefs, and behaviors. Group Activity exercises allow instructors to use collaborative learning in the classroom.

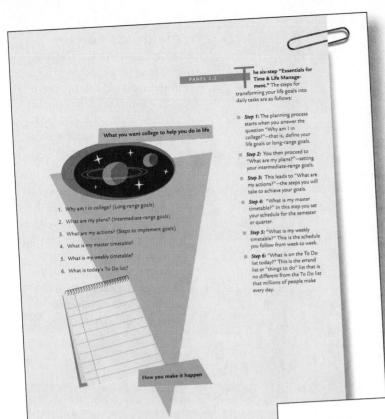

PANEL 2.2

The six-step "Essentials for Time & Life Management." The steps for transforming your life goals into daily tasks are as follows:

■ **Step 1:** The planning process starts when you answer the question "Why am I in college?"—that is, define your life goals or long-range goals.

■ **Step 2:** You then proceed to "What are my plans?"—setting your intermediate-range goals.

■ **Step 3:** This leads to "What are my actions?"—the steps you will take to achieve your goals.

■ **Step 4:** "What is my master timetable?" In this step you set your schedule for the semester or quarter.

■ **Step 5:** "What is my weekly timetable?" This is the schedule you follow from week to week.

■ **Step 6:** "What is on the To Do list today?" This is the errand list or "things to do" list that is no different from the To Do list that millions of people make every day.

What you want college to help you do in life

1. Why am I in college? (Long-range goals)
2. What are my plans? (Intermediate-range goals)
3. What are my actions? (Steps to implement goals)
4. What is my master timetable?
5. What is my weekly timetable?
6. What is today's To Do list?

How you make it happen

WHAT DO YOU WANT OUT OF COLLEGE? HOW WILL YOU GET WHAT YOU WANT? The first three chapters in *LEARNING SUCCESS* help you decide what you want out of your college education and how to reach your goals.

■ **Translating Your Life Goals into College Goals & Daily Tasks** The six-step plan in Chapter 2 called *Essentials for Time & Life Management* shows you how to translate your life goals into daily tasks.

Academic Help

PREVIEW People who can assist you with academic problems are academic advisors, instructors, librarians and media center staff, and tutors and study-skills staff. Other academic services include the computer center, music practice rooms, and the Dean of Students office. Academic advising—which is principally about degrees, majors, and courses—is extremely important because it affects your college, career, and life plans.

ome day you may return to college as a retired person and *actually take some courses for the fun of it.* Older people often do this. I assume, however, that you are the type of student for whom "fun" is not the main priority of the college experience. That is, you are here on the serious mission of getting a degree.

Obtaining a college degree—whether associate's, bachelor's, master's, or other—is the goal, of course, of the academic part of college. The degree signifies that you have passed certain courses with a minimum grade. Completing the courses means that you have passed tests, written research papers, done projects, and so on. To accomplish all these, you must have attended classes, listened to lectures, gone to the library, and read a lot. Hopefully, while you're having to jump through all these hoops, learning is also taking place.

POSSIBLE ACADEMIC DIFFICULTIES. The problem with accomplishing these tasks is that there are many places where hangups can occur—and where you might need some help. Here are some possibilities: You can't get the classes you want. You wonder if you can waive some prerequisites. You don't know what you still need to do to graduate. You're having trouble with your writing, math, or study skills. You're sick and can't finish your courses. You don't know how to compute your grade-point average. You need recommendations for an employer or a graduate school.

Knowing how to find help, get good advice, and cut through bureaucratic red tape aren't skills that become obsolete after college. They are part and parcel of being A Person Who Can Get Things Done, which is what we all wish to be. Learning how to find your way around the college academic system, then, is training for life. Outside college, these skills are called *networking* and *trouble-shooting—and they are invaluable in helping you get where you want to go.*

To get help or advice in college, you may need to consult the following academic services or people:

■ Academic advisors
■ Instructors
■ Librarians and media-center staff
■ Tutors and study-skills staff
■ Some other academic services
■ When all other help fails: the Dean of Students office

ACADEMIC ADVISORS. What people will you deal with the most for academic matters? Probably your instructors. But there is another individual who, in the grand scheme of things, could be *more* important: your academic advisor. Why? "For most freshmen, the first year of college is both exciting and crisis oriented," say one pair of writers. "New students are unfamiliar with college resources, their major field, the faculty, course work, academic expectations, and career applications of their major." [1] Thus, *academic advising is important because it affects your planning for college and beyond that for your career and for your life.*

The *academic advisor* counsels students about their academic program. The academic advisor is either a full-time administrative employee or a faculty member, often in the field in which you'll major. What does he or she do that I think is so important? There are two principal activities:

■ **Finding the Right Resources** All the campus resources available to help you realize your goals—including academic advisors—are described in Chapter 3.

MAKING WORK PLAY. There's another aspect to learning to manage time: Many people make distinctions between work and play. But probably what you really want is *to do work that feels like play*. (The alternative is doing work that is boring, even hateful, in order to support your play after work.) Indeed, college can be a great laboratory for experimenting to find out what kind of work seems most fun for you.

I don't mean to suggest that *all* the work you'll do will be enjoyable. Most jobs have aspects that are tedious or difficult or unsatisfying. I am suggesting, however, that an important goal of college is to strive to find work that, to the extent possible, feels like play.

GROUP ACTIVITY #4.1

WHAT IS HAPPINESS? EDUCATING YOURSELF FOR THE WAY YOU WANT TO LIVE

You're in higher education, presumably, in the pursuit of your ultimate happiness—or something that will make you happier than you are now. But what, in fact, *is* happiness? If your instructor requests it, go to the library and read an article or part of a book on the subject of happiness. Make notes of the ideas that seem to speak directly to you. (If there's no time for research, take 5 minutes to write what you think happiness is and what would make you happy.)

In small groups (three to five people) discuss what happiness is. What is the way you want to live? How will education help you accomplish it? How does your definition of happiness differ from others' definitions? Could you be happy under others' terms?

How to Improve Your Time Management

PREVIEW The six-step "Essentials for Time & Life Management" plan describes how to set daily tasks from your life goals. The steps are: (1) Determine your ultimate goals. (2) Identify your plans for achieving them. (3) State the actions needed to realize your plans. (4) Lay out your master timetable for the school term. (5) Set your weekly timetable. (6) Do a daily or weekly To Do list with reminders and priorities.

ou may hear a fellow student say offhandedly, "Yeah, I got an A in the course. But it was easy—I hardly had to study at all."

Don't believe it.

Sure, I guess there really are some people who can get by this way (or courses that are really that easy). However, most people who talk like that just want to look as though they are brainy enough not to need to study. In general, though, the reality is that either they *are* studying a lot or they are *not* getting top grades.

Here is clearly an area in which you have to be tough-minded: Most of the time, studying *is* hard work. It *does* take time. It *does* take personal commitment. Most students *don't* like to do it. Studying *isn't* usually something to look forward to (although learning and exploring may be fun).

You need not feel upset or guilty about this. Accept that studying is not always something you're going to do because you feel like it. Then you can begin to organize your time so that you can always get enough studying done.

ACADEMIC SUCCESS STRATEGIES.

Chapters 4–9 show you how to achieve academic success through better techniques in lecture note-taking, reading, test-taking, and making written and oral presentations. Mastering these techniques will enable you to better manage your time and your memory.

■ **Learning to Manage Your Time** Chapter 4 shows you how you can have more free time by managing your time effectively every day. You'll learn how to make a master timetable for the school term, do a weekly schedule, and use To Do lists to keep up. It also shows you how to recognize and avoid major time wasters.

■ **Learning to Manage Your Memory** How will you remember everything? Chapter 5 shows you how to retain material in long-term memory and how to use your favorite "learning style" to your advantage.

---

they have to sit still and who express enthusiasm by jumping up and down. "These learners want to act out a situation, to make a product, to do a project, and in general to be busy with their learning," say Ducharme and Watford. "They find that when they physically do something, they understand it and they remember it."

MIXED-MODALITY LEARNING STYLE. Modality (pronounced "moh-*dah*-ty") means style. As you might guess, *mixed-modality learners* are able to function in any three of these learning styles or "modalities"—auditory, visual, and kinesthetic. Clearly, these people are at an advantage because they can handle information in whatever way it is presented to them.

LEARNING STYLES, LECTURES, & READING. Lectures would seem to favor auditory learners. Textbooks would seem to favor visual learners. Lectures and readings are the two principal pipelines by which information is conveyed in college.

However, suppose one or both of these methods don't suit you? Since you don't usually have a choice about how a subject is taught, it's important to get comfortable with both methods. This means you need to be able to *extract* the most information out of a lecture or textbook—that is, take useful notes, for example—regardless of your learning preference and the instructor's style. Chapters 6 and 7 show how to do this.

How to Improve Your Memory Power

PREVIEW There are several principal strategies for converting short-term memory to long-term memory: (1) You can practice relaxation. (2) You can practice repeatedly, even overlearn material. (3) You can study a little at a time repeatedly (distributed practice) instead of cramming (massed practice). (4) You can avoid memory interference from studying similar material or being distracted. (5) You can make material personally meaningful to you. (6) You can use verbal memory aids—write out or organize information; use rhymes, phrases, and abbreviations; make up narrative stories. (7) You can use visual memory aids—make up a vivid picture or story of unusual images.

s should be clear by now, *success in college principally lies with a strategy in which you convert short-term memories into long-term memories.* Let me suggest a number of techniques for doing this.

1. RELAX & BE ATTENTIVE. You have certainly discovered that you easily recall those things that interest you—things to which you were *attentive*. "Attention is *conscious, not reflex,*" says one memory expert (the emphasis is hers). "It is indispensable to the controlled recording of information."[11]

The goal of improving your memory, then, is to improve your attention, as we explain in this section. The first means for doing this is through relaxation. Anxiety interferes with memorizing, distracting your recall abilities with negative worries. When you are relaxed, your mind captures information more easily.

things about yourself. For example, write down things you have done recently or in the past that are positive. When negative thoughts creep in, say "Stop," and think one of these good thoughts about yourself.

If you are the one being let down, don't spend a lot of time speculating *why*. The other person may not even know why he or she is no longer in love. It won't help to torture yourself trying to figure it out. A helpful strategy may be to simply put some distance between yourself and the other person.

If you are the one trying to disengage from the relationship, remember how it feels to be rejected. Try to be honest but gentle: "I no longer feel the way I once did about you." Don't promise to try to "work things out," and don't try to take care of or "rescue" the other person. Do try to mobilize your support group and get involved with activities you enjoy.

GROUP ACTIVITY #12.1

WHAT KINDS OF SUPPORTING RELATIONSHIPS DO YOU HAVE?

"No man is an island, entire of itself . . . ," the poet John Donne said. He might have said "man or woman," but the point is clear: we are not alone, isolated from other people.

Form a small group with other students in your class. Take turns describing people you know who will give you emotional and other support, if needed, to help sustain you. What kind of qualities do such people have? Are they good listeners? Do they express their feelings well? If you or others feel short on such support, where can it be found? How can one widen the circle of supportive friends?

Conflict & Communication: Learning How to Disagree

PREVIEW Committed couples must learn to address differences in several areas. They include unrealistic expectations, work and career issues, financial difficulties, problems with in-laws, sexual problems, and commitment. Communication consists of ways of learning to disagree. In bad communication, you become argumentative and defensive and deny your own feelings. In good communication, you acknowledge the other person's feelings and express your own openly. Expert listening consists of tuning in to your partner's channel. It means giving listening signals, not interrupting, asking questions skillfully, and using diplomacy and tact. Most important, it means looking for some truth in what the other person says. To express yourself, use "I feel" language, give praise, and keep criticism specific.

hy can't people get along better? Must there always be conflict in close relationships, as between lovers, family members, roommates or housemates? To see what your usual approach to conflict is, try the following Personal Exploration.

Chapters 10–13 cover strategies for personal success in the areas of money, health, relationships, and your major and career.

■ **Relationships: How to Communicate Effectively & Handle Conflict** How you relate to friends and lovers can directly affect your happiness and schoolwork. Chapter 12 shows how to learn to disagree, deal with rejection, express yourself positively, and develop assertiveness.

■ **The Future: Now's the Time to Decide What You Want to Do with the Rest of Your Life!** This is the time to figure out what career will be most fulfilling for you. In Chapter 13 you'll discover what resources are available to you—career counseling, vocational testing, job placement services, and resume-writing strategies.

THE "CAREER VIDEO" EXERCISE. John Holland is a psychologist at Johns Hopkins University who has developed a system that divides career areas into six categories based on different interests and skills.[14] Here let us suppose that

Holland's six career categories have been produced as a series by a "career introduction video service." (This is sort of a variation on those video dating services I'm sure you've seen ads for.) To see which careers appeal to you, try Personal Exploration #13.1.

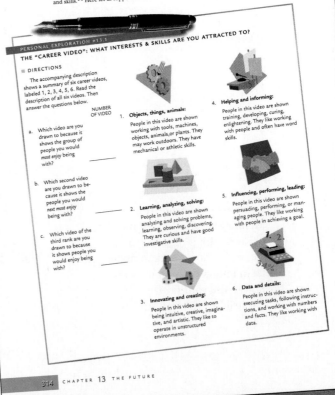

PERSONAL EXPLORATION #13.1

THE "CAREER VIDEO": WHAT INTERESTS & SKILLS ARE YOU ATTRACTED TO?

▶ **DIRECTIONS**

The accompanying description shows a summary of six career videos, labeled 1, 2, 3, 4, 5, 6. Read the description of all six videos. Then answer the questions below.

NUMBER OF VIDEO

a. Which video are you drawn to because it shows the group of people you would *most enjoy* being with? _____

b. Which second video are you drawn to because it shows the people you would *next most enjoy* being with? _____

c. Which video of the third rank are you drawn to because it shows people you would enjoy being with? _____

1. **Objects, things, animals:** People in this video are shown working with tools, machines, objects, animals, or plants. They may work outdoors. They have mechanical or athletic skills.

2. **Learning, analyzing, solving:** People in this video are shown analyzing and solving problems, learning, observing, discovering. They are curious and have good investigative skills.

3. **Innovating and creating:** People in this video are shown being intuitive, creative, imaginative, and artistic. They like to operate in unstructured environments.

4. **Helping and informing:** People in this video are shown training, developing, curing, enlightening. They like working with people and often have word skills.

5. **Influencing, performing, leading:** People in this video are shown persuading, performing, or managing people. They like working with people in achieving a goal.

6. **Data and details:** People in this video are shown executing tasks, following instructions, and working with numbers and facts. They like working with data.

LEARNING SUCCESS
BEING YOUR BEST
AT COLLEGE & LIFE

transition

becoming the best—
for now &
for life

learning how
to learn is
the key to college
& life success

Life is full of transitions and turning points, requiring us to take on new behaviors and responsibilities. Higher education is only one such experience. This chapter considers some of the changes you will face. We consider the following:

■ ***How college is different:*** Higher education is one of life's important turning points. It differs in many ways from high school.

■ ***How college can better your life:*** Compared to high-school graduates, college graduates usually make more money. They also experience gratifying personal growth during college. Finally, they probably have a better chance to discover what makes them happy.

■ ***How college improves your career skills:*** The skills that make you successful in college can make you successful in your career.

■ ***Why some people have trouble with college:*** We consider six reasons why students drop out of college.

■ ***How your values affect your college choices:*** We define *values*, discuss their three characteristics, and describe how your values determine your approach to college.

1. What is the *single most important thing* you think college could give you? Write it down here. (You can use personal shorthand to make it a private note to yourself. Example: "btr jb" for "better job.")

_____
_____
_____
_____
_____
_____
_____
_____

2. What is *one of the most important things* in the world *to you*? (Examples: family, religion, material success. Use personal shorthand, if you like.)

_____
_____
_____
_____
_____
_____
_____

■ SKIMMING FOR PAYOFFS

Skim through this chapter. Pick out *one single idea* that arouses your interest or that you know you can use. Put a big star (*) next to it in the margin.

I wish I had the opportunity to talk with you personally.

I wish that you and I could sit down together and discuss what you think about higher education—your hopes, concerns, and expectations.

However, a book is pretty much a one-way street, of course. I get to communicate with you, but you can't immediately communicate back, as we would in conversation.

Fortunately, there are two ways around this:

■ *This is an "interactive" book that you can use to gain important information about yourself:* By "interactive" I mean that the book is not meant to be read passively, like a novel. Rather, it is designed so that you can participate in it and get feedback—as if you were talking with another person.

■ *You have someone else to help you:* This book is meant to be used in a class on how to get the most out of college or other forms of higher education. That class, of course, is taught by an instructor. He or she can give you the assistance that this book cannot.

Without your involvement, however, this book is about as useful as a paperweight or a doorstop. The secrets of college survival can't simply be injected into you, like a shot of penicillin. Your participation is crucial. *The more you participate, in both the book and the class, the greater your chances for college success.* If you don't become actively engaged with the book, my efforts will have no more impact than a 30-second television commercial.

So, maybe we can't sit down and talk face to face. But we can try for the next best thing—a dialogue that you control through these pages.

The Transition to Higher Education

PREVIEW Throughout life one goes through stages of development—being a student in higher education is one of them—that require different behaviors and responsibilities and produce different stresses. First-year students often have to learn that higher education is not the same as high school. High school is a *structured* environment, offering less freedom but requiring less responsibility. College is a more *unstructured* environment, offering you more freedom but in turn requiring more responsibility. Some older returning students, however, may find college means less freedom for a while because studying gives them less leisure time.

I teach a course called *Transitions: The First-Year Experience* at a college in upstate New York. No doubt some of the students who come to these classes are much like you. I've seen students of every size and shape— and gender, age, race, religion, economic level, and physical ability. I have taught the class to high-school teachers, who in turn have taught the course to high-school students. I've taught it to foreign students of several different nationalities. I have gone to nearby prisons and taught the course to inmates.

Most of these students have one thing in common: they are *in transition.* They are in the midst of moving from one stage of their lives to another.

HIGHER EDUCATION: ONE OF LIFE'S IMPORTANT TURNING POINTS. Throughout life there are stages of development that most of us go through that represent major changes. We go from childhood to adolescence, to young adulthood, to middle age, and to old age. We go from grade school to middle school to high school to college or other forms of higher education. These changes of status are marked by a *rite of passage,* **some kind of associated ritual.** Sometimes the change is observed formally, as with a graduation ceremony, a first communion, a bar or bas mitzvah, a debutante ball. Sometimes it is observed informally, as in buying the first razor or lipstick. Such changes will continue throughout life. Some changes represent *gains:* getting one's own apartment or house, getting a job, getting a promotion, perhaps getting married, perhaps having children. Others represent *losses:* perhaps losing a job, perhaps getting divorced, and so on. The point is, *all such changes require us to take on new behaviors and new responsibilities.* They generate new stresses even as they open new doors.

Going to college is no exception. It will require you to act differently and will inject new kinds of tensions into your life. Yet it will also provide experiences and benefits you'll always be glad you had.

GROUP ACTIVITY #1.1

YOUR RITES OF PASSAGE

Some of the most powerful learning occurs during small-group discussion and projects. (A small group consists of about three to six students.) Thus, this book offers frequent suggestions for group activities. Here's the first one:

In a small group, you and others take turns describing rites of passage you have been through. (Examples: changing from a child to an adolescent, getting married, earning your first paycheck.) A *rite of passage* involves physical or emotional changes in your life, changes in how others view you, new behaviors, and new responsibilities. It is often accompanied by stress. One person in your group, acting as recorder or secretary, should make a list of the different rites of passage. Then all group recorders should copy their lists onto the classroom board.

With the whole class, discuss the lists developed by each group. What are the similarities? the differences? Were any possibilities overlooked? What are different ways of dealing with rites of passage (anger, avoidance, feelings of fight-or-flight, and so on)? Which of these ways are most appropriate?

HOW HIGHER EDUCATION DIFFERS FROM HIGH SCHOOL. What kinds of changes and tensions arise during the rite of passage known as college? Here's one example: I have observed—and other college instructors have frequently told me—that many first-year students have one overriding difficulty in common. This difficulty is: *getting used to the fact that higher education is not high school.*

Perhaps you're in your late teens or perhaps you're a returning student with considerable life experience. Either way, if your last academic stop was high school, you may have some assumptions about education that are now due for a change.

Here are some differences:

■ *Many rules versus few rules:* High schools run on rules. Remember those days you sat in class looking out the window and daydreaming about being in the active adult world outside? Getting there probably required a pass from the teacher. If you were out sick, you were supposed to bring a medical excuse.

With college, you are now in that adult setting—and there are fewer rules. You can leave class without a pass, cut class, or have a sick day and not need a doctor's note to prove it. No assistant principal or teacher will ask you where you were. You may, however, find it a struggle to stay current in the course if you've been absent too many times.

■ *Living with parents versus living on your own:* Most high-school students live with their parents. (Or, if they go to boarding school, their living circumstances may be tightly regulated.) In college, by contrast, most students find their behavior is no longer under the watchful eye of an adult figure. Students find they are at liberty to stay up all night or party every day, if that's what they want to do. Or they are free to work on their personal relationships rather than their school-work.

What will you do, then, when you are working on a paper and your friends urge you to go hear this great band that's in town for only one evening? Even if you're still living at home, you're at an age when probably no parent is going to stand over you and tell you what to do. In college, you're your own parent.

Note: If you are a returning adult student (called a "nontraditional" student), you are probably already experiencing the freedom of living on your own. However, you may have new habits to learn also. For instance, you may have to get used to *giving up* some leisure time in order to attend to your college work. And if you're married and/or have children, your family may have to get used to it, too.

■ *Teaching environment versus learning environment:* High-school teachers teach. College instructors teach also. However, unlike high-school teachers, few instructors have been required to take a course on teaching methods. In addition, many instructors, particularly those in universities, have been hired as much to do research as to do teaching. The upshot is that colleges, universities, and other such institutions put less emphasis on teachers teaching and more emphasis on learners learning. In other words, more effort is expected of you the student in grasping the subject matter than is expected of the instructor in teaching it.

In conclusion: In going from high school to college, you are going from a system with many rules to one with fewer rules. You are going from an educational structure that often restricts freedom to one that allows a good deal of freedom. And you are expected to actively participate in learning the subject matter in your courses.

But this new environment has a condition attached to it: You're expected to take more responsibility for your actions.

How Could Higher Education Make a Difference in Your Life?

PREVIEW College graduates usually make more money, are more knowledgeable and competent, and experience more personal growth than nongraduates. These factors may contribute to increased happiness in life.

uppose you decided right now not to continue in college. What would you be missing if you didn't finish?
　Let's take a look.

INCREASED INCOME. With the widespread competitive and technological changes of the last few years, it has become clear that the rewards go to people with skill and education. There is all kinds of supporting evidence for this. Some examples:

- *The more education, the more income:* The more education people have, the higher their income, according to studies by Princeton University economists Orley Ashenfelter and Alan Kreuger. From grade school through graduate school, every year spent in school adds 16% to the average person's lifetime earnings. This means that a two-year or community college degree, for instance, can be expected to increase an individual's earnings by about *one-third*. A four-year college degree would increase them by almost *two-thirds*.[1]

- *Widening income gap:* The gap between high-school graduates and college graduates has widened over the years. In 1979, for example, a male college graduate earned 49% more than a man with a high-school diploma. In 1992, the average male college graduate was earning 83% more than his high-school graduate

counterpart. "Well-educated and skilled workers are prospering," says Labor Secretary Robert Reich, while "those without education or skills drift further and further from the economic mainstream."[2] In 1993, young college graduates earned a whopping 75% more than comparable high-school graduates.[3]

- *Growth in employer demands:* In the 1990s jobs requiring college degrees will grow 1.5% per year, according to the head of one economic advisory firm. For high-school degrees, the demand will grow only 0.6% per year.[4]

- *Lifetime earnings:* According to the U.S. Census Bureau, a high-school graduate can expect to earn $821,000 over the course of a working life. By contrast, a college graduate with a bachelor's degree can expect to earn $1.4 million. And a person with a professional degree can expect to receive more than $3 million.[5]

　Although a college degree won't *guarantee* you higher earnings, it provides better odds than just a high-school degree. Moreover, I suspect, going to college will help you develop flexibility. With this, whatever happens in the job market, you'll probably be better able to stay on your feet.

INCREASED PERSONAL DEVELOPMENT. Money, however, is not the only reason for going to college. Do you envy those high-school friends who skipped college and went directly to work? Don't. They are missing some significant experiences of personal growth and change.

　The very fact that college serves up unfamiliar challenges and pressures can help you develop better adjustment skills, such as those of time management. The competition of different values and ideas—religious, political, and so on—can help you evaluate, modify, and strengthen your belief system.

　Some of the positive changes that studies show are characteristic of college graduates are as follows.[6]

- *Increase in knowledge, competence, and self-esteem:* The college experience increases people's knowledge of content, as you might expect. This in turn extends their range of competencies and provides them with a greater range of work skills. It also helps them develop their reasoning abilities. Finally, it increases their self-esteem.

■ *Increase in personal range:* College helps people to develop their capacity for self-discovery and to widen their view of the world. They become more tolerant, more independent, more appreciative of culture and art, more politically sophisticated, and more future-oriented. Finally, they generally adopt better health habits, become better parents, and become better consumers and citizens.

INCREASED HAPPINESS. Is there a relationship between educational level and happiness? A lot depends on what is meant by "happiness," which is hard to measure. Still, by many standards wealthy people tend to be happier than poor people, points out one psychologist. "Does that mean that money buys happiness," he asks, "or that happy people are likely to succeed at their jobs and become wealthy?"[7]

Whatever, better educated people do make more money, as we have seen. They also have the opportunity to explore their personal growth and development in a way that less educated people cannot. This gives them a chance to discover what makes them happy.

How the Work of Higher Education Can Improve Your Career Skills

PREVIEW The four principal ways of learning in college are via lectures, readings, writing, and laboratories. The skills you develop to perfect these learning activities can be used not only to improve your grades but also to further your career in the work world.

et's get down to basics: How is knowledge transferred to you in college? Can you apply the methods of learning in college courses—whatever the subject—to help you be successful in your career *after* college? The answer is: Absolutely!

THE FOUR PRINCIPAL WAYS OF INSTRUCTION. European and other systems of higher education operate somewhat differently. However, in the colleges, universities, and technical institutes of North America most first-year students acquire knowledge in four principal ways—through lectures, reading, writing, and laboratories. Let's consider these:

■ *Lectures:* Students attend lectures by instructors and are tested throughout the school term on how much they remember.

Relevance to your career: When you go to work in the business or nonbusiness world, this method of imparting information is called a "presentation," "meeting," or "company training program." And the "test" constitutes how well you recall and handle the information in order to do your job. (Sometimes there's an actual test, as in government civil service, to see if you qualify for promotion.)

■ *Readings:* Students are given reading assignments in textbooks and other publications and are tested to see how much they recall and understand. Quite often lectures and readings make up the only teaching methods in a course.

Relevance to your career: In the work world, comparable ways of communicating information are through reports, memos, letters, instruction manuals, newsletters, trade journals, and books. Here, too, the "test" constitutes how well you interpret and use the information to do your work.

- *Writing:* Students are given assignments in which they are asked to research information and write it into a term paper. Generally, you need not recall this information for a test. However, you must manage your time so that you can produce a good paper, which is usually an important part of the course grade.

   Relevance to your career: In the work world, a research paper is called a "report," "memo," "proposal," or "written analysis." Police officers, nurses, salespeople, lawyers, managers, and teachers all write reports. How well you pull together facts and present them can have a tremendous impact on how you influence other people. This factor in turn affects how you are able to do your job.

- *Laboratories:* Laboratories are practice sessions. You use knowledge gained from readings, and sometimes lectures, to practice applying the material, and you are graded on your progress. For example, in computer science or office technology, you may take a lab that gives you hands-on instruction in word processing. In learning to speak Japanese, you may go to a lab to listen to language tapes and practice the language. In chemistry, you may do experiments with various chemicals on a laboratory workbench.

   Relevance to your career: In the world of work, your job itself is the laboratory. Your promotions and career success depend on how well you pull together and practice everything you've learned to do the job.

There are also other instructional techniques. Instead of lectures, you may have *seminars*, or discussion groups, but you'll likely still be tested on the material presented in them. Instead of readings, you may have to *watch films, slides, or videotapes or listen to audiotapes*, on which you may be tested. Instead of term papers or laboratories, you may be assigned *projects*. For example, in psychology or geology, you may be asked to go on a field trip and take notes. In music or drafting, you may be asked to create something. Still, most of these alternative methods of instruction make use of whatever skills you bring to bear in lectures, reading, writing, and laboratory work.

HOW LEARNING HIGHER EDUCATION CAN HELP YOUR CAREER. I have pointed out that all these instructional methods or situations have counterparts in the world of work. This is an important matter. I have no doubt that from time to time you'll think what you're doing in college is irrelevant to real life (as I did in college). When that happens, remember that the *time-management methods* by which you learn are *necessary skills for success in the work environment*.

If you know how to take efficient notes of lectures, for example, you can do the same in meetings. If you know how to extract material from a textbook, you can do the same for a report. Moreover, these and other learning skills will be valuable all your life because they are transferable skills between jobs and between industries. They are even transferable between the for-profit (business) and nonprofit (education and government) sectors of the economy. They are also valuable in nonwork areas, as in volunteer activities.

Finally, let me point out that companies generally are looking to hire people who have good time-management abilities. My wife, who has worked for an insurance company, says this is one of the primary skills they try to uncover in new job applicants. After they are hired, if people are found not to have it, they are often let go. (Most companies don't train their employees in time management.)

In sum: If you perfect the skills for acquiring knowledge in college, these skills will serve you well in helping you live the way you want to live professionally and personally.

Why Do Some People Have Trouble in Higher Education?

PREVIEW Students who drop out of college sometimes do so for financial reasons but also for more personal ones. They include (1) academic underpreparedness, (2) academic overpreparedness, (3) feeling that higher education isn't useful, (4) unrealistic expectations about college, (5) uncertainty about major or career, and (6) lack of a personal support system.

ot everyone can handle the mix of freedom-with-responsibility that comes with higher education. About a third of entering full-time, first-year college students in the United States are not at the same institution one year later. (This does not necessarily mean they are gone forever. Perhaps they go elsewhere. Or they may drop out and return to college later.) After the first year, however, the chance of students staying in the college at which they started increases significantly.[8]

In addition, it's important to know that, of first-year students who quit during school (rather than between terms), half drop out in the first six weeks. Thus, you should be aware that *the first two to six weeks are a critical time of adjustment.*

Why do students drop out? For some people the causes are financial—lack of money. However, for most the causes are more personal.[9] If you should end up leaving school, it will probably be for one of the following reasons:

- **You are underprepared academically, which leads to frustration:** Some students are underprepared—in reading, writing, and math skills, for instance—and find themselves in college courses that are too difficult for them. *It's important to know what your college offers in the way of academic support services—for example, math tutoring. But it's best not to wait until you're in trouble to find them.*

If you sense even in the first couple of weeks of your first term that you're slipping, tell the instructor of the class for which you are reading this book. Or go to the student counseling center. Be honest also about telling your academic advisor if you're worried about being in over your head.

- **You are overprepared academically, which leads to boredom:** Some first-year students complain that their courses repeat work they already covered in high school. This is why good academic advising by a counselor is important. Don't do as I did and take first-year chemistry in college after already taking it in high school (unless your advisor recommends it). Look for courses that will challenge and stretch you. Don't go for the "easy A."

- **You perceive college as being not useful:** First-year students who don't think their college work will be useful beyond the classroom are likely candidates for dropping out. This may be particularly so for first-year students who have not chosen a major. However, it also happens to those who do have career goals but who consider general-education requirements (normally a big part of the first year) irrelevant. It's important, then, to nail down the reasons *why* you're in college.

- **You have unrealistic expectations about college:** Some first-year students don't have realistic expectations about themselves and college. For example, some come to college expecting great things to happen without much investment on their part. Thus, they devote little effort toward making higher education work for them.

- **You are uncertain about your major or your career:** It's okay to come to college undecided about your major or a career. Indeed, college is a great place to explore these possibilities. Even so, you should be aware that indecision about these important goals is a reason for dropping out. Thus, you need to be *actively* looking into your long-range reasons for being in college.

- **You don't have a personal support system:** Most first-year students have to start from scratch building a personal support system. This means making friends with other students, counselors, and instructors or otherwise finding support. Whoever you are, a support system *is* available (as I describe in Chapter 3).

Still, some students have difficulty seeking out support. Students who become only weakly involved in the college experience may stay in their rooms all the time, leave campus every weekend, or miss classes frequently.

In general, all these difficulties can be boiled down to three matters:

■ *Skills achievement*

■ *Motivation*

■ *Support*

This book gives a lot of attention to these issues.

I feel certain that most readers of this book will continue on to finish the first year. Why? Because the evidence seems to be that students who take Introduction-to-College courses are much less apt to drop out than students who don't. Since you're enrolled in such a course, you're already ahead of the game!

Values & Choices: Why Not Be the Best?

PREVIEW Values, the truest expression of who you are, are principles by which you lead your life. A value has three characteristics:

(1) It is an important attitude.

(2) It is matter on which you take action.

(3) It should be consciously chosen.

eing in college, some students have told me, makes them feel as though they exist in suspension, postponing real life.

But life cannot be postponed. It is lived today—not held off until the weekend, or vacations, or graduation. Or until you're in a relationship or settled in a career. Or until your children leave home or you retire.

Real life starts when you open your eyes in the morning, when you decide—that is, *choose*—what you will do today. And what you choose to do reflects your values.

WHAT VALUES ARE. Your values are the truest expression of who you are. **A *value* is a principle by which you lead your life. It is an important belief or attitude that you think "ought to be" (or "ought not to be"). Moreover, it is a belief that you feel strongly enough about to take action on and that has been consciously chosen.**

There are three important parts here:

1. *A value is an important attitude:* A value is an important attitude or belief that you hold. Examples: "College should help me get a good job." "Fairness means hiring according to ability, not family background." "Murder is wrong except in self-defense." "It's worth trying my hardest to get an A." ("Chocolate is better than vanilla", is a preference, generally not a value.)

2. *A value is a matter on which you take action:* You can *think* whatever you want. However, if you don't back up your

thought with some sort of action, it cannot be considered a value (for all practical purposes). If you stand by while watching someone cheat on an exam, your attitude that "cheating is wrong" is not really a value.

3. *A value should be consciously chosen:* Values are not very strong if they are not truly your own. Many first-year students hold values they obtained from their parents—values to which they may not have given much thought, such as religious beliefs. For an idea to be a value rather than just a belief, you have to have thought enough about it to consider accepting or rejecting it. You have to have made it yours. You can't just say "That's the way it is."

GROUP ACTIVITY #1.2

YOURS & OTHERS' VALUES

Before breaking into groups, you and your classmates should each take out a sheet of paper and make a list of 20 matters you consider important—your values. Then reduce the list to the five most important values. On joining your group (three to five people), appoint one person as a recorder or secretary. Go through and discuss your lists and agree (if possible) on what the top five values are for the group. The secretary should then write this list on the classroom blackboard.

In class discussion, consider what are the similarities and differences of values among the groups? How do your personal values compare to those of your group members? Did you find it difficult in your group to come to agreement, and, if so, why?

If you had only a month or year to live, how would that fact influence your choices?

BEING YOUR BEST—ONE OF THE PARAMOUNT VALUES. Most of us discover early on that we can't be the best at everything. However, *it's important to try to be the best at the PRIMARY THINGS WE DO*—otherwise, why do them? For instance, you might devote your best hours or your most hours to being an athlete, or a salesperson, or a parent. If this is the major focus of your time and energy, why do a mediocre job of it? *Why not be the best?*

No one *has* to attend college. This is not involuntary servitude. You can leave any time. Since you're here voluntarily—and presumably will be here for months and even years—why not decide to do it right?

To some extent, of course, this desire to do well means competing with others to see who's the best. However, it's more important that you decide to achieve your *personal best.* Compared to some other people, you may not be a great basketball player, mathematician, linguist, or whatever. But you can try to be the best that *you* can be in these endeavors. That is the paramount value.

Adopting the attitude that you will try to do your best in college will also help you outside college. Doing the best at whatever is the primary focus of your time and interests will give you a better chance of building the kind of life you want to live.

YOUR VALUES ABOUT HIGHER EDUCATION. What kind of values do you hold? These are not frivolous matters, since they have a great bearing on how you view the whole subject of higher education. To see how your values affected your actions in going to college, try Personal Exploration #1.1.[10]

YOUR VALUES ABOUT HIGHER EDUCATION

Take at least 10–15 minutes for this activity. The purpose is to see how your values and family background affected your actions in going to college.

■ A. FAMILY MATTERS

1. College is not a tradition in my family. (Family includes not only parents and grandparents or guardians but also uncles, aunts, and brothers and sisters.)

   ____ True ____ False
   ____ Somewhat true

2. My father/guardian completed (check one): ____ grade school ____ high school ____ college ____ graduate or professional school ____ other (identify)
   _____
   _____

3. My father/guardian (check one):
   ____ supports
   ____ does not support
   my decision to go to this college.

4. My mother/guardian completed (check one): ____ grade school ____ high school ____ college ____ graduate or professional school ____ other (identify)
   _____
   _____

5. My mother/guardian (check one):
   ____ supports
   ____ does not support
   my decision to go to this college.

6. My spouse/boyfriend/girlfriend (check one):
   ____ supports
   ____ does not support
   my decision to go to this college.

7. My spouse/boyfriend/girlfriend completed (check one):
   ____ grade school
   ____ high school ____ college
   ____ graduate or professional school ____ other (identify)
   _____
   _____

■ B. COLLEGE & FREE CHOICE

1. Regarding the influence of my parents/guardians or others, I'd say my going to college was the following (check one): (a) ____ It was mainly my decision but a little bit others' decision. (b) ____ It was mainly others' decision but a little bit my decision. (c) ____ It was about equally both mine and others' decisions. (d) ____ It was never talked about; it was just assumed I'd go.

2. If I wasn't going to college, I would do the following instead:
   _____
   _____
   _____
   _____
   _____
   _____
   _____
   _____
   _____

3. If I had the money and could do anything I wanted to this year, I would rather be doing the following:
   _____
   _____
   _____
   _____
   _____
   _____
   _____
   _____
   _____
   _____

4. Looking over my last three responses, I feel that I am going to college because of the following (check one): (a) ____ I am choosing to go and want to go. (b) ____ I don't really choose to go and don't really want to go, but others want me to. (c) ____ I don't feel I have a choice, but I want to go anyway. (d) ____ I don't know, I'm confused.

■ C. PUBLIC REASONS, PERSONAL REASONS

1. When people ask me why I chose this college, I tell them the following. (List three or four reasons.)

   a. _____
   _____

   b. _____
   _____

   c. _____
   _____

   d. _____
   _____

2. When people ask me why I am interested in a particular major or field of study (or why I am undecided), I tell them the following. (List three or four reasons.)

   a. _____
   _____

   b. _____
   _____

   c. _____
   _____

   d. _____
   _____

3. The reasons I chose (if I chose) the particular major or field of study mentioned in C.2 that I *don't* tell people about are as follows. (Examples: "My parents want me to do it." "I'm afraid I lack the talent or brains to do something else I might like better." "It's a matter of conscience.")

   a. _____
   _____

   b. _____
   _____

(continued on next page)

■ D. REASONS FOR GOING TO COLLEGE

The following is a list of reasons for attending college. Rank them in order of importance to you, with 1 meaning most important, 2 of secondary importance, 3 third in importance, and so on.

My reasons for going to college are . . .

a. ___ To please my parents.

b. ___ To have fun.

c. ___ To get a degree.

d. ___ To prepare for a career.

e. ___ To make friends.

f. ___ To better support my family/ help my children.

g. ___ To avoid having to work for a while.

h. ___ To find a girlfriend/ boyfriend/mate.

i. ___ To raise my economic level/ get a better job.

j. ___ To explore new ideas and experiences.

k. ___ To acquire knowledge.

l. ___ To gain maturity.

m. ___ To learn how to solve problems.

n. ___ To learn how to learn.

o. ___ To gain prestige.

p. ___ To become a better citizen.

■ E. IDENTIFYING YOUR VALUES REGARDING HIGHER EDUCATION

Look back over this Personal Exploration. Identify the top three values that influenced your decision to attend the college you are in. Write a brief essay in the following space. In the essay explain how each of the three values led you to take a particular kind of action in choosing the present college.

_____
_____
_____
_____
_____
_____
_____
_____
_____
_____
_____
_____
_____
_____
_____
_____
_____
_____
_____
_____
_____
_____
_____
_____
_____
_____

GROUP ACTIVITY OPTION

In a small group (three to five people), discuss some of the results of Personal Exploration #1.1. What role did your family or people close to you have in your decision to go to college? What would you do (or rather do, if you had the money) if you weren't going to college? What top three values influenced you to go to college? Discuss also your thoughts about "being the best" in the primary things you do. How do you feel about doing your "personal best" in college? What do you want to be? How would you like college to help you get there?

Onward: Applying This Chapter to Your Life

PREVIEW Learning how to learn can make all the difference not only in the success of your first college year but also to your survival in the expanding information economy.

By enrolling in this introductory course in how to succeed in college you'll learn all the shortcuts that I didn't learn until much later in my college career. They'll also be shortcuts that students not in the course may not learn except in a haphazard kind of way, if at all.

But there are greater benefits here than just learning tricks to helping survive your first college year. Consider this: In the year 1300, the Sorbonne library in Paris contained a mere 1338 volumes—which one person could have absorbed within a lifetime. Today, by contrast, the Library of Congress in Washington, D.C., has over 98 million books, manuscripts, and documents. Even people with narrow specialties are hard put to keep up with expanding knowledge. More new information was produced in the last 30 years than in all the previous 5000. Information today is doubling every five years. By the end of the century, *it will double every 20 months.*[11]

It's clear from these numbers that we live in the Information Age—and that the explosion in knowledge will continue throughout our lifetimes. Many people may take the deluge of data as an excuse that it's okay to be ignorant—indeed, they may even celebrate it—figuring they'll scrape by on luck and common sense. Of course, in some areas of life we may have to operate without full knowledge of the facts. However, as a general approach it's not very practical and probably is even dangerous.

How on earth are you going to be able to keep up with what's required of you? The answer is: by *learning how to learn.* By building your skills as a learner—as a gatherer and user of information—you not only help yourself do better in school; you also equip yourself to be an information manager in the global information economy.

A last thought before you leave this chapter: Was there anything you read that made you say, "I didn't know that!"? Did you see anything that helped you discover something new about yourself? Was it something that you could *make useful in your life?* If so, what is it, and how could you make use of it? Write it down here:

_____

_____

_____

_____

_____

_____

_____

_____

_____

_____

_____

_____

_____

_____

_____

_____

_____

_____

_____

"The unexamined life is not worth living," stated the great Greek philosopher Socrates. If ever there was a time to examine your life, it is now, during the first year of college.

As you take this course, you should be considering such basic questions as:

1. Why am I choosing the direction I've chosen?

2. How do I feel about the things I've seen, read, or heard?

3. What do I think of this idea, that person, those beliefs?

4. How can I *make use* of the new experiences?

The place to express these thoughts and to keep track of the progress you are making is in a *journal.* By writing in a journal, you come to a better understanding of yourself. The form of the journal probably doesn't matter, although your instructor may make some suggestions. It may be a notebook, loose-leaf sheets in a three-ring binder, typed pages, or on a computer.

Your journal may be entirely private. It's possible that, from time to time, your instructor will express interest in your thoughts or progress with the journal. However, you need not show him or her your actual journal, unless you want to. Rather, you can provide some sort of separate statement that summarizes some of those thoughts you feel like sharing.

At the end of each chapter, I will indicate some suggestions for your journal, although you need not feel bound by them. Here is the first suggestion.

■ At the top of the page, write your name, the date and time, and the place you are as you write this entry. Now consider the following questions: (1) What are your *strongest* motivations for attending college? (2) What are some other motivations for attending college—reasons that are less strong but that motivate you nonetheless? (3) What kinds of support do you have that will help you succeed?

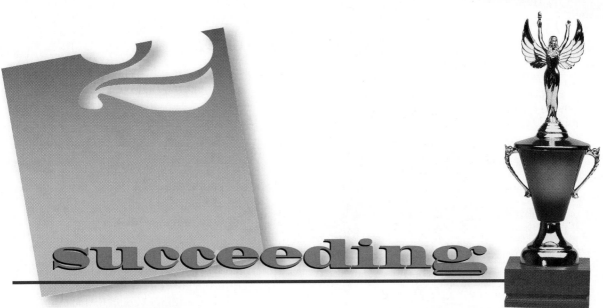

succeeding

making higher education work for you

determine why you're here, overcome your fear

IN THIS CHAPTER: If the first year of college is "punctuated by feelings of panic and incompetence," as one observer put it, that's normal.[1] This chapter begins to address those feelings. We consider the following subjects:

- **The "why" of college:** Why are you here? We explore this most fundamental question.

- **The fears of college:** What are your fears about college? You're not alone. They are probably mostly the same fears everyone else has—and they can be lessened.

- **Your strengths:** You bring certain strengths to college that will help you achieve success.

- **Life goals and college goals:** We look at six steps for translating your life goals into college goals and daily tasks.

1. If two things outside of yourself could make you happy, what would they be? Identify them here. (Examples: love relationship, lots of money. Use a secret code or shorthand, if you like—nobody else has to see this. Example: "TTW"—for "travel the world.")

_____

_____

_____

_____

_____

2. What are your principal doubts, worries, or anxieties about college? Write them down here. (Use a code, if you like. Example: "FOFO"—for "fear of flunking out.")

_____

_____

_____

_____

_____

_____

■ SKIMMING FOR PAYOFFS

How will you realize Question 1 and deal with Question 2? There is no point in reading this book if it's not useful to you. Thus, the trick is to *make it* useful—to find your own payoffs.

Skim through the chapter and look for ideas, tips, and resources that might address the concerns in Questions 1 and 2. Write personal notations in the margin if you find things that you think might be worth trying.

"Get a life!" everyone says.

ut what, exactly, is "a life," anyway? And how do you "get" it?

As the bumper sticker says, LIFE IS NOT A DRESS REHEARSAL. We pass this way only once. The calendar leaves fall away. And then it's over.

Some things just happen to us, but a lot of things we choose. How many people, though, wake up at the age of 60 or 70 and say: "I missed the boat; there were better things I could have chosen to do"?

Over a lifetime everyone acquires a few regrets. But the thing that people regret the most, according to a survey by Cornell University researchers, is not what they *have done* so much as what they *haven't done*. And chief among the regrets are (1) *missed educational opportunities* and (2) *failure to "seize the moment."* [2]

You are at a time and place to seize some splendid opportunities. College allows you to begin examining the choices available to you—about what you want your life to be. We're talking about the main event, the Big Enchilada— deciding what is *truly* important to you.

Why Are You Here, What Is Your Fear?

PREVIEW Is the ultimate purpose of college to make you happy? Aren't there easier ways to achieve happiness? In the end, motivation is everything.

Over the years I've heard a variety of thoughts, feelings, and opinions expressed about college. The issue I find most interesting, however, is the one that is at the heart of everything: *Why do people want to go to college?*

Before proceeding, I urge you to stop right here and try the following Personal Exploration #2.1 on page 18, identifying your reasons for going to college. This will expand on the insights you gained from Personal Exploration #1.1 in Chapter 1.

THE "WHY" OF HIGHER EDUCATION. On my first day of class for my *Transitions: The First-Year Experience* course, I begin by handing out the course outline and reading list. Then the students and I usually have a discussion that goes something like this. (My side of it is a set piece I've done for a few years.)

"Let me ask, Why are you here?" I begin. "Why did you come to college? Does anyone care to answer that?"

After an interval, someone usually says something like "I'm here to get an education."

"Terrific," I may say. "And maybe you could tell me why you want to get an education."

"Well, to get a college degree," the student may reply.

"Excellent. What will a degree do for you?"

"Help me get a decent job."

"And what will a good job allow you to do?"

"Earn money."

"All right. And what would you do with the money?"

"Buy things."

"What kinds of things? Does anyone else care to join in?" At this point, I often ask various people to name things that they'd like to buy.

"A car," one may say. "A house," says another. "A trip to Europe," says a third.

"What," I ask the classroom at large, "will buying things do for you?"

Here there may be an awkward silence. Finally, someone usually says: "Make me happy." Others in the class generally nod their agreement.

We've come to an interesting point. "Okay," I say, "Let's see what this means. You say that you're going to college in order to gain an education that will lead to a degree that in turn will help you get a good job so that you can earn money to buy things so that you can *be happy?*"

People nod affirmatively, but they're clearly waiting to see where these questions are leading.

"If it's *happiness* you want," I say, "I have a solution for you—and it's a whole lot easier than going to college. Let's pretend I have with me today a powerful mind-altering drug." At this point I whip out a piece of chalk or other prop from my pocket and hold it up. "It's guaranteed to make you happy. Take this, and you won't feel any stress or pain. As all of you know, there are plenty of pills and drugs like this around."

> *"If it's **happiness you want**, I have a solution for you—and it's a whole lot easier than going to college."*

Now people are usually listening attentively.

"On the other hand," I continue, "if you take this drug, you won't feel like *doing* anything. You'll just want to sit in a

GOING TO COLLEGE: WHY ARE YOU HERE?

Take 5–10 minutes for this activity, or even more time, if you can—it will probably provide you with the most important piece of self-knowledge you will get out of this book.

■ WHAT TO DO

For each of the following statements, circle the number below corresponding to how much you agree or disagree:

1 = strongly disagree
2 = somewhat disagree
3 = neither disagree nor agree
4 = somewhat agree
5 = strongly agree

1. College will help me get a better-paying or more prestigious job than I could get otherwise.
   1   2   3   4   5

2. College will help me get a more interesting or challenging job.
   1   2   3   4   5

3. College will help lead me to fulfilling work.
   1   2   3   4   5

4. College will help me explore what career I want to pursue.
   1   2   3   4   5

5. Going to college gives me an opportunity to continue to pursue interests (for instance, sports, music) I've already developed.
   1   2   3   4   5

6. Going to college gives me the opportunity to develop new interests.
   1   2   3   4   5

7. College allows me to take courses in areas that I would never have thought to explore.
   1   2   3   4   5

8. College helps me get away from home.
   1   2   3   4   5

9. College gives me the opportunity to explore who I am and try to understand myself.
   1   2   3   4   5

10. College will help me figure out what makes people (or the world) tick.
    1   2   3   4   5

11. College will provide me with skills that will be useful regardless of what I do in life.
    1   2   3   4   5

12. Being in college enables me to meet more interesting people than I could otherwise.
    1   2   3   4   5

13. Being in college may help me find a lover or mate.
    1   2   3   4   5

14. College will help me to become an interesting person.
    1   2   3   4   5

15. College will allow me to travel and see places I've never seen.
    1   2   3   4   5

16. College will help me build self-confidence.
    1   2   3   4   5

17. College seems a more interesting alternative to what I would most likely be doing otherwise as just a high-school graduate.
    1   2   3   4   5

18. College will help me learn how to interact with all kinds of people.
    1   2   3   4   5

19. College will help me to explore the meaning of life.
    1   2   3   4   5

20. I am in college because my friends are going.
    1   2   3   4   5

21. My parents expect me to go to college.
    1   2   3   4   5

22. I have an athletic scholarship or other kind of scholarship or veterans' benefits.
    1   2   3   4   5

23. I couldn't go when I was younger and now I want the experience.
    1   2   3   4   5

24. Being in college is a form of recreation or entertainment for me.
    1   2   3   4   5

25. College will . . . (write in other benefits):

    _____
    _____
    _____

    1   2   3   4   5

Add the number of points: _____

■ MEANING OF YOUR SCORE

100–125   *High*
You have a great number of motivations for attending and persevering in college.

75–99   *Average*
You have a fair number of motivations for attending and continuing in college.

74 or less   *Low*
You need to take a look at why you're here. Your score suggests you need to determine your motivations for attending college if you are to make a success of it.

▪ INTERPRETATION

The scores and interpretations of this activity are not absolutes. Repeat: *They are NOT absolutes.* They are merely meant to get you thinking about your motivations and concerns so that you can better clarify the goals of your college experience.

Key items: If you scored high on any or all of items 8, 13, 20, 21, and 24, read the following:

8   *"College helps me get away from home."* This is not the best motivator, especially if the reason is to spite your parents or get away from an unhealthy home environment.

13 *"Being in college may help me find a lover or mate."* For students in their late teens or early 20s, relationships can be a significant reason for experiencing academic difficulties, if their social life falls apart and brings down the entire college experience with it.

20 *"I am in college because my friends are going."* True motivation for going to college has to come from the inside (internal motivation versus external motivation). If peer pressure is the main reason you're in college, it can also make you party too much and neglect your academic work. Peer pressure may be a reason for starting out in college, but it won't keep you there.

21 *"My parents expect me to go to college."* This motivation is external rather than internal. Some students may really resent their parents' pressure and may not be ready for college yet.

24 *"Being in college is a form of recreation or entertainment for me."* Partying, sports, and so on are probably not sufficient to keep you in college. Having fun is fine, but you need to know that college *work* is planning and preparation for the rest of your life.

In a small group (three to five people), discuss some of the reasons for attending college. Which ones seem to apply to you? Are there any reasons that you feel shaky about but that you tell people anyway? Are there any private reasons you care to bring out that might benefit from group discussion?

corner. You'll be quite happy, but you'll have no wish to go out on dates, play games, or go to parties. Or view the sunset, eat pizza, be with your family, and so on. You'll just be a happy vegetable." I hold out the chalk. "So, let me ask you: Does anyone want to take this drug?"

Someone might jokingly raise a hand for a second, but basically there are no takers.

"Why not?" I ask. "Didn't you say you want to be happy?"

I then offer the stub of chalk to someone at random. "How about it—wouldn't you choose happiness if it's this easy?"

A shake of the head. "I don't want happiness that way," the student usually says. "I want to earn it on my own."

"Terrific! How many agree? Would you prefer the kind of happiness you have to earn on your own?"

There is a murmur of agreement.

"Okay," I say, "this is important. You don't want happiness that comes easily, like a magic pill. You want the kind of happiness that you have to *earn*. You want happiness that *you're responsible for.*"

I then go to the blackboard and write:

WHY AM I HERE?

TO ACHIEVE HAPPINESS THAT **I** AM RESPONSIBLE FOR.

THEREFORE, MY PURSUIT OF HAPPINESS REQUIRES

THAT **I** BE RESPONSIBLE FOR MY EFFORTS.

"The point is this," I then tell the class. "College can be difficult. I know it was for me when I was a student. When you're faced with weeks or months of term papers and tests, there will be times when you may wonder why you're doing it.

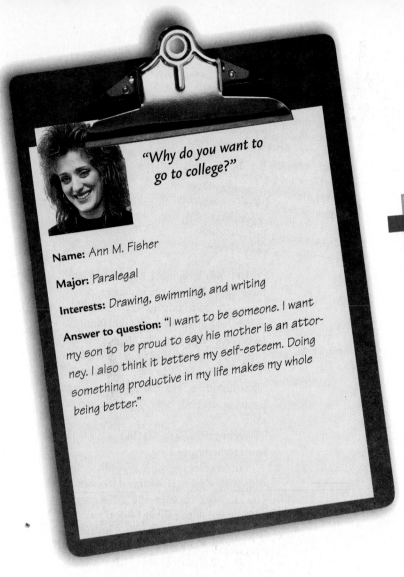

"Why do you want to go to college?"

Name: Ann M. Fisher

Major: Paralegal

Interests: Drawing, swimming, and writing

Answer to question: "I want to be someone. I want my son to be proud to say his mother is an attorney. I also think it betters my self-esteem. Doing something productive in my life makes my whole being better."

Or pay from a full-time job or time with your friends or family. You have to decide, then, that what you'll get in the future outweighs the sacrifices of the present.

Ultimately, then, you have to remember that you want college to lead to the kind of happiness that *you* are responsible for. No one else can give that to you. The pursuit of happiness is *your* responsibility."

Forgive me if that classroom dialogue turned into a bit of a lecture, but one thing that cannot be stressed enough is that *motivation* is everything. A college is not a correctional facility; you can walk away from it at any time. And no doubt there will be times when you will want to, particularly during the first quarter or semester. So what, ultimately, is going to motivate you not only to stay in but to do your best while you're there?

"Motivation depends not only on what you want to do," says a Columbia University psychiatry professor, "but what you think you'll have to *give up* to do it."[3] Going to college means giving up some things—some leisure time, for instance.

FEAR & CHANGE. Most people don't want to continue doing the same old thing because that gets boring. Yet when an opportunity for change comes along, they are often afraid of it. Indeed, fear of change seems to be more usual than unusual.

You're not abnormal if you have some concerns and fears about college, but it's important to identify them now so you can take steps to deal with them. Take a few minutes now to try Personal Exploration #2.2.

GOING TO COLLEGE: WHAT IS YOUR FEAR?

dentifying your fears about college is the first step in fighting them.

WHAT TO DO

For each of the following statements, circle the number below corresponding to how much you agree or disagree:

1 = strongly disagree
2 = somewhat disagree
3 = neither disagree nor agree
4 = somewhat agree
5 = strongly agree

I am afraid that . . .

1. College will be too difficult for me.   1 2 3 4 5

2. I will get homesick.   1 2 3 4 5

3. I might flunk out.   1 2 3 4 5

4. I won't be able to handle the amount of school work.   1 2 3 4 5

5. My study habits won't be good enough to succeed.   1 2 3 4 5

6. I'll get lost on campus.   1 2 3 4 5

7. I'll be a disappointment to people important to me, such as my parents, family, or children.   1 2 3 4 5

8. I won't have enough money and will have to drop out.   1 2 3 4 5

9. I won't be able to handle working and/or family responsibilities and college at the same time.   1 2 3 4 5

10. I will get depressed.   1 2 3 4 5

11. I won't be able to manage my time being on my own.   1 2 3 4 5

12. I'll oversleep or otherwise won't be able to get to class on time.   1 2 3 4 5

13. I won't be able to maintain the grade average I want.   1 2 3 4 5

14. The college will find out that I'm basically incompetent and will kick me out.   1 2 3 4 5

15. I won't be able to compete with other students.   1 2 3 4 5

16. I won't make any friends.   1 2 3 4 5

17. I won't be able to overcome my shyness.   1 2 3 4 5

18. I'll have problems with my roommates.   1 2 3 4 5

19. I won't be able to handle writing/spelling or math.   1 2 3 4 5

20. My professors will find out I'm inadequate.   1 2 3 4 5

21. There will be no one to help me.   1 2 3 4 5

22. I'll choose the wrong major.   1 2 3 4 5

23. I'll have to cheat in order to survive the tough academic environment.   1 2 3 4 5

24. My family or my job will complicate things, and I won't be able to keep up.   1 2 3 4 5

25. Other (write in):

_____
_____
_____
_____
_____
1 2 3 4 5

Add the number of points: _____

MEANING OF YOUR SCORE

100–125 *High*

You are very fearful or very concerned about your college experience. Although these concerns are not unusual, it would be a good idea to check into some college resources to assist you in dealing with your worries. Such resources include career and personal counseling, the college's learning center, and the financial aid office.

75–99 *Average*

You are somewhat fearful or somewhat concerned about your college experience. Welcome! Join the crowd! Your concerns are typical and are shared by the majority of college students. To assist you in addressing these issues, you may wish to identify the appropriate college resources— counseling center, learning center, financial aid—for assistance.

74 or less *Low*

You have few fears, perhaps are even laid back. Even so, it would be useful to identify college support services (such as counseling or learning center) in case you ever need them.

INTERPRETATION

We all tend to think that any one worry we have is unique, that it is ours alone, that no one else ever experiences it with the intensity that we do. This is not true! Indeed, the fears and concerns listed above are quite common. So also is the reluctance to seek help, to get support. But seeking support is probably what will help you overcome the fear. Resources such as counseling and financial aid are described in Chapter 3.

In a small group each student should discuss his or her top three concerns (unless they're considered too private to be shared), and others in the group should state whether they are experiencing the same concern. In addition, ask every person in the group to suggest (as tactfully as possible) a possible way to deal with each concern discussed.

In their first week or two in college, the students in my class mention all kinds of fears. Fear of flunking out is the biggest. Fear of loneliness, of not finding supportive friends, is another. Fears of the work required, of the pressure, of not being able to compete, of the responsibility, these are all commonplace. Then there are more specific fears—about being on one's own, about not finding one's way around, about not getting dates. Or about not having a good time, about running out of money, even about oversleeping. Adult returning students express concerns about not being able to balance college and family and/or job responsibilities. The kinds of worries students tell me personally are also fears students express to researchers.[4,5] With the help of this book and your instructor, however, you can get beyond those fears and make college the success you want it to be.

What Strengths Do You Bring to Higher Education?

PREVIEW Four qualities are helpful for achieving success in college—and in life: (1) Sense of personal control and responsibility. (2) Optimism. (3) Creativity. (4) Ability to take psychological risks.

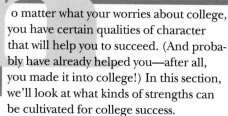

No matter what your worries about college, you have certain qualities of character that will help you to succeed. (And probably have already helped you—after all, you made it into college!) In this section, we'll look at what kinds of strengths can be cultivated for college success.

Successful people have the following qualities:

- Sense of personal control and responsibility

- Optimism

- Creativity

- Ability to take psychological risks

    Let's take a look at these.

PERSONAL CONTROL & RESPONSIBILITY. How much personal control do you feel you have over your destiny? **The term *locus of control* refers to your beliefs about the relationship between your behavior and the occurrence of rewards and punishment.**

    People are said to have either an external or an internal locus of control:

- *External:* Do you believe strongly in the influences of chance or fate or the power of others? **People who believe their rewards and punishments are controlled mainly by outside forces or other people are said to have an *external locus of control.***

- *Internal:* Do you believe that "I am the captain of my fate, the master of my soul"? **People who believe their rewards and punishments are due to their own behavior, character, or efforts are said to have an *internal locus of control.*[6]**

    You may wish to try Personal Exploration #2.3 to see what your locus of control is.

WHO'S IN CHARGE HERE?

Are you in charge of your fate, or is a great deal of it influenced by outside forces? Answer the following questions to see where you stand.

1. Do you believe that most problems will solve themselves if you just don't fool with them?
   ❏ Yes   ❏ No

2. Do you believe that you can stop yourself from catching a cold?
   ❏ Yes   ❏ No

3. Are some people just born lucky?
   ❏ Yes   ❏ No

4. Most of the time do you feel that getting good grades means a great deal to you?   ❏ Yes   ❏ No

5. Are you often blamed for things that just aren't your fault?
   ❏ Yes   ❏ No

6. Do you believe that if somebody studies hard enough he or she can pass any subject?
   ❏ Yes   ❏ No

7. Do you feel that most of the time it doesn't pay to try hard because things never turn out right anyway?   ❏ Yes   ❏ No

8. Do you feel that if things start out well in the morning, it's going to be a good day no matter what you do?   ❏ Yes   ❏ No

9. Do you feel that most of the time parents listen to what their children have to say?
   ❏ Yes   ❏ No

10. Do you believe that wishing can make good things happen?
    ❏ Yes   ❏ No

11. When you get punished, does it usually seem it's for no good reason at all?   ❏ Yes   ❏ No

12. Most of the time, do you find it hard to change a friend's opinion?
    ❏ Yes   ❏ No

13. Do you think cheering more than luck helps a team win?
    ❏ Yes   ❏ No

14. Did you feel that it was nearly impossible for you to change your parents' minds about anything?
    ❏ Yes   ❏ No

15. Do you believe that parents should allow children to make most of their own decisions?
    ❏ Yes   ❏ No

16. Do you feel that when you do something wrong, there's very little you can do to make it right?
    ❏ Yes   ❏ No

17. Do you believe that most people are just born good at sports?
    ❏ Yes   ❏ No

18. Are most other people your age stronger than you are?
    ❏ Yes   ❏ No

19. Do you feel that one of the best ways to handle most problems is just not to think about them?
    ❏ Yes   ❏ No

20. Do you feel that you have a lot of choice in deciding who your friends are?   ❏ Yes   ❏ No

21. If you find a four-leaf clover, do you believe that it might bring you good luck?   ❏ Yes   ❏ No

22. Did you often feel that whether or not you did your homework had much to do with the kind of grades you got?   ❏ Yes   ❏ No

23. Do you feel that when a person your age is angry with you, there's little you can do to stop him or her?   ❏ Yes   ❏ No

24. Have you ever had a good-luck charm?   ❏ Yes   ❏ No

25. Do you believe that whether or not people like you depends on how you act?   ❏ Yes   ❏ No

26. Did your parents usually help you if you asked them to?
    ❏ Yes   ❏ No

27. Have you ever felt that when people were angry with you, it was usually for no reason at all?
    ❏ Yes   ❏ No

28. Most of the time, do you feel that you can change what might happen tomorrow by what you do today?   ❏ Yes   ❏ No

29. Do you believe that when bad things are going to happen, they are just going to happen no matter what you try and do to stop them?   ❏ Yes   ❏ No

30. Do you think that people can get their own way if they just keep trying?   ❏ Yes   ❏ No

31. Most of the time, do you find it useless to try to get your own way at home?   ❏ Yes   ❏ No

32. Do you feel that when good things happen, they happen because of hard work?   ❏ Yes   ❏ No

33. Do you feel that when somebody your age wants to be your enemy, there's little you can do to change matters?   ❏ Yes   ❏ No

34. Do you feel it's easy to get friends to do what you want them to do?
    ❏ Yes   ❏ No

35. Do you usually feel that you have little to say about what you get to eat at home?   ❏ Yes   ❏ No

36. Do you feel that when someone doesn't like you, there's little you can do about it? ❏ Yes   ❏ No

37. Did you usually feel it was almost useless to try in school because most other children were just plain smarter than you were?
    ❏ Yes   ❏ No

38. Are you the kind of person who believes that planning ahead makes things turn out better?
    ❏ Yes   ❏ No

39. Most of the time, do you feel that you have little to say about what your family decides to do?
    ❏ Yes   ❏ No

40. Do you think it's better to be smart than to be lucky?
    ❏ Yes   ❏ No

(continued on next page)

■ SCORING

Place a check mark to the right of each item in the key when your answer agrees with the answer that is shown. Add the check marks to determine your total score.

1. Yes ❑   2. No ❑   3. Yes ❑
4. No ❑   5. Yes ❑   6. No ❑
7. Yes ❑   8. Yes ❑   9. No ❑
10. Yes ❑ 11. Yes ❑ 12. Yes ❑
13. No ❑   14. Yes ❑ 15. No ❑
16. Yes ❑ 17. Yes ❑ 18. Yes ❑
19. Yes ❑ 20. No ❑   21. Yes ❑
22. No ❑   23. Yes ❑ 24. Yes ❑
25. No ❑   26. No ❑   27. Yes ❑
28. No ❑   29. Yes ❑ 30. No ❑
31. Yes ❑ 32. No ❑   33. Yes ❑
34. No ❑   35. Yes ❑ 36. Yes ❑
37. Yes ❑ 38. No ❑   39. Yes ❑
40. No ❑

Total score: _____

■ INTERPRETATION

Low scorers (0–8):
Nearly one student in three receives a score of 0 to 8. These students largely see themselves as responsible for the rewards they obtain or do not obtain in life.

Average scorers (9–16):
Most students receive from 9 to 16 points. These students view themselves as partially in control of their lives. Perhaps they view themselves as in control academically but not socially, or vice versa.

High scorers (17–40):
Nearly 15% of students receive scores of 17 or higher. These students view life largely as a game of chance. They see success as a matter of luck or a product of the kindness of others.

GROUP ACTIVITY OPTION

What is *one area* in which you feel you can influence and control people and events? With others in a small group, discuss this area and the feelings of mastery and power it gives you. Discuss whether you think this control and influence could be applied to your academic work in college.

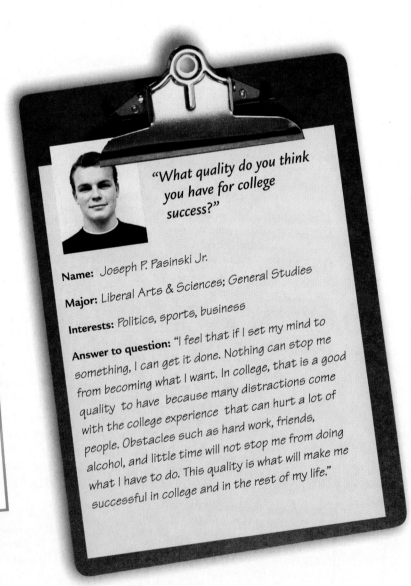

"What quality do you think you have for college success?"

Name: Joseph P. Pasinski Jr.

Major: Liberal Arts & Sciences; General Studies

Interests: Politics, sports, business

Answer to question: "I feel that if I set my mind to something, I can get it done. Nothing can stop me from becoming what I want. In college, that is a good quality to have because many distractions come with the college experience that can hurt a lot of people. Obstacles such as hard work, friends, alcohol, and little time will not stop me from doing what I have to do. This quality is what will make me successful in college and in the rest of my life."

Studies have shown that people who have an internal locus of control—that is, low scores in Personal Exploration #2.3—are able to achieve more in school than people with an external locus of control.[7] They are also able to delay gratification, are more independent, and are better able to cope with various stresses.[8] Some people may have both an internal and external locus of control, depending on their situation. For instance, they may feel they can control their lives at home but not in the workplace.

OPTIMISM. "Mom, where are all the jerks today?" asks the young girl as she and her mother are driving along. "Oh," says the mother, slightly surprised. "They're only on the road when your father drives."

Therapist Alan McGinnis tells this story to make a point: "If you expect the world to be peopled with idiots and jerks, they start popping up."[9]

Are you an optimist, or are you what some people like to call a "realist" when they actually mean a pessimist? Perhaps optimism is related to matters of personal control. Pessimists may be overwhelmed by their problems, whereas optimists are challenged by them, according to McGinnis, author of *The Power of Optimism*.[10] Optimists "think of themselves as problem-solvers, as trouble-shooters," he says. This does not mean they see everything through rose-colored glasses. Rather they have several qualities that help them have a positive attitude while still remaining realistic and tough-minded. *(See ■ Panel 2.1.)*

CREATIVITY. The capacity for creativity and spontaneity, said psychologist Abraham Maslow, is an important attribute of the psychologically healthy person. This attribute is not limited to some supposed *artistic* class of people; it is built into all of us. Creativity refers to the human capacity to express ourselves in original or imaginative ways. It may also be

PANEL 2.1

ptimism. Twelve characteristics of tough-minded optimists.

OPTIMISTS . . .

1. Are seldom surprised by trouble.

2. Look for partial solutions.

3. Believe they have control over their future.

4. Allow for regular renewal.

5. Interrupt their negative trains of thought.

6. Heighten their powers of appreciation.

7. Use their imaginations to rehearse success.

8. Are cheerful even when they can't be happy.

9. Believe they have an almost unlimited capacity for stretching.

10. Build lots of love into their lives.

11. Like to swap good news.

12. Accept what cannot be changed.

thought of as the process of discovery. As Nobel Prize–winning physician Albert Szent-Györgyi expressed it, "Discovery consists of looking at the same thing as everyone else and thinking something different."[11]

Being creative means having to resist pressure to be in step with the world. It means looking for several answers, not the "one right answer," as is true of math problems. As Roger von Oech, founder of a creativity consulting company, puts it: "Life is ambiguous; there are many right answers—all depending on what you are looking for."[12] It means forgetting about reaching a specific goal, because the creative process can't be forced. One should, in von Oech's phrase, think of the mind as "a compost heap, not a computer," and use a notebook to collect ideas.

ABILITY TO TAKE PSYCHOLOGICAL RISKS. I am not endorsing the kind of risk-taking (such as drug taking or fast driving) that might jeopardize your health. I'm only concerned with situations in which what is at risk is mainly your pride. That is, the main consequences of failure are personal embarrassment or disappointment. This kind of risk-taking—having the courage to feel the fear and then proceeding anyway—is a requirement for psychological health.

Consider failure: None of us is immune to it. Some of us are shattered but bounce back quickly. Others of us take longer to recover, especially if the failure has changed our lives in a significant way. But what is failure, exactly? Carole Hyatt and Linda Gottlieb, authors of *When Smart People Fail*, point out that the word has two meanings. First, it is a term for an event, such as failing a test or not getting a part in a play or not making the team. Second, it is a *judgment you make about yourself*—"so that 'failure' may also mean not living up to your own expectations."[13] The first type of failure—the actual event—you may not be able to do anything about. The second, however, is something you can do something about. For instance, you can use your own inner voice—your "self-talk"—to affect your judgment about yourself.

> ## "Discovery consists of looking at the same thing as everyone else and thinking something different."

(For example, "I didn't get the part because I'm better suited to playing comedies than tragedies.")

One characteristic of many peak performers, according to psychologist Charles Garfield, is that they continually *reinvent* themselves. The late jazz musician Miles Davis, for example, constantly changed his musical direction in order to stay fresh and vital. Novelist James Michener takes himself on a new adventure of travel and research with every book he writes.[14]

WHAT ARE YOUR POSITIVE QUALITIES?

Make a list of all the things you like about yourself. Recall instances where you really felt good about who you were and what you were doing. Then, in a small-group setting, discuss some of these qualities. See how they compare to the qualities for success described in the foregoing section.

Find something that you like about each person in the group and compliment that person. Because you may not know others in the group very well, you may want to make the compliments about the person's looks, clothes, or jewelry. Try to think of other things to compliment as well, such as posture, manner of speaking, or quality of ideas expressed.

Discuss how you feel about being complimented. Do you tend to discount a compliment because of feelings of weak self-esteem? Do you tend to brag about yourself—also because of low self-esteem?

Discuss whether your parents or others who raised you frequently praised you or frequently criticized or punished you. Do you think their general behavior toward you affected your positive or negative view of yourself?

Setting Higher-Education Goals from Life Goals

PREVIEW The six-step strategy called "Essentials for Time & Life Management" describes how to set daily tasks from life goals. The first step is to determine your ultimate goals.

We make decisions all the time. *Taking* action is making a decision. So is *not taking* action. There's nothing wrong with inaction and aimlessness, if that's what you want to do, but realize that aimlessness is a choice like any other. Most first-year students find out, however, that college works better if they have a program of aims. The following pages tell you how to set up such a program.

ESSENTIALS FOR TIME & LIFE MANAGEMENT: SETTING DAILY TASKS FROM LIFE GOALS. Essentials for Time & Life Management is a six-step program for translating your life goals into daily tasks. *(See ■ Panel 2.2, next page.)* The idea is to make your most important desires and values a *motivational force* for helping you manage your time every day.

In Chapter 4, you will see how you can apply these steps and employ them as strategies for time management. Here let us do just the first step.

STEP 1: WHY AM I IN COLLEGE? Why are you here? Even if you haven't picked a major yet—even if you're still a "searcher," which is perfectly all right—it's important to at least *think* about your long-range goals, your *life goals.*

These goals should be more than just "I want to get a college education" or "I want a degree so I can make a lot of money." You need ultimate goals but not goals that are too general. Better to state the goals not in terms of surpassing other people—for there will always be people yet to be surpassed—but rather

The six-step "Essentials for Time & Life Management." The steps for transforming your life goals into daily tasks are as follows:

- **Step 1:** The planning process starts when you answer the question "Why am I in college?"—that is, define your life goals or long-range goals.

- **Step 2:** You then proceed to "What are my plans?"—setting your intermediate-range goals.

- **Step 3:** This leads to "What are my actions?"—the steps you will take to achieve your goals.

- **Step 4:** "What is my master timetable?" In this step you set your schedule for the semester or quarter.

- **Step 5:** "What is my weekly timetable?" This is the schedule you follow from week to week.

- **Step 6:** "What is on the To Do list today?" This is the errand list or "things to do" list that is no different from the To Do list that millions of people make every day.

What you want college to help you do in life

1. Why am I in college? (Long-range goals)

2. What are my plans? (Intermediate-range goals)

3. What are my actions? (Steps to implement goals)

4. What is my master timetable?

5. What is my weekly timetable?

6. What is today's To Do list?

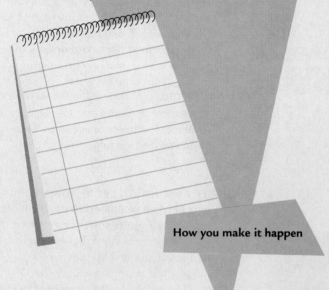

How you make it happen

in terms of fulfilling your own potential. These goals should express *your* most important desires and values—not necessarily what your family wants you to do or what you think society expects of you. (See ■ *Panel 2.3.*)

As I've mentioned, college is not an easy experience. To pull yourself through some difficult times, you will need to know *why* you are doing all this. Now, then, is the time to set down your long-range goals. See Personal Exploration #2.4 below.

PERSONAL EXPLORATION #2.4

WHAT ARE YOUR LONG-RANGE GOALS?

Look back over your lists of reasons for attending college. Do they include what might be considered *life goals*—things you hope college will help you achieve, say, 10 years from now? If not, add some life goals to the list below.

The top five goals I hope college will help me reach are . . .

1._____

_____

2._____

_____

3._____

_____

4._____

_____

5._____

_____

GROUP ACTIVITY OPTION

In a small group, take turns describing your life goals. How do your goals compare to, or differ from, those of others? How will going to college help you reach these goals?

How do the goals in your group compare with those of other small groups in your class?

PANEL 2.3   Examples of life goals.

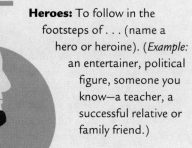

Heroes: To follow in the footsteps of . . . (name a hero or heroine). (*Example:* an entertainer, political figure, someone you know—a teacher, a successful relative or family friend.)

Sacrifice: What is worth sacrificing for and what the sacrifice is. (*Examples:* giving up making a lot of money in order to help people; giving up close family life in order to travel the world.)

Values: What you hold to be most important and dear to you.

Love: How you would express it and to whom.

Family: What its importance is to you at present and in the future.

Security: What the least security is you would settle for financially, emotionally.

Principles: What you would stand up for and base your life on.

Creativity: What things you would like to create.

Curiosity: What questions you want to satisfy.

Personal challenges: What abilities you need to prove about yourself.

Death: What you hope to accomplish in the face of your own mortality.

Onward: Applying This Chapter to Your Life

PREVIEW You are constantly changing.

oing to college is "like moving to a foreign country," says Karen Leven Coburn, an associate dean of students at Washington University in St. Louis. "There's a new landscape, a new culture, and a new language. . . . Even the food is different."[15] For many first-year students, college means making many decisions they have not had to think about much: what to study, who to hang out with, when to eat and sleep. There are anxieties about money, about succeeding in school, about finding new friends, about relations with their family. No wonder it has been said that the first college year "is punctuated by feelings of panic and incompetence."

The important thing to keep in mind is that, regardless of your present self-image, you are *constantly changing*. If you have negative beliefs about yourself, the way you see yourself today need not be the way you see yourself tomorrow or in future years. By keeping yourself open to new information and experiences, you can change your self-image so that most of the traits by which you identify yourself will be positive.

Now, before you wrap up the reading of this chapter, try to take something away from it so that you feel as though you "own" it—have made it yours. That is, if you were allowed to keep *only one idea*, what would it be and why would you want to keep it? Write it down here:

_____

_____

_____

_____

_____

_____

_____

THE EXAMINED LIFE:
YOUR JOURNAL

Why are you here? What is your fear? These are two of the most important questions you can consider in college. Write in your journal at least 25 words about each of these matters. Then write down what you consider to be the personal strengths that will help see you through.

3

resources

the campus gold mine

you can find assistance, opportunities, & diversity everywhere

IN THIS CHAPTER: In this chapter discover three treasure troves to be found on your campus:

■ *Assistance:* How to find help—for your studies, health, emotions, finances, and other matters.

■ *Opportunities:* How to get extra value with your education—in activities, student life, and living arrangements.

■ *Diversity:* How to see through the eyes of people different from you—in gender, age, race, ethnicity, nationality, religion, and ability.

MAKING THIS CHAPTER WORK FOR YOU

1. Think of two problems that might give you trouble in completing this college term. Identify them here (use shorthand, if you like):

_____

_____

_____

_____

2. Next, identify two situations that give you real pleasure:

_____

_____

_____

_____

3. Finally, describe an incident in which your age, race, religion, or nationality caused some difficulty. Write about it here:

_____

_____

_____

_____

SKIMMING FOR PAYOFFS

Now skim this chapter looking for payoffs. These might be resources, ideas, or insights that might help you with the areas you described above. For example, you might want help with money or child care. Put check marks in the margin near the things that interest you.

HELP!

That's a word we've all used at some point. Or certainly wanted to.

Often help is easy to ask for and easy to get. ("Am I in the right line?") At other times, however, *Help!* may be the silent cry of a student overwhelmed by homesickness, loneliness, test anxiety, family problems, or money worries. Is help available for these sorts of matters? The answer is: You bet!

Unfortunately, sometimes people with a problem can't imagine there's a way out. That's why I've put this chapter early in the book. Its purpose is to show what kind of assistance is available *before* you need it.

In addition, I wanted to give you the chance to find out what a gold mine college is outside of the classroom. Many college graduates treasure lifelong friendships they made while in school. Many also still practice athletic, musical, and other skills they developed at that time. To help you do the same, we will look at opportunities college gives you to make these connections.

Finally, people in the 21st century will be exposed to far more cultural diversity than was true in the past. Thus, we will look at ways you can use college to learn to get along with people different from you. By "different" I mean different in all ways—in dress, gender, age, religion, skin color, nationality, sexual preference, cultural tastes, and so on.

A Tour of the Campus: Let's Go on a Scavenger Hunt!

PREVIEW Finding out about campus services resembles going on a scavenger or treasure hunt. The orientation program and campus tour for new students is a good way to start. Helpful publications include the college catalog, campus map, student handbook, campus newspaper and bulletins, course lists and instructor evaluations, brochures and posters. Areas of assistance include academic help; physical, emotional, and spiritual help; other college help; activities and campus life; and community services.

erhaps you've heard of scavenger hunts, even if you've never been on one. A scavenger hunt is a party game. People are sent out to acquire, within a time limit and without paying money, items that take some difficulty to obtain. The list is provided by the party's host. The items might include a picture frame, a hotel DO NOT DISTURB sign, an old Grateful Dead LP, and a Christmas-tree ornament (in July).

In this chapter, let's pretend you're participating in a scavenger hunt. The goal of the hunt is to visit various campus facilities. The purpose? To demonstrate that all kinds of services and opportunities are available to help you survive, enjoy, and derive extra value from college. (It's up to your instructor to make this an actual scavenger hunt as a class assignment. He or she may ask you to do Personal Exploration #3.3, presented later in the chapter.)

THE ORIENTATION PROGRAM & CAMPUS TOUR. Many colleges offer an orientation program and tour of the campus for new students. However, some facilities and services may be left off the tour (because of time). Or you may not find some of them personally interesting or currently valuable to you. Still, if you have a chance to take the tour, I urge you to do so. You may sometime need to know where to go to get permission to skip a course or get into one already started. Or you may need to get information to resolve a tenant-landlord hassle or other problem.

Obviously, if you've already had a campus tour or orientation, you'll be better able to get through the scavenger hunt.

PUBLICATIONS: WHAT YOU NEED FOR THE HUNT. There are various publications that you'll need for the scavenger hunt, as well as for your college career:

- *College catalog:* Publications are a great way to learn about all aspects of campus life. Probably the most valuable is the college catalog, which is the playbook or rule book for the game of higher education. **The *college catalog* contains requirements for graduation, requirements for degree programs, and course descriptions.** It also may contain a history of the school, information about faculty members, and various programs and services. In addition, it may contain information about financial aid.

  The college catalog is most likely available in the Admissions Office, Counseling Office, or campus bookstore.

- *Campus calendar:* **Of particular value is the *campus calendar*, which lists the deadlines and dates for various programs.** You'll particularly want to note the last days to enroll in a new course and to drop a course without penalty. The campus calendar may be included in the college catalog.

- **Campus map:** Many college catalogs include a map of the campus, but if yours does not, pick up one. You might wish to have a one-page map anyway because it's easier to carry around.

- **Student handbook:** Some colleges publish a _student handbook_, **which summarizes many of the college's policies and regulations.** This may duplicate information in the catalog but be written so as to be more accessible to students.

- **College newspaper and campus bulletins:** **The _college newspaper_ is a student-run news publication that is published on some campuses.** The college newspaper may be the single best source of ongoing information. Depending on the campus, it may be published daily, twice a week, weekly, or every two weeks. Because its readership is the entire college community—students, staff, faculty, and possibly townspeople—the news may cover topics of broad interest. In addition, some colleges publish a special "Orientation Edition" of the paper as a service to new students.

  On some campuses, there may also be a student bulletin. **The _student bulletin_, or _campus bulletin_, is helpful in keeping you informed of campus activities and events,** as well as other matters. This periodical, appearing occasionally throughout the term, may be published by the student government or by an office of the administration.

- **Course lists and instructor evaluations:** **The _course list_ is simply a list of the courses being taught in the current school term.** Published before each new term, the course list states what courses are being taught. The list states on what days at what times courses are given, for how many units, and by what instructor.

  Sometimes the instructor is simply listed as "Staff." This may mean he or she is a teaching assistant (often a graduate student). Or it may mean that the instructor was simply unassigned at the time the course list was printed. Call the department if you want to know who the instructor is.

On some campuses, students publish instructor evaluations. **_Instructor evaluations_ consider how fairly instructors grade and how effectively they present their lectures.** If your campus does not have such evaluations, you may be able to sit in on a potential instructor's class. You can also talk with other students there to get a feel for his or her style and ability. In addition, you can find out what degrees an instructor has and from what institutions, usually by looking in the college catalog.

- **Brochures, flyers, and posters:** Especially during orientation or when registering, you may find yourself flooded with brochures. You may also see flyers and posters on campus bulletin boards.

  Some of these may be on serious and important personal subjects. Examples are security and night escorts to parked cars, alcohol and other drug abuse, and date rape. Some may be on campus events and club offerings. Some may simply list apartments to share or rides wanted. Some may list upcoming concerts, political rallies, or film festivals.

  Most of this kind of information has to do with the informal or extracurricular side of your college experience. Much of this is as important as the purely academic part. Indeed, many prospective employers look at this extracurricular side to see how well rounded a student's educational experience has been.

  To begin to get familiar with the college catalog, do Personal Exploration #3.1.

LEARNING TO USE YOUR COLLEGE CATALOG

O btain a copy of your college catalog. Fill in the answers in the following lines.

A. GENERAL

1. How many undergraduate students are enrolled?_____

2. When was the college founded?_____

3. What is the mission, orientation, or specialization of the college? (Examples: liberal arts, religious values, teacher training.)
_____
_____
_____
_____

4. How is the institution organized? (Example: schools, with divisions and departments.)
_____
_____
_____

5. What are three graduate or professional programs offered by the college, if any, that interest you? (Examples: teacher certification, business, law.)
_____
_____
_____

6. What are some other campuses or sites the college has, including extension divisions, if any?
_____
_____
_____

7. Look at the lists of majors and minors offered by the college. Which three majors might interest you?
_____
_____
_____

   Which three minors might interest you?
_____
_____
_____

8. Is it possible to graduate with more than one major? If so, which two might interest you?
_____
_____
_____
_____

B. THE CAMPUS CALENDAR

1. *Cut-off dates:* What is the last date this semester on which you may ... (specify month and day)

   Add a course?_____

   Drop a course?_____

   Drop a course and receive partial tuition refund?_____

   Ask for a grade of "Incomplete," if offered?_____

   Withdraw from a course?_____

2. *Holidays:* On what holidays is the college closed this semester?
_____
_____
_____

3. *Registration:* What are the dates for registration for next semester?
_____
_____

4. *Exams:* When are final exams scheduled for this semester?
_____
_____

5. *Class end and start dates:*

   What is the last day of classes for this semester?_____

   What is the first day of classes for next semester?_____

C. TUITION & FINANCIAL AID

1. What is the annual tuition for in-state students at the college? _____ For out-of-state students? _____

2. What financial aid is available? (Examples: loans, scholarships, work/study.)
_____
_____

D. GRADES

1. Grades instructors give (such as A, B, C, D, F) and what they mean:
_____
_____

2. Meaning of "Pass/fail," if offered:
_____
_____

3. Meaning of "Incomplete," if offered:
_____
_____

4. Meaning of "Audit":
_____
_____
_____

5. What minimum grade-point average do you need to maintain in order to be considered in satisfactory academic standing?
_____

6. What happens if you fall below that minimum?
_____
_____
_____

E. CREDITS

1. What is the definition of a credit (or unit)?
_____
_____
_____

2. Does your college give credit for advanced courses taken in high school? _____ For courses taken at other colleges? _____

   For some life experience outside of college? _____

(continued on next page)

■ F. GRADE-POINT AVERAGE & GRADUATION REQUIREMENTS

1. Explain the formula for comput-ing students' grade-point average:

    _____
    _____
    _____
    _____

2. List the courses you are taking this semester or quarter and the number of credits (units) for each.

    _____
    _____
    _____
    _____
    _____
    _____

    For each course assign a hypo-thetical grade according to the following formula: A = 4.0, B = 3.0, C = 2.0, D = 1.0, F = 0.0. Then compute the grade points earned for each course. (Example for one course: "First-Year Experi-ence, 3 credits, grade of A = 4.0; 4.0 x 3 credits = 12 grade points.")

    Now add up your grade points earned for all courses. Finally, divide them by the total number of credits (units) attempted to derive your hypothetical grade-point average for the semester or quarter.

_____
_____
_____
_____
_____

3. What minimum grade-point aver-age is required for graduation?

    _____
    _____

4. Besides completing a major, what are the other requirements for graduation?

    _____
    _____
    _____

■ G. MISCONDUCT

1. *Academic matters:* How does the college deal with cheating and plagiarism? (Plagiarism is passing off someone else's work as your own, as when writing a paper.)

    _____
    _____
    _____
    _____

2. *Nonacademic matters:* How does the college deal with nonacademic matters such as sexual harass-ment, drunkenness, property damage, or off-campus arrests?

_____
_____
_____
_____
_____

■ H. SPECIAL PROGRAMS

1. *Academic honors:* What forms of recognition does the college offer for academic excellence? What are the standards for achieving such honors? (Examples: honors programs, dean's list, Phi Beta Kappa, scholarships.)

    _____
    _____
    _____
    _____
    _____
    _____

2. *Other special programs:* What other special programs are offered, and what are the criteria for participa-tion? (Examples: study-abroad programs, internships.)

SOME PARTICULARLY IMPORTANT PLACES TO KNOW ABOUT. There are three places on campus that, in my opinion, a newcomer should get to know right away:

■ *The library:* Most new students don't understand how to use the library and are unaware of the scope of its services. When it comes to writing papers, this is the place to know about.

■ *The learning center:* This is the place for learning specific subjects or skills (for example, word processing or math help). You can also get tutoring in most subjects here. The learning center is an invalu-able resource.

■ *The career counseling center:* If you're undecided about your major, the career counseling center is the place to go. This can save you from going down a lot of blind alleys. Even students who have already chosen a major can benefit from this place, which can help them focus their efforts.

Complete Personal Exploration #3.1. Then on a separate piece of paper list a feature or two of the college that you're still not quite clear on. Also list some resources you might be interested in. They may include matters related to grades, majors, and graduation. They may also include nonacademic matters that will help you enjoy your college experience.

In a small-group setting discuss anything you're still unsure or confused about. Ask other members of the group what their understanding is. Also discuss those matters you'd like to investigate further.

Which things discussed by your group are particularly interesting or noteworthy? Designate someone to describe them to the class.

FIVE ADDITIONAL IMPORTANT SERVICES OR CENTERS. There are five additional areas of services or centers, as I will describe in this chapter.

- *Academic help:* Examples are instructors, academic advisors and counselors, librarians, and tutors.

- ***Physical, emotional, and spiritual help:*** Examples are health and fitness professionals, counselors, psychotherapists, security personnel, and chaplains. In addition, there are probably support groups (as for adult returning students or single parents, for example).

- *Other help:* Examples are financial affairs, housing office, career counseling and placement, child care, and legal services. There are also various community services, such as post office, laundry, and bank.

- ***Activities and campus life:*** Examples are athletics, clubs, bands and other musical groups, and fraternities and sororities.

- ***Multicultural centers:*** Examples are centers for racial and ethnic groups, women, international students, gays and lesbians, nontraditional students, and students with disabilities.

GOING ON A SCAVENGER HUNT—WHAT TO DO

Divide into teams of two. Visit at least one advisor, service, facility, or center from each of the five areas mentioned above. You're urged to follow your curiosity. Visit areas that you would probably not visit were it not for this opportunity. Find out what the facility or center offers or does.

Bring back evidence of your visit for your instructor. (For example, you might bring back a free leaflet, someone's business card, or a one-sentence note from someone you met.) Attach the evidence to a one-page report (composed by both of you) of where you went and what you learned.

Academic Help

PREVIEW People who can assist you with academic problems are academic advisors, instructors, librarians and media center staff, and tutors and study-skills staff. Other academic services include the computer center, music practice rooms, and the Dean of Students office. Academic advising—which is principally about degrees, majors, and courses—is extremely important because it affects your college, career, and life plans.

Some day you may return to college as a retired person and *actually take some courses for the fun of it.* Older people often do this. I assume, however, that you are the type of student for whom "fun" is not the main priority of the college experience. That is, you are here on the serious mission of getting a degree.

Obtaining a college degree—whether associate's, bachelor's, master's, or other—is the goal, of course, of the academic part of college. The degree signifies that you have passed certain courses with a minimum grade. Completing the courses means that you have passed tests, written research papers, done projects, and so on. To accomplish all these, you must have attended classes, listened to lectures, gone to the library, and read a lot. Hopefully, while you're having to jump through all these hoops, learning is also taking place.

POSSIBLE ACADEMIC DIFFICULTIES. The problem with accomplishing these tasks is that there are many places where hangups can occur—and where you might need some help. Here are some possibilities: You can't get the classes you want. You wonder if you can waive some prerequisites. You don't know what you still need to do to graduate. You're having trouble with your writing, math, or study skills. You're sick and can't finish your courses. You don't know how to compute your grade-point average. You need recommendations for an employer or a graduate school.

Knowing how to find help, get good advice, and cut through bureaucratic red tape aren't skills that become obsolete after college. They are part and parcel of being A Person Who Can Get Things Done, which is what we all wish to be. Learning how to find your way around the college academic system, then, is training for life. Outside college, these skills are called *networking* and *troubleshooting—and they are invaluable in helping you get where you want to go.*

To get help or advice in college, you may need to consult the following academic services or people:

- Academic advisors
- Instructors
- Librarians and media-center staff
- Tutors and study-skills staff
- Some other academic services
- When all other help fails: the Dean of Students office

ACADEMIC ADVISORS. What people will you deal with the most for academic matters? Probably your instructors. But there is another individual who, in the grand scheme of things, could be *more* important: your academic advisor. Why? "For most freshmen, the first year of college is both exciting and crisis oriented," say one pair of writers. "New students are unfamiliar with college resources, their major field, the faculty, course work, academic expectations, and career applications of their major." [1] Thus, *academic advising is important because it affects your planning for college and beyond that for your career and for your life.*

The _academic advisor_ counsels students about their academic program. The academic advisor is either a full-time administrative employee or a faculty member, often in the field in which you'll major. What does he or she do that I think is so important? There are two principal activities:

■ *Gives information about degrees, majors, and courses:* The academic advisor explains to you what courses are required in your degree program. The *degree program* **consists of all the courses you must take to obtain a college degree in a specific field.** Courses will be of two types:

(1) *General education courses* are those specified in the college catalog that all students have to take to obtain a degree. Examples are a choice of some courses in social science (as in sociology, political science) or in humanities (as in English, philosophy).

(2) *Courses in your major* will be those offered, from another list, that are needed for you to complete your major. **Your *major* is your field of specialization.** Perhaps a third of the courses you need to graduate will be in this category. Some colleges also require a *minor*, **a smaller field of specialization**, which will entail fewer courses.

Both general-education courses and the courses for your major are identified on a *curriculum worksheet*, available to you and your advisor. **The *curriculum worksheet* lists all the courses required for the major and the semesters in which it is recommended you take them**. It may also list additional courses you might have to take if you transfer from a community college to a university. The accompanying example shows a curriculum worksheet for Hotel Technology: Hospitality Management, which is offered at the college at which I teach. (See ■ *Panel 3.1.*)

■ *Provides information, advice, and support in general:* Academic advisors are usually also available to talk about other matters important to you. These include difficulty keeping up with course work, uncertainty about your major, worries about fair treatment by an instructor, and personal stresses. If an advisor does not feel capable of helping you directly, he or she can certainly suggest where to turn. (You may be directed to a counselor, who is different from an advisor.)

PANEL 3.1

A curriculum worksheet. This example, which shows the courses required and their recommended order, is for a major in Hotel Technology: Hospitality Management.

Using your advisor for college success.

Like everything else in college, you get out of academic advising what you put into it. Here are some tips for using your advisor to make college work best for you:

Be aware of the advising period—see the catalog: The college requires students at least once a semester or quarter to see their advisors about which courses they will take the next term. The period for doing this, often about two weeks, is usually listed on the academic calendar in the college catalog and is announced in the campus newspaper and elsewhere. *Put the dates of the advising period on your personal calendar and be sure to make an appointment to see your advisor.*

See your advisor more than once a term to establish a relationship: Your advisor is not just a bureaucrat who has to sign off on your courses and should not be treated as such. See him or her at least one other time during the semester or quarter to discuss problems and progress. Ask about interesting courses, interesting professors, any possible changes in major, and difficult courses and how to handle them. Discuss any personal problems affecting your life and work. *In short, if possible, make your advisor a mentor—a person you can trust.*

If your advisor isn't right for you, find another one: If you feel your advisor is distant, uncaring, arrogant, ignorant, or otherwise unsuitable, don't hesitate to make a change. You have this right, although you have to be your own advocate here. *To make a change, ask another instructor or staff person to be your advisor.* Depending on the arrangements on your campus, you may get another advisor by going to the Advisement Center, the Registrar, the Office of Student Services, or the Dean of Students.

■ Here's an important fact: *poor academic advising is a major reason students drop out of college.*[2] Conversely, students who receive good academic advising are not only more apt to graduate but also are happier while in college. For students in community colleges planning to go on to a university, seeing an academic advisor can save them headaches later. This is because different colleges and universities sometimes have different transfer requirements. Thus, it's possible to end up spending extra semesters taking courses at the junior or senior level that you could have completed earlier. An academic advisor can help you avoid such time wasters.

When you enter college, an academic advisor will be assigned to you. Later, if you change majors or if you go from being "Undecided" or "Undeclared" to declaring your major, you may change advisors. When I was in college, I changed from being a philosophy major to undeclared to sociology major. Each time I was assigned a new academic advisor.

Students should see their academic advisor *at least* once a semester or quarter. You should also see him or her whenever you have any questions or important decisions to make about your college career. *(See ■ Panel 3.2.)*

INSTRUCTORS. You will have many instructors, and they can be valuable resources to you. College instructors and high-school teachers have different kinds of training and different emphases on teaching, as follows.

■ *Training in teaching:* You may have been bored by some of your high-school teachers, but, believe it or not, all such teachers have actually had training in how to teach. College instructors, on the other hand, often have not, unless they are former high-school teachers. (Some graduate students are required to take a course in teaching.)

- **Years of study:** Most high-school teachers have earned a teaching credential on top of a bachelor's degree (B.A. or B.S.), representing a minimum of four to five years of schooling.

  Full-time college instructors usually have at least a master's degree (M.A. or M.S.), which represents one or two years of study after the bachelor's degree. Many professors—those you might address as "Doctor"—have a *doctorate* or Ph.D. or Ed.D. degree. (Ph.D. stands for "Doctor of Philosophy," although the degree is given for all subject areas in addition to philosophy. Ed.D. stands for "Doctor of Education.") To earn this degree, instructors must take additional courses and spend several years researching and writing a doctoral dissertation. This dissertation is a book-length investigation of a specific subject.

  Part-time college instructors may also have master's or doctoral degrees. Or they may be graduate students (called *teaching assistants*, or "T.A.'s"). Or they may be people from another campus or the nonacademic world (called *adjunct professors*) teaching special courses. Their years of study may be about the same as those of most high-school teachers. (These instructors may be addressed as "Mr." or "Ms." or "Professor.")

- **Mission—teaching or research?** High-school teachers teach—that's their principal job. That's also the principal mission of *some*, but not all, college instructors. It depends on what kind of institution of higher learning you're attending.

  For example, professors in two-year colleges—community colleges or junior colleges—are hired mainly to teach. A full-time instructor may teach four or five courses a week. The same is true in vocational-technical schools.

  However, the teaching demands for professors in four-year colleges may not be so explicit. Teaching may indeed be the main mission of an instructor at a private liberal-arts college or even at some state universities. (These are institutions that grant bachelor's and master's degrees and sometimes doctorates.) However, for the really large and/or top-flight state or private universities, teaching is *not* the main emphasis for professors. Rather, research, writing, and publishing are.

  The biggest difference between taking courses in high school and in college is: *more is expected of you in college.* College, after all, is designed more to treat you as an adult. Thus, you have more adult freedoms than were probably allowed you in high school. For example, many instructors do not take daily attendance. Moreover, they may not check your assignments on a daily basis. Thus, you are expected to do more of your work on your own.

  Still, instructors are among the academic resources available to you. All college faculty members are required to be in their offices during certain hours. (Hours are posted on their office doors and/or are available as course handouts or through the department secretary.) In addition, many are available for questions a minute or so after class. You may also be able to make appointments with them at other times. (Be sure to make a note of the time of the appointment. Telephone the instructor if you can't keep it.)

  The instructor is the one to see if you have a question or problem about the course you are taking. These include which books to buy, what readings a test will cover, anything you don't understand about an assignment or a test question. Don't be afraid to ask. And if you begin to have trouble in a course, don't wait until the test. See your instructor as soon as possible.

INTERVIEWING AN INSTRUCTOR

The purpose of this 10- to 15-minute Personal Exploration is to introduce you personally to one of your instructors. This will give you practice in talking to faculty members. The interview will enable you to see what kind of people they are and what their expectations are of students.

■ WHAT TO DO

Select one of the instructors at the college. It can be one in a course you are now taking. Or it can be someone in a field that you are thinking of majoring in. Or it can be your faculty advisor.

Telephone that instructor, and explain that you are doing a class assignment for the course. Ask if he or she can spare 10 or 15 minutes of time for a brief interview. Make an appointment to meet. Review the interview questions below and add two of your own.

Note: Instructors are busy people, so be sure to hold your interview to 10–15 minutes.

■ QUESTIONS FOR THE INTERVIEW

Fill in the following blanks.

Name of instructor being interviewed:

_____

_____

Department in which instructor teaches. (Example: Business.)

_____

_____

1. What is your particular discipline? (Example: Management.)

_____

_____

_____

2. What is your area of specialization or research?

_____

_____

_____

_____

_____

3. What are your other interests or hobbies?

_____

_____

_____

_____

_____

_____

_____

4. Why did you choose to teach in this particular discipline?

_____

_____

_____

_____

_____

_____

5. What kind of undergraduate and graduate degrees do you have, and where did you receive them?

_____

_____

_____

_____

_____

_____

6. Why did you decide to teach at this college?

_____

_____

_____

_____

_____

_____

7. Ask a question of your own. (Example: "What do you think are the characteristics of a good student?")

Your question:

_____

_____

_____

_____

_____

_____

The instructor's answer:

_____

_____

_____

_____

_____

_____

_____

_____

_____

8. If there's time, ask another question of your own. (Example: "What do you think are the characteristics of a bad student?")

Your question:

_____

_____

_____

_____

The instructor's answer:

_____

_____

_____

_____

_____

_____

_____

_____

Thank the instructor for his or her time.

GROUP ACTIVITY OPTION

Conduct Personal Exploration #3.2 in teams of two. Report back to the class two of the most interesting questions and their answers. Or write up your results as a report.

LIBRARIANS & MEDIA-CENTER STAFF. Perhaps you think the library is just a quiet place with books and magazines where you can go to study. Actually, there is more to it than that. *One of the first things you should do in college is find out how to use the library.* Often the library has a room or section in it called the *media center.*

The library is one of the most important buildings on campus. Don't be intimidated by all the staff, books, and machines (computer terminals, microfilm readers). Instead, I suggest doing the following:

■ *Tour the facilities:* Go to the library/media center and simply walk around every place you are allowed to go. *Actively* scan the titles on the shelves, looking for books or magazines you're interested in. *Actively* take note of the desks and study areas available, picking out a couple of spots you might favor using later. *Actively* read the directions on how to use machines, such as computers, microfilm readers, and copiers.

■ *Ask how to use the facilities:* Have you ever noticed how some people are so concerned with how they look to others that they never ask directions? Some drivers, for instance, would rather "figure it out for themselves" than stop and ask a local person how to get somewhere.

These folks really limit themselves. People shut off a major source of personal growth when they can't ask for assistance or help.

If you're the kind of person who's reluctant to seek help, here's a good exercise. Ask the librarians or media-center staff for a *demonstration* on how to use the facilities to do research. Sometimes there is a standard guided tour. Ask how to use the computer-based catalog for books and periodicals and how to use microfilm equipment. Ask how to play videotapes or audiotapes in the media center. Ask about other research libraries and facilities on campus.

■ We take a look at libraries and media centers in more detail in Chapter 9, "Communication."

TUTORS & STUDY-SKILLS STAFF. *This is an important, probably underused resource.* Most colleges offer courses or services for improving your reading, writing, math, or study skills. The place for doing this may be located in a learning center. **A *learning center*, or *learning lab*, is a special center where you go to learn a specific subject or skill.** Sometimes learning centers are located in a special building on campus. Sometimes they are attached to various departments, such as foreign-language departments. For example, some foreign-language learning centers have computer terminals or booths with television monitors and earphones for practice purposes.

In addition, you can arrange through the learning center or through academic departments (ask the department secretary) for tutoring help. **A *tutor* is essentially a private teacher or coach.** This person will help you, through a series of regularly scheduled meetings, to improve a particular skill.

SOME OTHER ACADEMIC SERVICES. Other on-campus resources are available to help you with your academic work, ranging from photocopiers to music practice rooms. For example, your campus may have several art resources: museums, art galleries, archives, and special libraries.

Some campuses have computers or a lab in which you may use a personal computer. Computers are useful for such tasks as writing papers (word processing), doing calculations (using spreadsheets), doing computer graphics, and the like. Courses that teach valuable computer skills, such as word processing, are offered through the computer center or academic courses.

WHEN ALL OTHER HELP FAILS: THE DEAN OF STUDENTS OFFICE. If you can't seem to find help for whatever your difficulty is, try the Dean of Students office. It is the *job* of the staff here to see that you are taken care of in college. If they can't handle the problem themselves, they will find someone who will.

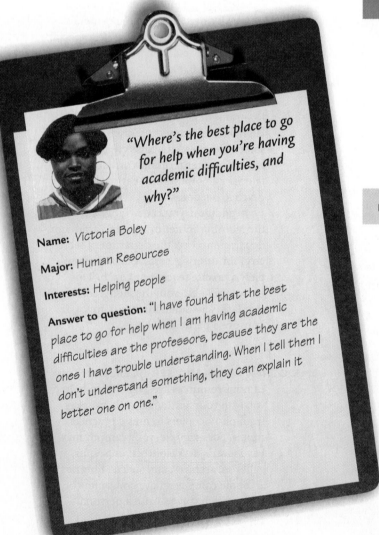

"Where's the best place to go for help when you're having academic difficulties, and why?"

Name: Victoria Boley

Major: Human Resources

Interests: Helping people

Answer to question: "I have found that the best place to go for help when I am having academic difficulties are the professors, because they are the ones I have trouble understanding. When I tell them I don't understand something, they can explain it better one on one."

Physical, Emotional, & Spiritual Help

PREVIEW People to help you take care of your physical, emotional, and spiritual well-being are found in several places. They include the health service, counseling center, security office, chapel, wellness/fitness services, and on-campus and off-campus support groups.

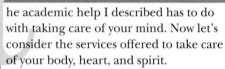

he academic help I described has to do with taking care of your mind. Now let's consider the services offered to take care of your body, heart, and spirit.

The basic facilities and services are:

- Health service
- Counseling center
- Security
- Chapels and religious services
- Wellness/fitness services
- Support groups

HEALTH SERVICE: THE CLINIC OR INFIRMARY. Most colleges have some sort of health or medical service. Treatment is often free or low-cost for minor problems.

If you are attending a large residential campus, there is probably a clinic, health-care center, or infirmary staffed by nurses and physicians. If you go to a college that mainly serves commuters, it may be just a nurse's office. The college assumes that most students' health care will be handled by community hospitals and other resources. However, you can at least get first aid, aspirin, and advice and referrals.

The health service is a good place to go to if you need help with physical problems, of course. In addition, it can help with anxiety, birth-control information, sexually transmitted diseases, and alcohol or other drug problems.

COUNSELING CENTER: PSYCHOLOGICAL SERVICES.

All of us have stresses in our lives, and going to college unquestionably adds to them. If you're sleeping through classes because you dread the subject or are panicky with test anxiety, *don't hesitate to seek help at the counseling center.* Certainly if you feel you're on the verge of flunking for whatever reason, get to the center as quickly as you can. Such counseling is often free or low-cost.

In addition, problems arise that may not have much to do with the academic side of college. These include love relationships, problems with parents and with self-esteem, "Who am I?" identity concerns, pregnancy, and worries about sexually transmitted diseases. Most psychological counselors are familiar with these problems and are able to help.

Psychological distress is as real as physical distress and should not be ignored. Some students worry that it is not cool or it will be seen as an admission of weakness to seek counseling help. Nothing could be further from the truth. People who are unwilling to admit they need help often find their problems "leak out" in other ways. These could include oversleeping, alcohol or other types of drug abuse, or anger toward family or roommates. By refusing to get help, they compound their problems until later they need help even more. Believe me, I speak from experience on this because, besides teaching first-year college-experience courses, I also work as a counselor.

SECURITY: CAMPUS POLICE.

Campus security personnel or police may be most visible in their roles of enforcing parking control—a problem on almost every college campus. However, they do far more than that.

Afraid to walk across campus to your car after a night class? Call campus security to ask for an escort. It's done all the time on many urban campuses. Locked out of your car, residence hall, or locker? Call the campus police. Lost your watch, discovered your room burglarized, been hassled by a drunk, or found yourself

dealing with someone who's been raped? Such problems are the reasons why, unfortunately, campus security exists. *(See ■ Panel 3.3 on page 46.)*

CHAPELS & RELIGIOUS SERVICES.

Residential campuses often have chapels that students may attend for religious services. Even nonreligious students are welcome to go in during quiet times just to meditate. Or they may wish to talk about personal or spiritual problems with the chaplain.

In addition, many campuses have organizations serving students of different religious affiliations. Examples are the Newman Club for those of the Catholic faith and Hillel House for those of the Jewish faith.

WELLNESS/FITNESS SERVICES: ATHLETIC & FITNESS CENTERS.

If you think gymnasiums, field houses, and athletic centers are just for athletes (as I did in my first year), think again. They are supposed to be available for all students, including physically challenged students.

You can use not only lockers, showers, and spas but also pools, fitness centers, weight equipment, racquetball courts, and basketball courts. If your campus is anything like mine, you'll see scores of students jogging or playing or working out every day. And many of them did not take up such activities until they got to college.

SUPPORT GROUPS.

Most colleges offer some sort of connection to support groups of all kinds. There are, for example, support groups for people having difficulties with weight, alcohol, drugs, gambling, incest, spouse abuse, or similar personal problems. There are also support groups or "affinity" groups. (They may exist for women, men, physically challenged, gays, ethnic and racial minorities, returning students, foreign students, and so on.) The counseling center can probably connect you with a support group of interest to you. Or you may see meeting announcements in campus publications.

Tips for staying safe.

Safety is a major issue on many campuses. At your college, you may see posters, brochures, and newspaper articles concerned with such matters as dormitory security, date rape, and use of nighttime escorts to parked cars. The basic piece of advice is: Use common sense about your safety; be alert for trouble. Other safety tips are as follows:

WHEN WALKING, TRAVELING, OR OUT IN PUBLIC:

1. At night or early morning, don't walk alone or jog alone. Stay with groups. Take advantage of campus escort services. Travel in well-populated, well-lighted areas.

2. Don't show money or valuables in public. Discreetly tuck away your cash after using an automated teller machine.

3. On foot: Walk rapidly and look as though you're going somewhere; don't dawdle. If someone makes signs of wanting to talk to you, just keep on going. It's less important that you be polite than that you be safe.

4. In a car: Make sure all doors are locked. Don't open them for anyone you don't know.

WHEN IN YOUR RESIDENCE OR CAMPUS BUILDINGS:

1. Lock your dorm-room or residence doors, even when you go to the shower. Theft is a big problem in some residence halls.

2. Don't let strangers into your residence hall. Ask any stranger the name of the person he or she wants to see.

3. Don't leave backpacks, purses, or briefcases unattended, even in your residence lounge.

IF YOU SENSE YOU MIGHT BE ATTACKED:

1. If you are facing an armed criminal, the risk of injury may be minimized by cooperating with his or her demands. Avoid any sudden movements and give the criminal what he or she wants.

2. If you sense your life is in immediate danger, use any defense you can think of: screaming, kicking, running. Your objective is to get away.

3. In a violent crime, it is generally ineffective for the victim to cry or plead with the attacker. Such actions tend to reinforce the attacker's feeling of power over the victim.

LOCK

Other Kinds of Assistance

PREVIEW Questions about your academic record can be resolved at the registrar's office. Other assistance is available to help with financial aid, housing, transportation, check cashing, job placement, career counseling, day care, and legal services. Alumni organizations can also be interesting resources. Finally, services not found on campus, ranging from post offices to gas stations to church-sponsored student centers, are available in the community.

hen you leave home, going to college can almost be like moving to another town—except that the town's main industry is education. Fortunately, the town's administrators also care about students. Thus, they have set up services to deal with those of your needs that are not academic, physical, emotional, or spiritual.

Among the departments and services available are the following:

- Registrar
- Financial aid
- Housing
- Transportation
- Cashier/Business office
- Job placement
- Career counseling
- Child care
- Legal services
- Community services

REGISTRAR. **The *registrar* is responsible for keeping all academic records.** This is the office you need to seek out if you have questions about whether a grade was recorded correctly. The people there can also answer your inquiries about transcripts, graduation, or transfer from or to another college.

FINANCIAL AID. This is one of the most important offices in the college. If you're putting yourself through school or your family can't support you entirely, you need to get to know this office. Just as its title indicates, **the *financial aid office* is concerned with finding financial aid for students.** Such help can consist of low-interest loans, scholarships, part-time work, and other arrangements.

The workings of financial aid are discussed in Chapter 10, "Money."

HOUSING. No doubt you already have a roof over your head for this semester or quarter. If you're living in a campus residence hall, you probably got there through the housing office when you accepted your admission.

The campus *housing office* helps students find rooms in campus housing (except fraternities and sororities). It also provides listings of off-campus rooms, apartments, and houses for rent in the community. Because landlords probably must meet standards for safety and cleanliness, the housing office may be a better source than advertisements for rentals.

TRANSPORTATION. The transportation office may be part of campus security or the campus police. **The *transportation office* issues permits for parking on campus and gives out information on public transportation and car pools.**

CASHIER/BUSINESS OFFICE. **The *cashier's office* or *business office* is where you go to pay college fees or tuition.** On some campuses you may also be able to cash checks here.

JOB PLACEMENT. **The *job placement office*, or *employment office*, provides job listings from local or campus employers looking for student help.** Most of the jobs are part time. They may range from waiting tables, to handing out equipment in the chemistry lab, to working behind a counter in a store.

CAREER COUNSELING. The _career counseling center_ is the place to find help if you're having trouble deciding on career goals or a major. (It may also be called the _career development center_ or the _career center._) We consider the process of selecting a major and a career in Chapter 13, "The Future."

CHILD CARE. Some colleges offer child-care or day-care facilities for children of adult students and faculty. The centers are usually staffed by professional child-care specialists. They may be assisted by student interns or helpers studying child-related disciplines, such as education or psychology.

LEGAL SERVICES. Larger colleges and universities have a legal-services office to provide information and counseling to students. Naturally, I hope you'll never have to use it. Still, it's good to know where to call if problems such as landlord-tenant disputes, auto accidents, drunk driving, or employment discrimination arise.

COMMUNITY SERVICES. You'll probably want such services as a post office, laundromats, copy centers, automated teller machines, eating places, service stations, and bicycle repair shops. These may exist right on campus, at least at larger colleges. In other places they exist in the community close by the college. You may also be able to find help in consumer organizations, political and environmental organizations, city recreation departments, and YMCAs and YWCAs. Finally, you may need to find such services as off-campus counseling, child care, and legal assistance.

Activities & Campus Life

PREVIEW A great deal of student life centers on the student union, the bookstore, college residences, and clubs and activities.

If colleges consisted only of lecture halls, laboratories, and libraries, they wouldn't be much fun. Much of the fun and energy on a college campus come from the places that are student-centered. These include the student union, the bookstore, student residences, and other centers of student life.

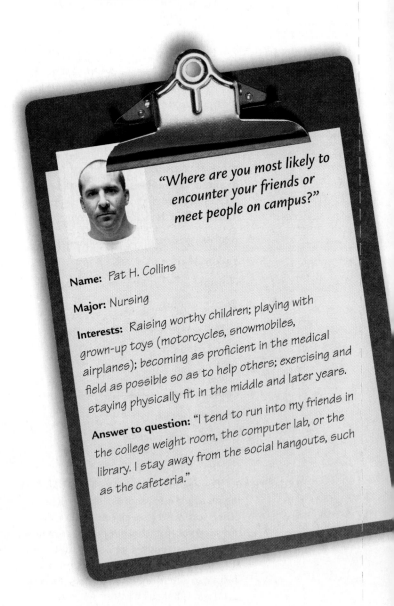

"Where are you most likely to encounter your friends or meet people on campus?"

Name: Pat H. Collins

Major: Nursing

Interests: Raising worthy children; playing with grown-up toys (motorcycles, snowmobiles, airplanes); becoming as proficient in the medical field as possible so as to help others; exercising and staying physically fit in the middle and later years.

Answer to question: "I tend to run into my friends in the college weight room, the computer lab, or the library. I stay away from the social hangouts, such as the cafeteria."

STUDENT UNION. This is often the "crossroads of the campus," the place where you go to hang out after class, to find your friends. **The *student union*, often called the *student center* or *campus center*, is different on every campus. However, it most certainly includes a cafeteria or dining hall and probably some recreation areas.** Recreation may include television rooms, Ping-Pong tables, pool tables, video games, and maybe even a bowling alley. There may also be a bookstore, study lounges, a post office, convenience store, barbershop or hairdresser, and bank or automated teller machine. Here's where you will find bulletin boards advertising everything from films to shared rides.

BOOKSTORE. Often located in the student center, the campus bookstore's main purpose is to make textbooks and educational supplies available for students. Beyond that, it may carry anything from candy, coffee mugs, and college sweatshirts to general-interest books and personal computers. The bookstore also often sells the *college catalog* and the *course list* (if these are not free).

In most college bookstores, you can find textbooks for the courses you're taking by looking for the course number on the shelves. Three tips I try to pass along to my students regarding textbooks are as follows:

- ■ *Check out the books for your courses:* If ever there was a way of getting a preview of your academic work, it is here. Want to know how hard that course in physics or German is going to be? Go to the bookstore and take a look through the textbooks.

- ■ *Buy the books early:* Many students do a lot of course adding and dropping at the beginning of the school term. Thus, they may wait to buy their textbooks until they are sure of what their classes are. Big mistake. Books may be sold out by the time they make up their minds, and new ones may take weeks to arrive. Better to buy the texts, but don't write in them. Hang on to your receipts so that you can return the books later and get your money back.

- ■ *Buy the right edition:* As material becomes outdated, publishers change the editions of their books. If you buy a used version of the assigned text, make sure you get the most recent edition. An out-of-date edition (even for a history book) won't have all the facts you need to know.

In some communities, off-campus bookstores also carry textbooks, both new and used.

COLLEGE RESIDENCES. Some first-year students live at home or in off-campus housing, particularly for commuter schools, such as many community colleges. However, at residential colleges, many first-year students—particularly those of the traditional student age of about 18 or so—live in a campus dormitory. **A *dormitory*, or *residence hall*, is a facility providing rooms, or suites of rooms, for groups of students.** In a typical case, you might share a room with another student. Each dormitory floor would have one community bathroom, if the dorm is single-sex, or two, if it's shared by both sexes.

One good source of advice is the resident assistant. **The *resident assistant*, or RA, is an advisor who lives in the residence hall and is usually a student also.** RAs have been through the same kinds of experiences you are presently undergoing, so they can readily relate to your problems.

Fraternities and sororities may be open to first-year students. However, you probably will have to have "pledged" (chosen to join) during the summer or by the end of the first fall term. I'd advise finding out the *purpose* of a fraternity or a sorority before joining, since they are not all alike. Some, for instance, are more service-oriented than others. Once you're in, however, you may have a network of friends and connections that will be invaluable later in life.

STUDENT LIFE. Whatever your background, there is probably some club, association, or activity on or near the campus that will interest you. Through these you can continue to develop talents discovered

CAMPUS SERVICES & EXTRACURRICULAR ACTIVITIES

This Personal Exploration has two parts. In Part A, you take a walking tour of the campus. In Part B, you explore extracurricular activities of possible interest to you.

A. A WALK AROUND CAMPUS: FINDING IMPORTANT SERVICES

Find the following places, and write down the location and the telephone number for contacting them. (If these places do not exist on your campus, indicate *None* in the space.) Unless your instructor asks you to turn this in, post the list over your desk or near your bed.

■ **LEARNING/TUTORING CENTER**

Building name & room number

_____

_____

Telephone _____

■ **LIBRARY/MEDIA CENTER**

Building name & room number

_____

_____

Telephone _____

■ **YOUR ACADEMIC ADVISOR**

Building name & room number

_____

_____

Telephone _____

■ **DEAN OF STUDENTS**

Building name & room number

_____

_____

Telephone _____

■ **HEALTH SERVICE OR INFIRMARY**

Building name & room number

_____

_____

Telephone _____

■ **COUNSELING CENTER**

Building name & room number

_____

_____

Telephone _____

■ **SECURITY OR CAMPUS POLICE**

Building name & room number

_____

_____

Telephone _____

■ **CHAPEL**

Building name & room number

_____

_____

Telephone _____

■ **REGISTRAR**

Building name & room number

_____

_____

Telephone _____

■ **FINANCIAL AID OFFICE**

Building name & room number

_____

_____

Telephone _____

■ **HOUSING OFFICE**

Building name & room number

_____

_____

Telephone _____

■ **TRANSPORTATION OFFICE**

Building name & room number

_____

_____

Telephone _____

■ **CASHIER/BUSINESS OFFICE**

Building name & room number

_____

_____

Telephone _____

■ **JOB PLACEMENT CENTER**

Building name & room number

_____

_____

Telephone _____

■ **CAREER COUNSELING CENTER**

Building name & room number

_____

_____

Telephone _____

■ **CHILD CARE**

Building name & room number

_____

_____

Telephone _____

■ **LEGAL SERVICES**

Building name & room number

_____

_____

Telephone _____

■ **STUDENT UNION OR CENTER**

Building name & room number

_____

_____

Telephone _____

■ **BOOKSTORE**

Building name & room number

_____

_____

Telephone _____

■ B. LOOKING INTO EXTRA-CURRICULAR ACTIVITIES

Choose three extracurricular activities that you are interested in getting involved in. They might be a club, an athletic event, a community-service organization. The catalog, student newspaper, bulletin, or other information will indicate what's available. Then, for one of the three activities, attend one event or meeting this week. In the following lines, describe what you did, including the names of club officers, performers, or other principals involved.

_____

_____

_____

_____

_____

_____

_____

GROUP ACTIVITY OPTION

Do the first part of this project with another person from your class—someone you don't know. Turn in your written results to your instructor.

before college, such as in music or sports. You can also use them to develop new talents and interests, such as those in theater, politics, or camping.

You can join groups not only simply to have fun but also for two other important reasons. The first is to make friends. The second is to get some experience related to your major. For instance, if you major in journalism, you'll certainly want to work in whatever media are available on campus—newspaper, radio, film, television. The same is true with other majors. This is not just "pretend" stuff. It is valid experience that you'll want to put on your career resume when you go job-hunting later.

Diversity of Genders, Ages, Cultures, Races, & So On: Preparing for the 21st Century

PREVIEW Because of the changing "melting pot," global economy, and electronic communications, you will live in a world that is increasingly culturally and racially diverse. College gives you the opportunity to learn to live with diversity in gender and sexual orientation, age, race and culture, and disabilities.

Three developments ensure that the future will not look the same as the past:

- **Changing "melting pot" (or "salad bowl"):** By the year 2000, it is estimated that white males will make up less than 10% of newcomers to the American workforce. Most new workers will be women, minorities, and recent immigrants.[3] America has always been considered a "melting pot"—or maybe "salad bowl" is a better description—of different races and cultures. However, it seems we will become more so in the near future.

- **Changing world economy:** The American economy is becoming more a part of the world economy. "We are in an unprecedented period of accelerated changes," point out futurists John Naisbitt and Patricia Aburdene. Perhaps the most breathtaking, they say, "is the swiftness of our rush to all the world's becoming a single economy."[4] The American economy is now completely intertwined with the other economies of the world—and therefore with the world's people.

- **Changing electronic communications:** Electronic communications systems—telephones, television, fax machines, computers—are providing a wired and wireless universe that is bringing the cultures of the world closer together. For example, 25 million people around the world already communicate with each other through the Internet. The *Internet* is a global computer-linked network tying together thousands of smaller computer networks.

Many people are not prepared for these changes. Fortunately, many colleges are *multicultural,* **or culturally and racially diverse places.** *Diversity* **means variety—in race, gender, ethnicity, age, physical abilities, and sexual orientation.** College gives you the opportunity to learn to study, work, and live with people different from you. In this way you prepare yourself for life in the 21st century.

In this section, we look at the following kinds of diversity:

- Gender and sexual orientation

- Age

- Race and culture

- Disabilities

GENDER & SEXUAL ORIENTATION. After steady increases over two decades, college enrollments of women now exceed those of men. In 1970 women made up 42% of college enrollment. By 1990 that figure had risen to 55%. Why the dramatic change? One reason, perhaps, is the surge of interest among older women who postponed or never considered college and now are enrolling. Indeed, 49% of women in college are more than 24 years old, compared with 24% of men.[5]

Women have reasons to feel proud of their accomplishments. They get higher grades on average than men do, are awarded more scholarships, and complete bachelor's degrees at a faster pace.[6] However, traditionally they also suffer lower pay and slower advancements after college. Still, with so many women in college, the increased numbers of female graduates could put pressure on employers to change.

Colleges have experienced considerable pressures to develop policies for countering sex stereotypes, sexism, and sexual harassment:

- *Stereotype:* **A** *stereotype* **is an expected or exaggerated expectation about a category of people, which may be completely inaccurate when applied to individuals.** For example, a stereotype is that men are better than women in math and science, or women are better than men in cooking.

- *Sexism:* *Sexism* **is discrimination against individuals based on their gender.** An example is instructors who call more often on men than women (as is frequently the case) to answer questions in class.

- *Sexual harassment:* *Sexual harassment* **consists of sexually oriented behaviors that adversely affect someone's academic or employment status or performance.** Examples are requests for sexual favors, unwelcome sexual advances, or demeaning sexist remarks.

Colleges and universities have also been trying to improve the climate for homosexuals, or gays and lesbians, on their campuses. In recent times, surveys

OBSERVING SEXIST BEHAVIOR

During the next week, write down five instances you've observed personally, or discovered in writing or films, of sexist behavior or attitudes. (Some examples: Males who talk principally to males when in conversation with a male-and-female couple. Male instructors who call on male students more often than female students or call on "good-looking" rather than average-looking female students.)

1._____
_____
_____
_____

2._____
_____
_____
_____
_____
_____

3._____
_____
_____
_____

4._____
_____
_____
_____

5._____
_____
_____
_____

have found freshmen more accepting of gay rights. For example, in 1987 60% of male freshmen said there should be laws prohibiting homosexuality. Four years later only 33% of them still supported such laws.[7]

Most students keep their views on homosexuality to themselves. However, on some campuses, homophobia still exists and may be expressed in active ways. *Homophobia* **is fear of, or resistance to, the idea of homosexuality or of homosexuals.** Students may express their opposition by harassing gay rights activists or even physically assaulting students whose sexual orientation they do not accept.

AGE. About 17 million Americans are taking college courses. However, only 6 million are so-called *traditional students*—**that is, between 18 and 24 years old.**[8] The dramatic shift from students in their late teens and early 20s occurred because of the rising number of nontraditional students. *Nontraditional students*—**sometimes called adult students or returning students—are those who are older than 24.** As mentioned, nearly half the women and a quarter of the men attending college are over 24. Many of these also attend part-time. (Actually, about 75% of college students, regardless of age, are enrolled part-time.)

Who are these nontraditional students? There is no easy way to catalog them. Large numbers are women entering the labor force, displaced workers trying to upgrade their skills, and baby boomers switching careers. Some are managers taking courses to gain advancement, others are people seeking intellectual stimulation. Some are retirees: In a recent year, 320,000 Americans age 50 and over were enrolled in college courses.[9]

Whatever their reasons, nontraditional students often bring a high level of motivation, much life experience, and a willingness to work hard. They also bring a number of concerns. They worry that their skills are rusty, that they won't be able to keep up with younger students. They worry that their memory is not as good, that their energy level is not as

FORM A STUDY GROUP WITH OTHERS LIKE YOU

Many students feel as if they are somehow "out of step" with other students. However, nontraditional students—those over age 24—are especially apt to feel this way. One effective morale-booster is to form study groups with other students who are like you. (This activity can also be done by students of any group, not just nontraditional students.)

Note: The principal reason for forming a study group with others like you is to get *support*. You want to be careful, however, that it doesn't lead to your isolating or "ghettoizing" yourself from the other students. A goal of college should be to *seek out* diversity, not avoid it.

■ WHAT TO DO

In this or any other course, approach two or more other students with whom you think you might feel comfortable. Ask them if they would like to set aside an hour or two once a week for a study group. Suggest that the purpose could be to share study techniques, compare lecture notes, practice math problems, or review for exams. In the course of your meetings you can also discuss the problems peculiar to being a nontraditional student. (Examples are holding a full-time job, child care, divorce, or whatever.)

■ YOUR STUDY GROUP OR GROUPS: MEMBERS & MEETING TIMES

For each class for which you've formed a study group, list members' names and telephone numbers below. Also list the day, time, and place where you've arranged to meet every week.

1. Name & phone
   _____
   _____
   Day, time, & place
   _____
   _____

2. Name & phone
   _____
   _____
   Day, time, & place
   _____
   _____

3. Name & phone
   _____
   _____
   Day, time, & place
   _____
   _____

4. Name & phone
   _____
   _____
   Day, time, & place
   _____
   _____

5. Name & phone
   _____
   _____
   Day, time, & place
   _____
   _____

---

high. Single parents worry that they won't be able to juggle school and their other responsibilities. Fortunately, most campuses have someone whose job it is to support adult students. There are also a number of other strategies that adult learners can employ. (See ■ *Panel 3.4.*)

RACE & CULTURE. Past generations of the dominant culture in the United States felt threatened by the arrival of Irish, Italians, Germans, Eastern Europeans, Catholics, and Jews. (And some people are still uncomfortable with them today.) Now the groups considered prominent racial minorities are people of African, Hispanic, and Asian descent or Native American and Alaskan Native. Indeed, four of these groups (African-Americans, Hispanic-Americans, Native Americans, and Alaskan Natives) presently make up

20% of Americans. By the year 2000 they are expected to make up nearly a third of the college population.

Let us briefly consider some of these groups.

■ *African-Americans:* The largest nonwhite minority, African-Americans make up 12% of the population of the United States, comprising 30 million people. By almost any measure, African-Americans continue to face disadvantages resulting from the burden of slavery and three centuries of racial discrimination. Indeed, one survey found that 80% of African-Americans who responded reported some form of racial discrimination during their college years.[10]

Gains in civil rights and voting rights during the 1960s increased the number of African-Americans in elective office sixtyfold during the last 30 years. Outlawing discrimination in education and

Strategies for adult learners.

Some strategies for students who are over age 24 or attending college part-time:

Ask for support: Get your family involved by showing them your textbooks and giving them a tour of the campus. Hang your grades on the refrigerator right alongside those of the kids. Or get support from friends (such as other adult students), a counselor, or an instructor. See if the college sponsors an adult support group.

Get financial aid: See Chapter 10, on money. You may be able to get loans, scholarships, or fellowships.

Enroll part-time: Going part-time will ease the stresses on your time and finances. Start with just one course to test the waters.

Arrange for child care: If you have young children, you'll need child care not only for when you're away at class but also when you're home doing homework.

Learn time-management skills: See the other chapters in this book, particularly Chapter 4, on how to manage your time.

Get academic support: If you're worried about being rusty, look for review courses, one-on-one free tutoring, and similar support services.

Avoid grade pressure: Unless you're trying to get into a top graduate school, don't put yourself under undue pressure for grades. Just do the best you can in the time you have to devote to school.

Have fun: College should also be enjoyable for itself, not just a means to a better life. If you can't spare much time for campus activities, at least spend some time with other nontraditional students. Some campuses, for example, even have a "resumers lounge." Or experiment with your image, dressing in ways (hip? professional? sexy?) that will allow you to reinvent yourself a bit.

Form or join a returning students group: Get together with others in your classes who seem to be in similar circumstances for study and other mutual support.

employment has helped establish a third of African-Americans in the middle class (up 10% from the 1960s). Still, unemployment rates for African-Americans continue to be double those of whites. Moreover, they continue to suffer disproportionately from serious health problems, crime, and poverty.

Many African-Americans go to school in the large system of black colleges and universities. Still, perhaps 80% of African-American students attend institutions of higher education in which the majority of students are white.[11]

■ *Hispanic-Americans:* People from Spanish-speaking cultures make up the second largest minority group in the United States (at 9% of the population, or 22 million). They make up more than 10% of the population of Colorado, Florida, and New York. They constitute nearly a fifth of Arizona, a quarter of California and Texas, and more than a third of New Mexico.

Two-thirds of Hispanics are Mexican-Americans, who, after African-Americans, represent the second largest disadvantaged minority group. Puerto Ricans and Cubans are the next largest groups of Hispanics, followed by others from Caribbean, Central American, and South American countries.

■ *Asian-Americans:* There are 28 separate groups of Asian-Americans, according to census studies, ranging from Chinese to Japanese to Pacific Islanders. Asian-Americans are the fastest-growing minority in the United States, with 40% living in California and most of the rest in Hawaii and New York.[12] The two largest groups are Chinese and Filipino who, along with the Japanese, are descendants of earlier tides of immigration. However, the fastest-growing groups of recent years have been those from Vietnam, India, Korea, Cambodia (Kampuchea), and Laos. Asian-Americans continue to suffer discrimination, as reflected in lower income levels compared to whites.

■ *Other races, cultures, religions:* Of course there are many other groups of ethnic and religious minorities. Indeed, many of them—blacks, Jews, Roman Catholics, and others—have established their own colleges to serve their special needs.

Those with the longest history of habitation in the United States are those considered native—Indians, Alaskans, and Hawaiians. In 1990, there were nearly 2 million Native Americans and Alaskan Natives, according to the U.S. census. Since 1968, 24 colleges have been established in the United States that are owned and operated by Native Americans.[13]

The dominant religion in the U.S. is Protestant. Nevertheless, there are numerous minority religions: Catholic, Jewish, Muslim, Buddhist, Hindu, and so on. And, of course, many people have no formal religion or no religion at all.

■ *International students:* Many campuses are enriched by the presence of international students. These are foreign visitors who have come to the United States to

TALKING TO OTHERS ABOUT PREJUDICE

Whatever group you belong to, majority or minority, this activity is intended to give you more information about cultural or racial prejudice.

■ IF YOU'RE A MEMBER OF THE MAJORITY CULTURE . . .

Find someone on campus who is of a *different* culture or race from yours. Ask if you may speak to him or her for a minute or so. This person may be a student in a class above you (sopho-more or junior) or an instructor or a staff member. Ask him or her the following two questions and write down the answers.

1. Can you give an example, large or small, of an instance of racial discrimination or prejudice on this campus? (Example: No white student has asked to borrow his or her notes.)

_____

_____

_____

_____

2. What advice do you have for members of the majority culture about dealing with members of the minority culture on this campus?

_____

_____

_____

_____

_____

_____

■ IF YOU'RE A MEMBER OF A MINORITY CULTURE . . .

Find someone on campus who is of the *same* culture or race as yours, if possible. Ask if you may speak to him or her for a minute or so. This person may be a student in a class above you (sophomore or junior) or an instructor or a staff member. Ask him or her the following two questions and write down the answers.

1. Can you give an example, large or small, of an instance of racial discrimination or prejudice on this campus? (Example: No white student has asked to borrow his or her notes.)

_____

_____

_____

_____

_____

_____

2. What advice do you have for members of your culture about how to succeed in college on this campus?

_____

_____

_____

_____

_____

_____

pursue a course of study. Some of them may find themselves especially welcomed. Others, however, may find that their skin color, dress, or accent exposes them to no less bias than American-born minorities experience. Some Americans worry that, with so much overseas talent in science and engineering programs, we are offering a kind of foreign aid. In fact, however, over half of all foreign graduate students in science and engineering choose to remain here after completing their schooling. Thus, they form an important part of our high-tech work force.[14]

GROUP ACTIVITY OPTION

Report some of your findings as the basis for class discussion.

WHAT IT IS LIKE HAVING A PHYSICAL DISABILITY

How does it feel to be physically handicapped? If you're young and healthy, you can try doing as students in a college class on aging and human development did. You can use earplugs to reduce hearing and use or discard glasses to impair eyesight. You can wrap your joints in elastic bandages to simulate stiffness.[15] Or you can do as medical students do in a program training them in better communication skills with the elderly. That is, you can try wearing wax earplugs and fastening splints to your joints. Or you can put raw peas in your shoes to simulate corns and callouses. Or you can don rubber gloves to diminish the sense of touch.[16]

■ WHAT TO DO

Devise a project you will undertake to simulate a disability, and describe how you will go about it. (Examples: Borrow a wheelchair and try getting around campus, wear earplugs all day, use duct or masking tape to immobilize your fingers.)

_____
_____
_____
_____
_____
_____
_____
_____
_____

■ REPORT YOUR EXPERIENCES

Briefly describe what you learned.

_____
_____
_____
_____
_____
_____
_____
_____
_____
_____
_____
_____

DISABILITY. Nearly one in eleven first-year college students report some kind of physical disability.[17] **A** *physical disability* **is a health-related condition that prevents a person from participating fully in daily activities,** including school and work. Because of the 1990 Americans With Disabilities Act, colleges have had to change policies to accommodate students with disabilities. For instance, the law bars discrimination against the disabled in public accommodations and transportation. This means that new and renovated buildings and buses must be accessible to people with handicaps.

Disabled people include not only those who are physically handicapped (for example, wheelchair-bound) or the visually or hearing impaired. They also include those with any type of learning disability. For example, people with dyslexia have difficulty reading. In any case, disabled people resent words that suggest they're sick, pitiful, childlike, or dependent or, conversely, objects of admiration. They also object to politically correct euphemisms such as the "differently abled," "the vertically challenged," or the "handi-capable."[18]

Report some of your experience to the rest of the class.

Onward: Applying This Chapter to Your Life

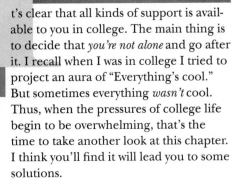

PREVIEW Don't always pretend "everything's cool" when it's not.

It's clear that all kinds of support is available to you in college. The main thing is to decide that *you're not alone* and go after it. I recall when I was in college I tried to project an aura of "Everything's cool." But sometimes everything *wasn't* cool. Thus, when the pressures of college life begin to be overwhelming, that's the time to take another look at this chapter. I think you'll find it will lead you to some solutions.

The principal lesson of this chapter has a great deal of value outside college. That lesson is: *find out everything you can about the organization you're in.* The more you understand about the departments and processes of your work world, for instance, the better you'll be able to take control of your own life within it. The same is true with the world outside of work.

What information in this chapter did you find most useful to you? How can you apply it to your own life? Write it down here:

1. What problem can you think of that might occur during your college career for which you might need help? It could be lack of money, conflicts in a personal relationship, dealing with child care, or difficulty keeping up with a course. What kind of assistance could you get to ease the problem?

2. If any extracurricular activity could be considered as important as your major, what would it be? How would you go about becoming involved, if you aren't already?

3. The chapter described several kinds of diversity. Which types (if any) do you represent? How has your experience as a member of a minority group affected you?

4 time

translating your life goals into task management

yes, it's possible to get everything done. here's how

- **Time and happiness:** How learning time management helps you achieve happiness.

- **Setting priorities:** How to set daily tasks from your life goals.

- **Beating time wasters:** How to avoid procrastinations and distractions and gain The Extra Edge.

1. What circumstances make you worry that you will waste time and not be able to get your school work done? (Examples: people dropping in to talk, family interruptions, too much partying.) Write two of them here (using your private shorthand):

_____

_____

_____

_____

2. What interesting circumstances might make you push aside other concerns? (Examples: pursuing a relationship, practicing a sport or musical instrument, hanging on to a good job.) Identify two here:

_____

_____

_____

_____

_____

■ SKIMMING FOR PAYOFFS

You can be alert to the circumstances you listed in #1 because you're already worrying they're problems. The information in #2 indicates that some things are important enough to you to make time for. Thus, you can probably do the same for college subjects.

Skim this chapter looking for payoffs. Look for things that address your worries and show you how to find time to do what you really want.

Use a different-colored pen from the one you usually use to make notations in the margin (for example, "This might work for me!").

What kinds of stories about college students appear in the newspapers and on TV?

It seems to me often they're college football stories, spring break head-for-the-beach stories, fraternity-partying stories. In short, they're about various forms of *having fun.* If this was all you knew about higher education, you'd think college was nothing but endless *play.*

Indeed, once you get into college and start classes, it looks as if you'll have ample time for fun. This is especially so at the beginning, because the demands at the start of a school term seem so light. "Hey, I only have 16 hours of class a week," students say. "With that I can do homework and work part time and *still* do what I want on weekends."

I have to make a special point of telling them what was once told to me:

Students are expected to devote 2 or 3 hours of study for every hour of class.

This is so important it bears repeating. *You need to study 2–3 hours for every hour you spend in class.* This is the generally universal advice given on all campuses. (By "study," I mean reviewing notes, reading assignments, writing papers—all the activity known as "homework.") Some classes will require less than 2–3 hours, but some might require *more.* Indeed, some might require 4–5 hours of study for every hour in class.

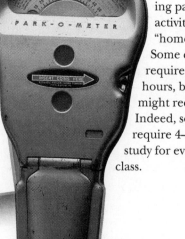

Thus, suppose you have 16 hours of class time, a standard full-time course load. If to this you add 32 hours of study time, then *at least* 48 hours a week should be devoted to college work. Compare that to the standard 40-hour week that your employed noncollege friends may be working. This means your *college work is more than a full-time job!*

"Oh, no!" you may say. "So where's the time for fun?" Consider, though, that there are 168 hours in a week, with 56 or so hours devoted to sleeping. Thus, most students usually find time enough left over for them to have fun and be with their friends. But let's be honest. Are you commuting long distances? Are you working as well as studying? Are you on an athletic scholarship? Are you an adult returning student with family responsibilities? Then you simply won't have as much time now for leisure as you may have had in the past.

The bottom line is this: you're hoping that, as a result of your college efforts, there'll be *more* time for play later. College requires some sacrifices now for increased happiness in the future. After all, as I said earlier, college is not prison; you don't have to be here. You're here, presumably, because you *want* to be here and hope the college experience will lead to your greater happiness later. Thus, you need to keep your ultimate goal in focus and see how you can get the most you can out of college while you're here.

Among several skills basic to mastering our system of higher education, two of the most important are:

- *Knowing how to manage your time*—discussed in this chapter;

- *Knowing how to use your memory*—discussed in the next chapter.

The Importance of Managing Time

PREVIEW People who learn to control their time learn to control their lives—and are thereby much happier than people who don't. Many people misuse free time when they have it and thus are unsatisfied. One of the most worthwhile goals is to find *work that feels like play.*

hink about what time is: it is really *life.* When you spend time, you spend another few minutes or hours of your life, a dwindling resource that you get to use only once. This idea has enormously important implications: you literally *are* what you *do.*

"What's the biggest advantage to managing your time?"

Name: Amy L. Verschage

Major: Liberal Arts & Sciences: General Studies

Interests: Reading, listening to music, dancing, travel, motorcycling, spending time outdoors, skiing, bicycle riding, swimming, walking, aerobics.

Answer to question: "By managing my time, I have time to do my schoolwork and also am able to do other things. If I didn't manage my time, I would never be able to see my boyfriend because I would have too much schoolwork to do."

TIME MANAGEMENT & HAPPINESS. Consider your future: How do you want to spend your life? Do you want to have control over your destiny and the freedom to do many of the things you want to do? Or do you want to have little control, being forced to do what others want?

You undoubtedly want more control. If so, you're already on the right track by going to college. Generally speaking, the more education people have, the more control they have over their lives and the happier they are. People in poverty, for instance, have fewer choices and feel they have little control over the circumstances of their lives.

Now consider the present. You might prefer to be watching television or being with friends. However, right now you have those tests to take, papers to write, requirements to fulfill. As a student, will you always *have* to be doing something school-related?

Actually, you'll probably have sufficient time for play, though you certainly won't be able to take it whenever you feel like it. That's true also of people who work, of course. In any case, *by learning to manage your time, you'll learn to take control over your life—and therefore be a happier person.* "Happy . . . are those," says David Myers, "who gain the sense of control that comes with effective management of one's time."[1] Myers, a psychologist, wrote these words in a book about the pursuit of happiness.

THE MISUSE OF FREE TIME. It's an interesting thing about free time. Those who have too much time on their hands, such as people out of work, find unoccupied time unsatisfying. "Sleeping late, hanging out, watching TV, leave an empty feeling," Myers points out.[2]

Indeed, most people don't seem to get much happiness out of their free time when they have it. Myers quotes another psychologist who was struck by "the relative poverty of experience in free time, the emptiness of most leisure." He says:

We all want to have more free time: But when we get it we don't know what to do with it. Most dimensions of experience deteriorate: People report being more passive, irritable, sad, weak, and so forth. To fill the void in consciousness, people turn on the TV or find some other way of structuring experience vicariously. These passive leisure activities take the worst edge off the threat of chaos, but leave the individual feeling weak and enervated.[3]

A great deal of this problem has to do with using free time for passive activity, most notably watching television. It has been found that Americans two years old and older spend an average of one-quarter of their waking hours watching television. (The average is 28 hours and 13 minutes a week.)[4] Researchers find that television relaxes people while they watch. Afterward, however, it leaves them feeling *less* relaxed, *less* happy, and *less* able to concentrate compared to participation in sports, reading, or gardening.[5]

The desirable course, then, seems clear. When you do have free time, try to get involved in something less vegetative than reclining in front of the TV. To quote Myers for the last time, we can put more happiness into our lives "by living more intentionally." This means "saying yes to the things that we do best and find most meaningful, and no to time-wasting demands. . . ."[6]

MAKING WORK PLAY. There's another aspect to learning to manage time: Many people make distinctions between work and play. But probably what you really want is *to do work that feels like play.* (The alternative is doing work that is boring, even hateful, in order to support your play after work.) Indeed, college can be a great laboratory for experimenting to find out what kind of work seems most fun for you.

I don't mean to suggest that *all* the work you'll do will be enjoyable. Most jobs have aspects that are tedious or difficult or unsatisfying. I am suggesting, however, that an important goal of college is to strive to find work that, to the extent possible, feels like play.

How to Improve Your Time Management

PREVIEW The six-step "Essentials for Time & Life Management" plan describes how to set daily tasks from your life goals. The steps are: (1) Determine your ultimate goals. (2) Identify your plans for achieving them. (3) State the actions needed to realize your plans. (4) Lay out your master timetable for the school term. (5) Set your weekly timetable. (6) Do a daily or weekly To Do list with reminders and priorities.

ou may hear a fellow student say offhandedly, "Yeah, I got an A in the course. But it was easy—I hardly had to study at all."

Don't believe it.

Sure, I guess there really are some people who can get by this way (or courses that are really that easy). However, most people who talk like that just want to look as though they are brainy enough not to need to study. In general, though, the reality is that either they *are* studying a lot or they are *not* getting top grades.

Here is clearly an area in which you have to be tough-minded: Most of the time, studying *is* hard work. It *does* take time. It *does* take personal commitment. Most students *don't* like to do it. Studying *isn't* usually something to look forward to (although learning and exploring may be fun).

You need not feel upset or guilty about this. Accept that studying is not always something you're going to do because you feel like it. Then you can begin to organize your time so that you can always get enough studying done.

GROUP ACTIVITY #4.1

WHAT IS HAPPINESS? EDUCATING YOURSELF FOR THE WAY YOU WANT TO LIVE

You're in higher education, presumably, in the pursuit of your ultimate happiness—or something that will make you happier than you are now. But what, in fact, *is* happiness? If your instructor requests it, go to the library and read an article or part of a book on the subject of happiness. Make notes of the ideas that seem to speak directly to you. (If there's no time for research, take 5 minutes to write what you think happiness is and what would make you happy.)

In small groups (three to five people) discuss what happiness is. What is the way you want to live? How will education help you accomplish it? How does your definition of happiness differ from others' definitions? Could you be happy under others' terms?

PANEL 4.1 The six-step program of "Essentials for Time & Life Management." Steps for transforming your life goals into daily tasks.

What you want college to help you do in life

1. Why am I in college? (Long-range goals)

2. What are my plans? (Intermediate range goals)

3. What are my actions? (Steps to implement goals)

4. What is my master timetable?

5. What is my weekly timetable?

6. What is today's To Do list?

How you make it happen

THE SIX-STEP PROGRAM OF ESSENTIALS FOR TIME & LIFE MANAGEMENT. Essentials for Time & Life Management, as I stated in Chapter 2, is a six-step program for translating your life goals into daily tasks. (*See* ■ *Panel 4.1.*) The idea is to make your most important desires and values a *motivational force* for helping you manage your time every day.

The steps are as follows:

■ *Step 1:* The planning process starts when you answer the question "Why am I in college?"—that is, define your life goals or long-range goals.

■ *Step 2:* You then proceed to "What are my plans?"—setting your intermediate-range goals.

▨ *Step 3:* This leads to "What are my actions?"—the steps you will take to achieve your goals.

■ *Step 4:* "What is my master timetable?" In this step you set your schedule for the semester or quarter.

■ *Step 5:* "What is my weekly timetable?" This is the schedule you follow from week to week.

▨ *Step 6:* "What is on the To Do list today?" This is the errand list or "things to do" list that is no different from the To Do list that millions of people make every day.

Two points need to be made before we proceed:

1. *Skipping steps:* It's possible you already know your life goals and how they translate into a college major and required courses. In that case, you may be interested only in how to get through the present quarter or semester most efficiently. If so, you will want to skip Steps 1–3 and go directly to Step 4. Alternatively, you may simply not feel like doing Steps 1–3 right now. At some point, however, you will have to, because they have everything to do with why you're in college in the first place.

2. *Planning and spontaneity:* Does the idea of making such detailed plans bother you because it seems to rob life of its free-

dom and spontaneity? I would say that planning gives you *more* freedom. Planning allows you to focus on what's really important. Then you're less apt to spin your wheels—and waste time—on insignificant matters. As a result, you'll have more time left over to do the spontaneous things you want. (Also, you can always *change* your plans, of course.)

Now let's look at the six-step program of "Essentials for Time & Life Management" in detail.

STEP 1: WHY AM I IN HIGHER EDUCATION? You already answered this question in Personal Exploration #2.4 in Chapter 2, when you defined your long-range goals. Repeat them in Personal Exploration #4.1. If you've changed your mind about a few matters since then, that's fine. Just modify them in the space below.

STEP 2: WHAT ARE MY PLANS? Maybe you don't know what you want to be, but you know that you want to explore areas that express your values:

- to help people,
- to make good products,
- to create,
- to educate,
- to exercise your curiosity,
- to entertain,
- . . . or whatever.

Or maybe you already know what you want to be: a journalist, an engineer, an actor, a nurse, a teacher, a lawyer, a businessperson. In any event, now you need a plan, a rough strategy, of how to achieve or figure out your life goals.

PERSONAL EXPLORATION #4.1

WHAT ARE YOUR LONG-RANGE GOALS?

The top five goals I hope college will help me reach are . . .

1. _____

2. _____

3. _____

4. _____

5. _____

We're talking here about career choices and your major field. "So soon?" you may say. "I just got here!" Nevertheless, you at least need to decide what you *don't* want to do. For example, a major in engineering, medicine, music, or mathematics requires a sequence of courses that begins in the first year of college. If you think you might want to pursue these or similar fields, you need to be thinking about it now. Otherwise, you'll be required to make up courses later.

In making a plan, you need to take your thoughts about your life goals or long-range goals and then do the following things:

■ *Decide on a major field (if only tentatively) and two or more alternatives:* Looking at the college catalog, state what major will probably help you realize your life goals. Also state two or more alternative majors you think you would enjoy pursuing.

■ *Think of obstacles:* You need to think of the possible problems that may have to be overcome. Money possibly running out? Job and family responsibilities? Uncertainty about whether you're suited for this path? (Lack of motivation can be a killer.) Deficient math or language or other skills necessary for that major? Lack of confidence that you're "college material"?

■ *Think of reinforcements:* Think of what you have going for you that will help you accomplish your goals. Burning desire? Sheer determination? Parental support? Personal curiosity? Relevant training in high school? Ability to get along with people? Acquaintance with someone in the field who can help you? It helps to have positive reinforcement over the long haul.

To begin this process, do Personal Exploration #4.2, on the opposite page.

STEP 3: WHAT ARE MY ACTIONS? Step 2 provides you with the general guidelines for your college career. Step 3 is one of *action.* You have a plan for college; now you have to act on it. (Or why bother doing the preceding steps?)

Let me say a few words on behalf of taking action. *If you don't feel as if you're a terrific student or time manager, just fake it.*

Seriously.

Even if you haven't done well in school in the past, pretend now that you're the ultimate student. Be a phony and "play at" being a scholar. Feign at being organized. Simulate being a good time manager.

There's a reason for all this. If you *act* like the person you want to become, you will *become* that person. This is true whether it's being less shy, having a more optimistic outlook, having more self-esteem, or being a better student. After you have gotten used to your new role, the feelings of discomfort that "this isn't natural for me" will subside. *You are more apt to ACT* your way into a new way of thinking than to think your way into it.[7]

If you don't believe this, just consider that people act their way into behavior change all the time. People may not feel as if they can handle the responsibilities of a promotion or a new job beforehand, but they usually do. Being a parent looks pretty awesome when you're holding a newborn baby, but most people in the world get used to it. I've taught a number of students at a nearby prison who had dropped out of high school, got into all kinds of trouble, and ended up behind bars. Yet they then earned bachelor's and master's degrees. You too, then, can remake your behavior—and consequently remake your thinking.

As part of taking action, you need to look at what areas need to be improved in order for you to excel. Are your math, reading, or writing skills a bit shaky? Take advantage of the (often free) assistance of the college and get tutorial help. This is not something to be embarrassed about. Lots of people find they need practice of this sort to upgrade their skills.

WHAT ARE YOUR PLANS? INTERMEDIATE-RANGE GOALS

The point of this exercise is not to lock in your decisions. You can remain as flexible as you want for the next several months, if you like. The point is to get you thinking about your future and what you're doing in college—even if you're still undecided about your major.

■ WHAT TO DO: DETERMINING YOUR INTERMEDIATE-RANGE GOALS

Look at the five goals you expressed in Personal Exploration #4.1. Now determine how these goals can be expressed relating to college.

Example: Suppose your life goals or long-range goals include:

1. "To enter a profession that lets me help people."

2. "To find out how I can become a world traveler."

3. "To explore my interest in health and science."

4. "To meet interesting people."

    You might list possible majors in Health, Nursing, and International Relations. In addition, you might list nonacademic activities—for instance, "Join International Club." "Go to a meeting of Premed Society" (for premedical students). "Look into study at overseas campus in sophomore or junior year."

Decide on Three or More Alternative Majors: Determine which major fields seem of particular interest to you. You can simply do this out of your head. However, it's better if you look through the college catalog.

Three possible majors that might help me fulfill my life goals are the following:

1. _____
   _____

2. _____
   _____

3. _____
   _____

Decide on Nonacademic Activities Supporting Your Goals: Determine what kind of extracurricular activities interest you. Again, you can make this up out of your head, or you can consult the college catalog or people in the campus community.

Five possible areas of extracurricular activities that might help me advance my college goals are the following:

1. _____
   _____

2. _____
   _____

3. _____
   _____

4. _____
   _____

5. _____
   _____

Identify Possible Obstacles: List the kinds of possible problems you may have to overcome in your college career.

Examples: Possible money problems. Conflict with job and family responsibilities. Temptation to pursue too active a social life. Uncertainty about a major. Lack of preparation in mathematics.

The five following obstacles could hinder me in pursuing my college career:

1. _____
   _____

2. _____
   _____

3. _____
   _____

4. _____
   _____

5. _____
   _____

Identify Reinforcements: List the kinds of things you have in your life that will support you in the achievement of your college goals when the going gets rough.

Examples: Support of your parents, husband/wife, or boyfriend/girlfriend. Personal curiosity. Knowing someone in a career you're considering. History of enjoying similar fields or activities in high school.

The five following facts or ideas could help sustain me in pursuing my college career:

1. _____
   _____

2. _____
   _____

3. _____
   _____

4. _____
   _____

5. _____
   _____

In a small-group situation, first report on your possible majors and extracurricular activities. Then take turns discussing the obstacles, followed by the positive things that will reinforce you in pursuing a college career. On a sheet of paper put the heading "I'M GOING TO MAKE IT BECAUSE . . ." Then list the things that will support you in realizing your college goals. Share some of your reasons with the class.

In Personal Exploration #4.3 you will need to accomplish the following:

■ **Determine the courses needed to accomplish your goals:** You need to know what courses you will probably take in what semester or quarter in order to make progress. Generally you can tell the courses you need to take for a particular major by looking in the college catalog. (Look for language such as the following: "Students seeking the bachelor of arts degree in Journalism must complete at least 128 credits, 40 of which will be in courses numbered 300 or higher . . ." Or, "The requirements for the degree of Associate in Applied Science in Criminal Justice are . . .")

Laying out course sequences will take some time. But, believe me, *students who don't do such planning could find themselves out of step on some course requirements. This could require extra semesters or quarters later on.* Such slippage is especially a hazard in colleges suffering from budget cutbacks, where it may be difficult to get the courses you want.

■ **Determine what extracurricular activities to pursue:** Some students, such as those on athletic scholarships, take their extracurricular activities as seriously as their coursework. (Some take them even *more* seriously than their courses.) Some students also are highly motivated to study at an overseas campus at some point in college. In any event, you need

to figure out how nonacademic activities fit with your academic activities, both in the short and long run.

■ **Determine how to overcome obstacles, if possible:** Money worries? Family problems? Work conflicts? See if you can identify some solutions or avenues that might lead to solutions (such as checking the Financial Aid Office).

■ **Get advice about your tentative plans, then revise them:** Take your plans (including your list of obstacles) to your academic advisor and discuss them with him or her. In addition, I strongly recommend taking them to a counselor in the career counseling center. Since all this advice is free (or included in your stu-dent fees or tuition), you might want to take advantage of it. You will end up with a reality-based plan that may help save you a semester or two of misdirection.

To identify your courses of action, do Personal Exploration #4.3 on pages 71–72.

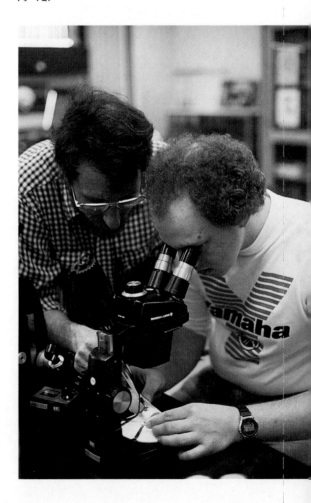

WHAT ARE YOUR ACTIONS? STEPS TO IMPLEMENT YOUR PLANS

This activity may take some time—perhaps an hour or so. However, *it is one of the most important Personal Explorations in this book*—maybe *the* most important.

■ WHAT TO DO

Here you list the *details* of how you will carry out your college plans. These include identifying courses to take, activities to pursue, and strategies for overcoming obstacles and getting appropriate advice.

Identify Courses to Take: Use the space below and/or a separate sheet of paper. List what courses (including prerequisites) you might need to take to realize your college degree and to fulfill your major and alternative majors. Indicate what years or semesters you will need to take them. These courses will be listed for the degree requirements in your college catalog. You may use a curriculum worksheet to complete this, as shown in Chapter 3, Panel 1.

The courses I will need to take to obtain my degree or degrees are as follows:

_____
_____
_____
_____
_____
_____
_____
_____
_____
_____
_____
_____
_____
_____
_____
_____
_____
_____
_____
_____

(Continue on a separate sheet of paper, if necessary.)

Identify Nonacademic Activities to Pursue: In the space below, list the nonacademic activities you want to try to pursue.

Examples: If you wish to play hockey, note how practice, game times, and travel may affect the rest of your schedule. If you wish to try to study abroad in your junior year, note the arrangements you need to make. (These include researching overseas programs, getting application forms, and noting deadlines for applying. In addition, note how overseas study will affect your course sequences on your home campus.)

The nonacademic activities I wish to pursue, and arrangements I will have to make, are as follows:

1. _____

2. _____

3. _____

4. _____

5. _____

(continued)

Identify Strategies for Overcoming Obstacles: If you're worrying about obstacles, now is the time to begin to deal with them. In the space below, indicate the steps you will take.

Examples: For "Possible money problems," you might state you will look into financial aid. For "Family conflicts," you might look into child-care possibilities.

The possible obstacles I need to overcome, and the steps I will take to begin to overcome them, are as follows:

1. _____
   _____
   _____
   _____
   _____
   _____

2. _____
   _____
   _____
   _____
   _____
   _____
   _____

3. _____
   _____
   _____
   _____
   _____
   _____

4. _____
   _____
   _____
   _____
   _____
   _____

5. _____
   _____
   _____
   _____
   _____
   _____

Get Advice About Your Plans: This section takes very little time, but it may involve using the telephone and then following up with a personal visit. The point of the activity is to identify and then follow through on courses of action you need to take.

Examples: With your list of prospective majors and course sequences in hand, call your academic advisor. Make an appointment to meet and discuss your concerns. If you're thinking about joining the student newspaper, call to find out what you have to do. If you're worried that money might be a problem, call the Financial Aid Office to discuss it. (Some kinds of action need not involve a telephone. For example, you could tell your family members that you need to sit down and talk about child-care arrangements and study time.)

Here are the telephone numbers I need to call, or people I need to see and when, about a certain matter. The date following signifies when I took the action.

1. PERSON TO CONTACT (AND PHONE NUMBER) AND MATTER TO BE DISCUSSED
   _____
   _____
   _____

   ACTION WAS TAKEN ON (DATE)
   _____
   _____

2. PERSON TO CONTACT (AND PHONE NUMBER) AND MATTER TO BE DISCUSSED
   _____
   _____
   _____
   _____

ACTION WAS TAKEN ON (DATE)
_____
_____

3. PERSON TO CONTACT (AND PHONE NUMBER) AND MATTER TO BE DISCUSSED
   _____
   _____
   _____
   _____

ACTION WAS TAKEN ON (DATE)
_____
_____

4. PERSON TO CONTACT (AND PHONE NUMBER) AND MATTER TO BE DISCUSSED
   _____
   _____
   _____

ACTION WAS TAKEN ON (DATE)
_____
_____

5. PERSON TO CONTACT (AND PHONE NUMBER) AND MATTER TO BE DISCUSSED
   _____
   _____
   _____

ACTION WAS TAKEN ON (DATE)
_____
_____

The exercise in Personal Exploration #4.3 is a take-home activity that involves working with another student from the class, if possible. Make arrangements with someone in your class to meet in the next day or so and do this Personal Exploration together. With that person's help, work through the course requirements for your respective majors and their alternatives. Also explore together the exercises on nonacademic activities, strategies for overcoming obstacles, and obtaining advice. Put your name and date at the top of the assignments and turn them in to your instructor for evaluation.

STEP 4: WHAT IS MY MASTER TIMETABLE?

Once you've determined your line-up of courses for the next few years, you need to block out your master timetable for the term you're now in.

"I already know my class times and meal times," I sometimes hear first-year students say. "Why is it necessary to plan anything else?"

I think the answer lies in one word: *priorities.*

People who don't set priorities always find themselves dealing with things on an improvised or emergency basis. Students who think setting priorities takes all the spontaneity and fun out of life are certainly entitled to that opinion. However, it also means that they're probably running from crisis to crisis.

Making up a timetable for the semester or quarter allows you to identify your priorities. This is what business and professional people do: they attend to their career responsibilities before anything else. Prioritizing allows you to do this as a student, which, of course, is *your* professional responsibility.

To make a master timetable for the semester or quarter, do the following:

- *Obtain a month-at-a-glance calendar with lots of writing room:* You should use the blank calendar shown on pages 75–76. (Or buy a month-at-a-glance calendar covering all the weeks in the school term. It should have big squares for all the days of the month, squares large enough to write 5–10 words in.) When filled in with due dates and appointments, this will become your master timetable for the semester or quarter.

- *Obtain your college academic calendar:* The college or university's academic calendar may be printed in the college catalog. Sometimes it is sold separately in the college bookstore. The academic calendar tells you school holidays, registration dates, and deadlines for meeting various college requirements. It usually also indicates when final exam week takes place.

- *Obtain the course outline for each course:* The course outline or course information sheet is known as the *syllabus* ("sill-uh-bus"). The syllabus tells you midterm and final exam dates, quiz dates (if any), and due dates for term papers or projects. The syllabus is given to you by your instructor, usually on the first day of class.

Now go through the college calendar and all your course outlines. Transfer to your master timetable calendar all class times, important dates, and deadlines. These include pertinent due dates, dates for the beginning and end of the term, and college holidays. Also add other dates and hours you know about. Examples are those for part-time job, medical

The master timetable. This illustration shows an example of one month of a student's semester or quarter. Note it shows key events such as deadlines, appointments, and holidays.

MONDAY 14

November

Sunday	Monday	Tuesday	Wednesday	Thursday	Friday	Saturday
			1	2	3 *Poli Sci test*	4
5	6 *English essay*	7	8 *Dentist 3 p.m.*	9	10	11 *Concert 8 p.m.*
12	13	14 *Math test*	15	16	17 *Poli Sci test*	18
19 *Tennis 3 p.m.*	20 *English essay*	21	22	23	24 ← *Holidays* → *Thanksgiving*	25
26	27 *Poli Sci paper due*	28 *Math test*	29	30		

9 MARCH

and dental appointments, concerts, football games, and birthdays. *(See ■ Panel 4.2.)* Leave enough space for any given day so that you can add other entries later, if necessary. *Note:* Consider using a different, highly visible color—flaming red, say—to record critical dates such as research-paper deadlines and exam dates.

To begin making up your own master timetable for the present semester or quarter, do the following Personal Exploration. After it is completed, you can three-hole-punch it and carry it in your binder or notebook. Or you can post it on the wall above the place where you usually study.

PERSONAL EXPLORATION #4.4

YOUR MASTER TIMETABLE FOR THIS TERM

Make up your own master timetable for the present school term, using a blank calendar. *(See ■ Panel 4.3 on pages 75–76.)*

GROUP ACTIVITY OPTION

This activity requires that you have (a) the college academic calendar for the present school term and (b) the course outline (syllabus) for each course you are taking. You should also have (c) knowledge of important extracurricular events (such as scheduled games if you are on a team).

Make up your own master timetable for this semester or quarter. Swap it with someone sitting next to you and discuss each other's efforts. Are there any circumstances to be particularly alert to, such as many deadlines coming all at once? What priorities should be established? (For example, what papers could be started early in order to avoid a crunch with exam preparation later on?)

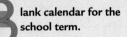

Blank calendar for the school term.

Sunday	Monday	Tuesday	Wednesday	Thursday	Friday	Saturday

Sunday	Monday	Tuesday	Wednesday	Thursday	Friday	Saturday

Sunday	Monday	Tuesday	Wednesday	Thursday	Friday	Saturday

Sunday	Monday	Tuesday	Wednesday	Thursday	Friday	Saturday

STEP 5: WHAT IS MY WEEKLY TIMETABLE? Now we get down to the business end of the Essentials for Time & Life Management: making up a weekly timetable. (*See* ■ *Panel 4.4.*) *The main point of creating a weekly timetable is to schedule your study time.*

Some first-year students aren't sure what I mean by "study time." They think of it as something they do a day or two before a test. By *study time* I mean *everything connected to the process of learning.* This means preparing for tests, certainly, but also reading textbook chapters and other required readings, doing library research, writing papers, and so on. Studying is *homework*, and it's an ongoing process.

PANEL 4.4

The weekly timetable. This illustration shows an example of the important activities in a student's weekly schedule. The most important purpose of this schedule is to program in study time. Some students, however, may wish to program in other fixed activities. Examples are workouts, church attendance, household responsibilities, and travel time to school.

	Monday	Tuesday	Wednesday	Thursday	Friday	Saturday	Sunday
7 a.m.							
8						Work	
9	English	Study	English	Study	English	Work	
10	History	Spanish	History	Spanish	History		
11							
Noon							Study
1 p.m.	Psych	Study	Psych	Study	Psych		Study
2	Study	Math	Study	Math	Study		Study
3	Study	Study	Study	Study	Study		
4							
5							Study
6	Study	Work	Study	Work			Study
7	Study	Work	Study	Work			Study
8	Study	Work	Study	Work			Study
9	Study	Work	Study	Work			Study
10		Work		Work			
11							

By actually creating a weekly timetable to schedule their study time, students are putting themselves on notice that they take their studying *seriously*. They are telling themselves their study time is as important as their classes, job, sports practice, band rehearsal, family meals, or other activities with fixed times.

They are also alerting others that they are serious, too. Some of my students post their weekly schedule on the doors of their rooms in their residence halls. Or on their bedroom doors, if they're living at home. (Thus, if someone drops into your room to talk, you can point to the schedule and say, "Unfortunately, I have to study now. Can I talk to you in another half hour?" More likely than not, they'll remember they have something to do, too.)

If you don't schedule your study time, you may well study only when something else isn't going on. Or you will study late at night, when your energy level is down. Or you will postpone studying until the night before a test.

The weekly master plan should include those activities that happen at fixed, predictable times. These are your classes, work, regularly scheduled student activities—and your regularly scheduled studying times. As mentioned, studying time should amount to about 2 hours of studying for every hour of class time, perhaps more.

If you want, you can add meals, exercise, church, and commuting or transportation times. However, I believe that the fewer things you have on your calendar, the more you'll pay attention to the things that *are* there. Otherwise, you may get to feeling overregulated. You shouldn't schedule break times, for instance; you'll be able to judge for yourself the best times to stop for a breather. (I describe extended study time and breaks later in the chapter.)

I repeat: the main purpose of developing a weekly timetable is to have a visible billboard of your hours for studying. *Stay with your scheduled study times.* Then during your free hours you won't always be feeling guilty about not hitting the books.

To begin making up your own weekly timetable for this semester or quarter, do Personal Exploration #4.5. This, too, may be three-hole-punched and carried in your notebook and/or prominently posted near your principal study place.

Blank timetable for the week.

	Monday	Tuesday	Wednesday	Thursday	Friday	Saturday	Sunday
7 a.m.							
8							
9							
10							
11							
Noon							
1 p.m.							
2							
3							
4							
5							
6							
7							
8							
9							
10							
11							

Examples of daily & weekly "To Do" lists. An "*" may be placed beside those activities that are most urgent.

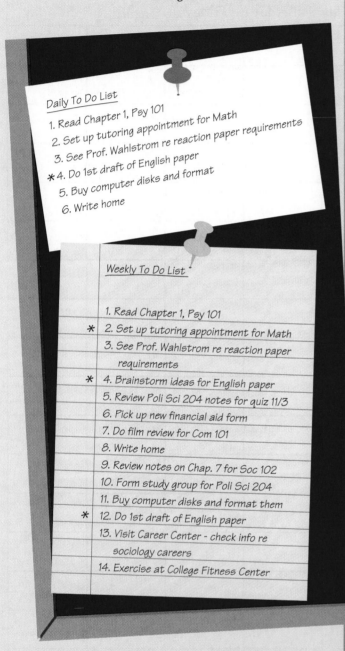

Daily To Do List
1. Read Chapter 1, Psy 101
2. Set up tutoring appointment for Math
3. See Prof. Wahlstrom re reaction paper requirements
*4. Do 1st draft of English paper
5. Buy computer disks and format
6. Write home

Weekly To Do List

1. Read Chapter 1, Psy 101
* 2. Set up tutoring appointment for Math
3. See Prof. Wahlstrom re reaction paper requirements
* 4. Brainstorm ideas for English paper
5. Review Poli Sci 204 notes for quiz 11/3
6. Pick up new financial aid form
7. Do film review for Com 101
8. Write home
9. Review notes on Chap. 7 for Soc 102
10. Form study group for Poli Sci 204
11. Buy computer disks and format them
* 12. Do 1st draft of English paper
13. Visit Career Center - check info re sociology careers
14. Exercise at College Fitness Center

STEP 6: WHAT IS MY DAILY "TO DO" LIST?

The final step is just like the informal "To Do" lists that many people have, whether students or nonstudents. (*See Panel ■ 4.6.*)

The To Do list can be made up every week or every evening, after referring to your master timetable and weekly timetable. The To Do list can be written on a notepad or on a 3×5 card. Either way, it should be easy to carry around so that you can cross things off or make additions. You can be as general or as detailed as you want with this list, but the main purpose of a To Do list is twofold:

■ *Reminders:* Remind yourself to do things you might otherwise forget. Examples are doctor's appointments, tennis dates, things to shop for, and books to return to the library. Don't forget to write down promises you made to people (such as to get them a phone number or a photocopy of your lecture notes).

■ *Priorities:* Set priorities for what you will do with your day. It may be unnecessary to list your scheduled classes, since you will probably go to them anyway. You might want to list an hour for exercise, if you're planning on it. (It's important to exercise at least three times a week for 20 minutes or more.) You may wish to list laundry, shopping, and so on.

However, *the most important thing you can do is to set priorities for what you're going to study that day.* Thus, your To Do list should have items such as "For Tues.— Read econ chapter 13" and "Wed. p.m.— Start library research for psych paper."

Most managers and administrators find a To Do list essential to avoid being overwhelmed by the information overload of their jobs. Since you, too, are on the verge of drowning in information and deadlines, you'll no doubt find the To Do list a helpful tool. Clearly also the To Do list is another application that you can carry over from your educational experience to the world outside of college.

Battling the Killer Time Wasters

PERSONAL EXPLORATION #4.6

YOUR "TO DO" LIST FOR THIS WEEK

On a separate piece of paper make up your own weekly To Do list for the present week.

GROUP ACTIVITY OPTION

Make up a To Do list for this week. Put your name at the top. Your instructor or another student will collect all the To Do lists in the class and put them in a hat (or box). The hat will be circulated throughout the classroom and everyone will draw someone else's To Do list. On the list that you get, write your reactions. When everyone is done, the lists are returned to their owners. A general discussion of To Do lists may follow.

PREVIEW There are four principal strategies to prevent wasting time. (1) Schedule study sessions that actually work. Study during the best times of day, don't schedule overly long sessions, allow short breaks, reward yourself afterward. (2) Fight procrastination. Concentrate on boring assignments intensively for short periods; study with a friend or in a study group. Break long tasks into smaller ones, tackle difficult tasks first, and meet unsettling tasks head on. (3) Fight distractions. Establish regular study sites, set up a good study environment, combat electronic and telephone distractions, and learn to handle people distractions. (4) Gain The Extra Edge. Use waiting time for studying, use spare time for thinking, listen to tapes of lectures.

TIME MANAGEMENT REVISITED. Determine what your life goals are. Figure out what major or exploration will help you realize them. See what courses are required to get there. Make a master timetable of due dates and appointments for the school term. Make a weekly timetable that programs study time into your life. Use a weekly or daily To Do list for reminders and priority setting for studying. All these make up a *strategy* that brings the force of your life goals to bear on your daily study time.

Is this enough to turn you into a good time manager? Perhaps. But life has a way of providing constant distractions and interruptions that can divert us from our course. Let us see how you can handle these.

"Even if you had 25 hours in a day," I sometimes ask my students, "could you manage the time any more efficiently? What about 26 or 27 hours?"

Everyone gets the same ration, a disappointingly small 24 hours a day. Although some people are indeed smarter, usually the ones who excel at school and at work simply *use* their time better. If you do try Personal Exploration #4.7—"How Do You Spend Your Time?"—for a week, you can begin to see where the holes, if any, are in your leaky rowboat. Once you've identified the time wasters, see if the ideas in this section help.

HOW DO YOU SPEND YOUR TIME?

The purpose of this activity is to enable you to see where your time goes. Honesty is important. The idea is to figure out how much time you *do* spend on studying. Then you can determine if you could spend *more* time.

■ KEEPING A LOG OF YOUR TIME

Record how many hours you spend each day on the following activities. (There are 168 hours in a week.)

	MON	TUES	WED	THUR	FRI	SAT	SUN
1. Sleeping							
2. Showering, dressing, and so on							
3. Eating							
4. Traveling to and from class, work, and so on							
5. Going to classes							
6. Working							
7. Watching television							
8. After-school activities (such as sports, band practice)							
9. Other leisure activities (such as movies, dating, parties)							
10. Other scheduled matters— church, tutoring, volunteering							
11. Other (such as "hanging out," "partying," "child care")							
12. Studying							
TOTAL HOURS							

■ YOUR INTERPRETATION

I put "Studying" at the bottom of the list so you can see how other activities in your life impinge on it.

Now consider the following:

1. Do you feel you are in control of your time? ____

2. Are you satisfied with the way you spend your time? ____

3. On what three activities do you spend the most time?

_____

_____

_____

_____

_____

_____

4. Do you feel you're giving enough time to studying? ____

5. If you had to give more time to studying, what two or three activities could you give up or cut down on?

_____

_____

_____

_____

This activity requires that you have kept an accurate record for a week on how you spent your time. In a group situation, large or small, discuss questions 1–5 in Personal Exploration #4.7.

SCHEDULE STUDY SESSIONS THAT ACTUALLY WORK. As I've said, creating a schedule for studying *and sticking with it* are terribly important. Indeed, this is probably the single most valuable piece of advice anyone can give you. As mentioned, you need to build into your week 2–3 or more hours of study time for every hour of class time.

There are, however, certain things to consider when you sit down to block out the master timetable that includes your study time:

■ *Make study times during your best time of day:* Are you a "morning person" or a "night person"? That is, are you most alert before breakfast or most able to concentrate in the evening when it's quiet? When possible, schedule some of your study time for the times of day when you do your best work. These are particularly good times for doing difficult assignments, such as writing research papers.

■ *Don't schedule overly long sessions:* Imagine how you're going to feel at the start of a day in which you've scheduled 10 hours for studying. You'll probably take your time getting to work and won't do more than 7–9 hours of actual studying that day anyway.

To avoid setting yourself up for failure, I suggest programming *no more than* 8 hours of studying in a day. Also, divide that time block into two 4-hour sessions separated by perhaps a couple of hours of time off. (Actually, many students will find they just can't stand 8 hours of studying in a single day.) And if you do schedule long blocks of study time, mix the subjects you're working on so you'll have some variety. The point, after all, is not how *long* you study but how *effectively* you study.

Perhaps an even better strategy, however, is to schedule *several short sessions* rather than a handful of long sessions. I find, for instance, that I perform much better when I have several short stints of work rather than one long one.

■ *Allow for 5- to 10-minute study breaks:* Some people are like long-distance runners and do better by studying for long sessions—for example, 50 minutes followed by a 10-minute break. Others (myself included) are like sprinters and perform better by studying for 25 minutes followed by a 5-minute break.

Of course, you don't have to go exactly by the clock, but you should definitely permit yourself frequent, regularly scheduled breaks. Taken at regular intervals, breaks actually produce efficiencies. They enable you to concentrate better while studying, reduce fatigue, motivate you to keep going, and allow material to sink in while you're resting.

Breaks should be small ways of *pleasuring yourself*—going for a soft drink, taking a walk outside, glancing through the newspaper. I don't recommend getting on the phone, picking up your guitar, or dropping in on a friend, however, unless you can keep it short. You don't want the diversion to be so good that it wrecks your study routine.

■ *Reward yourself when you're done studying:* The end of the course is weeks away, the attainment of a degree months or years. What's going to keep you going in the meantime?

You need to give yourself as many immediate rewards as you can for studying, things to look forward to when you finish. Examples are a snack, phone talk with a friend, some music or TV time. Parts of your college career will be a grind, but you don't want it to be *just* a grind. Rewards are important.

If, after scheduling in your study time, you find it still isn't enough, you need to see where you can make adjustments. Can you reduce the number of courses? Work fewer hours? Get help with chores from family members? Whatever, the main thing is to make your scheduled study time effective when you're doing it.

"What's the biggest time waster for you?"

Name: Kevin Carter

Major: Sports Management

Interests: Playing baseball, hanging out with friends, taking long trips alone

Answer to question: "The biggest time waster for me is the television. I tend to watch an excessive amount of TV when I know I should be studying. Or I watch TV while I'm trying to study."

FIGHT PROCRASTINATION! All of us put off doing things sometimes, but *procrastination* **is defined as putting off things intentionally and habitually.** This continual delay in doing your work can manifest itself in many small ways: You can't seem to get up when the alarm clock goes off. You're always a measly 5 or 10 minutes late getting to your desk. You take time "warming up" by sharpening pencils, adjusting the room temperature, getting coffee, and so on. You find you always need to get organized—pull your notes and books together and find the place where you left off. You wander away from

your work to take phone calls. You knock off early at the slightest convincing excuse.

Procrastination can result when your prospective task is *boring, long, difficult,* or *emotionally unsettling* to you. You need to look hard to see if one of these reasons applies, then fight back by applying the appropriate strategies:

- *Fight boring assignments with short concentrations of effort:* If the task is boring, you need to concentrate on seeing how fast you can get a portion of it done. That is, you need to concentrate on the benefits of completing it in a short time rather than on the character of the task itself.

  Thus, you can say to yourself, "I'm going to work on this for 15 minutes without stopping, applying my full concentration. Then I'm going to move along to something else." You can stand anything for 15 minutes, right? And this task may seem more acceptable if it's not seen as several hours of work—especially if you plan a mini-reward for yourself (getting a soft drink, say) at the end of that time.

- *Fight delaying tactics by studying with a friend or joining a study group:* Some students find that it helps to get together with a friend in the same course to study boring—or even nonboring—subjects. By exchanging ideas about the subject matter, you may find the time goes faster.

  An extremely valuable aid to learning is the study group, **in which a group of classmates get together to share notes and ideas.** In a study group you can clarify lecture notes, quiz each other about ideas, and get different points of view about an instructor's objectives. Being in a group also helps to raise everyone's morale. It makes you realize that you are not alone.

- *Fight long assignments by breaking them into smaller tasks:* Most people have a difficult time tackling large projects, such as research papers. Indeed, most of us tend to take on simple, routine tasks first, saving the longer ones for later when we'll supposedly "have more time."[8] Thus, we often delay so long getting going on large assignments that we can't do an effective job when we finally do turn to them.

The way to avoid this difficulty is to break the large assignments into smaller tasks. You then schedule each of these tasks individually over several days or weeks. (That's how this book got written—in small increments over several months.) For example, when reading a chapter on a difficult subject, read just five or seven pages at a time.

■ *Fight difficult tasks by tackling them first and by making sure you understand them:* If you have one particular area of study that's difficult or unpleasant, *do that one first,* when your energy level is higher and you can concentrate best. For instance, if you find math problems or language learning more difficult than reading a sociology text, tackle them first. The easiest tasks, such as list-making and copying-type chores, can be done late in the day, when you're tired.

If a task seems difficult, you may also take it as a warning signal: maybe there's something about it you don't understand. Are the directions clear? Is the material over your head? If either of these conditions is true, *run, do not walk,* to your instructor. Ask for clarification, if directions are the problem. Be frank with the instructor if you think the material (statistics? grammar? lab experiments?) is hard to comprehend or perform. It may be that what you need is to quickly get yourself the help of a tutor.

I cannot stress enough the importance of taking your own worries seriously if you find that what you're studying is too difficult. However, if you can deal with this before the semester or quarter is too far along, you'll probably be all right.

■ *Fight emotionally unsettling tasks by getting allies:* You may not be able to predict what some of these are. Let me just say, however, that I've seen students blow an assignment or a course because something about it was emotionally disagreeable or frightening.

Maybe, for instance, it's some aspect of *shyness,* so that you find making an oral presentation nearly unbearable. (Shyness, incidentally, is an extremely common condition, one afflicting 4 out of 10 people.)[9] Maybe it's some deep embarrassment about your writing or language skills. Maybe you think "I'm no good at math." Maybe you're queasy about doing biology lab experiments. Maybe there's a former boyfriend/girlfriend in the class whose presence is upsetting you. Maybe the instructor turns you off in some way.

These and most similar situations can be helped, but *you have to reach out and get the help.* If you don't feel you can take the problem up with your instructor, then *immediately* go to the student counseling center. Counseling and tutoring are open to you, normally without any additional charge, as part of the support system available to students. But try not to wait until you're overwhelmed.

FIGHT DISTRACTIONS! A phone call comes in while you're studying, and 25 minutes later you finish the conversation. Are you later going to tell yourself that you actually studied during your scheduled study time? Or are you going to pretend that you'll simply make up the work some other time?

There are many such possible intrusions, but it's important that you not delude yourself—that you not play games with your study time. The following are some strategies for preventing or handling various common distractions:

■ *Establish a couple of places where all you do is study:* When I was in college, I generally studied in two places—at a desk in my room, and here and there in the university library. This seems to be a reasonably common arrangement. I also sometimes studied in the laundry room of my residence hall. (It was warm in the winter and the machine noises blotted out the noise of people talking.)

You see students studying just about everywhere, which is fine. However, it's important that *you establish a couple of places for regular studying* and, if possible, do nothing else there. Unless you can't avoid it, don't routinely study on your bed, where you might fall asleep. Avoid studying at the kitchen table, where you may be inspired to eat. Don't work in the student lounge in front of the TV. If you use your study places only for studying, they will become associated just with that and will reinforce good study behavior.[10]

■ ***Establish a good study environment:*** For your principal study site, the best arrangement is a separate room, such as a spare room, that you treat as your home office. Otherwise, use a corner of your bedroom or dormitory room. Turn a desk or table to the wall to provide you with as much privacy as possible from others sharing the room.

Make this spot as comfortable and organized as you can. Make sure you have the right temperature, good lighting, and a comfortable chair. The desk should have room on it for a computer or a typewriter, as well as reading/writing space. Books and supplies should be within reach. Having a personalized bulletin board is useful. Adult returning students in particular may have to be somewhat assertive with others in their household about their need for a quiet space.

If your living area is too distracting, you can do as many students do and make the library your primary study place. Some libraries have small tables tucked away in quiet areas. Moreover, the entire atmosphere of quiet is supportive to studying.

■ ***Fight electronic distractions:*** Electronic equipment has completely taken over many student residence halls. Indeed, as one college administrator says, "the walls in some students' rooms look like the flight deck of the space shuttle."[11]

In some places, televisions, VCRs, powerful stereo systems, and CD players are considered basic furniture.[12] (This is in addition to computers, clock radios, microwave ovens, coffee machines, and refrigerators.) In fact, a two-person room at UCLA, for example, now requires 16 electrical outlets, compared to only three or four 25 years ago.[13]

One researcher found that, even though college students may have television in their rooms, they watch less of it than the average adult.[14] Even so, you may need to deal with it and the other forms of noise-producing electronics if they interfere with your studying.

If you have a roommate, you should make arrangements for each of you to have headphones for listening to music or watching TV. If the noise in the dormitory becomes too overwhelming and you can't get it turned down by common agreement, go elsewhere. Plan to do your studying in the library or other quiet place such as the laundry room or empty dining hall.

I realize this is a tricky matter, because so many students think that they can study better with television or music as background noise. Indeed, it may be possible to study to certain kinds of music, such as classical music. However, the evidence suggests that the best studying is done when it's quiet.

You can appreciate the importance of eliminating background noise if you recall what it's like to have two people talking to you at once. Your mind goes back and forth between them, and you're unable to get the complete message of either. The same is also true for studying to music, especially if you know the words to the song. One minute you're reading, and the next you're

singing the song to yourself. In sum: your mind can best attend to only one stream of information at a time.

■ *Fight telephone distractions:* Of course you don't have to make any outgoing calls during your scheduled study times, and you should resist doing so. As for incoming calls, there are four things you can do:

(1) Be disciplined and don't answer the phone at all. (What kind of power is it that the telephone has over us? When it rings, do we *have* to pick it up?)

(2) Answer the phone, but tell the caller you'll have to call back because "I have something important going on here."

(3) Tell whoever answers the phone to take a message for you. You can then call back on your 5-minute study break, if you can manage to keep the conversation short. Even better, you can call back after you're done studying.

(4) Let an answering machine collect your calls, then call back later. Whatever tactic you use, the idea is to minimize the interruption, of course.

I personally suggest letting another person or a machine take the calls. You're then like business people who have answering machines or secretaries hold their calls while they're doing important work, then return them all at once later.

■ *Fight people distractions:* I remember my freshman-year dorm had one guy who restlessly wandered up and down the hall, dropping in to students' rooms to make conversation. He drove me crazy because he never seemed to sense that I had other priorities.

Eventually I realized that, by not telling him I was too busy to talk, I was simply being too polite for my own good. I then hit on the idea of hanging a hotel-room DO NOT DISTURB sign on the door knob whenever I was studying. It worked. (If you do this, you need to remember to take in the sign when you're not studying. Otherwise, people won't pay any attention to it.)

People interruptions can be a real

problem, and eventually you have to learn to "Just say no." You shouldn't be complaining or accusatory, but polite and direct. There's a piece of advice that says, *Don't complain, don't explain, just declare.* So when interrupted, you just declare: "Sidney, this is interesting, but I have to study right now. Can we talk later?"

Early on you need to develop some understanding with your roommates or family members about your study requirements. Show them your study schedule. Tell them that when you're at your desk you're supposed to be doing your college work. Ask them for their assistance in helping you accomplish this. One writer says that a student he knows always wears a colorful hat when he wants to study. "When his wife and children see the hat, they respect his wish to be left alone."[15]

● ●

"There's a piece of advice that says, Don't complain, don't explain, just declare."

● ●

What if you're a parent and have nowhere to put a young child (not even in front of a television set or in a room full of toys)? In that case, just plan on doing the kind of studying that is not too demanding, expecting to be interrupted. Or use your study breaks to play with the child. Or take a few minutes to play attentively with the child before you hit the books, then say you have work to do. As long as the child feels he or she is getting *some* of your attention, you can still get some things done.

Of course, you can't control everything. Things will come up that will cut into your study time, as in the electricity going off or the flu wiping you out. That's why it's important to think of your scheduled study sessions as your main, inviolable study times. In addition, however, you need to be willing to study at various other, "fill-in" times. Let me explain how this works.

GAINING THE EXTRA EDGE. We often read of the superstar athlete who spends many extra hours shooting baskets or sinking putts. Or we hear of the superstar performer who endlessly rehearses a song or an acting part. These people don't have The Extra Edge just because of talent. (There's *lots* of talent around, but few superstars.) They have put in the additional hours because they are in a highly competitive business and they want to perfect their craft. Students are in the same situation.

What do you think when you walk across campus and see students studying on the lawn or in a bookstore line or at the bus stop? Perhaps you could think of them as doing just what the superstar basketball player shooting extra hoops does. *They are making use of the time-spaces in their day to gain The Extra Edge.*

Here are some techniques that can boost your performance:

■ *Always carry some school work and use waiting time:* Your day is made up of intervals that can be used—waiting for class to start, waiting for meals, waiting for the bus, waiting for appointments. These 5- or 10- or 20-minute periods can add up to a lot of time during the day. The temptation is to use this time just to "space out" or to read a newspaper. However, it can also be used to look over class notes, do some course-related reading, or review reading notes.

If you find yourself at times not carrying books or lecture notes, make a point of carrying 3×5 cards. These cards can contain important facts, names, definitions, formulas, and lists that you can pull out and memorize.

Students learning a foreign language often carry *flash cards*, with foreign words on one side and the English meaning on the other. **_Flash cards_ are cards bearing words, numbers, or pictures that are briefly displayed as a learning aid. One side of the card asks a question, the other side provides the answer.** Flash cards are also sold in college bookstores for other subjects, such as biology, to help you learn definitions. You can make up flash cards of your own for many courses.

The 5-minute ministudy session is far more beneficial than might first seem. The way to better memorizing is simply to *practice practice practice,* or *rehearse rehearse rehearse.* Just as the superstars do.

■ *Use your spare time for thinking:* What do you think about when you're jogging, walking to class, standing in a bank line, inching along in traffic? It could be about anything, of course. (Many people think about relationships or sex.) However, there are three ways your mind can be made to be productive:

(1) Try to recall points in a lecture that day.

(2) Try to recall points in something you've read.

(3) Think of ideas to go into a paper you're working on.

Again, the point of this use of idle time is to try to involve yourself with your college work. This is equivalent to football players working plays in their heads or singers doing different kinds of phrasing in their minds. The superstars are always working at their jobs.

Make tapes of lectures and listen to them: This advice is particularly suitable for students with a tape deck in the car or those with a portable tape player who ride the bus. At the end of a long day you might just want to space out to music. But what about at the beginning of the day, when you're fresh?

Making tapes of lectures is no substitute for taking notes. But listening to the tapes can provide you with *additional reinforcement*. This is especially the case if the lecture is densely packed with information, as, say, a history or biology lecture might be.

Special note: Be sure to ask your instructors for permission to tape them. Some are uncomfortable having tape recorders in their classes. Some institutions, in fact, *require* that you get the permission of instructors.

GROUP ACTIVITY #4.2

HOW DOES A STUDY GROUP WORK?

Research shows that students who study in groups often get the highest grades. The reasons are many. Students in a group fight isolation by being members of a social circle. They give each other support and encouragement. They help each other by working through lecture notes and readings and preparing for exams.

The purpose of this activity is to show you how to organize and perform in a study group. In the class for which you're reading this book, organize or join a group of three to five other students. (It's best if the group is not one you have been in before.) Introduce yourselves to one another, then consider the following questions, which have to do with this chapter. What are the biggest problems you have in studying? What are your principal distractions or time wasters? What time-spaces in your day could you use for mini-studying? What are the principal questions that will be asked about this chapter on the next exam? How do you feel about continuing this study group through the term for this course? What are some of your other, more difficult courses for which a study group would be helpful? Who would you ask to join in forming one?

Onward: Applying This Chapter to Your Life

PREVIEW Avoiding cramming is important, since it usually only produces stress without the grades to show for it.

erhaps you have a sneaky suspicion that all this time-management stuff really isn't necessary. After all, maybe in high school you put off a lot of studying, then at the last minute stayed up late *cramming*—studying with great intensity. Indeed, maybe you know that lots of college students seem to use this method.

Unfortunately, as a regular study technique, cramming leaves a lot to be desired. In fact, you'll probably find yourself greatly stressed without retaining much and without the grades to show for it. This is because in college there is so much more to learn.

In this chapter you looked at one of the two important techniques for being successful in college—time (and task) management. In the next chapter we'll consider the second one—*memorization*.

Learning time and task management is one of the skills that is essential for success not only in school but in life. What information in this chapter did you find most useful in helping you develop this skill? How can you apply it outside of college? Write it down here:

_____
_____
_____
_____
_____
_____
_____
_____
_____
_____
_____

THE EXAMINED LIFE: YOUR JOURNAL

1. How strongly motivated are you to pursue your life and college goals? What activities would you be willing to give up to achieve them?

2. Do you find, after keeping track of your time usage for a few days, that you waste time in certain specific ways? Do these time-wasting ways serve some other purposes in your life, such as alleviating stress or furthering friendships? How could these needs be addressed in some other ways to give you more time for college academic work?

3. Just as business and professional people often look for ways to improve their time-management skills, so can students. What kinds of things did you mark in this chapter that might help you manage your time better?

4. Some students get so deeply into "partying" that they find it has a major impact on their time. Often the kind of escape sought in partying is brought about by the stresses of the constant academic demands of college. Is this a possible area of concern for you? Explore it in depth.

5. If you're an adult returning student, what are some of the other responsibilities you have besides school? Are there some nonessential tasks that could be delegated to others?

memory

keystone to learning

so much to remember! how do people do it?

IN THIS CHAPTER: You discover one of the most valuable tools you own—your memory—and how to use it effectively. We consider three subjects:

■ *The importance of managing memory:* Understanding the drawbacks of cramming, the differences between short-term and long-term memory, and the "forgetting curve."

■ *Your learning style:* Which senses you tend to favor for learning—sound, sight, touch, or all three.

■ *How to improve your memory:* How to give your memory an extra push—through overlearning, studying a little at a time frequently, avoiding interference, making material meaningful to you, using verbal memory aids, and using visual memory aids.

1. What personal skills do you have? They could be anything from how to speak Spanish to how to shoot baskets, from how to drive a car to how to play a guitar. List two skills you feel especially good about.

_____

_____

_____

_____

_____

_____

2. Do some subject areas worry you because (to the extent you know anything about them) they seem to require lots of memorizing? Write down two of these areas here:

_____

_____

_____

_____

_____

■ SKIMMING FOR PAYOFFS

Both instances above involve use of your *memory*. Of course, you already have some skills that have involved lots of memorizing. You're capable of developing the same rich memory about subjects that you're now doubtful about.

Page through this chapter looking for payoffs—tips, methods, and ideas that might help you memorize terms and concepts in a new area.

Make notes ("Got to try this one!") in the margin opposite those things that interest you.

"What's a food you particularly like? Steak? Burgers? Ice cream?"

his is the beginning of a classroom routine I like to do once in a while that students seem to respond to.

People around the room volunteer a few favorite foods. ("Fudge!" "Piroshkis!" "Pepperoni pizza!")

I pick one of them. "Could you eat pizza every evening for a week?" I ask.

"Just about!" a couple of students may say.

"Okay, let's suppose I'm inviting you two over to my house for dinner tonight. And I'm going to order out for pizza, the best in town. All the toppings you like. Think you'd want to come?"

"Sure."

"I have just one qualification," I say. "You'll be required to eat a week's worth of pizza in one sitting."

"What!"

"Yep. It's the rule at my house."

"Well, I don't know . . ."

Then I explain what I'm driving at: Anyone would find it difficult to eat a week's worth of pizza at one meal. However, when it comes to schoolwork, many students think nothing of trying to stuff a week's worth of *studying* into a single evening.

The Importance of Managing Long-Term Memory

PREVIEW So much of college teaching consists of lectures and reading, which require memorization for testing. "Cramming" for exams—massive memorization at the last minute—is not advisable because there is so much to learn in college. Memory is principally *immediate, short-term,* and *long-term.* Boosting your long-term memory is better than favoring your short-term memory because of the "forgetting curve," whereby information retention drops sharply after 24 hours.

What would be your greatest wish to help you through college? Maybe it would be for a photographic memory, a mind that could briefly look at something just once and later recall it in detail. Perhaps 5–10% of school-age children have this kind of memory—it's called *eidetic imagery*—but it seldom lasts into adulthood.[1] You can see, though, why a photographic memory would be so valuable. *If so much of college instruction consists of lectures and readings and of testing you on how much you remember from them, your ability to memorize great quantities of information becomes crucial.*

How good is your memory? **Memory is defined as a mental process that entails three main operations: recording, storage, and recall.** The main strategy at work seems to be *association*—**one idea reminds you of another.**[2] Actually, even though you may worry that you have a weak memory because you immediately forget people's names after being introduced to them at a party, it's probably just fine. (Remembering names is a skill you can quite easily develop, as I'll show.) To see how good your memory is—and let me to prove a point—try Personal Exploration #5.1 on page 94.

"Do you regret it when you wait too long and have to cram for an exam?"

Name: Jennifer Boyce

Major: Human Services/Nursing

Interests: Reading, music, travel, sports

Answer to question: "Most definitely! I don't feel prepared, which makes me more frustrated and nervous, and then I forget what I've tried to cram in my brain in the first place! It's much easier for me to prepare for exams a little at a time; that way there is less pressure. Then, the night before the exam, all I have to do is look over my notes briefly and read chapter summaries. After I do this, I have a friend quiz me on the material. If all I wanted to do was pass the exam, cramming would be sufficient. But to get As and really learn the material, pacing yourself is a better alternative."

HOW'S YOUR MEMORY?

Honing your associative skills can boost short-term memory, says neurosurgeon Arthur Winter, director of the New Jersey Neurological Institute in Livingston and author of *Build Your Brain Power*.

■ WHAT TO DO

To test your powers of association, look at the following word list for just 5 seconds.

Dog	Stone
Cat	Winter
Bird	White
Shovel	Will
Skill	Went
House	Ten
Horse	Star
Crag	Stair
Robin	Life
Grant	Late
Elizabeth Taylor	Honor

Now cover the list and write down as many items as you can remember in the following space.

_____

_____

_____

_____

_____

_____

_____

_____

_____

_____

_____

_____

_____

_____

_____

_____

_____

■ INTERPRETATION

"How many did you write down?" asks Winter. Probably no more than 10, he guesses, although undoubtedly you remembered *Elizabeth Taylor*. The better you are at creating associations among words—such as making a sentence using most of them—the sharper your short-term memory will be.

Take a few minutes to make up a list of 15 terms (not people) related to *one* subject with which you are familiar. (Examples: cars, health, your school.) Now add the name of a famous person, such as a movie actor.

Swap lists face down with someone else in the class. When everyone has someone else's list, turn it over and take 10 seconds (looking at the classroom clock or being timed by your instructor) to try to memorize the 15 terms. Then turn the piece of paper over and write as many terms as you can on the back.

Discuss with others, in either a large or small group setting, how many terms you were able to remember in 10 seconds. What tricks, if any, did you use to recall terms? What does this experiment say about your ability to remember new terms you will need to memorize in a subject you've never studied before? Was the subject on which the terms were based (for example, health) one you were already familiar with? Were you therefore able to remember more terms than you probably would have otherwise?

"I CRAM, THEREFORE I AM." Your mind holds a wonderful mishmash of names, addresses, telephone numbers, pictures, familiar routes, words to songs, and thousands and thousands of other facts. How did you learn them—during several hours late one night or repeatedly over a long time? The answer is obvious.

When it comes to college, however, many students try to study for exams by doing a great deal of the work of a semester or quarter all in one night or in a couple of days. This is the time-honored memorizing marathon known as *cramming*. **Cramming is defined as preparing hastily for an examination.**

Many students have the notion that facts can be remembered best if they're *fresh*. There is indeed something to that, as I'll discuss. But does cramming work? Certainly it beats the alternative of not studying at all. Suppose, however, you crammed all night to memorize the lines of Hamlet. And suppose also that the next morning, instead of going to an examination room, you had to get up on a stage and recite the entire part. Could you do it? Probably not. Yet the quarter or semester's worth of material you have tried overnight to jam into your memory banks for a test may be even more comprehensive than all the lines Shakespeare wrote for his character.

In sum: Even if you found cramming a successful exam-preparation technique in high school, you should begin now to find other techniques for memorizing. In college there is simply too much to learn.

TYPES OF MEMORY: IMMEDIATE, SHORT-TERM, & LONG-TERM. To use your memory truly effectively to advance your college career—and your goals in life—it helps to know how it works. Memory is principally *immediate, short-term,* and *long-term.*

■ *Immediate perceptual memory:* **Immediate perceptual memory is defined as "a reflex memory in which an impression is immediately replaced by a new one."**[3] An example is in typing. As soon as a word is typed it is forgotten.

■ *Short-term memory:* **Short-term memory is defined by psychologists as recording seven elements for a maximum of 30 seconds.** This is about the number of elements and length of time required to look up a telephone number and dial it. Short-term memory has only limited capacity—for instance, about five to nine numbers for most people. To transfer such short-term information into your long-term memory requires reciting or other association techniques, as I'll discuss.

The details of short-term memories fade unless you rehearse them. Or unless some emotionally charged event happens at the same time.

■ *Long-term memory:* **Long-term memory entails remembering something for days, weeks, or years.** Long-term memory often requires that *some kind of change be made in your behavior* so that the information being learned makes a significant enough impression.

Remembering how to perform a musical piece, how to shoot a perfect free-throw, or how to do winning moves in chess require repetition. To achieve these things, you can't just "wing it" by learning something once. Of course, long-term memories also fade, but they do so more slowly.[4]

The forgetting curve.
Material is easily
forgotten if you are
exposed to it only once. The
retention of information drops
rapidly in the first 24 hours for
nonsense syllables, which are
not meaningful, and slightly less
so for prose, which is meaningful. Poetry is remembered best
because of helpful devices such
as rhyming. Even so, only 40% of
a poem is remembered after a
month's time.

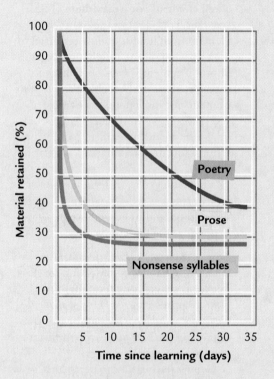

THE FORGETTING CURVE: FAST-FADING MEMORIES.

To understand why, from the standpoint of college learning, long-term memory is so much more important, consider what psychologists call the *forgetting curve*. In one famous experiment long ago, Hermann Ebbinghaus found that, in memorizing nonsense syllables, *a great deal of information is forgotten just during the first 24 hours,* then it levels out.[5] Although fortunately you need not memorize nonsense syllables, the rate of forgetting also occurs rapidly for prose and poetry. (*See* ■ *Panel 5.1.*) (Poetry is easier to memorize than prose because it has built-in memory cues such as rhymes.)

How good are people at remembering things in the normal course of events?

According to a survey from the National Institute for Development and Administration at the University of Texas, we remember only:

> *10% of what we read,*
> *20% of what we hear,*
> *30% of what we see,*
> *50% of what we see and hear,*
> *70% of what we say,*
> *90% of what we do and say.*[6]

Walter Pauk reports a study of people who read a textbook chapter in which it was found that they forgot:

> *46% of what they read after 1 day,*
> *79% of what they read after 14 days,*
> *81% of what they read after 28 days.*[7]

As for remembering what one has heard, Pauk describes an experiment in which a group of psychologists who attended a seminar forgot over 91% of what they had heard after two weeks.[8]

If you were tested every other day on the lectures you attended and textbooks you read, memorizing wouldn't be much of a problem. But that's not the way it usually works, of course. Ordinarily an instructor will give you an exam halfway or a third of the way into the course. There may be another exam later, followed by a final exam at the end of the course. Each time you will be held accountable for several weeks' worth of lectures and readings.

Memory is also important in writing papers. If you start your research or writing and then abandon it for a couple of weeks, it will take you some time to reconnect with your thoughts when you go back to it.

GROUP ACTIVITY #5.1

INTERVIEWING EACH OTHER: HOW'S YOUR MEMORY?

Divide into teams of two. Take 5 minutes or so apiece to interview each other, but *don't take notes*. Just try very hard to remember your team mate's answers.

Questions to ask: How good do you think your memory is? What subjects, hobbies, or interests are you able to memorize easily? What areas do you have trouble memorizing? Do you think cramming works? What memory tricks have you developed that you've found useful?

Now join with another team. Each of you reports to the group on what your partner said, then let your partner comment on how well you recalled his or her answers. What kinds of conclusions can you draw from this experience?

The Four Learning Styles: Which Fits You?

PREVIEW There are four types of learning styles, corresponding to the principal senses: auditory (hearing), visual (sight), kinesthetic (touch), and mixed modality (all three). You may favor one of these over the others.

Educators talk about differences in *learning styles*—**the ways in which people acquire knowledge.** Some students learn well by listening to lectures. Others learn better through reading, class discussion, hands-on experience, or researching a topic and writing about it. Thus, your particular learning style may make you more comfortable with some kinds of teaching and learning, and even with some kinds of subjects, than with others.

To find out the ways you learn best, try Personal Exploration #5.2.

HOW DO YOU LEARN BEST?

There are 12 incomplete sentences and three choices for completing each. Circle the answer that best corresponds to your style, as follows:

1 = the choice that is *least* like you.

2 = your second choice.

3 = the choice that is *most* like you.

1. When I want to learn something new, I usually . . .

   a. want someone to explain it to me. 1 2 3

   b. want to read about it in a book or magazine. 1 2 3

   c. want to try it out, take notes, or make a model of it. 1 2 3

2. At a party, most of the time I like to . . .

   a. listen and talk to two or three people at once. 1 2 3

   b. see how everyone looks and watch the people. 1 2 3

   c. dance, play games, or take part in some activities. 1 2 3

3. If I were helping with a musical show, I would most likely . . .

   a. write the music, sing the songs, or play the accompaniment. 1 2 3

   b. design the costumes, paint the scenery, or work the lighting effects. 1 2 3

   c. make the costumes, build the sets, or take an acting role. 1 2 3

4. When I am angry, my first reaction is to . . .

   a. tell people off, laugh, joke, or talk it over with someone. 1 2 3

   b. blame myself or someone else, daydream about taking revenge, or keep it inside 1 2 3

   c. make a fist or tense my muscles, take it out on something else, hit or throw things. 1 2 3

5. A happy event I would like to have is . . .

   a. hearing the thunderous applause for my speech or music. 1 2 3

   b. photographing the prize picture of an exciting newspaper story. 1 2 3

   c. achieving the fame of being first in a physical activity such as dancing, acting, surfing, or a sports event. 1 2 3

6. I prefer a teacher to . . .

   a. use the lecture method, with informative explanations and discussions. 1 2 3

   b. write on the chalkboard, use visual aids and assigned readings. 1 2 3

   c. require posters, models, or in-service practice, and some activities in class. 1 2 3

7. I know that I talk with . . .

   a. different tones of voice. 1 2 3

   b. my eyes and facial expressions. 1 2 3

   c. my hands and gestures. 1 2 3

8. If I had to remember an event so I could record it later, I would choose to . . .

   a. tell it aloud to someone, or hear an audiotape recording or a song about it. 1 2 3

   b. see pictures of it, or read a description. 1 2 3

   c. replay it in some practice rehearsal, using movements such as dance, play acting, or drill. 1 2 3

9. When I cook something new, I like to . . .

   a. have someone tell me the directions, a friend or TV show. 1 2 3

   b. read the recipe and judge by how it looks. 1 2 3

   c. use many pots and dishes, stir often, and taste-test. 1 2 3

10. My emotions can often be interpreted from my . . .

    a. voice quality. 1 2 3

    b. facial expression. 1 2 3

    c. general body tone. 1 2 3

11. When driving, I . . .

    a. turn on the radio as soon as I enter the car. 1 2 3

    b. like quiet so I can concentrate. 1 2 3

    c. shift my body position frequently to avoid getting tired. 1 2 3

12. In my free time, I like to . . .

    a. listen to the radio, talk on the telephone, or attend a musical event. 1 2 3

    b. go to the movies, watch TV, or read a magazine or book. 1 2 3

    c. get some exercise, go for a walk, play games, or make things. 1 2 3

■ SCORING

Add up the points for all the "a's," then all the "b's," then all the "c's."

Total points for all "a's": _____

Total points for all "b's": _____

Total points for all "c's": _____

(continued)

#5.2 CONTINUED

INTERPRETATION

If "a" has the highest score, that indicates your learning style preference is principally *auditory*.

If "b" has the highest score, your learning style preference is principally *visual*.

If "c" has the highest score, your learning style preference is *kinesthetic*.

If all scores are reasonably equal, that indicates your learning style preference is *mixed*.

See the text for explanations.

GROUP ACTIVITY OPTION

Do Personal Exploration #5.2. This activity could result in a real sense of discovery for you. Maybe you vaguely suspected that you learned better by one method than another, but now's the first time you've had it demonstrated. This is extremely important knowledge.

Read the text (pp. 97–100) for an explanation of what your scores mean. Then in a small group take turns discussing what you learned from this Personal Exploration. Does your learning style suggest you will learn some subjects more easily than you will others? Will you have difficulty learning from lectures or from reading, probably the two principal means by which knowledge is conveyed in college —and in life? What should you resolve to do if you've found out that you have a harder time learning by some methods than others?

People have four ways in which they favor learning new material: *auditory, visual, kinesthetic,* and *mixed modality.*[9] Let's consider these.

AUDITORY LEARNING STYLE. Auditory has to do with listening and also speaking. *Auditory learners* **use their voices and their ears as the primary means of learning.** They recall what they hear and what they themselves express verbally.

"When something is hard to understand, they want to talk it through," write professors Adele Ducharme and Luck Watford of Valdosta State University in Georgia. "When they're excited and enthusiastic about learning, they want to verbally express their response. . . . These learners love class discussion, they grow by working and talking with others, and they appreciate a teacher taking time to explain something to them."[10]

If you're this type of person, it's important to know that such learners are easily distracted by sounds. Thus, it's a good idea that they *not* listen to the radio while studying, because they attend to all the sounds around them. An effective study technique, however, is to repeat something aloud several times because that helps them memorize it. These types of learners may do well in learning foreign languages, music, and other subjects that depend on a strong auditory sense.

VISUAL LEARNING STYLE. Visual, of course, refers to the sense of sight. *Visual learners* **like to see pictures of things described or words written down.** "They will seek out illustrations, diagrams, and charts to help them understand and remember information," say Ducharme and Watford. "They appreciate being able to follow what a teacher is presenting with material written on an overhead transparency or in a handout." For visual learners, an effective technique for reviewing and studying material is to read over their notes and recopy and reorganize information in outline form.

KINESTHETIC LEARNING STYLE. *Kinesthetic* (pronounced "kin-es-*thet*-ik") has to do with the sense of touch and of physical manipulation. *Kinesthetic learners* **learn best when they touch and are physically involved in what they are studying.** These are the kind of people who fidget when

How to Improve Your Memory Power

PREVIEW There are several principal strategies for converting short-term memory to long-term memory: (1) You can practice relaxation. (2) You can practice repeatedly, even overlearn material. (3) You can study a little at a time repeatedly (distributed practice) instead of cramming (massed practice). (4) You can avoid memory interference from studying similar material or being distracted. (5) You can make material personally meaningful to you. (6) You can use verbal memory aids—write out or organize information; use rhymes, phrases, and abbreviations; make up narrative stories. (7) You can use visual memory aids—make up a vivid picture or story of unusual images.

they have to sit still and who express enthusiasm by jumping up and down. "These learners want to act out a situation, to make a product, to do a project, and in general to be busy with their learning," say Ducharme and Watford. "They find that when they physically do something, they understand it and they remember it."

MIXED-MODALITY LEARNING STYLE. Modality (pronounced "moh-*dal*-it-y") means style. As you might guess, **_mixed-modality learners_ are able to function in any three of these learning styles or "modalities"— auditory, visual, and kinesthetic.** Clearly, these people are at an advantage because they can handle information in whatever way it is presented to them.

LEARNING STYLES, LECTURES, & READING. Lectures would seem to favor auditory learners. Textbooks would seem to favor visual learners. Lectures and readings are the two principal pipelines by which information is conveyed in college.

However, suppose one or both of these methods don't suit you? Since you don't usually have a choice about how a subject is taught, it's important to get comfortable with both methods. This means you need to be able to *extract* the most information out of a lecture or textbook—that is, take useful notes, for example—regardless of your learning preference and the instructor's style. Chapters 6 and 7 show how to do this.

s should be clear by now, *success in college principally lies with a strategy in which you convert short-term memories into long-term memories.* Let me suggest a number of techniques for doing this.

1. RELAX & BE ATTENTIVE. You have certainly discovered that you easily recall those things that interest you—things to which you were *attentive*. "*Attention is conscious, not reflex,*" says one memory expert (the emphasis is hers). "It is indispensable to the controlled recording of information."[11]

The goal of improving your memory, then, is to improve your attention, as we explain in this section. The first means for doing this is through relaxation. Anxiety interferes with memorizing, distracting your recall abilities with negative worries. When you are relaxed, your mind captures information more easily.

Thus, when you sit down to read a textbook, write notes for a lecture, or take a test, take a few seconds to *become relaxed*. Close your eyes, take a deep breath, inhale, repeat. Say to yourself, "I plan to remember." If you're still tense, repeat this a few times.

The rule here, then, is: *Put yourself in a relaxed frame of mind when you're planning to absorb information you will have to remember later.* Some relaxation techniques are described in Chapter 11, "Health."

2. PRACTICE REPEATEDLY—EVEN OVERLEARN MATERIAL. How well could you play a part in a play after two readings? five readings? fifteen? Clearly, you can't just speed-read or skim the script. You have to actively practice or rehearse the material. The more you rehearse, the better you retain information. Indeed, it has been found that *overlearning*—continued study even after you think you have learned the material—will help you really commit it to memory.[12] **Overlearning is defined as continued rehearsal of material after you first appeared to have mastered it.**[13]

A good way to learn is to repeatedly test your knowledge in order to rehearse it. Some textbooks come with self-testing study guides to help you do this, but you can also make up the questions yourself or form a study group with friends to trade questions and answers.

The more you rehearse, in fact, the better you may also *understand* the material.[14] This is because as you review your mind begins to concentrate on the most important features, thus helping your understanding.

The rule, then, is: *Study or practice repeatedly to fix material firmly in mind.* You can apply this rule to your social life, too. If you meet someone new at a party, for instance, you can repeat the person's name on being introduced, then say it again to yourself; then wait a minute and say it again. There are also some other tricks of association. (*See* ■ *Panel 5.2 on page 102.*)

3. STUDY A LITTLE AT A TIME FREQUENTLY: DISTRIBUTED PRACTICE VERSUS MASSED PRACTICE. Learning experts distinguish between two kinds of learning or practice techniques: massed practice and distributed practice.

- *Massed practice:* Massed practice is what students do when they are cramming. **Massed practice is putting all your studying into one long period of time**—for example, one study session of 8 hours in one day.

- *Distributed practice:* Distributed practice takes no more time than cramming. **With distributed practice you distribute the same number of hours over several days**—for example, four days of studying 2 hours a day.

Distributed practice has been found to be more effective for retaining information than mass practice, especially if the space between practice periods is reasonably long, such as 24 hours.[15] One reason is that studying something at different times links it to a wider variety of associations.[16]

The rule here, therefore, is: *Study or practice a little at a time frequently rather than a lot infrequently.* This rule suggests you can make use of the time-spaces in your day for studying. You can look over your notes or books or flash cards while on the bus, for example, or waiting for class to start. You can mentally rehearse lists while standing in line. It's like the difference between lifting weights once for 5 hours or five sessions of 1 hour each: the first way won't train you nearly as well as the second way.

4. AVOID INTERFERENCE. Learning some kinds of information will interfere with your ability to recall other kinds of information, especially if the subjects are similar. **Interference is the competition among related memories.** For example, if you tried to memorize the names of the bones in the feet and then memorize the names of the bones in the hand, one memory will interfere with the other. (*Proactive interference* is the disruption an older memory produces on a newer one.

How to remember names. Stanford University memory expert Danielle Lapp offers these tips.

To put a name on a face, you can learn a mnemonic [memory device] based on the principle of image-association. At the time of recording, just do the following:

1. Choose one Prominent Feature in the face, and analyze it.
   (PF = Image #1)

2. Look for a Name Trans-formation (NT = Image #2) by "listening" to the sound of the name (or by dividing it analytically into syllables), answer-ing the question: "Does the name *mean* anything (or make me think of something) *easy to visual-ize?*"

3. Make an Image-Associa-tion by visualizing the two together.
   (PF + NT) . . .

Upon meeting someone, choose a Prominent Feature during your conversa-tion. At the time of parting, ask the person to repeat his/her name and visualize it in red graffiti on a white wall (visual trick). Then look for a Name Transformation. Practice makes a big difference in the matter. For example: Fenn = a fin, Grey = the fog, O'Neill = kneeling in front of an egg. Do not forget the last important step: Visualize the two together while repeating the name.

Retroactive interference is the disruption a newer memory produces on an older one.) And the more information you learn, such as lists of words, the more you may have trouble with new information on successive days, such as new lists of words.[17]

Interference can also come from other things, such as distractions from the people you share your living space with, background music, television, and so on. The notion of interference also suggests why you do better at recalling information when it is fresh in mind. In other words, though I don't recommend cramming for exams, I do recommend giving information a thorough last-minute review before you go into the test. A last-minute review puts the "frosting on the cake" of helping you absorb the material, but it's no substitute for studying the material earlier.

The lesson here is: *When you're trying to memorize material, don't study anything else that is too similar too soon.* This is why it is often a good idea to study before going to sleep: there is less chance of the new information getting competition from other information.[18] It also shows why it's a good idea to study similar material for different courses on different days. [19]

5. MAKE MATERIAL MEANINGFUL TO YOU: DEPTH OF PROCESSING. Information in memory may be stored at a superficial or at a deep level, depending on how well you understood it and how much you thought about it, according to the *depth-of-processing principle*.[20] **The *depth-of-processing principle* states that how shallowly or deeply you hold a thought depends on how much you think about it and how many associations you form with it.** The deeper the level of "processing" or thinking, the more you remember it.

This means that in memorizing something you shouldn't just mindlessly repeat the material; you are better able to remember it when you can make it meaningful.[21] It's important to somehow make the material your own—understand it, organize it, put it in your own words, develop emotional associations toward it, associate it with information you already know or events you have already experienced. For example, if you are trying to remember that business organizations have departments that perform five functions—accounting, marketing, production, personnel management, and research—you can look for relationships among them. Which departments do or do not apply to you? Which ones do your relatives work in? Indeed, one way to make material meaningful to you is to *organize* it in some way, which is why outlining your reading can be a useful tool.

To repeat, the rule here is: *Make learning personally meaningful to you.* This is also a trick you can use in your social life. If you meet someone new at a party, you can try to remember the new name by associating it with the face of someone else with that name. (When you meet someone named Kirk, remember that your uncle is named Kirk too, or think of actor Kirk Douglas or of *Star Trek*'s Captain Kirk.)

6. USE VERBAL MEMORY AIDS. One way to make information more meaningful, and so retain it better, is to use memory aids—and the more you are able to personalize them, the more successful they will be. Psychologists call memory aids *mnemonic* ("nee-*mahn*-ik") *devices*, **tactics for making things memorable by making them distinctive.**

Some verbal devices for enhancing memory are as follows:

- *Write out your information:* This advice may seem obvious. Still, the evidence is that if you write out a shopping list, for example, but lose it, you are more apt to remember the items than if you didn't write them out.[22] Clearly, this is a reason for taking notes during a lecture, quite apart from making a record: the very act of writing helps you retain information.

- *Organize your information:* People are better able to memorize material when they can organize it. This is one reason why imposing a ranking or hierarchy, such as an outline, on lecture notes or reading notes works so well, especially when the material is difficult.[23]

- **Use rhymes to remember important ideas:** You may have heard the spelling rule, "I before E except after C" (so that you'll be correct in spelling "receive," not "recieve"). This an example of the use of rhyme as a memory aid. Another is "Thirty days hath September, April, June, and November. . . ."

Most of the time, of course, you'll have to make up your own rhymes. It doesn't matter how silly they are. Indeed, the sillier they are, the better you may be able to remember them.

- **Use phrases whose first letters represent ideas you want to remember:** Probably the first thing music students learn is "*Every Good Boy Does Fine*" to remember what notes designate the lines of the musical staff: *E G B D F*. This is an example of using a phrase in which the first letter of each word is a cue to help you recall abstract words beginning with the same letter.

What kind of sentence would you make up to remember that business organizations have departments performing five functions—*Accounting, Marketing, Production, Personnel* management, and *Research*? (Maybe it would be, "*Any Man Playing Poker is Rich*"—this also plants a picture in your mind that will help your recall.)

- **Use a word whose first letters represent ideas you want to remember:** To remember the five business functions above, you could switch the words around and have the nonsense word *PRAMP* (to rhyme with "ramp," then think of, say, a wheelchair ramp or a ramp with a pea rolling down it), the letters of which stand for the first letters of the five functions.

A common example of the use of this device is the name "Roy G. Biv," which students use to memorize the order of colors in the light spectrum: *r*ed, *o*range, *y*ellow, *g*reen, *b*lue, *i*ndigo, *v*iolet. Another is "Mark's Very Elegant Mother Just Sent Us Nine Puppies" for the order of the planets in our solar system: *M*ercury, *V*enus, *E*arth, *M*ars, *J*upiter, *S*aturn, *U*ranus, *N*eptune, *P*luto.

- **Make up a narrative story that associates words:** In a technique known as the **narrative story method, it has been found that making up a narrative, or story, helps students recall unrelated lists of words by giving them meaning and linking them in a specific order.**[24]

Suppose you need to memorize the words *Rustler, Penthouse, Mountain, Sloth, Tavern, Fuzz, Gland, Antler, Pencil, Vitamin.* This is quite a mixed bag, but if you were taking a French class, you might have to memorize these words (in the foreign language). Here is the story that was constructed to help recall these unrelated words:

A Rustler *lived in a* Penthouse *on top of a* Mountain. *His specialty was the three-toed* Sloth. *He would take his captive animals to a* Tavern, *where he would remove* Fuzz *from their* Glands. *Unfortunately, all this exposure to sloth fuzz caused him to grow* Antlers. *So he gave up his profession and went to work in a* Pencil *factory. As a precaution he also took a lot of* Vitamin E.[25]

"What device or approach have you found most useful for helping you remember things you're trying to learn?"

Name: Walter Carney

Major: Liberal Arts & Sciences: General Studies

Interests: Weightlifting, exercise

Answer to question: "The past few months I have learned more from the First-Year Experience course about how to remember than ever before: How to take notes. What to look for from instructors. How to study. Reading my notes shortly after class, reciting them aloud, and relating them to something familiar has been most helpful to me. Also, I've made flash cards for math, psychology, and First-Year Experience—they have been a great help."

In using verbal memory tricks, then, the rule is: *Make up verbal cues that are meaningful to you to represent or associate ideas.* In social situations, as when you are introduced to several people simultaneously, you can try using some of these devices. For example, "LAP" might represent Larry, Ann, and Paul.

7. USE VISUAL MEMORY AIDS. Some psychologists theorize that using visual images creates a second set of cues in addition to verbal cues that can help memorization.[26] In other words, it helps if you can mentally "take photographs" of the material you are trying to retain.

There are two visual memory aids you may find useful—a single unusual visual image, or a series of visual images.

■ *Make up a vivid, unusual picture to associate ideas:* The stranger and more distinctive you can make your image, the more you are apt to be able to remember it.[27]

Thus, to remember the five business functions (research, accounting, marketing, personnel management, production), you might create a picture of a woman with a white laboratory coat (research) looking through a magnifying glass at a man a'counting money (accounting) while sitting in a food-market shopping cart (marketing) that is being pushed by someone wearing a letter sweater that says *Person L* (personnel) who is watching a lavish Hollywood spectacle—a production—on a movie screen (production). (If you wish, you could even draw a little sketch of this while you're trying to memorize it.)

■ *Make up a story of vivid images to associate ideas:* A visual trick called the *method of loci* ("method of places") is to memorize a series of places and then use a different vivid image to associate each place with an idea or a word you want to remember.[28]

For example, you might use buildings and objects along the route from your house to the campus, or from your residence hall to a classroom, each one associated with a specific word or idea.

Again, the image associated with each location should be as distinctive as you can make it. To remember the information, you imagine yourself proceeding along this route, so that the various locations cue the various ideas. (The locations need not resemble the ideas. For example, you might associate a particular tree with a man in a white laboratory coat in its branches—research.)

In short, when using visual memory tricks, the rule is: *the more bizarre you make the picture, the more you are apt to remember it.*

MEMORIZING TECHNIQUES REVISITED. Get relaxed. Rehearse repeatedly. Study small amounts of information frequently. Avoid interference from similar material or distractions. Make material personally meaningful to you. Use distinctive verbal and visual memory cues.

Perhaps you've noticed something I'm doing in these pages: I am using the trick of repetition, telling you the principles of memorization three times. Does this help you retain the information? If not, stop here and look back through the preceding pages.

GROUP ACTIVITY #5.2

FINDING EXAMPLES OF THE SEVEN MEMORIZING STRATEGIES

Divide into seven small groups with nearly equal numbers of people in each group. Each group should take one of the seven memorizing strategies discussed: relaxation, overlearning, distributed practice, avoiding interference, depth of processing, verbal memory aids, visual memory aids.

With others in your group, come up with as many ways as possible to illustrate how you could use the particular learning strategy. Share your best examples with others in the class. Invite discussion and other examples from the class.

Onward: Applying This Chapter to Your Life

PREVIEW Rehearse it often, make it meaningful.

In this chapter I described the general strategies of memorization. In general, they may be summarized as two principles: (1) *Rehearse it often.* (2) *Make it meaningful to you.* In the upcoming chapters, I'll show you some refinements, such as how to apply these strategies to your reading assignments, lecture notes, and test taking.

There was probably some piece of knowledge in this chapter that you will find you can use outside of college, as in your career or other aspects of your life. What was it? Write it down here:

_____

_____

_____

_____

_____

_____

_____

_____

_____

_____

_____

_____

_____

_____

_____

_____

_____

_____

_____

1. What subjects do you worry you will have the most trouble memorizing? Why is this? What tricks can you use from this chapter to change this?

2. In what kind of areas have you had to do extensive memorizing in the past? Examples might be music, athletic moves or plays, dramatic roles, or skills in conjunction with a job. What motivated you to remember? How did you go about doing the memorization?

3. Which is your predominant learning style—sight, hearing, or touch? What kind of work can you do to improve your skills with other learning styles?

4. Think of some nonacademic areas connected with college in which it might be useful to do extensive memorizing. For example, you might want to learn the names of everyone in your living group, or the department where you work, or on a team on which you play. How would you go about a program of memorizing?

lectures

important information pipeline #1

make notes that really work

IN THIS CHAPTER: Now we come to some techniques that will truly benefit you for the rest of your life:

■ **Making lectures work:** Whatever you think of lectures, they can be made to work for you.

■ **Memorizing material:** How to use the "5R steps" to memorize information from a lecture.

1. When you think of listening to a lecture, what negative feelings, if any, come to mind? Write them down here:

_____

_____

_____

_____

_____

_____

_____

2. Which is more important to you—doing enough in college to avoid flunking out or doing enough to pull As and Bs? Express your answer, using some sort of private shorthand.

_____

_____

_____

_____

_____

_____

■ SKIMMING FOR PAYOFFS

Because you will encounter the lecture method in one form or another all your life (for example, in meetings or speeches), you'll want to have a strategy for dealing with it. Look through this chapter and see what two things you can take away from it that will benefit you outside of college. Make some sort of note in the margin.

Lecturing may be an efficient way for instructors to convey information. Is it a good way for students to receive it?

I do a great deal of teaching through discussion and small-group activities, but I also do a fair amount of lecturing, as do most instructors. Lecturing is certainly an easy way for instructors to transfer knowledge—they talk and students listen. Perhaps this is why the lecture system is one of the mainstays of college teaching. Whether it is efficient for any given student, however, depends a lot on his or her preferred learning style.

Lectures, Learning Styles, & Life

PREVIEW Because you can't control the way information is conveyed to you, either in college or in your career, it's important to become comfortable with the lecture method. This means discovering how to extract material from the lecture and learn it.

f the four learning styles I described in Chapter 5—auditory, visual, kinesthetic, and mixed modality—lectures would seem to favor auditory learners. *Auditory learners,* you'll recall, use their voices and their ears as the primary means of learning.

But suppose you're not an auditory learner. That is, suppose you're a *visual learner* and favor pictures or words written down. Or you're *kinesthetic* and favor touching and physical involvement. (If you're *the mixed-modality type,* you can function in all three learning styles.)

In the work world, too, you don't always have a choice about the method by which information is conveyed to you. You may often have to attend a meeting, presentation, speech, or company training program. There, as I pointed out earlier, the "examination" will consist of how well you recall and handle the information in order to do your job.

It's important, therefore, that you learn to get comfortable with the lecture method of teaching. Thus, you have two tasks:

- *Be able to extract material:* You need to be able to *extract* the most information out of a lecture—that is, take useful notes, regardless of your learning preference and the instructor's style.

- *Be able to learn material:* You need to be able to *learn* the lecture material so that you can do well on tests.

The rest of this chapter shows you how to accomplish this.

GROUP ACTIVITY #6.1

HOW WELL DOES YOUR LEARNING STYLE SUIT THE LECTURE METHOD?

n a group situation, look back at Personal Exploration #5.2 in Chapter 5. Determine which learning style—auditory, visual, kinesthetic, or mixed-modality—you seem to favor. Then discuss the following questions.

What experiences have you had that make you think you like one learning style better than others (if that's the case)? How well does your learning style relate to the lecture method of presenting information? In a work situation, have you had any difficulty with retaining information from presentations and meetings? What kinds of strategies would you recommend for getting the most out of the lecture system?

Making Lectures Work: What They Didn't Tell You in High School

PREVIEW Cutting classes has been found to be associated with poor grades. Being in class, even a boring one, helps you learn what the instructor expects. It also reflects your attitude about your college performance—whether you want to get successfully through school or merely slide by. Being an active participant means bringing syllabus and textbooks to class and doing the homework and reviewing previous assignments in order to be ready for each new lecture.

ow do you approach the whole matter of going to class? Many of your classroom habits may have been picked up while you were in high school. Do you sit in the back, find yourself constantly

Successful and unsuccessful students' class attendance. According to one study, attendance was much better among successful students (B average or above) than unsuccessful students (C-minus or below).

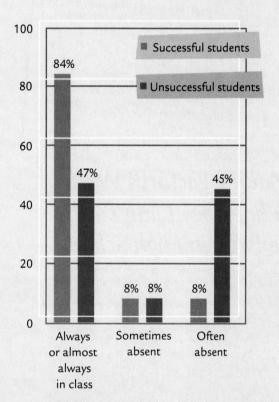

- Successful students
- Unsuccessful students

100

80

60

40

20

0

84%

47%

8% 8%

8%

45%

Always or almost always in class

Sometimes absent

Often absent

distracted during lectures, have difficulty taking notes? To get an idea of your present performance in the classroom, try Personal Exploration #6.1.

CLASS ATTENDANCE & GRADES. In high school, I was required to attend every class every school day. What a surprise, then, when I got to college and found that in many classes professors didn't even take attendance and that I was free to cut if I chose. Of course, it was easy to be selective about which classes to go to and which not. In the wintertime, for instance, it wasn't hard to choose between staying in a warm bed and getting up for an 8:00 A.M. class—particularly if I thought the instructor or the subject was boring.

However, in those early days I was not aware of an important fact: *poor class attendance is associated with poor grades.* According to one study, "unsuccessful" students—those defined as having grades of C-minus or below—were found to be more commonly absent from class than "successful" students, those with a B average or above.[1] *(See* ■ *Panel 6.1.)*

"But," students may say, "what if I find the lecture's practically useless? Why should I waste my time?"

There are two answers to this—things they don't usually tell you in high school:

- ■ *Being in class helps you learn what the instructor expects—and to anticipate exams:* Even if the instructor is so hard to follow that you learn very little from the lectures, it's still important to go to class. "If nothing else," one set of writers points out, "you'll get a feel for how the instructor thinks. This can help you to anticipate the content of exams and to respond in the manner your professor expects."[2]

- ■ *Going to class goes along with a successful attitude about college in general:* There are probably two kinds of students: passive students, or those who try to slide by in school, and active students, or those who try to triumph in school.

  Students who try to *slide* by in school are those who look for all the ways to pass their courses with the least amount

LISTENING QUESTIONNAIRE: HOW'S YOUR CLASSROOM PERFORMANCE?

Read each statement and decide how the habit reflects your listening. Answer as follows:

"Yes"—if you use the habit over half your listening time.
"No"—if you don't use the habit very much at all.
"Sometimes"—if you use the habit periodically.

1. Do you often doodle while listening?
   ❑ Yes
   ❑ No
   ❑ Sometimes

2. Do you show attending behaviors through your eye contact, posture, and facial expressions?
   ❑ Yes
   ❑ No
   ❑ Sometimes

3. Do you try to write down everything you hear?
   ❑ Yes
   ❑ No
   ❑ Sometimes

4. Do you listen largely for central ideas as opposed to facts and details?
   ❑ Yes
   ❑ No
   ❑ Sometimes

5. Do you often daydream or think about personal concerns while listening?
   ❑ Yes
   ❑ No
   ❑ Sometimes

6. Do you ask clarifying questions about what you do not understand in a lecture?
   ❑ Yes
   ❑ No
   ❑ Sometimes

7. Do you frequently feel tired or sleepy when attending a lecture?
   ❑ Yes
   ❑ No
   ❑ Sometimes

8. Do you mentally review information as you listen to make connections among points?
   ❑ Yes
   ❑ No
   ❑ Sometimes

9. Do you often call a lecture boring?
   ❑ Yes
   ❑ No
   ❑ Sometimes

10. Do you recall what you already know about a subject before the lecture begins?
    ❑ Yes
    ❑ No
    ❑ Sometimes

11. Do you generally avoid listening when difficult information is presented?
    ❑ Yes
    ❑ No
    ❑ Sometimes

12. Do you pay attention to the speaker's nonverbal cues?
    ❑ Yes
    ❑ No
    ❑ Sometimes

13. Do you often find yourself thinking up arguments to refute the speaker?
    ❑ Yes
    ❑ No
    ❑ Sometimes

14. Do you generally try to find something of interest in a lecture even if you think it's boring?
    ❑ Yes
    ❑ No
    ❑ Sometimes

15. Do you usually criticize the speaker's delivery, appearance, or mannerisms?
    ❑ Yes
    ❑ No
    ❑ Sometimes

16. Do you do what you can to control distractions around you?
    ❑ Yes
    ❑ No
    ❑ Sometimes

17. Do you often fake attention to the speaker?
    ❑ Yes
    ❑ No
    ❑ Sometimes

18. Do you periodically summarize or recapitulate what the speaker has said during the lecture?
    ❑ Yes
    ❑ No
    ❑ Sometimes

19. Do you often go to class late?
    ❑ Yes
    ❑ No
    ❑ Sometimes

20. Do you review the previous class lecture notes before attendin class?
    ❑ Yes
    ❑ No
    ❑ Sometimes

(continued)

#6.1 CONTINUED

SCORING

Count the number of "Yes" answers to *even-numbered* items: _____

Count the number of "Yes" answers to *odd-numbered* items: _____

INTERPRETATION: The even-numbered items are considered *effective* listening habits.

The odd-numbered items are considered *ineffective* listening habits.

If you answered an item as "Sometimes," determine how often and under what circumstances you find yourself responding this way. Identify the areas where you have written "Yes" or "Sometimes" to odd-numbered items and write an explanation here:

_____
_____
_____
_____
_____
_____
_____
_____
_____
_____

GROUP ACTIVITY OPTION

In a small group situation, go through Personal Exploration #6.1 and discuss some of the items you answered "Yes" to. What things are you doing right? What things need changing? Since changing one's behavior is not always easy, what kinds of prompts or reinforcement will you give yourself to help you change negative behavior to positive behavior?

of effort: they cut class, borrow other students' notes, cram the night before exams, and so on.

Students who try to *triumph* in school take the attitude that, sure, there are certain shortcuts or efficiencies to making one's way through college (this book is full of such tips). However, they realize that always trying to cut corners is not productive in the long run. Thus, among other things, they try to attend every class.

Which one would an employer want to hire? Here again we have the relevance of college to life outside college: A can-do attitude in higher education is the kind of quality needed for you to prevail in the world of work.

BEING AN ACTIVE PARTICIPANT: PREPARING FOR CLASS. Being an active rather than passive student means becoming involved in the course. Besides attending regularly and being on time for class, try to prepare for your upcoming classes, doing the following:

- *Use the course syllabus as a basic "roadmap":* The syllabus is a very important document. **The _syllabus_ (pronounced "*sill*-uh-buss") is a course outline or guide that tells you what readings are required, what assignments are due when, and when examinations are scheduled.** This basic roadmap to the course is a page or more that the instructor hands out on the first class day.

  It's a good idea to three-hole-punch the syllabus and include it in the front of your binder or staple it inside the front of your notebook. That way you will automatically bring it to class and can make any changes to it that the instructor announces (such as a new date for a test).

- *Do the homework before the lecture:* A syllabus will often show that certain readings coincide with certain lectures. It usually works best if you do the readings *before* rather than after the lectures. Like putting your toe in the water, this will help you know what to expect. If you do the homework first, you'll understand the instructor's remarks better.

- **Anticipate the lecture:** Not only will doing the required readings before class prepare you for the lecture, but so will reading over your lecture notes from the last class. Often the next lecture is a continuation of the last one. In addition, you can look at the syllabus to see what's expected.

  When doing the homework, develop questions on the readings. Bring these to class for clarification.

- **Bring the textbook to class:** Some people come to class carrying only a notebook and pen (and some don't even bring those). Are they the A and B students? If I had to guess, I would say they are not the top grade getters.

  Students who are successful performers in college don't feel they always have to travel light. Besides their notebook they also carry the principal textbook and other books (or supplies) relevant to the course. This is because instructors often make special mention of material in the textbook, or they draw on the text for class discussion. Some instructors even follow the text quite closely in their lectures. Thus, if you have the text in the classroom, you can follow along and make marks in the book, writing down possible exam questions or indicating points of emphasis.

GROUP ACTIVITY #6.2
PRACTICING GETTING READY FOR THE NEXT LECTURE

This activity requires that you have the syllabus for one of your other classes, along with the principal textbook and lecture notes from the most recent lecture. In a small-group situation, discuss what you need to do for the upcoming lecture in that course, following the guidelines above.

The 5R Steps: Record, Rewrite, Recite, Reflect, Review

PREVIEW Because the greatest amount of forgetting happens in the first 24 hours, you need not just a note-*taking* system but also a note-*reviewing* system. Five steps for committing lecture notes to long-term memory are: Record, Rewrite, Recite, Reflect, and Review.

Many students have the idea that they can simply take notes of a lecture and then review them whenever it's convenient—perhaps the night before a test. Certainly that was the way I started out doing it in college. And it's easy to think you are doing well when you attend every class and fill page after page of your notebook.

However, simply writing everything down—acting like a human tape recorder—by itself doesn't work. *The name of the game, after all, is to learn the material, not just make a record of it.* Writing things down now but saving all the learning for later is simply not efficient. As I mentioned elsewhere, research shows that the most forgetting takes place within the first 24 hours, then drops off. The trick, then, is to figure out how to reduce the forgetting of that first 24 hours.

Effective learning requires that you be not only a good note *taker* but also a good note *reviewer.* This may mean you need to change the note-taking and note-learning approach you're accustomed to. However, once these new skills are learned, you'll find them invaluable not only in college but also in your career. One method that has been found to be helpful in note taking and note learning consists of five steps known as **the _5R steps_, for Record, Rewrite, Recite, Reflect, Review**. They are:

Blank margins. Draw rules on your note paper as shown. (This is a variation on the "Cornell method" of note taking.)

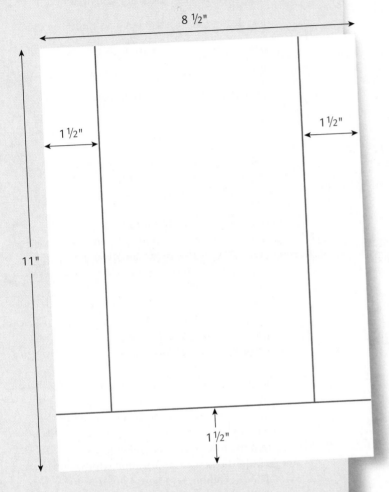

8 ½"

1 ½"   1 ½"

11"

1 ½"

■ *Step 1—Record:* Capture the main ideas.

■ *Step 2—Rewrite:* Following the lecture, rewrite your notes, developing key terms, questions, and summaries.

■ *Step 3—Recite:* Covering up the key terms, questions, and summaries, practice reciting them to yourself.

■ *Step 4—Reflect:* To anchor these ideas, make some personal association with them.

■ *Step 5—Review:* Two or three times a week, if possible, review your notes to make them more familiar.

"Too much!" I hear students say. "I've got a lot of things to do. I can't be forever rehashing one lecture!"

Actually, the system may not take as much time as it first looks. Certainly it need not take much more *effort* than if you try to learn it all by cramming—absorbing all the material in one sitting.

In any event, studies show that increased practice or rehearsal not only increases retention. It also improves your *understanding* of material, because as you go over it repeatedly, you are able to concentrate on the most important points.[3]

You probably can appreciate this from your own experience in having developed some athletic, musical, or other skill: the more you did it, the better you got. Like an actor, the more you practice or rehearse the material, the better you will be able to overcome stage fright and deliver your best performance on examination day.

Let's consider what these five steps are:

STEP 1: RECORD. You'll see many of your classmates with pens racing to try to capture every word of the lecture. Don't bother. You're not supposed to be like a court reporter or a secretary-stenographer, recording every word. You should be less concerned with taking down everything than in developing a *system* of note taking. Here is how the system works:

■ *Leave blank margins on your note page:* This is a variation on what is known as the *Cornell format* of note taking. *(See* ■ *Panel 6.2.)* Draw a vertical line, top to bottom, 1 ½ inches from the left edge of the paper, a similar line 1 ½ inches from the right side, and a horizontal line 1 ½ inches up from the bottom. As I explain below, you will use these blank margins for review purposes.

- **Take notes in rough paragraph form:** At some point you may have been told to take notes in outline form, using the standard "I, A, 1, a," format. If you're good at this, that's fine. However, most professors don't lecture this way, and you should not have to concentrate on trying to force an outline on the lecture material.

  Simply take your notes in rough paragraph form. Put extra space (a line or two) between new ideas and divisions of thought. Don't try to save on the cost of notepaper by cramming notes onto every line of the page.

- **Try to capture the main ideas:** Don't try to take down everything the instructor says. Not only will this create a mass of information that you will have to sort through later, it will also interfere with your learning. Instead of forcing you to pay attention and concentrate on what's important, you become simply a tape recorder. An extremely important part of your note-taking system, then, is to try to capture just the key ideas. More on this below.

- **Develop a system of abbreviations:** Some people take highly readable notes, as though preparing to let other people borrow them. You shouldn't concern yourself primarily with this kind of legibility. The main thing is that *you* be able to take ideas down fast and *you* be able to read them later.

  Thus, make up your own system of abbreviations. For example, "w.r.t" means "with regard to"; "sike" means "psychology"; "para" is borrowing the Spanish word for "in order to." *(See ■ Panel 6.3.)*

By adopting these practices, you'll be well on your way to retaining more information than you have in the past.

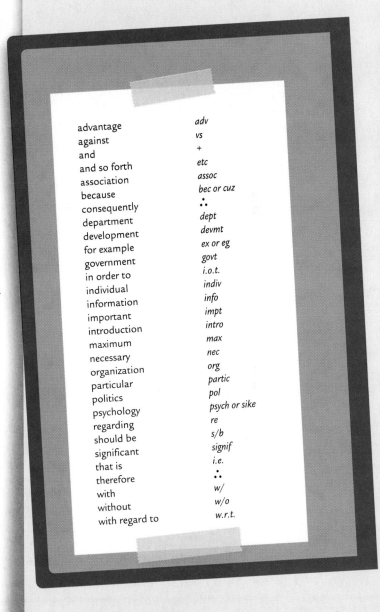

PANEL 6.3 **P**ersonal shorthand. These are some commonly used abbreviations. If you wish, you can tear out or photocopy this list and tape it inside the cover of your binder or notebook.

advantage	*adv*
against	*vs*
and	*+*
and so forth	*etc*
association	*assoc*
because	*bec or cuz*
consequently	*∴*
department	*dept*
development	*devmt*
for example	*ex or eg*
government	*govt*
in order to	*i.o.t.*
individual	*indiv*
information	*info*
important	*impt*
introduction	*intro*
maximum	*max*
necessary	*nec*
organization	*org*
particular	*partic*
politics	*pol*
psychology	*psych or sike*
regarding	*re*
should be	*s/b*
significant	*signif*
that is	*i.e.*
therefore	*∵*
with	*w/*
without	*w/o*
with regard to	*w.r.t.*

Soc. 101   1/25

deviance | Deviance
| – behavior that violates social norms
| – deviance is relative
| – varies from place to place
| – changes over time
|
| Negative consequences
| – social disorder
| – erosion of trust
| – expensive
| – may result in widespread
| nonconformity
|
| Positive consequences
| – clarifies social norms
social | – increases social solidarity
control | – may influence social change
|
internal | Social control — means to promote
social | conformity
control | internal   – as a result of socialization
| external   – rewards/punishments
external | – formal   – laws
social | – informal – gossip
control |

What is meant when deviance is referred to as a relative term?
What are the positive and negative consequences of deviance?

Deviance is a relative term that changes over
time and from place to place and has both positive
and negative consequences for society.

STEP 2: REWRITE. *This is extremely important.* The point of this step is to counteract the brain's natural tendency to forget 80% of the information in the first 24 hours.

As soon as possible—on the same day in which you took lecture notes—you should do one of two things:

1. *Either recopy/rewrite your notes,* or

2. *At least go over them to familiarize yourself and to underline key issues and concepts and make notations in the margins.*

Of course, it's not *necessary* to recopy your notes. The point I must emphasize, however, is that this very activity will give you the extra familiarization that will help to imprint the information in your mind.

Alternatively, if you don't have time or aren't strongly motivated to rewrite your notes, you should take 5 or 10 minutes to make use of the blank margins you left around your notes. (You should also do this if you rewrite your notes.) Whichever method you use, by rewriting and underlining you reinforce the material, moving it from short-term into long-term memory.

Here's what to do:

■ *Read, rewrite, and highlight your notes:* Read your notes over. If you can, rewrite them—copy them over in a separate notebook or type them up on a word processor—with the same margins at the left, right, and bottom as I described above. Now read the notes again, using highlighter pen or underlining to emphasize key ideas.

■ *Write key terms in the left margin:* In the left margins, write the key terms and main concepts. *(See ■ Panel 6.4.)* Reviewing these important terms and concepts is a good way of preparing for objective questions on tests, such as true-false or multiple-choice questions.

■ *Write one or two questions in the right margin:* On the right side of each page, write two questions about the material on the page. *(See ■ Panel 6.4 again.)* Reviewing these questions later will help you prepare for tests featuring essay questions or subjective questions.

■ *Write a summary on the last page:* At the bottom of the last page of that day's notes, summarize in a few words the material in the notes. *(See* ■ *Panel 6.4 again.)* Some students write these summaries in red or green ink. With this eye-catching color, they can then flip through their notes and quickly take in all the summary information.

I cannot stress enough how important it is to take time—*absolutely no later than one day after your class*—to go over your notes, rewriting them if you can but certainly writing key terms, questions, and summaries at the end. *Special note:* If you have a personal computer with a word processing program, the rewriting is not as time consuming as it sounds. *(See* ■ *Panel 6.5 on page 118.)*

STEP 3: RECITE. Another reinforcement technique is *recitation*. This consists of covering up your detailed notes and using the key terms or concepts in the left margin to say out loud (or under your breath to yourself) what you understand your notes to mean. You can also do this with the questions in the right margin and the summary in the bottom margin.

Recitation is an activity you can do at your desk when you're doing homework or when you have 5 or 10 minutes between classes. It is a particularly effective reinforcing technique because the activity of verbalizing gives your mind time to grasp the ideas and move them from short-term to long-term memory.

STEP 4: REFLECT. Reflecting is something you can do in the first few minutes you sit in class waiting for the next lecture to begin. Look over your notes from the previous class period in the course and try to make some *personal associations* in your mind with the material. Such personal associations will help to anchor the material. For example, if you're learning about European history, imagine how you might link some of these facts on a tour of Europe or to a movie you've seen that was set in that period.

STEP 5: REVIEW. Two or three times a week, review all your notes, using the techniques of recitation and reflection to commit the information to memory. At first you may find that the review takes longer, but as you get more familiar with the material the review will get easier. At the end of the semester or quarter you will then have perhaps 80% of the lecture information stored in your long-term memory. The remaining 20% can be learned in the days before the exam. Unlike the process of cramming, having this much material already memorized will give you much more confidence about your ability to succeed on the test.

GROUP ACTIVITY #6.3

STUDYING YOUR NOTES: PRACTICING THREE OF THE FIVE R'S

This activity requires that you have the notes of the last lecture from one of your other courses. Pair up with another student in your First-Year Experience class. Take your lecture notes and follow the procedures in Step 2, Rewrite. Then take a few minutes to follow Step 3, Recite, and Step 4, Reflect.

Now trade your rewritten notes with your partner. Take turns quizzing each other on your respective notes. How well does this experience help you retain information? Discuss with the class at large.

Using the computer to rewrite your notes.

If you have a personal computer with word processing capability on it, here's how to use it to rewrite your notes. As with the pen-and-paper method of rewriting notes, you should try to do this *within 24 hours* of the lecture, in order to head off the "forgetting curve."

Open a word processing file for each course: Open a file with a readily recognizable file name (such as "PSYCH101" or "ECON130") for each course you're taking.

Reset margins: After opening a new file, look in the instruction manual for the word processing program (or get assistance through the "Help" command) and find out how to reset the left and right margins. You want to have margins on both sides that are $1\frac{1}{2}$ inches wide. You may wish to reset the bottom margin to $1\frac{1}{2}$ inches also; otherwise, simply leave extra space at the bottom as you are typing in material.

Identify the lecture: At the top of the page, put the date of the lecture and a title that describes the topic or topics discussed that day (for example, "SCHOOLS OF PSYCHOLOGY: FREUD AND JUNG").

Type in your notes: Copy your handwritten notes from class into the computer. Don't just copy blindly, but focus on the main ideas and key questions. Use CAPITAL LETTERS, **boldface,** and <u>underlining</u> to emphasize important points.

Print out a copy and write in the margins: Print out a final version of the lecture—single space if you want to be able to see more things on a page or double space if you want to write between the lines. Then, using pencil or pen, write key terms and main concepts in the left margin. Write questions in the right margin. Write a summary in the bottom margin.

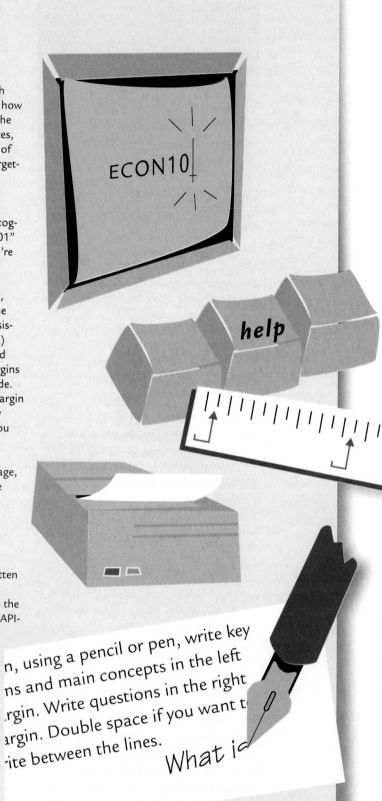

ECON10

help

n, using a pencil or pen, write key
ns and main concepts in the left
rgin. Write questions in the right
rgin. Double space if you want t
rite between the lines.

What i

Optimizing the Classroom Game

PREVIEW The best way to fight boredom and fatigue in the classroom is to make attending class a game. Three ways to improve your classroom game are to learn (1) to focus your attention, (2) to participate, and (3) to overcome classroom obstacles.

The way to deal with attending class is to treat it as a game. The point of the game is to struggle against two enemies to get the grade you want. The two enemies are *boredom* and *fatigue*:

- **Boredom:** Boredom is a very real factor. Television may have raised our expectations as to how stimulating education ought to be. However, many instructors—indeed, most people in general—can't be that interesting all the time.

- **Fatigue:** Fatigue can also be a real factor. This is particularly so for students who are struggling with other demands, such as those of work and family, or who short themselves on sleep.

As a student, then, you need to turn yourself into an active listener and active participant in the classroom to get past these two hurdles.

Let's consider three ways to improve your classroom game. They are:

- Learning to focus your attention

- Learning to participate

- Learning to overcome classroom obstacles

LEARNING TO FOCUS YOUR ATTENTION. Once you've come to class, what do you do then? You learn to pay attention. Being attentive involves *active listening,* which is different from the kind of passive listening we do when "listening" to television (sucking at the electric bottle, as they say). Active listening is, in one writer's description, "paying attention so that your brain absorbs the meaning of words and sentences."[4]

Being an active listener requires that you do the following:

- **Take listening seriously:**[5] Make up your mind you will listen. Everything begins with your attitude—hence this decision. Students can coast through the college classroom experience yawning, daydreaming, and spacing out, thereby missing a lot, or they can *decide* to listen.

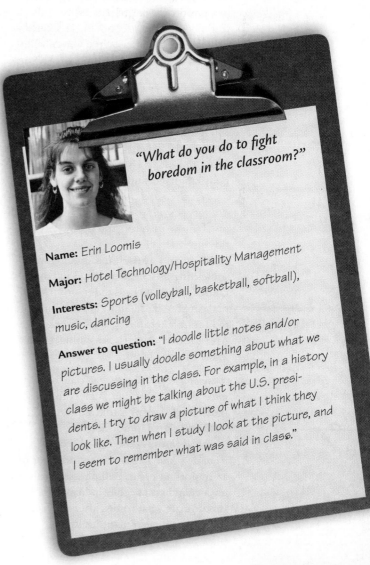

"What do you do to fight boredom in the classroom?"

Name: Erin Loomis

Major: Hotel Technology/Hospitality Management

Interests: Sports (volleyball, basketball, softball), music, dancing

Answer to question: "I doodle little notes and/or pictures. I usually doodle something about what we are discussing in the class. For example, in a history class we might be talking about the U.S. presidents. I try to draw a picture of what I think they look like. Then when I study I look at the picture, and I seem to remember what was said in class."

Making the commitment to learn and taking an active part in obtaining information also improves your ability to remember the material. If you find your mind wandering, pull your thoughts back to the present and review mentally what the speaker has been saying.

■ **Sit up front and center:** For a variety of reasons, some students don't want to sit at the front of the class. However, when you go to a musical event or stage performance, you probably *want* to sit down front—because you're interested and you want to see and hear better.

Sitting in the front and center rows in the classroom will also help you hear and see better, of course. Moreover, the very act of sitting in that place will actually stimulate your interest. This is because you have taken the physical step of *making a commitment*—of putting yourself in a position to participate more. (Also, you'll be less likely to talk to classmates, write letters, or fall asleep if you're where the instructor can see you.)

■ **Stay positive and pay attention to content, not delivery:** If you *expect* a lecture to be boring or lacking in content, I guarantee you it will be. By contrast, if you suppress negative thoughts, ignore distractions about the speaker's style of delivery or body language, and *encourage the instructor with eye contact, interested expression, and attentive posture,* you will find yourself much more involved and interested in the subject matter.

If you find yourself disagreeing with something the speaker says, don't argue mentally, but suspend judgment. (Maybe make a note in the margin and bring the matter up later during class discussion.) Assess the instructor's reasoning, then make up your mind.

■ **Listen for "bell" phrases and cues to determine what is important:** All lecturers use phrases and gestures that should "ring a bell" and signal importance.

A *bell phrase*—also called a *signal word* or *signal phrase*—is an indicator of an important point. Bell phrases are important because they indicate you should note what comes after them and remember them. Examples of bell phrases are: "Three major types . . .";

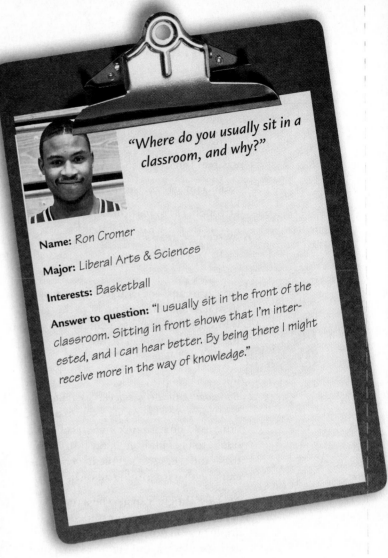

"Where do you usually sit in a classroom, and why?"

Name: Ron Cromer

Major: Liberal Arts & Sciences

Interests: Basketball

Answer to question: "I usually sit in the front of the classroom. Sitting in front shows that I'm interested, and I can hear better. By being there I might receive more in the way of knowledge."

"The most important result is . . ."; "You should remember . . ."; "Because of this . . ."; "First . . . second . . . third . . ." (See ■ *Panel 6.6.*)

A *bell cue* is an action or gesture that indicates important points. Examples are (1) diagrams or charts; (2) notes on the board; (3) pointing, as to something on the board or a chart; (4) underlining of, or making a check mark by, keywords; (5) banging a fist; and (6) holding up fingers.

When a class is long or tedious, you can turn it into a game by telling yourself you will try to detect as many bell phrases and cues as possible. Then, every time you pick up one, put a check mark in your notes. I've found when I do this I become more actively involved. Not only does it fight boredom and fatigue but it also increases the quality of my note taking.

Some bell phrases. Also known as "signal words" and "signal phrases," these indicate an important point that should be remembered.

Additive words: These say, "Here's more of the same coming up. It's just as important as what we have already said."
Examples:
also
and
besides
further
furthermore
in addition
moreover
too

Equivalent words:
They say, "It does what I have just said, but it does this too."
Examples:
as well as
at the same
equally important
likewise
similarly
time

Amplification words:
The author is saying, "I want to be sure that you understand my idea; so here's a specific instance."
Examples:
as
for example (e.g.)
for instance
like
specifically
such as

Alternative words:
These point up, "Sometimes there is a choice; other times there isn't."
Examples:
either/or
other than
otherwise
neither/nor

Repetitive words: They say, "I said it once, but I'm going to say it again in case you missed it the first time."
Examples:
again
in other words
that is (i.e.)
to repeat

Contrast-and-change words: "So far I've given you only one side of the story; now let's take a look at the other side."
Examples:
but
conversely
despite
even though
however
in spite of
instead of
nevertheless
notwithstanding
on the contrary
on the other hand
rather than
regardless
still
though
whereas
yet

Cause-and-effect words: "All this has happened; now I'll tell you why."
Examples:
accordingly
because
consequently
for this reason
hence
since
so
then
therefore
thus

Qualifying words:
These say, "Here is what we can expect. These are the conditions we are working under."
Examples:
although
if
provided that
unless
whenever

Concession words:
They say, "Okay, we agree on this much."
Examples:
accepting the data
granted that
of course

Emphasizing words:
They say, "Wake up and take notice!"
Examples:
above all
indeed
more important

Order words: The author is saying, "You keep your mind on reading; I'll keep the numbers straight."
Examples:
finally
first
last
next
second
then

Time words: "Let's keep the record straight on who said what and especially when."
Examples:
afterward
before
formerly
meanwhile
now
presently
previously
subsequently
ultimately

Summarizing words:
These say, "I've said many things so far; let's stop here and pull them together."
Examples:
for these reasons
in brief
in conclusion
to sum up

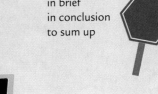

Even if you're somewhat shy and hate to get involved in class participation, the preceding suggestions will sharpen your listening skills, comprehension, and memorization, which will help you perform well on tests. If you *really* want to be a peak-performing student, however, you should go to the next step—participation.

LEARNING TO PARTICIPATE. Are you the type of person who prefers to be invisible in the classroom? No doubt you've noticed many students are. They sit in the back row, never ask questions, and can go an entire semester without talking to the instructor.

In doing this, one can probably scrape by. However, life does not reward the passive. If you ever need a reference from an instructor for a job or for graduate or professional school, how will you know whom to ask if you've never given the instructor an opportunity to know you? When you're starting on your career, what skills will you be able to draw on to speak up in meetings, give presentations, or persuade authority figures of your point of view? As I've said all along, the skills you practice in the college classroom, regardless of subject, really are practice for life outside of or after college.

For many students, shyness is a very real, even incapacitating problem. I deal with that elsewhere in the book (in Chapter 12), and if it's an important issue for you, I urge you to skip ahead

> *"If you can't let go of the fear of 'being laughed at,' there is a real question as to whether you'll be able to get what you want."*

and read that material soon. Even those who are not shy are often reluctant to "make a fool of myself," to risk being laughed at.

However, there comes a time in life when, *if you can't push beyond these limitations and let go of the fear of "being laughed at," there is a real question as to whether you'll be able to get what you want in your career and in your relationships.* Learning to participate in a public dialogue is simply part of the growth process.

Class participation, whether in a lecture or a discussion section, further reinforces memorization because it obliges you to become actively engaged with the material and to organize it in your mind. Some suggestions regarding participation are as follows:

- *Do your homework:* There is an understood contract—namely, that you should have kept up with the homework assignments, such as the textbook readings. That way you won't embarrass yourself by asking questions or making remarks about something you are already supposed to have read.

- *Respect the opinions of others:* If the questions or remarks of others seem off-the-wall or biased, don't try to trash them. A spirit of cordiality and absence of intimidation is necessary to keep learning channels open and tempers cool.

- *Follow your curiosity:* We've all had the experience of holding back on asking a question, then hearing someone else raise it and be complimented by the professor with "That's a very good question!" Follow your instincts. You have a right to ask questions, and the more you do so, the more you will perfect this particular art.

LEARNING TO OVERCOME CLASSROOM OBSTACLES.

You now know what to do if the instructor or subject matter is boring. What do you do if the instructor speaks too fast or with an accent? If your shorthand or ear is not good enough to keep up, here are some strategies:

- *Do your homework before class:* If you keep up with the reading assignments, doing them before the lecture rather than afterward, you'll often be able to mentally fill in gaps and select key points.

- *Leave holes in your notes:* Whenever you miss something important, leave spaces in your notes, with a big question mark in the margin. Then seek to fill in the missing material through other methods, as explained below.

- *Trade notes with classmates:* If you and others in class take readable notes (even using private shorthand), you can easily make photocopies of your notes and exchange them. Two or three students may find that among them they are able to pick up most of a lecture.

- *Use a tape recorder:* The trick here is not to make a tape recorder a *substitute* for note taking. Then you'll merely be taking the same amount of time to listen to the lecture again—and perhaps still be confused. Use the tape recorder as a backup system, one in which you can use the fast-forward and reverse buttons to go over material you had trouble following in class. (Remember to get permission from the instructor to use a tape recorder in his or her class.)

- *Ask questions—in class or after:* If the instructor has a question period, you can ask questions to clarify what you missed. Or see the instructor after class or during his or her office hours.

Note: Some students are reluctant to talk to instructors during office hours for fear of "bothering" them. But you're not bothering them; that's what they're there for. Instructors are *paid* to be available for your questions.

GROUP ACTIVITY #6.4

DECODING YOUR INSTRUCTORS

This activity requires that you monitor two of your lectures in other classes this week. What bell phrases and bell cues do you observe your instructors using? Write them down (in your lecture notes) as you hear and see them. Observe what effect, if any, paying attention to these cues has on your levels of boredom and fatigue.

In your First-Year Experience class, share with the class or with a small group some of the bell phrases and bell cues you observed. How did putting yourself in a state of alertness to these cues affect your levels of boredom and fatigue? What are some questions you might see on an exam that are suggested by these cues?

Onward: Applying This Chapter to Your Life

You'll be exposed to lectures all your life.

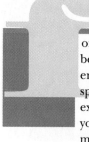

or your entire life the lecture format will be enacted over and over again in different settings. If it's not a college professor speaking, it could be your boss, or an expert in an area of particular interest to you, or a speaker at a neighborhood meeting, or a political leader on television. Thus, the skills you've learned in this chapter will be of value well beyond your time in college.

What is the single most important thing you learned in this chapter that you can "own" and use for the rest of your life? Write it down here:

_____

_____

_____

_____

_____

_____

_____

_____

_____

_____

_____

_____

_____

_____

_____

_____

_____

_____

_____

_____

THE EXAMINED LIFE: YOUR JOURNAL

1. How should you change your note-taking habits from your accustomed methods?

2. What kinds of instructors, or what particular instructors, do you have trouble following when they lecture? Why, and what can you do about it?

3. Are you afraid other students will laugh at you for being too obviously engaged in the lecture and learning process? Are you afraid they will consider you some sort of wimp because you're not obviously detached, indifferent, or supposedly cool? Why does this bother you? What does this self-consciousness—this tremendous concern about how people think about you—imply for your future in college or in a career?

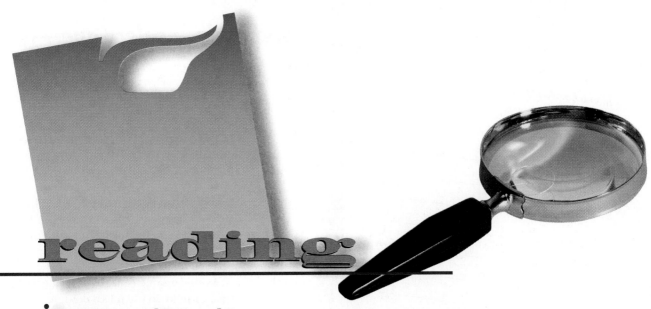

reading

important information pipeline #2

get everything you need to know from what you read

IN THIS CHAPTER: It's possible you won't have to do much reading after you complete your higher education, except for pleasure or curiosity. More likely, however, because of the explosion of facts caused by information technology, you will have to keep reading to continually update your skills and keep ahead in your career. In this chapter, then, you will learn a valuable skill—namely, *how to read to remember.*

The chapter offers three kinds of reading systems:

Reading System #1: The *SQ3R Method* consists of surveying, questioning, reading, reciting, and reviewing.

Reading System #2: The *3Rs Method* consists of reading, recording, and reciting.

Reading System #3: The *Textbook–to–Study Guide Method* consists of previewing and questioning, reading actively, writing keywords/questions in the margins, reciting, reflecting, and reviewing.

1. Think of two subjects (not fiction) that you really *liked* reading about (for instance, playing a guitar, fixing a car). Write them down here:

_____

_____

_____

_____

_____

_____

_____

_____

2. Identify a couple of areas that frustrate, bore, or upset you when you try to read about them. Use shorthand, if you like.

_____

_____

_____

_____

_____

_____

_____

_____

■ SKIMMING FOR PAYOFFS

Skim the chapter looking for *just two things* (and no more than two) that you could put to practical use. If you can't find them on the first pass, look again. Write in the margin: "This might be useful to me."

Reading is—select one—
(a) fun
(b) boring
(c) difficult

Which describes your feelings? Myself, I always thought reading was fun when I was growing up—provided it was a novel, a magazine, or a newspaper.

Textbooks? Well . . .

As a beginning college student, here's what I would do when I sat down to read a textbook: I would plow through a chapter the way I went through a novel, reading it just one time. I would also deliberately skip over any pictures and tables and charts and chapter summaries, which I thought were "just extra stuff." Thus, I could tell myself "This chapter is really only 24 pages, not 35."

See what I was doing? I was more intent *on simply getting through the assignment as quickly as possible* than on trying to learn it. However, this supposed time-saving method didn't work, for it certainly didn't help me do well on tests.

What are your thoughts about the whole business of reading in higher education? To get an idea, try Personal Exploration #7.1.

WHAT DO YOU KNOW ABOUT THE READING PROCESS?

Perhaps you regard the reading of textbooks as a reasonably straightforward activity. Or perhaps you find the whole process dreary or mysterious or scary. Answer "Yes" or "No" depending on whether you agree or disagree with the following statements.

1. Reading makes unusual or unique demands on a reader.

   _____ Yes   _____ No

2. Reading is a form of the thinking process. You read with your brain, not your eyes.

   _____ Yes   _____ No

3. Reading is a one-step process.

   _____ Yes   _____ No

4. Effective readers constantly seek to bring meaning to the text.

   _____ Yes   _____ No

5. Many comprehension problems are not just reading problems.

   _____ Yes   _____ No

6. Good readers are sensitive to how the material they are reading is structured or organized.

   _____ Yes   _____ No

7. Speed and comprehension are independent of each other.

   _____ Yes   _____ No

■ ANSWERS

1. *False.* Reading actually does not make unusual demands on a reader. The same mental processes you use to "read" people's faces or grasp the main idea of a situation you observe are used when you read.

2. *True.* Your eyes simply transmit images to the brain. Improving your reading means improving your thinking, not practicing moving your eyes faster or in a different way.

3. *False.* Reading includes three steps: (a) preparing yourself to read (thinking about what you already know about a subject and setting purposes for reading); (b) processing information; and (c) reacting to what you read.

4. *True.* When they are not comprehending, they take steps to correct the situation.

5. *True.* If you fail to understand something you are reading, it could be because it is poorly written. More likely, however, you lack the background information needed to comprehend—you wouldn't understand it even if someone read it aloud to you. Perhaps you need to read an easier book on the same subject first.

6. *True.* Good readers know the subject matter and main idea of each paragraph and understand how each paragraph is organized (for example, sequence, listing, cause and effect, comparison and contrast, definition).

7. *False.* The more quickly you can understand something, the faster you can read it. However, "speed" without comprehension is meaningless. Reading is more than just allowing your eyes to pass over lines of print.

GROUP ACTIVITY OPTION

In a group-discussion situation, consider which answers surprised you. Why did you think the opposite was true? Does anything you've learned change your previous attitude toward reading?

Reading for Pleasure Versus Reading for Learning

PREVIEW Reading for pleasure is different from reading for learning. With most pleasure reading you need only remember the information briefly, holding it in your short-term memory. With reading for learning, the information must be stored in your long-term memory, so that you can recall it for tests. This means you must read material more than once. Accordingly, you need to treat textbooks seriously. You also need to understand what their basic features are—title page, copyright page, table of contents, preface, glossary, appendix, bibliography, and index. Finally, you need to know what "advance organizers" are for purposes of surveying material.

aybe you already think you read pretty well. After all, you've been doing it for most of your life.

Or maybe you don't feel comfortable about reading. You prefer television to print. Or you think you get information better when someone tells it to you. Or you find English a hard language to follow.

Whatever your skills, *there are techniques to improve your reading abilities so that you can better handle subjects at the level of higher education.* Some of them I'll describe in this chapter. If you don't find what you need here (for example, you feel you need help in reading English as a second language), you can get assistance through the school's learning center or lab.

TWO TYPES OF READING. Reading is principally of two types—for pleasure and for learning:

- *For pleasure:* You can read action-adventure, romances, sports, and similar material just one time, for amusement. This is the kind of material that appears in many novels, magazines, and newspapers. You don't have to read it carefully, unless you want to.

- *For learning:* Most of the other kind of reading you do is for learning of some sort, because you *have* to understand it and perhaps retain it. For instance, you certainly have to pay close attention when you're reading a cookbook or instructions on how to fix a car.

Reading for learning is something you will have to do all your life, whether it's studying to get a driver's license or finding out how much medicine to give an infant. Indeed, what many managers and administrators are doing all day, when they read reports, letters, and memos, is reading to learn.

But here's the difference between those kinds of reading for learning and reading textbooks: *In higher education, you'll often have to read the same material more than once.* The reason, of course, is that in higher education you have to *understand and memorize* so much of what you read.

READING TO FEED YOUR LONG-TERM MEMORY. "Oh, boy," you may think. "You mean there's no way I can just read stuff once and get it the first time?"

Perhaps you can if you're the sort who can memorize the code to a bicycle or locker combination lock with just one glance. Most people, however, need more practice than that.

This has to do with the notion of short-term memory versus long-term memory. As I described in Chapter 5, the retention of information drops rapidly in the first 24 hours after you've been exposed to it (the "forgetting curve"). Short-term memory is roughly anything you can't hold in mind for more than 24 hours.

Long-term memory refers to information you retain for a good deal longer than 24 hours.

Some students might try to make these facts an argument for cramming—holding off until the last day before a test and then reading everything at once. However, there is no way such postponement can really be effective. Many instructors, for instance, have *cumulative* final exams. They test you not just on the new material you're supposed to have learned since the last exam. Rather, they test you on *all* the material back to the beginning of the course. If you opt for cramming, this puts you in the position of having to cram for the *whole course*. In sum: you need to do the kind of reading that will feed your long-term memory.

TREAT TEXTBOOKS SERIOUSLY. Some students regard their textbooks as troublesome or uninteresting but unfortunately necessary (and expensive) parts of their instruction. Or they think of the books as being perhaps useful but not vital (and so they try to avoid buying them).

There's a likelihood, however, that *half or more of your study time will be devoted to such books.* Thus, when you think about what your college education *is,* half of it is in your books. You need, then, to treat them as the tools of your trade (your trade being a student)—just as you would an instruction manual if your job required you, say, to tear down and fix motorcycles or to lead a tour group of Great Britain.

With that in mind, here are a few tips for extracting some benefits from your textbooks:

- *Look the text over before you take the course:* If you have any doubts about a course you're contemplating taking, take a look in the bookstore at the textbook(s) and any other reading materials that will be required for it. This way you can see what the course will cover and whether it is too advanced or too low-level in the light of your previous experience.

- *Buy your books early:* In my first couple of semesters as a first-year student, I would dawdle as long as a week or 10 days before buying some of my books. Not a good idea. The school term flies by awfully fast, and I lost the advantage of a head start. (Also, sometimes when I waited too long the books were sold out.)

- *Look the text over before the first class:* The reason, of course, is that in higher education you have to understand and memorize so much of what you read. If you are familiar with the principal text before you walk into your first class, you will know what the course is going to cover and know how to use the book to help you. Taking a couple of minutes to go from front to back—from title page to index—will tell you what resources the book offers to help you study better.

BECOME FAMILIAR WITH THE BASIC FEATURES. To get a sense of what a book is like, you need to look for eight particular features in the front and back of the book. *(See ■ Panel 7.1.)*

- *Title page:* At the front of the book, **the title page tells you the title, edition number (if later than the first edition), author, and publisher.** Often the title can give you a sense of the level of difficulty of the book—for example, *Introduction to Business* (introductory level) versus *Intermediate Accounting* (higher level).

- *Copyright page:* **The copyright page (on the back of the title page) tells you the date the book was published.** With some of the more rapidly changing fields, such as computer science, you hope for as recent a book as possible.

- *Table of contents:* **The table of contents lists the principal headings in the book.** Sometimes a "brief contents" will list just parts and chapters, and a "detailed contents" will list other major headings as well.

- *Preface:* **The preface tells you the intended audience for the book, the author's purpose and approach, why the book is different, and perhaps an overview of the organization.** (The preface—which may also be called "Introduction" or "To the Student"—may go in front of the table of contents.)

- *Bibliography:* Appearing at the back of the book or at the end of each chapter, **the bibliography, or "Notes" section, lists sources or references used in writing the text.** This section can be a good resource if you're writing a term paper for the course. Scanning the textbook's bibliography may suggest some valuable places to start.

- *Glossary:* In the back of the book, **the glossary is an alphabetical list of key terms and their definitions, as found in the text.** Quite often the same terms appear within the main body of the text in **boldface** (dark type) or *italics* (slanted type).

- *Appendix:* Also in the back of the book, **the appendix contains supplementary**

Looking over a textbook. Principal features to look for in a textbook.

▼ Title page

POPULATION
An Introduction to Concepts and Issues
Fifth Edition

John R. Weeks
San Diego State University

Wadsworth Publishing Company
Belmont, California
A Division of Wadsworth, Inc.

▼ Copyright page

To Deanna

Editor: Serina Beauparlant
Editorial Assistant: Marla Nowick
Production: Greg Hubit Bookworks
Print Buyer: Randy Hurst
Permissions Editor: Peggy Meehan
Copy Editor: Kathleen McCann
Manuscript Editor: Deanna Weeks
Cover: Henry Breuer
Compositor: Bi-Comp, Incorporated
Printer: Arcata Graphics Fairfield

The cover illustration shows countries in proportion to population. Adapted by the author from United Nations data.

This book is printed on acid-free paper that meets Environmental Protection Agency standards for recycled paper.

© 1992 by Wadsworth, Inc. All rights reserved. No part of this book may be reproduced, stored in a retrieval system, or transcribed, in any form or by any means, without the prior written permission of the publisher, Wadsworth Publishing Company, Belmont, California 94002.

1 2 3 4 5 6 7 8 9 10—96 95 94 93 92

Library of Congress Cataloging in Publication Data

Weeks, John Robert, 1944—
  Population : an introduction to concepts and issues / John R. Weeks. — 5th ed.
    p.   cm.
  Includes bibliographical references and index.
  ISBN 0-534-17346-2
  1. Population. I. Title.
HB871.W43 1992
304.6—dc20   92-6251
                                          CIP

▼ Table of Contents

DETAILED TABLE OF CONTENTS

▼ Preface

PREFACE

Population growth in the 1950s and 1960s could have been likened to a runaway train without an engineer, veering perilously close to a collision course with shortages of food and resources. That specter was altered somewhat by the events of the 1970s, especially by a few hopeful signs of a downturn in the birth rates of several large developing nations. In the 1980s and the 1990s the imagery has changed from the collision course to something equally terrifying. We are faced with a situation analogous to an immense locomotive hurtling down the track at a speed faster than the roadbed can tolerate. The engineer is groping for the brakes, but if and when those brakes are fully applied, the train will still cover a huge distance before it comes to a halt. How much havoc will the charging locomotive of population wreak before it stops, and what condition will we be in at that point? These are two of the most important questions that face the world.

Over the years I have found that most people are either blissfully unaware of the enormous impact that population growth and change have on their lives, or else they have heard so many horror stories about impending doom that they are nearly overwhelmed whenever they think of population growth. My purpose in this book is to shake you out of your lethargy (if you are one of those types), without necessarily scaring you in the process. I will introduce you to the basic concepts of population studies and help you develop your own demographic perspective, enabling you to understand some of the most important issues confronting the world. My intention is to sharpen your perception of population growth and change, to increase your awareness of what is happening and why, and to help prepare you to cope with (and help shape) a future that will be shared with billions more people than there are today.

▼ Bibliography

BIBLIOGRAPHY

Abelson, P.
14   1975a "The world's disparate food supplies." Science 187: editorial.
14   1975b "Food and nutrition." Science 188 (4188):501.
11   Adamchak, D., A. Wilson, A. Nyanguru, and J. Hampson
     1991 "Elderly support and intergenerational transfer in Zimbabwe: an analysis by gender, marital status, and place of residence." The Gerontologist 31:505–13.
4   Adelman, C.
     1982 "Saving babies with a signature." Wall Street Journal, 28 July.
5   Adlakha, A., and D. Kirk
     1974 "Vital rates in India 1961–71 estimated from 1971 census data." Population Studies 28(3):381–400.
7   Agassi, J., and I. C. Jarvie
     1959 Hong Kong. London: Oxford Press.
8   Ahlburg, D., and M. Schapiro
     1984 "Socioeconomic ramifications of changing cohort size: an analysis of U.S. postwar suicide rates by age and sex." Demography 21(1):97–105.
6   Ahonsi, B.
     1991 "Report on the seminar on anthropological studies relevant to the sexual transmission of HIV, Sonderborg, Denmark, 1990." IUSSP Newsletter 41:79–103.
4   Akin, J., R. Bilsbarrow, D. Guilkey, B. Popkin, D. Benoit, P. Cantrelle, M. Garenne, and P. Levi
     1981 "The determinants of breast-feeding in Sri Lanka." Demography 18(3):287–308.

4   Akpom, C., K. Akpom, and M. Davis
     1976 "Prior sexual behavior of teenagers attending rap sessions for the first time." Family Planning Perspectives 8:203–6.
12   Alba, R., and J. Logan
     1991 "Variations on two themes: racial and ethnic patterns in the attainment of suburban residence." Demography 28:431–53.
16   Allan, C.
     1981 "Measuring mature markets." American Demographics 3(3):13–17.
1,12 Alonso, W., and P. Starr
     1982 "The political economy of national statistics." Social Science Research Council Items 36(3):29–35.
16   Alsop, R.
     1984 "Firms still struggle to devise best approach to black buyers." Wall Street Journal, 25 October.
     American Demographics
16   1982 "The demographic future." The Monthly Report of International Demographics (brochure).
16   1983 "Here comes 1984." American Demographics 5(6):11.
16   Anderson, B., and B. Silver
     1989 "Patterns of cohort mortality in the Soviet population." Population and Development Review 15:471–502.
     Ankrah, E. M.
6   1991 "AIDS and the social side of health." Social Science and Medicine 32:967–80.
6   Aries, P.
     1962 Centuries of Childhood. New York: Vintage Books.

530

▼ Glossary

GLOSSARY

This glossary contains words or terms that appeared in boldface type in the text. I have tried to include terms that are central to an understanding of the study of population. The chapter notation in parentheses refers to the chapter in which the term is first discussed in detail.

abortion the expulsion of a fetus prematurely; a miscarriage—may be either induced or spontaneous (Chapter 4).

abridged life table a life table (see definition) in which ages are grouped into categories (usually five-year age groupings) (Appendix).

accidental death loss of life unrelated to disease of any kind but attributable to the physical, social, or economic environment (Chapter 6).

achieved characteristics those sociodemographic characteristics such as education, occupation, income, marital status, and labor force participation, over which we do have some degree of control (Chapter 9).

age/sex pyramid graph of the number of people in a population by age and sex (Chapter 8).

age/sex-specific death rate the number of people of a given age and sex who died in a given year divided by the total number of people of that age and sex (Chapter 6).

age-specific fertility rate the number of children born to women of a given age divided by the total number of women that age (Chapter 4).

age stratification the assignment of social roles and social status on the basis of age (Chapter 11).

age structure the distribution of people in a population by age (Chapter 8).

Agricultural Revolution change that took place roughly 10,000 years ago when humans first began to domesticate plants and animals, thereby making it easier to settle in permanent establishments (Chapters 2 and 14).

alien a person born in, or belonging to, another country who has not acquired citizenship by naturalization—distinguished from citizen (Chapter 7).

Alzheimer's disease a disease involving a change in the brain's neurons, producing behavioral shifts; a major cause of senility (Chapter 11).

ambivalence state of being caught between competing pressures and thus being uncertain about how to behave properly (Chapter 5).

amenorrhea temporary absence or suppression of the menstrual discharge (Chapter 4).

amino acids building blocks from which proteins are formed (Chapter 14).

anovulatory pertaining to a menstrual cycle in which no egg is released (Chapter 4).

antinatalist based on an ideological position that discourages childbearing (Chapter 3).

arable describes land that is suitable for farming (Chapter 14).

ascribed characteristics sociodemographic characteristics such as gender and race and ethnicity, with which we are born and over which we have essentially no control (Chapter 9).

average age of a population one measure of the age distribution of a population—may be calculated as either the mean or the median (Chapter 8).

521

(continued next page)

▼ Appendix

APPENDIX
The Life Table,
Net Reproduction Rate,
and Standardization

▼ Index

INDEX

material, material of optional or specialized interest. Examples are tables, charts,
and more detailed discussion than is
contained in the text. Often there is
more than one appendix. Engineering
or business students, for instance, will
often find time-saving tables contained
in appendixes.

■ *Index:* **The _index_ is an alphabetically
arranged list of names and subjects that
appear in the text, giving the page
numbers on which they appear.** Sometimes there are two indexes—a name
index and a subject index. The index is
an *extremely* useful tool. If you're not sure
a topic is discussed in the book, try looking it up in the index.

UNDERSTAND WHAT "ADVANCE ORGANIZERS" ARE.
As I discuss shortly, one concept
underlying many reading strategies is that
of surveying. **A _survey_ is an overview.** That
is, you take a couple of minutes to look
through a chapter to get an overview of it
before you start reading it.

Surveying a chapter has three
purposes:

1. *It gets you going:* Getting started reading
   on a densely packed 35-page chapter can
   be difficult. Surveying the material gets
   you going, like a slow warm-up lap
   around the track.

2. *It gives you some familiarity with the material:* Have you ever noticed that when
   you're reading on a subject with which
   you're familiar you read more rapidly?
   For example, you might read slowly
   about an event reported in the morning
   paper but read more rapidly a story
   about that same event in the evening
   paper or a different newspaper. When
   you survey a chapter in a textbook, you
   begin to make it familiar to you. Notice,
   then, that the survey is not a waste of
   time. *It enables you to read faster later.*

3. *It gives you "advance organizers" to help
   you organize information in your mind:* As
   you do your overview you pick up what
   are called "advance organizers." *Advance
   organizers* **are mental landmarks under
   which facts and ideas may be grouped
   and organized in your mind.** Thus, when

you go to read the chapter itself, you already have some advance information about it.

Textbooks provide some or all of the following *advance organizers*. It's a good idea to pay attention to these when doing a survey of a chapter.

- *Chapter table of contents:* You can find a breakdown of the headings within the chapter at the front of the book (in the table of contents). Some textbooks repeat this outline of the contents at the beginning of each chapter.

- *Learning objectives:* Not all books have this, but many texts have learning objectives. **Learning objectives** are topics you are expected to learn, which are listed at the beginning of each chapter. This usually starts out with a sentence something like: "After you have read this chapter, you should be able to . . ." The list of objectives then follows.

  For example, learning objectives in an introductory computer book might be: "Explain what desktop publishing is" or "Discuss the principal features of word processing software."

- *Chapter summary:* Many textbooks have a summary at the end of the chapter, describing key concepts of the chapter. *Be sure to read the chapter summary FIRST,* even though you probably won't understand everything in it. It will help you get an overview of the material so it will seem somewhat familiar to you later.

  In this book, instead of having a summary at the end of each chapter, I have put a summary (called "PREVIEW") following every main section heading. This section-head summary describes the material you are about to read in the section.

- *Review or discussion questions:* These, too, may appear at the end of the chapter. Sometimes review or discussion questions can be quite important because *they ask some of the questions that will be asked on the test.* Be sure to skim through them.

- *List of key terms:* Key terms may appear in **boldface** type (dark type) or *italics* (slanted type) within the text of the chapter. Sometimes key terms also appear in a list at the end of the chapter.

- *Headings, subheadings, and first sentences:* Read anything that appears as a heading; then read the first sentence following the heading.

Of course, a lot of the advance organizers that you read during the survey step are not going to make complete sense. But some of them will. And most of the material will have a familiar, hence somewhat comfortable, feeling to it when you come back to it on subsequent steps.

In the rest of this chapter I describe three reading systems devised to help students get the most out of textbooks.

GROUP ACTIVITY #7.1

WHAT DO YOU THINK OF TEXTBOOKS?

If half of your education is in your textbooks, it's important to determine what your attitude is toward them. First list three negative things that come to mind about textbooks. Then list three positive things.

In class discussion, describe some of your feelings about textbooks, then consider some of the following questions. If you didn't have textbooks, what would you use instead to get the same information? Would it be more efficient? How much money in a quarter or term do you spend on recreation and how does that compare to the money spent on books? When you're learning something for work or personal interest, what kinds of sources of information do you use?

Reading System #1: The SQ3R Method

PREVIEW The five-step SQ3R method stands for: *Survey, Question, Read, Recite, Review.* Its advantage is that it breaks down reading into manageable segments that require you to understand them before proceeding.

here's a war on! We must teach them to read faster!"

Maybe that's what psychologist Francis P. Robinson was told in 1941. In any event, Robinson then set about to devise an intensified reading system for World War II military people enrolled in special courses at Ohio State University. Since then, many thousands of students have successfully used his system or some variation. The reason the system is effective is that it *breaks a reading assignment down into manageable portions that require you to understand them before you move on.*

Robinson's reading system is called the SQ3R method. **The *SQ3R reading method* stands for five steps: *Survey, Question, Read, Recite, Review.*** [1] Let's see how you would apply these to the chapter of a textbook you are assigned to read.

STEP 1: S—SURVEY. As I said, a *survey* is an overview. You do a quick 1- or 2-minute overview of the entire chapter before you plunge into it. Look at the advance organizers—the chapter outline or learning objectives, if any; the chapter headings; and the summary, if any, at the end of the chapter. The point of surveying is twofold:

- *You establish relationships between the major segments:* Surveying enables you to see how the chapter segments go together. Understanding how the parts fit in with the whole helps you see how the chapter makes sense.

- *You see where you're going:* If you know where you're going, you can better organize the information as you read. This is just like reading over directions to someone's house before you leave rather than bit by bit while traveling.

Next you apply Steps 2 through 4—Question, Read, Recite—*but only to one section at a time, or to an even smaller segment.* That is, you apply the next three steps section by section, or even paragraph by paragraph, if the material is difficult. You apply the last step, Step 5, Review, after you have finished the chapter.

STEP 2: Q—QUESTION. Take a look at the heading of the first section and turn it into a question in your mind. For example, if the heading (in a book about computers) is "Basic Software Tools for Work and Study," ask "What does 'Basic Software Tools' mean?" If the heading is to a subsection, do the same. For example, if the heading is "Word Processing," ask, "How does word processing work?"

Questioning has two important effects:

- *You become personally involved:* By questioning, you get actively involved in your reading. And personal involvement is one of the most fundamental ways to commit information to memory.

- *You identify the main ideas:* Giving the heading this kind of attention pinpoints the principal ideas you are now going to read about. And it is the main ideas that are important, after all, not the supporting details.

If you are proceeding on a paragraph-by-paragraph basis because the material is difficult (as in technical courses, such as physics), there may not be any heading that you can convert to a question. In that case, you'll need to put Step 3, Read, before Step 2: you read the paragraph, then create a question about that paragraph.

Incidentally, it's perfectly all right (indeed, even desirable) at this stage to move your lips and ask the question under your breath.

STEP 3: R—READ. *Now* you actually do the reading—but only up to the next section heading (or paragraph). Note, however, that you do not read as though you were reading a popular novel. Rather, *you read with purpose—actively searching to answer the question you posed.* If you don't seem to understand it, reread the section until you can answer the question.

What is the difference between passive and active reading? If you were reading a murder mystery *passively*, you would just run your eyes over the lines and wait, perhaps mildly curious, to see how things came out. If you were reading that mystery novel *actively*, you would constantly be trying to guess the outcome. You would be asking yourself such questions as: Who was the killer? What was that strange phone call about? What motive would she have for the murder? What was that funny business in his background? And you would be searching for the answers.

You don't need to do that with recreational reading. Reading a textbook, however, should *always* be an active process of asking questions and searching for answers. That's why you have to take study breaks from time to time (perhaps 5 minutes every half hour), because this type of reading is not effortless.

In addition, especially if the segment is somewhat long, you should read (perhaps on a second reading) for another purpose:

■ *You should determine whether the section asks any other questions:* The question you formulated based on the section heading may not cover all the material in the segment. Thus, as you read, you may see other questions that should be asked about the material.

■ *Ask those questions and answer them:* You probably get the idea: the Question and Read steps are not completely separate steps. Rather, you are continually alternating questions and answers as you read through the segment.

Some examples of questions you might frame in your mind as you read a textbook are:

What is the main idea of this paragraph?

What is an example that illustrates this principle?

What are the supporting facts?

Who is this person and why is he or she considered important?

What could the instructor ask me about this on the exam?

What is there about this that I don't understand?

If necessary, as you stop and think about key points, you may want to write brief notes to trigger your memory when you get to Step 5, Review.

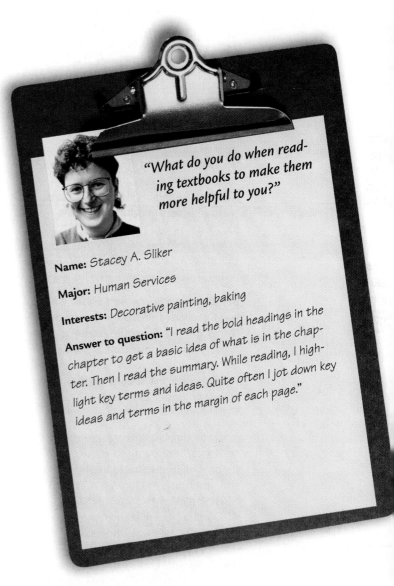

"What do you do when reading textbooks to make them more helpful to you?"

Name: Stacey A. Sliker

Major: Human Services

Interests: Decorative painting, baking

Answer to question: "I read the bold headings in the chapter to get a basic idea of what is in the chapter. Then I read the summary. While reading, I highlight key terms and ideas. Quite often I jot down key ideas and terms in the margin of each page."

STEP 4: R—RECITE. When you reach the end of the section, stop and look away from the page. *Recite* the answer you have just discovered for the question you formulated. You should practice this in two ways:

- *Recite the answer aloud:* When I say "aloud," I don't mean so loud that you have other students in the library looking at you. But there's nothing embarrassing about talking subvocally to yourself—that is, moving your tongue within your mouth while your lips move imperceptibly. When you move the muscles in your lips and mouth and throat, this vocalizing or subvocalizing helps lay down a memory trace in your mind.

  I can't stress enough the importance of reciting aloud or nearly aloud. As Walter Pauk writes, "Reciting promotes concentration, forms a sound basis for understanding the next paragraph or the next chapter, provides time for the memory trace to consolidate, ensures that facts and ideas are remembered accurately, and provides immediate feedback on how you're doing. . . ."[2] Pauk also mentions experiments that show that students who read and recite learn much better than students who just read.

- *Say the answer in your own words:* When you formulate the answer in your own words (perhaps using an example), rather than just repeating a phrase off the page, you are required to *understand* it rather than just memorize it. And when you understand it, you *do* memorize it better.

  If you did not take any notes for review earlier, you may wish to at this point. The notes should not be extensive, just brief cues to jog your memory when you move to Step 5, Review.

  Don't move on to the next segment until you're sure you understand this one. After all, if you don't get it now, when will you? Once you think you understand the section, move on to the next section (or paragraph) and repeat steps 2, 3, and 4.

STEP 5: R—REVIEW. When you have read all the way through the chapter (or as far as you intend to go in one study session), section by section in Question-Read-Recite fashion, you are ready to test how well you have mastered your key ideas. Here's how to do it:

- *Go back over the book's headings or your notes and ask the questions again:* Repeat the questions and try to answer them without looking at the book or your notes. If you have difficulty, check your answers.

- *Review other memory aids:* Read the chapter summary and the review questions. Then skim the chapter again, as well as your notes, refreshing your memory.

GROUP ACTIVITY #7.2

PRACTICING THE SQ3R METHOD

At the instructor's discretion, this activity may be performed all in class, or partly out of class and partly in class.

Divide into two teams of two people each. Select two earlier chapters from this book on which to practice the SQ3R method. One team practices the method on one chapter, the other team on the other chapter. (Or use two chapters from another text on which the four of you can agree.) The method may be performed in or outside of class as the instructor suggests.

Next, without looking at the text, have the other team quiz you on the chapter you studied. Then take turns quizzing them on the chapter they studied. Finally, in class discuss how well the method worked for you. What would you do differently?

Reading System #2:
The 3Rs Method

PREVIEW The three-step 3Rs method stands for: *Read, Record, Recite.* The method has no survey step, but it helps you retain material through reading, rereading, underlining, making questions, and self-testing.

he *3Rs reading system* **has three steps for mastering textbooks: *Read, Record, Recite.*** This system was described by Walter Pauk, who says it "is perfect for students who like to move quickly into a textbook chapter, or for those who face exams with little time for intensive study."[3] In other words, if (against all advice) you have to resort to cramming, use this method.

STEP 1: READ. There is no surveying or questioning of material first, as in the SQ3R method. Rather, you just start reading and read a section or several paragraphs. Then do as follows:

- *Ask what you need to know:* Return to the first paragraph and ask yourself, "What do I need to know in this paragraph?"

- *Read and reread for answers and say aloud:* Read and reread the paragraph until you can say aloud what you need to know about it.

STEP 2: RECORD. The SQ3R method, previously discussed, says nothing about making marks or writing in the book, although you can do so if it helps. However, in Step 2 of the 3Rs method you are *required* to mark up the book. Here's how:

- *Underline key information:* Once you can say aloud what you need to know, you should underline the key information in the book. It's important that you *underline just the key information—terms, phrases, and sentences*—not line after line of material. This is so that when you come back to review, you will see only the essential material.

- *Write a brief question in the margin:* After underlining, write a *brief question* in the margin that asks for the information you've underlined. Forming questions is extremely important to the 3Rs System, so you must be sure to do this.

After you finish this step for these paragraphs, proceed to the next segment or paragraphs and again Read and Record.

Incidentally, a word about underlining: I've sat in libraries and watched students reading a chapter for the first time, underlining the text as they go. At the end, if they are using a green pen, say, the entire chapter looks like a mess of green paint. Obviously, this kind of underlining doesn't work. The point is to use your pen or highlighter to mark only *important things*, not *everything*. This is why it's best to read the chapter (or section) first without underlining, then reread it, doing your underlining on the second reading. (Note: Be sure to use pen or highlighter. If you use felt-tip markers or Magic Markers, the ink will go through the paper—indeed, perhaps through five or more pages.)

STEP 3: RECITE. After you've finished doing Steps 1 and 2 for the chapter, go back to the beginning. Now you will do the Recite step for the entire chapter, as follows:

- *Cover the page and ask yourself each question:* Use a folded piece of paper or your hand to cover the printed page of the text except for the questions you've written in the margins. Ask yourself the questions.

- *Recite aloud and check your answers:* Recite *aloud* the answer to each question. ("Aloud" can mean talking to yourself under your breath.) Then lift the paper and check your answer. If you're not clear on the answer, ask and answer again. Put a check mark in the margin if you need to come back and review again.

Continue the Recite step until you get to the end of the chapter. Then go back and look at the places where you've left a check mark.

Reading System #3: The Textbook–to–Study Guide Method

PREVIEW The Textbook–to–Study Guide method is a seven-step system that produces a study guide you can use to prime yourself before exams. The seven steps are (1) Preview and question; (2) Read actively; (3) Reread and underline; (4) Write keywords/questions in margins; (5) Recite; (6) Reflect; and (7) Review.

After several years of looking at various reading systems and how well they prepare students for exams, I've come up with a system adapted from others' contributions, such as Walter Pauk's "Questions-in-the-Margins" method.[4] The principal benefit of this system is that *it produces an efficient study guide that you can use to effectively prime yourself the night before an exam.* You may find that the SQ3R method works just fine for most reading assignments and that the 3Rs system will do the job when you're short on time. However, if you really want to imprint the reading material on your memory and get a grade of A on the exam, consider trying the Textbook–to–Study Guide method. Or consider mixing and matching steps from all these methods until you find something that works for you.

The *Textbook–to–Study Guide method* **consists of seven steps: (1) Preview and question, (2) Read actively, (3) Reread and underline, (4) Write keywords/questions in margins, (5) Recite, (6) Reflect, and (7) Review.**

STEP 1: PREVIEW & QUESTION. A *preview* is the same as a survey. You do a 2-minute or 5-minute overview of the entire chapter to establish relationships between major segments and to establish sign posts so you can see where you're going.

At the same time you skim through the chapter, you make up *questions*. That is, you use a pen or pencil to turn every heading into a question, adding words such as "What" or "How." For example, you might turn the heading "Characteristics of Floppy Disks" into the question, "What are the characteristics of floppy disks?" Turning headings into questions prepares you to read actively to answer questions—the kind of mindset you need to have when you go into a test.

STEP 2: READ ACTIVELY. After previewing and questioning, you read the chapter. Or you read a section at a time, then return to the beginning.

This reading is not just moving your eyes over the page. Rather, you are *reading to answer the questions* you posed in the headings. Once you have answered a question, ask another.

As you read, then, you should hold a continuing question-and-answer dialogue with yourself, a kind of ongoing muttering under your breath. *And if you don't comprehend something, stop right there and go back and reread.*

STEP 3: REREAD & UNDERLINE. Now reread the material and use your highlighter or pen selectively to:

- Mark key terms
- Mark main ideas
- Mark conclusions

Don't mark examples or other supporting material. Don't mark tables or illustrations, unless they are especially important and contain many key terms or concepts.

STEP 4: WRITE KEYWORDS/QUESTIONS IN MARGINS. "Look at all this white space," I've heard students say about the margins in their textbooks. "What a waste of paper!"

Actually, though, the more space you have, the more helpful it is. It's what you will use to turn your textbook into a study guide.

Now you make yet another pass through the chapter or section. This time you use a pen to write two things in the margin—keywords and questions. (*See ■ Panel 7.2.*) *This is a particularly important step.* Here's how it's done:

■ *Keywords:* Write key-words in the margin. *Keywords* **are important terms or names that you are expected to understand and be able to define.** As mentioned, keywords may be **bold-faced** or *italicized* key terms appearing in the text, or they may be other words that your two previous readings have shown you to be important. For example, in a history book, keywords might be names, dates, or titles of important documents.

■ *Short questions:* Write short-answer types of questions, the kinds of questions that might appear on a test. The answers, of course, appear in the text (where you have previously underlined) opposite where you write the questions.

When you're writing these keywords and questions, don't use a scrawl or abbreviations, if they might give you trouble reading them later. What you are doing in this step is creating a study guide that you will use later to prepare for tests.

PANEL 7.2

Keywords & questions. In Step 4, you write keywords and ques-tions in the margin.

How Television Works

What are 8 depts of TV station?

a TYPICAL television station has eight departments: ① sales, ② programming (which includes news as well as entertain-ment), ③ production, ④ engineering, ⑤ traffic, ⑥ promotion, ⑦ pub-lic affairs, and ⑧ administration.

People in the *sales* department sell the commercial slots for the programs. Advertising is divided into *national* and *local* sales. Advertising agencies, usu-ally based on the East Coast, buy national ads for the products they handle. Ford Motor Company, for instance, may buy time for a TV ad that will run simultaneously all over the country. But the local Ford dealers who want you to shop at their showrooms buy their ads directly from the local station. These ads are called local (or spot) ads. For these sales, salespeople at each station negotiate packages of ads, based on their station's rates. These rates are a direct reflection of that station's position in the ratings.

① Sales – what duties? What are 2 types of advertising?

The *programming* department selects the shows that you will see and develops the station's schedule. Network-owned stations, located in big cities (KNBC in Los Angeles, for example), are called O & O's, which stands for owned-and-operated. Stations that carry network programming but are not owned by the networks are called affiliates.

② Programming – what duties? O & O – define affiliates – define How differ?

O & O's automatically carry network programming, but affiliates are paid by the network to carry its programming, for which the network sells most of the ads and keeps the money. The affiliate is allowed to insert into the network programming a specific number of local ads, for which the affiliate keeps the money.

Because affiliates can make money on network programming and don't have to pay for it, many stations choose to affiliate themselves with a network. When they aren't running what the network provides, affiliates run their own programs and keep all the advertising money they collect from them.

More than one-third of the nation's commercial TV stations operate as independents. Independent stations must buy and program all their own shows, but independents also can keep all the money they make on advertising. They run some individually produced programs and old movies, but most of their programming consists of reruns of shows that once ran on the networks. Independents buy these reruns from program services called syndicators.

Independents – define

Syndicators also sell independently produced programs such as *Donahue*, *The Oprah Winfrey Show*, and *Wheel of Fortune*. These programs are created and

What are syndicators?

180

What if the textbook publisher provides a separate study guide to go along with the text? Could you use that instead?

Indeed you could. I'm a great believer in the effectiveness of study guides. The point is, however, you have to *use* them, and use them more than once. One reading of the text and one reading of the study guide is not going to do it.

STEP 5: RECITE. This step is a self-test. After you have written all the marginal keywords and questions, you return to the beginning of the chapter (or section). You cover the text with a piece of paper or your hand, leaving the keywords and questions exposed. You then make another pass, this time asking yourself aloud:

■ *"What does the keyword mean?"* Here you test yourself to see how well you can define the keyword.

■ *"What is the answer to the question?"* You try to guess the answer to the short-answer question you have written.

As you state the definitions and answers, you then check yourself by lifting or sliding your paper or hand and looking at the text.

This reciting should be done aloud. If you can, try to recite without mumbling, framing complete sentences, as though you were dictating your answers to the test. Or, if you are in a public place, try to make your recitation as close to being aloud as you can manage without embarrassment.

STEP 6: REFLECT. As you conclude the recitation for each section or each chapter, you should raise your eyes and reflect on the knowledge you've acquired. Reflecting means thinking it over, bringing your own ideas to what you've learned, making your own personal associations with it.

You can, for instance, visualize yourself in the classroom, writing the answers on the exam. Or you can imagine yourself at a party telling someone else what you've just learned. You can think about how this material is related to another course or to other aspects of your life. Reflection makes your own personal connections to the knowledge, which helps to establish the memory trace.

By this point, you have gone over the material five times. (1) You have given it an overview. (2) You have read it once actively. (3) You have reread and underlined it. (4) You have written marginal keywords and questions. (5) You have tested yourself by reciting and reflecting on the definitions and answers. These five passes should be done in one sitting.

"Five passes!" you may think. "What a drag!" Remember, though, *this is not recreational reading*. Moreover, you're supposed to be taking little study breaks, a few minutes every half hour or hour. And when you're done with the chapter, you'll know the material far better than

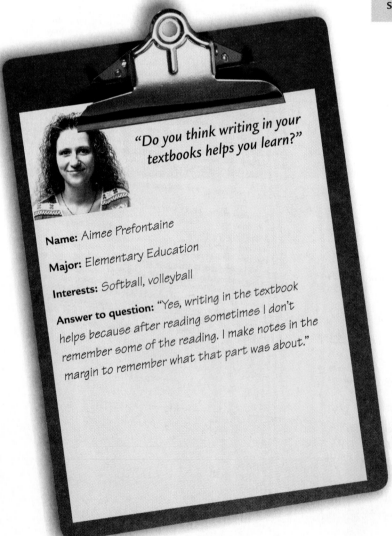

"Do you think writing in your textbooks helps you learn?"

Name: Aimee Prefontaine

Major: Elementary Education

Interests: Softball, volleyball

Answer to question: "Yes, writing in the textbook helps because after reading sometimes I don't remember some of the reading. I make notes in the margin to remember what that part was about."

the people who've read it just once or twice. You've also created a study guide for yourself that will help you review later.

Moreover, when you're done, you'll *deserve* your reward of conversation, snack, TV, or whatever. You won't be doing these activities just to escape from anxieties about studying.

STEP 7: REVIEW. As I said earlier, the retention of information drops considerably in the first 24 hours after you've been exposed to it (the "forgetting curve"). Imagine that what you read was a life-and-death matter—that you're a doctor supposed to do surgery on someone three weeks from now based on what you've read. Could you do it?

Reviewing, like any form of practice, is what makes you better, whether it's performing surgery, playing a guitar, or taking a test. So, add to the five passes you've done of the material at least one or two more.

Reviewing is of two sorts:

■ *Immediate reviewing:* Before you close your book for the night, do one last leisurely sweep through the chapter. Use your newly created study guide: look at the keywords and questions you've written and visualize the definitions and answers. If you have difficulty, say the answer over one extra time, then put a check mark in the margin, so you'll know to pay particular attention to this question in the future.

■ *Later reviewing:* If you really want to crack the exam and get an A—particularly if this course is in your major—you'll want to do more reviewing. If you did your first reading of the chapter three weeks before the test, I certainly wouldn't wait until the night before the test to review again. It's better to look it over once or so a week. Then, of course, right before the test you'll want to do a refresher review again.

When you do the later reviews, do the following:

■ *Recite:* Cover the text with a piece of paper and go page by page looking at the keywords and questions in the margins. Recite *aloud* the definitions for the keywords and answers to the questions; then check your results by looking at the text. If you're still having trouble with those near which you put a check mark, put another check mark down.

■ *Reflect:* Pause on each page or at the end of each section and try to make a personal connection in your mind to the material you have just recited. Think particularly about material near which you've placed a check mark.

You hear people say, "I could do that with my eyes closed" or "I could do that half asleep." No doubt there are some things you could do in these states because you've practiced them over and over: find your way home, bake a cake, throw a football, play a song, whatever you have done repeatedly. Now the question is: How badly do you want to ace the exam in this course? The answer will determine how much practice you're willing to put into reading your textbooks.

GROUP ACTIVITY #7.3

WHAT ARE THE PRINCIPAL MISTAKES MADE IN READING FOR LEARNING?

Along with others in a small group, make a list of examples of mistakes you have made in reading for learning (such as doing too much underlining or reading only once). Then identify specific techniques for correcting these mistakes. (These may be whole systems such as SQ3R or specific techniques such as making diagrams.) It's important that you show, through use of example, how the technique is being used.

With your group pick the best example of the use of a technique and share it with the class as a whole. Discuss which techniques appear to work best in which situations.

Dealing with Special Subjects: Math, Science, Languages, & Others

PREVIEW Mathematics, science, social science, history, foreign languages, and literature may be areas of study that require more study effort than you're accustomed to. The first step is to reduce your anxiety, using positive self-talk. The second step is to devote enough time and practice to the subject. The third step is to avail yourself of such tools as flashcards or index cards; diagrams, charts, and maps; and cassette tapes.

ome students, even though they may be smart in many ways, go into a panic when confronted with a particular subject—technical subjects such as math or chemistry or detail-oriented subjects such as foreign languages, history, or literature. The specific advice for coping here is:

- *Take steps to reduce your anxiety.*
- *Devote more time and practice to your assignments, and don't fall behind.*
- *Use special tools for information organizing and study.*

Let's consider these matters.

REDUCING YOUR ANXIETY. "Math anxiety" is very real for a number of people, as is anxiety about the other subjects mentioned. Students may believe that math requires a logical ability or special knack that they don't think they have. With science they may think there is only one way to solve problems. With history, literature, or foreign languages, they may think they don't have a good enough memory for details.
Here's what to do:

- *Learn your inner voice:* The first step is to learn what your inner voice is saying, to pinpoint those inhibiting pronouncements from within. This inner voice, the *Voice Of Judgment (VOJ),* is the internal broadcast that goes on in all of us.

  As one book describes it, the Voice Of Judgment "condemns, criticizes, attaches blame, makes fun of, puts down, assigns guilt, passes sentence on, punishes, and buries anything that's the least bit unlike a mythical norm."[5]

- *Pinpoint your negative thoughts:* Once you've identified the negative thoughts ("I'm not smart enough to grasp this stuff"), speak them aloud or write them down. Usually, such thoughts come down to two matters:

(1) *"I don't understand it now, so I never will."* If you think about this, however, you'll realize that there have been many times in the past when you haven't understood something but eventually did. After all, there *was* a time when you couldn't read, ride a bicycle, drive a car, or whatever.

(2) *"Everybody else is better at this subject than I am."* If you do a reality check—by asking your classmates—you'll find that this just isn't so. Probably a number of people will, if they're honest, say they aren't confident about this subject.

- *Replace your negative thoughts with positive self-talk:* Now try to replace the VOJ and use your inner voice as a force for success. You do this by using *positive self-talk,* which can help you control your moods, turn back fear messages, and give you confidence.[6,7] **Positive self-talk consists of giving yourself positive messages.**

  The messages of positive self-talk are not mindless self-delusions. Rather they are messages such as "You can do it. You've done it well before" that correct errors and distortions in your thinking and help you develop a more accurate internal dialogue.[8]

  Stop and try Personal Exploration #7.2 to identify your negative thoughts, then figure out how to make them positive, using positive self-talk.

NEGATIVE THOUGHTS & POSITIVE THOUGHTS

Think of certain subjects you are anxious about and listen to what your inner voice (your Voice Of Judgment) says about you. (*Examples:* "My mind is always in confusion when I'm confronted with math problems." "I'm the kind of person who can barely change a light bulb, let alone operate a microscope." "I'm not as good as other people at figuring how a foreign language works." "If I ask the question I want to ask, people will think I'm dumb.")

1. _____

2. _____

3. _____

4. _____

Now try to replace these negative thoughts with positive self-talk. (*Examples:* "I can solve math problems when I approach them calmly and deliberately and give myself time." "Just as I've learned [basketball, weaving, or some other skill] in the past, so I can learn a foreign language without having to compare myself to others." "Smart people ask questions rather than withhold questions.")

1. _____

2. _____

3. _____

4. _____

With others in a group of three, develop a list of negative thoughts. Then replace them with a list of positive thoughts. Post a couple of examples of each on the board for class discussion. Are there some negative thoughts that seem to be fairly common? How are they hindrances to doing well in school and in life? What do you think of the idea of replacing "negative inner voices" with "positive inner voices"?

- **Deal with the stresses:** The sense of unpleas-antness that the anxiety-provoking subject evokes may be felt in a physical way—as clammy hands, constricted breathing, headache, or other kinds of panicky reactions. In Chapters 8 and 11 I describe ways to deal with stress, such as techniques of relaxation and visualization.

  For now, however, just try this: Every time you have to deal with a troublesome subject, take a slow, deep breath and slowly exhale; then repeat. Then tell yourself, "Now I'm ready to deal with this subject calmly and methodically, taking however long it takes." If the anxiety begins to resurface, repeat the slow, deep breathing twice.

DEVOTE ENOUGH TIME. Once you've dealt with the emotional barriers, then be prepared to spend more time on the subject. It doesn't matter that it takes you longer to learn math, physics, French, or whatever than it will some other students; you're doing this for yourself. (The chances are, however, that a difficult subject for you is also a difficult subject for many others.)

Spending more time on the subject involves the following:

- **Keep up with the assignments:** Don't fall behind. Subjects such as math and foreign languages are *cumulative* or *sequential* kinds of knowledge: it's difficult to understand the later material if you don't understand the earlier material.

  Thus, if you feel yourself slipping, *get help right away.* Seek assistance from a classmate, the instructor, teaching assistant, or a tutor. If you're worried about confiding your anxieties to someone involved with the subject, see your faculty advisor. Or go to the campus counseling center and seek the advice of a counselor.

- **Review the previous assignment before starting the present one:** Precisely because later skills depend on having mastered earlier skills, it's a good idea to review the previous assignment. Being confident you understand yesterday's material will give you the confidence to move on to today's assignment.

> ## "If you feel yourself slipping, get help right away."

- **Apply the SQ3R, 3Rs, or other reading method:** Difficult subjects are precisely the kinds of subjects in which you need to go over things several times, constantly asking questions and marking up the text. The reading methods described earlier in this chapter will help here.

- **Work practice problems:** Math and foreign languages require that you learn specific skills as well as information. Accordingly, you should work all practice problems that are assigned, whether math problems or language exercises. For example, you should work practice problems at the end of every section within the book and also those at the end of every chapter.

- **Take frequent breaks—and remind yourself of why you're doing this:** Needless to say, studying difficult material is a frustrating business. Go easy on yourself. If you feel you're beating your head against the wall, take frequent breaks. Study some other material for awhile.

  When you come back to your original work, remind yourself why you're studying it—for example, "I need to study chemistry because it's important to my nursing career."

- **Do lab assignments:** Some subjects require use of a laboratory. For biology or chemistry, for example, there is often a lecture portion, in which you take notes about concepts from a lecturer, and a lab portion, in which you do experiments or other hands-on tasks. *The two kinds of classes are not independent of each other:* what's learned in the lab reinforces what's learned in the lecture.

  Foreign language classes also have laboratories, usually places to practice listening to audiocassette tapes. Since repetition is essential for learning languages, language labs can be very effective.

USE SPECIAL TOOLS FOR STUDYING. A whole bag of tools is available for helping to organize information and make special study guides to help you learn difficult subjects. Some of these tools, such as diagrams and charts, may be especially helpful if your learning style tends to be more visual than verbal.

The tools are as follows:

■ *Flashcards or index cards:* **A** *flashcard* **is a card bearing words, numbers, or pictures that is briefly displayed as a learning aid.** A flashcard may be a 3 × 5 index card that you make up yourself. Or it may be part of a set of cards that you buy in the bookstore to use to study biological terms, foreign language vocabulary, or whatever.

If you're making up a flashcard yourself, write the key term, concept, or problem that you are trying to grasp on the front and the explanation or answer on the back. Don't forget that you can put several terms on one side and their answers on the reverse. For example, for a history course you might list the name of a treaty followed by such questions as "Year?" "Signers?" "Purpose?" "Consequences?" You would list the answers on the back of the card.

Flashcards can be used for all kinds of subjects. For literature classes, you can write the name of a short story or poem on one side and its meaning on the other. For history, you can write the name of an important person or document on the front and the chief characteristics on the back. For math, you can write a term or formula on one side and its definition, meaning, or calculations on the other. In science, you can state the theory or scientist on the front and the important principles or hypothesis associated with it or him/her on the back.

When you use flashcards, you can sort them into three piles according to how well you've memorized them: (1) cards you know well; (2) cards you know but respond slowly to or are vague about; (3) cards you don't know. You'll find it's pleasing to watch the "I know" pile grow.

Carry a few flashcards with you wherever you go. Then when you find yourself with a few minutes to spare you can take them out and practice answering the questions on them.

- **Diagrams, charts, and maps:** Drawing diagrams of concepts helps reinforce learning in two ways: (1) It helps your *visual sense*, because you can see the ideas. (2) It helps your *kinesthetic sense,* or sense of touch, because you are actually creating something with your hand.

There are all kinds of ways to sketch out concepts and information. What follows are only a few ideas.

(a) **Study diagrams are literal representations of things from real life, which you have rendered in your own hand.** This type of artwork is especially useful in the biological sciences: You can draw and label the parts of a cell, the bones in the head, the arteries and veins of the circulatory system. *(See ■ Panel 7.3a.)*

(b) **Process diagrams are useful for representing the steps in a process and thus are useful in such subjects as biology, geology, or environmental science.** For example, you might sketch the process of photosynthesis, the process of global warming, or the geological formation of an ancient lake. *(See Panel ■ 7.3b.)*

(c) **Concept maps are visual diagrams of concepts.** For example, you can make a drawing of psychologist Abraham Maslow's famous hierarchy of needs, the parts of a symphony, or the five departments of a typical business organization. *(See Panel ■ 7.3c.)*

(d) **Time lines are sketches representing a particular historical development.** They are useful in memorizing historical processes, such as the buildup to the Civil War or the growth of computer technology. A time line consists of simply a vertical line with "tick marks" and labels, each indicating the year and its important event. *(See Panel ■ 7.3d.)*

(e) **Comparison charts are useful for studying several concepts and the relationships among them.** Headings are listed across the top of the page and down the left side of the page; the concepts are then briefly described in a grid in the middle of the page. For example, you might compare various religions by listing their names across the top (such as *Christianity, Buddhism, Hinduism*), the principal categories of comparison down the side (*Deity, Holy book, Principal countries*), and then the specifics within the grid. *(See Panel ■ 7.3e.)*

- **Cassette tapes:** Elsewhere I mentioned that taping lectures can provide a kind of reinforcement, particularly if the lecturer is hard to follow (though taping is no substitute for note taking). Listening to cassette tapes is also valuable for certain specific subjects such as language study. Since the heart of learning a foreign language is repetition and practice, during spare moments in your day you can use a Sony Walkman, for example, to listen to tapes on which you have recorded new vocabulary terms, verb forms, and idioms.

GROUP ACTIVITY #7.4

USING DIAGRAMS, CHARTS, & MAPS AS STUDY AIDS

Join other students in a group of three in selecting part or all of a previous chapter in this book (or in any other text on which you can agree, if you're sharing other courses). Use a diagram, chart, or map, as discussed above, to illustrate the use of a visual aid in learning. Share with the class why you selected this particular method and what other visual aids might prove useful for learning the same material and why. Describe how your individual choice of a particular visual aid relates to your preferred learning style.

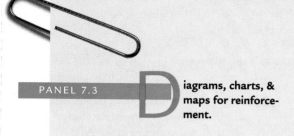

PANEL 7.3 **D**iagrams, charts, & maps for reinforcement.

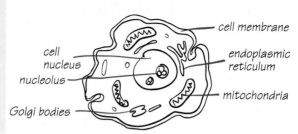

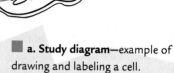

a. Study diagram—example of drawing and labeling a cell.

Space

solar energy

③ About 30% of infrared radiation escapes back into space

④ Greenhouse gases trap heat and radiate it back to earth

Atmosphere

Earth ① Sun's heat absorbed by earth ② Earth radiates heat back into atmosphere

Gases: CFCs from air conditioning; CO_2 from industry, deforestation, & burning of fossil fuels; methane & nitrous oxide from cattle

b. Process diagram—example of representing steps in global warming.

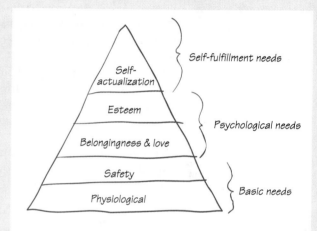

c. Concept map—example of visual diagram of concepts in Maslow's hierarchy of needs.

1832	1843	1890	1930	1946	1952	1964	1970	1977	1981
Babbage's analytical engine	First programmer – Ada Lovelace publishes notes	Electricity used with punched cards	General theory of computers	ENIAC – first computer in U.S.	UNIVAC predicts presidential election (Eisenhower)	IBM 360 line of computers introduced	Micro-processor chips	Apple II computer – first personal computer in assembled form	IBM introduces PC

d. Time line—example of historical development of the computer.

	Hinduism	Judaism	Christianity	Islam
Principal geographic locations	India	Israel, Europe, Americas	Especially Europe & Americas; adherents worldwide	Asia, North Africa, Central Africa
Type (number of gods)	Polytheistic	Monotheistic	Monotheistic	Monotheistic
Holy book(s)	Mahabharata, Ramayana	Torah	Bible	Koran

e. Comparison chart—example of concepts of various world religions.

Onward: Applying This Chapter to Your Life

PREVIEW Reading is half your education.

Reading, as I said, may well constitute half your education during the next few terms or years—reading textbooks, that is. There is also reading of another sort that you will do—namely, reading your lecture notes. Thus, some of the reading skills you have learned in this chapter will apply to the previous chapter on lectures.

In the next chapter, we will put together what you've learned from the lecture and the reading chapters and show you how to apply the knowledge to tests.

Consider two things you can take away from this chapter that you think will be useful lifelong. Describe them here:

_____

_____

_____

_____

_____

_____

_____

_____

_____

_____

_____

_____

_____

_____

_____

_____

_____

_____

_____

THE EXAMINED LIFE: YOUR JOURNAL

1. Be honest: After reading this chapter, do you still think there is some shortcut for absorbing all the volumes of material you'll need to read? Is there some "speed reading" trick that hasn't been mentioned? How do you think this might work? If you are still searching for shortcuts, do some research

2. No doubt at some point in the past you had to learn a lot of material from reading. What was it? How did you go about absorbing it?

3. What is your present system for marking up and reviewing textbooks? How could it be improved?

4. Do you do anything different in studying more challenging material—such as mathematics, foreign language, or history—than you do in studying "regular" subject matter? How is your approach different? What does your Voice Of Judgment tell you about your inadequacies in handling certain types of material (math, for example)?

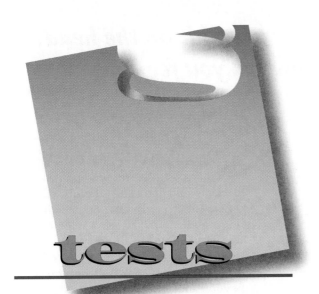

tests

facing & acing the challenge

there's a knack for succeeding at exams

IN THIS CHAPTER: Often people assume they have to be *really smart* to pull As on tests. Actually, it's not so much a matter of one's basic intelligence as it is other things, which this chapter shows you how to do.

- **Test preparation:** You learn how to become as ready as possible for tests.

- **Anxiety management:** You learn how to cope with anxiety during tests.

- **Test-taking strategy:** You learn a six-step approach to test-taking.

- **Coping with various types of tests:** You learn to deal with different types of tests, both objective and subjective.

■ MAKING THIS CHAPTER WORK FOR YOU

Recall an instance in which you really suffered when taking a test. Describe all your feelings of anxiety, both mental and physical (use private shorthand):

_____

_____

_____

_____

_____

_____

_____

_____

_____

_____

■ SKIMMING FOR PAYOFFS

Skim the chapter looking for three things you can do to reduce your anxieties. Describe them here:

_____

_____

_____

_____

_____

_____

_____

_____

Ever been hit on the head? How did you feel?

hen I ask students this, they give similar replies. They say, "I was shocked, confused, scared."

That's also how some students feel when they look at the first question on an exam—and don't know the answer. Certainly that was the case with me when I was a student. It's like being hit on the head. You're stunned, disoriented, frightened.

And if you then look at the second question and draw a blank on *that*, you may feel you've been hit with a one-two combination punch—and suddenly be overcome with panic.

Sound familiar? You'll be glad, then, to have read this chapter if that time comes again. *Even if you don't immediately know the answers to the initial questions on a test, you'll know what to do.* You won't be thrown into a panic and be tempted to bolt from the room.

This chapter shows you how to handle tests of all kinds—quizzes, midterms, final exams. We'll cover the following strategies:

- How to take charge of taking tests

- How to cope with test anxiety

- How to use the six-step examination approach

- How to handle different kinds of tests— from true-false to long-answer essay

- How to deal with the important matter of academic honesty

Taking Charge
of Taking Tests

PREVIEW Becoming expert at tests means psyching out the instructor, learning how to prepare for specific tests, knowing what to bring to the test, and getting off to the right start in the testing room.

aking charge of taking tests begins with assuming the right attitude. Recall why you're in college in the first place: because you think it will help you be your best and lead to your ultimate happiness. You are not a conscript or victim; you are here by choice. You are not being led to exams like cattle to the slaughterhouse. Exams may not be fun, but they are simply part of the experience of higher education—an experience you have *chosen* to undertake. Thus, perhaps the attitude to take is "Since I'm here in school voluntarily and want it to enhance my life, I might as well become good at one of the important things school requires—taking tests."

Taking charge of taking tests has four components:

- Psyching out the instructor
- Learning how to prepare for specific tests
- Knowing what to bring to the test
- Getting started right in the testing room

PSYCHING OUT THE INSTRUCTOR. Instructors not only have different ways of teaching, they also have different ways of testing. Some will test mainly on the textbook, some mainly on the lecture material, some on both. It's up to you to be a *detective*—to figure out the instructor's method of operating and to plan accordingly. Actually, this is usually not hard to do. The aim of an instructor, after all, is not to trick you with questions on the test but to find out what you know.

Following are some ways to get a jump on the test by finding out what the instructor will do:

- ***Look at the course syllabus:*** The syllabus handed out by the instructor on the first class day is often a good guide for test preparation. As I mentioned elsewhere, the syllabus is a course outline or guide that tells you what readings are required, when assignments are due, and when examinations are scheduled.

    This basic roadmap to the course may tell you a lot about testing. It may tell you what kind of weight testing has in the overall course grade. It may indicate if low grades may be made up. It may describe what happens if the test is missed. It may indicate if the lowest grade on a series of tests is dropped when the instructor is determining your average grade for all tests.

- ***Look at instructor handouts:*** Frequently instructors hand out potential essay questions in advance, or they prepare study guides. Handouts show what the instructor thinks is important. Like an actor learning your lines, you can use such material to practice taking the test. This can not only help prepare you by giving you sample material, it may also help reduce that kind of stage-fright-like condition known as test anxiety.

- ***Ask about the specific test:*** Particularly before the first test in a class, when you don't know what's coming, make a point to ask the instructor (in class or during office hours) the following:

(1) How long will the test last?

(2) How much will the test results count toward the course grade?

(3) What types of questions will appear on the test? Will they be true-false? multiple-choice? fill-in? essay? all of these? Different questions require different test-taking strategies, as I'll show in a few pages.

It's also fair to ask the instructor what is most important for you to know. Some instructors may emphasize certain subject areas over others, or they may emphasize the lecture material over the textbook.

- *Ask to see copies of old tests:* Some instructors may be willing to provide you with copies of old tests or with the kinds of questions they are inclined to ask. Don't feel it's somehow impolite or incorrect to ask to see old tests. (Sometimes old tests are on file in the library.)

- *Consult students who have taken the course:* If you know others (such as roommates) who have already taken the course, ask them about their test experiences. See if you can get them to share old exams so you can look at what kinds of questions the instructor likes to ask. Indeed, an item from an old test may even reappear on the one you will take, since there are only so many ways to ask a question. (But don't count on it.)

- *In lectures watch for "bell phrases" and "bell cues":* As I mentioned in Chapter 6, all lecturers use phrases and gestures that should "ring a bell" and signal importance.

    A _bell phrase_ is a verbal indicator of an important point. Examples of bell phrases are: "Three major types . . . ," "The most important result is . . . ," and "You should remember. . . ."

    A _bell cue_ is an action or gesture that indicates important points. Examples are pointing, as to something on the board or a chart; underlining keywords or making a check mark by them; and holding up fingers.

LEARNING HOW TO PREPARE FOR A SPECIFIC TEST. In addition to the foregoing suggestions, there are strategies to employ when preparing for a specific test.

- *Rehearse study-guide or other practice questions:* Some textbook publishers produce a separate study guide, which you can buy at the campus bookstore. **A _study guide_ is a booklet that contains practice questions, along with their answers, covering material in the textbook.** Available for a fairly modest price, the study guide represents an excellent investment because *it gives you a trial run at various types of questions similar to those that are apt to be asked on the test.*

A variation on the paper-and-print study guide now being seen more frequently is the electronic study guide. **An _electronic study guide_ is a floppy disk that students can use on their personal computer (IBM-style or Apple Macintosh) to rehearse practice questions and check their answers.**

Some textbooks also have practice questions at the end of the chapters, with answers to some or all of them in the back of the book.

- *Form study groups with other students to generate practice questions:* Forming study groups with some of your classmates is an excellent way to generate possible test questions—especially essay questions—and quiz one another on answers. Moreover, study groups offer reinforcement and inject a bit of social life into your studying.

- *Develop self-study practice sessions:* Besides study guides and study groups, a useful preparation strategy is simply to have your own periodic practice sessions. Every week set aside time to go through your notes and textbooks and compose practice tests. Specifically:

(1) Practice reviewing material that is emphasized. This includes anything your instructor has pointed out as being significant. Practice defining key terms, the terms presented in *italics* or **boldface** in the text. This is an area, incidentally, where you can make excellent use of flashcards. **A _flashcard_ is a card bearing words, numbers, or pictures that is briefly displayed as a learning aid.**

(2) Practice reviewing material that is enumerated, presented in numbered lists (such as the 13 vitamins or warning signs for heart disease). Enumerations often provide the basis for essay and multiple-choice questions.

(3) Practice answering questions on material on which there are a good many pages of coverage, either in the text or in the lecture notes. Answer questions you've written in the text margins and in your lecture notes. Formulate essay questions and outline answers.

- *Study throughout the course:* The best way to prepare for exams is *not* to play catch-up. Elsewhere (Chapter 5) I mentioned the idea of overlearning. *Overlearning* **is continuing to repeatedly review material even after you appear to have absorbed it.** Of course, to overlearn, you must first have learned. This means keeping up with lecture notes and textbooks, rereading them so that you really get to know the material. Space your studying rather than cramming, since it is *repetition* that will move information into your long-term memory bank.

- *Review the evening and morning before the test:* The night before a test, spend the evening reviewing your notes. Then go to bed without interfering with the material you have absorbed (as by watching television). Get plenty of rest—there will be no need to stay up cramming if you've followed the suggestions of this book. The next morning, get up early and review your notes again.

KNOWING WHAT TO BRING TO THE TEST. Asking to borrow a pencil or pen from the instructor on exam day because you forgot to bring one will not get you off to a good start. It makes you feel and look as though you're not exactly in charge. Thus, be sure to bring some sharpened pencils (#2 if the tests are machine-scored) or pens (preferably blue or black ink; no red, a color instructors often use for grading).

Besides pencils or pens, other items you should bring are:

- *A watch:* If the examination room has no clock, you'll need a watch to be able to budget your time during the test.

- *Blue book or paper and paper clips:* Some instructors will hand out "blue books" for examinations or require that you bring some along. (They're usually for sale in the campus bookstore.) Otherwise, bring some paper to write on and some paper clips (or small stapler) to attach pages together.

- *Calculator, dictionary, formulas, or other aids:* Some instructors allow you to bring items to assist test-taking. Be sure to give yourself the extra edge by availing yourself of these learning aids if they're permitted!

  In math, business, and science courses, you may be allowed to have a calculator.

  In foreign language or literature courses, you may be permitted access to a dictionary.

  In some math, statistics, business, engineering, and science courses, instructors may allow you to jot down formulas on index cards and bring them to the test.

GETTING STARTED RIGHT IN THE TESTING ROOM. It's important to extend the feeling of "taking charge" to the environment of the testing room. Here's how:

- *Arrive on time:* Have you ever been sitting in an exam room and watched some fellow students arrive late, perhaps having overslept? You have to feel sorry for them. They're clearly starting at a great disadvantage, and their faces show it.

  Arrive early. Or if arriving early makes you nervous, because it means listening to other students talk about the test, then arrive on time.

- *Find a good test-taking spot:* Find a spot where you won't be distracted. Sitting near the front of the room is good, where you won't see a lot of other people. Or sitting in your normal spot may make you feel comfortable. Some people like the back of the room because other people can't see them—or see how nervous they are.

How to Cope with Test Anxiety in the Classroom

PREVIEW Five short-term strategies exist for coping with test anxiety in the classroom. (1) Press fists against your closed eyes and squint. (2) Drop your head forward and slowly roll it left and right. (3) Alternately tense your muscles, then let go. (4) Concentrate on breathing slowly in and out. (5) Try positive self-talk.

Dry mouth. Rapid breathing. Quickened pulse. Taut muscles. Sweating. Nausea. Headache. These are just some of the *physical* symptoms—which I well recall myself—associated with test anxiety. Then there are the *mental* aspects: panic, mental blocks, foreboding, dread. "You're going to freeze up," the inner Voice Of Judgment says. "You *know* you're going to flunk!"

Test anxiety consists of thoughts and worries (the mental component) and feelings and sensations (the physical component) of stress linked to test taking. Test anxiety has much in common with other kinds of *performance anxiety*—the stresses associated with first dates, public speaking, job interviews, pregame nervousness, stage fright, and the like.

Anxiety is an indicator of the importance we attach to an event and of our concern that we will not succeed. Thus, anxiety is *normal* under these circumstances. In fact, a certain amount of anxiety can actually be *helpful.* As you've probably noticed in other kinds of challenges (games, for example), some anxiety makes you focus your attention and gets yourself "up" to perform. The problem lies in the kind of test anxiety that hinders your performance. What can be done about it?

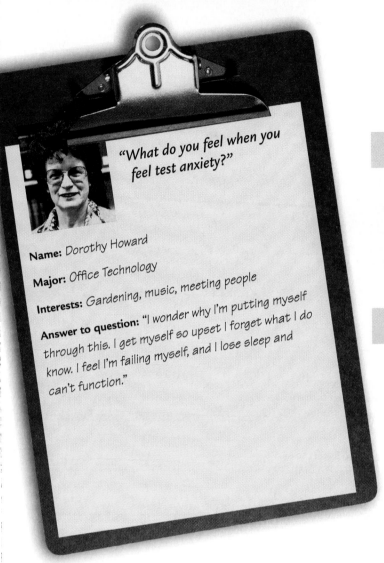

Squint or tightly close your eyes at the same time.

After a few seconds, take your hands away and open your eyes.

2. DROP YOUR HEAD FORWARD & SLOWLY ROLL IT LEFT & RIGHT. Do the following exercise five times:

Drop your head forward on your chest.

Roll it slowly over to your left shoulder, then slowly over to your right shoulder.

3. ALTERNATELY TENSE YOUR MUSCLES & THEN LET GO. If a particular part of your body, such as your shoulders, is tense, try this tense-and-relax activity. The effect is to make you aware of the relaxed feeling after you have released the tension.

Take a deep breath and hold it.

Make the muscles in the tense place even more tense. Hold tightly for a few seconds.

Then let out your breath and release the tension.

You can do this for other parts of your body (chest, neck, and so on) or for all parts simultaneously.

The best recipe for alleviating feelings of panic is to be prepared. If you've reviewed the material often enough, you can have butterflies in your stomach and still feel confident that you'll pull through. Beyond that, there are various techniques for coping with stress (such as relaxation training and visualization, which I describe in Chapter 11).

Five techniques for handling test anxiety in the classroom are the following.

1. PRESS FISTS AGAINST YOUR CLOSED EYES & SQUINT. This exercise will give you a moment to blank out tensions and distractions. Here's how it works (best not to try this if you wear contact lenses):

Press your fists against your closed eyes.

4. CONCENTRATE ON BREATHING SLOWLY IN & OUT. This activity will calm some of the physical sensations in your body. Do this for 2–5 minutes.

Focus your mind on your breathing.

Breathe slowly through your nose.

Deeply and slowly inhale, filling your lungs.

Then slowly exhale through your mouth.

Avoid taking short breaths.

Once your breathing is calm and regular, you can concentrate on the test.

5. TRY POSITIVE SELF-TALK. When the Voice Of Judgment within you says "You're going to flunk!" make an effort to replace this and other negative thoughts with positive ones. Say to yourself: "Nonsense! I studied enough, so I know I'll be okay."

MORE ON NEGATIVE THOUGHTS & POSITIVE THOUGHTS

What kinds of negative thoughts do you have during tests? Pretend you are sitting in an examination room. Listen to what your inner voice (the Voice Of Judgment) is saying, and write down the thoughts below. *Examples:*

"My mind is a blank; I can't remember anything!"

"I'm going to flunk, and my life will be ruined!"

"Everyone else is leaving early; they're smarter than I am!"

1. _____

   _____

   _____

2. _____

   _____

   _____

3. _____

   _____

4. _____

   _____

   _____

Now try to replace these negative thoughts with positive thoughts, using positive self-talk. Write your responses below. *Examples:*

"Breathe easy, and you'll start to remember some things. If not, come back to the question later."

"Even if you flunk, you'll survive. But don't get distracted. Just concentrate on each step of the test."

"Leaving early doesn't mean they're smarter, maybe the reverse. Just focus on the test, not other students."

1. _____

   _____

   _____

2. _____

   _____

   _____

   _____

3. _____

   _____

   _____

4. _____

   _____

   _____

With others in a small group write down a list of negative thoughts, like those above, that you sometimes have during test situations. Also describe the circumstances that generate such negative thoughts.

Next generate a list of positive thoughts, like those above, to replace the negative thoughts. Share your responses and conclusions with the class and with your instructor.

The Six-Step Examination Approach

PREVIEW The six-step examination approach consists of the following: (1) Unload. (2) Review subjective questions. (3) Do objective questions. (4) Do subjective questions. (5) Do questions left undone. (6) Proofread.

Once you have settled your nerves with some of the exercises described in the previous section, you need to apply a strategy for taking the test itself. The six-step system discussed here has three purposes. First, it is a very efficient method for tackling a test. Second, it helps you stave off panic because it gives you a plan to follow. Third, it helps you build confidence.

The six steps are:

1. Unload on the back of the test.

2. Review, but don't answer, the subjective questions.

3. Answer the objective questions.

4. Answer the subjective questions.

5. Answer questions left undone.

6. Proofread the examination.

STEP 1: UNLOAD ON THE BACK OF THE TEST. The first thing you should do after getting the test from your instructor is to *put your name on it.* (You'd be surprised how many students simply forget to sign their examination sheet, baffling the instructor and delaying posting of the final grade.)

After signing it, *without looking at any of the questions,* flip the examination sheet over and simply *unload.* **Unloading means taking 2–3 minutes to jot down on the back of the exam sheet any keywords, concepts, and ideas that are in your mind.** These are things that you think might be on the test. They may also be things that you feel a bit shaky about— that is, things you've only recently studied and need to get down on paper while you still have them in mind.

Unloading is important for two reasons:

■ *It relieves anxiety:* Just "blowing out" all the information pent up in you at the outset of the test can be extremely useful in helping overcome test anxiety.

■ *It helps prevent forgetting:* One term or one idea can be like a string attached to a whole train of ideas that make up an entire essay. Unloading may well produce a key term or idea that leads to a string that you can pull on later in the test.

There is nothing illegal or unethical about unloading. It is not cheating so long as the things you unload are the product of your own brain and not cribbed from somewhere.

STEP 2: REVIEW, BUT DON'T ANSWER, THE SUBJECTIVE QUESTIONS. After unloading, flip the test over. Skip over any objective questions (true-false, multiple-choice) and go to the subjective questions. **Subjective questions are those that generally require long answers, such as essay-type questions or those requiring lists as answers.** Examples of such questions are:

Describe the principal causes of the Civil War.

List the four operations of a computer system.

Compare and contrast the main schools of psychology.

You should also take 2–3 minutes to do a form of unloading: Write *keywords* in the margins next to each question. These keywords will help to serve as a rough outline when you start answering. Don't, however, immediately begin writing answers to the subjective questions (unless these are the only kinds of questions on the exam). Rather, proceed next to the objective questions on the test.

STEP 3: ANSWER THE OBJECTIVE QUESTIONS.

Objective questions **are those that are true-false, multiple-choice, matching, and fill-in.** There's a good reason for answering these objective questions before answering any subjective questions: *the very process of answering may help supply you with extra details for helping you answer your subjective questions.* It may also help you answer a subjective question that you didn't know when you reviewed it in Step 2.

This method of operating shows how you can use the test as a tool. That is, your recognition of the answer to an objective question may help you to recall other material that may help you later in the test.

Answer the objective questions as quickly as you can. Don't spend any time on questions you're not sure of. Rather, circle or star them and return to them later.

STEP 4: ANSWER THE SUBJECTIVE QUESTIONS.

When grading the test, instructors often assign more importance to some subjective questions than to others. That is, they will judge the answer to one question to be worth, say, 30% of the test grade and another to be worth 10%. Quite often the point values may be mentioned on the examination sheet. If they are not, raise your hand and ask the instructor or test giver. It's your right as a student to know.

To make efficient use of your time, do the following:

- *Read the directions!* This is obvious advice, and it applies to all types of test questions. However, since subjective questions usually have more point values than objective questions do, you want to be sure you don't misunderstand them.

- *Either answer the easiest first . . . :* Answer the *easiest* subjective questions first.

- *. . . Or answer the highest-value questions first:* Alternatively, answer the subjective questions with *the greatest point values* first.

STEP 5: ANSWER QUESTIONS LEFT UNDONE.

By this point you will have answered the easiest questions or the ones that you have most knowledge about. As you get toward the end of the test period, now is your chance to go back and try answering the questions you left undone—those you circled or starred.

A word about guessing: *Unless the directions say otherwise,* often an *unanswered* question will count off just as much as an *incorrectly answered* question, especially on objective questions. Thus, *unless the instructor or test says there's a penalty for guessing,* you might as well take a guess.

STEP 6: PROOFREAD THE EXAMINATION.

If you get through all your questions before the end of the examination period, it's tempting to hand in your test and walk out early. For one thing, you'll be dying to find relief from the pressure cooker. Secondly, you may think it somehow looks as if you're smarter if you're one of the first to leave. (However, it's not so. Often it's the ones who don't know, and who have given up, who leave early.)

The best strategy, however, is: If you have any time left, use it. By staying you give yourself the extra edge that the early leavers don't. During this remaining time, look over the test and *proofread* it. Correct any misspellings. Reread any questions to make sure you have fully understood them and responded to them correctly; make any changes necessary to your answers.

Mastering
Objective Questions

PREVIEW Different strategies may be employed for the different types of objective questions— for true-false, multiple-choice, matching, or fill-in-the-blank questions.

s mentioned, *objective questions* are true-false, multiple-choice, matching, or fill-in-the blank questions. Objective questions can often be machine-scored. Such questions are called "objective" because, for the instructor or teaching assistant who is doing the grading, there is no need for interpretation or "judgment calls." By contrast, with "subjective," essay-type questions, the grader has some leeway in how to judge the worth of the answer.

Here are three general strategies to apply to objective questions:[1]

- *Guess, unless there's a penalty:* With objective questions, *never leave an answer blank,* unless the instructor or test indicates there's a penalty for guessing. Note: Some instructors have grading systems for objective tests that penalize guessing. (For example, a correct answer may count +1, a nonresponse −1, and a wrong answer −2.) Thus, be sure you know the ground rules before you guess.

- *If penalty exists, guess after eliminating half of the choices:* If the instructor does take points off for guessing, take a guess anyway when you can eliminate half or more of the options—for example, two out of four choices on a multiple-choice test.

- *Allow second thoughts, if you've prepared:* Answer objective questions reasonably quickly, and make a check mark for any answer that you're unsure about. You may decide to change the answer when you do a final survey, based on information suggested to you by later items on the test.

"Contrary to the popular advice about never changing answers, *it can be to your advantage to change answers,*" say educators Tim Walter and Al Siebert (the emphasis is theirs, not mine). "The research evidence shows that when students have prepared well for an examination, the number of students who gain by changing answers is significantly greater than the number of students who lose by changing answers."[2]

The key here is "prepared well." If you've studied well for the test, your second thought may be more apt to be correct.

HANDLING TRUE-FALSE QUESTIONS. *True-false questions* **are statements that you must indicate are either "true" or "false."** With such items, you have a 50% chance of getting each one right just by guessing. Thus, instructors may try to put in statements that seem true but on close reading actually are not.

Here are some strategies for handling true-false questions:

- *Don't waste a lot of time:* Go through the true-false items as quickly as you can. Don't spend time agonizing over those you don't know; they usually aren't worth a lot of points compared to other parts of the test. Moreover, later questions may jog your memory in a way that suggests the correct answers.

- *Be aware that more answers are apt to be true than false:* True-false tests generally contain more true answers than false ones. Thus, mark a statement true unless you know for sure it is false.

- *Be aware longer statements tend to be true:* Statements that are longer and provide a lot of information *tend* to be true, though not always so. Read the statement carefully, however, to be sure no part of it is false.

- **Read carefully to see that every part is true:** For the answer to be true, every part of the statement must be true. That is, a statement is false if *any part of* it is false. (Example: "The original Thirteen Colonies included Massachusetts, Virginia, and Illinois" is a false statement because the last state was not a member, though the first two were.)

- **Look for qualifier words:** Qualifier words include the following: *all, none, always, never, everyone, no one, invariably, rarely, often, usually, generally, sometimes, most.*

  Two suggestions to follow are these:

(1) Statements that use *absolute* qualifier words, such as "always" or "never," are usually false. (Example: "It's always dry in Nevada" is false because it does rain there some times.)

(2) Statements that use *moderating* qualifier words, such as "usually" or "often," tend to be true more often than not. (Example: "It's generally dry in Nevada" is true.)

HANDLING MULTIPLE-CHOICE QUESTIONS. *Multiple-choice questions* **allow you to pick an answer from several options offered,** generally between three and five choices. The question itself is called the *stem*. The choices of answers are called the *options*. Incorrect options are known as *distractors* because their purpose is to distract you from choosing the correct option. Usually only one option is correct, but check the test directions (or ask the instructor) to see if more than one answer is allowed.

There are two kinds of strategies to apply to multiple-choice questions— *thinking strategies* and *guessing strategies*. Here are some *thinking strategies:*

- **Answer the question in your head first:** Read the question and try to frame an answer in your mind before looking at the answer options. This will help you avoid being confused by "distractor" options.

- **Eliminate incorrect answers first:** Read *all* the options, since sometimes two may be similar, with only one being correct. (Beware of trick answers that are only partly correct.) Eliminate those options you know are incorrect. Then choose the correct answer from those remaining.

- **Return to questions that are difficult:** Mark those questions that are difficult and return to them later if time permits. Spending time mulling over multiple-choice questions may not pay off in the points the instructor allows per question. Moreover, later questions in the test may trigger a line of thought that may help you with answers when you come back.

- **Try out each option independently with the question:** If you're having trouble sorting out the options, try reading the question and just the first option together. Then try the question and the second option together. And so on. By taking each one at a time, you may be able to make a better determination.

- **Be careful about "All of the above" or "None of the above":** The options "All of the above" or "None of the above" are often the correct choices. However, you have to examine the alternatives carefully. Make sure that *all* of the other options apply before checking "All of the above." Make sure *no one* other option is correct before marking "None of the above."

- **Look for opposite choices:** If two choices are opposite in meaning, one is probably correct. Try to eliminate other choices, then concentrate on which of these two opposite options is correct.

Here are some *guessing strategies* for multiple-choice questions:

- **Guess, if there's no penalty:** Unless the instructor has indicated he or she will take points off for incorrect answers, you might as well guess, if you don't know the answer.

- **Choose between similar-sounding options:** If two options have similar words or similar-sounding words, choose one of them.

- **If options are numbers, pick in the middle:** If the alternative options indicated consist of numbers, high and low numbers tend to be distractors. Thus, you might try guessing at one of the middle numbers.

- **Consider that the first option is often not correct:** Many instructors think you should have to read through at least one incorrect answer before you come to the correct answer. Thus, when you're having to guess, consider that there's a high probability that the first option will be incorrect.

- **Pick a familiar term over an unfamiliar one:** An answer that contains an unfamiliar term is apt to be a distractor, although many students tend to assume otherwise. If you're having to make a guess, try picking an option with a familiar term.

As I said with the true-false questions, when you go back and review your answers, don't be afraid to change your mind, if you realize that you could have made a better choice. The idea that you should always stick with your first choice is simply a myth.

HANDLING MATCHING QUESTIONS. *Matching questions* require you to associate items from one list with items from a second list. For example, on a history test you might be asked to associate eight famous political figures listed in Column A with the time period in which each one lived, as listed in Column B.

Strategies for handling matching questions are as follows:

- **Ask if items can be used more than once:** With most matching-questions tests, each item in one column has its unique match in the other column. However, it's *possible* that items can be used for more than one match. That is, an item in Column B may fit several items in Column A. If you're not sure, ask the instructor.

- **Read all choices before answering, then do the easy matchings first:** Before making your choices, read all options in both columns. Then work the easy items first. Matching the easier items first may help you match the tougher ones later by a process of elimination.

If you may use an item only once, cross off each item as you use it. (If items can be used more than once, put a check mark next to the ones you have used, rather than crossing them out.)

Put a question mark next to the matchings you're not sure about. If time permits, you can go back later and take another look at them.

HANDLING FILL-IN-THE-BLANK QUESTIONS. Also known as *sentence-completion questions*, **fill-in-the-blank questions require you to fill in an answer from memory or to choose from options offered in a list.** Often the answers are names, definitions, locations, amounts, or short descriptions. Frequently there are clues contained within the incomplete sentence that will help you with your answer.

Strategies for working fill-in-the-blank tests are as follows:

- **Read the question to determine what kind of answer is needed:** Reading the question carefully will tell you what kind of fact is needed: a key term? a date? a name? a definition? By focusing on the question, you may be able to trigger an association from your memory bank.

- **Make sure the answer fits grammatically and logically:** Be sure that subject and verb, plurals, numbers, and so on, are used grammatically and logically. For example, if the statement says "a _____," don't put in "hour" and if it says "an _____," don't put in "minute." "*A* hour" and "*An* minute" are not grammatical.

As I've suggested with the other types of objective questions, you should put a star or question mark beside those items you're not sure about. Later material on the test may prompt your memory when you come back to review them.

Mastering Written Examinations: Short & Long Essays

PREVIEW Two types of written examinations are short-answer essay and long-answer essay. The strategy for the short-answer essay is to determine the amount of detail needed, depending on time available, point value, and your knowledge. The strategy for the long-answer essay is to meet the standards for relevance, completeness, accuracy, organization, logic, and clarity. This means reading the directions, looking for guiding words; determining choice of essay question; brainstorming ideas and making an outline of your position, supporting details, and summary; writing the three parts of the essay; making sure the essay is clear; and watching your time.

I**n *written examinations* you are generally required to write essays, either short or long.** Both types of essays may be on the same exam. In either case, the point values for answers usually count more than those for answers to objective questions.

- *Short-answer essay:* **A *short-answer essay* may be a brief one-word or one-sentence answer to a short-answer question, a one- or two-paragraph essay, or a list or diagram.** Usually you are asked to write a response to just one question.

- *Long-answer essay:* **A *long-answer essay* generally requires three or more paragraphs to answer.** You may be required to answer one question or several questions, all in the same essay.

    Let's consider strategies for both of these.

HANDLING THE SHORT-ANSWER ESSAY.

Frequently tests contain questions that require only a short answer—anywhere from a single word to two or three paragraphs. Examples:

   State the name of a particular theory. (This might be a one- or two-word answer.)
   Define a certain term. (Could be done in a sentence.)
   List the basic steps in a process. (Could be several words or sentences or a list.)
   Describe a particular scientific study. (Might require a paragraph.)
   Identify and describe three causes of a particular event. (Might be done in two or three paragraphs.)

   Your strategy here is to provide the instructor with enough information (but not an excessive amount) to show that you understand the answer—whether it's a list, some brief sentences, or a few paragraphs.

   How much detail should you provide? This is sometimes difficult to determine. After all, the question "Identify and describe three causes of the Civil War" could run to several pages. To decide how much detail is appropriate, you need to make a judgment based on three factors:

- *Time available:* How much time do you have for other questions on the exam? You may need to allow for an upcoming long essay question, for example.

- *Point value:* What is the relative weight (number of points) that the instructor assigns to short-answer questions compared with other questions?

- *Your knowledge:* How much do you know about the topic? The instructor might take points off if you volunteer information that is erroneous.

   In general, it's best to write down just the minimum you think necessary. If you're in doubt, write out a response to one short-answer question, then take it up to the instructor and ask if it's long enough.

HANDLING THE LONG-ANSWER ESSAY. The long-answer essay (and to some extent the short-answer essay) is sometimes considered a *subjective* test. This notion would seem to imply there are no "objective" facts and that it's up to the grader to determine how good your answer is. Actually, there usually *are* objective facts, and the instructor looks for them in your answer.

What strategy should you follow on a long-answer question? According to one clinical psychologist and instructor of first-year seminar courses, research shows that instructors award the greatest number of points when an essay answer meets the following six standards:[3]

1. *Relevance:* The answer sticks to the question. That is, the facts and points set down are relevant to the question.

2. *Completeness:* The question is answered completely.

3. *Accuracy:* The information given is factually correct.

4. *Organization:* The answer is organized well.

5. *Logic:* The answer shows that the writer can think and reason effectively.

6. *Clarity:* Thoughts are expressed clearly.

Basically, then, two things are important in answering essay questions: First, *you need to know your facts.* Second, *you need to present them well.*

. . . .

"Two things are important in answering essay questions: you need to know your facts and you need to present them well."

. . . .

Let us now proceed to outline a strategy for answering long-answer essay questions.

■ *Read the directions!* This instruction is important for *all* test questions, of course. However, it is especially important here because of the amount of time you're required to invest in responding to long-answer essay questions and the high point values attached to them.

In failing to read the directions carefully, students may answer only one question when three have been asked. Or they may answer three when only one has been asked (thereby depriving themselves of time to respond adequately to later test questions). Or they may go off on a tangent with an answer that earns no credit. I don't know how many times I've written in the margin of a test, "Nice response, but it misses the point. Did you read the directions?"

Reading the directions will help you stay on the topic, thereby helping you to meet Standard #1 above—making the answer *relevant.*

■ **Look for guiding words in the directions:** When you read the directions, look for guiding words—key task words such as *discuss, define,* or *compare*—which may guide your answer. **Guiding words are common words that instruct you in the task you are to accomplish in your essay-question answer.**

Common guiding words are *analyze, compare, contrast, criticize, define, describe, discuss, enumerate, explain, evaluate, illustrate, interpret, outline, prove, relate, state, summarize,* and *trace.* A list of guiding words and their definitions appears in in the box on the opposite page. *(See* ■ *Panel 8.1.)*

As you read the directions, *circle or underline the guiding words* so that you know exactly what is required of you. This will help you achieve Standards #2 and #3—making your answer *complete* and *accurate.*

Often, for instance, I will ask students to "compare and contrast" two ideas. However, some students will show only the similarities ("compare") and not the differences ("contrast"), thus answering only half the question and getting only half the points. Circling guiding words will help you avoid such oversights.

■ **If you have a choice of essay questions, read them all:** Some tests will allow you to choose which of, say, two or three essay questions you want to answer. In order to take your best shot, read all such questions, circling the guiding words. Then pick the essay question you think you can answer best.

■ **Brainstorm ideas:** Now it's time to go to work—by doing some brainstorming and then making an outline. It's best to make your notes on a separate sheet of scratch paper. (If you use a part of the exam-questions sheet or blue book, be sure to cross them out afterward. You don't want

to confuse the grader and have your notes figured into your point values—unless you're attaching the outline because you've run out of writing time.)

Here's how to proceed:

(1) Do a little brainstorming. **Brainstorming means jotting down all the ideas that come to mind in response to the directions in the question.** Just blow out as many ideas as you can that seem to be pertinent. Do this for a minute or two. This will help ensure that you haven't left anything out—helping you to achieve Standard #2, *completeness.*

(2) Next read through your notes and *underline the important ideas.* These will become the basis for your outline and your essay.

Guiding words. These key words appear in essay-question directions as part of the examination vocabulary. As you read the instructions, circle or underline such words so that you will be sure to focus your answer.

When an examination states . . .	You should . . .
Analyze	Explain the major parts or process of something.
Apply	Show function in a specific context.
Compare	Show similarities.
Contrast	Show differences.
Criticize (Critique) (Evaluate) (Examine)	Present your view (positive or negative) of something, giving supporting evidence for your position.
Define	Give the meaning of a word or expression. (Giving an example often helps.)
Demonstrate	Show function.
Describe	Present major characteristics.
Differentiate	Distinguish between two (or more) things.
Discuss (Review)	Give a general presentation of the question. (Give examples or details to support the main points.)
Enumerate	Present all the items in a series, as on a numbered list or outline.
Experiment	Try different solutions to find the right one.
Explain	Show how and why; clarify something.
Formulate	Devise a rule workable in other situations; put together new parts in several ways.
Identify	Label or explain.
Illustrate	Present examples of something.
Interpret	Explain the meaning of one thing in the context of another.
Justify	Give reasons why; argue in support of a position.
Organize	Put together ideas in an orderly pattern.
Outline	Present main points and essential details.
Perform (Solve) (Calculate)	Work through the steps of a problem.
Propose	Suggest new idea of your own for consideration.
Restate	Express the original meaning of something in new words.
Revise	Put together items in new order.
Sketch (Diagram)	Outline; draw picture or graph.
Summarize	Present core ideas.
Trace	Present a sequence; start at one point and go backward or forward in order of events.
Translate	Convert from one system to another.

Some examples:

Identify the parts of the cell.	[On a drawing of a cell, label the nucleus, cytoplasm, cell membrane, etc.]
Define seasonal affective disorder.	[Give the meaning of the term—for example, "Condition in which people become seriously depressed in winter and normal or slightly manic in summer."]

PANEL 8.2

Outline of the parts of a long-answer essay. The answer consists of three parts: Your Position, Supporting Details, and Summary.

The essay question:
Criticize or defend the proposition that capital punishment benefits society.

Possible outline for answer:

Part 1, Your Position:
State your position in response to essay question.

1. Doesn't benefit.

Part 2, Supporting Details:
List keywords representing 3 or so facts supporting your position.

2. Why not:
   a. Doesn't deter murders (FBI stats—compare states)
   b. Innocent executed (names)
   c. C.P. applied more to poor than rich (names)

Part 3, Summary:
Restate your position; include supporting "mini-fact."

3. C.P. not mark of civilized society. Canada, England, Japan lower murder rate, no C.P.

■ *Make an outline of your prospective answer:* At this point you may feel yourself under extreme pressure to simply begin writing. However, by taking another minute to make an outline you will help achieve Standard #4—your answer will be *organized.*

My students have found that a certain formula for an outline seems to help them organize their thoughts and touch on the main points of the answer. The outline formula consists of three parts— Your Position, Supporting Details, and Summary. *(See* ■ *Panel 8.2.)*

Part 1, *Your Position,* states your position or viewpoint in response to the question being asked. It says what you are going to write about.

Part 2, *Supporting Details,* lists the supporting evidence for your position. These might be three or more facts. In your outline, jot down keywords that represent these facts.

Part 3, *Summary,* restates your position. It may include an additional supporting "mini-fact."

One reason for making an outline is that *if you run out of time and can't finish, you can attach the outline to your test answer and get partial credit.*

■ *Do Part 1, Your Position, by rewriting the test question, stating your position, and listing the evidence:* Now begin writing Part 1 of the essay, Your Position. If you follow the formula for the first paragraph that I describe, you will show your instructor that you are achieving Standard #5—your answer is *logical*.

(1) In the first sentence, include part of the examination question in your answer (without using the exact same words the instructor used). This will help you overcome inertia or anxiety and get going.

(2) Next state the position or point of view you will take.

(3) Then list, in sentence form, the facts you will discuss as evidence to support your position, starting with the strongest points in order to make a good impression.

Your first paragraph might read as shown in the example to the right. *(See ■ Panel 8.3.)*

PANEL 8.3

Example of a first paragraph for a long-answer essay. The first sentence restates the examination question or direction. The second sentence states the position you will take. The third, fourth, and fifth list the facts you will discuss as evidence to support your position.

The essay question or direction:

Criticize or defend the proposition that capital punishment benefits society.

The first paragraph of your long-answer essay:

Whether capital punishment actually benefits society has long been a controversial issue in the United States.

[This first sentence somewhat restates the test question.]

I will argue that in the long run it does not.

[This second sentence states your position.]

As evidence, I offer the following supporting facts: First, capital punishment has not been found to deter future murders. Second, some innocent prisoners have been executed by mistake. Third, capital punishment is applied disproportionately to poor people.

[These last three sentences list the supporting facts for your position, which you will develop in subsequent paragraphs.]

Let us consider these three facts . . .

[This is a transition sentence. You will now develop each of the three facts into a full paragraph.]

Example of expansion of supporting fact into a paragraph.

Let us consider these three facts. One of the strongest arguments for capital punishment is that the example of execution of murderers deters others from committing murders themselves. Thus, we would expect homicide rates to be lower in states with capital punishment laws than in states without them. However, this is not always the case. According to FBI crime statistics,

[Notice the supporting detail.]

homicide rates in Southern states, most of which feature capital punishment, are higher than they are in many states in the Midwest, in which the strongest penalty for a homicide conviction is a life sentence. For instance, Georgia, which has capital punishment, has a higher murder rate than Minnesota, which does not.

[Notice additional supporting detail.]

Proponents of capital punishment also assume that the criminal justice system doesn't make mistakes . . .

[Notice the transition sentence to the next paragraph of supporting evidence.]

■ ***Do Part 2, Supporting Details, by expanding each fact into a paragraph:*** Now you take the supporting facts you stated in sentence form in the first paragraph and address them separately. Take each fact and expand it into a full paragraph with supporting details. *(See* ■ *Panel 8.4 at left.)* Use transitional sentences to connect the supporting details so that the reader can follow the progress of your discussion.

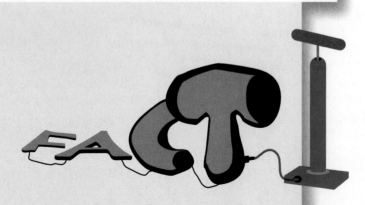

■ **Do Part 3, Summary, by writing a paragraph summarizing your position and adding a supporting mini-fact:** The conclusion is basically a summary paragraph in which you simply restate your position. If you have an additional supporting mini-fact (or a supporting detail you've forgotten until now), this can "punch up" your ending a bit and bring your essay to a dramatic close. *(See* ■ *Panel 8.5 at right.)*

■ **As you write your essay, make sure it's clear:** Here are some tips to help you achieve Standard #6—*clarity.*

(1) *Write legibly,* using a pen rather than a pencil (which is difficult to read) and writing neatly rather than using a frantic scrawl. Because, as I said, grading of essay questions is somewhat subjective, you don't want to irritate the instructor by making your answer hard to read and risking lowering your points.

(2) *Write on one side of the paper only.* Writing on both sides will make the ink show through. Writing on one side also leaves you the opposite side of the page as a place to write an insert later in case you've forgotten something.

(3) *Leave generous space between paragraphs and in the margin.* Leaving space gives you an opportunity to add material later in such a way that you don't have to cram it in and make it hard to read.

(4) *Proofread.* If you have time, go back over your answer and check for grammar, spelling, and legibility so as to boost the clarity of your effort.

PANEL 8.5 Example of summary paragraph.

In conclusion, I believe capital punishment is not the mark of a civilized society but rather its opposite.

[This first sentence restates your position.]

Other nations of the developed world, with far lower homicide rates than ours—Canada, England, Japan—have long since abolished this extreme form of punishment.

[This second sentence adds a last supporting mini-fact.]

It's time that we join them.

■ *Watch your time:* Throughout the test you should keep track of your time, periodically checking to see how much time you have left. Answer the easy questions first, to build confidence, but after that give more time to questions that are worth more points.

As a student I used to think test-taking was often a matter of luck or having some sort of inherited smarts. However, you can see from the foregoing that it's pretty much a *learned* skill. And there's no question you're capable of learning it.

The Important Matter of Academic Honesty

PREVIEW Academic honesty is very important. Types of dishonesty include the following:

(1) Cheating, or using unauthorized help.

(2) Plagiarism, or presenting someone else's ideas as one's own. (3) Fakery, or inventing material. (4) Lying, by omission or commission.

People will commit such dishonest behaviors for several reasons:

(1) They think what they're doing is a "white lie that won't hurt anyone."

(2) They are in a crisis and are desperate.

(3) They think "everyone does it." You can determine whether behavior is ethical by looking at yourself in the mirror, asking what your parents or friends would say, or asking if you could defend the behavior in court. Penalties for dishonesty in higher education could be a failing grade, suspension, or expulsion. Alternatives to cheating are (1) being prepared or (2) negotiating with the instructor.

At some point in this book we need to consider the matter of academic honesty. This is as good a place as any, since one of the areas where problems arise is cheating on tests.

There are all kinds of ways to be less than honest in higher education: use crib sheets for tests, exchange signals with other test takers, give instructors false reasons for being late ("I was ill"; "I had car problems"), plagiarize term papers (pass off others' material as your own), buy "canned" term papers already prepared by commercial firms—the devices are endless.

HOW WOULD YOU RESPOND TO CHALLENGES TO HONESTY?

College can throw you into situations that pose basic ethical conflicts. To see how you might fare, answer the following "Yes" or "No":

1. If I were in a classroom taking a final exam and saw two *friends* exchanging secret signals about the answers, I would do the following:

   a. Tell them afterward that I was ticked off because I'd studied hard and they hadn't, and their cheating might affect my grade.

      ❏ Yes   ❏ No

   b. Probably say nothing to them.

      ❏ Yes   ❏ No

   c. Report them in an unsigned (anonymous) note to the instructor.

      ❏ Yes   ❏ No

   d. Complain personally to the instructor.

      ❏ Yes   ❏ No

2. If I saw two students who were *unknown* to me exchanging secret signals in a test situation, I would do the following:

   a. Do nothing about it, although I might be contemptuous of them or even upset.

      ❏ Yes   ❏ No

   b. Report them in an unsigned (anonymous) note to the instructor, identifying their location in the classroom and what I saw.

      ❏ Yes   ❏ No

   c. Complain personally to the instructor.

      ❏ Yes   ❏ No

3. I wouldn't cheat on a test myself, but I would not turn in a friend who cheated.

   ❏ Yes   ❏ No

4. Lying about why I am late with a paper or missed a class is just a "white lie" that harms no one.

   ❏ Yes   ❏ No

5. Higher education (and the world) is so competitive that sometimes you have to bend the rules just to survive.

   ❏ Yes   ❏ No

6. So many people cheat. Cheating is wrong only if you get caught.

   ❏ Yes   ❏ No

7. If you don't cheat, you're just an honest loser in a world where other people are getting ahead by taking shortcuts.

   ❏ Yes   ❏ No

8. I try to be honest most of the time, but sometimes I get in a jam for time and am forced to cheat.

   ❏ Yes   ❏ No

9. There's nothing wrong with buying a term paper written by someone else and passing it off as my own.

   ❏ Yes   ❏ No

10. If instructors look the other way or don't seem to be concerned about cheating, then I'd be a fool not to take advantage of the system and cheat.

    ❏ Yes   ❏ No

■ MEANING OF THE RESULTS

See the discussion in the text.

GROUP ACTIVITY OPTION

The class is divided into small groups. Each group is asked to consider a different question from this Personal Exploration. After debating the question, share your conclusions and reasoning with the rest of the class.

A good place to examine one's values is in the area of academic honesty. To get a sense of some of the areas you may well encounter, take a look at Personal Exploration #8.2 above.

TYPES OF ACADEMIC DISHONESTY. Academic dishonesty is of several principal types—cheating, plagiarism, fakery, and lying:

- *Cheating: Cheating* **is using unauthorized help to complete a test, practice exercise, or project.** This can mean writing crib notes of critical dates and names for a history test on one's shirt cuff or under the bill of a baseball cap. It can mean arranging a signal with other test takers to exchange answers. It can mean stealing a look at someone else's exam booklet or of a copy of the test before it is given out. It can mean copying someone else's laboratory notes, or field project notes, or computer project.

- *Plagiarism: Plagiarism* **means presenting another person's ideas as one's own.** For example, some students, having no opinions of their own about, say, a novel they've been assigned to write a report about, may try to pass off the comments of a literary critic as their own ideas. (If you can't come up with any ideas of your own but you simply agree with the critic's ideas, that's okay. Only be sure to *cite* the critic.)

- *Fakery: Fakery* **is when a person makes up or fabricates something.** Inventing data for a science experiment, for example, would be fakery.

- *Lying: Lying* **is simply misrepresentation of the facts.** Lying may be by omission or commission.

   In lying by *omission*, crucial facts are simply left out. For example, a student might explain a late paper with "I had computer problems," when what she really means is that the person whose computer she often borrows had to use it.

   In lying by *commission*, facts are simply changed. For example, a student might say his paper was late "because I was sick," when in fact he was just partying.

   The most outrageous, and risky, form of lying is passing off work as your own on which you have expended very little or no effort—for example, a term paper bought from a commercial firm or dug out of a fraternity-house file.

WHY DO PEOPLE LIE OR CHEAT? According to Sissela Bok, professor of ethics at Brandeis University and author of the book *Lying,* people lie or cheat for one of three principal reasons:[4]

- *Just a little white lie:* People say to themselves they're just telling a little white lie. "It doesn't hurt anybody," they say, "so who cares?" Often, however, the lie *does* hurt somebody. In a course in which students are graded on a curve, for example, the honest term-paper writers who gave up their weekends to meet a course deadline may be hurt by the person who stayed up partying, then lied about being sick when handing in the paper late.

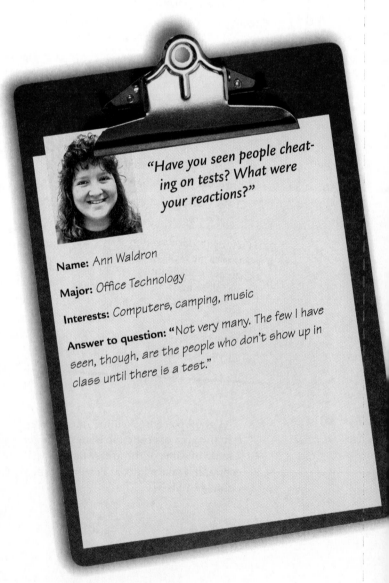

"Have you seen people cheating on tests? What were your reactions?"

Name: Ann Waldron

Major: Office Technology

Interests: Computers, camping, music

Answer to question: "Not very many. The few I have seen, though, are the people who don't show up in class until there is a test."

- **Desperation:** People may feel obliged to cheat because of a crisis. To save face with themselves they may say, "I don't usually do this, but here I really have to do it." This is the rationalization of students handing in a phony research paper bought from a term-paper factory because they didn't allow themselves enough time to research and write the paper themselves.

- **"Everyone does it":** This is a very common excuse. As one graduate student at the Massachusetts Institute of Technology said, commenting on a 1991 cheating scandal attributed to extreme academic pressures, students see cheating take place, and "they feel they have to. People get used to it, even though they know it's not right."[5]

People who cheat in higher education, suggests University of Southern California psychology professor Chaytor Mason, are those "who don't think they're smart enough to make it by themselves. One of the greatest threats people feel is being considered unacceptable or stupid."[6]

Many people who are bent on cheating, then, are probably less concerned with looking like a crook than with looking like a schnook. And that certainly shows *their* values. Clearly, this dilemma can be avoided by developing adequate study skills and scheduling enough time for studying.

• • • • • • • • • • • • • • • • • • •

"One of the greatest threats people feel is being considered unacceptable or stupid."

• • • • • • • • • • • • • • • • • • •

IMAGINING YOU'RE FOUND OUT. If cheating seems to have been widespread in some places, ethics appear to be making a comeback. According to Michael Josephson, head of the Los Angeles-based Joseph and Edna Josephson Institute for the Advancement of Ethics, studies show that "90% of adults say they want to be considered ethical."[7] According to an executive for The Roper Organization, polls show that students in higher education are deeply concerned with "the moral and ethical standards in our country."[8] Thus, the place for ethics and morality starts with you.

If you have any doubt about the ethical question of something you're doing, you might put yourself through a few paces recommended by a crisis-management expert for business people who are worried about whether they are committing fraud:[9]

- **The Smell Test:** Can you look yourself in the eye and tell yourself that the position you have taken or the act you are about to undertake is okay? Or does the situation have a bad smell to it? If it does, start over.

- **The What-Would-Your-Parents-Say Test:** This is far more demanding. Could you explain to your parents (or friends) the basis for the action you are considering? If they are apt to give you a raised eyebrow, abandon the idea. (You might actually have to deal with your parents, of course, if you were found to be cheating and were expelled from school.)

- **The Deposition Test:** A deposition is testimony taken under oath by lawyers. Could you swear in court that the activity you are doing is right? Or if a future employer or graduate or professional school asked if your grades were satisfactory, could you show them a transcript of your courses containing no Fs—the automatic failing grade given students caught cheating?

THE PENALTIES FOR CHEATING. No matter how much you might be able to rationalize cheating to yourself or to anyone else, ignorance of the consequences is not an excuse. Most colleges spell out the rules somewhere against cheating or plagiarizing. These may be embodied in student codes handed out to new students at the beginning of the year. Where I teach, instructors frequently give students a handout, as I do, at the beginning of the course that states that "If reasonable evidence exists that indicates you have cheated, you will receive a failing grade."

In general, the penalties for cheating are as follows:

■ *Failing grade:* You might get a failing grade on the test, the course, or both. This is the slap-on-the-wrist punishment. Actually, it's usually automatic with a cheating or plagiarism offense and is given out *in addition to* other penalties.

Of course, if you think you might fail the course anyway, you might be inclined to think, "Why not take the chance and cheat?" The reason not to do it is the additional penalties, which could vitally affect your future—as well as your feelings about yourself.

■ **Suspension:** Suspension **means you are told you cannot return to school for a given amount of time, usually a semester or quarter or a year.**

■ **Expulsion:** Expulsion **means you are kicked out of school permanently; you are not allowed to return.** This penalty is especially bad because it could make it very difficult to transfer to another school.

ALTERNATIVES TO CHEATING: PREPARATION & NEGOTIATION. Some students cheat routinely, but most do so only once, probably because they are desperate.[10] Let me make some suggestions on how one can avoid cheating:

■ *Be prepared:* Some pretty obvious advice is simply: Be prepared. This usually comes down to a matter of developing your time-management and study skills. Overcoming bad habits such as procrastination or spending too much time on nonacademic things will probably eliminate even the thought of cheating. Getting the assistance of a tutor may also help.

■ *Negotiate with the instructor for more time:* So your instructor is an intimidating figure? You assume he or she won't listen to an explanation of your situation? As an instructor myself, I understand how it's possible to fall behind and I'm always open to a reasonable explanation from my students. (On the other hand, my college administrators would not look fondly on me if I simply announced that slacking off is permissible—nor, in the long run, would this be helpful to the students.)

Note that there may be other times in your life when you'll have to nervously explain to some authority figure why something you were responsible for didn't work out. Explaining to an instructor why you need more time to study for a test or to write a paper is simply practice for those other occasions. It's possible you could push back the deadline a couple of days, which may be all you need. Or you might need to take an "Incomplete" in the course, which would allow you to make it up the following term. (Some schools, however, allow "Incompletes" only for medical reasons.)

Of course it's possible the instructor may deny your request, but at least you made the effort. If that's the case, grit your teeth, pull an all-nighter, do the best you can in the short time you have, and make a resolution never to put yourself in this bind again. Learning from experience is the first step toward change.

But don't cheat. That could really mess up your future. And it certainly reflects poorly on the values you would like to think you hold.

HAVE YOU EVER CHEATED? WHAT DO YOU THINK OF CHEATERS?

This is a classwide discussion activity. On a piece of scratch paper (preferably one handed out by the instructor, so that all pieces of paper look alike), describe in 25 words or less one of the following: (a) An incident in which you cheated in school. (b) An incident of cheating you observed in school. (c) An incident of cheating you observed in some other situation.

Don't put your name on the paper. Carefully fold up your answer, which will be collected along with those of everyone else in the class. Students will then take turns coming up to the front of the class, drawing one of the folded comments from a hat or box, then reading it aloud. Discuss the comments. Are there any circumstances under which cheating is excusable?

What are the rules of your school's academic integrity standards? (If you don't know, look them up in the school's catalog.)

Onward: Applying This Chapter to Your Life

PREVIEW If you still have high levels of anxiety about testing, you can try other stress-busting techniques.

If, after reading this chapter, you get into a testing situation and find that your anxiety is still much too high, don't give up hope. One way to deal with such tensions is with relaxation training, as I discuss in Chapter 11, using creative visualization and similar methods. Another way, which has been found to be effective in alleviating anxiety-producing situations, is with systematic desensitization. This consists of replacing one's anxiety with relaxation. A visit to the counseling department of your school may show you how to avail yourself of such techniques.

This was an important chapter because it showed you valuable techniques for being successful on tests. It also asked you to take a hard look at matters of academic honesty and how they relate to your core values. What did you find in this chapter that you can apply in the world outside of higher education? Write it down here:

_____

_____

_____

_____

_____

_____

_____

_____

_____

1. How have you prepared for tests in the past? How successful has your routine been? Which techniques would you take from this chapter that you would use in the future?

2. How big a roadblock is test anxiety for you? Which techniques will you try to employ to reduce it next time?

3. What kinds of tests do you do the worst on—true-false, multiple-choice, matching, fill-in-the-blank, short-answer essay, or long-answer essay? How will you change your approach in the future?

4. Are you used to cramming for tests? How do you feel about this method? How will you break this habit in the future?

communication

making powerful written & oral presentations

think & express yourself creatively & critically— successfully

IN THIS CHAPTER: Does the idea of having to write a paper (or give a speech) make you ill? Maybe that's because you don't have a formula for doing it. You'll probably have to write a number of papers in school— and in your career (when they're called "reports"). Now's your chance, then, to develop a strategy for writing papers.

This chapter considers the following:

■ *How to target your audience:* What instructors look for in a written presentation, such as a research paper

■ *Making a written presentation:* The five phases of conceptualizing, researching, and writing a paper—including employment of creative thinking

■ *Critical thinking:* Guides to clear thinking

■ *Making an oral presentation:* Giving a talk or a speech

1. If you're the kind of person who hates doing papers, write down why. Describe some reasons and describe the kinds of feelings that go along with them.

_____

_____

_____

_____

_____

_____

2. If you can't stand the idea of giving a speech, state why.

_____

_____

_____

_____

_____

_____

SKIMMING FOR PAYOFFS

Browse through the chapter looking for three things you can say "Aha!" about—something that strikes you as a technique you can probably use lifelong. Describe them here:

_____

_____

_____

_____

Writing papers and giving oral reports is mainly just academic busywork and not required much outside of college—right?

hat's what I used to think. I thought these were just temporary skills I had to learn so instructors would have some basis for grading me.

After I graduated, however, I found out otherwise. The training I had developed in doing researching, writing, and speaking, I discovered, was *very* important in building a career. If you need to research a business report, make a presentation to clients, or contribute to a newsletter, for instance, you'll be glad you learned how.

For now, though, it's a great benefit to learn how to think creatively and critically. It's also a benefit to learn how to use the library, pull information together, and present your research well. These are vital skills for success in higher education. In this chapter, we'll consider the following:

- What instructors look for in a term paper

- How to write a paper

- How to tap into creative thinking and employ critical thinking

- How to give an oral presentation

What Do Instructors Look for in a Term Paper?

PREVIEW Instructors grade term papers according to three criteria: (1) Demonstration of originality and effort. (2) Demonstration that learning took place. (3) Neatness, correctness, and appearance of the presentation.

riting may be something you do for yourself. For instance, you can keep a journal or diary about your feelings, observations, and happenings (as I've urged throughout this book); this is *personal writing*. Or you can write songs or poetry or musings; this is *expressive writing*. Or you can keep private notes about something you're working on, to help you sort out what you think. Here, however, let us consider a kind of writing you do for other people—specifically term papers for instructors.

Think about the meaning of the word "term" in *term paper*. Doing the paper is supposed to take the greater part of a school *term*—that is, a semester or quarter. Thus, it is supposed to be a paper based on extensive research of a specific subject. When finished it should probably run 10 or more double-spaced pages done on a typewriter or word processor. (This is equivalent to about 20 handwritten pages.) Sometimes you may have to give an oral presentation instead of writing a paper, but much of the work is the same. Because so much effort is required, no wonder instructors often consider the term paper to be worth *50% of the course grade*. This suggests why it's worth giving it your best shot, not just knocking it out over a weekend. (This is the equivalent of cramming for a test.)

Perhaps the best way to get oriented is to ask, *How do instructors grade term papers?* There are probably three principal standards:[1]

- Demonstration of originality and effort

- Demonstration that learning took place

- Neatness, correctness, and appearance of the presentation

1. DEMONSTRATION OF ORIGINALITY & EFFORT. *Are the ideas in your paper original and does the paper show some effort?* Instructors are constantly on the lookout for papers that do not represent students' own thoughts and efforts. These papers can take three forms, ranging from most serious (and dangerous to the student) to least serious:

- *"Canned" or lifted papers:* Papers known as "canned" papers may be *bought from commercial term-paper-writing services.* Or they may be *rewritten or lifted from old papers*, as from those in a fraternity-house file.

  Beware of submitting a paper that is not your own. The instructor might recognize it as the work of a student who was there before you or suspect the style is not yours. If you're found out, you'll not only flunk the course but probably will be put on some form of academic probation. This means you might be suspended or expelled from school.

- *Plagiarized papers:* The ideas and/or expression in a paper may be **plagiarized; that is, another person's ideas are passed off as one's own.** For instance, a student may copy passages from another source without giving credit to the source.

  Most instructors have developed a sensitivity to plagiarism. They can tell when the level of thought or expression does not seem appropriate for student writing. Moreover, lifting others' ideas goes against the very nature of why you're supposed to be in higher education to begin with. That is, you're supposed to be here to help yourself learn ways to meet challenges and expand your competence. In any case, plagiarism can also result in an F in the course and possible suspension from school.

■ *Unoriginal, no-effort papers:* Quite often students submit papers that *show no thought and effort.* They consist of simply quoting and citing—that is, rehashing—the conflicting ideas of various experts and scholars. There is no evidence that the student has weighed the various views and demonstrated some critical thinking. A 10-page paper that shows original thinking is always better than a 20-page paper with lots of footnotes but no insights of your own.

This leads us to point 2, about learning.

2. DEMONSTRATION THAT LEARNING TOOK PLACE.

Instructors want to see you demonstrate the very reason why you're supposed to be in an institution of higher learning in the first place: *Does the paper show that you've learned something?*

How do you show that you're learning? My suggestion is this: *Ask a question for which the term paper provides the answer.* Examples of questions are as follows.

"Do men and women view 'date rape' differently?"

"Are alcohol and cigarettes really 'gateway' drugs to illegal drug use?"

"How did the Vietnam War affect the U.S. approach to the war in Bosnia?"

"What's the best way to dispose of radioactive waste?"

Always try, if you can, to make the question one that's important or interesting to you. That way you'll be genuinely motivated to learn something from the answer. At the end of your paper, you'll be able to demonstrate that learning took place. For example, you might conclude "When I first looked into the question of date rape, I wondered whether men and women view the matter differently. As the research in this paper has shown, I have found that. . . ."

3. NEATNESS, CORRECTNESS, & APPEARANCE OF PRESENTATION.

Like most readers, instructors prefer neatness over messiness, readability over unreadability. Studies show that instructors give papers a higher grade if they are neat and use correct spelling and grammar. The third standard, then, involves form. *Is your paper typed and proofread and does it follow the correct form for footnotes and references?*

Let's consider these points:

■ *Typed versus handwritten:* All instructors *prefer*—and many *require*—that you hand in a paper that has been produced on a typewriter or word processor rather than handwritten. Even if you're only a hunt-and-peck typist, try to render the final version of your term paper on a typewriter or word processor. (A word processor is easier for people who make lots of typing mistakes.) Or hire someone else to type it.

■ *Correct spelling and grammar:* As you write, look up words in the dictionary to check their spelling. Proofread the final version to correct any mistakes and bad grammar. (And if you're using a word processor, run the final draft through a spelling-checker program, in addition to proofreading it yourself.)

You may be sick and tired of your paper when you finally get done with it. Nevertheless, you would hate to blow it at the end by allowing the instructor to mark it down because you overlooked the small stuff.

■ *Follow correct academic form:* Different academic disciplines (English and psychology, for example) have their preferred footnote and bibliography styles. Be sure to follow any directions your instructor gives for these and any other requirements for the form of the paper.

Now you know what you're aiming for. Let's see how to achieve it.

Writing a Term Paper: Five Phases

PREVIEW The five phases of producing a term paper are as follows. (1) Pick a topic. (2) Do initial research and develop an outline. (3) Do further research. (4) Sort notes, revise the outline, and write a first draft. (5) Revise, type, and proofread the paper.

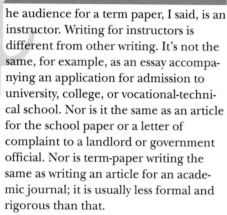

he audience for a term paper, I said, is an instructor. Writing for instructors is different from other writing. It's not the same, for example, as an essay accompanying an application for admission to university, college, or vocational-technical school. Nor is it the same as an article for the school paper or a letter of complaint to a landlord or government official. Nor is term-paper writing the same as writing an article for an academic journal; it is usually less formal and rigorous than that.

In this section, I'll explain how to prepare a term paper for an instructor. There are five principal phases:

- ***Phase 1:*** Picking a topic—employing creative thinking

- ***Phase 2:*** Doing initial research and developing a preliminary outline

- ***Phase 3:*** Doing your research—using the library

- ***Phase 4:*** Sorting your notes, revising the outline, and writing a first draft of the paper

- ***Phase 5:*** Revising, typing, and proofreading your paper—employing critical thinking

Be mindful of the fact that the grade on the term paper will count heavily toward the grade in the course. Thus, you should try to spread these phases over the semester or quarter—not do them all in one week or a few days.

Phase 1: Picking a Topic—Employing Creative Thinking

PREVIEW The first phase, *picking a topic,* has five parts. (1) Set a deadline for picking a topic. (2) Pick a topic important to the instructor and interesting to you. (3) Generate ideas, employing creative thinking. Creative thinking consists of being receptive to messiness, avoiding conceptual blocks such as stereotypes, not being afraid of making mistakes, and other techniques. (4) Refine proposed topics into three questions. (5) Check topics with the instructor.

hase 1 consists of picking a topic. This has five parts:

- Set a deadline for picking the topic
- Pick a topic important to the instructor and interesting to you
- Generate ideas—employ creative thinking
- Refine your proposed topics into three questions
- Check with your instructor

SET A DEADLINE FOR PICKING YOUR TOPIC. Students often procrastinate on this first step. However, the most important advice I can give you about writing papers is: START EARLY. By beginning early, you'll be able to find a topic that interests you. Moreover, you'll avoid pitfalls such as picking a subject that is too narrow or too large.

Thus, *as soon as you get your instructor's guidelines for the term paper, set a deadline for picking the topic.* In your lecture notes, on a page by itself, write a big note to yourself:

*** DEADLINE: PICK TERM PAPER TOPIC BY TUESDAY NOON! ***

In addition, put this on your To Do list and on your weekly planner.

PICKING A TOPIC: TWO CRITERIA. There are two criteria for picking a topic. You should pick something that is (1) important to your instructor and (2) interesting to you.

- *Topics important to the instructor:* You need to determine what is important to your instructor because he or she is the sole audience for your paper.

  How do you find out what the instructor believes is significant? First, if he or she has provided any written guidelines, read them carefully. If the assignment is given verbally, take precise notes. You'll also get a better idea of what's important when you meet with the instructor to discuss your proposed topics, as I describe.

- *Topics interesting to you:* Motivation is everything. Thus, whenever possible, try to choose a topic that interests you. It also helps if you already know something about it. To determine what might be suitable, look through your lecture notes to see what things pop out at you.

GENERATING IDEAS: EMPLOYING CREATIVE THINKING. If you're having trouble nailing down a topic idea, it's good to know how to stimulate creative thinking. *Creative thinking* **consists of imaginative ways of looking at known ideas.** Creative thinking not only helps you to dream up topics for term papers but also to solve problems for which traditional problem-solving methods don't work.

So how do you come up with ideas? The following are some suggestions:

- *Be receptive to disorder and messiness:* Creativity is a messy process. There are people with an excessive fondness for order who cannot abide misleading and ill-fitting data and opinions. However, by allowing yourself to be receptive to such untidiness, you give yourself the chance for a new kind of order.

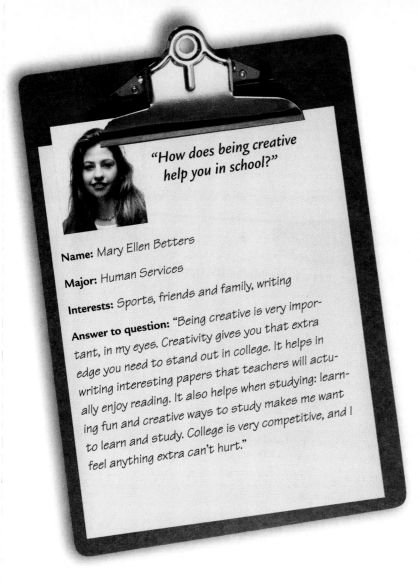

consider information you'd normally ignore. Judgment and criticism are necessary later in the problem-solving process. However, if they occur too early, you may reject many ideas, some of which are fragile and imperfect but may be made mature later.

■ ***Try brainstorming:*** The word *brainstorming* was coined by advertising man Alex Osborn for a type of group problem solving in which several people work simultaneously on a specific problem. However, you can use this method by yourself. Four rules govern the procedure, according to Osborn:

(1) No evaluations or judgments are permitted, which might cause people to defend rather than generate ideas.

(2) Think of the wildest ideas possible, in order to decrease individual judgment among individual members.

(3) The more ideas the better—quantity is more important than quality and, in fact, quantity leads to quality.

(4) Build on and modify the ideas of others whenever possible, which will lead to ideas superior to the original ones.[2]

■ ***Surrender to your unconscious:*** The unconscious mind can be a terrific problem-solver, point out Michael Ray and Rochelle Myers, authors of *Creativity in Business*. They suggest that when you're trying to solve something (such as picking a term-paper topic), you should let go of anxious striving. Instead, ask a clear question about the key issue, then turn the problem over to your unconscious, as in your sleep.[3] Relaxation allows the mind to wander over "silly" ideas that may prove to deliver the "Aha!" you are looking for.

■ ***Ask dumb questions:*** Ask questions the way a child would: "What's behind a rainbow?" "What color is the inside of my brain?" "Why are my toes in front of my feet?"[4] Such "dumb" questions have no expectations, assumptions, or illusions. Once you begin, questions will lead to more questions.

■ ***Watch out for conceptual blocks such as stereotyping:*** Conceptual blocks, or "mental walls" on creativity, keep you from correctly perceiving a problem or conceiving of its solution. One such block is *stereotyping*, or selective perception. This is when you see only what you expect to see. (When you see someone wearing a grey business suit, what kind of person do you expect? What about someone with a diamond in his or her nose?)

■ ***Don't be afraid of mistakes:*** The fear of making a mistake, of failing, is quite common. It occurs because most of us have been rewarded while growing up for producing "right" answers. However, sometimes you *want* to permit yourself mistakes because that allows you to come up with fresh ideas.

By saying that no ideas are too risky or embarrassing, you allow yourself to

- **Be receptive to all your senses:** Some people are resistant to using *all* their senses—smell, taste, and touch, as well as the more favored sight and hearing. Or some think verbally rather than visually, or vice versa. It's important to have access to all areas of imagination—to be able to smell and hear a ball park as well as visualize it. In addition, one must be able to manipulate and recombine ideas in the imagination—imagining a volcano in a ball park, for instance.

To see how creative you are in this respect, try Personal Exploration #9.1.

CREATIVITY: HOW GOOD ARE YOU AT DIFFERENT TYPES OF SENSORY IMAGES?

Rate the following to find out how good you are at different types of sensory images.

- c = Clear
- v = Vague
- n = Nothing

This activity may help you develop your sensory imagery ability, if used extensively. Sight tends to be the predominant sense. However, it should not be allowed to overpower other modes—smell, sound, taste, and touch—which can increase the clarity of one's imagery.

■ IMAGINE:

	c	v	n
1. The laugh of a friend.	c	v	n
2. The sound of thunder.	c	v	n
3. The sound of a horse walking on a road.	c	v	n
4. The sound of a racing car.	c	v	n
5. The feel of wet grass.	c	v	n
6. The feel of your wife's/husband's/girlfriend's/boyfriend's/pet's hair.	c	v	n
7. The feel of diving into a cold swimming pool.	c	v	n
8. The feel of a runny nose.	c	v	n
9. The smell of bread toasting.	c	v	n
10. The smell of fish.	c	v	n
11. The smell of gasoline.	c	v	n
12. The smell of leaves burning.	c	v	n
13. The taste of a pineapple.	c	v	n
14. The taste of Tabasco sauce.	c	v	n
15. The taste of toothpaste.	c	v	n
16. The muscular sensation of pulling on a rope.	c	v	n
17. The muscular sensation of throwing a rock.	c	v	n
18. The muscular sensation of running.	c	v	n
19. The muscular sensation of squatting.	c	v	n
20. The sensation of being uncomfortably cold.	c	v	n
21. The sensation of having eaten too much.	c	v	n
22. The sensation of extreme happiness.	c	v	n
23. The sensation of a long attack of hiccups.	c	v	n

With others in a small group share your findings from this Personal Exploration. Discuss which senses seem to be most fully developed. List some sensations, similar to those above, that represent some of your less developed senses. Share them with the class at large.

- *Stuff your brain, keep idea notes, and cultivate lucky accidents:* Stuff your brain with all kinds of words, pictures, and sounds, whether or not they seem useful at the time. When in the library or before a magazine rack, pick up a magazine or journal you're not familiar with and scan it. Do anything that feeds the mind.

Keep a clipping file of articles and pictures that just strike your fancy. Carry a notepad or 3 × 5 cards and jot down ideas. Write down anything that interests you: insights, jokes, poems, quotes, songs, book titles, possible money-making ideas, and so on. Put in sketches, too, and cartoons.

The point of all this is to create a lot of lucky accidents, an event known as serendipity. *Serendipity,* according to the dictionary, is "the faculty of finding valuable or agreeable things not sought for." If you review your notes and idea files now and then, you'll be surprised how many turn out to be useful.

EXPRESSING PROPOSED TOPICS AS THREE QUESTIONS. By the time your self-imposed deadline arrives for choosing your topic, you should have three alternative ideas. Because your purpose is to demonstrate that you're learning, these should be expressed as questions.

For example, for an introductory health course, you may decide on the following possible topics.

> *"What diets are most effective for weight loss?"*

> *"Does meditation prolong life in cancer patients?"*

> *"Does wearing helmets reduce motorcycle injuries?"*

Are some of these questions too broad (diets) or too narrow (helmets)? In the next step, you'll find out.

CHECKING TOPIC IDEAS WITH YOUR INSTRUCTOR. It's now a good idea to take your topic questions and show them to your instructor (after class or during office hours). Questions to ask are the following:

- *Is it important enough?* Ask "Do you think any of these topics are important enough to be worth exploring in a term paper?" The answer will indicate whether you are meeting the first criterion in selecting a topic—does the instructor think it's significant?

- *Is the scope about right?* Ask "Do you think the topic is too broad or too narrow in scope?" The instructor may suggest ways to limit or vary the topic so you won't waste time on unnecessary research. He or she can also prevent you from tackling a topic that's too advanced. Equally important, the instructor may be able to suggest some books or other resources that will help you in your research.

What if you're in a large class and have difficulty getting access to your instructor (or teaching assistant)? In that case, go to the library and ask a reference librarian for an opinion on the topic's importance and scope. In addition, of course, he or she will be able to steer you toward some good sources of information for your research.

GROUP ACTIVITY #9.1

GETTING GOING ON A RESEARCH PAPER

With three to five other students you are to select one of the following topics. They are: *horse racing, magnetic resonance imaging (MRI), information literacy, population control, Christmas-tree farming, long-distance running, retirement planning, Mayan ruins.* (Or consult with your instructor about another topic.) Develop a number of questions on the topic. Now use the questions to produce an outline. Write your names at the top of the outline and turn it in to the instructor.

Phase 2: Doing Initial Research & Developing an Outline

PREVIEW The beginning of Phase 2, *doing initial research,* consists of using the library's card catalog and guide to periodicals to determine the scope of research material. The second part of Phase 2, *developing an outline,* means doing a tentative outline suggesting the paper's beginning (introduction), middle (body), and end (conclusion). The beginning and middle pose questions you hope your research will answer.

hase 2 consists of doing initial research and developing an outline. If it took you one week to decide on a topic, it should take you another week to do Phase 2. Here, too, you should write a big note to yourself (and also put it on your weekly calendar and To Do list):

*** DEADLINE: CHECK OUT RESEARCH FOR TERM PAPER BY WEDNESDAY 5 P.M.! ***

The idea here is to satisfy yourself about two things:

- **Research material:** Is enough material available to you so that you can adequately research your paper?

- **Rough outline:** Do you have a rough idea of the direction your paper will take?

INVESTIGATING RESEARCH MATERIAL. This step need not take long—perhaps a half hour in the library. The idea is to look in a handful of places to get a sense of the research material accessible to you. Two places to look. in particular, are:

- **Card or online catalog:** Look under the subject listing in the library's card catalog or online catalog to see what books exist on your topic. Don't assume, however, that just because the books are listed that they are easily available. (They may be checked out, on reserve, or in another campus library. An online catalog may tell you if they're checked out.) Look up some call letters for relevant titles, then visit the shelves and see what books you can find.

- **Guide to periodicals:** Magazines and journals are apt to be more up to date than books. Check the *Reader's Guide to Periodical Literature* or computerized catalog to see what articles are available in your topic area. Jot down the names of the periodicals, then check with the reference librarian to see if they are available to you.

Further information about the library, including use of the card catalog and guide to periodicals, is given in Phase 3, Research. This preliminary investigation, however, gives you an overview of the subject.

DEVELOPING AN OUTLINE. While you're in the library doing your first research you should also do a preliminary outline.

Many people resist doing an outline because they think "I don't know where I'm going until I've been there." That is, they think they won't know their direction until they've done all the research and thought about the material. Or they think an outline is somehow going to lock them in to an approach that might not work out.

The purpose of doing a preliminary outline now is twofold. First, it will save you time later. Second, it will provide you with a general road map. You can always change the outline later. But if you set out without one, you may waste time wandering around before you get a sense of direction.

Take a sheet of paper and write *OUTLINE #1* across the top. Then fill in the following three parts—*I. Beginning, II. Middle, and III. End.* [5]

I. *BEGINNING—the introduction*

The beginning or introduction describes the *one or two main questions your paper will try to answer.* In the final paper, the beginning will be one or two paragraphs.

Example: "How smart are college athletes?" "Are college athletics dominated by 'dumb jocks'?"

II. *MIDDLE—the body*

The middle or body of the outline describes *some specific questions your paper will try to answer.* These are detailed questions that will help you answer the main questions.

Examples: "What's the grade-point average (GPA) of college football, baseball, and basketball players?" "What's the GPA of competitive swimmers, gymnasts, and tennis players?" "What percentage of athletes graduate compared to most students?" "What percentage drop out?" "What proportion of athletes in pro sports are college graduates?" "Are top athletes usually top scholars, such as Phi Beta Kappa, magna cum laude, Rhodes Scholars?" And so on.

III. *END—the conclusion*

You won't know the end or conclusion, of course, until you've done the research and answered your questions. For now, *just state that you will write a conclusion based on your answers.*

Here are some techniques for developing your outline:

■ *Write questions on index cards:* Get a stack of 3 × 5 index cards or cut sheets of notepaper into quarters. On each card or quarter-page, write a question you want to answer about your topic. *Write as many questions as you can think of, both general and detailed.*

■ *Organize index cards into categories:* Now sort your 3 × 5 cards into stacks. The stacks represent whatever categories come to mind. One stack might contain a few general questions that will make up your introduction. The others will make up specific categories for the body of the outline.

What kinds of categories might you have? Some might be stacks of similar kinds of questions. Some might be advantages and disadvantages, or cause and effect, or compare and contrast. Do whatever kind of grouping seems sensible to you.

■ *Write out your outline:* Copy out the categories and questions into the outline form shown above. You now have a road map to follow to begin your research.

Note: If you are used to a computer, you may find an *outlining program* useful rather than 3 × 5 cards. This kind of software allows you to brainstorm and sort out ideas onscreen.

After developing it, show your outline to your instructor.

He or she will be able to determine at a glance whether you seem to be headed in the right direction.

Phase 3: Doing Your Research—Using the Library

PREVIEW Phase 3, *doing research,* usually means using the library. This requires learning the parts of the library; discovering how to use librarians and the catalog; knowing how to locate books, periodicals and journals, and reference materials; and finding out how to use other libraries. Low-tech ways of collecting information involve use of 3 × 5 cards. High-tech ways involve the use of photocopiers and computers.

hase 3 consists of doing your research, which usually means making use of the library. In this section, let us consider these aspects:

- Parts of the library

- Using librarians and the catalog

- Locating books

- Finding periodicals and journals

- Finding reference materials

- Using other libraries

- Low-tech ways to collect information: 3 × 5 cards

- High-tech ways to collect information: photocopiers and personal computers

FINDING YOUR WAY AROUND THE LIBRARY.
Particularly at a large university, you may find that the library is a lot larger than those you're accustomed to. Indeed, there may be several libraries on campus, plus access to libraries elsewhere. The most important one for first-year students is the *central library,* the principal library on campus.

The central library has several parts:

■ *Main section:* The main section includes six parts:

(1) The desk where you check books out

(2) The catalog (card or computerized) listing books

(3) A reference section, with dictionaries, encyclopedias, and directories

(4) A periodicals section displaying current newspapers, magazines, and journals

(5) A section (perhaps called the "stacks") housing books

(6) A section housing back issues of periodicals

■ *Other sections:* In addition, the central library usually has some special sections:

(1) A media center, or section containing audiotapes and videotapes

(2) A section for reserve books, which have been set aside by instructors for certain courses

(3) A vertical file containing pamphlets on special topics

(4) A government documents section

■ *Other services—study areas and machines:* Most campus libraries also provide study areas. Indeed, because the whole purpose of the library is to enable students to do serious work, there are relatively few distractions there.

Finally, there may be several kinds of machines available for your use. Examples are machines for reading microfilm and microfiche (materials on film), terminals for accessing databases and indexes, and machines for making photocopies. Some libraries provide typewriters or word processors. Some also have machines providing access to audiotapes, CDs, videotapes, slides, films, filmstrips, videodisks, computer floppy disks, and/or CD-ROM disks.

If you have not had a formal orientation to the library, whether videotaped presentation or actual tour, now is the time. If possible, do it before you're under a tight deadline for a research paper, so you won't have to do your research under panic conditions. Some institutions offer a credit course in how to use the library—something I would recommend to anyone.

The principal resource, the trained navigators, as it were, are the *reference librarians.* Don't hesitate to ask for their help. That's what they're there for. They can tell you if the library has what you need and show you how to get started. Reference librarians are also the people to hunt up when you have exhausted other resources. They may refer you to special sources within the library or to different libraries on or off campus.

- *The card catalog:* A library *card catalog* contains information about each book typed on a 3-by-5-inch card, stored in wooden file drawers. This is the system that has been used by libraries for decades.

  Libraries have three kinds of card catalog listings for books: *title, author,* and *subject.* Thus, you can find *The Right and the Power: The Prosecution of Watergate* by Leon Jaworski in three ways. The first is by title—under "R." (Words such as "The," "A," and "An" are omitted if they are the first word in a title.) The second is by author's last name—under "J." The third is by subject—under "United States, petitioner"; "Nixon, Richard Milhous"; or "Watergate Affair." *(See* ■ *Panel 9.1, opposite page.)*

  When doing research papers, you'll probably often use the subject catalog. Standardized subject headings are listed in the reference work *Library of Congress Subject Headings,* which the reference librarian can help you find.

- *CD-ROM computerized catalog: CD-ROM catalogs* look like music compact disks (CDs), except that they are used to store text and images. CD-ROM stands for Compact Disk—Read Only Memory. To use a CD-ROM, you put the disk into the microcomputer's CD-ROM drive, then follow directions (perhaps on Help screens) for searching by title, author, or subject.

  An advantage of CD-ROMs is that you can use keywords to search for material. *Keywords* are any words you use to find specific information. For example, you could use the keywords "National Socialism" to look for books about Hitler and the Nazi Party.

  A drawback of CD-ROMs, however, is that a disk cannot be updated. Instead a new disk must be produced, which your library may do every month or so. Thus, any CD-ROM catalog you consult may lag slightly behind the library's acquisitions.

HOW TO FIND WHAT YOU WANT IN BOOKS.
Books may be found on open shelves in the main section of the library. In some places, they may also be back in the "stacks," requiring a library page or runner to go get them. Or they may be in special libraries located elsewhere on campus, such as those attached to the business school or the law school. Or they may be available by means of *interlibrary loan,* **a service that enables you to borrow books from other libraries.** Allow extra time—several days or even a couple of weeks—and perhaps a small fee, when you're obtaining a book through interlibrary loan.

To find a book, you may use a *card catalog, CD-ROM computerized catalog,* or *online computerized catalog:*

Three kinds of card catalog listings: title, author, subject. The same book may be found on cards in the three separate catalogs. Note the subject headings at the bottom of the card. These offer more categories that could produce other books pertinent to your area of research.

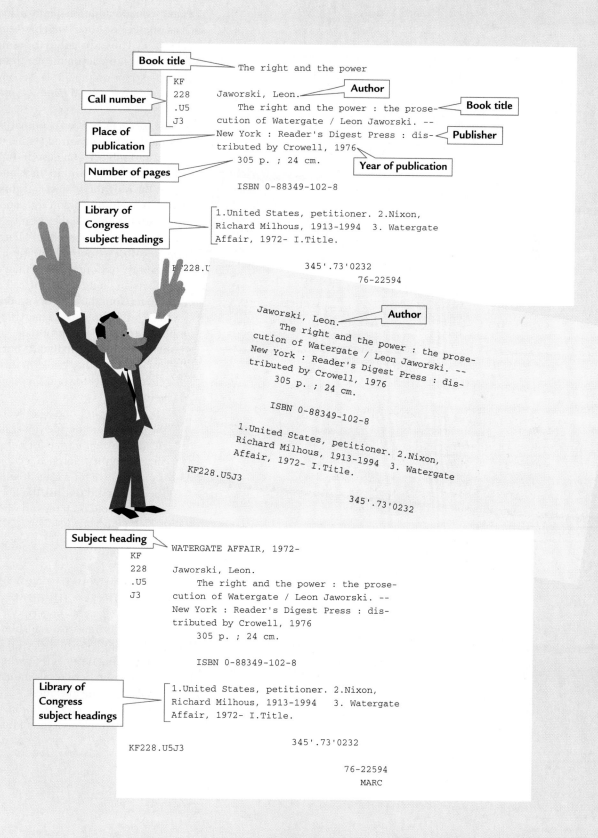

Book title — The right and the power

Call number
```
KF
228        Jaworski, Leon.        Author
.U5            The right and the power : the prose-    Book title
J3         cution of Watergate / Leon Jaworski. --
```
Place of publication — New York : Reader's Digest Press : dis-   **Publisher**
tributed by Crowell, 1976   **Year of publication**

Number of pages — 305 p. ; 24 cm.

ISBN 0-88349-102-8

Library of Congress subject headings
```
1.United States, petitioner. 2.Nixon,
Richard Milhous, 1913-1994  3. Watergate
Affair, 1972- I.Title.
```

KF228.U   345'.73'0232
                                         76-22594

Jaworski, Leon.   **Author**
    The right and the power : the prose-
cution of Watergate / Leon Jaworski. --
New York : Reader's Digest Press : distributed by Crowell, 1976
    305 p. ; 24 cm.

ISBN 0-88349-102-8

1.United States, petitioner. 2.Nixon,
Richard Milhous, 1913-1994 3. Watergate
Affair, 1972- I.Title.

KF228.U5J3

                                345'.73'0232

Subject heading — WATERGATE AFFAIR, 1972-
```
KF
228        Jaworski, Leon.
.U5            The right and the power : the prose-
J3         cution of Watergate / Leon Jaworski. --
```
New York : Reader's Digest Press : dis-
tributed by Crowell, 1976
    305 p. ; 24 cm.

ISBN 0-88349-102-8

Library of Congress subject headings
```
1.United States, petitioner. 2.Nixon,
Richard Milhous, 1913-1994   3. Watergate
Affair, 1972- I.Title.
```

KF228.U5J3   345'.73'0232

                                    76-22594
                                      MARC

Online computerized library catalog.
Example of a screen showing response to subject or keyword search—in this case, the keywords are "National Socialism."

- **Online computerized catalog:** _Online computerized catalogs_ **require that you use a computer terminal or microcomputer that has a wired connection to a database.** Online catalogs have all the advantages of CD-ROMs, including the ability to do keyword searches. However, they are more quickly updated. Moreover, they may contain additional information, such as whether or not a book has been checked out. The instructions for using online catalogs appear on the computer keyboard and/or on the display screen (in Help screens). _(See ■ Panel 9.2, left.)_

Note: _Books in Print_ is an annual reference work—organized by title, author, and subject—that lists most books currently in print in the United States. By using the subject category you can also find books in your area of research, although they won't necessarily be in your school's library.

Most schools' libraries use the Library of Congress system of call numbers and letters. Get the call numbers from the card or computerized listing, then use a map of the library to find the appropriate shelves. Once you've found your book, look at other books in the general vicinity to see if they could be useful.

If you can't find a book on the shelves and decide you really need it, ask a librarian for help. It may be in the reference section or on reserve for a class. If it has been checked out, ask the library to put a hold on it for you when it's returned. Or ask for help getting another copy through interlibrary loan.

```
                                                              LIBCAT

Your search: S=NATIONAL SOCIALISM                              Date
LINE                                                           1965
#     ---------Author---------    ----------------Title----------------    1961
1   Allen, William Sherida    The Nazi seizure of power; the experience    1968
2   Bossenbrook, William J    The German mind.                             1986
3   Butler, Rohan d'Olier.    The roots of national socialism, 1783-1933   1970
4   Engelmann, Bernt, 1921    In Hitler's Germany : daily life in the Th   1978
5   Fest, Joachim C., 1926    The faces of the Third Reich; portraits of   1988
6   Glaser, Hermann.          The cultural roots of national socialism /   1965
7   Herzstein, Robert Edwi    Waldheim : the missing years / Robert Edwi   1966
8   McRandle, James Harrin    The track of the wolf; essays on national    1959
9   Mosse, George L. (Geor    Nazi culture: intellectual, cultural, and
10  Snell, John L., ed.       The Nazi revolution: Germany's guilt or Ge
(More)

Enter:  Line #    (1, 2, 3, etc.) to see more information.    P   to see previous screen.
        N         to see Next screen.                         ST  to start over.
        B         to Backup.
        (UP ARROW) to view previous commands.

                                                      Enter ? for HELP

>>
```

HOW TO FIND WHAT YOU WANT IN NEWSPAPERS, MAGAZINES, & JOURNALS.

You can see what general newspapers, magazines, and journals are available by simply looking at the open shelves in the periodicals reading room. A list of the library's holdings in periodicals should also be available at the main desk.

Here are some avenues for finding articles in the research area you're interested in. _(See ■ Panel 9.3, opposite page.)_

Sources for research.

Newspaper indexes: Examples of newspapers printing indexes about articles appearing in their pages are *The New York Times Index* and *The Wall Street Journal Index.* Look also for *Newspaper Abstracts* and *Editorials on File.*

Examples of computerized databases providing information about newspaper articles are *Data Times, Dialog, CompuServe, America Online, Prodigy,* and *Nexis.*

Magazine indexes: The *Readers' Guide to Periodical Literature* lists articles appearing in well-known American magazines.

Other indexes, available in printed, microfilm, or CD-ROM form, are *Magazine Index, Newsbank, InfoTrac, Business Index,* and *Medline.*

Journal indexes and abstracts: Examples of indexes and databases for specialized journals are *Accountants' Index, Applied Science and Technology Index, Art Index, Business Periodicals Index, Computer Data Bases, Education Index, Engineering Index Monthly, General Science Index, Humanities Index, Medline,* and *Social Science Index.*

Examples of indexes called abstracts are *Biological Abstracts, Chemical Abstracts, Historical Abstracts, Psychological Abstracts,* and *Sociological Abstracts.*

Some computerized online indexes to journals are available, such as *PsycLit,* a bibliographic database to *Psychological Abstracts.*

Specialized dictionaries: Examples of specialized dictionaries for technical subjects are *Dictionary of Biological Sciences, Dictionary of Film Terms, Dictionary of Quotations, Dorland's Illustrated Medical Dictionary, Grove's Dictionary of Music and Musicians, Mathematical Dictionary,* and *Webster's New World Dictionary of Computer Terms.*

Encyclopedias, almanacs, and handbooks: Examples of encyclopedias on specialized subjects are *Cyclopedia of World Authors, Encyclopedia of Associations, Encyclopedia of Banking and Finance, Encyclopedia of Bioethics, Encyclopedia of Religion and Ethics, Encyclopedia of Sports, Encyclopedia of World Art, Thomas Register of American Manufacturers,* and *The Wellness Encyclopedia.*

Examples of specialized almanacs, handbooks, and other reference sources are *The Business Writer's Handbook, Comparisons, The Computer Glossary, Facts on File, The Guinness Book of World Records, Keesing's Record of World Events, Literary Market Place, The Pacific Rim Almanac,* and *The Secret Guide to Computers.*

Government literature: Publications published by the U.S. Government are listed in *The Monthly Catalog* and *PAIS (Public Affairs Information Service).*

Computer networks: Examples of guides to computerized information networks are *Directory of Online Databases, Encyclopedia of Information Systems and Services,* and *Guide to the Use of Libraries and Information Services.*

- *Newspaper indexes:* In the United States, the newspapers available nationally and in many campus libraries are *The New York Times, The Wall Street Journal,* and *USA Today.* Some schools may also subscribe to other respected newspapers such as *The Washington Post* or *The Los Angeles Times.* Some newspapers print indexes that list information about the articles appearing in their pages. Examples are *The New York Times Index* and *The Wall Street Journal Index.* Look also for *Newspaper Abstracts* and *Editorials on File.*

  In addition, your library may subscribe to computerized databases providing bibliographical information about articles appearing in hundreds of magazines and newspapers. Ask the librarian how you can use *Data Times, DIALOG,* or the reference services of *CompuServe, America Online, Prodigy,* or *Nexis.*

- *Magazine indexes:* The index for the 100 or so most general magazines, many probably available in your library, is the *Readers' Guide to Periodical Literature.* This lists articles appearing in such well-known magazines as *Time, Newsweek, Reader's Digest, Psychology Today,* and *Business Week.*

  Other indexes, available in printed, microfilm, or CD-ROM form, are *Magazine Index, Newsbank, InfoTrac, Business Index,* and *Medline.*

- *Journal indexes and abstracts:* Journals are specialized magazines, and their articles are listed in specialized indexes and databases. Examples range from *Applied Science and Technology Index* to *Social Science Index.*

  In addition, there are indexes called *abstracts,* **which present paragraphs summarizing articles along with bibliographical information about them.** Examples range from *Biological Abstracts* to *Sociological Abstracts.*

  Some journal indexes are accessed by going online through a computer. For example, *PsycLit* is a bibliographic database to *Psychological Abstracts.*

HOW TO FIND OTHER REFERENCE MATERIALS.

All kinds of wonderful other reference materials are also available to you. Here's a short list:

- *Dictionaries, thesauruses, style books:* Need to look up specialized terms for your paper? The reference section of the library has not only standard dictionaries but also specialized dictionaries for technical subjects. Examples range from *Dictionary of Biological Sciences* to *Webster's New World Dictionary of Computer Terms.*

  In addition, you may find a thesaurus helpful in your writing. **A *thesaurus* lists synonyms, or words with similar meanings.** This is a great resource when you can't think of the exact word you want when writing.

  Finally, there are various style books for helping you do footnotes and bibliographies, such as *The Chicago Manual of Style.*

- *Encyclopedias, almanacs, handbooks:* No doubt the library has various kinds of standard encyclopedias, in printed and CD-ROM form. As with dictionaries, there are also encyclopedias on specialized subjects. Examples range from *Cyclopedia of World Authors* to *The Wellness Encyclopedia.*

  There are also all kinds of specialized almanacs, handbooks, and other reference sources. Examples range from *The Business Writer's Handbook* to *The Secret Guide to Computers.*

- *Government literature:* A section of the library is probably reserved for information from both the federal government and state and local governments. The most prolific publisher in the world is the United States government. To find out publications pertinent to your subject, look in *The Monthly Catalog* and *PAIS (Public Affairs Information Service).*

- *Computer networks:* This is a vast subject in itself. Now many libraries subscribe to computerized information networks, such as DIALOG, ERIC, ORBIT, and BSR. Directories and guides exist to help you learn to use these services. Examples are *Directory of Online Databases, Encyclopedia of Information Systems and Services,* or *Guide to the Use of Libraries and Information Services.*

  In addition, there are many online information services: America Online, CompuServe, Delphi, and GEnie. Prodigy, and MicroSoft Network. Many schools also provide access to the Internet, the so-called network of networks, which unifies over 11,000 individual computer networks.

HOW TO USE OTHER LIBRARIES.

In big universities, various departments and schools often have their own libraries. Thus, the libraries of, say, the business school or medical school will have material that the main library does not. In addition, you may find a visit to local city or county libraries worthwhile or the libraries of other colleges nearby. Although you probably won't be allowed to check out materials, you can certainly use the materials available to the general public.

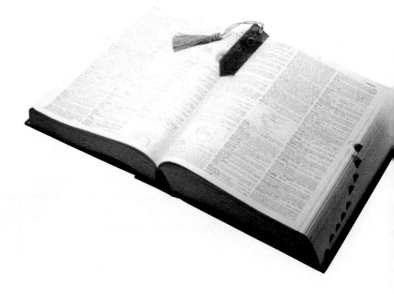

Three uses of 3 × 5 cards: sources, information, ideas.

a. Source card: Use source cards to keep track of bibliographical information.

Anderson, Dave. "Real College Champions Are the Ones Who Graduate."
New York Times   July 6, 1995, p. B5.

b. Information card: Use information cards to write down information to be used in the paper; put quoted material in quotation marks.

Anderson 1995 p. B5   Graduation Rates
NCAA issued graduation rates at its 302 Division I
schools for all 1st-year students compared with student-
athletes (men & women) who entered college in 1988-89
school year. No breakdown of sports documented.

"Based on its graduation numbers, Penn State (77%
student-athletes, 79% all students) deserved to be the
top-ranked football team last season..."

"Of basketball's Final Four teams, North Carolina had the
best rates (76% student-athletes, 85% all students)."

c. Idea card: Use idea cards to jot down ideas that occur to you.

IDEA #1

Find out: Do many college athletes not graduate
because they don't have time-management
skills to handle both studies and sports?

LOW-TECH WAYS TO COLLECT INFORMATION:

3 × 5 CARDS. Some materials (principally books) you'll be able to check out and have access to at your usual writing desk. However, most libraries won't let you take out magazines, encyclopedias, and general reference materials. Thus, you'll need to be able to take notes in the library.

Traditional 3 × 5 index cards are useful because you can write one idea on each card, then later sort the cards as you please. Index cards should be used in three ways—as *source cards, information cards,* and *idea cards.* (See ■ *Panel 9.4.*)

■ **Source cards:** Use *source cards* to keep track of bibliographical information. At the time you're looking up your sources, you can jot down the call letters on these cards. Specifically:

(1) For each *journal article:* Write down the author's last and first name (for example, "Wahlstrom, Carl"), title of article, title of journal, month and year, volume and issue number, and page numbers.

(2)   For each *book:* Write down the author's (or editor's) name, book title, edition, city and state of publication, name of publisher, year of publication (listed on the copyright page), and pages you referred to, if necessary.

Later, when you type your references, you'll be able to arrange these source cards in alphabetical order by authors' last names.

■ **Information cards:** Use *information cards* to copy down information and quotations. This is the actual research material you will use. The card will have three areas:

(1) *Source abbreviation:* At the top of each card, put an abbreviated version of the source, including the page number. (Example: "Wahlstrom 1995, p. 23." If you have two 1995 Wahlstrom references, label them *a* and *b*.) If you use more than one card for a single source, number the cards.

(2) *Information:* In the lower part of the card, write the information. If it's a direct quote, enclose it in quotation marks.

(3) *Keyword zone:* Reserve the top right corner of the card as a "keyword zone." In this area put one or two keywords that will tie the card to a place on your outline. (Example: "Graduation rates.") The keyword can also tie the card to a new subject, if it is not on the outline.

■ **Idea cards:** Use *idea cards* to jot down ideas that occur to you. To make sure you don't mix them up with information cards, write "IDEA #1," "IDEA #2," and so on, at the top.

To keep the cards organized, keep them in three separate stacks each wrapped in a rubber band.

HIGH-TECH WAYS TO COLLECT INFORMATION: PHOTOCOPIERS & PORTABLE COMPUTERS. Using 3×5 cards is a traditional though low-tech way of collecting information. They can also be somewhat time-consuming, since you're required to write out everything by hand.

Two high-tech ways to collect information in the library are the use of photocopiers and portable computers.

■ **Photocopiers:** When you find an article from which you'd like to quote extensively, it may make sense to simply use the library's photocopying machines. Sometimes this means feeding the machine a lot of dimes, but the time saving may still be worth it. Some libraries allow students to open charge accounts for use of these machines.

For organizing purposes, you can then take scissors and cut up the photocopied material. Then write the source abbreviation and page number in one margin and the "keywords" in the other.

■ **Portable computers:** Having a portable computer with a word processing program can be a godsend in collecting library information. (If your library has desktop word processors installed on the premises, you might also be able to use them.) Some researchers also use hypertext programs. An example is the Hyper-Card software on the Apple Macintosh, which electronically simulates 3×5 "cards" and "stacks" that can be manipulated.

Even if you're not very fast on the keyboard, it may still be faster than writing out your information by hand. Follow the same format as you would for 3×5 cards.

Personal Exploration #9.2 lets you try your hand at researching a topic or author.

RESEARCH: LOOKING UP A TOPIC IN THE LIBRARY

Think of a topic that you are required to research for another class or just for your own interest. (Or, if your instructor assigns this as a group activity, you might use the topic you developed in Group Activity #9.1.) Then use three methods to locate three different sources of information about it.

A. YOUR TOPIC

The topic for which I am doing research is _____
_____

B. FINDING SUBJECT HEADINGS

Check the *Library of Congress Subject Headings* for two subject headings that will lead to information about your topic. Write them down here:

1. _____
_____
_____

2. _____
_____
_____

C. FINDING BOOKS

Look in the subject section of the library's card catalog or electronic catalog. Write down information for three books on your subject. Information should include authors' names, book titles, city and name of publisher, year of publication (look on copyright page), call number.

1. Book #1:
_____
_____
_____
_____

2. Book #2:
_____
_____
_____
_____

3. Book #3:
_____
_____
_____
_____

D. FINDING MAGAZINE, JOURNAL, AND NEWSPAPER ARTICLES

Use three sources to find three different articles. One should be from a magazine, one from a journal, and one from a newspaper.

1. **Article from a Magazine:** Use the *Reader's Guide to Periodical Literature* to find an article on your topic. Write down the author's names, article title, name and date of magazine, volume number, article page numbers, and call number. Find the article and write down the first and last sentence in it.

_____
_____
_____
_____
_____
_____

2. **Article from a Journal:** Use another periodical index to find another article on your subject, this time from an academic journal. (An example is *Applied Science and Technology Index*; see other examples in Panel 9.3.) Write down the periodical index used,

the authors' names, article title, name and date of journal, volume and issue number, article page numbers, and call number. Find the article and write down the first and last sentence in it.

_____
_____
_____
_____
_____
_____

3. **Article from a Newspaper:** Use a newspaper index to find an article on your topic. (Examples are the *New York Times Index* and the *Wall Street Journal Index*.) Write down the newspaper index used, the author's names, article title, name and date of newspaper, section and page numbers, and call number. Find the article and write down the first and last sentence in it.

_____
_____
_____
_____
_____
_____

E. FINDING OTHER SOURCES

Use other sources to find more information—for example, government literature, encyclopedias, or computer networks.

1. _____
_____
_____

2. _____
_____
_____

This activity involves out-of-class time because it requires a visit to the library. You may develop the topic agreed on by your group in Group Activity #9.1 or use a topic required for a paper in another class.

In the library research the sources requested above, either by yourself or with other students in your team from Group Activity #9.1. In class discuss the following questions. What types of information were the easiest to locate and why? Which the most difficult? Is your approach to locating sources low-tech or high-tech and how? How could searching for information be improved? What did you learn about the library?

Phase 4: Sorting Your Notes, Revising the Outline, & Writing the First Draft

PREVIEW In Phase 4, you first determine your writing place, then sort your notes, revise your outline, and write a thesis statement and working title. You next write your first draft—middle first, then beginning, then end. In writing, you should make your point and give support, quoting experts, avoiding irrelevancies, and giving sources.

hase 4 consists of sorting your notes, revising your outline, and writing a first draft of the paper. The research phase may have taken a lot of work, but now it's time to put it all together.

ESTABLISHING YOUR WRITING PLACE. What kind of writing environment suits you best is up to you. The main thing is that it *help you avoid distractions.* You may also need room to spread out, even be able to put 3×5 cards and sources on the floor. If you write in longhand, a table in the library may do. If you write on a typewriter or word processor, you may need to use the desk in your room.

Some other tips:

- *Allow time:* Give yourself plenty of time. A first draft of a major paper should take more than one day.

- *Reread instructions:* Just before you start to write, reread the instructor's directions regarding the paper. You would hate to find out afterward that you took the wrong approach because you overlooked something.

Ready? Begin.

SORTING YOUR NOTES & REVISING YOUR OUTLINE. In gathering your information, you may have been following the questions that appeared on your preliminary outline. However, the very process of doing research may turn up some new questions and areas that you hadn't thought of. Thus, your 3 × 5 cards or source materials may contain information that suggests some changes to the outline.

Here's what to do:

- **Sort your information cards:** Keeping your eye on the keywords in the upper right corner of your 3 × 5 cards (or other source material), sort the information material into piles. *Each pile should gather together information relating to a similar question or topic.*

  Now move the piles into the order or sequence in which you will discuss the material, according to your preliminary outline.

- **Revise your outline:** The piles may suggest some changes in the order of your outline. Thus, you should now take a fresh sheet of paper, write *OUTLINE #2* at the top, and redo the questions or categories.

  By now you will be able to write answers to some or all of your questions. *As you rework the outline, write answers to the questions you have listed.* Refer to the sources of your information as you write. For example, suppose you have the question "What percentage of basketball players graduate compared to most students?" You might write:

  "NCAA 1995 study: No breakdown by sports. However, at basketball Final Four schools, graduation rates were as follows: North Carolina 76% student-athletes, 48% all students; UCLA 56% and 77%; Arkansas 39% and 41%; Oklahoma State 38% and 40% (Anderson 1995, p. B5)."

  Resequence the topics so that they logically seem to follow, with one building on another.

- **Write a thesis statement and working title:** When you get done with reworking and answering questions in *II. Middle* of your outline, go back up to *I. Beginning*. Revise the main question or questions into a thesis statement. **A _thesis statement_ is a concise sentence that defines the purpose of your paper.** For example, your original main questions were "How smart are college athletes?" and "Are college athletics dominated by 'dumb jocks'?" These might now become your thesis statement:

  "Though graduation rates of college athletes are lower than those for other students, some individual athletes are among the best students."

  The thesis statement will in turn suggest a working title. **A _working title_ is a tentative title for your paper.** Thus, you might put down on your outline: *Working title: "How Smart Are College Athletes?"*

WRITING YOUR FIRST DRAFT. The first draft has one major purpose: *to get your ideas down on paper.* This is not the stage to worry about doing a clever introduction or choosing the right words or making transitions between ideas. Nor should you concern yourself about correct grammar, punctuation, and spelling. Simply write as though you were telling your findings to a friend. *It's important not to be too judgmental about your writing at this point.* Your main task is to get from a blank page to a page with *something* on it that you can refine later.

Proceed as follows:

■ *Write the middle:* Skip the beginning, letting your thesis statement be the introduction for now. Instead, follow Outline #2 for *II. Middle* to write the body of your paper, using your information cards to flesh it out. Set down your answers/ideas one after the other, without worrying too much about logical transitions between them. Use your own voice, not some imagined "scholarly" tone.

Follow some of the writing suggestions mentioned in the next section, "Some Writing Tips."

■ *Write the beginning:* When you have finished setting down the answers to all the questions in the middle, go back and do *I. Beginning.* By starting with the middle, you'll avoid the hang-up of trying to get your paper off the ground or of writing an elegant lead. Also, having done the middle, you'll have a solid idea, of course, of what your paper is about. You'll know, for instance, which questions and answers are the most important. These may be different from the questions you asked before you did your research.

Now, then, you'll be able to write the introduction with some confidence. An example might be:

"A common image many people have of college athletes is that they are 'dumb jocks.' That is, they may be good on the playing field but not in the classroom. Is this true? The facts vary for different sports, colleges, class levels, and other factors. This paper examines these differences."

■ *Write the end:* Finally, you write *III. End.* The end is the conclusion. It does not include any new facts or examples. It provides just the general answer or answers to the main question or questions raised in the beginning. This is the answer you've arrived at by exploring the questions in the middle section. It's possible, of course, that your conclusion will be tentative. It's all right to state that further research is needed.

An example of the end of a paper might be as follows:

"As we have seen, although the dropout rate is higher for players in some sports and in some schools, it is not in others. Moreover, college athletes often graduate with honors, and some go on not only to professional sports but also to Rhodes scholarships, Fullbright and Wilson fellowships, and graduate and professional schools. Today the 'strong-back, weak-brain' athlete of yesteryear is largely a myth."

SOME WRITING TIPS. In writing the first draft of the middle, or body, of the paper, you should try to get something down that you can revise and polish later. Thus, don't worry too much if this initial version seems choppy; that's why a first draft is called a "rough" draft.

As you write, follow these guidelines:

■ *Make your point and give support:* The "point" you want to make is the answer to each question. (For example, your question might be "Does football require more intelligence than other major sports?") In your writing, this answer will become a statement. Example:

"It's possible that football requires greater intelligence than other major sports do."

Then support the statement with evidence, data, statistics, examples, and quotations. Example:

"Memorizing and executing scores or hundreds of different plays, for instance, takes a lot of intelligence. When scouts for pro football teams look over college players, one question they ask is, 'How is he at learning the playbook?'" (Then footnote the source.)

- **Quote experts:** It makes your statements or arguments much more convincing when you can buttress them with brief quotes from experts. Quoting authorities also can make your paper much more interesting and readable to the instructor. One caution, however: don't overdo it with the quotations. Keep them brief.

- **Avoid irrelevancies:** Don't think you have to use all your research. That is, don't feel you have to try to impress your instructor by showing how much work you've done in your investigation. Just say what you need to say. Avoid piling on lots of irrelevant information, which will only distract and irritate your reader.

- **Give the source of your data and examples:** Your instructor will want to know where you got your supporting information. Thus, be sure to provide sources. These can be expressed with precision on the final draft, following the particular footnote and bibliography ("works cited") style you've decided on. For now put some sort of shorthand for your sources in the first draft.

  For instance, at the end of the sentence above about the football playbook, you could provide the author, year, and page for the source in parentheses. Example: " '. . . learning the playbook?' (Wahlstrom 1996, p. 23)."

- **Jot down ideas:** As you proceed through the first draft, jot down any ideas that come to you that don't immediately seem to fit anywhere. You may find a place for them later.

- **Take breaks:** Professional writers find that physical activity gives the mind a rest and triggers new ideas. The brain needs to disengage. Take short breaks to relax. Go get a soda, stroll down the corridor, take a walk outside, or otherwise move your body a bit. Take pen and paper and jot down thoughts.

LETTING THE DRAFT SIT. Many students write papers right up against their deadlines. It's far, far better, however, if you can get the first draft done early and let it sit in a drawer for a day or so. This will allow you to come back and revise it with a fresh perspective.

Phase 5: Revising, Finalizing, & Proofreading Your Paper— Employing Critical Thinking

PREVIEW Ideally the fifth phase should take as much time as the first four. This final phase consists of seven parts. (1) Read the paper aloud or have someone else read it. (2) Delete irrelevant material. (3) Write transitions and do reorganizing. (4) Do fine tuning and polishing. (5) Type the paper. (6) Proofread the paper. (7) Make a copy.

The last phase, Phase 5, consists of revising, finalizing, and proofreading your paper. How much time should revising take? One suggestion is this: Phases 1–4 should take half your time, and Phase 5 should take the other half of your time. This rule shows the importance that is attached to revision.

The steps to take in revision are as follows:

- Read the paper aloud or get someone else to read it

- Delete irrelevant material

- Write transitions and do any reorganizing

- Do fine tuning and polishing

- Type the paper

- Proofread the paper

- Make a copy

Also, whereas at the beginning of the term-paper process you needed to do creative thinking, now you need to do critical, or analytical, thinking. I explain how in a few pages (in the section "Critical Thinking: What It Is, How to Use It").

READ ALOUD OR HAVE SOMEONE ELSE READ DRAFTS OF YOUR PAPER. It's hard for us to spot our own mistakes, particularly during a silent reading. To better catch these, try the following:

- *Read your draft aloud to yourself:* If you read aloud what you've written, whether first draft or revised draft, you'll be able to spot missing words, awkward usage, and missing details.

- *Get feedback from another person:* By having a friend, family member, or the instructor read any of your drafts, you can get the help of an "editor." (You can offer to read friends' papers in exchange.) Any additional feedback can be valuable.

  SPECIAL NOTE: *Don't take the criticism personally.* If your readers say your paper is "illogical" or "vague," they are not implying you're stupid. When people criticize your draft, they are not criticizing you as a human being. Moreover, remember you don't have to do what they say. You're looking for suggestions, not commandments.

DELETE IRRELEVANT MATERIAL. The best way to start the revision is to take a pencil and start crossing out words. Like a film maker cutting scenes so a movie won't run too long (and bore the audience), you should cut your paper to its essentials.

This is what editors call "blue penciling." Strive for conciseness and brevity. As a mental guideline, imagine someone writing "Repetitious!" or "Redundant!" or "Wordy!" in the margin. Be ruthless. First cut unnecessary sections, pages, and paragraphs. Then cut unnecessary sentences, phrases, and words. Cut even your best ideas and phrases—those gems you're proud of—if they don't move the essay along and advance your case.

WRITE TRANSITIONS & DO ANY REORGANIZING. You may have written the first draft fairly rapidly and not given much thought to making transitions—logical connections—between thoughts. You may also have deleted such connections when you blue-penciled material above. Now's the time to make sure the reader is able to move logically from one of your ideas to another.

You may well discover while doing this that your paper needs to be reorganized, that your outline isn't working right. There are two ways to handle this:

- *Low-tech reorganizing—scissors and glue:* You can use scissors to cut up your paper, then move the cut-up sections around. Use glue (paste) or transparent tape to attach the sections to blank pieces of paper. This activity is known as "cutting and pasting."

- *High-tech reorganizing—word processing:* The same kind of resequencing can be done electronically with a word processing program by using the "block move" function. You use the "block" command to mark the beginning and end of a section. Then you go to another location in the document and use the "move" command to transfer that marked-off section to it.

PANEL 9.5

Documentation. The preferred style of documentation is to identify the author's last name with the page reference within parentheses in the text. The complete source is then presented at the end of the paper in a "Works Cited" section.

Example of citation in text:

One <u>New York Times</u> sportswriter points out that extenuating factors were ignored in the NCAA's survey comparing student athlete and nonathlete graduation rates. "No breakdown of courses was presented, either pre-med or pre-unemployed," he says. "No breakdown of sports was documented, either football or field hockey" (Anderson B5).

Example of "Works Cited" section:

<u>WORKS CITED</u>

Anderson, Dave. "Real College Champions Are the Ones Who Graduate." <u>New York Times</u> 6 July 1995, B5.

Hyatt, Carole and Linda Gottlieb. <u>When Smart People Fail</u>. New York: Simon and Schuster, 1987.

Rice, Phillip L. <u>Stress and Health</u>. 2nd ed. Pacific Grove, CA: Brooks/Cole, 1992.

DO FINE TUNING & POLISHING. Now you need to take a pencil and do a final editing to make sure everything reads well.

Some suggestions:

- *Have a thesis statement:* Make sure the introduction to the paper has a thesis statement that says what the main point of your paper is.

- *Guide the reader:* Tell the reader what you're going to do. Introduce each change in topic. Connect topics by writing transitions.

- *Present supporting data:* Make sure you have enough examples, quotations, and data to support your assertions.

- *Don't be wordy:* Don't be infatuated with the exuberance and prolixity of your own verbosity. Don't use big words when short ones will do. Delete unnecessary words.

- *Check grammar and spelling:* Check your paper for grammatical mistakes. Also check for spelling. Look up words you're not sure about.

- *Follow correct style for documentation:* Follow the instructor's directions, if any, for documenting your sources. The humanities, for example, follow the style developed by the Modern Language Association. The social sciences follow the style developed by the American Psychological Association. Guidebooks are available in the campus bookstore.

In general, the preferred style nowadays is to identify the author's last name and the page reference within parentheses. For example:

"One sportswriter points out that extenuating factors were ignored in the NCAA survey (Anderson B5)."

You then present a complete description of each source in an alphabetical listing at the end of the paper entitled "Works Cited." (See ■ Panel 9.5 at left.)

THE PRESENTATION: TYPE YOUR PAPER.

Presentation is important. Some instructors accept handwritten papers, but they'd rather not, since they're harder to read. In a job interview situation, you have to sell yourself not only with your experience but also by the way you dress and present yourself. Similarly, you have to sell your paper not only by its ideas but by its presentation.

Thus, you should type your paper or have it typed. You need not be expert; using two fingers instead of ten just means typing will take a little longer. If you have access to a personal computer, you'll find typing is even less of a chore, because it's easier to fix mistakes. You can type (keyboard) on the machine, print out a draft, and make corrections on the draft with a pencil. Then you can type in the corrections and print out a clean draft.

PROOFREADING.

In the past have you had papers come back from the instructor with red ink circling spelling and grammatical mistakes? Those red circles probably negatively affected your final grade, marking you down from, say, an A– to a B+.

With your paper in beautiful final-typed form (and the hand-in deadline perhaps only hours away), it may be tempting not to proofread it. You may not only be supremely tired of the whole thing but not want to "mess it up" by making handwritten corrections. Do it anyway. The instructor won't have any excuse then to give you red circles for small mistakes. (If you're using a word processor, providing a completely clean final draft is very easy.)

MAKE A COPY.

Papers do get lost or stolen after they've been handed in (or on a student's way to handing it in). If you typed your paper on a word processor, make sure you save a copy on a floppy disk. If you typed it on a typewriter or handwrote it, use a photocopying machine at the library or an instant-printing shop to make a copy.

Important note: Another good reason for retaining a copy of your paper is that you may be able to expand on the subject in subsequent papers later. I've known students who gradually explored a particular topic to the point where in graduate school it finally became the subject of their doctoral dissertation.

GROUP ACTIVITY #9.2

HANDLING FOOTNOTES & REFERENCES

Finding the correct form for footnotes and/or references may seem somewhat daunting. With a bit of out-of-class time for research and in-class time for discussion, however, you can learn to feel comfortable with these important matters.

You need to be able to do correct references for three kinds of source material: (1) books, (2) articles from periodicals, and (3) other sources (such as encyclopedias and government publications). Different academic disciplines have their own preferred reference and footnote styles. In the library, find and copy footnote and reference styles for books, articles, and other sources. Find sources that will appear in (a) papers you will submit in most of your courses and (b) papers you will submit in courses in your major or prospective major.

The instructor will select some examples to put on the board. Discuss the differences between the various forms.

Critical Thinking: What It Is, How to Use It

PREVIEW Critical thinking is clear or skeptical thinking. It uses the tools of reasoning, as in determining when arguments are deductive or inductive. There are several types of incorrect reasoning, or fallacies. They include *jumping to conclusions, false cause, appeal to authority, circular reasoning, irrelevant attack on opponent, straw man argument, slippery slope, appeal to pity,* and *use of questionable statistics.*

throughout the first-draft and second-draft stages of writing, you'll be required to exercise critical thinking. ***Critical thinking* means skeptical thinking or clear thinking. It is actively seeking to understand, analyze, and evaluate information in order to solve specific problems.** You need to exercise critical thinking, for example, when you're trying to analyze the correctness of someone's point of view.

The opposite of critical thinking is, obviously, uncritical thinking. Uncritical thinking is all around us. People run their lives on the basis of horoscopes, numerology, and similar nonsense. They believe in "crystal healing" and "color therapy." They think cranks and quacks can cure cancer with apricot-pit extract or alleviate arthritis with copper bracelets. Otherwise intelligent people believe that mind power alone can be used to bend spoons.

These are not just bits of harmless goofiness, like wearing your "lucky" shirt to your final exam. James Randi, a debunker of claims made by supporters of the paranormal, suggests just why such uncritical thinking is dangerous. "We live in a society that is enlarging the boundaries of knowledge at an unprecedented rate," he says, "and we cannot keep up with more than a small portion of what is made available to us. To mix our data input with childish notions of magic and fantasy is to cripple our perception of the world around us. We must reach for the truth, not for the ghosts of dead absurdities."[6]

The enemy of clear thinking is our *mindsets.* By the time we are grown, our minds have become "set" in patterns of thinking that affect how we respond to new ideas. These mindsets are the result of our personal experiences and the various social environments in which we grew up. Such mindsets determine what ideas we think are important and, conversely, what ideas we ignore.

As one book on clear thinking points out, we can't pay attention to all the events that occur around us. Consequently, "our minds filter out some observations and facts and let others through to our conscious awareness."[7] Herein lies the danger: "As a result we see and hear what we subconsciously want to and pay little attention to facts or observations that have already been rejected as unimportant."

Having mindsets makes life comfortable. However, as the foregoing writers point out, "Familiar relationships and events become so commonplace that we expect them to continue forever. Then we find ourselves completely unprepared to accept changes that are necessary, even when they stare us in the face."[8]

> **"To mix our data input with childish notions of magic and fantasy is to cripple our perception of the world around us. We must reach for the truth, not for the ghosts of dead absurdities."**

THE REASONING TOOL: DEDUCTIVE & INDUCTIVE ARGUMENTS. The tool for breaking through the closed habits of thought called mindsets is reasoning. ***Reasoning*—giving reasons in favor of this assertion or that**—is essential to critical thinking and solving life's problems. Reasoning is put in the form of what philosophers call *arguments*. **Arguments consist of one or more _premises_, or reasons, logically supporting a result or outcome called a _conclusion._**

An example of an argument is as follows:

Premise 1: All instructors must grade students.
Premise 2: I am an instructor.
Conclusion: Therefore, I must grade students.

Note the tip-off word "Therefore," which signals that a conclusion is coming. In real life, such as arguments on TV or in newspapers, the premises and conclusions are not so neatly labeled. Still, there are clues: the words *because* and *for* usually signal premises. The words *therefore, hence,* and *so* signal conclusions. Not all groups of sentences form arguments. Often they may form anecdotes or other types of exposition or explanation.[9]

The two main kinds of correct or valid arguments are inductive and deductive:

■ ***Deductive argument:* A _deductive argument_ is defined as follows: If its premises are true, then its conclusions are true also.** In other words, if the premises are true, the conclusions cannot be false.

■ ***Inductive argument:* An _inductive argument_ is defined as follows: If the premises are true, the conclusions are PROBABLY true, but the truth is not guaranteed.** An inductive argument is sometimes known as a "probability argument."

An example of a deductive argument is as follows:[10]

Premise 1: All students experience stress in their lives.
Premise 2: Reuben is a student.
Conclusion: Therefore, Reuben experiences stress in his life.

This argument is deductive—the conclusion is *definitely* true if the premises are *definitely* true.

An example of an *inductive argument* is as follows:[11]

Premise 1: Stress can cause illness.
Premise 2: Reuben experiences stress in his life.
Premise 3: Reuben is ill.
Conclusion: Therefore, stress may be the cause of Reuben's illness.

Note the word "may" in the conclusion. This argument is inductive. The conclusion is not stated with absolute certainty; rather, it only suggests that stress *may* be the cause. The link between premises and conclusion is not definite because there may be other reasons for Reuben's illness.

SOME TYPES OF INCORRECT REASONING. **Patterns of incorrect reasoning are known as _fallacies._** Learning to identify fallacious arguments will help you avoid patterns of faulty thinking in your own writing and thinking. It will also help you identify them in others' thinking.

Some principal types of incorrect reasoning are as follows:

■ ***Jumping to conclusions:*** Also known as *hasty generalization,* the fallacy called ***jumping to conclusions* means that a conclusion has been reached when not all the facts are available.**
Example: Cab drivers may (illegally) refuse to take certain passengers merely on the basis of their skin color or looks, assuming they will end up in a dangerous neighborhood. But what if that person turns out to be a city councilman, as happened in Boston not long ago?

■ ***False cause or irrelevant reason:*** The faulty reasoning known as non sequitur (Latin for "It does not follow"), which might be better called ***false cause* or *irrelevant reason*, means that the conclusion does not follow logically from the supposed reasons stated earlier.** There is no *causal* relationship.
Example: You receive an A on a test. However, because you felt you hadn't been well prepared, you attribute your success to your friendliness with the instructor. Or to your horoscope. None of these "reasons" has anything to do with the result.

- *Appeal to authority:* Known in Latin as *argumentum ad verecundiam,* **the _appeal to authority_ argument uses an authority in one area to pretend to validate claims in another area in which the person is not an expert.**

  Example: You see the appeal-to-authority argument used all the time in advertising. But what *does* a champion golfer really know about real-estate developments?

- *Circular reasoning:* **The _circular reasoning_ argument rephrases the statement to be proven true. It then uses the new, similar statement as supposed proof that the original statement is in fact true.**

  Examples: You declare that you can drive safely at high speeds with only inches separating you from the car ahead. After all, you have driven this way for years without an accident. Or you say that paying student-body fees is for the common good because in the long run paying student-body fees benefits everyone.

- *Irrelevant attack on opponent:* Known as an *ad hominem* argument (Latin for "to the person"), **the _irrelevant attack on an opponent_ attacks a person's reputation or beliefs rather than his or her argument.**

  Example: Politicians will frequently try to attack an adversary's reputation. Someone running for student-body president may attack an opponent's "character" or intelligence rather than the opponent's stand on the issues.

- *Straw man argument:* **The _straw man argument_ is when you misrepresent your opponent's position to make it easier to attack, or when you attack a weaker position while ignoring a stronger one.** In other words, you sidetrack the argument from the main discussion.

  Example: A politician might attack an opponent as a "socialist" for supporting aid to mothers with dependent children but not for supporting aid to tobacco growers. (This is because the first politician also favors supporting tobacco growers.)

- *Slippery slope:* **The _slippery slope_ is a failure to see that the first step in a possible series of steps does not lead inevitably to the rest.**

  Example: The "domino theory," under which the United States waged wars against Communism, was a slippery slope argument. It assumed that if Communism triumphed in Nicaragua, say, it would inevitably spread to the rest of Central America and finally to the United States.

- *Appeal to pity:* **The _appeal to pity_ argument appeals to mercy rather than an argument on the merits of the case itself.**

  Example: Begging the dean not to expel you for cheating because your impoverished parents made sacrifices for your education exemplifies this fallacy.

- *Questionable statistics:* Statistics can be misused in many ways as supporting evidence. The statistics may be unknowable, drawn from an unrepresentative sample, or otherwise suspect.

  Examples: Stating that people were less happy 10,000 years ago than today is an example of unknowable or undefined use of statistics. Stating how much money is lost to taxes because of illegal drug transactions is speculation because such transactions are hidden or underground.

  Fallacies such as these are used every day in promotional pitches, legal arguments, news analysis, and appeals for money. Clearly, then, being aware of them will serve you well lifelong.

GROUP ACTIVITY #9.3

CRITICAL THINKING

Letters to the editor in newspapers (particularly locally published dailies or weeklies) can be a rich source of faulty reasoning. In the library see if you can find examples of logical fallacies in these or any other written material. Photocopy or copy out the examples and bring them to class for handing in to the instructor. He or she may read them aloud and ask the class to identify the particular types of incorrect reasoning.

Making an Oral Presentation

PREVIEW An oral presentation can involve the same kind of research and writing as is required for a written presentation (term paper). Beyond that, an oral presentation has the following aspects. (1) You need to prepare readable speaker's notes, either full text or notes only. (2) You need to prepare a beginning that goes right to the point, a middle that expands on that, and an ending that repeats the middle points. (3) You need to understand the attention cycle of the audience. (4) You need to know how to reduce your nervousness through rehearsal and preparation, breathing, and mind control. (5) You need to make the delivery while coping with your nervous energy, focusing on the audience, and pacing yourself.

The material you've gathered and organized for a written paper can also be used for an oral presentation. If you're one of the millions of people who are anxious—indeed, panicked—about speaking on your feet before several other people, take heart. I used to be that way myself, but I've since found some ways to make it easier—and to reduce the panicky feelings.

It's possible to go all the way through school and not have to make an oral presentation. Some instructors, however, may require it. More important, outside school, the ability to speak to a room full of people is one of the greatest skills you can have. This is supported by a study conducted by AT&T and Stanford University. It found that the top predictor of success and professional upward mobility is how much you enjoy public speaking and how effective you are at it.[12]

PREPARING YOUR NOTES: TWO METHODS.

Obviously, your notes have to be readable. If you have to squint or bend over to read them, you'll be undermining the effect of your presentation. Thus, unless you'll be sitting down when you deliver your speech, assume you'll be reading your notes from about 2 feet away.

Whether your speech takes 10 minutes or an hour, there are two ways to prepare your notes:

■ *On 4 × 6 cards:* You can prepare your final text or your notes on 4 × 6 note cards (better than the smaller 3 × 5 cards). Number the cards so that you can put them back in order if they are dropped. Move the cards from front to back of the stack as you go through them.

If you'll be standing up while you speak (or if your vision is not perfect), print your notes in large block letters. If you'll be sitting down, type them in all-capital letters.

■ *Outlined on paper:* You can also prepare your text or notes on standard size (8 ½ × 11) paper. The advantage of this method is that you won't distract your audience by shuffling cards.

When you type your text, type all capital letters, triple-spaced, and allow generous margins to the left and right. One public-speaking expert, Ed Wohlmuth, recommends using standard proofreader's marks in red for emphasis. Put "a triple underline under the first letter of each sentence and circle around each period," he says. "This will help you find the location of each complete sentence very quickly. . . ."[13]

If you use a word processor for typing, some programs will allow you to enlarge the type. Thus, to enhance readability, you can produce notes in a type size two or three times as large as normal typewriter type.

FULL TEXT OR NOTES ONLY? Should you type out the full text of the speech or should you just do notes? Wohlmuth recommends that you write out the entire speech, even if later you convert to notes-only. The reason is that doing a word-for-word text will help you ingrain the speech in your memory.[14]

A full text is particularly recommended if you are doing a stand-up speech to an audience of 30 people or more. If you're talking to a small group, whether you're standing up or sitting down, a full-text delivery is probably inappropriate. You want to *interact with* the people in the audience, not talk to them.

THE BEGINNING, MIDDLE, & END. Speech writer Phil Theibert says a speech comprises just three simple rules:[15]

1. *Tell them what you're going to say.*

2. *Say it.*

3. *Tell them what you said.*

These correspond to the three parts of a paper—beginning, middle, and end (or introduction, body, and conclusion).

- *Beginning:* The introduction should take 5–15% of your speaking time, and it should prepare the audience for the rest of the speech.

  Should you begin with a joke? Probably not. If it bombs, your audience will be uncomfortable (and will wonder if more mediocre material is to come) and so will you. Unless you're David Letterman or Jay Leno—whose jokes fail surprisingly often, you'll notice—it's best to simply "tell them what you're going to say."

  Also I suggest avoiding phrases such as "I'm honored to be with you here today. . . ." Because everything in your speech should be relevant, try to go right to the point. For example:

  "Good afternoon. The subject of computer security may seem far removed from the concerns of most of us. But I intend to describe how our supposedly private computerized records are routinely violated, who's doing it, and how you can protect yourself."

If you wish, you might tell a *true* story (not a joke) as a way of hooking your audience.[16] For example:

"My topic this morning is computer security. In a few seconds I'm going to explain how our supposedly private computerized records are routinely violated, who's doing it, and how you can protect yourself. First, however, I'd like to tell you a true story about a student, his father, and a personal computer. . . ."

- *Middle:* In the main body of the speech, the longest part, which takes 75–90% of your time, you "say what you said you were going to say."

  The most important thing to realize is this: Your audience won't remember more than a few points anyway. Thus, you need to decide *what three or four points must be remembered.*[17] Then cover them as succinctly as possible.

  The middle part generally follows the same rules as were explained for the middle part of a term paper. Use examples, quotations, and statistics (don't overdo it on the statistics) to support your assertions and hold your listeners' attention.

  Be particularly attentive to transitions. Listening differs from reading in that the listener has only one chance to get your meaning. He or she cannot go back and reread. Thus, be sure you constantly provide your audience with guidelines and transitional phrases so they can see where you're going. For example:

  "There are four ways the security of computer files can be compromised. The first way is. . . ."

- *End:* The end might take 5–10% of your time. Don't drop the ball here. You need a wrap-up that's strong, succinct, and persuasive. Indeed, many professional speakers consider the conclusion to be as important as the introduction.

  The conclusion should "tell them what you told them." You need some sort of signal phrase that cues the audience you are heading into your windup. For example:

"Let's review the main points we've covered. . . ."

"In conclusion, what CAN you do to protect against unauthorized invasion of all those computerized files with your name on them? I pointed out three main steps. One. . . ."

Give some thought to the last thing you're going to say. It should be strongly upbeat, a call to action, a thought for the day, a quotation, a little story. In short, you need a solid finish of some sort. For example:

"I would like to leave you with one last thought. . . ."

"Finally, let me close by sharing something that happened to me. . . ."

"As Albert Einstein said, 'Imagination is more important than knowledge.'"

Then say "Thank you" and stop talking.

UNDERSTANDING THE AUDIENCE. As you know yourself, your attention can wander when you're a member of an audience. Thus, you have to understand the basics of the attention cycle and tailor your speech accordingly—particularly the middle part. As Tony Alessandra and Phil Hunsaker, authors of *Communicating at Work*, point out:

Studies have shown that material at the beginning and end of a presentation will be remembered more than the material in the middle. Our attention span lasts only for a short time and then it tapers off. When we sense the end of a message, we pull back in time to catch the last material. Fluctuation of the attention cycle is one of the main reasons we put such emphasis on the introduction and conclusion.[18]

So how do you hold people's attention during the middle of your speech? Alessandra and Hunsaker recommend putting in a lot of mini-cycles with beginnings, middles, and ends, changing the pace every 10–15 minutes. You can do this by including appropriate humor, stories, analogies, examples, comparisons, personal testimony, and variation in tone of voice. You can even have activities and exercises that ask for the audience's involvement.

HOW TO REDUCE YOUR NERVOUSNESS: REHEARSAL & PREPARATION. It may be true that the number one fear of most adults—even more than death—is speaking in public.[19] You can't do anything about death, of course, but you can about your fear of public speaking.

Professional speaker Lilly Walters suggests that 75% of your fear can be reduced by rehearsal and preparation. The remaining 25%, she says, can be reduced by breathing and mind control.[20] Stage fright is *normal*. Every professional speaker, actor, musician, and performer gets that feeling of weak

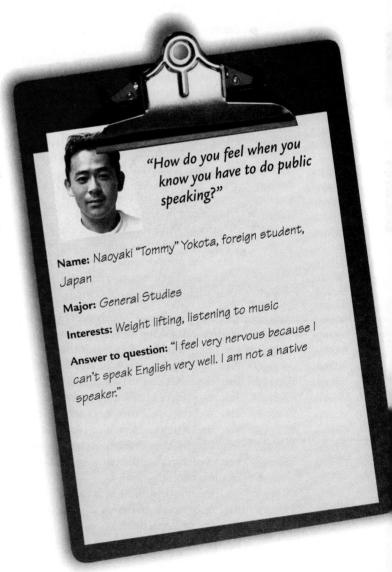

"How do you feel when you know you have to do public speaking?"

Name: Naoyaki "Tommy" Yokota, foreign student, Japan

Major: General Studies

Interests: Weight lifting, listening to music

Answer to question: "I feel very nervous because I can't speak English very well. I am not a native speaker."

knees, sweaty palms, and butterflies in the stomach. The best way to reduce this nervousness is through rehearsal and preparation—in other words, practice practice practice.

Here are some tips for rehearsing the speech:

- **Read silently:** Read the speech over several times silently. Edit the manuscript as you go to smooth out awkward passages.

- **Read aloud:** Read the speech several times aloud. Use a loud voice (unless you'll be using a microphone when you speak). Your voice sounds different to you when you talk loudly; you want to be used to this when you give your address. Time yourself so you won't run too long.

- **Memorize the opening:** Memorize the opening *word for word*. This is essential.

- **Practice on a spot:** Practice your speech while staring at a spot on the wall. This is particularly good advice for the opening. You are most nervous during the first few minutes. Thus, one professional speaker suggests, you should memorize a dynamite opening and practice it while staring at a spot on the wall. As a result, he says, "you develop such fantastic confidence that it carries you through the rest of the speech."[21]

- **Practice in a mirror:** Practice delivering the speech while standing in front of a mirror. Observe your gestures, expressions, and posture. Don't worry too much about gestures: the main thing is to do whatever comes naturally.

- **Practice on audiotape, videotape, or in front of friends:** Any other rehearsal activities can't help but help. Read your speech into an audiotape recorder and listen to the results. Or do the same thing with a videotape recorder, which may be available at the school's media center. Notice voice inflections and mannerisms (such as *you knows, umms, ahs*). Watch for your voice trailing off at the end of sentences or phrases.

Try out your address in front of friends or family members. It's possible they will be heavy on the positive ("I think your speech is quite good").

However, you should solicit and listen to any criticism ("Do you know you rock from side to side a lot?").

HOW TO REDUCE YOUR NERVOUSNESS: BREATHING & MIND CONTROL.

When we're nervous, we forget to breathe normally, which makes us more nervous. To control your breathing, Lilly Walters suggests the following 5-second exercise:

Think, "Deep breath and hold, 1, 2, 3, 4, 5." (Add a "Mississippi" onto the end of each number—it's pretty tough to figure out how long a second is when your adrenaline is racing.) Tell yourself, "Slow release, and inhale 1, 2, etc." [22]

Mind control consists of self-talk. Your inner Voice Of Judgment may be saying a lot of negative things. ("They're going to *hate* me." "I'm going to look like a *fool*." "I'll look *fat*.") You can take comfort, then, from what Walters says:

Have you ever gone to a presentation and really wanted the presenter to be terrible? Most of the time you'd much rather have a good time than a bad time. The same is true for your audience. Most listeners are sitting there, ready and willing to make allowances for your mistakes. In fact, a few mistakes make you human and just that much more lovable. [23]

Instead of letting negative thoughts take over, try positive affirmations that are important to you: "I know what I know." "I'm glad I'm here." "I can do it!" Using self-talk, let your thoughts direct you to success!

DELIVERING THE ORAL PRESENTATION. Come the day of the big speech there are a few things to concentrate on:

■ *Dress appropriately:* Dress to look your best—or at least appropriate to the occasion. Even if you're just doing a report in a classroom, audiences like it when you look a little special (though not out of place).

■ *Deal with your nervous energy:* Almost every speaker—even professionals—experiences stage fright. This is actually your body preparing for a big event; in fact, you need the edge in order to be your best. The trick is to manage your nervous energy—foot tapping, fiddling with eyeglasses, swaying back and forth—which can be annoying to an audience.

Ed Wohlmuth suggests buying a kid's rubber ball that's large enough to cover most of your palm. During your waking hours before the speech, squeeze it frequently in each hand. From then on, when you feel nervous energy start to mount, think of the rubber ball.[24]

Whatever you do, don't use tranquilizers or alcohol. Eat in moderation before your talk. Drink some water (but not gallons) before the speech to ease the dryness in your mouth.

■ *Try out the speaker's position:* Get to the classroom or hall early, or go a day or two before. Step behind the podium or wherever the speaker's position is. If the room is empty, speak your introduction aloud, aiming it at the last seat in the room. You might even deliver the entire speech.

If you plan on using audiovisual aids, flip charts, or a microphone, it's especially recommended you do a dry run. (Do this with the help of others managing the equipment.)

■ *Focus on the audience:* When your speech is under way, focus on the audience. Maintain eye contact, shifting your attention among a few friendly faces in the room. When you look at people, the audience becomes less intimidating.

■ *Pace yourself and watch your time:* Try to stick to the timetable you set during your rehearsals. You can lay a watch face up on the podium. Or you can position it on the inside of your wrist, where it's easier to glance at it without calling attention to the act.

Pace yourself. Your instinct may be to rush through the speech and get it over with. However, your listeners will appreciate a pause from time to time.

Remember that it's better to end early than to run long. Because the conclusion is so important, you don't want to have to be rushed at the end because you're squeezed for time.

It may be that you won't have to do much in the way of stand-up oral presentations. But it's important to learn to speak in public anyway. By learning to speak up in class, for example, you'll become comfortable with getting answers to questions that come to mind during lectures. Through your involvement and interaction you'll increase your learning ability—and probably your grades.

GROUP ACTIVITY #9.4

THE 1-MINUTE ORAL PRESENTATION

Perhaps the prospect of giving a half-hour oral presentation to a large group fills you with terror. A way to begin to overcome your fears is to start by doing something very short before a small group. The instructor may ask you to take some time to prepare this 1-minute oral presentation ahead of time, speaking on whatever topic you choose. Or you may be asked to speak without preparation—doing what is called "extemporaneous" speaking.

The class will be divided into groups of seven or eight people each. The groups will assemble in corners of the room. Give your 1-minute speech to this group. When it's your turn to listen to others, take notes listing positive and negative points about each person's speech. After everyone has finished speaking, take turns giving a brief analysis of the presentation. *Important:* Begin your analysis by giving *positive feedback,* then give *negative feedback,* then conclude with *more positive feedback.* This is the best form in which to give criticism.

Onward: Applying This Chapter to Your Life

PREVIEW Education is more than memorizing subjects.

earning to conceive, research, and write papers and speeches is learning how to think. American education has been criticized because students are required to memorize subjects rather than to understand and analyze them. However, as Wisconsin student James Robinson points out, future survival lies in knowing how to solve problems. "If we do not know how to analyze a problem," he says, "how are we ever going to compete in the real world? The problems we are going to face are not all going to be written down in a textbook with the answers in the back. . . . As students, we must realize that we need to come up with our own solutions."[25]

Robinson is right. And the final payoff is this: It has been found that students who learn how to think do better not only in school but in life.[26]

Writing and speaking are among the most useful skills you will ever learn. What two specific things did you find in this chapter that you can use during your career? Write them down here:

_____

_____

_____

_____

_____

_____

_____

_____

_____

_____

_____

_____

_____

1. Write about something that is very important to you, such as a particular person or event that profoundly affected you. Describe how writing helps you understand it.

2. Write down any remaining questions you have about the library not answered in this chapter. How would you go about finding answers to them?

3. One subject that might have been discussed in more detail in this chapter was the proper form for footnotes and bibliographies. Is this an area in which you need further help? Who can give you the assistance you need?

4. In what ways can you employ the techniques of creative thinking besides thinking up subjects for term papers?

5. What worries do you have about public speaking? Besides the techniques described in this chapter, what other means are available to help you do better at giving stand-up speeches? For instance, the counseling service may offer assistance, or you could join the group known as Toast Masters, which helps amateur speakers achieve proficiency.

money

how to get it, how to use it

you can master your finances, not let them master you

■ MAKING THIS CHAPTER WORK FOR YOU

What bothers you about your current financial circumstances? Not enough money? Inability to handle money? Describe your feelings about money.

_____
_____
_____
_____
_____
_____
_____
_____
_____
_____
_____

■ SKIMMING FOR PAYOFFS

Skim the chapter and find two pieces of advice that make you think "That's a good idea! I should try that!" Describe them here.

_____
_____
_____
_____
_____
_____
_____
_____

Several years ago I picked up a book called "Getting By on $100,000 a Year."

hat?" I said to myself. "One hundred thousand dollars a year *just to GET BY?*"

Granted, the book was published in 1980, and there's been some inflation since then.[1] Even so, to put this figure in perspective, today less than 2% of the millions of workers in America earn more than $100,000 a year. (The average American *family*—which nowadays usually includes more than one income earner—takes in an annual income of just $40,000.)[2]

It turns out, however, that many people who are earning $100,000 a year feel they are barely making ends meet. Clearly, feeling "well off" or "rich" is partly a matter of perception. Indeed, a lot about money has to do with *psychology*—needs, wants, perceptions, feelings, fears, envy, self-worth. For some people, $100,000 is enough to make them feel rich. For others, it does not even come close—because "wealth" for them represents a psychological state of mind that is far different.

Money & Emotions

PREVIEW Because our emotions can cause us to do strange things in relation to money, it's important to keep two pieces of advice in mind. Moral #1 is that you should *pay attention* to your money. Moral #2 is that, in perceptions about money, *feelings aren't facts.*

Feelings about money are important because they can twist people's lives and make them do things that often they shouldn't be doing. (And I don't mean just robbing banks.) A high-school student reports that most of his friends work after school. However, it's not because they need the money, he says, just "to get what we want." To be in style, he says, "you have to have a job."[3] A woman attending a self-help group for people deep in debt says, "I *lusted* after money. I was arrogant and overbearing when I had it. I was totally miserable when I didn't. I always needed more. . . . I was constantly in debt."[4]

Even the well-off seem to have trouble with money. Journalist Gail Sheehy, suddenly wealthy as the author of her best-selling book *Passages*, spoke of "that classic American trap." Sudden wealth should mean that you can live "pretty much as you have, only a little better and with a lot more security behind you— with money there to do something amazing every once in a while when it really counts." Instead, she says, "you suddenly leap up to meet that [new] income level and always bubble up over it. . . ."[5]

Isn't something wrong here? I think so. These observations seem to reflect irrational perceptions about money. Why should middle-class high-school kids work 30 hours a week just to acquire music CDs and car insurance when they don't have to? Especially when it causes them to fall asleep in class, jeopardizing the very education that will provide them with a financially comfortable future. Why should 20 million Americans be only one paycheck ahead of disaster, their debts nearly destroying them? Why

should financial success not benefit but actually distort people's lives, producing disappointment and emotional turmoil?

There seem to be at least two morals that can be drawn here.

- You need to pay attention to your money.

- When it comes to money, feelings aren't facts.

MORAL #1: PAY ATTENTION TO YOUR MONEY.

As an economist and former banker put it, you have to *pay attention*. "Our inattentiveness toward money is enough of a misperception of reality that it can lead us into trouble," he says. In this way it is dangerous in the same sense that "any misperception of reality can lead to trouble."[6]

Thus, he says, the most important rule is that "you have to keep track of your money. You have to know approximately how much you have, how much you are spending, how much is coming in, what the general direction of your dollar flow is."[7] This chapter shows you how to do this.

MORAL #2: FEELINGS AREN'T FACTS.

All of us are susceptible to various emotions about money, but *feelings about money are not the same as facts about money.*

For example, it's easy to begin to worry about or get depressed over bills and debts. But as former debtor Jerrold Mundis points out, such emotions come "because you're projecting into the future. You're responding to what you think is going to happen next week, next month, next year." In actuality, you don't know what's going to happen; nobody does. "So, in truth, all you're reacting to is your own imagination. There is nothing real in that."[8]

Right at this moment, Mundis points out, you probably have a roof over your head, clothes to wear, and food to eat. "So right now, today, you are perfectly all right—you have everything you need, you don't lack for anything essential." Debt is simply a *fact*, a temporary situation. How you *feel* about debt is another matter altogether—and something you can begin to exert control over. But feelings themselves are not facts.

Can You Afford Higher Education?

PREVIEW Although the cost of higher education is high, a great many students feel the sacrifices are worth it. The increased income of college graduates is generally sufficient to repay student loans.

igher education isn't cheap. Indeed, for many people, college is the second major expense of their lives, after buying a house. When students tell me they are thinking of dropping out because of the expense of college, I can certainly sympathize. Meeting the costs of college wasn't easy for me either. (I had to work my way through.) However, I try to point out a couple of facts.

- Financial struggles are commonplace.

- College graduates make more money.

FINANCIAL STRUGGLES ARE COMMONPLACE.

Many students are doing whatever it takes financially to get a college education. More first-year students than ever before are now basing their choice of college not on educational reasons but on financial reasons. For example, they may choose an institution because it charges low tuition, offers financial aid, or enables them to live at home.[9] Many students are also having to borrow in order to meet their college expenses. Half the students graduating from college have debts, such as student loans, that have to be repaid.[10] Indeed, the number of students in debt has doubled over the past 10 years.[11]

In addition, more and more students are taking longer than four years to graduate from college. In part this is because many need to work and go to school part-time. At the University of Texas in Austin, for instance, less than half of the first-year students graduate in four years. At San Francisco State University in California, less than a quarter of students graduate within *five* years.[12]

These facts are evidence that a lot of students are willing to go to great lengths to get a college education. Are the sacrifices worth it?

GRADUATES MAKE MORE MONEY.

Most college graduates make incomes sufficient to repay their investment in college. As a group, college graduates have always done better than high-school graduates, but in recent years they have widened the gap significantly. (See ■ *Panel 10.1.*) During the 1980s, college grads earned about 30% more than high-school graduates. Now they earn *60% more.*[13]

Thus, even if you leave school owing $10,000—the debt of the average student finishing today—you'll probably be able to handle it. Indeed, a year after graduation, college graduates will be making an average (median) annual income of $18,600.[14,15]

Add to this the fact that college graduates usually have happier, more fulfilled lives than noncollege graduates, and the costs seem worth it.

GROUP ACTIVITY #10.1

WHAT ARE COMMON CONCERNS ABOUT MONEY?

On a sheet of paper, write down some things that come to mind about money—your five principal thoughts or worries. Don't put your name on the paper, but fold it up for collection by the instructor. The instructor will read aloud some of the responses to the class for discussion purposes. How common are some of these concerns? What can you do about them? Does it make you feel better knowing that others have the same worries you have?

Money: the increasing advantage for college grads. Since 1979, real wages for low-skilled workers have greatly declined. For those with more education and skills, they have vastly increased. (Figures are for full-time year-round workers, ages 25–64, corrected for inflation.)

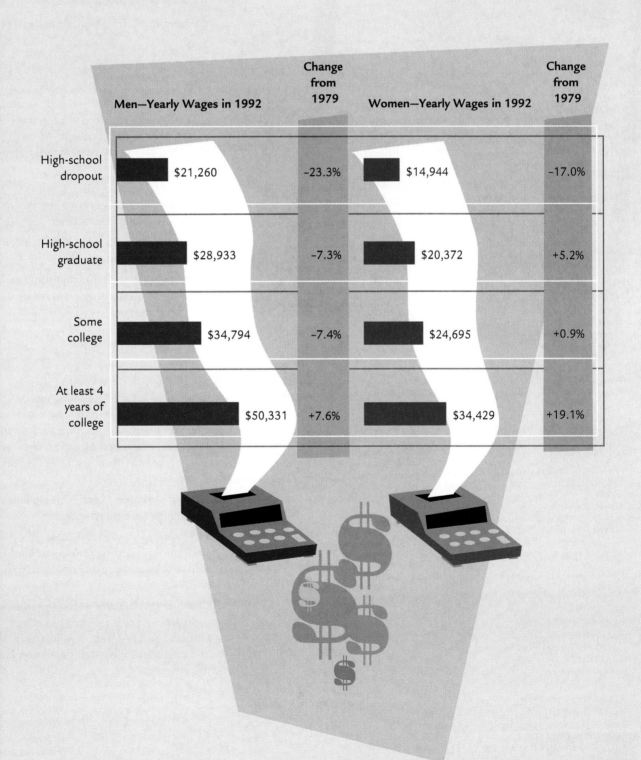

	Men—Yearly Wages in 1992	Change from 1979	Women—Yearly Wages in 1992	Change from 1979
High-school dropout	$21,260	–23.3%	$14,944	–17.0%
High-school graduate	$28,933	–7.3%	$20,372	+5.2%
Some college	$34,794	–7.4%	$24,695	+0.9%
At least 4 years of college	$50,331	+7.6%	$34,429	+19.1%

Managing Costs: Getting & Spending

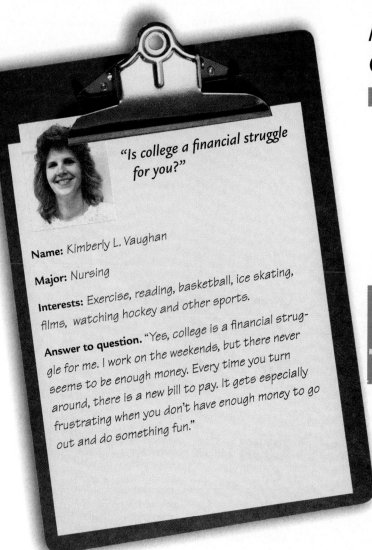

"Is college a financial struggle for you?"

Name: Kimberly L. Vaughan

Major: Nursing

Interests: Exercise, reading, basketball, ice skating, films, watching hockey and other sports.

Answer to question. "Yes, college is a financial struggle for me. I work on the weekends, but there never seems to be enough money. Every time you turn around, there is a new bill to pay. It gets especially frustrating when you don't have enough money to go out and do something fun."

PREVIEW Students get their money from parents, jobs, grants and loans, and other sources. They spend it not only on college and living expenses but also in some unpredictable ways. Handling your money is a matter of constantly balancing your income and your expenses.

I f you can do addition and subtraction, that's all that's required to keep track of your money while in college. After all, there are only three parts to basic money management:

- **Getting**—determining your *income,* or **where the money comes from**
- **Spending**—determining your <u>outgo,</u> or **what your expenditures are**
- **Balancing**—determining that you have the income *when you need it* to balance the spending

Let's take a look at these.

THE GETTING: YOUR INCOME. Most people would not consider gambling and robbery efficient sources of income. (Neither are predictable nor look good on a career resume.) However, there are a variety of other sources. Most students have a mix, as follows:[16]

- **Parents' assistance:** Nearly three-quarters of students have this resource.
- **Employment:** More than half of all students work during summers. Nearly a third work part-time during the school year.
- **Grants or scholarships:** A good portion of college costs are supported by college, federal, or state grants or scholarships, and nearly half of students have access to this resource.

- **Loans:** Many college costs are supported from the Guaranteed (Stafford) Student Loan.

- **Other sources:** Savings not derived from summer or part-time work earnings and other sources make up the rest of the income sources. More than a quarter of all students draw on non-work-related savings as a resource.

Do you have more control over your sources of income than your expenses? That's up to you to decide. Some students get a regular allowance from their parents. Others, such as many adult returning students, may have to earn or borrow every cent they get—more evidence of how the world is unfair. On the other hand, those who must go out and scrape up their income themselves have one advantage. They often develop a better sense of the value of money than those who simply have it given to them.

THE SPENDING: YOUR OUTGO. A corollary to Moral #2 ("Feelings are not facts") is: *It's important to distinguish between your needs and your wants.* Sure, you might want to go out and party, to dress right, to treat your friends, but do you need to? You might like to move off campus or away from home and have your own apartment, but do you have to? With the constant drumming of advertising on us from television and other mass media (18,000 messages a day, supposedly), we are always being made to *want* all kinds of things. But, when you think about it, we *need* very little. This can be a healthy point of view to take when you consider your expenses.

Expenses are of the following types:

- **One-time educational expenses:** These are one-shot expenses for items that you need to buy only once and that might serve you for most of your college years. Examples are bicycle (for getting to or around campus), computer or type-writer, furniture and linens, and dictionary and other reference books. Some of these you (or your family) may already have at home.

> *"In spending it's important to distinguish between your needs and your wants."*

- **Recurring educational expenses:** These are educational expenses that are repeated every quarter or semester. Examples are tuition, registration fees, books and educational supplies, and laboratory fees. Many of these figures you can get from your college catalog.

- **Room, board, and clothing expenses:** These are the expenses that it takes just to live: housing, utilities, food. Don't forget to add insurance, such as fire and theft insurance of your possessions. You also need to determine your clothing expenses—even if you wear only T-shirts and jeans half the time.

  Note: Don't underestimate the cost of food. Besides the college-cafeteria ticket, if that's your arrangement, you'll need to allow for meals out and snacks—possibly a big item.

- **Transportation:** If you have a car, this can be a big expense, because you'll need to allow for car insurance, maintenance, and repairs, as well as gas and oil. Parking fees can also be a big item. Many students don't have cars, of course, but need to allow for bus or other commuting fees.

- *Personal and health expenses:* These include expenses for your laundry, toothpaste and other personal-care products, medicines, and health insurance or health-center fees.

- *Telephone expense:* This expense can get tricky, depending on your living arrangements, but it should be budgeted for.

- *Entertainment:* If you didn't budget under "room and board" for expenses for snacks and eating out, put them here. Dating, going to musical or athletic events, movies or theater, skiing, whatever seems to be fun—add these expenses here. Also add as many other entertainment expenses as you can think of. These include CDs and tapes, athletic gear, musical instruments, travel and hotels during spring break, and so on.

- *Emergencies and other expenses:* Bad stuff happens, and you need to allow for it. I'm talking about car breakdowns, emergency trips home, roommates skipping out and sticking you with their telephone bills, and so on. You may also want to plan for some good stuff—a summer trip, for example.

THE BALANCING ACT. What if you get most of your money at the beginning of the fall term, but your expenses will go on for the next nine months? One of my students, on picking up his financial-aid money at the start of the school year, thought the check looked so big that he went and bought an expensive CD player. Later he found himself short when the telephone bill came in.

One problem that people who don't have a regular allowance or paycheck have to face is *uneven cash flow.* That is, many bills (rent, phone, credit cards) tend to come due at regular intervals. However, the income does not flow in on the same timely basis. Thus, some short-range saving is necessary. Of course, saving money may not be as much fun as spending it. However, short-range saving sure beats the desperate feeling of not having the funds there when the rent is due. Managing your money, in short, is a constant balancing act between income and outgo.

For many of us, money has a way of just dribbling through our fingers, and we're not really sure where it goes. That's why credit counselors, who help people in debt, have clients keep detailed records of all expenses, even for candy bars and newspapers. Even if you don't have money troubles, before you can *plan* how to manage your money, you need to *observe* your present money patterns. To do this, I suggest doing the Personal Exploration #10.1 for a week, longer if you can. From this information, you can draw up some spending categories and projections, as I will show.

THE MONEY DIAGNOSTIC REPORT: WHERE DOES IT COME FROM, WHERE DOES IT GO?

Tear out or photocopy the following page and carry it around with you in an accessible place for a week.

Every time you receive a check or cash (*Money in*), write down its source and the amount. (Example: "Loan from Susie, $10.") Every time you

spend money—whether cash, check, or credit card (*Money out*)—write down the expenditure and the amount. (Example: "Movie, food: $12.")

■ **MONEY IN:** Examples of sources of funds: job, parents, grant, savings, loan, friend, tax refund.

MONEY IN FROM	SUNDAY	MONDAY	TUESDAY	WEDNESDAY	THURSDAY	FRIDAY	SATURDAY

Total received for week: _____

■ **MONEY OUT:** Examples of expenditures: books, meals, bus fare, snacks, phone, rent, entertainment, clothes, laundry.

MONEY OUT FOR	SUNDAY	MONDAY	TUESDAY	WEDNESDAY	THURSDAY	FRIDAY	SATURDAY

Total spent for week: _____

Bring your completed Money Diagnostic Report to class. In a small group or with the class at large, share any impressions you've gained during the week. Are there any surprises? In what unexpected areas do you find yourself spending too much money?

Money Plans & Expense Record

PREVIEW A money plan, or budget, is of two types. The *yearly money plan* helps you look at the big picture of your income and outgo. The *monthly money plan* helps project ordinary monthly expenses. The money *expense record* tells you what your expenses actually were.

o effectively balance your getting and spending, you need to know where you're going. This requires formulating a *money plan,* the name I prefer rather than *budget,* although they are the same. **A money plan, or budget, is simply a plan or schedule of how to balance your income and expenses. It helps you see where your money is going to come from and where it is going to go.**

Most students find it useful to have two kinds of money plans:

- *Yearly:* A yearly money plan helps you visualize the big picture for the school year.

- *Monthly:* A monthly money plan, which includes "Money in" and "Money out" columns, helps you keep track of your ongoing financial situation.

Let's take a look at these.

THE YEARLY MONEY PLAN. The yearly money plan is your big-picture estimate of your income and expenses for the academic year (for example, September to June). You may be able to obtain much of your financial information from the college catalog. Examples of sources of "Money in" are loans or grants. Examples of kinds of "Money out" are tuition and dormitory room and board.

Other information you may have to estimate. If you have already established a record of expenses, as in Personal Exploration #10.1, you can use that. You can also collect a month or two of old bills and receipts, cancelled checks, and credit card statements. Then you can estimate what these expenses would amount to over the course of the school year. If you have not already made out a Yearly Money Plan, I strongly suggest you spend some time on Personal Exploration #10.2.

THE MONTHLY MONEY PLAN. The monthly money plan is a smaller version of the yearly one. It is particularly useful if you don't live in an on-campus dormitory or residence hall (thus appropriate for adult returning students). Then you are more apt to have several monthly bills, such as rent, phone, water, electricity, gas, and garbage. Even students living on campus, however, may have monthly credit-card and telephone bills for which they need to plan.

Developing a monthly money plan requires three steps:

- *Subtract large one-time expenses from yearly income:* First you need to take your *yearly* income and subtract all your *large one-time* expenses: college tuition, registration fees, housing fees, meal ticket, textbooks and supplies (total for all terms), and insurance premiums. Some students also subtract their transportation from home to campus and back at the beginning and end of the school terms.

  Example: Using round figures, suppose you have $18,000 coming in from all sources. This includes loans, grants, part-time and summer work, and parents' help. Suppose your tuition and registration fees are $10,000. Add your on-campus housing fee ($3000), meal ticket ($1500), insurance ($300), and textbooks and supplies ($300 for two semesters). Add your round-trip plane ticket from home ($400). The total comes to $15,500. You then subtract $15,500 from $18,000, which leaves $2500.

- *Divide the remaining sum by the number of months to determine how much you have to spend on everything else:* After subtracting one-time large expenses from your yearly income, you can see how much you have left for other requirements.

THE YEARLY MONEY PLAN: HOW MUCH MONEY COMES IN & GOES OUT DURING A SCHOOL YEAR?

■ INCOME (FOR 10 MONTHS)

Examples of money sources: grants/scholarships, loans, salary, parents, refunds, sale of unneeded belongings, other.

INCOME	SEP	OCT	NOV	DEC	JAN	FEB	MAR	APR	MAY	JUN

Total income: _____

■ OUTGO (FOR 10 MONTHS)

Examples of expenses: rent/mortgage, food, tuition, college fees, books/supplies, transportation (including parking), clothes, phone, insurance, medical, child care, personal items, entertainment, other.

OUTGO	SEP	OCT	NOV	DEC	JAN	FEB	MAR	APR	MAY	JUN

Total outgo: _____

Example: Suppose you figure you had $2500 left over after subtracting one-time expenses from yearly income. You would divide that by the number of months in the academic year—that is, nine months (September and June are partial school months). This would give you about $278 a month to spend. This may seem like a lot if you just need to cover snacks and an occasional movie or meal out. However, if you have to support a car or buy a lot of clothes and heavy entertainment, it may not be enough.

■ **Determine other categories of expenses and decide how much to spend each month:** Only you can determine the expenses remaining after your one-time "big ticket" expenses are taken out. The cost of your monthly transportation expenses will differ depending on whether you drive a car or ride a bicycle to class. Expenses for clothing, phone calls, CDs,

video rentals, and meals off campus can vary tremendously, depending mainly on your personal restraint.

One category many students are glad they've created: savings. This category will help you keep a fund for emergencies or special expenses. It may also help you restrain your spending.

Example: Your monthly categories for spending $278 might be as follows, ranging from large to small expenses. *Car* (gas and oil, repairs, parking—insurance is included above): $80. *Entertainment* (including dates): $45. *Personal* (personal-care products): $33. *Meals out:* $30. *Clothes:* $30. *Snacks:* $25. *Phone:* $25. *Savings:* $10.

To set up your Monthly Money Plan, spend a few minutes with the "A. To Plan" portion of Personal Exploration #10.3.

PERSONAL EXPLORATION #10.3

YOUR MONTHLY MONEY PLAN—& YOUR RECORD OF ACTUAL INCOME & OUTGO

Tear out or photocopy the form on the opposite page. Use this form (1) to plan and (2) to record your income and outgo for the next month.

■ The left side of the form is for *planning and recording Income*—money in.

■ The right side of the form is for *planning and recording Outgo*—money out.

■ A. TO PLAN

On the left side of the form ("Income") indicate your predicted sources and amounts of money you expect to receive. *Examples:* "Family," "Job," "Loan," "Grant," "Scholarship," "Tax refund," "Aunt Gladys." Put the amounts in the column headed *Planned.*

On the right side of the form ("Outgo"), first indicate your categories of expenses, from left to right. *Examples:* "Rent," "Phone," "Utilities," "Credit card," "Car payments," "Food," "Transportation," "Clothing," "Entertainment," "Savings," "Miscellaneous." For each category, put in the *predicted* expenses. Put these amounts in the columns headed *Planned.*

■ B. TO RECORD

On the left side ("Income"), record the date/source and amount of money coming in. Example: "9/30 job— $200." Record these data in the *Actual* column.

On the right side ("Outgo"), record the date/expenses, amounts, and method of payment ($$ for cash,

CK for check, CC for credit card) of your expenditures within each category. *Example:* Within the category of "Entertainment," you could record "10/15 video rental—$6.00 CK"; "10/18 dinner Amelio's—$12.30 CC"; "10/18 crackers—$1.10 $$."

■ AT MONTH'S END

Total up your *predicted* Income and Outgo and compare it with the *actual* Income and Outgo. Use the information to adjust your predicted Money Plan for the next month.

MONTHLY MONEY PLAN & RECORD

INCOME: MONEY IN

Date/Source	Planned Amount	Actual Amount

OUTGO: MONEY OUT

Category Date/Expense/Amount	Category Date/Expense/Amount	Category Date/Expense/Amount	Category Date/Expense/Amount	Category Date/Expense/Amount

MONTHLY MONEY PLAN & RECORD

INCOME: MONEY IN

Date/Source	Planned Amount	Actual Amount

OUTGO: MONEY OUT

Category Date/Expense/Amount	Category Date/Expense/Amount	Category Date/Expense/Amount	Category Date/Expense/Amount	Category Date/Expense/Amount

THE EXPENSE RECORD. How do you know if you're overspending in some expense categories? In accordance with Moral #1 ("Pay attention to your money"), you keep an expense record. The expense record has two parts, daily and monthly:

- **The daily expense record:** This can be very simple and can be carried around as a shirt-pocket spiral-bound notebook or even as a 3 × 5 card in your wallet or purse. The point is to make this easy so you won't mind doing it.

    You need write down only three things: *date, item, cost.* (If you wish, you can also indicate if you paid with cash, check, or credit card—$$, CK, CC.) Examples are:

3/15	*Snack*	*1.50*
3/15	*Gas*	*8.33*
3/16	*Toothpaste*	*2.00*
3/16	*Movie & popcorn*	*6.50*

- **The monthly expense record:** At the end of the month, you can sort the daily expenses into the different categories of your Monthly Money Plan under the "Actual" column. The categories might be: *Housing & utilities, Meals & snacks, Transportation, Entertainment, Personal supplies, Books & supplies, Savings,* and *Other.* When you add up the different columns, you can then see if you are staying within your budget.

    To record your expenses in the coming month, follow the "B. To Record" portion of Personal Exploration #10.3.

    Does all this record keeping seem like a lot of boring work? Actually, it's just a series of easy mechanical tasks. The whole reason for doing them is to give you *peace of mind.* After all, disorganization around money and consequent financial problems can affect your emotional well-being in other ways, making it difficult to study. Using these tools can help you avoid those difficulties.

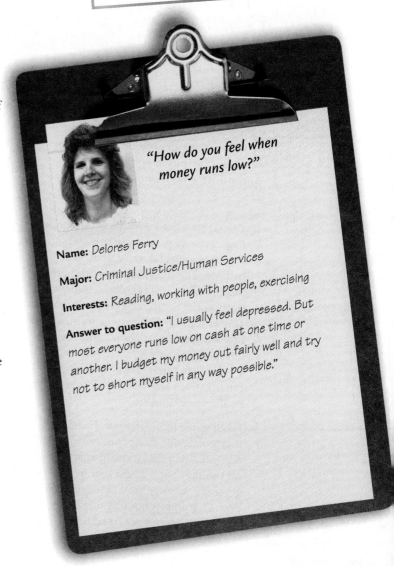

GROUP ACTIVITY #10.2

HOW CAN WE REDUCE EXPENSES?

Bring completed Personal Explorations #10.2 and #10.3 to class. With others in a small group, generate a list of largest monthly expenses. Also list expenses that you might be able to reduce. Share the lists and money-saving strategies with the rest of the class. Which areas are the easiest to reduce spending in and why? Which areas most difficult? What have you learned about your needs and your wants? Do you control your emotions or do they control you regarding spending? What can you do to exercise more control over your financial affairs?

"How do you feel when money runs low?"

Name: Delores Ferry

Major: Criminal Justice/Human Services

Interests: Reading, working with people, exercising

Answer to question: "I usually feel depressed. But most everyone runs low on cash at one time or another. I budget my money out fairly well and try not to short myself in any way possible."

A Crash Course in
Money Handling

PREVIEW Controlling spending starts with managing big-ticket purchases, such as housing and transportation, which are often tradeoffs. You can also find ways to get inexpensive furniture and computers. Tactics exist for controlling telephone charges and food and clothing purchases. Students need to investigate good banking and ATM sources. They need to know how to manage charge cards and credit cards. They also need to make arrangements to be covered by insurance—health, tenant's, and automobile.

There's more to money management in college than the occasional artful phone call home requesting replenishment of funds. For some first-year students, however, it's an opportunity to learn what sooner or later we all have to learn—the skills of money handling.

CONTROLLING YOUR SPENDING. It's almost impossible to grow up in this society and not want to spend more than one's income. The television and print ads just never let us forget life's endless possibilities for parting with our money. Maybe you can't increase your income, but you can almost always find ways to cut spending.

Here are some money-saving tips, ranging from big-ticket items to everyday small expenditures:

■ *Housing and transportation:* Housing and transportation often represent a trade-off. You might find a cheap apartment off campus, but it might require a car to get there, an expensive mode of transport. On-campus housing might cost more, but you can get around on foot or bicycle.

If you desperately want a car, maybe you can swing it by living at home or by sharing living space with roommates. For short periods of time, you might even live rent-free by house-sitting someone's place, taking care of plants and pets. A good place to look for these connections is the campus housing office.

When comparing prospective rents, be sure to determine if the rent does or doesn't include utilities, such as electricity, water, and garbage collection. Try to take care of your rental unit, by fixing things yourself when possible and making sure to keep up the yard. This will help you get back any security deposits when you move out. It will also help you get a favorable reference from the landlord that will assist you in lining up the next rental.

Cars can be expensive. I remember turning a deaf ear to my father's warning that the purchase price of a car was only the beginning. It wasn't until a year later that I knew how expensive my powerful Chevy was in the way of gas, oil, tires, repairs, insurance, and parking. It was then I realized I could have commuted to campus by bus and even taken dates out in a taxi for a whole lot less. On a daily basis, a bus or a bicycle may turn out to be a real bargain.

Note: If you own a car, join a motor club such as the American Automobile Association. Then if you have a breakdown or a dead battery, someone will give your car a tow or jump-start without your handing over wads of cash. This is especially important if you're going to be making long trips.

■ *Computers, furniture, refrigerators:* Things that cost the most are also those on which you can cut costs. Remember you won't be in college forever. Thus, you don't need to go first class on such big-ticket items as computers and furniture. Do you need a television set, CD player, radio, heater, or fan? Check with your housemates or roommates, who may have these. Do you need a bed, a desk lamp, a dresser? All of these may be bought used.

You don't need *both* a typewriter and a computer, but you're well advised to have one or the other. (You might be able to borrow someone else's machine. But what if he or she needs it when you're up against a tight deadline to get a paper done?) Computers may be bought used, especially if all you need them for is typewriter-like purposes, such as writing papers.

Some students like to have a refrigerator in their rooms, either the 2.8 cubic-foot size or the smaller 1.6 cubic-foot size. These may be rented from local organizations (for perhaps $50–$75) or bought outright for $100–$150 from local discount appliance stores.[17] When these costs are shared with housemates, they become manageable.

■ **The telephone:** Probably there's not much hazard in making a lot of local calls— unless you're tying up your family or housemates' phone, too. However, homesickness, cross-country love affairs, and talks with friends at other schools can produce massive long-distance charges.

If you're the one originating the calls, you may find a telephone timer will help you hold calls to 10–15 minutes instead of 2 hours. Also, don't feel you have to answer every incoming call, especially if you're studying. Tell others in your living unit to take a message, then call back later.

■ **Food and clothing:** Food can be a great hidden magnet for cash. Consider what the minimum wage is in this country ($4.25 an hour at the moment). Then consider how *little* that will buy in the way of soft drinks, potato chips, and other packaged snacks. Even meals at fast-food places can rapidly drain your money. Meals at fancier restaurants can be a major hit on your wallet.

Clearly, learning how to cook will save you money, even if it's just spaghetti. So will learning how to shop. Shop from a list, which keeps you disciplined. Don't shop when you're hungry; it tends to make you reach for convenience foods and snacks. Shop for fresh fruits, vegetables, grains, and other foods that are not processed; they are less expensive. Use clip-out coupons from newspapers if they will really save you money. (Don't use them to buy expensive processed foods you would not otherwise buy.)

Some people are hyper-conscious about the way they dress, which is fine, so long as they aren't hooked into following every fashion. There are ways to buy clothes cheaply: at the end of the season, at other sale times, or at used-clothing stores. If you build your wardrobe around one or two colors, you can do a lot of mixing and matching.

You might consider entering into a contest with housemates to find ways of saving money: turning down the thermostat, turning off unnecessary lights, keeping doors and windows closed in winter, buying toilet paper and paper towels in large lots at discount prices

If you want to get into money saving in a big way, take a look at *Skinflint News*, a monthly journal of frugality and practical advice. (A free copy is available from P.O. Box 818, Palm Harbor, FL 34682; 813-785-7759. Subscriptions are $12 a year.) The college library also undoubtedly carries *Consumer Reports* magazine, a valuable, unbiased guide for all kinds of purchases.

BANKS & ATMS. One student who, with friends, wrote a guide to college survival, suggests keeping two things in mind when choosing a bank.[18] First, find a bank that has automated teller machines (ATMs) that are handy for you. Second, consider all possible hidden costs of the bank in question.

You can always stay with your hometown bank (or parents' bank). However, if you're going to college some distance away, this may be inconvenient, especially if you want an ATM card. Moreover, local merchants may prefer a check drawn on a local bank.

There are many kinds of checking and savings accounts. On standard checking accounts, some banks charge you a monthly fee, some a fee for every check you write, some both. Some checking accounts pay interest if you maintain a high balance, but often the fees will eat up the interest. If you don't write a lot of checks, you might do better with a savings account, which pays interest. Finally, some banks offer a basic banking account, geared to low-income or retired customers. This allows you to write six or so checks per month without additional charge.

ATMs are popular with those who want fast spending money. Indeed, customers who are 18–24 years old conduct a higher share of their transactions at ATMs than any other age group. Most of the youngest ATM users are college students.[19] Clearly, there are some advantages to having an ATM card. For example, with shared banking networks, family members can make a deposit in one state and you can make a withdrawal in another. In addition, you can do transactions during evenings and weekends, when most banks are closed.

CHARGE CARDS, CREDIT CARDS, & DEBIT CARDS. Studies have shown banks and credit-card companies that students are as responsible with credit as most adults. Consequently, campuses have been deluged with ads and applications, trying to entice thousands of students into The Way of Plastic. Indeed, credit-card companies often waive credit histories and income requirements.[20] As a result, 82% of college students have at least one credit card.[21]

***Charge cards* are those that require that the bill be paid off every month.** Examples are charge cards given out by American Express and many oil companies.

***Credit cards* are those that allow the charges to be paid off in installments plus interest, provided you make a minimum payment every month.** Examples are those given out by MasterCard, Visa, and Discover.

A third kind of card is the debit card, which can be used at certain stores such as some grocery chains. **The *debit card* enables you to pay for purchases by withdrawing funds electronically directly from your savings or checking account.** That is, the debit card acts in place of a paper check.

The advantage of all three types of cards is convenience: you don't have to carry cash. Such cards also allow you to rent cars, buy plane tickets, and book hotel rooms, transactions difficult to do with cash or check. Credit cards can also give you a loan when you need it.

There are, however, some disadvantages:

- ***It's easy to forget you're spending money:*** "We'll just put it on plastic," I hear students say. Somehow it's easy to spend $80 on that great coat in the store window when you only have to sign a charge slip. It's a lot more difficult when you have to hand over four Andrew Jacksons. With plastic, you get what you want now without the pain of feeling as if you're paying for it.

- ***Debts can pile up:*** With debit cards, the money is gone from your checking account as soon as you use it. With American Express and other charge cards, you have to pay the bill every month, just like the phone bill. With Visa, Discover, MasterCard, and other credit cards, however, debts can be carried over to the next month. Credit limits for students typically start at $500. Many students find this line of credit too much of a good thing.

A survey of students at three Michigan universities found that 10% had outstanding credit-card bills of more than $700. A handful had bills as high as $5000 or $6000.[22] One student was reported to have an $1100 bar tab on his Visa. One first-year law student was $40,000 in debt but unable to stop using her cards.[23]

■ *Interest rates can be high:* Credit-card interest rates can be much higher than the rates banks charge for other kinds of loans, such as car loans. (And that's all that a credit card is—a loan.) Many cards charge 18–20% a year. And every month interest is added to the interest.

Note: If you carry a $2000 credit-card balance and make only the minimum payment every month, you'll be paying off that $2000 for—the next 33 years! (And that cost could include over $7000 in interest.)[24]

If you have trouble restraining yourself on your credit cards, there's only one solution: take some scissors and cut them in half.

INSURANCE. A dull subject, you may think, but it's important. Murphy's Law states, "If anything can go wrong, it will." When you buy insurance, the insurance company is hoping nothing will go wrong, so they can simply collect your premiums. If it does, they have to give you something back. You're hoping nothing will go wrong too. However, if it does, holding an insurance policy will make you ready for it.

For a college student, there are two or three important kinds of insurance:

■ *Health insurance:* This is absolutely essential. The United States is not a country where it's wise to be without health insurance. If something goes wrong, a hospital somewhere (maybe not a good one) will probably admit you. However, without health insurance you might not get the level of care you need. Moreover, the hospital's business office will bill you anyway. This could lead to financial disaster, either for yourself or, if you're a minor, for your parents.

Parents' employer health plans can often be extended to cover college-age children up until the age of around 24. In addition, most colleges offer student health plans, and you should check to see what their benefits cover. Are lab tests, surgery, hospital stays, long-term care included? If necessary, pay for supplemental health insurance to cover care not provided on campus.

I repeat: Adequate health insurance should not be thought of as optional; it's *absolutely necessary* in our society. Don't forego it.

■ *Tenant's insurance:* Thefts aren't going to happen to you? I certainly hope not. Many college residences, however, are such open living situations that theft can be a problem. Fires are less likely but always a possibility.

Probably the best piece of advice I've heard is not to bring to college anything you would really miss if it disappeared. This includes jewelry, family heirlooms, and similar valuables. Don't bring important photographs of which you have only one copy. In addition, don't leave money or favorite items lying around your room. Lock your bike, lock your desk, lock your doors. Put (inscribe, if possible) your name and phone number on major equipment.

Still, you should make sure your possessions are covered by insurance against fire and theft. Students who are still dependents of their parents may be covered by their parents' insurance. This is so even if the students live in a dormitory or off-campus apartment. It assumes, however, that they still live at home during the summer, are registered to vote there, or carry a driver's license with parents' address. Your coverage usually amounts to 10% of your parents' coverage, minus the deductible. Thus, if your parents' plan covers $150,000 and has a $250 deductible, you are covered up to $15,000. If a $2000 computer system is stolen out of your room, you'll get that amount back minus $250. Check with your insurance company to make sure you're covered as you should be. If not, you should be able to get a special policy for additional premiums.

If you're self-supporting or emancipated or older than about 23, you'll need to get your own tenant's policy.

■ *Car insurance:* If you have a car and are under age 25 (especially if you're an unmarried male), perhaps you've already found that car insurance is one of the most expensive things you can buy. Indeed, it and all other car expenses should seriously make you think about whether you really need a car at school.

If you have an older car, as so many students do, it may not be worth carrying collision insurance. This is the kind of insurance that covers any repairs (usually with a deductible) should anyone run into you. However, you'll want to carry as much comprehensive insurance as you can in case you run into another car, bicyclist, or pedestrian. You should also be covered for hospitalization for any passengers riding in your car.

With car insurance it's worth getting on the phone with the telephone-book Yellow Pages and doing some comparison shopping. Be sure to ask if you can get a discount on your premiums for maintaining good grades. Some companies offer this.

Financial Aid

PREVIEW Financial aid may consist of gifts, such as grants and scholarships. Or it may consist of self-help assistance, such as loans, part-time work, and college work-study. Most financial aid is considered "need-based," in which you show economic need. However, some aid is "merit-based," such as academic, music, or sports scholarships. To demonstrate financial need, you or your family must fill out a needs analysis document. Aid is available for parents of students, self-supporting students under 24, and older students.

ife," the saying goes, "is what happens to you while you're making other plans."

There you are, going along with what you think are adequate financial resources. Suddenly you're faced with some sort of reversal—family illness, loss of job—that requires you to scramble for additional funds. Or perhaps you realize that you'd like to become a professional person—doctor, lawyer, college professor, for example. Such a goal will require years of graduate training for which you need to find financial support. That is the purpose of this section: to show you the different sources of financial aid available to you.

GIFTS & SELF-HELP, NEED-BASED & MERIT-BASED. The term *financial aid* refers to any kind of financial help you get to enable you to pay for college. There are two ways to distinguish financial aid:

- *Gifts versus self-help assistance: Gift assistance* is financial aid you do not have to pay back. It includes grants and scholarships.

  Self-help assistance is financial aid that requires something in return. *Loans,* which must be repaid, are one example. *Part-time work* and *college work-study* are others.

- *Need-based versus merit-based:* Most financial aid is need-based. With *need-based financial aid,* you or your parents fill out forms stating your resources. The college then determines how much aid needs to be made up from somewhere else.

  Merit-based financial aid is based on some sort of superior academic, music, sports, or other abilities.

CAN YOU SHOW YOU NEED IT? *Demonstrated financial need* means that you have proven you need financial aid according to a certain formula, such as the Congressional Methodology. To begin to apply for need-based financial aid, you must ask your institution for an application form called a needs analysis document. **The *needs analysis document* is a form for helping people prove their financial need to colleges.** The *two federal forms you are most likely to encounter are the FAF and the FAFSA.* Financial aid is available whether you are or are not getting money from your family. It is also available whether you are going it alone as a young person or are going back to school as an older person.

- *Aid for parents of students:* The Congressional Methodology formula considers your family's size, income, net worth, and number of members now in college. It then considers your anticipated costs of attending a particular college. From these two factors, the formula arrives at an estimated family contribution. Colleges then make their own calculations based on this formula. If the results show your family's resources insufficient, you'll get some help.

- *Aid for self-supporting students under 24:* If you're self-supporting, the Congressional Methodology formula counts just your income and assets, not your family's. You must show that you are single, under age 24, and without dependents. You must also show you have not been claimed as a dependent by your parents for two years. Finally, you must show you have had annual resources of at least $4000 during each of these two years.[25]

- *Aid for returning adult students:* Even returning adult students can obtain financial aid based on need. It's a matter of minimizing one's income and assets. (For example, older people can move their savings into retirement plans, which are sheltered from financial aid computations.) Believe it or not, it may also help to apply to an expensive college, according to one piece of advice. The reason is that the more expensive the college is, the more aid one is eligible for.[26]

TYPES OF FINANCIAL AID. We may classify financial aid as grants, scholarships, loans, and work. These are available from several sources: federal, state, college, and private.

- *Grants: Grants* **are gifts of money;** they do not have to be repaid.

  One large need-based grant program from the federal government is the *Pell Grants*, given to undergraduates on the basis of need. Normally Pell Grants are given to families with an annual income of less than $25,000, although there are special exceptions. You should apply in any case. Many colleges will not consider you for other grants unless you've been turned down for a Pell Grant.

  Another need-based federal grant program is the *Supplemental Educational Opportunity Grants (SEOG),* which are designed to augment other forms of financial aid.

  Some companies also offer their employees grants in the form of educational benefits that allow them to attend school while working. For example, a hospital may pay one of its employees to go to nursing school while he or she continues working.

- *Scholarships: Scholarships* **are usually awarded on the basis of merit**, often academic merit. Sometimes the scholarships are for merit in other areas as well, such as proficiency in a certain sport or musical activity. Examples are various *Reserve Officer Training Corps (ROTC)* scholarships.

  Sometimes scholarships are available for reasons you couldn't possibly predict, and they seem to have nothing to do with merit. For instance, you have a certain last name, have a parent who worked for a certain organization, or are from a certain geographical area. You'll never know what these are unless you start looking. Go to the financial aid office or library and ask for help.

- *Loans:* **A *loan* is money you have to pay back, either as money or in some form of work.** There are three well-known federal loan programs.

  The *Perkins Loans* allow students to borrow up to $4500 for their first and second years. They can borrow up to $9000 for all undergraduate years. The interest rate is 5%. Repayment begins nine months after graduation (unless you quit or become a student less than half time). The repayment may be spread over 10 years.

  The *Stafford Loan Program,* also known as the Guaranteed Student Loans, allows you to borrow money up to $2625 per year for the first and second year. You can borrow up to $4000 for the third year and beyond. Thus, you can accumulate up to $17,250 for your undergraduate years. Loans are made by banks or other private lenders. Repayment doesn't start until six months after you graduate, quit, or drop below half-time student status.

  The *Parent Loans for Undergraduate Students (PLUS)* program allows parents to borrow from a private lender for their children's education. They can borrow up to $4000 a year, up to $20,000 for each student and at a rate up to 12%. To be eligible, you have to have applied for a Pell or Stafford first. Parents begin repayment 60 days after receiving the money. Students taking out the loan may wait until 60 days after quitting or graduating from college before beginning repayment.

  A more recent kind of loan, which was to have included 1500 campuses in 1995, is a direct-loan program by the U.S. Government, designed to cut out bankers' profits, streamline procedures, and help students predict and organize their debts. Depending on their circumstances, graduates can repay their debt over 10 to 30 years. (Most student loans are structured for repayment over 10 years.)[27]

■ **Work:** Many colleges offer part-time work opportunities, usually on campus, for money or for room and/or board. Of course, you may also be able to line up part-time work off-campus. In addition, a federally funded need-based program called *College Work-Study* helps colleges set up jobs for students. Typically College Work-Study covers 12–15 hours a week, or up to 40 hours a week during the summer.

Cooperative education programs **allow you to improve your marketability upon graduation by giving you work experience in your major.** The work may go on at the same time as the course work or as part-time school and part-time work. Or the work may alternate with course work—for example, one semester in school and the next semester at work. Pay is often modest, but the experience is what counts. Cooperative education programs are offered at about 1000 schools (such as Boston's Northeastern University and Ohio's Antioch College).

GETTING GOING. Even if you don't think you're eligible for financial aid right now, it might be advisable to go through the application process. At least then you'll know where you stand. And you'll be prepared if something happens to the college funds that you're presently counting on. Help in obtaining financial assistance is offered through a couple of toll-free numbers. Call the Federal

Student Aid Information Center at 800-4-FEDAID or the Federal Student Aid Advisory Center at 800-648-3248.

One caution, however: allow *lots* of time. No one's going to give you any money if you didn't follow their rules and apply within the deadlines posted. Applying for money is just like applying to get into college itself—these things do not happen instantaneously. It will take time for you (or your parents) to fill out the forms and meet a filing deadline (usually far in advance of the first day of the school term). Then it will take college officials time to approve the paperwork before they can send you a check.

Applying for financial aid is just as much a test of adult responsibility as filing an income-tax return. Just as the burden is on you to meet the deadlines and proofs of the tax collector, so it is with financial aid. Thus, be sure to keep copies of all your paperwork in case something gets lost.

GROUP ACTIVITY #10.4

THERE'S MONEY OUT THERE SOMEWHERE

This activity, which requires some out-of-class time, is to be done in a group with three to five other students. Many students are familiar with the basic state and federal programs offering financial aid. The purpose of this exercise is to locate less obvious sources of financial assistance. With your group members, use the campus library to identify *five* new potential sources of financial aid. (If possible, prepare a typed list of potential resources, to be distributed to each person in the class.)

In class, report on your findings or distribute your list. What were your reactions to the sources of financial assistance available? Do you feel these funds are readily accessible? Have you identified new sources of monetary aid that are directly applicable to your own financial situation?

Onward: Applying This Chapter to Your Life

PREVIEW Money concerns are usually lifelong.

nless they come into a large inheritance or otherwise strike it rich, most people find that money concerns continue after they're out of college. Thus, like other skills in this book, the techniques described here are not just things you need to know for the short run. They are lifelong skills that will benefit you no matter what kind of degree you hold.

I hope you have found at least one thing in this chapter that you didn't know about money matters. If so, write it down here:

_____

_____

_____

_____

_____

_____

_____

_____

_____

_____

_____

_____

_____

_____

_____

_____

_____

_____

_____

_____

THE EXAMINED LIFE: YOUR JOURNAL

1. What do you find particularly upsetting to you about money? What does this chapter suggest you might be able to do about it?

2. Some students are only vaguely aware of how much money they owe, including both student loans and credit-card debts. Indeed, they may be off by as much as $5000. Do you know how much you need to repay? How long would it be before you're debt free?

3. Some students talk almost like bankers, computing which loans and repayment schedules are better than others. Have you done comparisons of the various loans available? If not, what kind of action might you take here?

health

taking care of yourself mentally & physically

manage stress, look good, & feel good

1. Regarding your health, what single thing that you do or don't do bothers you the most? (*Examples:* don't exercise, eat too much, party too much.) What feelings do you have about this matter?

_____

_____

_____

_____

_____

2. How do you react to stress? (Examples: stomach problems, sleeplessness.) How do you deal with stress?

_____

_____

_____

_____

_____

_____

_____

■ SKIMMING FOR PAYOFFS

Flip through the chapter and find one area that you think you can benefit from concentrating on in the coming school term. Write a big note to yourself: "Try this" or something similar. Describe the area of interest here:

_____

_____

_____

_____

_____

Don't eat this. Don't drink that. Do more of this. Do less of that.

We are all exposed to conflicting messages about health, and I'll be the first to tell you I get confused myself. Still, a great deal of agreement exists about many aspects of health.

One of the things I recall when I was a student was feeling almost invulnerable. "Hey, I'm young, what could happen?" Health professors tell me this attitude drives them crazy. It's extremely frustrating, they say, to convince students of traditional college age that the habits they are establishing now will affect them in the future.

For example, many students whose drinking behavior is pretty excessive seem to think their alcohol consumption will be reduced once they are out of college. This will be true for many, but others will have established drinking patterns that will be tough to change. Many students say their alcohol and other drug use is related to *stress,* which college provides in abundance. What they may not know, however, is that the overuse of alcohol and other drugs only leads to *more* stress.

In this chapter, I describe some health practices that have several benefits: they are stress-busters, they make you look good, and they make you feel better.

Stress: Causes & Manifestations

PREVIEW Three principal worries of college students are: (1) anxiety over wasting time, (2) anxiety over meeting high standards, and (3) feelings of being lonely. *Stress* is the body's reaction, *stressors* are the source of stress. Stressors may be small irritating hassles, short-duration crises, or long-duration strong stressors. A source of stress may be negative and cause "distress" or positive and cause "eustress." Stress may produce certain physical reactions: skin problems, headaches, gastrointestinal problems, and high blood pressure. Stress may also produce emotional reactions such as nervousness and anxiety, and burnout.

great deal of the college experience, unfortunately, consists of *stress*. Indeed, at one point for me in college, things were so stressful—because of academic pressures, financial worries, and my stormy love life—that I considered dropping out. I'm glad I didn't, because of course I've found since that stress certainly doesn't end with graduation. Indeed, I've learned there's even a good kind of stress, one that propels you to accomplish the things you want to do.

I've read that stress or burnout is one of the greatest causes of students leaving school without graduating.[1] I say that not to alarm you but simply so you'll know that any feelings of anxiety or tension you have are *commonplace* for college students.

THE WORRIES OF STUDENTS. College students, says one psychologist, are most hassled by three things:[2]

- *Anxiety over wasting time:* To be in college is to always feel like you should be studying—particularly if you haven't yet set up a time-management system. Students who don't draw up a schedule of their study times and stick to it are particularly apt to suffer constant anxiety over wasting time.

- *Meeting high standards:* Another worry for students is whether or not they can meet the high standards of college. They may worry that they won't do well enough to get top grades. Or they may worry that they won't do well enough even to get passing grades and will flunk out.

- *Being lonely:* Many college students feel lonely from time to time. They may be lonely because they presently have no friends with common interests, no one with whom to share their worries, or no current love relationship.

To these three stresses you can probably add a few of your own, such as those related to work or family.

TYPES OF STRESSORS: THE CAUSES OF STRESS. To understand how to fight stress, you need to understand the difference between *stress* and *stressors*. **Stress is the reaction of our bodies to an event. The source of stress is called a _stressor_.** Stressors may be specific and may range from small to large. That is, they may cover everything from a question you don't understand on a test all the way up to a death in your family.

Some characteristics of stressors are as follows:

- *Three types:* There are three types of stressors—*hassles, crises,* and *strong stressors.* **A _hassle_ is simply a frustrating irritant,** such as a term-paper deadline.

  A _crisis_ is an especially strong source of stress, such as a horrible auto accident.

Though it may be sudden and not last long, it may produce long-lasting psychological (and perhaps physical) effects.

A *strong stressor* is a powerful, ongoing source of extreme mental or physical discomfort, such as a back injury that keeps a person in constant pain. It can dramatically strain a person's ability to adapt.

From these terms, it would appear the stressors of college aren't so bad compared to other things that can happen. That is, your main experience is one of *hassles* rather than crises or strong stressors.

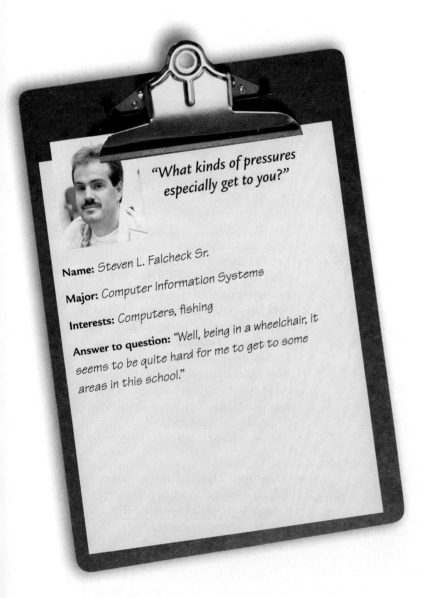

"What kinds of pressures especially get to you?"

Name: Steven L. Falcheck Sr.

Major: Computer Information Systems

Interests: Computers, fishing

Answer to question: "Well, being in a wheelchair, it seems to be quite hard for me to get to some areas in this school."

■ *Distressors or eustressors:* One famous expert on stress, Canadian researcher Hans Selye, points out that stressors can be either negative or positive.[3]

When the source of stress is a negative event, it is called a *distressor* and its effect is called *distress*. An example of a distressor is flunking an exam or being rejected in love. Although distress can be helpful when one is facing a physical threat, too much of it may result in depression and illness.

When the source of stress is a positive event, it is called a *eustressor* and its effect is called *eustress* (pronounced "you-stress"). An example of a eustressor is getting an A on an exam or falling in love. Eustress can stimulate a person to greater coping and adaptation.

We can't always prevent distressors. However, we can learn to recognize them, understand our reactions to them, and develop ways of managing both the stressors and the stress. Eustressors, on the other hand, are what impel us to do our best. Examples are the pressure to win games, to make the dean's list, to try out a new activity, to ask out someone new for a date.

■ *The number, kind, and magnitude of stressors in your life can affect your health:* When stressors become cumulative they can lead to depression and illness. Several years ago, physicians Thomas Holmes and Richard Rahe devised a "future illness" scale.[4] The scale, known as the Holmes-Rahe Life Events Scale, identifies certain stressors (life events), both positive and negative. These are stressors that the physicians found could be used to predict future physical and emotional problems.

You may wish to try Personal Exploration #11.1, which contains a version of this scale, the Student Stress Scale. This was designed for people of the traditional student age, 18–24 (although anyone can take it). Note that the scale includes both negative and positive sources of stress.

THE STUDENT STRESS SCALE

In the Student Stress Scale, each event, such as beginning or ending school, is given a score that represents the amount of adjustment a person has to make in life as a result of the change. In some studies, people with serious illnesses have been found to have high scores on similar scales.

■ DIRECTIONS

Check off the events you have experienced in the past 12 months.

POINTS

1. Death of a close family member	❐ 100
2. Death of a close friend	❐ 73
3. Divorce of parents	❐ 65
4. Jail term	❐ 63
5. Major personal injury or illness	❐ 63
6. Marriage	❐ 58
7. Firing from a job	❐ 50
8. Failure of an important course	❐ 47
9. Change in health of a family member	❐ 45
10. Pregnancy	❐ 45
11. Sex problems	❐ 44
12. Serious argument with close friend	❐ 40
13. Change in financial status	❐ 39
14. Change of scholastic major	❐ 39
15. Trouble with parents	❐ 37
16. New girl- or boyfriend	❐ 37
17. Increase in workload at school	❐ 36
18. Outstanding personal achievement	❐ 36
19. First quarter/semester in school	❐ 31
20. Change in living conditions	❐ 30
21. Serious argument with an instructor	❐ 30
22. Lower grades than expected	❐ 29
23. Change in sleeping habits	❐ 29
24. Change in social activities	❐ 29
25. Change in eating habits	❐ 28
26. Chronic car trouble	❐ 26
27. Change in the number of family get-togethers	❐ 26
28. Too many missed classes	❐ 25
29. Change of college	❐ 24
30. Dropping of more than one class	❐ 23
31. Minor traffic violations	❐ 20

Total points: _____

■ SCORING

To determine your stress score, add up the number of points corresponding to the events you checked

■ INTERPRETATION

If your score is 300 or higher, you are at high risk for developing a health problem.

If your score is between 150 and 300, you have a 50-50 chance of experiencing a serious health change within two years.

If your score is below 150, you have a 1-in-3 chance of a serious health change.

The following can help you reduce your risk:

■ Watch for early signs of stress, such as stomachaches or compulsive overeating.

■ Avoid negative thinking.

■ Arm your body against stress by eating nutritiously and exercising regularly.

■ Practice a relaxation technique regularly.

■ Turn to friends and relatives for support when you need it.

GROUP ACTIVITY OPTION

On a sheet of paper list your Top Ten Stressors, drawing on the Personal Exploration, if necessary. Then, in a small group (three to five students), designate a secretary or recorder and develop a master list from your separate lists. Identify the top five stressors for the group. Discuss how the stressors affect your behaviors and feelings and how you have ineffectively coped with such stressors in the past. Discuss how you would hope to deal with them in the future. If time permits, share your experiences with the class as a whole.

TYPES OF STRESS: YOUR PHYSICAL & PSYCHOLOGICAL REACTIONS TO THE STRESSORS. Stress—your internal reactions to the stressor—has both physical and emotional sides. Physically, according to researcher Selye, stress is "The nonspecific response of the body to any demand made upon it."[5] Emotionally, stress is the feeling of being overwhelmed. According to one authority, it is "the perception that events or circumstances have challenged, or exceeded a person's ability to cope."[6]

Specifically, the stress reactions, for you and for most other students, could take the following forms:

■ *Physical reactions:* All diseases are to some extent disorders of adaptation.[7] Often, however, an adaptation to stress appears in a particular part of the body—what doctors call a person's *"stress site."* My own stress site, for instance, is the neck or back, when tension is felt as a knot in the muscles there—a familiar stress reaction for many people. Some people I know grind their teeth. Others develop nervous tics and or perspire excessively.

Do you have a "stress site"? Some physical reactions to stress are *skin problems, headaches, gastrointestinal problems, susceptibility to colds and flus,* and *high blood pressure.* [8–11]

■ *Psychological reactions:* Individual emotional reactions to stress cover a wide range. Among them are *nervousness and anxiety,* expressed as irritability, difficulty concentrating, and sleep disturbances. Nervousness and anxiety also are expressed in feelings of dread, overuse of alcohol and other drugs, and mistakes and accidents. Another emotional reaction is *burnout,* a state of physical, emotional, and mental exhaustion. [12,13]

Managing Stress

PREVIEW You can adapt to or cope with stress.

Adaptation is not changing the stressor or stress. Some ways of adapting are use of drugs and other escapes such as television watching, junk-food eating, or sleeping.

Coping is changing the stressor or your reaction to it. There are five strategies for coping: (1) Reduce the stressors.

(2) Manage your emotional response.

(3) Develop a support system. (4) Take care of your body. (5) Develop relaxation techniques.

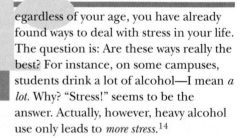

egardless of your age, you have already found ways to deal with stress in your life. The question is: Are these ways really the best? For instance, on some campuses, students drink a lot of alcohol—I mean *a lot.* Why? "Stress!" seems to be the answer. Actually, however, heavy alcohol use only leads to *more stress.*[14]

DO YOU CONTROL STRESS OR DOES STRESS CONTROL YOU? Unfortunately, we can't always control the stressors in our lives, and so we will experience stress no matter what we do. Not long ago, for example, I had an accident while playing basketball that put me in an ankle cast for 11 weeks. This was a form of stress I definitely didn't plan on. Thus, which is more important—what happens to you, or how you handle it? Clearly, learning how to *manage* stress—minimize it or recover from it—is more important.

There are two principal methods of dealing with stress—adaptation and coping.

■ *Adaptation:* **With _adaptation_, you do not change the stressor or the stress.** An example is getting drunk. Adaptation is the *bad* way of handling stress.

- **Coping:** **With _coping_, you do change the stressor or change your reaction to it.** For example, if you're feeling stressed about handing in a paper late, you go talk to the instructor about it. This is the _good_ way of handling stress.

ADAPTATION: THE NONPRODUCTIVE WAYS OF HANDLING STRESS.

Some of the less effective ways in which people adapt to stress are as follows:

- **_Drugs, legal and illegal:_** Coffee, cigarettes, and alcohol are all legal drugs. However, too much coffee can make you tense, "wired." Cigarettes also speed up the heart rate and may make it difficult to get going in the morning. Moreover, they put you under the stress of always having to reach for another cigarette.

    Alcohol is perceived as being a way of easing the strain of life temporarily, which is why it is so popular with so many people. The down side, however, is what heavy drinking makes you feel like the next morning—jittery, exhausted, depressed, all conditions that _increase_ stress.

    Other legal drugs, such as tranquilizers, and illegal drugs, such as marijuana and cocaine, may seem to provide relaxation in the short run. However, ultimately they complicate your ability to make realistic decisions about the pressures in your life.

- **_Food:_** Overeating and junk-food snacking are favorite diversions of many people. The act of putting food in our mouths reminds us of what eased one of the most fundamental tensions of infancy: hunger.

- **_Sleep and social withdrawal:_** Sleep, too, is often a form of escape from exhaustion and depression, and some individuals will spend more than the usual 7–9 hours required in bed. Withdrawal from the company of others is also usually an unhealthy form of adaptation.

    How do you adapt to stress now? Consider the kinds of responses you habitually make to the tensions in your life.

COPING: THE PRODUCTIVE WAYS OF HANDLING STRESS—FIVE STRATEGIES.

Now let me turn from negative adaptations to stress to positive coping mechanisms. There are five strategies for coping with stress, as follows:

1. Reduce the stressors.
2. Manage your emotional response.
3. Develop a support system.
4. Take care of your body.
5. Develop relaxation techniques.

STRATEGY NO. 1: REDUCE THE STRESSORS.

Reducing the source of stress is better than avoidance or procrastination.

"Reducing the stressors" seems like obvious advice. However, it's surprising how long we can let something go on being a source of stress—usually because dealing with it is so uncomfortable.

Examples: Falling behind in your work and having to explain your problem to your instructor. Having misunderstandings with your family, your lover, or people sharing your living space. Running up debts on a credit card.

It may not be easy, but all these problems are matters you can do something about. Getting the advice of a counselor may help. Avoidance and procrastination only make things worse.

STRATEGY NO. 2: MANAGE YOUR EMOTIONAL RESPONSE. *You can't always manage the stressor, but you can manage your reactions. Techniques include understanding and expressing your feelings, acting positively, and keeping your sense of humor and having hope.*

Learning how to manage your emotional response is crucial. Quite often you can't do anything about a stressor (being stuck having to read a dull assignment, for example). However, you can do something about your *reaction* to it. (You can tell yourself that resentment gets you nowhere, or choose to see a particular stressor as a challenge rather than a threat.)

Some techniques for managing your emotional response are the following:

- **Understand and express your feelings:** Understanding pent-up feelings is imperative. This advice is supported by a study of students at Southern Methodist University. It was found that those who kept a journal recounting traumatic events and their emotional responses had fewer colds and reported fewer medical visits.[15]

  Are you one who believes it's not appropriate to cry? Actually, crying helps. In one study, 85% of women and 73% of men reported that crying made them feel better.[16]

- **Act positively:** To keep their spirits up, some people put up signs of positive affirmation on their bathroom mirrors or over their desks. For example:

DON'T SWEAT THE SMALL STUFF.

ONE DAY AT A TIME.

"NEVER GIVE UP" —Winston Churchill

Can you actually *will* yourself to feel and act positively and affirmatively? There is some evidence this is so. Some studies have found that putting a smile on your face will produce the feelings that the expression represents—facial action leads to changes in mood.[17–19]

You can also make your "inner voice" a force for success. Positive "self-talk" can help you control your moods, turn back fear messages, and give you confidence.[20,21] Positive self-talk is not the

> *"Can you actually will yourself to feel and act positively and affirmatively? There is some evidence this is so."*

same as mindless positive thinking or self-delusion.[22] Rather, it consists of telling yourself positive messages—such as "You can do it. You've done it well before"—that correct errors and distortions in your thinking and help you develop a more accurate internal dialogue.

- **Keep your sense of humor and have hope:** There has been a growing body of literature that seems to show that humor, optimism, and hope can help people conquer disease or promote their bodies' natural healing processes.[23–26] There is some disagreement as to how much effect laughter and hope have on healing. Still, so many accounts have been written of the positive results of these two qualities that they cannot be ignored.

STRATEGY NO. 3: DEVELOP A SUPPORT SYSTEM. *Finding social support is vital for resisting stress. Sources of support are friends—in the true sense—counselors, self-help, and other support groups.*

It can be tough to do things by yourself, so it's important to grasp a lesson that many people never learn: *You are not alone. No matter what troubles you, emotional support is available—but you have to reach out for it.*

Some forms of support are as follows:

- **Talk to and do things with friends:** True friends are not just people you know. They are people you can trust, talk to honestly, and draw emotional sustenance from. (Some people you know quite well may actually not be very good friends in this sense. That is, the way they interact with you makes you feel competitive, anxious, or inferior.) Friends are simply those people you feel comfortable with, regardless of age or social grouping.

It's vital to fight the temptation to isolate yourself. Studies show that the more students participate in activities with other students, the less they suffer from depression and the more they have feelings of health.[27]

■ **Talk to counselors:** You can get emotional support from counselors. Paid counselors may be psychotherapists, ranging from social workers to psychiatrists. Unpaid counselors may be clergy or perhaps members of the college student services.

Sources of free counseling that everyone should be aware of are telephone "hot lines." Here, for the price of a phone call, callers can find a sympathetic ear and various kinds of help. (Hot lines are listed under the heading of CRISIS INTERVENTION SERVICE in the telephone-book Yellow Pages. Other forms of stress counseling are listed under the heading STRESS MANAGEMENT AND PREVENTION.)

■ **Join a support group:** This week an estimated 15 million Americans will attend one of about 500,000 meetings offered by some form of support group.[28] Self-help organizations cover all kinds of areas of concern. There are many on various types of drug addiction and offering help to adult children of alcoholics. Others range from single parenting to spouse abuse to compulsive shopping to "women who love too much" to various forms of bereavement. Some of these groups may exist on or near your campus.

In the true self-help group, membership is limited to peers. There is no professional moderator, only some temporarily designated leader who makes announcements and calls on people to share their experiences. This is in contrast with group-therapy groups, in which a psychologist or other therapist is in charge.

STRATEGY NO. 4: TAKE CARE OF YOUR BODY. *Taking care of the body helps alleviate stress in the mind. Techniques include eating, exercising, and sleeping right and avoiding drugs.*

The interaction between mind and body becomes particularly evident when you're stressed. If you're not eating and exercising well, or are short on sleep, or are using drugs, these mistreatments of the body will only make the mind feel worse.

STRATEGY NO. 5: DEVELOP RELAXATION TECHNIQUES. *There are three relaxation techniques for de-stressing yourself. One is progressive muscular relaxation, which consists of tightening and relaxing muscle groups. A second is mental imagery, which consists of visualizing a change. A third is meditation, which consists of focusing on removing mental distractions.*

There is an entire body of extremely effective stress reducers that most people in North America have never tried at all.[29] They include the following:

■ **Progressive muscular relaxation:** The technique of _progressive muscular relaxation_ **consists of reducing stress by tightening and relaxing major muscle groups throughout your body.** If you like, take 10 minutes to try the following.

(1) *Get comfortable and quiet.* Sit down or lie in a comfortable setting where you won't be disturbed. Close your eyes.

(2) *Be aware of your breathing.* Breathe slowly in through your nose. Exhale slowly through your nose.

(3) *Clench and release your muscles.* Tense and relax each part of your body two or more times. Clench while inhaling. Release while exhaling.

(4) *Proceed through muscles or muscle groups.* Tense and relax various muscles, from fist to face to stomach to toes. (A good progression is: Right fist, right biceps. Left fist, left biceps. Right shoulder, left shoulder. Neck, jaw, eyes, forehead, scalp. Chest, stomach, buttocks, genitals, down through each leg to the toes.)

Mental imagery. It's recommended that you devote 10 minutes or so to this procedure.

Get comfortable and quiet: Remove your shoes, loosen your clothes, and sit down or lie in a comfortable setting, with the lights dimmed. Close your eyes.

Breathe deeply and concentrate on a phrase: Breathe deeply, filling your chest, and slowly let the air out. With each breath, concentrate on a simple word or phrase (such as "One," or "Good," or a prayer). Focus your mind on this phrase to get rid of distracting thoughts. Repeat.

Clench and release your muscles: Tense and relax each part of your body, proceeding from fist to face to stomach to toes.

Visualize a vivid image: Create a tranquil, pleasant image in your mind—lying beside a mountain stream, floating on a raft in a pool, stretched out on a beach. Try to involve all five senses, from sight to taste.

Visualize a desired change: If you're trying to improve some aspect of your performance, such as improving a tennis serve, visualize the act in detail: the fuzz and seam on the ball, the exact motion of the serve, the path of the ball, all in slow detail.

- *Mental imagery:* *Mental imagery* is also known as *guided imagery* and *visualization.* It is a procedure in which you essentially daydream an image or desired change, anticipating that your body will respond as if the image were real. The accompanying box shows how to do mental imagery. (See ■ *Panel 11.1.*)

- *Meditation:* *Meditation* is concerned with directing a person's attention to a single, unchanging or repetitive stimulus. It is a way of quelling the "mind chatter"—the chorus of voices that goes on in the heads of all of us. An age-old technique, the purpose of meditation is simply to eliminate mental distractions and relax the body. The accompanying box shows one method.[30] (See ■ *Panel 11.2.*)

GROUP ACTIVITY #11.1
PRACTICING A RELAXATION TECHNIQUE

How self-conscious are you? How aware are you of others around you? To practice a relaxation technique, you need to learn to shut out distracting thoughts. Although it's not easily done, this is an opportunity to try such a technique.

The instructor will select *one* of the three relaxation techniques—*progressive muscular relaxation, mental imagery,* or *meditation*—for 10 minutes of practice by the class. He or she will read aloud from this book the steps for the particular method. *Important: Whenever everyday thoughts occur, disregard them and return to the relaxation procedure.*

After the 10 minutes are up, discuss your experience. Do you actually feel more relaxed? Did you almost fall asleep? Was it difficult to disregard the intrusion of everyday thoughts? Were you too aware of others in the room? Do you think the technique might work in private?

Meditation. Meditation includes the repetition of a word, sound, phrase, or prayer. Whenever everyday thoughts occur, they should be disregarded, and you should return to the repetition. The exercise should be continued for 10 minutes or so.

Herbert Benson, M.D., author of *The Relaxation Response* and *Your Maximum Mind*, offers the following simple instructions for meditation:

- Pick a focus word or short phrase that is firmly rooted in your personal belief system. For example, a Christian person might choose the opening words of Psalm 23, "The Lord is my shepherd"; a Jewish person, "Shalom"; a nonreligious individual, a neutral word like "One" or "Peace."

- Sit quietly in a comfortable position.

- Close your eyes.

- Relax your muscles.

- Breathe slowly and naturally, and as you do, repeat your focus word or phrase as you exhale.

- Assume a passive attitude. Don't worry about how well you're doing. When other thoughts come to mind, simply say to yourself, "Oh, well," and gently return to the repetition.

Legal Drugs: Caffeine, Tobacco, & Alcohol

PREVIEW Caffeine, found in coffee and soft drinks, can make you anxious and won't help academic performance. Smoking has many unpleasant consequences, both immediate and long-range, both to smokers and the people around them. Since alcohol—and alcohol abuse—is a big part of campus life, one needs to learn the art of drinking. This includes learning what "a drink" is and what "BAC" means, how to reduce the effects of alcohol, and what the risks of drinking are.

I like a cup of coffee in the morning and occasionally a beer before dinner. In that respect, I'm like a lot of people. Sometimes I think all of North America feels it needs "something to get going" to start the day and "something to wind down" toward the end of it.

Coffee gets you going because the caffeine in it is a type of drug known as a stimulant. **A *stimulant* stimulates the central nervous system, speeding up brain activity.** Alcohol winds you down because (for most people) it is a depressant. **A *depressant* slows down the central nervous system, making you feel relaxed, even anesthetized.** Some people are on a regular cycle with these mind-altering substances (for that's what they are). They get wound up on coffee throughout the day and wound down on alcohol during the evening.

Of course, there are many other kinds of mind-altering substances, as the media are forever reminding us. The news is full of accounts of cocaine smuggling, marijuana busts, the upsurge in heroin and LSD use, and so on. However, three kinds of drugs, experts say, have had a greater effect on human civilization than all the other mood-altering drugs combined.

These drugs are caffeine, nicotine, and alcohol.[31] Yes, they are legal, but that doesn't make them healthful or even safe. Let's take a brief look at them.

CAFFEINE: THE KICK FROM COFFEE & COLAS.

Most people associate caffeine, a stimulant, with coffee. (Caffeine is also found in many kinds of tea.) Recently, however, soft drinks have overtaken coffee as primary sources of caffeine, particularly among people ages 18–24.[32,33] If you drink a six-pack of regular Coke or Pepsi a day, you are getting the equivalent of 4 cups of instant coffee. On the average, caffeine drinkers consume 280 milligrams a day, equivalent to 3 cups of coffee.[34]

Although caffeine can be physiologically addictive, most people I know don't find it much of a problem. Indeed, studies show it may help people fight boredom and stay with a boring task longer. Still, you should be aware that caffeine does not noticeably increase your ability to perform complex intellectual tasks.[35] In fact, the opposite may be true. An association has been found between high intakes of caffeine and *lowered* academic performance.[36]

A common complaint of students who visit college health service professionals is anxiety, breathlessness, and headaches. One of the first questions the doctors usually ask is, "How much coffee do you drink?"[37] These students are showing signs of *caffeinism,* or "coffee nerves," which generally develop on 4–6 cups of coffee a day.[38,39] One study of college students found that moderate and high consumers of caffeine were more likely to be depressed and anxious than those who abstained.[40] In fact, too much caffeine may even trigger anxiety disorders and panic attacks.[41–43]

If you think you are presently drinking too much caffeine, the best course is to stop slowly. Stopping all at once can produce headaches for several days.[44–46]

TOBACCO: DANGEROUS TO SMOKERS & NONSMOKERS.

Think of all those cigarette ads showing sexy, healthy cowboys, swimmers, and volleyball players. Despite their clear hazards, as documented in over 50,000 studies, cigarettes are not only legal, they are aggressively promoted. Still, the good news is that college students are less likely to smoke than other people of the same age.[47]

Why do people smoke? The stimulation, handling, and relaxation are part of it. So is the wish to be different—that's why cigarette ads try to appeal to smokers' sense of being adventurous and independent.[48] Cigarettes also act as a tension reducer, particularly for young people. "A cigarette covers embarrassment, lifts depression, restores youthful cool," one expert states. However, he adds an important observation: "What the smoking adolescent never has the chance to learn is that, like his nonsmoking friends, he would have acquired that knack of [emotional] control anyway. It is called growing up and nearly everyone does it, with or without the help of cigarettes."[49]

If you're a smoker, you've probably discovered some of the immediate drawbacks of the habit: It makes your clothes and hair smell. It turns your fingers yellow. It cuts down your wind. It's expensive. It makes you uncomfortable when you have to go somewhere where you can't smoke.

Although tobacco ads like to suggest that smoking is sexy, cigarettes produce some unsexy results. Examples are premature facial wrinkles, decreased sexual arousal, and possible damage to sperm.[50–52] The long-range consequences are increased risk of lung cancer, heart disease, stroke, and respiratory disorders.[53–56] About half the people who smoke today and who began as teenagers will die prematurely in middle age. That is, they will lose 20–25 years of their life expectancy.[57] No wonder 70% of cigarette smokers say they want to stop.[58] Incidentally, smokeless tobacco—chewing tobacco and snuff—is not much of an improvement over cigarettes, leading to a higher risk of oral cancer.[59,60]

Nonsmokers sharing space with smokers don't own the air they breathe. A smoker inhaling directly on a cigarette may take in smoke for only about half a minute. However, everyone else may be doing *passive smoking*—breathing in so-called sidestream smoke—for the entire 12 minutes or so that the cigarette is burning. Exposed nonsmokers have increased risk of lung cancer, heart disease, and breast cancer.[61]

Cigarette smoking is one of the toughest of drug addictions. However, it can be beaten. There is no one right way to quit. All methods are useful for some people, useless for others. The methods include: tapering off, quitting cold turkey, joining a stop-smoking group, and such other methods as nicotine patches, nicotine gum, and hypnosis. Some smokers can quit regardless of the techniques they use. Others have great difficulty quitting regardless of what they try.[62,63] Either way, this is a clear case in which being a quitter is being a winner.

ALCOHOL: ARE YOU PARTIAL TO PARTYING?

People in general—and college students in particular—tend to equate drinking with relaxation, good times, fellowship, and the easing of pain and problems. *(See ■ Panel 11.3.)* Drinking is a big fact of life on a lot of campuses. "Partying starts on Thursday nights," wrote a recent graduate of one major eastern university. He went on to explain: "you must understand that partying and getting drunk are synonymous to a college student."[64]

Actually, campus drinking is said to be less than it used to be. "Fewer college students are drinking now than in the past 15 years," writes one researcher who has investigated campus drinking for over a quarter century. "And those who choose to drink are consuming less than in the past."[65] However, a 1993 Harvard University study of 17,592 students on 140 campuses found some depressing news. It reported that 50% of male college students and 39% of female students were *binge drinkers*.

Binge drinking is defined as consuming five (for men) or four (for women) or

PANEL 11.3   **W**hy college freshmen drink.

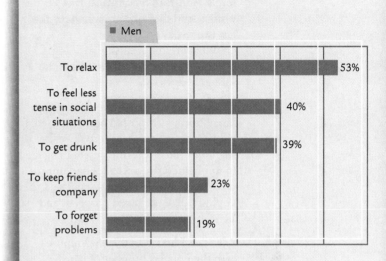

■ Men

To relax	53%
To feel less tense in social situations	40%
To get drunk	39%
To keep friends company	23%
To forget problems	19%

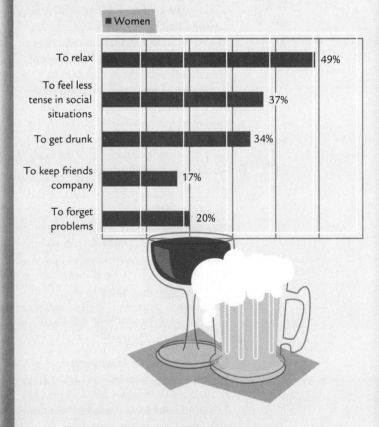

■ Women

To relax	49%
To feel less tense in social situations	37%
To get drunk	34%
To keep friends company	17%
To forget problems	20%

more drinks in a row one or more times in a two-week period. [66] White male students were found to drink far more than white females and more than blacks and Hispanics of both sexes. (There was positive news, however: 35% of men and 45% of women drank at nonbinging levels. And 15% of men and 16% of women said they had abstained for the last two weeks.)

What are the results of excessive drinking on campus? Here's what the research says:

- **Effects on selves:** Nearly two-thirds of binge drinkers reported having missed a class. Over half forgot where they were or what they did. Forty-one percent engaged in unplanned sex, and 22% had unprotected sex. Twenty-three percent said they got hurt, 22% damaged property, and 11% got into trouble with police.

- **Effects on others:** On the 43 campuses with the greatest number of heavy drinkers, 68% of the lighter drinkers said they had had their study or sleep interrupted by an intoxicated student. Over half had to care for a drunken student. About a third said they had been "insulted or humiliated." One in four women said she had experienced an unwanted sexual advance. Other sober students reported serious arguments, having property damaged, or having been pushed or assaulted.

- **Suicides, accidents, and violence:** According to other sources, two-thirds of student suicides were legally drunk at the time, and 90% of fatal fraternity hazing accidents involved drinking. In addition, 95% of violent crime on campus has been found to be related to alcohol or other drugs. Moreover, 73% of assailants and 55% of victims of rape had used alcohol or other drugs. [67]

- **Lower bank account, lower grades:** Students spend $5.5 billion on alcohol annually, *more than they spend on nonalcoholic drinks and books combined.*[68] Students with D or F grade averages drink, on average, three times as much (nearly 11 drinks a week) as A students (3.4 drinks a week). [69]

Interestingly, in the 1993 Harvard study of college drinking, few students reported themselves as having a drinking problem. Asked to characterize their alcohol use, only 0.2% of all students surveyed and only 0.6% of the binge drinkers designated themselves as problem drinkers.

What about you? What are your drinking habits like? You might want to try Personal Exploration #11.2.

Being part of a hard-drinking social circle is difficult because of the powerful influence of the group over the individual. Still, throughout life we will always have to deal with the power of the group, and certainly this power is not always worth giving in to. Here, then, are some suggestions on how to drink successfully:

- **Understand what a "drink" is:** Think some drinks are stronger than others—whiskey more than beer, for example? That may be so, but a typical *serving* of the major types of alcoholic beverages—beer, wine, distilled spirits—contains about the same amount of alcohol. That is, 1 beer = 1 glass of table wine = 1 glass of fortified wine = 1 shot of distilled spirits. In terms of pure 100% alcohol, they're all about the same.

We're talking about a *standard* size drink here, the kind a bartender would serve. A standard drink is equivalent to the following:

(1) A 12-ounce can of light beer that is 4.8% alcohol. (*Total alcohol content per serving: 0.58 ounce.*)

(2) A 4-ounce glass of table wine, such as chablis or burgundy, that is 12% alcohol. (*Alcohol content: 0.48 ounce per serving.*)

(3) A 1-ounce shot of distilled spirits ("hard liquor"), such as scotch, bourbon, vodka, gin, rum, or tequila, that is 50% (100 proof) alcohol. (*Alcohol content: 0.50 ounce per serving.*)

Many drinks, however, are not standard: Distilled liquors or spirits can range from 40% to 75% alcohol. Mixed drinks or poured drinks may have more alcohol than those in bottles or cans.

WHAT KIND OF DRINKER ARE YOU?

Answer each of the following questions by placing a check next to the appropriate answer.

1. Do you feel you are a normal drinker? (If you are a total abstainer, check "Yes.")

   ❑ Yes   ❑ No

2. Have you ever awakened the morning after some drinking the night before and found that you could not remember a part of the evening before?

   ❑ Yes   ❑ No

3. Does your spouse [boyfriend/girlfriend] (or a parent) ever worry or complain about your drinking?

   ❑ Yes   ❑ No

4. Can you stop drinking without a struggle after one or two drinks?

   ❑ Yes   ❑ No

5. Do you feel bad about your drinking?

   ❑ Yes   ❑ No

6. Do friends or relatives think you are a normal drinker?

   ❑ Yes   ❑ No

7. Do you ever try to limit your drinking to certain times of the day or to certain places?

   ❑ Yes   ❑ No

8. Are you always able to stop drinking when you want to?

   ❑ Yes   ❑ No

9. Have you ever attended a meeting of Alcoholics Anonymous (AA)?

   ❑ Yes   ❑ No

10. Have you gotten into fights when drinking?

    ❑ Yes   ❑ No

11. Has drinking ever created problems with you and your spouse [boyfriend/girlfriend]?

    ❑ Yes   ❑ No

12. Has your spouse [boyfriend/girlfriend] (or other family member) ever gone to anyone for help about your drinking?

    ❑ Yes   ❑ No

13. Have you ever lost friends or dates because of drinking?

    ❑ Yes   ❑ No

14. Have you ever gotten into trouble at work because of drinking?

    ❑ Yes   ❑ No

15. Have you ever lost a job because of drinking?

    ❑ Yes   ❑ No

16. Have you ever neglected your obligations, your family, or your work for two or more days in a row?

    ❑ Yes   ❑ No

17. Do you ever have a drink before noon?

    ❑ Yes   ❑ No

18. Have you ever been told you have liver trouble? Cirrhosis?

    ❑ Yes   ❑ No

19. Have you ever had delirium tremens (DTs) or severe shaking, heard voices, or seen things that weren't there after heavy drinking?

    ❑ Yes   ❑ No

20. Have you gone to anyone for help about your drinking?

    ❑ Yes   ❑ No

21. Have you ever been in a hospital because of drinking?

    ❑ Yes   ❑ No

22. Have you ever been in a psychiatric hospital or on a psychiatric ward of a general hospital where drinking was part of the problem?

    ❑ Yes   ❑ No

23. Have you ever gone to a psychiatric or mental health clinic or to a doctor, social worker, or clergy

man for help with an emotional problem in which drinking had played a part?

   ❑ Yes   ❑ No

24. Have you ever been arrested, even for a few hours, because of drunk behavior?

    ❑ Yes   ❑ No

25. Have you ever been arrested for drunk driving or driving after drinking?

    ❑ Yes   ❑ No

■ SCORING

Give yourself points for your answers as follows.

QUESTION NUMBER	"YES" ANSWER	"NO" ANSWER
1	0	2
2	2	0
3	1	0
4	0	2
5	1	0
6	0	2
7	0	0
8	0	2
9	5	0
10	1	0
11	2	0
12	2	0
13	2	0
14	2	0
15	2	0
16	2	0
17	1	0
18	2	0
19	2	0
20	5	0
21	5	0
22	2	0
23	2	0
24	2	0
25	2	0

continued next page

■ INTERPRETATION

0–3
You are most likely a nonalcoholic.

4
You may be an alcoholic.

5 or more
You almost definitely are an alcoholic.

[The interpretation is what the original screening test says. I would say, however, that 4–5 or more points means mainly that alcohol is severely affecting your life. If this is the case for you, you should talk to a health professional about it.]

GROUP ACTIVITY OPTION

Form a group with two to four other students. Use the questions in this test to discuss *someone you know* (don't use names) who seems to have a drinking problem. Which "yes" answers seem to apply to him or her? Does that person admit to having a drinking problem? Why or why not, in your opinion? What is there about alcohol that makes problem drinkers so unwilling to admit they have a problem?

■ *Understand how to determine when you're legally drunk:* The *blood alcohol concentration (BAC)* is a measure of the amount of alcohol in the blood. Thus, 10 drops of alcohol in 1000 drops of blood is expressed as .10% BAC. (Think of 10 black marbles in 1000 red marbles.) *If you have a .10% BAC, you are legally drunk in most places. In many places, you are considered drunk at a .08% BAC.* These are the levels, for example, at which the police establish whether someone is guilty of drunken driving ("driving under the influence").

How long will it take you to achieve these BACs? To determine that, you need to know how much you weigh and the number of drinks you've consumed in a 1-hour period. Find your approximate weight on the right side of the accompanying chart. (*See* ■ *Panel 11.4.*) Then look down the corresponding color line to see what your estimated BAC would be for a given number of drinks consumed in 1 hour.

For example, if you weigh 160 pounds and you have four drinks in an hour, your BAC will be .12%—which makes you legally drunk in most places. (Important note: In general, for men and women of equal weight, *women* will experience a higher BAC after the same number of drinks.)

Of course, the effects of drinking go way beyond just being intoxicated. During the several hours of sobering up afterward—in the period known as the hangover—your body's and mind's efficiency will be severely impaired. (You won't be able to study as well, for example.)

Calculating your BAC. This table presents the approximate blood alcohol concentration (BAC) according to your body weight and the number of drinks consumed during 1 hour. A drink is defined as any of the following: (1) A can or bottle (12 ounces) of beer. (2) A glass (4 ounces) of wine. (3) A 1-ounce shot of 100-proof liquor. (4) A 1½-ounce shot of 80-proof liquor.

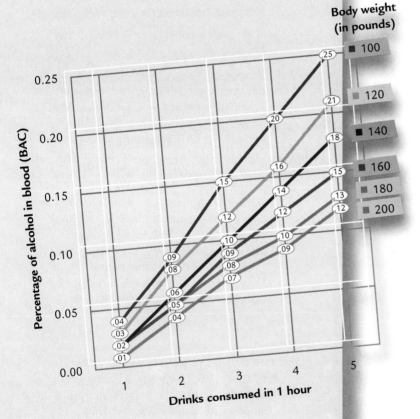

■ **Know how to reduce the effects of alcohol:** Although all the people around you at a party may be intent on getting roaring drunk, you can have a fine time without doing this. Some ideas:

(1) *Eat before and while drinking.* Food in the stomach will coat the areas of the stomach and small intestine through which alcohol is absorbed and slow it down. Meat, cheese, and milk are particularly good.

(2) *Avoid fizzy drinks, which get you drunk faster.* Alcohol mixed with carbonated beverages—cola, club soda, tonic water, ginger ale—will speed the delivery of alcohol through the bloodstream to the brain.

(3) *Use ice, drink slowly, mix your own drinks.* Letting ice melt in your glass will slow down your alcohol consumption. So will sipping rather than gulping. Take charge of making your own drinks, which gives you a chance to fill up your glass or beer can with water or nonalcoholic beverage.

(4) *Try nonalcoholic, or dealcoholized, beer or wine.* The nonalcohol beer named Kaliber, for example, has only .01% alcohol. Some of these nonalcoholic alternatives have been found to taste as good as their alcoholic counterparts.[70,71]

I realize I am being rather persistent in suggesting one go easy on alcohol. However, besides the fact that hangovers don't go well with academic performance, there are several other nasty effects from heavy drinking. Consider:

■ **Alcohol is heavily implicated in fatal accidents and suicides:** Car accidents account for the overwhelming majority of alcohol-related deaths. Suicides and homicides run a close second. Deaths from alcohol-related injuries, mainly automobile accidents, rise sharply through adolescence and peak at 6000 a year in the 20–24 age group.[72] As for suicides, it has been found that in four out of five suicide attempts, the individual has been drinking.[73]

■ **Heavy alcohol use produces sexual difficulties:** Ads like to show that drinking is sexy, but is it? Among men, heavy drinking affects the male sex hormones, producing a loss of sexual desire and difficulty in sexual performance. It also produces decreased sperm production and risk of conceiving defective offspring.[74] Among women, heavy drinking may produce impaired sexual functioning, different menstrual disorders, and halting of the menstrual period.[75]

For both men and women, drinking is also associated with high-risk sexual behavior. That is, people drink too much and then find themselves having sex in ways they wouldn't when sober. Thus, drinking becomes a risk factor in exposing people to infection from sexually transmitted diseases, such as HIV/AIDS.[76]

■ **Heavy alcohol use produces other difficulties:** In time heavy drinkers develop all kinds of physical and mental problems. The liver, which cannot regenerate itself, may be irreversibly damaged.[77] Heavy drinking also leads to gastrointestinal problems, heart and blood-vessel problems, and various kinds of cancer.

Some students may need to address a fundamental question: How badly do you need alcohol to change your mood? The belief that drinking is necessary as a basic pleasure in your life or as a stress and pain reliever may be central to alcohol becoming a difficulty. No one who gets involved with alcohol (or any other drug) ever thinks it is going to take over his or her life. Unfortunately, addictions creep up on people. The last to know they are addicted are the addicted.

Illegal Drugs: Marijuana, Cocaine, & Others

PREVIEW Drug dependence, the reliance on a substance, may give way to addiction, requiring increased dosages. Marijuana may lead to psychological dependence, lung problems, and other unpleasant side effects. Cocaine usually produces depression and anxiety after the high, as well as addiction and other hazards. Other drugs are stimulants (such as amphetamines), depressants (such as tranquilizers and sedatives), hallucinogens (such as LSD and PCP), and narcotics (such as heroin).

ore than a third of Americans over the age of 12 have used an illicit drug at least once.[78] The largest group of users are those in the 18–25 age group.[79] However, the message discouraging drug use *does* seem to have gotten through. "The proportion of college students who smoked marijuana at least once in 30 days went from one in three in 1980 to one in seven" in 1993, says one report. Moreover, "cocaine users dropped from 7% to 0.7% over the same period."[80] Even so, many students still do use illegal drugs, particularly marijuana. (*See* ■ *Panel 11.5.*)

WHAT'S THE REAL STORY ON DRUG USE?
In 1990 some University of California, Berkeley, researchers created an uproar among drug counselors when they released the results of a 15-year study. The investigators found that teenagers who had experimented casually with drugs appeared to be better adjusted than adolescents who either abstained or regularly abused drugs.[81,82] The teenagers the researchers labeled "experimenters" used no drug more than once a month, and no more than one drug other than marijuana. The frequent users used marijuana regularly, at least

PANEL 11.5

Drugs in college. A study by Harvard University's School of Public Health of 17,592 students on 140 U.S. campuses in 1993 found this picture of alcohol and other drug use.

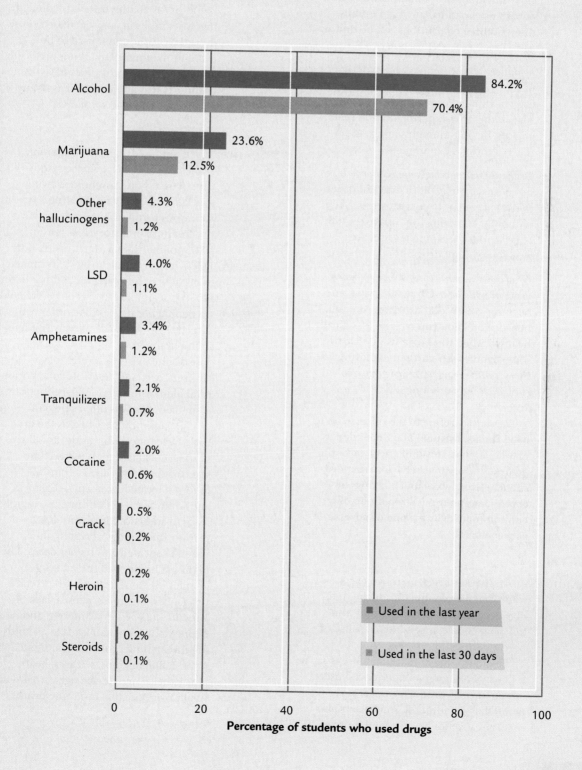

Percentage of students who used drugs

■ Used in the last year

■ Used in the last 30 days

Alcohol — 84.2% / 70.4%
Marijuana — 23.6% / 12.5%
Other hallucinogens — 4.3% / 1.2%
LSD — 4.0% / 1.1%
Amphetamines — 3.4% / 1.2%
Tranquilizers — 2.1% / 0.7%
Cocaine — 2.0% / 0.6%
Crack — 0.5% / 0.2%
Heroin — 0.2% / 0.1%
Steroids — 0.2% / 0.1%

once a week, and had tried several stronger drugs such as cocaine. The frequent users showed evidence early in life of psychological maladjustments, emotional mood swings, inattentiveness, stubbornness, insecurity, and other signs of emotional distress.

The Berkeley researchers insisted they did not mean to advocate drug experimentation, but many drug counselors were horrified anyway. Perhaps, though, three conclusions can be drawn:

- **Drug experimenters are not necessarily healthier:** Young people who experiment with drugs aren't necessarily psychologically healthier. Rather, the healthiest can survive the drug-experimentation years and are flexible enough to right themselves if they do experiment.

- **Drug experimentation is unnecessary:** It is not necessary to explore drugs in order to explore life or to combat stress. Techniques for achieving the "optimal experience" and for escaping tension are available without drugs.

- **Drug experimentation MAY lead to dependence or addiction:** Unfortunately, some beginning users don't survive. After all, how do you know you're "psychologically healthy" when you begin using? Clearly, some people who start out exploring life by experimenting with drugs do get caught in the trap of dependence or addiction.

    Dependence refers to the reliance on or need for a substance. The dependence may be physical, psychological, or both. **Addiction refers to a behavioral pattern characterized by compulsion, loss of control, and continued repetition of a behavior or activity in spite of adverse consequences.**

MARIJUANA. In the short run, marijuana acts somewhat like alcohol, producing feelings of relaxation and tranquility and, for some people, a heightened sense of perception.

The down side of marijuana use is as follows: (1) Among inexperienced users, marijuana may produce anxiety and paranoia.[83] In addition, some users also report headaches, nausea, and muscle tension. (2) It impairs psychomotor performance, so it's best not to drive a car while under the influence. (3) It may produce some psychological dependence. Heavy users who stop show such signs as sleep disturbance, irritability, and nausea.[84] (4) It may cause respiratory problems, such as chronic bronchitis and pulmonary disease.[85] (5) Some regular marijuana users have shown such behaviors as apathy, difficulty concentrating, lost ambition, and decreased sense of goals.[86] Although it used to be thought that marijuana is not physically addicting, some individuals have been found to be as addicted to it as to any other mind-altering substance.

COCAINE. "Even among drugs of considerable addiction potential, cocaine stands apart," writes one psychologist who specializes in studying the drug. "It is, in its various forms, the most destructive drug in human history. Not heroin, not LSD, not marijuana, not alcohol, not PCP—none of these drugs is as capable as cocaine of grabbing on and not letting go."[87] Cocaine exerts this powerful hold on people because, unlike other drugs, it directly stimulates the pleasure circuits in the brain.

Cocaine exists in several forms—regular, free-base, and crack. Regular cocaine is inhaled or injected. Free-base cocaine is smoked. Crack is often smoked.

The euphoria provided by the drug has a tremendous downside, as follows. (1) The cocaine high is followed by severe depression called a "crash," followed by anxiety, fatigue, shakiness, and withdrawal. (2) Cocaine use rapidly leads to addiction: In an attempt to recover the feelings of ecstasy, users require repeated and higher doses. The highs get higher, but the valleys get deeper. (3) Repeated use can produce headaches, shakiness, nausea, lack of appetite, loss of sexual interest, and depression. Addiction leads to all kinds of life-threatening problems: paranoid delusions, hallucinations, seizures, heart attack, heart-muscle damage, stroke—and finally overdose that can cause death.[88]

OTHER DRUGS. There is a whole host of other drugs, legal and illegal, which I don't have room to cover here in depth but which you may nevertheless come across:

■ **Stimulants:** I mentioned that *stimulants* stimulate the nervous system, raising the level of arousal. These drugs can be legal, such as coffee and nicotine, or illegal, such as cocaine.

  Amphetamines ("speed") are prescription drugs available illegally on the street. They may temporarily produce feelings of attentiveness and elation but later can produce paranoid delusions and disorganized behavior.

■ **Depressants:** *Depressants* are drugs such as tranquilizers (Valium) and sedatives (sleep-inducers, such as barbiturates), which slow down or sedate the nervous system. Available legally by prescription, depressants also are sold illegally on the street. They first produce a relaxation of inhibitions, then drowsiness. In heavy dosages they can lead to anesthesia (absence of pain) and then to coma and death.

■ **Hallucinogens: *Hallucinogens*, or "psychedelics," are drugs that produce visual hallucinations.** Examples are *LSD* and *psilocybin*, which produce visual hallucinations. An extremely dangerous variant of hallucinogen is *PCP*, whose effects are unpredictable.

  Most hallucinogens do not seem to produce physical dependence. However, tolerance develops quickly, so that more of a drug is required to achieve the same effect. Reactions are highly individual, with some people suffering "bad trips" associated with paranoia and panic.

■ **Narcotics: *Narcotics* are drugs that produce numbness and euphoria and relieve pain and that are also highly addictive.** Examples are *morphine* and *heroin*. A milder variant is *codeine*, found in cough medicines, which is less addictive.

  Clearly, if one wants to escape pain or feel euphoric, there is no end to the artificial ways of doing so. But how many people who are "successful" using drugs seem to be successful in other aspects of their lives?

"What's a good alternative to drug and alcohol use?"

Name: Rachelle Boitschenko
Major: General Studies/Psychology
Interests: Medical field
Answer to question: "Well, I learned that alcohol puts on weight. People just do it because they enjoy the buzz and it's very sociable. But when I quit drinking to get back in shape, I didn't miss it at all. The best part of it is when you're drinking your cold ice tea, your friends are gaining weight and acting like animals. You're sitting there looking great and have much better judgments. For drugs, well, they're addicting. So if you don't try them, you won't miss a thing!"

Some Other Dependencies: Gambling, Spending, Codependency

PREVIEW "Process dependencies" or "process addictions" cover compulsive gambling, compulsive spending, and codependency.

In recent years, the words "dependence" and "addiction" have become broadly generalized to behavior other than drug use. That is, some experts are now applying these terms to "processes" rather than chemicals—areas such as compulsive gambling, spending, eating disorders, and sexual obsessions.[89] (Not all health-care professionals agree that these are true dependencies, however.)

Two important process dependencies are gambling and spending.

COMPULSIVE GAMBLING. The rates of gambling by college students seem to be higher than among the adult population. A survey of 2000 college students in six states found that 87% had gambled. Moreover, 25% had gambled weekly, and 11% had gambled more than $100 in one day. Some amounts ranged up to $50,000 in one week![90] About 5.7% were described as having pathological gambling behavior, including repeatedly betting in hopes of winning big to make up for losses and continuing to gamble despite inability to pay debts. The study found that several students frequently gambled money set aside for college tuition.[91]

Once-in-a-while gamblers can have a little fun without spending a fortune, as I do when I visit my friends in Nevada. The trick is to designate a certain sum for betting purposes only (whether $10 or $50) and when that is gone, to spend no more. Compulsive gamblers may find help with Gamblers Anonymous.

COMPULSIVE SPENDING. Like other people, I occasionally make impulsive purchases for reasons that have nothing to do with the need for the specific object purchased. Maybe it's to cheer myself up when I'm feeling a bit down, for example. However, compulsive spenders repeatedly engage in impulse buying. Buying things becomes an activity used to provide feelings of self-assurance and self-worth and to help the buyer escape feelings of anxiety and despair. Not surprisingly, compulsive spenders often become compulsive debtors, who continually borrow money from institutions, family, and friends to pay their bills.

Characteristics of compulsive buyers are the following.[92]

(1) They are very anxious and depressed.

(2) They often buy for other people.

(3) They may be "binge buyers," "daily shoppers," or "multiple buyers." People who are binge buyers may go off on a shopping binge only occasionally, perhaps triggered by an upsetting event. Daily shoppers go shopping every day and become upset if they do not. Multiple buyers, a less common type, repeatedly buy several of the same item (perhaps because they like the sales clerk).

Many people have trouble handling money, and with credit cards now so easily available to students, the temptations also affect those of traditional college age. To guard against excess expenditures, you need to inject rationality into the shopping process. For example, you can draw up plans for shopping, ask others to do the shopping, shop only when feeling calm, or destroy all credit cards. Resources such as Debtors Anonymous are also available.

CODEPENDENTS. *Codependents* were originally considered to be spouses of alcoholics, but the term now covers others close to an alcoholic family member. The chief characteristic of codependents is that they tend to accommodate themselves to the alcoholic. In the last few years, the term "codependents" has been extended to people in families troubled by other addictions or compulsions, such as gambling or food.

Codependency rests on the idea that the *family* is more important than the *individual* within that family. Alcoholism and other addictions are considered family illnesses because of the tremendous impact that addicts have on those around them.

Some of the characteristics associated with codependents are as follows.

(1) They become concerned with others and neglect themselves. They base their self-esteem on what others think of them and organize their lives according to others' expectations of them. They become supporting actors to the major player, the addict. Their urge to help others becomes subsumed in an obsession with other people, so that they lose their own identity and self-worth.

(2) Failing to control the addiction itself, they become obsessed with protecting the family and the addict from intervention or knowledge by others outside the family. By becoming "enablers" of the addict and sparing him or her from the consequences of addiction, they actually allow the cycle of pain to persist.

Probably nothing will change in the family system until the codependent realizes that rescuing the addict isn't really helping either of them. Once the codependent stops making excuses, the addict will have to face his or her own problem. Some codependents may be able to establish their independence by themselves, but many will need to reach out and get help. The principal self-help Twelve-Step group is Co-Dependents Anonymous (CoDA). Other groups, such as Al-Anon, Nar-Anon, and Gam-Anon, are designed for codependents involved with specific types of addicts and addictions.

> **"Probably nothing will change until the codependent realizes that rescuing the addict isn't really helping either of them."**

GROUP ACTIVITY #11.2

IDENTIFYING SOME LEGAL DEPENDENCIES

With other students in a small group, identify as many *legal* dependencies as possible. (Don't list illegal drugs.) Also identify the reasons you think people develop such dependencies. Select two from the list and develop plans for reducing their dependence. Share your first list and your strategy with the rest of the class.

What are the major dependencies identified by the class? What do you think of the reasons suggested for why people develop dependencies? Do you think people choose dependencies of their own free will?

Feelings about parts of the body. This chart shows the percentage of respondents in a sampling of college students who reported very strong negative feelings about specific parts of their bodies. Women reported negative feelings at a significantly higher rate than men.

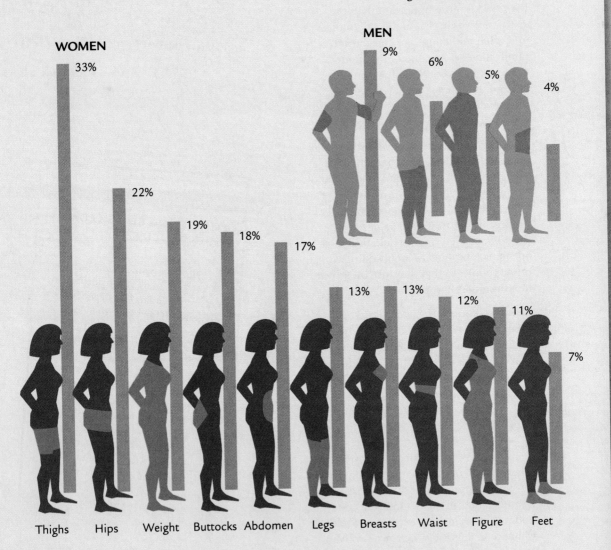

WOMEN

33%

22%

19%

18%

17%

13%

13%

12%

11%

7%

MEN

9%

6%

5%

4%

Thighs   Hips   Weight   Buttocks   Abdomen   Legs   Breasts   Waist   Figure   Feet

Looking Good: Weight & Energy Balance

PREVIEW Most women are self-critical of their looks, men are less so. Important factors in body image are size and weight. Standards for "cosmetically desirable" weight have changed. Obsessions with dieting often produce "yo-yo" (repetitious) ineffective weight loss and gain cycles. To maintain desirable weight, you need to understand the concept of energy balance.

I f you're like most people, you think you're less than perfectly attractive. Even handsome people feel they're flawed.

You have only to look to advertising and the mass media for comparison. Today the average model, dancer, and actress, for example, weighs 23% less than the average American woman. Moreover, she is thinner *than 95% of women.*[93] Is that what ordinary people are supposed to aspire to? Fortunately, the standard seems to be changing again. In recent years, a new look has become popular, among both women and men. It is no longer desirable to be thin but rather to be *muscular and fit.*[94]

HOW DO YOU FEEL ABOUT YOUR BODY?

Women and men college students have been found to have different kinds of feelings about their bodies. *(See Panel 11.6.)*

■ *Women:* In general, college women are highly self-critical, especially about their thighs, hips, and weight. Men are actually less critical of women than women are of themselves. Indeed, men actually prefer women who are heavier than women think is attractive.[95,96]

■ *Men:* College men tend to overestimate their own attractiveness or are relatively tolerant of their physical drawbacks, such as being overweight.

When it comes to their looks, people may be self-conscious about their skin, hair, teeth, having to wear glasses, or other attributes. In general, however, the most important matters bearing on body image appear to be *size and weight.*

What about you? Do you worry about your weight? Before reading on, look at Personal Exploration #11.3 and see how much you *should* weigh.

PERSONAL EXPLORATION #11.3

HOW MUCH SHOULD YOU WEIGH?

T he following heights (feet and inches) and weights (in pounds) are without clothes or shoes. Higher weights generally apply to men, lower to women. These guidelines allow for weight gain as you grow older.

■ DIRECTIONS

Weigh yourself without clothes and shoes. Write here how much you weigh: _____

Then look at the table. Write here how much you should weigh: _____

HEIGHT	19–34 YEARS	35 YEARS AND OVER
5'0"	7–128	108–138
5'1"	101–132	111–143
5'2"	104–137	115–148
5'3"	107–141	119–152
5'4"	111–146	122–157
5'5"	114–150	126–162
5'6"	118–155	130–167
5'7"	121–160	134–172
5'8"	125–161	138–178
5'9"	129–169	142–183
5'10"	132–174	146–188
5'11"	136–179	151–194
6'0"	140–184	155–199
6'1"	144–189	159–205
6'2"	148–195	164–210
6'3"	152–200	168–216
6'4"	156–205	173–222
6'5"	160–211	177–228
6'6"	164–216	182–234

THE CONCERN WITH WEIGHT. *Half* of all Americans (particularly women) think they are overweight, although only a fourth actually are.[97] As you read this, half of American women (50% not even overweight) and a quarter of American men are dieting to lose weight.[98] Nearly a third of American women ages 19–39 diet *at least once a month.*[99] This means that a significant proportion of the rest must be *putting on* weight, because up to 95% of dieters are unable to keep their weight off.

This cycle of weight loss and weight gain is called the <u>*yo-yo syndrome*</u>**, and it shows that dieting doesn't really work.** Indeed, yo-yo dieters may lose fat from one part of the body, but they tend to gain it back somewhere else.[100] Other obsessions and behavior patterns with food and weight can be even more hazardous. (*See* ■ *Panel 11.7.*)

HOW TO LOOK GOOD: THE CONCEPT OF ENERGY BALANCE. *"Low on calories!"* We seem to see that claim wherever we go—in food ads and on the grocery shelves. A few years ago, however, I realized I wasn't sure what a "calorie" was, so I did a little research.

A *calorie* is the unit of heat used to measure the energy potential of food. *Energy* is defined as "the capacity to do work." What this means is simply this: *The body takes in calories from food and expends them in "work"—namely, physical activity.*

Ideally, you should have what is called "energy balance." <u>**Energy balance**</u> **is the state in which the calories expended are the same as the calories consumed.** If the calories you eat are not expended in activity, you will *gain* weight. If you don't consume enough calories for the energy you expend, you will *lose* weight.

No doubt, some people are obese because they eat too much. But that's only half the story. As we see from the concept of energy balance, the calories expended are as important as the calories consumed. Not being physically active enough, in fact, may be *the* most important reason that one out of four adults in the United States is obese.

So how many calories do you actually need from food in order to look good? That depends on your sex, age, frame, percentage of body fat, and level of activity. For example:

■ *For women:* If you are 20 years old, 5 feet 4 inches tall, weigh about 120 pounds, and generally engage in only light activity, you need 1700–2500 calories a day to maintain your weight.

■ *For men:* If you are 20 years old, 5 feet 10 inches tall, weigh about 154 pounds, and engage in only light activity, you need 2500–3300 calories a day.

"Light activity" means that you spend 2 hours a day in light physical activity, ranging from putting on your clothes to fixing dinner. Beyond that, it is assumed you walk for 2 hours a day, stand for 5, sit for 7, and sleep or lie down for 8. People who are more active will need more calories than the above; so will people who are taller. Shorter people will need less; so will older people.

Here, finally, is the bottom line—the formula for looking good.

1. Don't think you have to look thinner or weigh less than is appropriate for your height and size.

2. Observe the concept of *energy balance:* don't eat any more in calories than you can expend in physical activity.

3. To achieve the "new look" of being muscular and fit, take part in physical activity.

Obsessing about food, weight, and looks. Food is supposed to bring us pleasure, but for some people it brings pain. This is clear with the principal eating disorders—obesity, anorexia nervosa, and bulimia.

Obesity: Obesity is being 20% or more over normal weight for your height and frame. About one out of four Americans is obese: 15% of adolescents and 26% of adults. These people experience not only the social and psychological problems resulting from people's rejection but also a range of health difficulties (from back and knee problems to heart and blood-vessel disorders to respiratory problems to diabetes and cancer).

Joining a self-help group, such as Overeaters Anonymous, is often a useful way of doing something about the problem while simultaneously alleviating feelings of isolation.

Anorexia: Some people (about 1% of women, but also some men) suffer such a fear of fatness that they starve themselves in order to be thin, sometimes going down 15% from normal body weight. This self-starvation is called anorexia nervosa, or simply "anorexia" (pronounced "an-uh-*reck*-see-uh"). Anorexia characteristically develops during the teen years or the twenties and can lead to malnutrition and even death. Anorexics are often rigid and perfectionistic, are often model students and daughters, and are highly achievement-oriented.

Although they frequently deny their symptoms and resist doing anything about them, about 70% of anorexics who are treated with psychotherapy, drug therapy, and behavior-change techniques recover or are improved.

Bulimia: Bulimia nervosa, or simply "bulimia" (pronounced "buh-*lim*-ee-uh"), consists of episodes of binge eating alternating with purging. (Purging means self-induced vomiting or use of laxatives or pills.) The group at greatest risk is women, mostly in their teens and twenties, though some men are also bulimic. Bulimics are inclined to be people-pleasers who do not deal easily with their feelings.

Although bulimics wait an average of 5 $\frac{1}{2}$ years before seeking help, they may be successfully treated with techniques similar to those used to fight anorexia.

Fitting in fitness. Fitness can be worked into your daily life. A 150-pound person following a program that mixes physical activity with chores can expend an extra 1500–2000 calories per week.

Activities	Calories
Monday	
Brisk walking, to and from work, 30 minutes	160
Stair climbing, 5 minutes	35
Tuesday	
Cycling, stationary, 15 minutes (10 mph)	105
Wednesday	
Brisk walking, to and from work, 30 minutes	160
Thursday	
30 minutes at gym:	
Stair climbing, fast, 10 minutes	85
Rowing, on machine, 10 minutes	65
Running, treadmill, 10 minutes	95
Friday	
Swimming, 20 minutes	180
Cycling, 20 minutes	135
Saturday	
Brisk walking, 15 minutes	80
Gardening, 20 minutes	110
Housecleaning, 20 minutes	80
Sunday	
Brisk walking, 15 minutes	80
Mowing lawn, 20 minutes	150
Raking grass and yard work, 20 minutes	135
Washing car, 20 minutes	65
Grand total (in about 5 hours)	**1800**

How much physical activity is required? Energy-expenditure requirements vary for each person. Nevertheless, a study of men who expended only 2000 *extra* calories per week in physical activity than their inactive counterparts found they were healthier and lived longer.[101] My guess is they also looked a whole lot better.

An extra 2000 calories a week isn't a lot, and this kind of activity can easily be worked into your life. For instance, a 150-pound person could burn about this many calories just by mixing physical exercise and chores over the course of 5 hours in a week. Physical activity could be walking or bicycling to class. Chores could be housecleaning or gardening. (*See* ■ *Panel 11.8.*)

Feeling Good: The Benefits of Being Active

PREVIEW Physical activity can enhance your mood, energy, and creativity; keep weight down; and reduce heart-disease and cancer risks.

I stated that being in college can be very stressful. But I also know from my experience that this is where physical activity can truly help. Indeed, I find activity a feel-good pill that can lift my spirits and my energy level.

HOW ACTIVITY MAKES YOU FEEL GOOD.

Some of the benefits of activity are as follows:

- **Anxiety and tension relief:** Physical activity provides a means of releasing yourself from anger, anxiety, and tension.[102–104] One study investigated men and women ages 30–49 who walked at slow, medium, fast, and self-selected paces. The researchers found that, regardless of the pace, all the walkers felt "immediate and significant decrease in anxiety and tension." Moreover, the improved moods lasted up to 2 hours after the workout ended.[105]

- **Alleviation of depression:** In one experiment, a group of mildly and moderately depressed patients were assigned randomly to one of two groups—those who would receive psychotherapy and those who would take up running. The runners felt better after only a week, and were declared "virtually well" within three weeks, with the benefits lasting at least a year. The runners were reported to do as well as the patients receiving short-term psychotherapy and to do better than those receiving long-term psychotherapy.[106–109]

- **Increased energy:** Even just a brisk 10-minute walk can increase energy and decrease fatigue for as long as 2 hours.[110] Thus, when you have an afternoon slump, you'll probably find a short, vigorous walk will pick you up better than, say, a candy bar.[111]

- **Stimulation of creative thinking:** Some people who exercise are able to let their minds "take a vacation" from the worries at hand.[112] (I find this happening to me.) Studies suggest that exercise can sharpen mental skills and enhance creativity. Even a single 20-minute session of aerobic dance can increase creative problem-solving abilities.[113]

Physical activity is the principal way to keep your weight at its desirable levels. It also has a whole bunch of health benefits: It probably reduces the risk of heart disease.[114–118] It may reduce the risk of cancer and diabetes.[119] Among women, it may reduce the risk of osteoporosis, a bone-crumbling disorder that often leads to hip fractures in later life.[120]

FITNESS & FUN.

You notice that, in general, I have used the term "physical activity" rather than "exercise" throughout. A lot of people think that exercise is an "odious, sweat-soaked endeavor," to quote two writers on the subject. Physical activity, on the other hand, "can be any daily undertaking, work or play, that involves movement."[121]

Actually, exercise need not be unpleasant. Indeed, whatever you choose to call it, this kind of activity should be something you *want* to do. Personal fitness is not about punishment—forget the expression "No pain, no gain." Rather, it's about *fun* and *feeling good*. The idea is not to think of exercise as training for "how far, how fast." Rather, you need to build in a strong component of fun. You need to remind yourself that exercise not only improves your health but also makes you *feel better*.

Perhaps, however, you want to go beyond various kinds of movement and into a *program* of physical fitness. **Physical fitness is defined as having above-average (1) flexibility, (2) aerobic endurance, and (3) muscle strength and endurance.** Here's what I mean:

- *Flexibility: Flexibility* is suppleness of movement—your ability to touch your toes or twist your body without discomfort, for instance. Flexibility is achieved through various stretching exercises.

- *Aerobic endurance: Aerobic endurance* describes how efficiently your body uses oxygen and is able to pump blood through your heart and blood vessels. Aerobic endurance is achieved by high-intensity workouts such as jogging or running or vigorous swimming, rowing, dancing, or bicycling. (I enjoy jogging and cross-country skiing myself.)

- *Muscle strength and endurance: Muscle strength* is the ability to exert force against resistance, whether standing up from a chair or lifting a free weight. *Muscle endurance* is the ability to keep repeating those muscle exertions, so that you can scoop not just one but several shovels full of snow. Muscle strength and endurance is achieved through *resistance training:* doing sit-ups, lifting free weights, working out on weight machines.

If you're interested in getting into some of these activities, consider signing up for some classes.

Peak Performance with a Power Diet

PREVIEW Avoid fats and oil, which lower energy and make you gain weight. Avoid sugar, which provides energy but no nutrients. Eat complex carbohydrates, such as vegetables and fruits. Eat a variety of foods. Avoid salt and junk foods; women should take calcium and iron.

College takes a lot of energy and stamina. Physical activity helps, but a power diet will boost your productivity or athletic performance even further. It will also lower your chances of getting heart disease or cancer.

How good is your diet now? To find out, try Personal Exploration #11.4.

THE EATING SMART QUIZ: HOW HEALTHY IS YOUR DIET?

How do you rate? This is a quick, simple eating quiz for all ages which looks at how your eating patterns compare to the American Cancer Society's guidelines. Below each category of food are examples. When rating yourself, think of foods similar to those listed that are in your diet.

■ DIRECTIONS

Circle the number of points for the answer you choose in the points column at the far right. Total your points. Compare your score with the analysis at the end of the quiz.

YOUR POINTS

Oils and fats: butter, margarine, shortening, mayonnaise, sour cream, lard, oil, salad dressing.

■ I always add these to foods in cooking and/or at the table.   0

■ I occasionally add these to foods in cooking and/or at the table.   1

■ I rarely add these to foods in cooking and/or at the table.   2

■ I eat fried foods 3 or more times a week.   0

■ I eat fried foods 1–2 times a week.   1

■ I rarely eat fried foods.   2

Dairy products:

■ I drink whole milk.   0

■ I drink 1%–2% fat-free milk.   1

■ I drink skim milk.   2

■ I eat ice cream almost every day.   0

■ I eat ice milk, low-fat frozen yogurt, and sherbet.   1

■ I eat only fruit ices, seldom eat frozen dairy desserts.   2

■ I eat most high-fat cheese (jack, cheddar, Colby, Swiss, cream).   0

■ I eat both low- and high-fat cheeses.   1

■ I eat mostly low-fat cheeses (2% cottage, skim milk mozzarella).   2

Snacks: potato chips, corn chips, nuts, buttered popcorn, candy bars.

■ I eat these every day.   0

■ I eat some occasionally.   1

■ I seldom or never eat these snacks.   2

Baked goods: pies, cakes, sweet rolls, doughnuts.

■ I eat them 5 or more times a week.   0

■ I eat them 2–4 times a week.   1

■ I seldom eat baked goods or eat only low-fat baked goods.   2

Poultry and fish:*

■ I rarely eat these foods.   0

■ I eat them 1–2 times a week.   1

■ I eat them 3 or more times a week.   2

Low-fat meat:* extra-lean hamburger, round steak, pork loin, roast, tenderloin, chuck roast.

■ I rarely eat these foods.   0

■ I eat these foods occasionally.   1

■ I eat mostly fat-trimmed red meats.   2

High-fat meat:* luncheon meats, bacon, hot dogs, sausage, steak, regular and lean ground beef.

■ I eat these every day.   0

■ I eat these foods occasionally.   1

■ I rarely eat these foods.   2

Cured and smoked meat and fish:* luncheon meats, hot dogs, bacon, ham and other smoked or pickled meats and fish.

■ I eat these foods 4 or more times a week.   0

■ I eat some 1–3 times a week.   1

■ I seldom eat these foods.   2

Legumes: dried beans and peas: kidney, navy, lima, pinto, garbanzo, split-pea, lentil.

■ I eat legumes less than once a week.   0

■ I eat these foods 1–2 times a week.   1

■ I eat them 3 or more times a week.   2

Whole grains and cereals: whole-grain breads, brown rice, pasta, whole-grain cereals.

■ I seldom eat such foods.   0

■ I eat them 2–3 times a day.   1

■ I eat them 4 or more times daily.   2

Vitamin C–rich fruits and vegetables: citrus fruits and juices, green peppers, strawberries, tomatoes.

■ I seldom eat them.   0

■ I eat them 3–5 times a week.   1

■ I eat them 1–2 times a day.   2

Vegetables of the cabbage family: broccoli, cabbage, brussels sprouts, cauliflower.

■ I seldom eat them.   0

■ I eat them 1–2 times a week.   1

■ I eat them 3–4 times a week.   2

Alcohol:

■ I drink more than 2 ounces of 80-proof liquor daily. (Alcohol equivalents: 2 oz. of 80-proof liquor = $6\frac{1}{2}$ oz. wine OR 18 oz. beer OR 25 oz. 3.2 beer.)   0

■ I drink alcohol every week, but not daily.   1

■ I occasionally or never drink alcohol.   2

Personal weight:

■ I'm more than 20 pounds over my ideal weight.   0

■ I'm 10–20 pounds over my ideal weight.   1

■ I'm within 10 pounds of my ideal weight.   2

*If you do not eat meat, fish, or poultry, give yourself a 2 for each meat category.

Total score: _____

■ HOW DO YOU RATE?

0–12 points: A warning. Your diet is too high in fat and too low in fiber-rich foods. It would be wise to assess your eating habits to see where you could make improvements.

13–17 points: Not bad! You're partway there. You still have a way to go.

18–36 points: Good for you! You're eating smart. You should feel very good about yourself. You have been careful to limit your fats and to eat a varied diet. Keep up the good habits and continue to look for ways to improve.

■ REMEMBER

A poor score does not mean you will get cancer, nor does a high score guarantee that you won't. But your score will give you a clue as to how you eat now and where you need to improve to reduce your cancer risks.

■ IMPORTANT

This eating quiz is for self-information and does not evaluate your intake of essential vitamins, minerals, protein, or calories. If your diet is restricted in some ways (for example, you are a vegetarian or have allergies), you may want to get professional advice.

GROUP ACTIVITY OPTION

In either large or small groups, discuss the results of this Personal Exploration. How much of your diet is based solely on the fact that "I only eat what tastes good"? How much is based on factors of cost? of availability? Suppose you were going to give up just *one* unhealthy food that you eat regularly (such as candy bars). What would you try to eat instead that would come close to providing the same reward?

There are really no secrets to eating right, and the rules are not very hard. They have been summarized by the federal government in an illustration known as the Food Guide Pyramid. *(See* ■ *Panel 11.9.)*

Here are some recommendations for a power diet.

1. GO EASY ON FOODS OF ANIMAL ORIGIN. Meat and dairy products are responsible for dietary fat, artery-clogging cholesterol, and a great many weight-adding calories. Try to revise your food choices so you eat less meat (particularly red meat), cheese (try low-fat cheese), greasy potato chips, ice cream (which contains fat), and the like.

Particularly to be avoided are *fats and oils.* Too much fat also makes people overweight and lowers their energy level. Fats and oils have been linked to cancer and heart and blood-vessel disease. Nutritionists feel strongly about the undesirability of fats and oils. Indeed, the Food Guide Pyramid shows these foods to not even be considered a "food group" and should be eaten only sparingly.

Different foods have different amounts of fat. Fat is low or nonexistent in fruits, vegetables, and grain products and high in foods of animal origin. *Visible fats* are fairly easy to spot. They are almost anything greasy—butter, margarine, shortening, cooking and salad oils, and the "marbling" in steak and other red meat. *Invisible fats* are harder to identify. The major sources are meat, poultry, fish, and dairy products. Invisible fats are also frequently added during the preparation of food. Examples are fried foods, butter on baked potatoes, foods in cream sauces, or anything deep-fried in batter.

2. GO EASY ON SUGAR. Sugar provides energy but no nutrients. Moderate sugar intake with meals is all right. However, most of it should come not from high-sugar foods such as candy but from "natural sugar" sources, such as fruits. In addition, you should drink water, not sugary soft drinks.

3. EAT PERFORMANCE FUEL: COMPLEX CARBOS. **Complex carbohydrates** **are foods such as whole grains, barley, whole-wheat pasta, vegetables, and fruit.** Athletes of all sorts eat large quantities of these to provide the body's main energy fuel, glycogen, to sustain intense physical activity. Fat and protein do not produce glycogen; carbohydrates do. (Complex carbos also provide *fiber,* helpful in preventing and alleviating constipation and certain intestinal disorders.) Sports nutritionists recommend a high-performance diet that is less protein and fat and principally carbohydrates—bread, cereal, pasta, vegetables, and fruits.[122,123]

4. EAT A VARIETY OF FOODS. Unless you have a highly imbalanced diet, you probably won't need vitamin and mineral supplements. Even athletes and other high-energy individuals can get needed vitamins from a low-fat, high-complex-carbohydrate diet—provided they eat a *variety of foods.* (This is what is called a "balanced diet.")

5. AVOID SALT, TAKE CALCIUM & IRON, AVOID JUNK. A few other tips round out the the recommendations for a power diet:

■ *Avoid salt:* Too much salt may raise blood pressure, at least in some people. High blood pressure is an indicator of potential heart disease.

■ *Women—take calcium and iron:* To avoid the bone disorder of osteoporosis in later life, women should take calcium supplements. To forestall anemia, they should also take iron.

■ *To avoid fatigue, eat frequently but avoid junk foods:* You may prefer five or six smaller meals to three large ones, if you expend a lot of energy. "Grazing" on low-fat, nutritious foods may help avoid that drowsy letdown that often follows a big lunch.[124] If you eat every few hours and eat before you get too hungry, it will keep you from being overwhelmed by hunger and gorging.

However, chips, ice cream, cookies, and the like are not low-fat and are not performance boosters. Better are fruit, vegetables, yogurt, bread sticks, unbuttered popcorn, juices, whole-grain crackers, and similar high-complex-carbohydrate items.

PANEL 11.9

The Food Guide Pyramid: How to eat. The food groups you need the least of are at the top; those you can use more of are in the bigger areas at the bottom. You can use lots of bread, cereal, and pasta, and plenty of fruits and vegetables. You need a certain amount of protein—milk, cheese, meat, and beans. Fats and sweets (top layer) are not even considered a food group and are to be eaten sparingly.

Fats, oils, and sweets
—*Not a food group*—
Use sparingly

Milk, yogurt, and cheese
2–3 servings

Meat, poultry, fish, dry beans, eggs, and nuts
2–3 servings

Vegetables
3–5 servings

Fruits
2–4 servings

Bread, cereal, rice, and pasta
6-11 servings (per day)

Recharging Time: Sleep & Rest

PREVIEW Your body's built-in sleep and energy cycle is an important factor in alertness. Many people neglect the sleep and rest they need, suffering a "sleep deficit" resulting in lowered performance. To get enough rest, you should follow regular sleep habits and bedtime rituals.

hat's the best way to pull an all-nighter? This is a question I hope you won't have to address, because the whole purpose of this book is to make it so you don't have to. Nevertheless, suppose you find that you have roughly 24 hours to prepare for a test or write a paper. Should you plug in the coffeemaker, hit the books, and then catch a 4:00 A.M. snooze before going to class? Actually, if you take a short nap before staying awake all night, you'll avoid sleepiness and your performance will be better.[125]

This is an example of how a little knowledge can enable you to manipulate your internal clock to further your performance.

UNDERSTANDING YOUR BODY'S INNER RHYTHMS. An important physiological cycle in your life is your body's built-in clock (called your *circadian* clock) that determines your individual sleep-wake cycle. This internal clock explains why you may feel a gradual rise in energy through the morning, with a peak around noon, and a drop in energy in mid-afternoon. You may then feel a rise in early evening, followed by a decline in energy until sleep.[126] The internal clock also explains why you may get sleepy after lunch, which is often halfway between your usual wake-up and bedtime hours. Finally, it may explain the Sunday afternoon blues. This is a mild depression that may happen because people disrupt their inner rhythms on weekends by staying up late and rising later.[127]

If you get a sense of your own body's rhythms, you can match your most demanding tasks (such as studying) to your peak-performance hours. Because of their internal rhythms, many people feel they are "night people," who do their best work at night. These are usually people under 40; as people grow older, most turn into "morning people."[128]

USING SLEEP TO YOUR ADVANTAGE. Sleep researchers say that people's sleep needs vary, although most adults seem to do their best work by sleeping 7–8 hours.[129] In general, most people need $7\frac{1}{2}$ to $8\frac{1}{2}$ hours of sleep per night. A small percentage, however, can get by on 5 or 6 hours and another small percentage need 9 or 10.

More than 100 million Americans get by with insufficient sleep—nearly every other adult and teenager.[130] Indeed, sleep experts have found that most people get 60–90 minutes less sleep each night than they should. However, this kind of "sleep deficit" can have important consequences. Even one night's loss of 2 hours' sleep is supposedly not made up during the following 5–6 days of normal sleep.[131] Sleep deprivation can lead to difficulty in concentration, fatigue, and poor performance on a variety of tasks.[132]

There are a number of things you can do to sleep better, as described in the accompanying box. *(See ■ Panel 11.10.)* If you have chronic insomnia, however, you should see a doctor.

GROUP ACTIVITY #11.4

SHARING SLEEP PROBLEMS & TIPS

Make a list of situations that cause you sleep difficulty. Then with others in a small group, share your list. Which problems seem to be commonplace? What are ways of dealing with them?

Tips for sleeping better.

Follow a regular sleep schedule: You don't have to go to bed at the same time every night, but you should try to get up at the same time every morning.

Save your bed for sleeping: The idea is to make sure bed is associated in your mind with sleep and not with such activities as studying or afternoon snacks.

Develop a bedtime routine: Develop bedtime rituals to allow yourself to wind down before sleep. Soak in a bath. Read a book. After turning out the light, give yourself 15 minutes to drift off to sleep. If you don't become drowsy, don't stay in bed; get up and go into another room and read for a while until you feel sleepy.

Watch what and when you drink and smoke: Caffeine is a stimulant, so drinking coffee or caffeinated soft drinks after midday may affect your sleep. Nicotine is also a stimulant and won't help you sleep. Alcohol, even in small amounts, can make you sleep less soundly. A glass of warm milk before bedtime may help you relax.

Deal with worries before you go to bed: If you find yourself lying awake worrying about a problem, write down what you can do about it in the morning. Also write down a list of reasons why it's not worth being upset about it now.

Exercise at regular times: Try to get at least some exercise every day. Although vigorous exercise is not recommended just before bedtime, a short evening walk may be helpful.

Minimize distractions: Try to eliminate distracting bedtime noises, or mask them with a soothing noise, such as music or the hum of a fan. Use heavy shades to darken your bedroom so you won't be awakened prematurely by the morning's first light.

Minimize use of sleeping pills: The effects achieved by most sleeping pills usually last only 2–4 weeks. Moreover, they only help you fall asleep faster, but do not help you achieve deep sleep. They also leave a hangover effect in the morning and decrease your alertness. Thus, if you must take a sleeping pill, try to limit yourself to one per week.

11:00pm

Onward: Applying This Chapter to Your Life

PREVIEW Your body is not expendable.

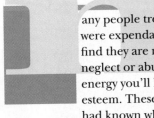

any people treat their bodies as if they were expendable, but in the end they find they are not. Probably the more you neglect or abuse your health, the less energy you'll have as well as less self-esteem. These are facts I certainly wish I had known when I was in college. Sooner or later, we all learn we have to take care of Number One.

Of course, on some level of consciousness you probably know this. Now's the time to put this knowledge into practice. What two specific things did you learn in this chapter that you could adopt for better taking care of yourself? Write them down here:

_____

_____

_____

_____

_____

_____

_____

_____

_____

_____

_____

_____

_____

_____

_____

1. What kind of psychological reactions do you have to stress (for example, irritability, impatience, depression)? What kind of physiological reactions do you have to stress (for example, insomnia, upset stomach, tiredness)? List your reactions and compare them to those of other students. What kinds of things can you do to reduce the feelings of stress?

2. Give some thought to the whole matter of "partying," or heavy drinking (and drugging). How much of it do you see around you? Have you been affected by it? How about your own drinking/drugging habits? Do you routinely get intoxicated or high? Has it affected your academic work or relations with others?

3. Consider your eating habits. Do you have a balanced diet? Is it high in fats? Do you weigh too much? What is *one thing* you could do every day that would put you onto a healthier diet?

4. Do you exercise regularly? If not, list all the reasons why you don't, such as feelings of embarrassment, don't know how to begin, and so on. What *one thing* could you do this week that would get you started?

relationships

the important other side of life

can you deal successfully with other people?

IN THIS CHAPTER: Some students think as much—or more—about their relationships as they do about their academic work. How you deal with other people—particularly love relationships—can have a lot of bearing on your happiness. In this chapter, we consider the following:

■ **Relationships and communication:** The nature of intimate relationships and how to handle conflict

■ **Assertiveness:** Assertiveness versus aggressiveness and nonassertiveness

■ **Unwanted sex:** From sexual harassment to rape

■ **Sexually transmitted diseases:** Especially HIV and AIDS

■ **Safer sex and contraception:** Rules for safer sex and birth control

What are the two most important personal issues in life?

ove and work, said psychologist Sigmund Freud. Or *"romance and finance,"* as I've heard other people put it.

What about you? Are relationships and career issues important matters in *your* life? I know they certainly are for me. Ending war, poverty, and disease are certainly of greater significance for humankind in general, of course. However, for most people the two most important *personal* issues are love and work.

We considered money issues in Chapter 10 and take up career matters in the final chapter. Here let's look at that important other side of life: relationships.

Intimate Relationships: From Being a Friend to Being in Love

PREVIEW Intimate relationships include friendship but also various kinds of intimacy. Love may be of five types: passionate (romantic), erotic (sexual), dependent (addictive), friendship (companionate), and altruistic (unselfish). Loss of love means having to deal with feelings of rejection and rebuilding self-esteem.

many psychologists seem to measure mental well-being by the success of our relationships with others. Let us examine the range of relationship possibilities.

FRIENDSHIP & INTIMACY. *Friendship* **is a relationship between two people that involves a high degree of trust and mutual support.** Friendship is important throughout your life. People's well-being seems to depend on the quality of social interaction they have with friends as well as with family.[1]

Many studies find better health among people who can turn to friends or family for affection, advice, empathy, assistance, and affirmation. They are more likely to survive major life challenges such as heart attacks and major surgery than those without such support. They are also less likely to develop cancer, respiratory infections, and other diseases.[2] Friends can help reaffirm your self-worth when you suffer life's disappointments or your good opinion of yourself is challenged.

Friendships can be close and may or may not involve intimacy. To some people, the word "intimate" means having sex. However, *intimacy* **is defined as a close, familiar, affectionate, and loving relationship with another person.**[3,4] Intimacy can take many forms.

People may share interests, ideas, or recreational activities. They may share closeness of feeling or closeness developed through physical contact.

Many adult returning students are fortunate because they already have family who support their efforts. Others, however, find that school in fact negatively affects their relationships with family members, who may resent the time being taken away from them. Still others, such as the divorced or widowed, may look for supportive friends on campus, perhaps with students in similar circumstances. Regardless of age, going to college generally changes the nature of existing relationships.

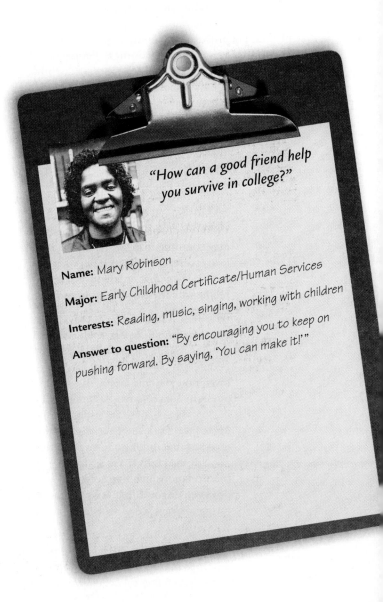

"How can a good friend help you survive in college?"

Name: Mary Robinson

Major: Early Childhood Certificate/Human Services

Interests: Reading, music, singing, working with children

Answer to question: "By encouraging you to keep on pushing forward. By saying, 'You can make it!'"

LOVE. What is love? The reason there is so much confusion about love is that this one word is used to describe a multitude of feelings.

Professor F. Philip Rice describes five types of love—*romantic, erotic, dependent, friendship,* and *altruistic.* Together they make up what he calls *complete love.*[5]

■ *Infatuation, passionate, or romantic love:* When we experience that dizzying ecstasy and joy known as "falling in love," we are infatuated. *Infatuation* **is passionate love, or romantic love: passionate, strong feelings of affection for another person.** This kind of love is real enough in its physiological manifestations: pounding heart, breathlessness, sometimes the inability to eat or sleep.[6]

The reasons people fall in love are probably proximity, commonality, and perceived attractiveness. People become attracted to those they see frequently and who share similar attributes.[7] Physical attractiveness is also often important at first. Attractiveness is sometimes heightened by the perception of dangerous circumstances (which is why secret love may be so intense).[8,9]

In the end, infatuation or romantic love cannot be sustained. It becomes less wildly romantic and more rational, although deepening of feelings of love may continue to grow. Wildly emotional love evolves into the more low-keyed *companionate love* or friendship love, with **feelings of friendly affection and deep attachment.**[10,11]

■ *Erotic love: Erotic love* **is sexual love,** but not necessarily romantic love. Many people can have sex without romantic love; indeed, some are unable to handle emotional involvement. Others find that having sex actually diminishes the feelings of romantic love. Yet others find that tensions that diminish loving feelings also adversely affect the sexual aspect of their relationship. Many couples, however, discover that their sexual and loving feelings blend and enhance their relationship.

■ *Dependent love: Dependent love* **is love that develops in response to previously unmet psychological needs.** For instance, someone who got little praise as a child may have an intense psychological need for appreciation met by the beloved. Or a studious person may welcome appreciation for his or her playfulness.[12]

At its extreme, this kind of love can become an addiction to another person as the source of security. Then love becomes a "mutual protection racket." The two people continue to hang on to avoid loneliness or to meet an extreme need for approval.

■ *Friendship love:* As mentioned, *friendship* or *companionate love* is more low-key than romantic love is. Friendship love is genuine *liking* for the other person, which results in a desire to be together. Despite the mass media's emphasis on romance and sexuality, companionate love may be the most common and frequently experienced aspect of love.[13]

■ *Altruistic love: Altruistic love* **is unselfish concern for the welfare of another.** An example is a parent willingly and happily assuming care for a child. In a relationship such as marriage, altruistic love means accepting the beloved without insisting that he or she change.

THE END OF LOVE. Relationships can be a source of great joy, their loss a source of great pain. One difficulty in coping with the end of love is dealing with *rejection.* Rejection can be unreciprocated love in an attempted relationship or love that "grows old and waxes cold."

In *How to Fall Out of Love,* Debora Phillips suggests some steps for recovering from the loss of love:[14]

■ *Stop thoughts of the person:* You can learn to spend less and less time thinking about the loved one. Make a list of positive scenes and pleasures that do not involve the former beloved. When a thought about the person enters your mind, say "Stop," then think about one of the best scenes on your list.

■ *Build self-esteem:* Just as a love relationship builds self-esteem, being rejected lowers it. To raise your self-esteem, Phillips suggests you use index cards on which every day you write two good things about yourself. For example, write down things you have done recently or in the past that are positive. When negative thoughts creep in, say "Stop," and think one of these good thoughts about yourself.

If you are the one being let down, don't spend a lot of time speculating *why*. The other person may not even know why he or she is no longer in love. It won't help to torture yourself trying to figure it out. A helpful strategy may be to simply put some distance between yourself and the other person.

If you are the one trying to disengage from the relationship, remember how it feels to be rejected. Try to be honest but gentle: "I no longer feel the way I once did about you." Don't promise to try to "work things out," and don't try to take care of or "rescue" the other person. Do try to mobilize your support group and get involved with activities you enjoy.

Conflict & Communication: Learning How to Disagree

PREVIEW Committed couples must learn to address differences in several areas. They include unrealistic expectations, work and career issues, financial difficulties, problems with in-laws, sexual problems, and commitment. Communication consists of ways of learning to disagree. In bad communication, you become argumentative and defensive and deny your own feelings. In good communication, you acknowledge the other person's feelings and express your own openly. Expert listening consists of tuning in to your partner's channel. It means giving listening signals, not interrupting, asking questions skillfully, and using diplomacy and tact. Most important, it means looking for some truth in what the other person says. To express yourself, use "I feel" language, give praise, and keep criticism specific.

Why can't people get along better? Must there always be conflict in close relationships, as between lovers, family members, roommates or housemates? To see what your usual approach to conflict is, try the following Personal Exploration.

WHAT ARE YOUR FEELINGS ABOUT CONFLICT?

Check which *one* of the following statements best describes your feelings when you approach a conflict with someone close to you.

1. ❑ I hate conflict. If I can find a way to avoid it, I will.

2. ❑ Conflict is such a hassle. I'd just as soon let the other person have his or her way so as to keep the peace.

3. ❑ You can't just let people walk over you. You've got to fight to establish your point of view.

4. ❑ I'm willing to negotiate to see if the other person and I can meet halfway.

5. ❑ I'm willing to explore the similarities and differences with the other person to see if we can solve the problem to both our satisfaction.

■ INTERPRETATION

Whichever one you checked corresponds to a particular style of dealing with conflict. They are: (1) avoidance, (2) accommodation, (3) domination, (4) compromise, (5) integration. For an explanation, read on.

In a small or large group, discuss the style of conflict that you seem to gravitate to. How well does this seem to work for you? As a regular way of operating, what kinds of frustrations does it produce for you, if any? for the people with whom you're in conflict? What alternative style of conflict can you see yourself using?

Researchers have identified five styles of dealing with conflict, one of which is probably closest to yours.

1. *Avoidance: "Maybe It Will Go Away."* People who adopt this style find dealing with conflict unpleasant and uncomfortable. They hope that by ignoring the conflict or by avoiding confrontation the circumstances will change and the problem will magically disappear. Unfortunately, avoiding or delaying facing the conflict usually means it will have to be dealt with later rather than sooner. By then, of course, the situation may have worsened.

2. *Accommodation: "Oh, Have It Your Way!"* Accommodation does not mean compromise; it means simply giving in, although it does not really resolve the matter under dispute. People who adopt a style of easily surrendering are, like avoiders, uncomfortable with conflict and hate disagreements. They are also inclined to be "people pleasers," worried about the approval of others. However, giving in does not really solve the conflict. If anything it may aggravate the situation over the long term. Accommodators may be deeply resentful that the other person did not listen to their point of view. Indeed, the resentment may even develop into a role of martyrdom, which will only irritate the person's partner.

3. *Domination: "Only Winning Matters."* The person holding the winning-is-everything, domination style should not be surprised if he or she some day finds an "I'm gone!" note from the partner. The dominator will go to any lengths to emerge triumphant in a disagreement, even if it means being aggressive and manipulative. However, winning isn't what intimate human relationships are supposed to be about; that approach to conflict produces only hostility and resentment.

4. *Compromise: "I'll Meet You Halfway."* Compromise seems like a civilized way of dealing with conflict, and it is definitely an improvement over the preceding styles. People striving for compromise

recognize that both partners have different needs and try to negotiate to reach agreement. Even so, they may still employ some gamesmanship, such as manipulation and misrepresentation, in an attempt to further their own ends. Thus, the compromise style is not as effective in resolving conflict as the integration style.

5. *Integration: "Let's Honestly Try to Satisfy Both of Us."* Compromise views solution to the conflict as a matter of each party meeting the other halfway. The integration style, on the other hand, attempts to find a solution that will achieve satisfaction for both partners.

Integration has several parts to it:

■ *Openness for mutual problem solving:* The conflict is seen not as a game to be won or negotiated but as a problem to be solved to each other's mutual benefit. Consequently, manipulation and misrepresentation have no place; honesty and openness are a necessary part of reaching the solution. This also has the benefit of building trust that will carry over to the resolution of other conflicts.

■ *Disagreement with the ideas, not the person:* There is an important part of integration, which I expand on below. This is that partners must be able to criticize each other's ideas or specific acts rather than each other generally as persons. It is one thing, for instance, to say "You drink too much!" It is another to say "I feel you drank too much last night." The first way is a generality that disparages the other's character. The second way states that you are unhappy about a particular incident.

■ *Emphasis on similarities, not differences:* Integration requires more work than other styles of dealing with conflict (although the payoffs are better). The reason is that partners must put a good deal of effort into stating and clarifying their positions. To maintain the spirit of trust, the two should also emphasize the similarities in their positions rather than the differences.

AREAS OF CONFLICT. It is said that no married couple hasn't thought about divorce. Likewise no other committed couple hasn't thought about splitting up. The number of subjects over which two people can disagree is awesome. One area about which couples must make adjustments are unrealistic expectations, such as who should do which household chores. Other matters have to do with work and career, finances, in-laws, sex, and commitment/jealousy.[15] Most of the foregoing problems can be overcome with effective communication. Indeed, good communication—to handle conflict and wants—is critical to the success of a committed relationship.

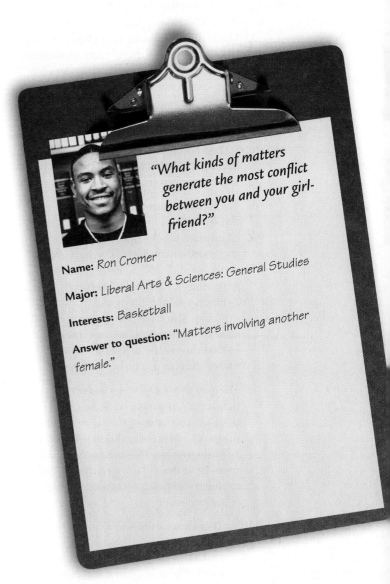

"What kinds of matters generate the most conflict between you and your girlfriend?"

Name: Ron Cromer

Major: Liberal Arts & Sciences: General Studies

Interests: Basketball

Answer to question: "Matters involving another female."

COMMUNICATION: THERE ARE WAYS TO LEARN HOW TO DISAGREE. The fact that conflict is practically always present in an ongoing relationship does not mean that it should be suppressed. When handled constructively, conflict may bring problems out into the open, where they can be solved. Handling conflict may also put an end to chronic sources of discontent in a relationship. Finally, airing disagreements may lead to new insights through the clashing of divergent views.[16] The key to success in relationships is the ability to handle conflict successfully, which means the ability to communicate well.

BAD COMMUNICATION. Most of us *think* communication is easy, points out psychiatrist David Burns, because we've been talking since we were children.[17] And communication *is* easy when we're happy and feeling close to someone. It's when we have a conflict that we find out how well we really communicate—whether it's good or bad.

Bad communication, says Burns, author of *The Feeling Good Handbook,* has two characteristics:

- *You become argumentative and defensive:* The natural tendency of most of us when we are upset is to argue with and contradict others. The habit of contradicting others, however, is self-defeating, for it creates distance between you and them and prevents intimacy. Moreover, when you are in this stance you show you are not interested in listening to the other person or understanding his or her feelings.

- *You deny your own feelings and act them out indirectly:* You may become sarcastic, or pout, or storm out of the room slamming doors. This kind of reaction is known as *passive aggression.* However, it can sometimes be as destructive as *active aggression,* in which you make threats or tell the other person off.

There are a number of other characteristics of bad communication. One is *martyrdom,* in which you insist you're an innocent victim. A second is *hopelessness,* in which you give up and insist there's no point in trying to resolve your difficulties. A third is *self-blame,* in which you act as if you're a terrible, awful person (instead of dealing with the problem). A fourth is *"helping,"* in which instead of listening you attempt to take over and "solve" the other person's problem. A fifth is *diversion,* in which you list grievances about past "injustices" instead of dealing with how you both feel right now.

GOOD COMMUNICATION. "Most people want to be understood and accepted more than anything else in the world," says Burns.[18] Knowing that is taking a giant first step toward good communication.

Good communication, according to Burns, has two attributes:

- *You listen to and acknowledge the other person's feelings:* You may be tempted just to broadcast your feelings and insist that the other agree with you. It's better, however, if you encourage the other to express his or her emotions. Try to listen to and understand what the other person is thinking and feeling. (I expand on listening skills below.)

- *You express your own feelings openly and directly:* If you only listen to the other person's feelings and don't express your own, you will end up feeling short-changed, angry, and resentful. When you deny your feelings, you end up acting them out indirectly. *The trick, then, is to express your feelings in a way that will not alienate the other person.*

BECOMING EXPERT AT LISTENING. If communication is listening, how is that done? Some ideas are offered by Aaron Beck, director of the Center for Cognitive Therapy at the University of Pennsylvania. In his book *Love Is Never Enough,* he suggests the following listening guidelines:[19]

■ *Tune in to your partner's channel:* Imagining how the other person might be feeling—putting yourself in the other's shoes—is known as *empathy*, trying to experience the other's thoughts and feelings. The means for learning what the other's thoughts and feelings are can be determined through the other steps.

■ *Give listening signals:* Use facial expressions, subtle gestures, and sounds such as "uh-huh" and "yeah" to show your partner you are really listening. Beck particularly urges this advice on men, since studies find that women are more inclined to send responsive signals. Talking to someone without getting feedback is like talking to a wall.

■ *Don't interrupt:* Although interruptions may seem natural to you, they can make the other person feel cut off. Men, says Beck, tend to interrupt more than women do (although they interrupt other men as often as they do women). They would do better to not express their ideas until after the partner has finished talking.

■ *Ask questions skillfully:* Asking questions can help you determine what the other person is thinking and keep the discussion going—provided the question is not a *conversation stopper.* "Why" questions can be conversation stoppers ("Why were you home late?"). So can questions that can have only a yes-or-no answer.

Questions that ask the other's opinion can be *conversation starters.* (Example: "What do you think about always having dinner at the same time?") Questions that reflect the other's statements help convey your empathy. (Example: "Can you tell me more about why you feel that way?") The important thing is to ask questions *gently,* never accusingly. You want to explore what the other person is thinking and feeling and to show that you are listening.

■ *Use diplomacy and tact:* All of us have sensitive areas—about our appearance or how we speak, for example. This is true of people in intimate relationships as much as people in other relationships. *Problems in relationships invariably involve feelings.* Using diplomacy and tact in your listening responses will help build trust to talk about difficulties.

An especially wise piece of advice about listening comes from David Burns: *Find SOME truth in what the other person is saying and agree with it.* Do this even if you feel that what he or she is saying is totally wrong, unreasonable, irrational, or unfair. This technique, known as *disarming*, works especially well if you're feeling criticized and attacked.

If, instead of arguing, you agree with the other person, it takes the wind out of his or her sails. Indeed, it can have a calming effect. The other person will then be more open to your point of view. Adds Burns: "When you use the disarming technique, you must be genuine in what you say or it will backfire. You can always find some valid way to agree, no matter how illogical the person's accusations might seem to you. If you agree with them in a sincere way, they will generally soften and will be far more willing to listen to you."[20]

BECOMING EXPERT AT EXPRESSING YOUR-SELF. It is often tempting to use the tools of war—attacking and defending, withdrawing and sulking, going for the jugular. However, these will never take you as far in resolving conflicts in intimate relationships as will kinder and gentler techniques.

In expressing yourself, there are two principal points to keep in mind:

■ *Use "I feel" language:* It's always tempting to use accusatory language during the heat of conflict. (Examples: "You make me so mad!" or "You never listen to what I say!") However, this is sure to send the other person stomping out of the room.

A better method is simply to say "I feel" followed by the word expressing your feelings—"frustrated"; "ignored"; "attacked"; "nervous"; "unloved." This way you don't sound blaming and critical. (Compare this to saying "You make me . . ." or "You never . . .") By expressing how you feel, rather than defending the "truth" of your position, you can communicate your feelings without attacking the other person.

■ *Express praise and keep criticism specific:* Most of us respond better to compliments than to criticism, and most of us seek appreciation and fear rejection. In any conflict, we may disagree with a person's *specific act or behavior.* However, we need not reject the other as a person.

For example, you might want to say, "When we go to parties, you always leave me alone and go talk to other people." It's better, however, to combine criticism with praise. For example: "I'm proud to be with you when we go to parties, and I hope you are of me. However, I think we could have even more fun if we stay in touch with each other when we're at a party. Does this seem like a reasonable request?"[21]

Assertiveness: Better than Aggressiveness or Nonassertiveness

PREVIEW Aggressiveness is expressing yourself in a way that hurts others. Nonassertiveness is not expressing yourself, giving in to others and hurting yourself. Assertiveness is expressing yourself without hurting either others or yourself. Both men and women have assertiveness problems, women sometimes being too passive, men too aggressive, although the reverse is also true. Developing assertiveness means observing your own behavior in conflict situations, visualizing a model for assertiveness, and practicing assertive behavior.

t's important to learn to express your disappointments, resentments, and wishes without denying yourself. Yet you also don't want to put other people down or make them angry. This means learning to be *assertive*.

Assertiveness doesn't mean being pushy or selfish but rather being forthright enough to communicate your needs while respecting the needs of others. Being assertive is important in intimate relationships, of course. However, it's also important in many other social interactions in which speaking out, standing up for yourself, or talking back is necessary.

AGGRESSIVE, NONASSERTIVE, & ASSERTIVE BEHAVIOR. Let us consider three types of behavior: aggressiveness, nonassertiveness, and assertiveness. (Distinctions among these behaviors have been put forth in two interesting books by psychologists Robert Alberti and Michael Emmons. They are *Your Perfect Right* and *Stand Up, Speak Out, Talk Back!* [22,23]) The definitions are as follows:

- *Aggressiveness—expressing yourself and hurting others:* Aggressive behavior means **you vehemently expound your opinions, accuse or blame others, and hurt others before hurting yourself.**

- *Nonassertiveness—giving in to others and hurting yourself:* Nonassertive behavior — also called submissive or passive behavior —means **consistently giving in to others on points of difference. It means agreeing with others regardless of your own feelings, not expressing your opinions, hurting yourself to avoid hurting others.** Nonassertive people have difficulty making requests for themselves or expressing their differences with others. In a word, they are *timid*.

- *Assertiveness—expressing yourself without hurting others or yourself:* Assertiveness is **defined as acting in your own best interests by expressing your thoughts and feelings directly and honestly. It means standing up for yourself and openly expressing your personal feelings and opinions, yet not hurting either yourself or others.** Assertiveness is important in enabling you to express or defend your rights.

It's important to learn to *ask for what you want in a civilized way, without hurting the feelings of the other person.* This is what assertive behavior is all about. Consider what happens if you try aggressive or nonassertive behavior. Aggressive behavior probably won't help you get what you want because your pushiness or anger creates disharmony and alienates other people. It may also make you feel guilty about how you treated others. Nonassertive behavior also may not help you get what you want. Though it may be an attempt to please others by not offending them, it may actually make them contemptuous of you.[24] In addition, nonassertive behavior leads you to suppress your feelings, leading to self-denial and poor self-esteem.

You need to know, however, that assertive behavior will not always get you what you want. Probably no one form of behavior will. Still, if performed correctly, it may improve your chances. The reason is that assertive behavior is not offensive to other people. This makes them more willing to listen to your point of view.

ASSERTIVENESS & GENDER STEREOTYPES.

It has been suggested that behaving assertively may be more difficult for women than men. This is because many females have supposedly been socialized to be more passive and submissive than men.[25] For example, some women worry that acting boldly in pursuing success will make them appear unfeminine.[26] Indeed, by the college years, women may view an act of assertive behavior as more aggressive when done by females than by males.[27]

However, many men have assertiveness problems, too. Some males have been raised to be nonassertive, others to be aggressive rather than assertive. Some researchers suggest that actually more males than females need to be trained in assertiveness to modify their typically more aggressive behavior.[28]

To get an idea of your assertiveness, try Personal Exploration #12.2.

DEVELOPING ASSERTIVENESS. There are different programs for developing assertiveness, but most consist of four steps:[29]

- *Learn what assertive behavior is:* First you need to learn what assertive behavior is, so that you know what it is supposed to be like. You need to learn how to consider both yours and others' rights.

- *Observe your own behavior in conflict situations:* You then need to monitor your own assertive (or nonassertive) behavior. You need to see what circumstances, people, situations, or topics make you behave aggressively or nonassertively. You may find you are able to take care of yourself (behave assertively) in some situations, but not in others.

- *Visualize a model for assertiveness:* If possible, you should try to find a model for assertiveness in the specific situations that trouble you and observe that person's behavior. Role models are important in other parts of life, and this area is no exception. If possible, note how rewarding such behavior is, which will reinforce the assertive tendencies.

- *Practice assertive behavior:* Of course the only way to consistently behave assertively is to practice the behavior. You can do this as a rehearsal, carrying on an imaginary dialogue in private with yourself. Or you can actually role-play the behavior, practicing the assertive behavior with a good friend, counselor, or therapist.

GROUP ACTIVITY #12.3

PRACTICING ASSERTIVENESS

In a group of three people, take turns describing situations in which you were *nonassertive* (passive). Describe who was involved in the interaction and how you felt about the person or persons. Describe also your feelings about yourself as a result of your nonassertiveness. Now give the same attention to situations in which you behaved *aggressively*. Finally, apply the same considerations to situations in which you were *assertive* in your communication style.

Choose one of the incidents in which you behaved nonassertively or aggressively. With a second group member role-playing the other person, practice behaving assertively in that situation. The third person in your group should act as observer, monitoring eye contact, voice tone, body posture, and other signs of assertiveness.

In your group or with the class as a whole, discuss what situations give you the most trouble in being assertive. State whether they involve authority figures, strangers, or people close to you. Identify role models who might help you become assertive. What do you notice about their behavior?

HOW ASSERTIVE ARE YOU?

Answer "Yes" or "No" to each of the following statements.

1. When a person is blatantly unfair, do you usually fail to say something about it to him or her?

   ❏ Yes   ❏ No

2. Are you always very careful to avoid all trouble with other people?

   ❏ Yes   ❏ No

3. Do you often avoid social contacts for fear of doing or saying the wrong thing?

   ❏ Yes   ❏ No

4. If a friend betrays your confidence, do you tell him or her how you really feel?

   ❏ Yes   ❏ No

5. Would you insist that a roommate do his or her fair share of cleaning?

   ❏ Yes   ❏ No

6. When a clerk in a store waits on someone who has come in after you, do you call his or her attention to the matter?

   ❏ Yes   ❏ No

7. Do you find that there are very few people with whom you can be relaxed and have a good time?

   ❏ Yes   ❏ No

8. Would you be hesitant about asking a good friend to lend you a few dollars?

   ❏ Yes   ❏ No

9. If someone who has borrowed $5 from you seems to have forgotten about it, would you remind this person?

   ❏ Yes   ❏ No

10. If a person keeps on teasing you, do you have difficulty expressing your annoyance or displeasure?

    ❏ Yes   ❏ No

11. Would you remain standing at the rear of a crowded auditorium rather than look for a seat up front?

    ❏ Yes   ❏ No

12. If someone kept kicking the back of your chair in a movie, would you ask him or her to stop?

    ❏ Yes   ❏ No

13. If a friend keeps calling you very late each evening, would you ask him or her not to call after a certain time?

    ❏ Yes   ❏ No

14. If someone starts talking to someone else right in the middle of your conversation, do you express your irritation?

    ❏ Yes   ❏ No

15. In a plush restaurant, if you order a medium steak and find it too rare, would you ask the waiter to have it recooked?

    ❏ Yes   ❏ No

16. If a landlord of your apartment fails to make certain necessary repairs after promising to do so, would you insist on it?

    ❏ Yes   ❏ No

17. Would you return a faulty garment you purchased a few days ago?

    ❏ Yes   ❏ No

18. If someone you respect expresses opinions you strongly disagree with, would you venture to state your own point of view?

    ❏ Yes   ❏ No

19. Are you usually able to say no when people make unreasonable requests?

    ❏ Yes   ❏ No

20. Do you think that people should stand up for their rights?

    ❏ Yes   ❏ No

■ INTERPRETATION

There is no scoring system. You can figure out what the answers *should* be.

Now it becomes a matter of rehearsing the response so you'll be able to act assertively the next time it's required. What will you do the next time the landlord fails to make repairs? Or the people in your household don't do their fair share of cleaning? Or you need to ask the waiter to have your steak cooked some more?

Unwanted Sex: From Sexual Harassment to Rape

PREVIEW Members of either sex may be victims of forced or unwanted sexual attentions or actions. Unwanted sex ranges from sexual harassment to sexual assault, including statutory, acquaintance, and date rape. It's important to learn techniques for preventing, resisting, or coping with acquaintance or stranger rape.

grave problem for both sexes, but particularly for women, is that of dealing with unwanted sexual attention or demands. This may range from listening to sexual remarks to experiencing rape.

SEXUAL HARASSMENT. Your instructor or supervisor puts a hand on your shoulder. "Can we discuss your coursework/possible promotion over dinner?" he or she says, then gives you a wink and glides away. You don't want to do it, but you're worried about your grade or promotion. This really isn't about sex, it's about power. What do you do?

Sexual harassment **is unwelcome sexual attention, whether physical or verbal, that creates an intimidating, hostile, or offensive learning or work environment.** Such harassment may include sexual remarks, suggestive looks, pressure for dates, letters and calls, deliberate touching, or pressure for sexual favors. The U.S. Supreme Court has ruled that sexual harassment constitutes employment discrimination as serious and illegal as racial or religious discrimination.[30]

Men and women may see each of these matters differently. For instance, in one study, 95% of women felt that "deliberate touching" by a supervisor constituted sexual harassment. However, only 89% of men felt this was so.[31] These differences seem to reflect a sexual double standard. However, men, too, occasionally experience harassment by women (or men).

So what do you do if you're confronted with sexual harassment by someone who has power over your college or work career? Proving harassment in court is difficult, and other institutional arrangements are predisposed to protect the harasser.[32,33] Thus, one needs to proceed deliberately. First keep a log, recording dates, times, nature of incidents, and any witnesses. According to one survey, just asking or telling the person to stop worked for 61% of the women. Telling co-workers, or threatening to, worked 55% of the time. Pretending to ignore the offensive behavior usually didn't work at all.[34] If the harassment persists, stronger measures may be required. *(See ■ Panel 12.1.)*

RAPE: DATE RAPE & OTHER SEXUAL ASSAULTS. Sex may be pleasurable, but forced sex is in the same category as any other attack. Assault is assault, whether it is with a gun, a club, a fist—or a penis. *Rape* **is defined as sexual penetration of a male or female by intimidation, fraud, or force.** Most rape victims are women. However, one study of 3000 randomly chosen Los Angeles residents found that one third of victims of attempted sexual assault were men.[35] In one survey of Stanford University students, 1 in 3 women and 1 in 8 men reported having unwanted sexual activity.[36]

Rape victims can be of all ages. However, it's a shocking fact that 61% of rape victims were under 18 when attacked, according to the National Victim Center.[37] In almost 80% of cases, the victim knew her rapist.

Three kinds of rape are particularly worth mentioning:

■ *Statutory rape: Statutory rape* **is unlawful sexual intercourse between a male over age 16 and a female under age 12 or 21.** (The exact definition depends on the state.) As the National Victim Center report showed, 3 out of 10 rape victims had not reached their 11th birthdays.

If sexual harassment persists, here are some steps to take:

Document: Keep a detailed written record of the incidents, with dates, times, places, names, and quotes. Keep any notes you receive.

Confide in co-workers or friends: You may tell trusted co-workers, friends, family members, a minister, or others, saying you may have to file a grievance and that you want them to know what is happening.

Find witnesses or supporting evidence: If there are witnesses, ask them to write a statement for you. If you are receiving harassing phone calls, have someone be an "ear witness" by listening in and taking notes. Look for other people in your same situation who may have been harassed by the same person.

Confront the harasser: Say the behavior must stop immediately, and let him or her know you will file a complaint if it does not. If necessary, write a letter—or follow up your conversation with a memo summarizing your talk—and hand it to the harasser in the presence of a witness. Keep a copy.

Talk to the harasser's supervisor: Talk to an appropriate third party such as the harasser's supervisor or someone in the human resources department or equal opportunity office.

File a complaint: If your institution or company does not take steps to stop the harassment, file a legal complaint based on state or federal antidiscrimination laws. Your state may have a department of fair employment or you may take your case to the U.S. Equal Employment Opportunity Commission (call 800-USA-EEOC).

- *Acquaintance rape:* *Acquaintance rape* is rape by a person known by the victim, whether related or unrelated. The National Victim Center report found that 78% of rapists were known to their victims.

- *Date rape:* In *date rape*, the rapist is someone with whom the victim has had a date, as on a college campus. At one time nonconsensual sex between men and women on dates was thought to be a form of female error or lack of resistance. Today, however, sexual activity that is abhorrent to females is considered assault by males.[38]

Some college students are still uncertain as to when sex is considered consensual or rape. One student, asked whether his date had consented to sex, replied, "No, but she didn't say no. So she must have wanted it, too."[39] He added that both had been drunk and the woman had struggled initially. The man's behavior may have been reinforced by pressure from other men to "score." Many men also assume that when a woman enters their bedroom it is an unspoken invitation to sex. Regardless, whatever one person's assumptions about the other or the state of intoxication, it is *always* rape if sex is not consensual.

AVOIDING & COPING WITH RAPE. Men and women interpret sexual cues differently. For instance, researchers asked students to judge several activities: going to a date's room, kissing, French kissing, removing one's shirt. More men than women interpreted these behaviors as indicating a willingness to have sex.[40] These are the kinds of misinterpretations of nonverbal cues that can hurt someone.

To cope with rape, here are some suggestions:

- *To avoid acquaintance or date rape:* Be aware of your surroundings and intentions. Stay out of ambiguous situations (such as bedrooms) and be clear in communicating what you want and don't want. Learn to listen carefully to your partner's messages about what he or she wants and doesn't want. Use a neutral tone and speak in "I" statements—for example, "I want to be taken home."

  Trust your instincts. If you're uncomfortable with a situation, follow your intuition. Don't be afraid of hurting somebody's feelings.

- *To avoid stranger rape:* When on the street, be aware of your surroundings. Anticipate how you would respond to an attack. Look behind you, stay in the middle of the sidewalk, and walk with a confident stride. Use extra caution in parking garages. If you're alone on an elevator, get out if a stranger gets on and pushes the button for the basement. Have your keys in hand when you approach your car so you won't have to stand there fumbling.

- *To resist rape of any kind:* Don't be too polite to fight. Be loud, be rude, cause a scene. Attackers count on the fear of embarrassment. Research shows that women who fight back have a better chance of escaping rape than those who plead or cry.[41] This is especially true if the person attempting rape is an acquaintance.

- **To cope with rape:** Call the police and a rape crisis center or rape treatment center. Don't bathe or wash yourself or your clothes or touch anything in the location of the rape. If a condom was used, try to remember where it was discarded. Try to remember everything about the rapist: his car, clothing, scars, haircut, and things he said and did. Report any weapons or restraints used, and if bruises show up later, have photographs taken by the police. Go to a hospital and be tested and/or treated for sexually transmitted diseases.

Afterward, expect emotional aftershocks, even if you weren't hurt physically. Tell your physician and try to institute a health strategy that includes psychological as well as physical factors. Confide your feelings to a friend.[42] Many women at first blame themselves, especially if they were attacked by men they trusted. Then later—perhaps years later—they may decide they were sexually assaulted.[43]

GROUP ACTIVITY #12.4

AMBIGUOUS SITUATIONS

Form small groups divided equally between males and females. Discuss situations that you are aware of (or can conceive of) in which a man and woman might have different understandings about whether one is interested in having sex. (Don't feel you have to participate in this discussion if you'd rather not. Practice your assertiveness and say "I'd rather just listen.") Describe how you might have handled such situations in the past. Then suggest how they should be handled now.

Sexually Transmitted Diseases: HIV & AIDS

PREVIEW HIV (Human Immunodeficiency Virus) may progress over about 10 years into AIDS (Acquired Immune Deficiency Syndrome). HIV is diagnosed through an antibody test, but the test cannot predict if the virus will become AIDS. HIV may infect both sexes and is principally transmitted by unprotected sex and by shared drug needles.

ormerly called venereal diseases, *sexually transmitted diseases (STDs)* **are infectious diseases that are transmitted as a result (usually) of sexual contact.** Although AIDS is the most serious, there are many other STDs. They include hepatitis B, herpes, human papilloma virus (HPV), chlamydia, gonorrhea, syphilis, and parasite infections. These are growing rapidly, bringing considerable suffering and even death.

HIV & AIDS: THE MODERN SCOURGE. We will focus on HIV and AIDS because they are recent threats and because they have produced all kinds of misunderstandings. HIV and AIDS are two different things:

- **HIV:** *HIV*, or *human immunodeficiency virus*, **the virus causing AIDS, brings about a variety of ills. The most important is the breakdown of the immune system, which leads to the development of certain infections and cancers.**

  Two variants of the virus are HIV-1 and HIV-2. *HIV-1* causes most of the AIDS cases in the United States. *HIV-2* is the dominant strain in Africa; cases are now showing up in the United States.

- **AIDS:** *AIDS* **stands for** *acquired immune deficiency syndrome*, **a sexually transmitted disease that is caused by HIV. It is characterized by irreversible damage to the body's immune system.** As a result, the body is unable to fight infections,

Four important facts about HIV and AIDS.

1. AIDS itself comes only at the end of a long, slow collapse—averaging 8–10 years in adults—of the body's immune system.

2. Often there are *no symptoms of illness* during the development of the disease, which means for perhaps 7–9 years.

3. So far *no one has ever recovered from AIDS.*

4. Yet *not everyone who has been exposed to HIV has gotten AIDS—so far*—just as not everyone exposed to the polio virus develops paralysis.

making it vulnerable to many diseases, such as pneumonia. So far, AIDS has proven to be always fatal.

Because HIV and AIDS are life-and-death matters, it's important that you have *accurate knowledge* about them. Doing Personal Exploration #12.3 will help you determine what you know.

HIV now affects about 1 million Americans, about a fifth of whom have developed AIDS.[44] In the early years, the epidemic in the United States was primarily an affliction of homosexual men and intravenous drug users. It also affected others, such as surgery patients and people with hemophilia (a blood disorder), who received infected products from blood banks.[45] Since then, the disease has spread in the United States along with epidemics of drug use and other sexually transmitted diseases. Today heterosexually acquired AIDS is rising—indeed, such cases are now doubling every 15 months.[46]

A very small proportion of people with HIV have not developed AIDS themselves. (They may yet, however—the disease has not been around long enough for us to know.) Still, all are contagious. They can transmit the disease to their sexual partners or those sharing hypodermic needles with them, such as drug users. The really scary thing is that people with HIV *often show no outward symptoms of illness*—FOR PERHAPS AS LONG AS 9 YEARS! Thus, a person can be a carrier and infect others without anyone knowing it.[47] The estimated average time from HIV infection to first symptom is 5 years and to AIDS 8–10 years.[48] *(See ■ Panel 12.2.)*

TESTING FOR HIV. How does a person find out whether he or she has HIV? The answer is by taking a standard blood test called the *HIV antibody test*. The test does not detect the virus itself. Rather it detects the antibodies that the body forms in response to the appearance of the virus. (Antibodies are molecules that are secreted into the bloodstream, where they bind to the invading virus, incapacitating it.)

WHAT DO YOU KNOW ABOUT HIV & AIDS?

Answer "Yes" or "No" to each of the following statements:

1. There is no known cure for AIDS.

    ❏ Yes   ❏ No

2. AIDS is caused by inheriting faulty genes.

    ❏ Yes   ❏ No

3. AIDS is caused by bacteria.

    ❏ Yes   ❏ No

4. A person can "carry" and transmit the organism that causes AIDS without showing symptoms of the disease or appearing ill.

    ❏ Yes   ❏ No

5. The organism that causes AIDS can be transmitted through semen.

    ❏ Yes   ❏ No

6. Urinating after sexual intercourse makes infection with AIDS less likely.

    ❏ Yes   ❏ No

7. Washing your genitals after sex makes infection with AIDS less likely.

    ❏ Yes   ❏ No

8. Sharing drug needles increases the chance of transmitting the organism that causes AIDS.

    ❏ Yes   ❏ No

9. The organism that causes AIDS can be transmitted through blood or blood products.

    ❏ Yes   ❏ No

10. Donating blood makes it more likely you will be exposed to HIV.

    ❏ Yes   ❏ No

11. You can catch AIDS like you catch a cold because whatever causes AIDS can be carried in the air.

    ❏ Yes   ❏ No

12. You can get AIDS by being in the same classroom as someone who has AIDS.

    ❏ Yes   ❏ No

13. You can get AIDS by shaking hands with someone who has AIDS.

    ❏ Yes   ❏ No

14. A pregnant woman who has HIV can give AIDS to her baby.

    ❏ Yes   ❏ No

15. Having a steady relationship with just one sex partner decreases the risk of getting AIDS.

    ❏ Yes   ❏ No

16. Using condoms reduces the risk of getting AIDS.

    ❏ Yes   ❏ No

17. A test to determine whether a person has been infected with HIV is available.

    ❏ Yes   ❏ No

18. A vaccine that protects people from getting AIDS is now available.

    ❏ Yes   ❏ No

■ CORRECT ANSWERS

1.	Yes
2.	No
3.	No
4.	Yes
5.	Yes
6.	No
7.	No
8.	Yes
9.	Yes
10.	No
11.	No
12.	No
13.	No
14.	Yes
15.	Yes
16.	Yes
17.	Yes
18.	No

GROUP ACTIVITY OPTION

In a group situation, large or small, discuss your feelings about the HIV/AIDS crisis. What did you not know that this Personal Exploration has taught you? Does HIV/AIDS seem like a real danger to people you know (perhaps including yourself)? What should people be doing to reduce their risk? Do you think heavy use of alcohol or other drugs could play a role in increasing one's risk? What do you think of the kind of sex-soaked culture portrayed in the mass media in relation to the AIDS epidemic? Since AIDS has grabbed so many of the headlines, what do you think of the hazards of other sexually transmitted diseases?

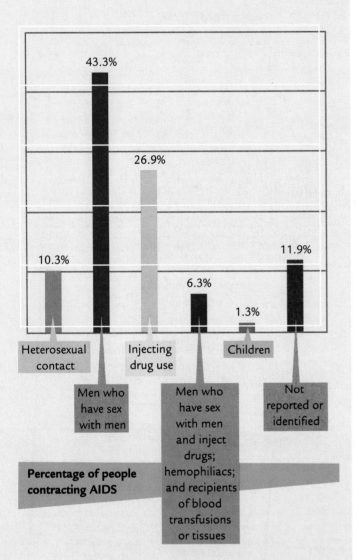

Where AIDS comes **from.** Percentage of people in the United States who contracted AIDS in 1994 by type of exposure.

43.3%

26.9%

10.3%

11.9%

6.3%

1.3%

Heterosexual contact

Injecting drug use

Children

Men who have sex with men

Men who have sex with men and inject drugs; hemophiliacs; and recipients of blood transfusions or tissues

Not reported or identified

Percentage of people contracting AIDS

Negative test results *can* mean positive news: the HIV may not be present. *Positive* test results *can* mean negative news: the HIV may be present. Still, anyone taking these tests needs to be aware of certain cautions:

■ *Antibodies to the virus may not develop immediately:* If the test results are negative, it may mean the body has not been exposed to HIV. But it may also mean that antibody formation has not yet taken place. The time it takes for most people to develop antibodies is about 1–3 months, though it varies. Some people do not develop antibodies until 6–12 months have elapsed since exposure to the organism. (Meanwhile the person may be infected and continue to infect others.)

■ *Be aware that testing labs can make errors:* If performed correctly, the tests themselves can be highly accurate, detecting antibodies in 99.6% of HIV-infected people. The problem is that some medical labs have problems with high error rates in their testing.[49]

■ *Tests cannot predict AIDS:* Currently, tests can show that a person has HIV. They cannot predict whether that HIV will develop into AIDS.

WHO GETS HIV/AIDS & HOW. Most recent figures show that the predominant number of reported U.S. AIDS cases were transmitted by male homosexual sex (43%). This was followed by those transmitted by intravenous drug use (27%). A small percentage of men (6%) fell into both categories. Heterosexual sex, as a means of transmission, was only 10%. (The remaining percentage resulted from blood transfusions, treatments for blood-clotting disorders, transmission from mothers to infants, and accidental contacts.) (*See* ■ *Panel 12.3.*)

However, the number of women infected with HIV through heterosexual intercourse is on the rise. Among women in the United States in the first six months of 1994, 38% of AIDS cases resulted from heterosexual transmission. This was up 8% from 1988. By contrast, the 43% of AIDS cases among women that resulted from drug use (sharing of infected needles) was down 10% from 1988.[50]

In fact, there is some evidence that *men are more efficient at infecting women than women are at infecting men.*[51] Studies seem to show that increasingly women are becoming HIV-infected through unprotected sex with bisexual men or male intravenous drug users.[52] Indeed, women are the fastest-growing category of people affected by the epidemic, particularly women of color.[53]

HIV is no longer spreading explosively among gay men, as it was in the recent past. Even so, *AIDS is still the second leading cause of death for men ages 25–44* in the United States.[54] Part of the reason for the epidemic among males is that men are more apt to engage in risk-taking behavior.[55]

HIV/AIDS is also transmitted by intravenous drug use. AIDS has dropped in Canada, where clean needles have been distributed free to drug addicts in large Canadian cities.[56,57] In the United States such programs were resisted for years on the grounds that free needles would increase drug use. The Canadian experience, however, found that there was no such increase in drug abuse. That is, participants have almost always been long-term abusers, not new recruits.

WHY IT'S IMPORTANT TO BE CONCERNED ABOUT STDS. The sexually transmitted diseases caused by viruses—HIV, hepatitis B, herpes, genital warts—cannot be cured, although they can in many cases be controlled. STDs caused by bacteria—chlamydia, gonorrhea, and syphilis—can be cured. Unfortunately, however, they are often difficult to detect, because many have no obvious symptoms, and thus may lead to grave difficulties later. Clearly, then, the wisest course is to do what's necessary to avoid getting STDs in the first place. (*See* ■ *Panel 12.4*)

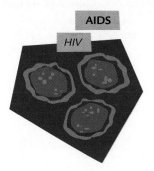

AIDS

HIV

Sexually transmitted diseases. Although it's the most recent (and perhaps most dangerous) STD, HIV/AIDS is by no means the only one. Others are hepatitis B, herpes, human papilloma virus (HPV), chlamydia, gonorrhea, syphilis, and parasite infections.

Hepatitis B: A Disease of the Liver

Hepatitis covers five virus-caused inflammatory diseases of the liver (A, B, C, D, and E), which have similar symptoms but otherwise are different. Hepatitis B is transmitted through infected blood (or saliva, mucus, and semen),

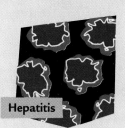

Hepatitis

typically by sexual contact or sharing of drug needles. Symptoms include fever, chills, headache, nausea, diarrhea, loss of appetite, skin rashes, and sometimes the yellowing of skin and eyes called jaundice.

Among Americans at risk for hepatitis B are the 10 million heterosexuals who have multiple partners or whose partners have multiple partners. Adolescents are particularly at risk because they tend to have sex more often with more partners, and many do not use condoms.

The disease lasts 2–6 months. People usually recover on their own, although in a small percentage of cases (1–3%) there are fatalities from liver failure. A drug called alpha interferon has shown promise of being effective in treatment. A vaccine has been available for about a decade which has been found to be 80–95% effective.

Herpes: The Secret Virus

Herpes is a viral infection that evades the body's immune defenses by hiding in the nervous system until reactivation of the virus occurs. A great number of people—30 million, or perhaps 16% of all Americans ages 15–74—have been infected with herpes, and perhaps as many as 1 million more join their ranks every year.

The most common strains are the *herpes simplex virus, types 1 and 2,* which are sexually transmitted and which produce cold-sore-like

(continued on next page)

blisters in the areas of the genitals and mouth. In both types, one may experience numbness, itching, or tingling in the area where there has been contact with the virus, followed by an often painful eruption of water-filled blisters. Within 10 days of an initial exposure to the virus, people may feel flu-like symptoms: fever, chills, nausea, headaches, fatigue, and muscle aches. The eruption crusts and scabs over, and then in about 2 weeks the skin appears normal.

After the first episode, the virus seems to disappear. Thereafter it emerges from time to time—sometimes as frequently as four or more times a year. Sometimes it will produce no symptoms. At other times it will produce outbreaks of blistering sores. As time goes on, many people find **Genital warts** that the duration of symptoms becomes shorter and less severe.

Among adults, apparently the principal effects of herpes are feelings of desperation and social inhibition. A great many herpes victims feel isolated and depressed and fear rejection in social situations.

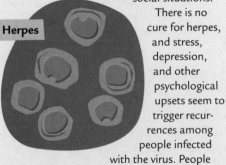

Herpes

There is no cure for herpes, and stress, depression, and other psychological upsets seem to trigger recurrences among people infected with the virus. People with herpes who have learned relaxation and other coping techniques seem to suffer fewer outbreaks. In addition, a prescription drug called *acyclovir,* if taken during the initial herpes outbreak, can ease the symptoms.

Human Papilloma Virus (HPV): The Fastest-Spreading STD

HPV, short for *human papilloma virus,* which causes genital warts, is the fastest-spreading STD in the United States. There are presently an estimated 12–24 million cases of HPV in the United States, with 750,000 new cases being added every year. Indeed, some researchers found that nearly *half* of a sample of sexually active college women, each of whom had had sexual relations with an average of four lifetime partners, were HPV positive.

HPV should not be taken lightly. At one time, it was thought that HPV caused only *genital warts*—unpleasant but supposedly harmless fleshy growths in the areas of the genitals and mouth. However, some types of HPV have also been found to be associated with cancer (of the anus, penis, vulva, and cervix). Unfortunately, HPV also may be painless and show no symptoms, both in males and females.

HPV is very contagious, being readily transmitted by sexual contact. On average the incubation period is 2–3 months after contact. One test for HPV infection is called the Southern blot technique.

Genital warts are treated by freezing, heat, cauterization, laser therapy, chemicals, or surgical removal. Treatment is required for one's sexual partner as well, who may otherwise reinfect the patient.

Chlamydia: The Most Common STD

If HPV is the fastest-growing STD in the United States, chlamydia is perhaps the most common, with as many as 4 million new cases appearing in the U.S. every year. *Chlamydia*—or more accurately *chlamydial infections*—consists of a family of sexually transmitted diseases caused by a bacterium (*Chlamydia trachomatis*). A major problem associated with this STD is that the organism *often does not cause any symptoms.* Yet if it is untreated it can cause lifelong damage, such as pelvic inflammatory disease in women, urinary tract infections in men, and sterility and blindness in both sexes.

About 50–70% of infected females and 30% of infected males show no signs of early symptoms. Those that do show signs may experience itching and burning during urination two to seven days after infection. Diagnosis of chlamydia must be made by a health-care professional, and the standard treatment is antibiotics.

Gonorrhea: An Old Enemy Comes Back

Once upon a time, when the phrase "venereal disease" was in use, when people thought of sexually transmitted diseases they thought principally of gonorrhea and syphilis. For a time, in the 1970s and early 1980s, the incidence of these two diseases declined. Recently, unfortunately, both the old enemies gonorrhea and syphilis have had a resurgence.

Gonorrhea is caused by the sexual transmission of a bacterium (*Neisseria gonorrhoeae*). It is an organism that is easily transmitted. A man who has had sexual intercourse *once* with an infected woman has a 20–25% risk of getting the disease; a woman who has intercourse *once* with an infected man has a 50% chance of getting it.

Because the gonorrhea bacterium needs warmth and humidity to thrive, it is harbored principally in warm, moist areas of the human body. Thus, one may contract gonorrhea from an infected person through genital, anal, and oral contact. Toilet seats may harbor the gonorrhea bacterium for a few seconds; however, the evidence does not show this to be a means of transmission.

Symptoms appear two to eight days after one has been infected. Some men, perhaps 10–20%, show no signs of infection at all. Otherwise, the main manifestation is burning pain during urination and later discharge (pus) from the urinary tract. Although the burning sensation may subside in 2–3 weeks, if the disease is not treated it spreads throughout the urinary and

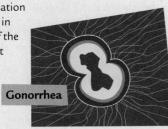

Gonorrhea

reproductive systems, causing scarring, obstructions, and sterility.

Early gonorrhea symptoms in women may be so slight that they are apt to be overlooked. Indeed, up to 80% of women show no symptoms at all, and women may only begin to suspect they have a problem when their partners are diagnosed. When symptoms appear, they may take the form of irritation of the vagina and painful and frequent urination.

Gonorrhea is primarily diagnosed through laboratory tests. The principal treatment is use of antibiotics, especially penicillin.

Syphilis: The "Great Imitator" Returns

Syphilis

Syphilis, another old enemy like gonorrhea, is known as the "great imitator" because its sores and other symptoms mimic other disorders and diseases, such as cancers, abscesses, hemorrhoids, and hernias. Once thought to be under control in the United States, syphilis has returned with a vengeance: in 1990 it reached its highest level since 1949, zooming 75% in just 5 years. One reason for this epidemic, experts say, is the surge in crack cocaine use, which promotes high-risk sexual behavior, such as trading anonymous sex for money or drugs.

Syphilis is a sexually transmitted disease caused by a bacterium (a long, slender, spiral bacterium, or spiro-

chete, called *Treponema pallidum*). Syphilis is serious because it can become a systemic infection, leading to possible brain damage, heart failure, and death.

Syphilis appears in four stages:

■ *Primary stage:* Within 10–90 days of infection, one or more pink or red dime-sized or smaller sores called *chancres* appear on the sex organs, mouth, or other parts of the body. Because the sores do not cause pain, they may not be noticed. The chancres disappear by themselves in 3–6 weeks, but this does not mean the disease has disappeared.

■ *Secondary stage:* About 6–8 weeks later, symptoms appear that may be mistaken for the flu: swollen lymph nodes, sore throat, headache, and fever. There may also be loss of hair. In addition, the disease produces a rash, which may appear on the hands or feet or all over the body and which does not itch. Finally, large, moist sores may appear around the mouth or genitals. The sores disappear in 2–6 weeks, but this only means the disease has entered the next stage.

■ *Latent stage:* In this stage, which may last from a few months to a lifetime, the disease goes underground. Although 50–70% of those with untreated syphilis remain in this latent stage for the rest of their lives and experience no further problems, the rest develop late-stage syphilis.

■ *Tertiary stage:* Years after the initial exposure, the effects of untreated syphilis may result in damage to the heart and major blood vessels, the central nervous system, or other organs. This may cause blindness, paralysis, and death.

Syphilis is diagnosed by means of

blood tests. Penicillin is the most common treatment and can be highly effective if given during the primary stage.

Parasite Infections: Pubic Lice & Scabies

The STDs described so far are dangerous. However, the two parasite infections transmitted by sexual contact are mainly just annoying.

Called "crabs," because of their crablike appearance, *pubic lice* are wingless, gray insects, about 1/16th inch long, that live in human hair. Pubic lice feed on blood, causing itching and skin discoloration. Female lice lay eggs, or *nits,* that are attached to the hair. *Scabies* are tiny mites that burrow under the skin and lay eggs, producing itching and discolored lines on the skin.

Besides being transmitted by sexual contact, both pubic lice and scabies may be picked up from infected clothing and bedding, which should be washed. Treatment is by washing oneself and others in the household with insecticide-containing shampoos and soaps available at pharmacies.

Some Rules for Safer Sex

PREVIEW One way to reduce the risk of exposure to STDs is to ask the right questions of prospective sexual partners. The answers, however, provide no guarantees. The safest form of sex for preventing transmission of STDs is abstinence and other behavior in which body fluids are not exchanged. The next least risky is protected sex, such as that using condoms. High-risk behavior involves sexual exchange of body fluids or use of intravenous needles. Long-term mutually monogamous relationships are an especially important consideration.

now your sexual partner," medical authorities advise. Concerned about STDs, many students have taken the advice to heart.

Unfortunately, they may go about it the wrong way, says psychologist Jeffrey D. Fisher.[58] Students try to gauge their risks by asking other students about their home town, family, and major. Or they try to judge their sexual chances on the basis of the other person's perceived "social class," educational level, or attractiveness.[59]

Do such external clues work? No, says Fisher. These are useless and irrelevant facts, not guides to safe sex.

How can you be sure that sex is really safe? The answer is: you can't. However, there are things that you can do to reduce your risks.

ASKING PROSPECTIVE PARTNERS ABOUT THEIR SEXUAL HISTORY. However embarrassing the conversation, it can be helpful for people to explore their prospective partners' sexual histories before getting involved. Here are some questions to ask:[60]

- **STD tests:** "Have you ever been tested for HIV or for other STDs? Would you be willing to have an HIV test?"

- **Previous partners:** "How many sexual partners have you had?" (The more partners, the higher the STD risk.)

- **Prostitution:** "Have you ever had sex with a prostitute?" Or, "Have you ever exchanged sex for money or drugs?" (If so, was protection used?)

- **Bisexuality:** For a woman to ask a man: "Have you ever had a male sexual partner?" For a man to ask a woman: "Have you ever had a sexual partner who was bisexual?"

- **IV drug use:** "Have you—*or your sexual partners*—ever injected drugs?" (Previous sexual partners can transmit HIV or hepatitis they got by sharing needles.)

- **Blood transfusion:** "Have you ever had a transfusion of blood or blood products?" (This fact is particularly important if the transfusion occurred before 1985, when blood wasn't screened for HIV.)

Even if you ask all the right questions, however, you still can't be sure of the answers. Someone may state with absolute honesty and sincerity that he or she has never had a genital infection or HIV. But that person may have an infection and not know it.

Even people who have had an HIV test can't prove they are HIV negative. The test measures the presence of antibodies (which fight HIV) that can take 6 months or more to develop. So a person can become infected and infect others during

"Truth is the first casualty in war. Some think it is also the first casualty in sexual behavior."

the 6 months required for the antibodies to show. He or she can also, of course, become infected after taking the test.

Truth is the first casualty in war, it is said. Some think it is also the first casualty in sexual behavior.[61] Clearly, the bottom line is that simply asking a prospective sexual partner about HIV does not by itself guarantee safer sex.[62]

THREE LEVELS OF RISK: HIGH-RISK SEX, SAFER SEX, SAVED SEX. In general, there are three levels of risk in sexual behavior:

- *Very risky—unprotected sex and other behavior:* Behavior that is high-risk for the transmission of STDs includes all forms of sex in which body fluids may be exchanged. By body fluids, I mean semen, vaginal secretions, saliva, or blood (including menstrual blood). These are transmitted through unprotected vaginal, oral, or anal sex.

  High risks also include behavior having to do with the intravenous injection of drugs, a prime means of transmitting STDs. Certainly you shouldn't share IV needles yourself. Moreover, you should avoid sexual contact with someone who is an IV drug user or whose previous partner was. Avoid having sexual contact with people who sell or buy sex, who are often IV drug users.

- *Somewhat risky—"safer" sex:* The next best step to ensuring safe sex—actually, only saf*er* sex—is to use *latex condoms.* "Safer" sex is still somewhat risky, but at least it minimizes the exchange of body fluids. One example of safer-sex behavior is deep (French) kissing. Another is vaginal intercourse using latex condoms with **nonoxynol-9, a spermicide that kills STD organisms.** (Condoms are described in detail in a few pages.)

- *Lowest risk—"saved sex":* The safest kind of sex avoids the exchange of semen, vaginal secretions, saliva, or blood. The principal kind of "saved sex" is abstinence. **Abstinence is the voluntary avoidance of sexual intercourse and contact with a partner's body fluids.**
  Saved sex includes massage, hugging, rubbing of bodies, dry kissing (not

exchanging saliva), masturbation, and mutual manual stimulation of the genitals. In all cases, contact with body fluids is avoided. *The trick in practicing safe-sex activity is not to get swept away and end up practicing unsafe sex.*

SOME SEX, SOME RISK. If you've decided that abstinence is not for you, what should you do? The principal kinds of advice are as follows:

- *Use precautions universally:* If you choose to have sex, then CONSISTENTLY use safer-sex measures, such as a condom and spermicide, with ALL partners. This means all sexual partners, not just those you don't know well or those you think may be higher risk. Doing this means you'll have to learn to overcome any embarrassment you may feel about talking with your partner about using condoms.

- *Keep your head clear:* Be careful about using alcohol and other drugs with a prospective sexual partner. Drugs cloud your judgment, placing you in a position of increased vulnerability.

- *Practice mutual monogamy:* Having multiple sexual partners is one of the leading risk factors for the transmission of STDs. Clearly, mutual monogamy is one way to avoid infection.

  Be aware, however, that even apparent monogamy may have its risks. If one partner has a secret sexual adventure outside the supposedly monogamous relationship, it does not just breach a trust. It endangers the other's life—especially if the unfaithful partner is not using condoms.

  In addition, you may be in a monogamous relationship but have no idea if your partner was infected previously. To be on the safe side, it's suggested the two of you wait several weeks while remaining faithful to each other. Then both of you should take a test to see if HIV antibodies are present. This gives some indication (though not absolutely) that the partner is currently free of infection.

ALL ABOUT CONDOMS. A _condom_ is a thin sheath made of latex rubber or lamb intestine. (Though called "natural skin," lamb intestine is not as safe as latex.) A condom comes packaged in rolled-up form. It should then be unrolled over a male's erect penis, leaving a little room at the top to catch the semen. Some condoms are marketed with a "reservoir" at the end for this purpose.

A condom provides protection for both partners during vaginal, oral, or anal intercourse. It keeps semen from being transmitted to a man's sexual partner and shields against contact with any infection on his penis. It also protects the male's penis and urethra from contact with his partner's secretions, blood, and saliva.

These thin, tight-fitting sheaths of latex rubber or animal skin are available in all kinds of colors, shapes, and textures. They also come with or without a reservoir tip and are available dry or lubricated. Spermicide-coated condoms, including those with nonoxynol-9, have been shown to be effective in killing sperm.[63] When buying condoms, always check the expiration date. Also, don't store them in places where they might be exposed to heat (wallets, glove compartments), which causes latex to deteriorate.

Unfortunately, _condoms are not perfect protection._ They only _reduce_ the risk of acquiring HIV infection and other STDs. Note that _reducing the risk is not the same as eliminating the risk._ If the condom is flawed or it slips off or breaks, there is suddenly 100% exposure. (And possibly to a disease that is 100% fatal.)

Condoms break most frequently when couples use oil-based lubricants or engage in prolonged sex. A condom may also be weakened if couples attempt their own "quality testing" (such as blowing up condoms to test for leaks). There are several precautions people can take to ensure that condoms are used properly. (See ■ _Panel 12.5._)

How to buy and use condoms.

■ _How to Buy_

Materials: Buy latex, not natural membrane or lambskin. Latex is less apt to leak and better able to protect against HIV transmission. Inexpensive foreign brands are suspect.

Sizes: The FDA says condoms must be between 6 and 8 inches in length when unrolled. (The average erect penis is $6\frac{1}{2}$ inches.)
Condoms labeled _Regular_ are $7\frac{1}{2}$ inches. Instead of "Small" for condoms under $7\frac{1}{2}$ inches, manufacturers use labels such as _Snug Fit._ Instead of "Large" for condoms over $7\frac{1}{2}$ inches, manufacturers use labels such as _Max_ or _Magnum._

Shapes: Most condoms are _straight-walled._ Some are labeled _contoured,_ which means they are anatomically shaped to fit the penis and thus are more comfortable.

Tips: Some condoms have a _reservoir_ at the end to catch semen upon ejaculation. Others do not have a reservoir, in which case they should be twisted at the tip after being put on.

Plain or Lubricated: Condoms can be purchased _plain_ (unlubricated) or _lubricated,_ which means they feel more slippery to the touch. There are four options:
1. Buy a plain condom and don't use a lubricant.
2. Buy a plain condom and use your own lubricant, preferably water-based (such as K-Y Jelly or Astroglide).
3. Buy a lubricated condom pregreased with silicone-, jelly-, or water-based lubricants.
4. Buy a _spermicidally lubricated_ condom, which contains _nonoxynol-9,_ a chemical that kills sperm and HIV. This is probably the best option.

Strength: A standard condom will do for vaginal and oral sex. Some people believe an *"extra-strength"* condom is less apt to break during anal sex, although this is debatable.

Gimmicks: Condoms come with all kinds of other features:

1. *Colors:* Red, blue, green, and yellow are safe. Avoid black and "glow in the dark," since dyes may rub off.
2. *Smell and taste:* Latex smells and tastes rubbery, but some fragranced condoms mask this odor.
3. *Adhesive:* Condoms are available with adhesive to hold them in place so they won't slip off during withdrawal.
4. *Marketing gimmicks:* Condoms are sold with ribs, nubs, bumps, and so on, but unless the additions are at the tip and can reach the clitoris they do no good whatsoever.

■ *How to Use*

Storage: Condoms should be stored in a cool, dry place. Keeping them in a hot glove compartment or wallet in the back pocket for weeks can cause the latex to fail.

Opening package: Look to see that the foil or plastic packaging is not broken; if it is, don't use the condom. Open the package carefully. Fingernails can easily damage a condom.

Inspection: Make sure a condom is soft and pliable. Don't use it if it's brittle, sticky, or discolored. Don't try to test it for leaks by unrolling, stretching, or blowing it up, which will only weaken it.

Putting on: Put the condom on before any genital contact to prevent exposure to fluids. Hold the tip of the condom and unroll it directly onto the erect penis. (If the man is not circumcised, pull back the foreskin before rolling on the condom.) Gently pinch the tip to remove air bubbles, which can cause the condom to break. Condoms without a reservoir tip need a half-inch free at the tip.

Lubricants: *Important!* If you're using a lubricant of your own, *don't use an oil-based lubricant.* Oil-based lubricants—examples are hand lotion, baby oil, mineral oil, and Vaseline—can reduce a latex condom's strength by 90% in as little as 60 seconds. Saliva is not recommended either.

Use a water-based or silicone-based product designed for such use, such as K-Y Jelly or spermicidal compounds containing nonoxynol-9.

Add lubricant to the outside of the condom before entry. If not enough lubricant is used, the condom can tear or pull off.

Slippage and breakage: If the condom begins to slip, hold your fingers around the base to make it stay on. If a condom breaks, it should be replaced immediately. If ejaculation occurs after a condom breaks, apply a foam spermicide to the vagina at once.

After ejaculation: After sex, hold the base of the condom to prevent it from slipping off and to avoid spillage during withdrawal. Withdraw while the penis is still erect. Throw the used condom away. (Never reuse condoms.) Wash the genitals.

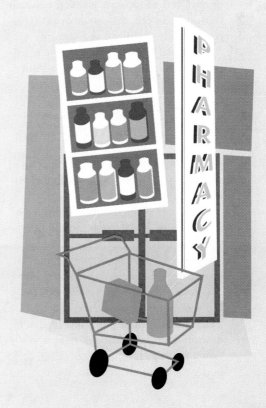

Choosing Among Birth-Control Methods

PREVIEW Methods of contraception vary greatly in effectiveness, side effects, cost, and other matters.

hat are the chances of becoming pregnant? For a couple having unprotected intercourse over a 1-year period, the odds are 85–90%. About 1 million unplanned adolescent pregnancies occur every year in the United States. In addition, every year about 1.5 million abortions are performed. It's clear from these figures, then, that the gambling casino of reproduction all too frequently works in nature's favor.[64]

CONCEPTION & CONTRACEPTION. Avoidance of unwanted pregnancies requires the practice of *contraception* **or birth control, the prevention of fertilization or implantation.** Fertilization and implantation are two different matters. *Fertilization,* **or** *conception,* **occurs when the male reproductive cell, the sperm, meets the female reproductive cell, the egg or ovum.** This produces the fertilized egg (zygote). *Implantation* **is the act in which the fertilized egg burrows into the lining of the uterus.** In this location it grows into a fetus.

Only one method of birth control is *guaranteed* to avoid pregnancy—*complete abstinence.* All others have *some* risk of pregnancy, although some (such as tubal sterilization or vasectomy) are extremely low-risk.

There are many different contraceptive methods, and no one can tell others which method is best for them. Today, however, concerns about preventing pregnancy often have to be linked with concerns about protection from STDs. For nonmonogamous, sexually active heterosexuals, these two concerns come down to a single method of contraception and protection: *condoms.* (Even better are condoms combined with

nonoxynol-9, an antiviral, antibacterial spermicidal agent.) Heterosexual couples who need not worry about STDs, however, have a great many choices in contraception.

CHOICES AVAILABLE: THE VARIETIES OF BIRTH CONTROL. There are many criteria for choosing a method of contraception: availability, effectiveness, cost, personal comfort, effect on health, and religious beliefs. The accompanying box shows the effectiveness (or lack thereof) of various contraceptive methods in terms of preventing pregnancy. *(See Panel 12.6.)* The various methods of contraception are explained within the box.

Effectiveness of contraceptive methods. The following are the principal types of birth-control methods, in order of effectiveness.

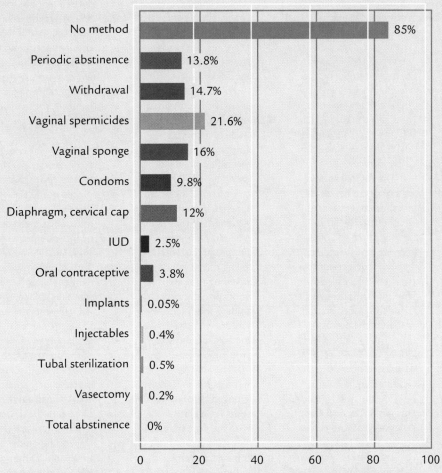

Method	Percent
No method	85%
Periodic abstinence	13.8%
Withdrawal	14.7%
Vaginal spermicides	21.6%
Vaginal sponge	16%
Condoms	9.8%
Diaphragm, cervical cap	12%
IUD	2.5%
Oral contraceptive	3.8%
Implants	0.05%
Injectables	0.4%
Tubal sterilization	0.5%
Vasectomy	0.2%
Total abstinence	0%

Percent women pregnant within 1 year

No Method at All. Intercourse in which no method of contraception at all is used has the highest failure rate for birth control. In one study, 85% of women ages 15–44 who didn't think they were infertile were estimated to have become pregnant within 1 year.

Douching. *Douching* is the practice of rinsing out the vagina with a chemical right after sexual intercourse. From the standpoint of birth control, it is almost worthless. Douching is an attempt to "wash out" the ejaculate. Instead, however, it often brings the sperm into contact with the cervix. Moreover, some sperm are able to enter the uterus within seconds of ejaculation, before a woman has a chance to begin douching.

Periodic Abstinence. *Abstinence* is the voluntary avoidance of sexual intercourse. *Complete abstinence* is the surest form of birth control. *Periodic abstinence* is another matter—it is not sure at all. Periodic abstinence refers to the avoidance of sexual intercourse during perceived fertile periods of the woman's menstrual cycle. Periodic abstinence goes under the names of *fertility awareness, natural family planning,* and the *rhythm method.*

This method cannot be used by women who have irregular menstrual cycles or who are at risk for STD exposure owing to unprotected intercourse. Moreover, using this method to prevent pregnancy requires a motivated, knowledgeable couple who has undergone training. The couple must be able to abstain or use another contraceptive method during those times the woman is estimated to be at risk for fertility.

Withdrawal. *Withdrawal* consists of removing the penis from the vagina prior to ejaculation, so that no sperm are deposited in or around the vagina. This method also seems to be flawed: nearly 15% of women are estimated to become pregnant with the technique. Not only does withdrawal require unusual willpower, but all it takes is the little bit of fluid released from the penis *prior* to ejaculation to send sperm into the vagina.

(continued next page)

Vaginal Spermicides Alone. *Vaginal spermicides* are sperm-killing chemicals—such as spermicidal foam, cream, jelly, film, or suppositories—which are placed in the vagina within 30 minutes before intercourse. Some require the use of an applicator. Others, such as the suppositories, require a waiting time of 10–15 minutes after insertion before intercourse can take place.

Spermicides can be effectively used as lubricants during sexual intercourse. Those that contain nonoxynol-9 also kill bacteria and viruses in addition to sperm. It is recommended that these agents be used with other methods such as condoms and diaphragms. Spermicides can be purchased without a physician's prescription in many drugstores and supermarkets. Some people are sensitive to these agents. If burning or itching occurs, you may find switching to another brand will often alleviate the problem.

One of the newer spermicide contraceptives is the *vaginal contraceptive film (VCF)*, which consists of a thin, small (2-inch × 2-inch) film impregnated with nonoxynol-9. From 5 to 90 minutes before intercourse, the woman inserts the VCF into her vagina, where it dissolves into a gel-like material over the cervix. It is effective for up to 2 hours.

Vaginal Sponge. The *vaginal contraceptive sponge* is a soft, mushroom-shaped spongy disk saturated with spermicide (nonoxynol-9). Moistened and inserted into the vagina over the cervix up to 24 hours before intercourse, the device blocks sperm from entering the uterus and kills the sperm. The sponge must be left in place for 6–8 hours after intercourse.

The vaginal sponge is a one-size-fits-all method that is available in pharmacies without prescription and does not require individual fitting. It does require that users be able to feel that the sponge is properly placed so that it covers the cervix.

Condoms. *Condoms* are discussed in the text and in Panel 12.5.

Diaphragm & Cervical Cap. Diaphragms and cervical caps are barrier contraceptives that are always used with spermicidal creams or jellies. They are available only by prescription. Both come in various sizes and require a fitting by a health-care professional to determine correct size and style.

Diaphragms and cervical caps can be inserted up to 6 hours before intercourse (although a shorter time between insertion and intercourse may afford better protection) and must remain in place for 6–8 hours afterward. Both should be checked for holes

after every use (just hold them up to the light). Both increase the woman's risk of *toxic shock syndrome*—a severe, potentially life-threatening bacterial infection—if they remain in the vagina for prolonged periods of time.

To distinguish between the two devices:

■ *Diaphragms:* A *diaphragm* is made of a soft latex rubber dome stretched over a flexible metal spring or ring. The size varies from 2 inches to 4 inches, depending on the length of the vagina. When in place, the diaphragm covers the ceiling of the vagina, including the cervix. It works primarily by holding spermicide in contact with the cervix and by blocking sperm from entering the cervix.

If possible, diaphragms should be removed before 24 hours have elapsed from the time of insertion. They should not, however, be removed within 6 hours of the last act of intercourse. Diaphragms can be reused for a period of up to 1 year.

■ *Cervical caps:* The *cervical cap* operates in much the same way as the diaphragm. This is a much smaller, thimble-shaped rubber or plastic cap that fits directly onto the cervix. Insertion of the cervical cap tends to present more of a challenge to first-time users than does the diaphragm.

Unlike diaphragm users, cervical cap users do not need to reapply spermicide with each subsequent intercourse after insertion. In addition, they can leave the cap in place for up to 48 hours. Not all women can use the cap, owing to fitting problems or problems with cervical damage.

IUD. The *IUD* (for *intra-uterine device*) is a small plastic device that is placed inside the uterus. The IUD, which must be inserted by a health-care professional, may prevent fertilization in some women. Or, if fertilization takes place, the IUD prevents the fertilized egg from being implanted in the lining of the uterus. Once inserted, the IUD string must be located after every menstrual period to be sure the device remains in place. Depending on the type used, an IUD may remain in the uterus for 1–6 years.

Oral Contraceptives. The *oral contraceptive* or *birth-control pill*, famously known as simply The Pill, consists of synthetic female hormones that prevent ovulation or implantation. It is the most effective *reversible* birth control method available (surgery, for instance, may not be reversible). Nearly 14 million women use the pill in the United States, and it appears to be the contraceptive of choice among women ages 15–24.

The three basic types of pills are as follows:

■ **Combination pill:** The *combination pill* contains two hormones, estrogen and progesterone. These hormones, independently or together, prevent pregnancy in three ways: (1) They primarily prevent ovulation. (2) They change the mucus in the cervix, making it difficult for the sperm to enter the cervix. (3) They change the lining of the uterus, preventing implantation.

The combination pill provides a steady dosage of the two hormones, estrogen and progesterone. The pill is taken for 21 days, with 7 days off.

■ **Multiphasic pill:** The multiphasic pill is a variation on the combination pill. Whereas the combination pill provides a steady dosage of the two hormones, the *multiphasic pill* provides a changing dosage of estrogen and progesterone that more nearly mimics the body's natural cycle of hormones.

Like the combination pill, the multiphasic pill is taken for 21 days, with 7 days off.

■ **Minipill:** The *minipill* contains progesterone only. It thus has fewer side effects than the other two, but it is also less effective in preventing pregnancy. Because it contains no estrogen, the minipill does not consistently prevent ovulation. It does,

however, change cervical mucus and change the lining of the uterus.

Unlike the combination and multiphasic pills, the minipill is taken every day.

It is important for users to check with their health-care practitioner regarding the pill-taking schedule and find out what to do in the event a pill is missed.

Women who are not good candidates for oral contraceptive use are those with a history of blood clots, stroke, heart disease, impaired liver function, or cancer. Those with diabetes, migraine headaches, hypertension, mononucleosis, or other problems should discuss the risks with a health-care practitioner.

Implant Contraceptives (Norplant). *Implants,* marketed under the brand name *Norplant,* consist of small, removable silicone-rubber rods or capsules filled with synthetic progestin, which are embedded in a woman's arm or leg. The capsules, which can be implanted surgically by a physician in 15 minutes using a local anesthetic, release low levels of synthetic progestin, preventing ovulation and restricting sperm from entering the uterus. The implants may stay in place for 5 years and can be removed surgically if a woman wants to become pregnant. Implants are considered

extremely effective, with less than one-half of 1% of women becoming pregnant in the first year.

Injectable Contraceptives (Depo-Provera). An *injectable contraceptive* known as *Depo-Provera* consists of a long-lasting progestin that is administered once every 3 months. During the time between injections, a woman has no menstrual periods or irregular ones. Fertility returns after the use of injectables is discontinued.

The risk of pregnancy from injectable contraceptives is extremely low—only 0.4% of women are estimated to become pregnant within the first year.

Tubal Sterilization—Female Sterilization. *Sterilization* is the surgical—and generally permanent—interruption of a person's reproductive capacity, whether male or female, preventing the normal passage of sperm or ova. Sterilization is the most popular contraceptive method among American couples.

In females, the procedure is called *tubal sterilization* and is accomplished by blocking or cutting the egg-carrying tubes called the fallopian tubes, thus preventing the passage of the egg from ovary to the uterus. Tubal sterilization may take the form of either *tubal ligation,* the cutting

and tying of the fallopian tubes, or *tubal occlusion,* the blocking of the tubes by cauterizing (burning) or by use of a clamp, clip, or band of silicone.

Vasectomy—Male Sterilization. Male sterilization is accomplished by means of a vasectomy. A *vasectomy* is a surgical procedure that involves making a pair of incisions in the scrotum and cutting and tying two tubes (called the vas deferens) that carry sperm from the testes to the urethra, through which semen is ejaculated. After a vasectomy, sperm continue to form, but they are absorbed by the body. The man continues to be able to have erections, enjoy orgasms, and produce semen, but the ejaculate contains no sperm cells.

Vasectomies, which can be performed as a 20-minute procedure in a doctor's office with local anesthetic, are considered extremely effective: only 0.2% of women whose mates have had vasectomies are estimated to become pregnant in the first year.

A man contemplating a vasectomy should proceed as though the procedure were irreversible. Although 90% of the operations to reopen the tubes are successful, only 40–70% of these reversals result in the ability to father children.

Onward: Applying This Chapter to Your Life

PREVIEW Ignorance about love and sex is not bliss.

ove and sexual passion are among the most powerful human forces. So powerful are they, in fact, that they lead people sometimes to take chances or make decisions they might not otherwise make. For instance, students who did not use a condom during sex often report they got carried away, "out of control." Or they say they did not plan ahead when they became sexually involved.[65]

We are surrounded by words and images about love and sex. However, a great many people, including many college-educated people, are surprisingly uninformed about these subjects. Unfortunately, we live in a time when ignorance in relationship and sexual matters can no longer be considered bliss.

Probably we all think we know quite a bit about human relationships. After all, we've grown up having relationships (of some sort) with other humans. Did you learn something new in this chapter? Write it down here:

_____

_____

_____

_____

_____

_____

_____

_____

_____

_____

_____

_____

THE EXAMINED LIFE: YOUR JOURNAL

1. Write a page or two of detail about an important relationship (such as with parents, boyfriend/girlfriend, spouse, children, professor, boss). Are you satisfied with this relationship? What have you learned in this chapter that might help you to improve it?

2. Do you feel you're inclined to be aggressive or to be passive in conflict situations? Imagine yourself having a disagreement with someone (perhaps an instructor about a grade on a paper or a roommate about living arrangements). Write out a little script about some things you might say. How would you express your point of view without hurting the other person or hurting yourself?

3. Have you ever had a dating experience in which another person seemed to misunderstand the nature of the occasion? That is, you may have thought there was/was not an invitation to have sex, but the other person thought the opposite. Describe the situation. (Note, incidentally, if there was any alcohol or other drugs involved.)

4. Do you often feel lonely, unloved, unwanted? Why do you think that is? Who might you talk to about this? (An example is someone at the college counseling service.)

5. Because we live in the Age of AIDS, more and more students are abstaining from sexual relationships. Do you know anyone who has announced this? How do you feel about his or her decision?

6. How difficult emotionally is it for you to buy condoms or to discuss their use with a prospective sexual partner? What are the impediments?

7. What method of birth control seems appropriate for you? Why?

13 the future

finding a major & a career

when will you decide what to do with the rest of your life? now is the time!

IN THIS CHAPTER: What will you do when you get out of college? What would you *like* to do? Is there necessarily a relationship between your major and your prospective career, and which should you decide on first? These are some of the most important questions you'll ever have to consider. And you're in the unique position of *being able* to consider them now. In this chapter, we consider the following:

■ *Your future:* What is the purpose of work? What do you want to do when you get out of college, and how can you get career advice?

■ *Vocational tests:* What vocational tests can help point you toward a career?

■ *Job hunting:* What are the best ways to find a good job? How can you use a computer to help you in a job search? What are the best ways to write a resume?

■ MAKING THIS CHAPTER WORK FOR YOU

Even if you're undecided about your major, your career dreams could well determine the kinds of majors you should consider. List here *five occupations*, fanciful or not, that you would like to consider entering. Also list *five possible majors* you might consider. (Careers and majors need not be related.)

_____

_____

_____

_____

_____

_____

_____

_____

_____

■ SKIMMING FOR PAYOFFS

Look through this chapter and check the one most important thing that seems to leap out at you. Write down here why it's of importance to you:

_____

_____

_____

_____

_____

_____

_____

_____

_____

"*Everyone wants a clear reason to get up in the morning.*"

o points out journalist Dick Leider. He goes on: "As humans we hunger for meaning and purpose in our lives. At the very core of who we are, we need to feel our lives matter . . . that we do make a difference."[1]

What is that purpose?

"Life never lacks purpose," says Leider. "Purpose is innate—but it is up to each of us individually to discover or rediscover it. And, it must be discovered by oneself, by one's own conscience."

Why Work?

PREVIEW Whatever you do to make money, you are trading your "life energy." To figure out the answer to the question "why work" is to figure out the purpose of your life.

What is the purpose of your life? For most people, Freud said, the two biggest things that provide meaning and purpose are *love,* as we discussed in the previous chapter, and *work.* For many students, in fact, the main reason they are going to college is because it will determine their future work.

Let us, however, consider a fundamental question: *Why work?*

Most people *think* they know the answer. To put bread on the table. To support their families. To afford to do the things they want to do when they're *not* working. In other words, they work for money.

But what is it, exactly, that we are giving up in return for money?

MONEY & YOUR LIFE ENERGY. Joe Dominguez and Vicki Robin are authors of a wonderful book called *Your Money or Your Life.* In it they point out that money is something we choose to trade our "life energy" for. They write:

Our life energy is our allotment of time here on earth, the hours of precious life available to us. When we go to our jobs we are trading our life energy for money. . . .

This definition of money gives us significant information. Our life energy is more real in our actual experience than money. You could even say money equals our life energy. So, while money has no intrinsic value, our life energy does—at least to us. It's tangible, and it's finite. Life energy is all we have. It is precious because it is limited and irretrievable and because our choices about how we use it express the meaning and purpose of our time here on earth.[2]

Thus, they say, in considering what to do for a living, two questions become important:

- Are you receiving satisfaction and value in proportion to your life energy expended?

- Is the expenditure of life energy in alignment with your values and purpose?

Considering all the ways you might spend your future days, then, what would make you *feel most fulfilled while trading your irretrievable life energy?*

WORK & YOUR LIFE'S PURPOSE. Philosopher Jacob Needleman is the author of *Money and the Meaning of Life.*[3] He also gives frequent seminars about people and money. The most common question he hears, he reports, is "How do I engage in making a living and still keep my soul?"[4] Thus, to figure out the answer to "Why work?" is to begin to figure out the purpose of your life.

Unfortunately, for a great many people, work does not give them that sense of purpose. According to a Gallup poll, only 41% of the respondents consciously chose the job or career they are in. Of the rest, 18% got started in their present job through chance circumstances, and 12% took the only job available. The remainder were influenced by relatives or friends. Perhaps the most important finding was this: *Nearly two thirds said that, given a chance to start over, they would try to get more information about career options.*[5]

Maybe, then, you are in a good position to take advantage of others' hindsight. Get as much information as you can about careers and jobs. Try to avoid aimlessness.

What Do You Want to Be After You Graduate?

PREVIEW You'll probably change jobs and even careers often. Though people dream about glamorous jobs, in college they usually focus on careers with some connection to their abilities and interests. Some careers have a relationship to one's major, but many others do not. Often the additional training needed can be acquired in graduate school. Other competencies needed for a career are related work experience, personal discipline, information-handling skills, and political and networking skills. It's best to decide on a career before a major; advice can be obtained at the college career counseling and job placement center.

I n urging you to get career information, I also need to say this: Don't be afraid about making a mistake in a career choice. People make career changes all the time, in all phases of life. Moreover, in the beginning it's natural to go through some trial and error until you find what suits you. Indeed, columnist and business consultant Jack Falvey points out that most people do some casting about: "It is a rare person who knows with certitude what he [or she] wants to be and then follows that dream into the sunset for a lifetime. It is unrealistic to set that [ideal] as a standard."[6]

In fact, in the future the average person is expected to have *four career changes*—and several job changes within each career.[7] Statistically, people change jobs or assignments every 2 $\frac{1}{2}$ years.[8] The best approach you can take, then, is to be flexible.

GROUP ACTIVITY #13.1

IF YOU DIDN'T HAVE TO WORK . . .

O n a sheet of paper, write down three things you would prefer to spend your life doing. Assume you'd be getting a reasonably modest income and didn't have to work. (These are your dreams, so make them as detailed as possible.) Now write down three more things you would like to do as work or career if money were no object.

In a small group or classroom setting, discuss your choices. Why would you choose these directions? Do you think you could achieve any of these? How might you go about it?

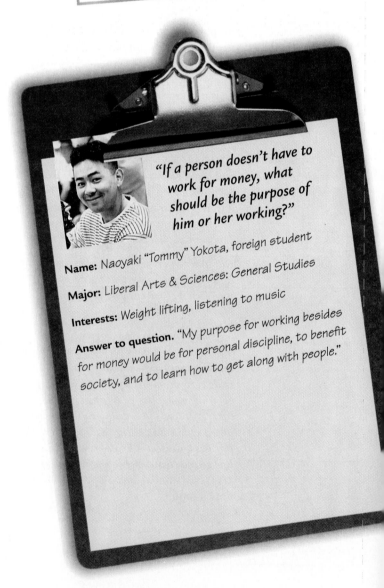

"If a person doesn't have to work for money, what should be the purpose of him or her working?"

Name: Naoyaki "Tommy" Yokota, foreign student

Major: Liberal Arts & Sciences: General Studies

Interests: Weight lifting, listening to music

Answer to question. "My purpose for working besides for money would be for personal discipline, to benefit society, and to learn how to get along with people."

"I WISH I WERE A . . ." Television tends to give us a false impression of the work world. (For instance, one study of 90 programs watched by children found that 58% of the TV characters didn't have occupations. Or they had unrealistic occupations, such as vampire hunter and ghostbuster.[9]) Maybe this in part explains why the professions men and women say they choose in a *fantasy* life consist of the following:[10]

> *Men:*
> Athlete—48%
> Business leader—38%
> Musician—29%
>
> *Women:*
> Singer—35%
> Author—31%
> Doctor—29%

Of course, there's nothing wrong with aspiring to one of these occupations. One has to realize, however, that to reach the *top* of one of these professions—to achieve fame and fortune—is another matter altogether. The stars in their fields stand at the summit of a pyramid. But the nature of a pyramid, as Falvey points out, is that the further you climb, the less space remains. Thus, the majority of pyramid climbers never get to the top.[11]

No wonder people have mid-life career crises in their mid-forties after having climbed as far as they're going to go. Clearly, then, the rewards of work should come not just from scaling the heights but from doing the job itself.

In any event, most first-year students think more about careers that are connected to their abilities and interests rather than are glamorous.

IS THERE A RELATIONSHIP BETWEEN MAJORS & CAREERS? Many students assume that to enter most careers you must have the appropriate major. There are three possibilities here:

- *Relationship between career and major:* For some fields, there clearly is a relationship between the major and the career. To be an engineer, nurse, or musician, for example, you should major in engineering, nursing, or music, respectively. This is because the training for the occupation is so specific.

- *No relationship between career and major:* A great many fields require no specific major at all. You can be a sales representative, a store manager, a police officer, or the like with almost any major.

- *Relationship between career and graduate training:* For some fields—even seemingly specialized and technical ones—training can be obtained at the graduate level. For example, you could major in history as an undergraduate, then get a master's degree in business, journalism, librarianship, or social work. The master's will enable you to enter one of these fields as a profession. (Some graduate programs may insist that you go back and make up particular undergraduate prerequisite courses that you might have missed.)

Quite apart from considering your career, however, is another important question: What do you want to *study*? For most people, college is a once-in-a-lifetime activity. Regardless of what you're going to do for a living, now's the time to study those things that truly interest you. Philosophy, English literature, ethnic studies, history of science, fine arts, and physical education might not seem directly connected to your career interests. But if you're interested in any of these subjects, the college years are the time to investigate them.

OTHER COMPETENCIES NEEDED FOR A CAREER. It's important to realize that a major and a college degree are only a start toward a career. Besides these, you need other competencies appropriate to the work you choose. Examples are:

■ *Related work experience:* It greatly helps to have acquired some skills related to the line of work you're entering. Such skills may be obtained from part-time work, internships, work-study programs, cooperative educational experiences, and co-curricular activities. These are matters I would strongly recommend looking into with a career counselor.

■ *Personal discipline:* You need to know how to dress appropriately, get to work on time, and be pleasant to co-workers and clients. You also need to be able to persist in completing your assignments come hell or high water. (You might not *want* to make 100 telephone calls a day, but it might be required in your job.)

■ *Information-handling skills:* Most jobs these days that have a future to them require that you know how to handle information. This means knowing how to write a report, give a speech or presentation, and run a meeting. It probably also means knowing how to handle a computer (to do word processing or spreadsheets, for example).

■ *Political and networking skills:* Knowing how to handle organizational dynamics, otherwise known as office politics, is an important aspect of most career building. So is networking—the making, nurturing, and maintaining of personal contacts with people who can assist you. Indeed, developing these skills while in college can help you get your foot in the door for a new career. (For example, you might get to know an instructor or fellow student who has connections to an industry you're interested in.)

WHAT DO YOU WANT TO DO FOR A CAREER?

Students often wonder what kind of work they can do with their major. A better question to ask—especially during your first year of college—is "What do I want to do for a career?" By taking the time to explore this question, you can then decide what majors (and minors) might be appropriate for you.

There are, of course, thousands of vocations. The *Dictionary of Occupational Titles,* published by the U.S. Department of Labor, lists over 20,000 occupations.

How do you find which might be best for you? You can just leave things to chance, as many people do. Indeed, one out of three students puts off making a career decision until after graduation.[12] Then you can take whatever comes along, hoping everything will just work out for your future happiness.

But consider what it is that makes people want to succeed. University of Rochester psychology professor Edward L. Deci has studied human motivation for many years. According to his research, people do better when they are encouraged to pursue a task for its own sake. They also enjoy it more than those told to do the task for a reward. Or those told they will be punished if they don't perform correctly.[13] Clearly, then, it's worth your while to seek out a career that you really want to do.

And remember what I said earlier about the working people interviewed for a Gallup poll: *Nearly two thirds said that, given a chance to start over, they would try to get more information about career options.*

Now's your chance.

CAREER COUNSELING & JOB PLACEMENT CENTER.

Career guidance starts with a visit to the career counseling center, which most colleges have. Often this is coupled with the job placement office.

Basically the career counseling and job placement center offers the following services:

■ *Vocational testing:* Tests such as those described in the next section ask you questions about your interests, abilities, and values. They also make suggestions about possible career areas that might interest you.

■ *Career counseling:* Career counseling offices usually have lots of information about what occupational fields are expanding. They also can tell you where the jobs tend to be concentrated geographically, the salary levels, and the training required. In addition, they can advise on transferring, as from community college to university.

You may get one-on-one advice from career advisors. Or you may be steered to job fairs attended by prospective employers or be introduced to alumni working in fields you're considering.

■ *Information about graduate school:* Some careers may require an advanced degree. Often the career counseling office provides information on graduate and professional programs and their admissions requirements and costs.

■ *Job placement:* Students of the 18–24 traditional college age range may think of part-time or summer jobs as simply ways of making money to help get them through college. However, they can also provide valuable work experience that you can leverage later when you're trying to obtain a career-path type of job. The job-placement office can also help you find out about internships or fieldwork jobs associated with your major.

Tests to Help Establish Career Interests

PREVIEW Vocational tests can help people establish their career interests and abilities. One presented here is the "career video" exercise. More formal tools include the Strong/Campbell Interest Inventory and the Edwards Personal Preference Schedule. Visiting the career counseling and job placement office can be a valuable and ultimately time-saving experience.

ow can you identify which occupations might suit your abilities and interests? One way to do this is through tests.

Most of the tests you have been required to take during school were to establish what you know. There are other kinds of tests, however, that you are not required to take—unfortunately. Such tests might be even *more* beneficial to you because they can point you in the direction of a satisfying career (or careers). Moreover, they can help you avoid wasting years of college pursuing goals that ultimately may not suit you. I'm talking about the kind of vocational testing offered by career counselors. Let's consider some of these tests.

THE "CAREER VIDEO" EXERCISE. John Holland is a psychologist at Johns Hopkins University who has developed a system that divides career areas into six categories based on different interests and skills.[14] Here let us suppose that Holland's six career categories have been produced as a series by a "career introduction video service." (This is sort of a variation on those video dating services I'm sure you've seen ads for.) To see which careers appeal to you, try Personal Exploration #13.1.

PERSONAL EXPLORATION #13.1

THE "CAREER VIDEO": WHAT INTERESTS & SKILLS ARE YOU ATTRACTED TO?

■ DIRECTIONS

The accompanying description shows a summary of six career videos, labeled 1, 2, 3, 4, 5, 6. Read the description of all six videos. Then answer the questions below.

NUMBER OF VIDEO

a. Which video are you drawn to because it shows the group of people you would *most enjoy* being with? _____

b. Which second video are you drawn to because it shows the people you would *next most enjoy* being with? _____

c. Which video of the third rank are you drawn to because it shows people you would enjoy being with? _____

1. **Objects, things, animals:**

People in this video are shown working with tools, machines, objects, animals, or plants. They may work outdoors. They have mechanical or athletic skills.

2. **Learning, analyzing, solving:**

People in this video are shown analyzing and solving problems, learning, observing, discovering. They are curious and have good investigative skills.

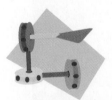

3. **Innovating and creating:**

People in this video are shown being intuitive, creative, imaginative, and artistic. They like to operate in unstructured environments.

4. **Helping and informing:**

People in this video are shown training, developing, curing, enlightening. They like working with people and often have word skills.

5. **Influencing, performing, leading:**

People in this video are shown persuading, performing, or managing people. They like working with people in achieving a goal.

6. **Data and details:**

People in this video are shown executing tasks, following instructions, and working with numbers and facts. They like working with data.

THE "CAREER VIDEO": WHAT INTERESTS & SKILLS ARE YOU ATTRACTED TO?

INTERPRETATION

The numbers represent the following:

1 = *Realistic*

2 = *Investigative*

3 = *Artistic*

4 = *Social*

5= *Enterprising*

6 = *Conventional*

In general, the closer the types, the less the conflict among the career fields. Here's what the six fields mean.

1. **Realistic:** People in this video consider themselves "doers." They are practical, down-to-earth, mechanically inclined, action-oriented, interested in physical activity.

   Interests may be mechanical or scientific. Examples of occupations: coach, computer graphics technician, electrical contractor, electronics technician, farmer, fitness director, health and safety specialist, industrial arts teacher, jeweler, navy officer, physical education teacher.

2. **Investigative:** If you're this type, you consider yourself a problem solver. You're probably rational and analytical, valuing intellectual achievement. You're thought-oriented rather than action-

oriented. You may not be very people-oriented, indeed may be a loner.

   Sample occupations: cattle breeder, college professor, computer programmer, engineer, environmentalist, flight engineer, physician, scientist, urban planner.

3. **Artistic:** As might be expected, artistic people describe themselves as creative. They also consider themselves independent, unconventional, and emotional, valuing self-expression and disliking structure.

   Careers are apt to be in visual or performing arts. Examples of occupations: actor, architect, cartoonist, communications specialist, editor, illustrator, interior decorator, jewelry designer, journalist, librarian, orchestra leader, photographer, public relations person, sculptor.

4. **Social:** Social people value helping others and consider themselves socially concerned and caring and understanding of other people. They are drawn to associating with others in close personal relationships.

   Some careers: career specialist, caterer, convention planner, counselor, home economist, insurance claims specialist, minister, nurse, teacher, travel agent.

5. **Enterprising:** If you consider yourself adventurous, assertive, risk-taking, outgoing, and persuasive, you may be of the enterprising type. Power and prestige are important to you, and you prefer leadership to supporting roles.

   Examples of occupations: banker, city manager, FBI agent, labor negotiator, lawyer, marketing specialist, politician, promoter, real-estate developer, sales representative, television announcer or producer.

6. **Conventional:** Conventional types see themselves as enjoying routine, order, neatness, detail, and structure, as well as prestige and status. They are self-controlled and skilled in planning and organizing.

   Some occupations: accountant, auditor, database manager, hospital administrator, indexer, information consultant, insurance administrator, legal secretary, office manager, personnel specialist, statistician.

Most people are not one distinct type but rather a mixture of types. This is why this Personal Exploration offers second and third choices.

With everyone else in your class, complete Personal Exploration #13.1. When everyone is done, join with others in a group corresponding to your first choice of career video. (If you find yourself the only one in a group, join the group of your second choice.)

Discuss the following questions: What qualities led you to this choice? What kinds of occupations mentioned above seem attractive to you? Does the major (or majors) you're contemplating lead in this direction?

Now join with others in your second choice of career video. Discuss the same questions. If there's time, join the group of your third choice. Do you find yourself assembling with most of the same people as before? If not, what seems to account for the differences? What information of personal value to you can you take away from this?

■ *The Strong/Campbell Interest Inventory (SCII):* Widely used in college counseling offices, this test enables students to compare their interests to those of people in various occupations.

■ *The Edwards Personal Preference Schedule (EPPS):* This test allows students to discover what their personal needs and preferences are—such as need for order, dominance, helping others, and social orientation.

GOING FOR AN APPOINTMENT AT CAREER COUNSELING. A visit to a career counseling center and the taking of a vocational test might take the better part of an afternoon. But the experience may well save you months or even years of wasted effort. In order to get started on establishing your career path—and the right major—do Personal Exploration #13.2.

OTHER TESTS FOR CAREER DECISION-MAKING. A more sophisticated version of the "career video" test is available under the name of the *Vocational Preference Inventory,* developed by John Holland. Holland has also written a *Self-Directed Search Assessment Booklet.* This contains a self-marking test that you can use to examine what occupations you might begin to investigate.

Two other tests favored by career counselors are the following:

WHAT CAN YOU LEARN FROM A VISIT TO THE CAREER COUNSELING & JOB PLACEMENT OFFICE?

The purpose of this assignment is to get you into the Career Counseling and Job Placement Office and have you talk to one of the counselors.

■ DIRECTIONS

Call the Career Counseling Center (or its equivalent on your campus) and make an appointment to come in. Explain to the counselor that you are doing a class assignment for this course. Ask if he or she can spare 15–20 minutes of time for a brief interview. Make an appointment to meet.

My appointment is at (date and time)

_____

_____

with (name of counselor)

_____

_____

at (location)

_____

_____

■ QUESTIONS FOR THE VISIT

Review the interview questions below and add two of your own. Ask the following questions and fill in the blanks.

■ GROUP ACTIVITY OPTION

After completing this Personal Exploration, discuss the results of your investigations in class. Then make an appointment to follow up on one of the components (such as taking a vocational test). Write a one-page report on your follow-up investigation to turn in to the instructor.

1. What kind of career counseling services do you offer?

2. What kind of information do you have about occupational fields?

3. What kind of vocational tests do you offer? How long do they take?

4. What kind of information do you have, if any, about graduate and professional schools?

5. If this office has a job placement component, what kind of services does it offer? Does it help students get internships or field-work placements?

The Job of Looking for a Job

PREVIEW Everyone should train in the job of looking for a job. Two ways to investigate jobs are via the informational interview and internships. The computer can also be a job-search tool, as in hunting for online job openings and putting your resume in an online database. It helps to know techniques for writing resumes, both recruiter-friendly and computer-friendly, chronological and functional. It's also important to know how to write a cover letter to accompany the resume and how to behave in an interview.

he average person will go job hunting *eight* times in his or her life," says Richard Bolles. A former clergyman, Bolles is author of *What Color Is Your Parachute?* and other writings about career searching.[15–17] Thus, today one needs to train for the task of *finding and getting* a job as much as for the ability to do the job itself.

Bolles offers several insights on finding that "lucky" job.[18] Luck, he says, favors people who:

- Are going after their dreams—the thing they really want to do most in the world.

- Are prepared.

- Are working hardest at the job hunt.

- Have told the most people clearly and precisely what they are looking for.

- Treat others with grace and dignity, courtesy and kindness.

WAYS OF LOOKING FOR JOBS. Listing the various ways of finding jobs would take a book in itself. My suggestion is to go through the Career Counseling Center and find out everything you can about this subject. I would agree with Jack Falvey, however, when he says that contacts are everything. This means developing relationships with people.

Some unique ways of establishing contacts are as follows:

"What's the best way to find the job you want?"

Name: Jennifer Chiaino

Major: Business Administration

Interests: Reading, skiing, camping, movies

Answer to question: "Cover all bases. Send resumes, make phone calls, send follow-up letters, attend job fairs, and sign up for civil service exams. Last but not least, tell your network of friends, colleagues, and people you use as references to keep their eyes open and put in a good word for you. Nobody is going to hand you your job or your dreams—you have to grab them yourself!"

THE INFORMATIONAL INTERVIEW

Look back at the heading "Ways of Looking for Jobs" and the discussion of informational interviews. Obtain an informational interview with someone, preferably an executive or administrator. He or she should be in an organization you're interested in working for, either as an intern or in a possible career capacity. Prepare a list of questions to ask the person you'll be interviewing. After the interview, write a one-page paper reporting your experience to your instructor.

WRITING A RECRUITER-FRIENDLY RESUME. Writing a resume is like writing an ad to sell yourself. However, it can't just be dashed off or follow any format of your choosing. It should be carefully designed to impress a human recruiter, who may have some fairly traditional ideas about resumes. (It should also be designed to be put into an employer's computerized database, as I'll describe.)

Some tips for organizing resumes, offered by reporter Kathleen Pender, who interviewed numerous professional resume writers, are as follows.[20] *(See ■ Panel 13.2.)*

■ *The beginning:* Start with your name, address, and phone number.

Follow with a clear objective stating what it is you want to do. (Example: "Sales representative in computer industry.")

Under the heading "Summary" give three compelling reasons why you are the ideal person for the job. (Example of one line: "Experienced sales representative to corporations and small businesses.")

After the beginning, your resume can follow either a *chronological* format or a *functional* format.

■ *The chronological resume:* The chronological resume works best for people who have stayed in the same line of work and have moved steadily upward in their careers. Start with your most recent job and work backward, and say more about your recent jobs than earlier ones.

The format is to list the dates you worked at each place down one side of the page. Opposite the dates indicate your employer's name and your job title. You can also list a few of your accomplishments, using action words ("managed," "created," "developed"). Omit accomplishments that have nothing to do with the job you're applying for.

■ *The functional resume:* The functional resume works best for people who are changing careers or are re-entering the job market. It also is for people who want to emphasize skills from earlier in their careers or their volunteer experience. It is particularly suitable if you have had responsibilities you want to showcase but have never had an important job title.

The format is to emphasize the skills, then follow with a brief chronological work history emphasizing dates, job titles, and employer names.

■ *The conclusion:* Both types of resumes should have a concluding section showing college, degree, and graduation date and professional credentials or licenses. They should also include professional affiliations and awards if they are relevant to the job you're seeking.

■ *The biggest mistakes on resumes:* The biggest mistake you can make on a resume is to *lie*. Sooner or later a lie will probably catch up with you and may get you fired, maybe even sued.

> *"The biggest mistake you can make on a resume is to lie."*

- **The informational interview:** Students have somewhat of a privileged status just by being students. That is, everyone knows that they are in a temporary position in life, that of *learning*. Consequently, it is perfectly acceptable for you to write a letter to a high-level executive asking for an *informational interview*. The letter should be written on high-quality paper stock, perhaps even on a letterhead printed with your name and address. *(See ■ Panel 13.1.)*

  "You may find it hard to believe that some senior management types would clear their calendars for an hour or two just to talk to a student," Falvey observes, "but they do it all the time.[19] After sending the letter, you can make the follow-up phone call. This will probably connect you with a secretary who handles the appointment calendar. Simply remind him or her that you had written to set up a meeting and ask how the executive's calendar looks.

- **Internships:** Essentially an *internship* gives you the chance to gain inside professional experience within a particular company or organization. What the company gets in return is your labor (sometimes for a modest salary, sometimes for no salary). It also gets the opportunity to bid for your services after college if the people there decide they like you. Internships may be as short as a few days during semester break or as long as a complete summer or school term.

  Internships—sometimes called field experiences or cooperative educational experiences—are found everywhere. You can locate these through the Career Counseling Center, of course. You can also simply ask guest speakers or other campus visitors. You might even be able to create your own internship, as by asking an executive during an informational interview.

PANEL 13.1   Example of letter requesting informational interview.

> I need your help. I am researching _____ industry (profession). If I could meet with someone of your experience, I am sure I could get enough information in a half hour to give me the direction I need to begin finding out how _____ really works.
>
> As a first-year student studying _____, I find it difficult to understand how everything applies or fits together.
>
> I will call your office in hopes of scheduling an appointment.

E xample of a basic
resume.

771 Randall Avenue   (713) 123-4567
Houston, TX 77027

WILLIAM W. WILLIAMS

OBJECTIVE:

Sales representative in a publishing or communications company in an entry-level position.

SUMMARY OF QUALIFICATIONS:

Experienced with working with general public and in retail selling during summer and Christmas jobs. Superb writing skills developed through college courses and extracurricular activities. Active speaker on behalf of environmental causes. Knowledge of Spanish, some French.

BUSINESS EXPERIENCE:

Nov. 22–Dec. 24, 1995   THE SPORTSMAN, Reno, Nevada.

                               SALESPERSON, skiing equipment for sporting goods store.

Nov. 22–Dec. 24, 1994   TOYS R US, Reno, Nevada.

                               SALESPERSON, video games for leading toy store.

SUMMER JOBS:

1990–1994   DEPT. OF PARKS & RECREATION, Houston, Texas.

June to Sept. 1994, GATE ATTENDANT, pool area; June to Sept. 1993, GATE ATTENDANT, pool area; June to Sept. 1992, LOCKER ROOM ATTENDANT; June to Sept. 1991, LOCKER ROOM ATTENDANT; June to Sept. 1990, PARK ATTENDANT. Collected tickets, checked residency, painted, cleaned pool area.

EDUCATION:

B. A. in International Relations, minor in Journalism, Sierra Nevada College,

          Incline Village, Nevada, 1996. Dean's List, 2 years.

          Courses in International Relations: U.S., European, Latin America.

Additional courses in: Principles of Journalism, Feature Writing,

          Fundamentals of Public Speaking, Principles of Economics, Introduction

          to Business.

Spent summer session in Guadalajara, Mexico, 1995.

EXTRACURRICULAR ACTIVITIES:

Editor and reporter, college newspaper.

Member, championship ski team.

Volunteer, Sierra Search & Rescue Team. Speaker for League to Save Lake Tahoe.

REFERENCES AVAILABLE ON REQUEST

Resume dos and don'ts.

There are no hard and fast rules to resume writing, but these are a few points on which the majority of experts would agree.

■ DO . . .

- ■ Start with a clear objective.
- ■ Have different resumes for different types of jobs.
- ■ List as many relevant skills as you legitimately possess.
- ■ Use jargon or buzzwords that are understood in the industry.
- ■ Use superlatives: biggest, best, most, first.
- ■ Start sentences with action verbs (organized, reduced, increased, negotiated, analyzed).
- ■ List relevant credentials and affiliations.
- ■ Limit your resume to one or two pages (unless you're applying for an academic position).
- ■ Use standard-size, white or off-white heavy paper.
- ■ Use a standard typeface and a letter-quality or laser-jet printer.
- ■ Spell check and proofread, several times.

■ DON'T . . .

- ■ Lie.
- ■ Sound overly pompous.
- ■ Use pronouns such as I, we.
- ■ Send a photo of yourself.
- ■ List personal information such as height, weight, marital status or age, unless you're applying for a job as an actor or model.
- ■ List hobbies, unless they're directly related to your objective.
- ■ Provide references unless requested. ("References on request" is optional.)
- ■ Include salary information.
- ■ Start a sentence with "responsibilities included:"
- ■ Overuse and mix type styles such as bold, underline, italic, and uppercase.

The second biggest mistake is to have *spelling errors*. Spelling mistakes communicate to prospective employers a basic carelessness.

Other resume dos and don'ts appear in the accompanying box. *(See ■ Panel 13.3.)*

WRITING A COMPUTER-FRIENDLY RESUME.

Once upon a time, an employer would simply throw away old resumes or file them and rarely look at them again. Now a company may well use a high-tech resume-scanning system such as Resumix.[21] This technology uses an optical scanner to input 900 pages of resumes a day, storing the data in a computerized database. The system can search for up to 60 key factors, such as job titles, technical expertise, education, geographic location, and employment history. Resumix can also track race, religion, gender, and other factors to help companies diversify their workforce. These descriptors can then be matched with available openings.

Such resume scanners can save companies thousands of dollars. They allow organizations to more efficiently search their existing pool of applicants before turning to advertising or other means to recruit employees. For applicants, however, resume banks and other electronic systems have turned job hunting into a whole new ball game. The latest advice is as follows:

- *Use the right paper and print:* In the past, job seekers have used tricks such as colored paper and fancy typefaces in their resumes to catch a bored personnel officer's eye. However, optical scanners have trouble reading type on colored or gray paper and are confused by unusual typefaces. They even have difficulty reading underlining and poor-quality dot-matrix printing.[22] Thus, you need to be aware of new format rules for resume writing. *(See* ■ *Panel 13.4.)*

- *Use keywords for skills or attributes:* Just as important as the format of a resume today are the words used in it. In the past, resume writers tried to clearly present their skills. Now it's necessary to use, in addition, as many of the buzzwords or keywords of your profession or industry as you can.

    Action words ("managed," "developed") should still be used, but they are less important than nouns. Nouns include job titles, capabilities, languages spoken, type of degree, and the like ("sales representative," "Spanish," "B.A."). The reason, of course, is that a computer will scan for keywords applicable to the job that is to be filled.

    Because resume-screening programs sort and rank keywords, resumes with the most keywords rise to the top of the electronic pile. Consequently, it's suggested you pack your resume with every conceivable kind of keyword that applies to you. You should especially use those that appear in help-wanted ads.[23]

    If you're looking for a job in desktop publishing, for instance, certain keywords in your resume will help it stand out. Examples might be *Aldus Pagemaker, Compugraphics, DCF, Harvard Graphics, Page Perfect, Quark.*

Tips for preparing a computer-scannable resume. Resumix Inc., maker of computerized resume-scanning systems, suggests observing the following rules of format for resume writing:

- Exotic typefaces, underlining, and decorative graphics don't scan well.

- It's best to send originals, not copies, and not to use a dot-matrix printer.

- Too-small print may confuse the scanner; don't go below 12-point type.

- Use standard $8\frac{1}{2} \times 11$-inch paper and do not fold. Words in a crease can't be read easily.

- Use white or light-beige paper. Blues and grays minimize the contrast between the letters and the background.

- Avoid double columns. The scanner reads from left to right.

USING THE COMPUTER TO LOOK FOR JOBS.

Today there are many computer-related tools you can use to help you in your job search. These range from resume-writing software to "online" databases on which you can post your resume or look for job listings.[24-32] *(See ■ Panel 13.5.)* Two types of online job-hunting tools are as follows:

■ *Online job openings:* You can search online for lists of jobs that might interest you. This method is called the "armchair job search" by careers columnist Joyce Lain Kennedy, co-author of *Electronic Job Search Revolution.* [33] With a computer you can prowl through online information services, online job ad services, or newspaper online information services. (Examples of online information services are America Online, Prodigy, and CompuServe.)

■ *Resume database services:* You can put your specially tailored resume in an online database, giving employers the opportunity to contact you. Among the kinds of resources for employers are databases for college students and databases for people with experience.

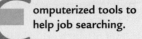

Computerized tools to help job searching.

■ **ONLINE JOB LISTINGS**

Lists of job openings are posted online through three types of services:

■ **Online information services:** CompuServe, America Online, Prodigy, and GEnie offer help-wanted listings, forums to discuss career issues, and networking groups. America Online, for instance, offers the Career Center, which allows viewers to look at sample resumes, peruse help-wanted ads, or have private career counseling sessions with the "CareerDoc."

■ **Online job ad services:** Also called "job bulletin boards," online job ad services are job notices posted by companies specializing in electronic job ads, government agencies, professional societies and trade associations, industry publications, recruiting agencies, and others.

For example, Help Wanted USA, a database of 4000 listings, appears on America Online and the Internet. The Career Network, a nonprofit venture backed by 40 major corporations, offers a wealth of information for students and graduates at many colleges. Job Ads USA displays help-wanted ads, collected from over 100 newspapers, which are of interest to human resource professionals.

■ **Newspaper online information services:** Many newspapers (for example, the *Atlanta Journal* and *Constitution*, the *Chicago Tribune*, and the *St. Louis Post-Dispatch*) offer, for a small fee, many of the same things online that they do in newsprint, including help-wanted ads.

RESUME DATABASE SERVICES

By putting your resume in one of the following types of online databases, you give employers the opportunity to find you:

■ **Databases for college students:** Colleges sometimes have or are members of online database services on which their students or alumni may place electronic resumes. For example, several universities have formed University ProNet, which provides online resumes to interested employers; students and alumni pay a one-time lifetime fee of $35.

The Career Placement Registry (available through the online service DIALOG) allows college students or recent graduates to post resumes for $15.

■ **Databases for people with experience:** Resumes for experienced people may be collected by private databases. An example is Connexions, which charges experienced professionals $40 a year to post their resume.

Some databases serve employers in particular geographical areas or those looking for people with particular kinds of experience. HispanData in Santa Barbara, California, specializes in marketing Hispanic professionals to employers seeking to diversify their workforces.

RESUME-WRITING & JOB-SEARCH SOFTWARE

Programs for the personal computer are available that will help you turn out resumes, generate cover letters, and similar tasks. Some features are as follows:

■ **Various resume formats:** Programs will help you tailor your resume in various ways, as in organizing a chronological, functional, or other type of resume. They also offer a choice of formats for best presenting your experience and strengths and tailoring the resume for particular jobs. Some offer special forms for people in technical, military, and academic fields.

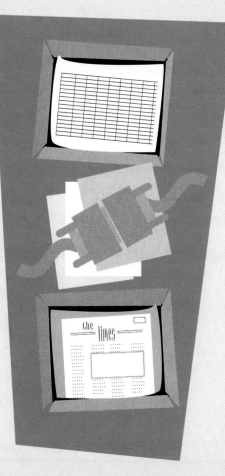

■ **Resume extras:** Some programs offer a glossary of action words to add marketable keywords. If you're not sure what to include in the resume, a program may "interview" you by taking you through a series of tasks and providing menus from which to choose information. A word processor and spellchecker is built into some programs.

■ **Cover letters:** You can get software that will provide professional letters by selecting from paragraphs written by experts, personalizing the letters with your own data. There may even be a module for printing envelopes.

■ **Databases of contacts, appointments, activity logs:** Some packages have rather sophisticated contact managers and calendars for keeping track of calls and appointments during a search. These can help you create a database of names and addresses of companies and do mass mailings. They can also remind you to send thank-you notes and follow-up letters. An activity log can help you plan your strategy.

■ **Expert advice and tutorials:** Some programs provide advice and practice in how to target a job search and practice for interviews. Others show you how to express your interests, research potential employers, and form a network of contacts.

There are even some programs that cater to niche markets; a package called Quick and Easy 171's produces a filled-out version of the SF-171 form required of applicants for government work. DataTech's PowerWords software converts English into bureaucratic words (instead of having "filed" documents, you "classified" documents) to alert government personnel officers.

You may wish to try Personal Exploration #13.3 to draft a resume using some of the principles just described.

WRITING A GOOD COVER LETTER. Write a targeted cover letter to accompany your resume. This advice especially should be followed if you're responding to an ad.

Most people don't bother to write a cover letter focusing on the particular job being advertised. Moreover, if they do, say San Francisco employment experts Howard Bennett and Chuck McFadden, "they tend to talk about what *they* are looking for in a job. This is a major turn-off for employers."[34] Employers don't care very much about your dreams and aspirations, only about finding the best candidate for the job.

Bennett and McFadden suggest the following strategy for a cover letter:

■ *Emphasize how you will meet the employer's needs:* Employers advertise because they have needs to be met. "You will get much more attention," say Bennett and McFadden, "if you demonstrate your ability to fill those needs."

How do you find out what those needs are? *You read the ad.* By reading the ad closely you can find out how the company talks about itself. You can also find out what attributes it is looking for in employees and what the needs are for the particular position.

■ *Use the language of the ad:* In your cover letter, use as much of the ad's language as you can. "Use the same words as much as possible," advise Bennett and McFadden. "Feed the company's language back to them." This will produce "an almost subliminal realization in the company that you are the person they've been looking for."

■ *Take care with the format of the letter:* Keep the letter to one page and use dashes or asterisks to emphasize the areas where you meet the needs described in the ad. Make sure the sentences read well and— very important—that no word or name is misspelled.

THE INTERVIEW. The intent of both cover letter and resume is to get you an interview. The act of getting an interview itself means you're probably in the top 10–15% of candidates. Once you're into an interview, a different set of skills is needed.

You need to look clean and well-groomed, of course. Richard Bolles suggests you also you need to say what distinguishes you from the 20 other people the employer is interviewing. "If you say you are a very thorough person, don't just say it," suggests Bolles. "Demonstrate it by telling them what you know about their company, which you learned beforehand by doing your homework."[35]

HOW CAN YOU BUILD AN IMPRESSIVE RESUME?

For this exercise, it doesn't matter whether you're of traditional college age or are a returning adult student. Its purpose is to get you accustomed to thinking about one important question: *What kinds of things might you be doing throughout your college years in order to produce a high-quality resume?*

Fill in the lines below with your *present* experience. Then add ideas about *experience you might acquire* that would help you in the next few years.

1. MY PRESENT EDUCATION:

_____
_____
_____
_____
_____

Highlights of my present education (your most impressive accomplishments):

_____
_____
_____
_____
_____

MY FUTURE EDUCATION:

_____
_____
_____
_____
_____

Highlights of my education (impressive accomplishments you would like to be able to list):

_____
_____
_____
_____

2. MY PRESENT WORK EXPERIENCE:

_____
_____
_____
_____

_____
_____
_____
_____

Highlights of my present work experience (your most impressive accomplishments):

_____
_____
_____
_____

MY FUTURE WORK EXPERIENCE:

_____
_____
_____
_____
_____

Highlights of my work experience (impressive accomplishments you would like to be able to list):

_____
_____
_____
_____

3. MY PRESENT CO-CURRICULAR ACTIVITIES:

_____
_____
_____
_____
_____

Highlights of my present co-curricular activities (your most impressive accomplishments):

_____
_____
_____
_____
_____

MY FUTURE CO-CURRICULAR ACTIVITIES:

_____
_____
_____
_____

Highlights of my co-curricular activities (impressive accomplishments you would like to be able to list):

_____
_____
_____
_____

4. MY PRESENT HONORS AND AWARDS:

_____
_____
_____
_____
_____

MY FUTURE HONORS AND AWARDS:

_____
_____
_____
_____

GROUP ACTIVITY OPTION

Brainstorming may help in putting together your resume. In a small group, talk through your responses to the directions above. Ask for feedback and suggestions. Then listen to others read their responses to this Personal Exploration and offer your own comments.

Onward: Applying This Chapter to Your Life

PREVIEW Life is an endless process of self-discovery.

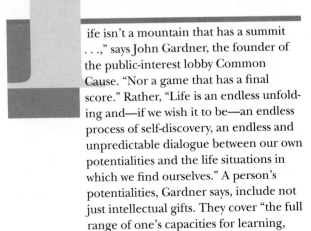

ife isn't a mountain that has a summit . . .," says John Gardner, the founder of the public-interest lobby Common Cause. "Nor a game that has a final score." Rather, "Life is an endless unfolding and—if we wish it to be—an endless process of self-discovery, an endless and unpredictable dialogue between our own potentialities and the life situations in which we find ourselves." A person's potentialities, Gardner says, include not just intellectual gifts. They cover "the full range of one's capacities for learning, sensing, wondering, understanding, loving, and aspiring."[36]

This, then, is not the end. It is the beginning. Explain what you can take from this chapter to help you on your journey:

_____

_____

_____

_____

_____

_____

_____

_____

_____

_____

_____

_____

_____

_____

_____

_____

_____

1. The best way to start thinking about your prospective major is to dream your dreams. Your journal is the place to do this. Take 15 minutes to free-associate. Write as quickly (but legibly) as you can all your desires about things you're curious about or enjoy and would like to study. Then state what majors might best serve your wishes.

2. You go through life only once. Yet it's possible to have more than one career. You could be a physician/musician, a writer/attorney, a social worker/social activist, for example. Or you might have successive careers, each one different. When you "dream the impossible dream," what careers come to mind?

3. Interviewing for jobs is a skill all by itself. This book did not have space to give this subject the coverage it deserves. What kinds of skills do you think are needed for interviewing? What books can you find in the library that might help you refine your interviewing techniques? (A classic one is *Sweaty Palms.*)

special section: productivity tools for your future

The old ways are changing, and changing fast.

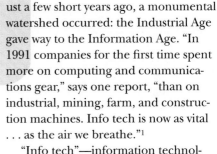

just a few short years ago, a monumental watershed occurred: the Industrial Age gave way to the Information Age. "In 1991 companies for the first time spent more on computing and communications gear," says one report, "than on industrial, mining, farm, and construction machines. Info tech is now as vital . . . as the air we breathe."[1]

"Info tech"—information technology—has brought new kinds of productivity tools into the workplace: calculators, copiers, word processors, personal computers, fax machines, cellular phones, voice mail, electronic mail, online services, the Internet and its World Wide Web, and so on. Learning to use tools like these can also increase your productivity as a student while simultaneously giving you skills that will help you advance your career.

This special section considers the following:

- Word processors

- Computer hardware

- Computer software

- Notebooks and subnotebooks

- Communications tools—electronic bulletin board systems (BBSs), online services, and the Internet

Word Processors

The typewriter, that long-lived machine, has gone to its reward. Today your choice is generally to buy (1) a word processing typewriter, (2) a personal word processor, or (3) a microcomputer-plus-printer that runs word processing software.[2]

WORD PROCESSING TYPEWRITER. The *word processing typewriter* is like the old typewriter in that it can be made to type directly on paper. Yet it can also let you see and edit your words on a small display screen before they are printed on paper. It can automatically check your spelling. It can also store a few pages of text that you can retrieve and print later. This machine prints with a daisy wheel, the petals of which stamp characters directly onto the paper.

Priced at around $200, the word processing typewriter is probably fine, experts say, if you do only short reports and routine correspondence. Models are available from Brother, Sears, and Sharp.

PERSONAL WORD PROCESSOR. The *personal word processor* is really a personal computer with a built-in word processing program, but it usually cannot run other types of programs. The machine is dedicated to creating, editing, and printing documents, and it can also store your written materials on diskettes. Display screens are usually easier to read than those on word processing typewriters.

Prices are higher than for typewriters, starting at about $300. Models are available from Brother, Panasonic, and AEG Olympia. Personal word processors are preferable if you do long reports.

MICROCOMPUTER, PRINTER, & WORD PROCESSING SOFTWARE. Microcomputers run not only word processing programs but also many other kinds of software. This is their principal advantage. *Word processing software* allows you to use computers to create, edit, revise, store, and print text material. Most current programs provide a number of menus for manipulating aspects of your document. The three leading programs for IBM-style Windows computers are WordPerfect, Microsoft Word, and Ami Pro; for Macintoshes they are Word and MacWrite.

Word processing software allows microcomputers to do what the other two types of machines do—namely, maneuver through a document with a cursor and *delete, insert,* and *replace* text, the principal correction activities. However, word processing software offers additional features that the other machines lack, such as Search, Replace, Block Move commands; spell checking; and thesaurus. *(See ■ Panel A.1, p. 332.)*

Opting for a microcomputer for word processing means you have to make three decisions:

- *Expense:* You have to be prepared to spend more than you would for a word processing typewriter or personal word processor. Microcomputers start at $500, and a state-of-the-art system that includes software and printer may cost $3000–$4000.

- *Software:* You have to determine what word processing software you want to use. For students, the easiest choice is to use that used by most other students, especially those in your major. That way you can easily borrow someone else's system if yours breaks down.

- *Portability:* You have to make some decisions about portability and printers. A desktop machine is often cheaper than a laptop, but a laptop is more easily carried around. Printers are a problem, since (with some exceptions) they are not built into the computer—and, indeed, are often bigger than the computer itself. Transporting both a microcomputer and a printer can be cumbersome, although most people find they don't need to move a printer around. Some small, portable printers (about the size of a cigarette carton) are available, but they are slow to operate.

Features of a word processing program.

Word processing software offers features such as the Search, Replace, and Block Move commands; spell checking; and thesaurus.

With a word processor, unlike with a typewriter, you can maneuver through a document and do the principal correction activities—*delete, insert,* and *replace*—with ease. In addition, word processing software offers these other features:

Search and replace: The *Search command* allows you to find any word or number that you know exists in your document. The *Replace command* allows you to automatically replace it with something else.

"Cut and paste" (block and move): Typewriter users were accustomed to using scissors and glue to "cut and paste" to move a paragraph or block of text from one place to another in a manuscript. With word processing, you can exercise the *Block command* to indicate the beginning and end of the portion of text you want to move. Then you can use the *Move command* to move it to another location in the document. (You can also use the *Copy command* to copy the block of text to a new location while also leaving the original block where it is.)

Report format: The *report format* is the layout of the printed page, including print columns, line spacing, justification, and headers or footers. It is easy to have one, two, or three columns of type on the page; to make the lines single-, double-, or triple-spaced (or all three within a document); or to have the text justified or unjustified.

Justify means to align text evenly between left and right margins, as, for example, is done with most newspaper columns. *Unjustify* means to not align the text evenly, as is done with the right side of many business letters ("ragged right").

A *header* is a small piece of text (such as a date) that is printed at the top of every page. A *footer* is the same thing printed at the bottom of every page.

You can also make format changes within a document, such as by centering or indenting headings or by emphasizing text with **boldface**, *italics*, or underlining.

Spelling and grammar checking, thesaurus, outlining, mail-merge: The principal word processing packages have some separate programs or functions that can really reduce your work.

Many writers automatically run their completed documents through a *spelling checker,* which tests for incorrectly spelled words. Another program is a *grammar checker,* which flags poor grammar, wordiness, incomplete sentences, and awkward phrases.

If you find yourself stuck for the right word while you're writing, you can call up an on-screen *thesaurus,* which will present you with the appropriate word or alternative words.

If you need assistance with organizing your thoughts, you might use an outline processor. An *outline processor* allows you to type in thoughts and then tag the topics with numbers and letters and organize them in outline form, with Roman numerals, letters, and numbers.

If you want to send out the same letter to different people, you can use the *mail-merge program* to print customized form letters, with different names, addresses, and salutations for each letter.

Computer Hardware

Students who come to college with a personal computer as part of their luggage are certainly ahead of the game. If you don't have one, however, there are other options.

IF YOU DON'T OWN A PERSONAL COMPUTER.

If you don't have a PC, you may be able to borrow someone else's sometimes. However, if you have a paper due the next day, you may have to defer to the owner, who may also have a deadline. When borrowing, then, you need to plan ahead and allow yourself plenty of time.

Virtually every campus now makes computers available to students, either at minimal cost or essentially for free as part of the regular student fees. This availability may take two forms:

- *Library or computer labs:* Even students who have their own PCs may sometimes want to use the computers available at the library or campus computer lab. These may have special software or better printers that they don't have themselves.

- *Dormitory computer centers or dorm-room terminals:* Some campuses provide dormitory-based computer centers (for example, in the basement). Even if you have your own PC, it's nice to know about these for backup purposes.

Some campuses also provide computers or terminals within students' dormitory rooms. These are usually connected by a campus-wide local area network (LAN) to lab computers and administrative systems. Often they also allow students to communicate over phone lines to people in other locations, including outside the country.

Of course, if the system cannot accommodate a large number of students, all the computers may be in high demand come term-paper time. Clearly, owning a computer offers you convenience and a competitive advantage.

IF YOU DO OWN A PERSONAL COMPUTER.

Perhaps someone gave you a personal computer, or you acquired one, before you came to college. It will probably be one of two types: (1) an IBM or IBM-compatible, such as an AST, Compaq, DEC, Dell, Gateway, Hewlett-Packard, NCR, NEC, Packard-Bell, Radio Shack, Toshiba, or Zenith; or (2) an Apple Macintosh or similar system. (Others, such as the Apple II or Commodore, are not used in college.) The question then is: Is it adequate?

If all you need to do is write term papers, nearly any microcomputer, new or used, will do. Indeed, you may not even need to have a printer, if you can find other ways to print out things. The University of Michigan, for instance, offers "express stations" or "drive-up windows." These allow students to use a floppy disk or connect a computer to a student-use printer to print out their papers. Or, if a friend has a compatible computer, you can ask to borrow it and the printer for a short time to print your work.

You should, however, take a look around you to see if your present system is appropriate for your campus and your major.

- *The fit with your campus:* Some campuses are known as "IBM" (or IBM-compatible) schools, others as "Mac" (Macintosh) schools. You should call the dean of students or otherwise ask around to find which system is most popular.

Why should choice of machine matter? The answer is that floppy disks generally can't be read interchangeably among the three main types of microcomputers. Thus, if you own the system that is out of step for your campus, you may find it difficult to swap files or programs with others. Nor will you be able to borrow their equipment to finish a paper if yours breaks down. (There are some conversion programs, but these take time and may not be readily available.)

- *The fit with your major:* Speech communications, foreign language, physical education, political science, biology, and English majors probably don't need a fancy computer system. Business, engineering, architecture, and journalism majors may have special requirements. For instance, an architecture major doing computer-aided design (CAD) projects or a journalism major doing desktop publishing will need reasonably powerful systems. A history or nursing major, who presumably will mainly be writing papers, will not.

Of course you may be presently undeclared or undecided about your major. Even so, it's a good idea to find out what kinds of equipment and programs are being used in the majors you are contemplating.

BUYING A PERSONAL COMPUTER: THE TRADEOFF BETWEEN POWER & EXPENSE.

Buying a personal computer, like buying a car, often requires making a tradeoff between *power* and *expense*.

The word *power* has different meanings when describing software and hardware:

- *Powerful software:* Applied to software, "powerful" means that the program is *flexible*. That is, it can do many different things. For example, a word processing program that can print in different type styles (fonts) is more powerful than one that prints in only one style.

- *Powerful hardware:* Applied to hardware, "powerful" means that the equipment (1) is *fast* and (2) has *great capacity*.

  A fast computer will process data more quickly than a slow one. With an older computer, for example, it may take several seconds to save, or store on a disk, a 50-page term paper. On a newer machine, it might take less than a second.

  A computer with great capacity can run complex software and process voluminous files. *This is an especially important matter if you want to be able to run newer forms of software.*

If your major does not require a special computer system, a microcomputer can be acquired for relatively little. You can probably buy a used computer, with software thrown in, for under $500 and a printer for under $200. (An IBM

AT may start for as low as $150 and a Mac Plus for $400; both of these are old but still-serviceable machines.)

Will computer use make up an essential part of your major, as it might if you are going into engineering, business, or graphic arts? If so, you may want to try to acquire powerful hardware and software. People who really want (and can afford) their own desktop publishing system, for instance, might buy a top-of-the-line Macintosh Power Mac with LaserWriter printer, scanner, and PageMaker software. This might well cost $7000. Most students, of course, cannot afford anything close to this.

What's the *minimum* you should get? Probably an IBM-compatible or Macintosh system, with 512K–640K of memory and two floppy-disk drives or one floppy-disk and one hard-disk drive. However, 8 megabytes of memory is preferable if you're going to run many of today's programs. Dot-matrix printers are in widespread use on all campuses (24-pin printers are preferable to 9-pin). To be sure, the more expensive laser printers produce a better image. However, you can always use the dot-matrix for drafts and print out the final version on a campus student-use printer.

WHERE TO BUY NEW.

Fierce price wars among microcomputer manufacturers and retailers have made hardware more affordable. One reason why IBM-compatibles have become so widespread is that non-IBM manufacturers early on were able to copy, or "clone," IBM machines and offer them at cut-rate prices. For a long time, Apple Macintoshes were considerably more expensive. In part this was because other manufacturers were unable to offer inexpensive clones. In recent times, however, Apple has felt the pinch of competition and has dropped its prices also. In addition, Apple has allowed other computer makers to clone its machines, resulting in lower prices.

There are several sources for inexpensive new computers:

- *Student discount:* With a college ID card, you're probably entitled to student discounts (usually 10–20%) through the campus bookstore or college computer resellers. In addition, during the first few weeks of the term, many campuses offer special sales on computer equipment. Campus resellers also provide on-campus service and support and, says one expert, can help students meet the prevailing campus standards while satisfying their personal needs.[3]

- **Computer superstores:** These are big chains such as Computer City, CompUSA, and Microage. Computers are also sold at department stores, warehouse stores (such as Costco and Price Club), Wal-Mart, Circuit City, Radio Shack, and similar outlets.

- **Mail-order houses:** Companies like Dell Computer Corp. and Gateway 2000 found they could sell computers inexpensively by mail order while offering customer support over the phone. Their success inspired IBM, Compaq, and others to plunge into the mail-order business.

The price advantage of mail-order companies has eroded with the rise of computer superstores.[4] Moreover, the lack of local repair and service support can be a major disadvantage. Still, if you're interested in this route, look for a copy of the phone-book-size magazine *Computer Shopper,* which carries ads from most mail-order vendors.

When buying hardware, look to see if software, such as word processing or spreadsheet programs, comes "bundled" with it. *Bundled* means that software is included in the selling price of the hardware. This arrangement can be a real advantage, saving you several hundred dollars.

Because the computers are somewhat fragile, it's not unusual for them to break down, some even when newly purchased. Indeed, nearly 25% of 45,000 PC users surveyed by one computer magazine reported some kind of problem with new computers.[5] (The failure rates were: hard drive—21%, motherboard—20%, monitor—12%, floppy-disk drive—11%, and power supply—10%.) The PCs (Apple was not included) that had the fewest problems were those from AST Research, Compaq, Epson, Everex, Hewlett-Packard, IBM, and NCR (AT&T).

WHERE TO BUY USED. Buying a used computer can save you a minimum of 50%, depending on its age. If you don't need the latest software, this can often be the way to go. The most important thing is to buy *recognizable* brand names, examples being Apple and IBM or well-known IBM-compatibles: Compaq, NCR, Tandy, Toshiba, Zenith. Obscure or discontinued brands may not be repairable.[6]

Among the sources for used computers are the following:[7]

- **Retail sources:** A look in the telephone-book Yellow Pages under "Computers, Used" will produce several leads. Authorized dealers (of IBM, Apple, Compaq, and so on) may shave prices on demonstration (demo) or training equipment. Also, colleges and universities may sell off their old equipment when it is being replaced.

- **Used-computer brokers:** There are a number of used-computer brokers, such as American Computer Exchange, Boston Computer Exchange, Damark, and National Computer Exchange.

- **Individuals:** Classified ads in local newspapers, shopper throwaways, and (in some localities) free computer newspapers/magazines provide listings of used computer equipment. Similar listings may also appear on electronic bulletin board systems (BBSs).

One problem with buying from individuals is that they may not feel obligated to take the equipment back if something goes wrong. Thus, you should inspect the equipment carefully. *(See* ■ *Panel A.2, p. 336.)* For a small fee, a computer-repair shop can check out the hardware for damage.

How much should you pay for a used computer? This can be tricky. Some sellers may not be aware of the rapid depreciation of their equipment and price it too high. The best bet is to look through back issues of the classified ads for a couple of newspapers in your area until you have a sense of what equipment may be worth.

Tips for buying used computers. Buying from an individual means you have little recourse if something goes wrong. The following tips should help you to buy carefully.

- If possible, take someone who knows computers with you.

- Turn the computer on and off a few times to make sure there are no problems on startup.

- Use the computer and, if possible, try the software you want to use. Listen for strange sounds in the hard drive or the floppies.

- Turn the computer off and look for screen burn-in, a ghost image on the screen after the machine has been turned off. It can be a sign of misuse.

- Ask about the warranty. Some companies, including Apple and IBM, permit warranties to be transferred to new owners (effective from the date of the original purchase). A new owner can usually have the warranty extended by paying a fee.

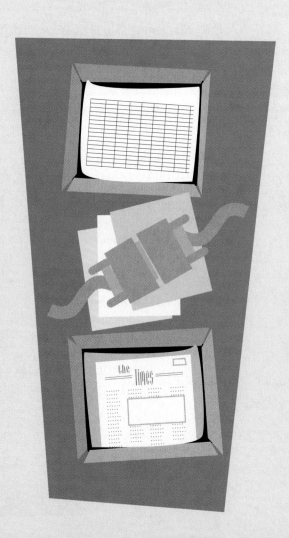

CHECKLIST. Here are some decisions you should make before buying a computer:

- ***Do I want a desktop or a portable?*** Look for a computer that fits your work style. For instance, you may want a portable if you spend a lot of time at the library. Some students even use portables to take notes in class. If you do most of your work in your room, you may find it more comfortable to have a desktop PC. Though not portable, the monitors of desktop computers are usually easier to read.

  It's possible to have both portability and a readable display screen. Buy a laptop, but also buy a monitor that you can plug the portable into. Computers are also available with "docking" systems that permit a portable to fit inside a desktop computer or monitor.

  We consider portables (notebooks and subnotebooks) in more detail in a few pages.

- ***What software will I need?*** Although it may sound backward, you should select the software before the hardware.[8] This is because you want to choose software that will perform the kind of work you want to do. First find the kind of programs you want—word processing, spreadsheets, communications, graphics, or whatever. Check out the hardware requirements for those programs. Then make sure you get a system to fit them.

  The advice to start with software before hardware has always been standard for computer buyers. However, it is becoming increasingly important as programs with extensive graphics come on the market. Graphics tend to require a lot of memory, hard-disk storage, and screen display area.

- ***Is upgradability important?*** The newest software being released is so powerful (meaning flexible) that it requires increasingly more powerful hardware. That is, the software requires hardware that is faster and has greater main memory and storage capacity. If you buy an outdated used computer, you probably will not be able to *upgrade* it. That is, you will be unable to buy internal parts, such as additional memory, that can run newer software. This limitation may be fine if you expect to be able to afford an all-new system in a couple of years. If, however, you are buying new equipment right now, be sure to ask the salesperson how the hardware can be upgraded.

■ *Do I want an IBM-style or a Macintosh?* Although the situation is changing, until recently the division between IBM-style personal computers on the one hand and Apple Macintoshes on the other was fundamental. Neither could run the other's software or exchange files of data without special equipment and software. We mentioned that some campuses and some academic majors tend to favor one type of microcomputer over the other. Outside of college, however, the business world tends to be dominated by IBM and IBM-compatible machines. In a handful of areas—graphics arts and desktop publishing, for example—Macintoshes are preferred.

If you think there's a chance you will need to become familiar with both IBMs and Macs, you might consider buying a high-end Macintosh PowerBook. This microcomputer can handle disks and programs for both systems.

■ *Do I want a modem?* A *modem* is needed to send messages from one computer to another via a phone line. About 40% of personal computers these days have a modem. The speed at which a modem can transmit data is measured in baud and bps (bits per second) rates. A slow modem, 2400 bps, can be bought for as little as $50; a faster modem, 9600 bps, which is becoming the standard, is available for $200; a high-speed modem, 14,400 bps, which is recommended by many users, can be purchased for only a few score dollars more. The faster your modem, the more you will save in telephone charges and in fees paid to any online organizations that charge by the minute.

Computer Software

There are thousands of software programs, available on floppy disks, that will run on computer hardware. The best way to consider the kind of software that might be useful to you is to visualize yourself sitting at a desk in an old-fashioned office: You have a calendar, clock, and name-and-address file. You have a typewriter. You have a calculator. You have desk drawers full of files. You have a telephone. You have an In-box and an Out-box to which someone delivers and from which someone takes your interoffice and outside mail. Many of these items could also be found on a student's desk. How would a computer and software improve on this arrangement?

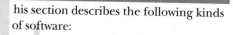

his section describes the following kinds of software:

- Desktop accessories and personal information managers
- Spreadsheets
- Database management systems
- Graphics
- Communications
- Integrated programs and suites
- Groupware

DESKTOP ACCESSORIES & PERSONAL INFORMATION MANAGERS. Is there any need to have an electronic version of the traditional appointment calendar, clock,

Characteristics of a spreadsheet program.

Spreadsheets can be used to display data in graphic form, such as in pie charts or bar charts, which are easier to read than columns of numbers. Spreadsheets can even be linked to more exciting graphics, such as digitized maps.

Columns, rows, and labels: *Column headings* appear across the top; *row headings* appear down the left side. Column and row headings are called *labels*. The label is usually any descriptive text, such as APRIL, PHONE, or GROSS SALES.

Cells, cell addresses, values, and spreadsheet cursor: The place where rows and columns intersect is called a *cell,* and its position is called a *cell address.* For example, "A1" is the cell address for the top left cell, where column A and row 1 intersect.

A number entered in a cell is called a *value.* The values are the actual numbers used in the spreadsheet—dollars, percentages, grade points, temperatures, or whatever. A *cell pointer* or *spreadsheet cursor* indicates where data is to be entered. The cell pointer can be moved around like a cursor in a word processing program.

Formulas and recalculation: Now we come to the reason the electronic spreadsheet has taken business organizations offices by storm. *Formulas* are instructions for calculations. For example, a formula might be SUM CELLS A5 TO A15, meaning "Sum (add) all the numbers in the cells with cell addresses A5 through A15."

After the values have been plugged into the spreadsheet, the formulas can be used to calculate outcomes. What is revolutionary, however, is the way the spreadsheet can easily do recalculation. *Recalculation* is the process of recomputing values *automatically*, either as an ongoing process as data is being entered or afterward, with the press of a key.

The "what-if?" world: The recalculation feature has opened up whole new possibilities for decision making. As a user, you can create a plan, put in formulas and numbers, and then ask yourself "What would happen if we change that detail?"—and immediately see the effect on the bottom line.

and file of phone numbers and addresses? A lot of people with computers still use old-fashioned paper-and-pencil calendars and To Do lists. However, others find ready uses for the kind of software called *desktop accessories* or *personal information managers (PIMs).*

- **Desktop accessories: A desktop accessory, or desktop organizer,** is a software package that provides an electronic version of tools or objects commonly found on a desktop: calendar, clock, card file, calculator, and notepad. Some desktop-accessory programs come as standard equipment with some systems software (such as on Microsoft's Windows). Others, such as Borland's SideKick or Lotus Agenda, are available as separate programs to run in your computer at the same time you are running other software. Some are principally *scheduling and calendaring programs;* their main purpose is to enable you to do time and event scheduling.

  Suppose, for example, you are working on a word processing document and someone calls to schedule lunch next week. You can simply type a command that "pops up" your appointment calendar, type in the appointment, save the information, and then return to your interrupted work. Other features, such as a calculator keypad, a "scratch pad" for typing in notes to yourself, and a Rolodex-type address and phone directory (some with automatic telephone dialer), can be display on the screen when needed.

- **Personal information managers:** A more sophisticated program is the *personal information manager (PIM),* a combination word processor, database, and desktop accessory program that organizes a variety of information.[9] Examples of PIMs are Ascend, CA-UpToDate, DayMaker Organizer, DateBook Pro, Dynodex, Instant Recall, Lotus Organizer, OnTime for Windows, and Personal Reminder System.

  Lotus Organizer, for example, looks on the screen much like a paper datebook—down to simulated metal rings holding simulated paper pages. The program has screen images of section tabs labeled Calendar, To Do, Address, Notepad, Planner, and Anniversary. The Notepad section lets users enter long documents, including text and graphics, that can be called up at any time.[10] Whereas Lotus Organizer resembles a datebook, the PIM called Dynodex resembles an address book, with spaces for names, addresses, phone numbers, and notes.

SPREADSHEET SOFTWARE. What is a spreadsheet? Traditionally, it was simply a grid of rows and columns, printed on special green paper, that was used by accountants and other financial types to produce financial projections and reports. A person making up a spreadsheet often spent long days and weekends at the office penciling tiny numbers into countless tiny rectangles. When one figure changed, all the rest of the numbers on the spreadsheet had to be recomputed—and ultimately there might be wastebaskets full of jettisoned worksheets.

In the late 1970s, someone got the idea of computerizing all this. The *electronic spreadsheet* allows users to create tables and financial schedules by entering data into rows and columns arranged as a grid on a display screen. The electronic spreadsheet quickly became the most popular small-business program. Today the principal spreadsheets are Excel, Lotus 1-2-3, and Quattro Pro. *(See ■ Panel A.3, opposite page.)*

DATABASE MANAGEMENT SYSTEMS. In its most general sense, a database is any electronically stored collection of data in a computer system. In its more specific sense, a *database* is a collection of interrelated files in a computer system. These computer-based files are organized so that those parts that have a common element can be retrieved easily. The software for maintaining a database is a *database manager* or *database management system (DBMS)*, a program that controls the structure of a database and access to the data. *(See ■ Panel A.4.)*

Characteristics of a database management system.

Organization of a database: A database is organized—from smallest to largest items—into *fields*, *records*, and *files*.

A *field* is a unit of data consisting of one or more characters. Examples of a field are your name, your address, or your driver's license number.

A *record* is a collection of related fields. An example of a record would be your name *and* address *and* driver's license number.

A *file* is a collection of related records. An example of a file could be one in your state's Department of Motor Vehicles. The file would include everyone who received a driver's license on the same day, including their names, addresses, and driver's license numbers.

Select and display: The beauty of database management programs is that you can locate records in the file quickly. For example, your college may maintain several records about you—one at the registrar's, one in financial aid, one in the housing department, and so on. Any of these records can be called up on a computer display screen for viewing and updating. Thus, if you move, your address field will need to be changed in all records. The database is quickly corrected by finding your name field. Once the record is displayed, the address field can be changed.

Sort: With a database management system you can easily change the order of records in a file. Normally, records are entered into a database in the order they occur, such as by the date a person registered to attend college. However, all these records can be sorted in different ways. For example, they can be rearranged by state, by age, or by Social Security number.

Calculate and format: Many database management programs contain built-in mathematical formulas. This feature can be used, for example, to find the grade-point averages for students in different majors or in different classes. Such information can then be organized into different formats and printed out.

Today the principal database manager for computers running the DOS operating system is dBASE. The major ones that run under Microsoft Windows are Access and Paradox, followed by Filemaker Pro for Windows, FoxPro for Windows, Q&A for Windows, and Approach for Windows. A multimedia program called Instant Database allows users to attach sound, motion, and graphics to forms.

Databases have gotten easier to use, but they still can be difficult to set up. Even so, the trend is toward making such programs easier for both database creators and database users.

GRAPHICS SOFTWARE. Computer graphics can be highly complicated, such as those used in special effects for movies. Here we are concerned with microcomputer applications useful for work and study—namely, analytical graphics and presentation graphics.

■ *Analytical graphics: Analytical graphics* are graphical forms that make numeric data easier to analyze than when it is in the form of rows and columns of numbers, as in electronic spreadsheets. The principal examples are bar charts, line charts, and pie charts.

Most analytical graphics are features of spreadsheet programs, such as Lotus 1-2-3. Whether viewed on a monitor or printed out, analytical graphics help make sales figures, economic trends, and the like easier to comprehend and analyze.

■ *Presentation graphics: Presentation graphics* are graphics used to communicate or make a presentation of data to others, such as clients or supervisors. Presentations may make use of analytical graphics, but they look much more sophisticated. They use different texturing patterns (speckled, solid, crosshatched), color, and three-dimensionality. Examples of well-known graphics packages are Curtain Call, Freelance Plus, Harvard Graphics, Hollywood, Persuasion, PowerPoint, and Presentation Graphics.

Some presentation graphics packages provide artwork ("clip art") that can be electronically cut and pasted into the graphics. These programs also allow you to use electronic painting and drawing tools for creating lines, rectangles, and just about any other shape. Depending on the system's capabilities, you can add text, animated sequences, and sound. With special equipment you can do graphic presentations on slides, transparencies, and videotape. With all these options the main problem may be simply restraining yourself.

COMMUNICATIONS SOFTWARE. Many microcomputer users feel they have all the productivity they need without ever having to hook up their machines to a telephone. However, having communications capabilities provides you with a great leap forward that vastly extends your range. This leap is made possible with communications software.

Communications software manages the transmission of data between computers. For most microcomputer users this sending and receiving of data is by way of a modem and a telephone line. As mentioned, a *modem* is an electronic device that allows computers to communicate with each other over telephone lines. When you buy a modem, you often get communications software with it. Popular microcomputer communications programs are Smartcom, Crosstalk, ProComm, PC-Dial, Blast, and PC Talk.

With communications software and a modem in your computer, you can connect with friends by e-mail (electronic mail), tap into so-called electronic bulletin-board systems (BBSs), and make use of the research possibilities of information services (America Online, CompuServe, Prodigy) and the Internet. These are described in more detail in another few pages.

INTEGRATED PROGRAMS & SUITES. What if you want to take data from one program and use it in another—say, call up data from a database and use it in a spreadsheet? You can try using separate software packages, but one may not be designed to accept data from the other. *Integrated packages* combine the features of several applications programs into one software package. Usually these capabilities are the ones we have described: electronic spreadsheets, word processing, database management, graphics, and communications. Thus, if you were a sales manager, you could use a database to get various sales figures for different parts of the country. Then you could compare them using a spreadsheet and graphics program, write a memo about them using a word processing program, and send your memo to the sales representatives using communications software.

Examples of integrated packages are ClarisWorks, Eight-in-One, Lotus Works, Microsoft Works, PFS:First Choice, and WordPerfect Works. In general, integrated packages are less powerful than separate programs used alone, such as a word processing or spreadsheet program used by itself. Moreover, systems software such as Windows make integrated programs unnecessary, since the user can easily shift between applications programs that are *completely different.* Finally, integrated programs are largely being replaced by *software suites.*

Suites are applications—like spreadsheets, word processing, graphics, and communications—that are bundled together and sold for a fraction of what the programs would cost if bought individually. Examples of suites are Microsoft Office, Smart Suite, and Perfect Office.

Although cost is what makes suites attractive to many corporate customers, they have other benefits as well. Manufacturers have taken pains to integrate the "look and feel" of the separate programs within the suites to make them easier to use.

GROUPWARE. Most microcomputer software is written for people working alone. *Groupware* is software that is used on a network and serves a group of users working together on the same project. Groupware improves productivity by keeping you continually notified about what your colleagues are thinking and doing, and they about you. "Like e-mail," one writer points out, "groupware became possible when companies started linking PCs into networks. But while e-mail works fine for sending a message to a specific person or group—communicating one-to-one or one-to-many—groupware allows a new kind of communication: many-to-many."[11]

With groupware, technology has changed the kind of behavior that is required for success in an organization. For one thing, such software requires workers to take more responsibility. Obviously, when your contribution to a group project is clearly visible to all, you need to do your best. For another thing, using e-mail or groupware means learning to be sensitive to the manners of being online.

Notebooks & Subnotebooks

Although currently the vast majority of American students who buy computers get the larger desktop models, many are finding that mobile computing makes a difference. Because they can take the computers to their residence halls or home, to the cafeteria, to a campus bench, or on a bus, many students praise the portables for their convenience.

There are four categories of portables:

1. *Laptops*—8–20 pounds
2. *Notebooks*—4–7.5 pounds
3. *Subnotebooks*—2.5–4 pounds
4. *Handhelds (palmtops)*—1 pound or less

Portables, especially 7-pound notebooks and under-4-pound subnotebooks, represent the best intersection of power and convenience. The 8-pound-plus laptops probably have no advantages over the notebook size, except perhaps in price. The under-1-pound handhelds are too limited for regular student use; they have no floppy-disk drive, no hard-disk drive, and no easy way to swap files with other computers.

Among the factors to consider in buying a notebook or subnotebook are: price, display screen, keyboard and mouse, portability, battery life and weight, disk drive, software, and expandability.

PRICE. Affordability is always important, of course. New desktops generally cost less than new portables. In general, however, a *top-of-the-line* notebook or subnotebook—one costing in the $5000 range and featuring a color display screen—will be just as suitable as a desktop microcomputer. For many people, though, that price is out of reach.

DISPLAY SCREEN. Price of a portable is affected by the kind of display screen: color or no-color (called *monochrome*). Color is nice but not necessary unless you plan on doing desktop publishing or lots of graphics work. Still, color is becoming an increasingly popular feature in notebooks and subnotebooks.

Lightweight portables have two principal types of color screens:

- *Active-matrix color:* In this version each little dot on the screen is controlled by its own transistor. The advantage of active-matrix screens is that colors are much brighter than those in the other version, passive matrix.

- *Passive-matrix color:* In this version a transistor controls a whole row or column of dots. The advantage of these screens is that they are less expensive and less power-hungry than active-matrix screens.

The display screens of most notebooks/subnotebooks measure 9.5 inches diagonally, and some are as small as 7.4 inches. This compares with the much more readable 14- or 15-inch (or even 17- or 20-inch) monitors that are standard with most desktop computers. Thus, if you do a lot of graphics work, you will probably want to get a portable with an external video connector that will attach it to a big color monitor on your desk. Several portables come with optional docking stations (described below).

KEYBOARD & MOUSE. You should try out the keyboard on the notebook or subnotebook to see if you can realistically touch-type on it. (This is very much a problem with the pocket or palmtop PCs.)

Notebooks and subnotebooks offer many variants on the mouse, the pointing device. Some devices must be unlimbered and clipped onto the side of the keyboard, which means you have yet another piece of paraphernalia to tote along. The IBM ThinkPad's pointing controller resembles a pencil eraser stuck among the G, H, and B keys. Other portables use a trackball built into the right side of the screen or centered below the spacebar.

PORTABILITY. How portable is that advertised "portable" computer? That depends on how deep a groove you're willing to let the strap put in your shoulder. It also depends on the computer itself:

- **Notebook versus subnotebook:** If you opt for desktop capability and bright screens, you will probably want the notebook, which will weigh about 7.5 pounds. Bright screens, however, require heavy batteries. Subnotebooks are lighter and smaller, although they may not provide some other features you want.

- **Accessories and AC adapter:** Notebooks usually have built-in floppy-disk drives. Subnotebooks do not, which means you may want to carry an external drive as an accessory. For both notebooks and subnotebooks, you will also always want to carry an AC adapter. This enables you to plug your machine into a wall plug for recharging after the battery runs down. (When doing weight comparisons, always include the AC adapter, since you may find yourself frequently hauling this around. Generally, you can count on 7.5–8.5 pounds with the adapter.)

- **Battery life and weight:** Portables vary in how long their batteries will hold a charge. Thus, battery life may be a short 1 hour and 34 minutes, in the case of the Compaq LTE Lite 4/25C, a notebook. Or it may be a long 3 hours and 40 minutes—some say up to 9 hours, although this seems unlikely—for the Hewlett-Packard OmniBook 300. This subnotebook runs on four flashlight-type AA batteries.[12,13]

  It's possible to take a backup battery—provided you've charged it first, of course—on, say, a long plane trip. So far, planes, buses, and cars offer no way of plugging in an AC adapter so that you can continue working after your battery runs down. (People used to try to recharge their batteries in airplane lavatories, but the airlines do not allow this.) Amtrak trains offer AC outlets, but they're best used for recharging your unit rather than for computing.

  An essential question to ask: How long do you need to plug in to charge the battery up? Some computers take only a couple of hours, but others need overnight.

  Another essential question: Are the battles nickel-cadmium (once the standard), which are relatively heavy, or nickel/metal hydride or lithium-ion, which offer lighter weight and longer life?

FLOPPY-DISK DRIVE, DOCKING STATION, OR PC CARD? One way manufacturers were able to make notebooks into the even lighter subnotebooks was, as mentioned, by leaving out the internal floppy-disk drive.

What if you need a floppy in order to transfer a file between computers or to install a new program? Or what if you want to make a backup copy of some material in case your hard disk fails?

There seem to be three choices:

- **Separate drive:** You buy a separate, external floppy-disk drive that plugs directly into your subnotebook. Make sure this is at least available for the machine you buy, in case you decide to get it later.

- **Docking station:** You buy a *docking station* that includes a floppy-disk drive. Docks have been described as "home bases the subnotebooks can attach to."[14]

  Some docks are far more complicated than the subnotebooks. They have not only floppy drives but also their own hard disks, network interfaces, add-on slots for expanding the computer's capabilities, and so on. In addition, docks may be somewhat portable themselves. The docking station for the IBM ThinkPad 750C includes CD-ROM drive and stereo speakers, yet its total traveling weight is less than 12 pounds—including the 9-pound notebook computer itself.[15]

  Other docking stations, called *mini-docks* or *ramps,* add an inch or so to the back of the subnotebook and provide additional connectors. These may be used to connect external floppy drives, networks, color monitors, and the like.

- **PC cards:** You buy a subnotebook that has one or two slots to hold *PCMCIA cards* or *PC cards.* These credit-card size circuit boards can hold extra memory, programs, hard drives, modems, sound

Going mobile: a buyer's checklist. Questions to consider when buying a notebook or subnotebook.

1. Is the device lightweight enough so that you won't be tempted to leave it behind when you travel?
   ❏ Yes   ❏ No

2. Does it work with lightweight nickel-hydride batteries instead of heavier nickel-cadmium batteries?
   ❏ Yes   ❏ No

3. Is the battery life sufficient for you to finish the jobs you need to do, and is a hibernation mode available to conserve power?
   ❏ Yes   ❏ No

4. Can you type comfortably on the keyboard for a long stretch?
   ❏ Yes   ❏ No

5. Is the screen crisp, sharp, and readable in different levels of light?
   ❏ Yes   ❏ No

6. Does the system have enough storage for all your software and data?
   ❏ Yes   ❏ No

7. Can the system's hard disk and memory be upgraded to meet your needs?
   ❏ Yes   ❏ No

8. Does the system provide solid communications options, including a fast modem, so you can send files, retrieve data, and plug into a local area network?
   ❏ Yes   ❏ No

9. Can you get service and support on the road?
   ❏ Yes   ❏ No

cards, and even pagers. The hard-drive cards may provide you with some additional backup storage that you can use in lieu of floppy disks.

There are different sizes of PC cards, and issues of compatibility are still being worked out. Thus, you may not be able to exchange files with your friends.

SOFTWARE, PERFORMANCE, & EXPANDABILITY. If you're buying an IBM-compatible portable, you'll probably want to use applications software that at least runs under Microsoft Windows 3.1 (though not necessarily the more recent Windows 95).

How fast a processor you want for your portable is up to you. Presentation graphics and financial modeling may require more advanced chips. Notebooks and subnotebooks generally now come with the latest in powerful chips (such as Pentium or Power PC chips).

You should also check out how expandable the portable is. That is, find out how easily it will take add-ons such as extra storage or devices such as a modem or larger hard-disk drive. Some subnotebooks allow add-ons only in the form of PC cards.

Communications is an area that definitely should not be overlooked. "A notebook is not just an island by itself," says Andrew Watson, a marketing manager for Compaq Computer; "the whole point is to communicate with other systems."[16] Thus, you should look for a portable that offers options for adding modems, fax boards, or even wireless communications features, so that you can stay connected.

Some other issues to consider in buying a notebook or subnotebook are addressed in the accompanying checklist. *(See* ■ *Panel A.5.)*

Communications Tools

The first wave of computing, 30 years ago, was driven by the huge computers known as mainframes. Twenty years later came the second wave, which produced the desktop personal computer. Now we are into the third wave, which is being driven by communications networks among computers. Communications technology, then, is vital to your future. The options include the following.

TELEPHONE-RELATED COMMUNICATIONS SERVICES. Services available through telephone connections, whether the conventional wired kind or the wireless cellular-phone type, include the following:

- **Fax messages:** Asking "What is your fax number?" is about as common a question in the work world today as asking for someone's telephone number. *Fax* stands for "facsimile transmission" or reproduction. A fax may be sent by dedicated fax machine or by fax modem.

  Dedicated fax machines are specialized devices that do nothing except send and receive documents over transmission lines from and to other fax machines. These are the stand-alone machines nowadays found everywhere, from offices to airports to instant-printing shops.

  A *fax modem,* which is installed as a circuit board inside a computer's cabinet, is a modem with fax capability. It enables you to send signals directly from your computer to someone else's fax machine or fax modem.

- **Voice mail:** Like a sophisticated telephone answering machine, *voice mail* digitizes incoming voice messages and stores them in the recipient's "voice mailbox" in digitized form. It then converts the digitized versions back to voice messages when they are retrieved.

  Unlike conventional answering machines, voice-mail systems allow callers to direct their calls within an office by pressing numbers on their touch-tone phone. They also allow callers to deliver the same message to many people within an organization. They can forward calls to the recipient's home or hotel.

  The main benefit is that voice mail helps eliminate "telephone tag." That is, two callers can continue to exchange messages even when they can't reach each other directly.

- **E-mail:** E-mail, or *electronic mail,* links computers by wired or wireless connections and allows users, through their keyboards, to post messages and to read responses on their display screens. E-mail allows "callers," or users, to send messages to a single recipient's "mailbox," which is simply a file stored on the computer system. Or they can send the same message to multiple users on the same system.

  As with voice mail, e-mail helps users avoid playing "telephone tag." It also offers confidentiality. Recipients cannot get into their "mailboxes" to pick up messages unless they enter a *password,* a secret word or numbers that limit access.

  To send a message, you dial the e-mail system's telephone number through your computer keyboard. You next type in the number of the recipient's mailbox, and then type in the message. The same message can be delivered to several other mailboxes on the system at the same time.

  To gain access to your mailbox, you dial the e-mail system's telephone number and type in the number of your mailbox and your password. The display screen will then show a list of the senders, subjects, and dates and times of messages sent. You can then read messages of interest, delete those not of interest, and transfer ("download") to your own computer those messages you want to keep.

  E-mail has jumped in use, especially in large organizations, where it helps to speed the exchange of memos and scheduling of appointments. Often a company will use its own specialized computer network. However, the Internet or outside online information

Online services. These are the principal mainstream online services.

America Online (800-827-6364). $9.95/month for 5 hours, then $2.95/hour. Easy-to-use interface; ideal for hobbyists and families wanting low-cost access to online features.

CompuServe (800-848-8199). $4.95/month for 5 hours, then $2.95/hour. Easy-to-use interface; ideal for people wanting to combine academic or business with hobbyist and family-type activities.

GEnie (800-638-9636). $8.95/month for basic services, then $3/hour 5 p.m. - 9 a.m. Offers ease in extensive database searches; well-known for variety of games and special-interest forums.

Microsoft Network (MSN) (800-386-5550) $4.95/month for 3 hours, then $2.50/hour. Access is built in to the Windows 95 operating system, allowing users to connect with an easy mouse click; splashy graphics; still expanding offerings

News Corp./MCI Online Ventures (formerly Delphi Internet) (800-695-4005). $10/month for 4 hours, then $4/hour. Ideal for more technologically oriented computer user; offers software sampling, weather, sports scores.

Prodigy (800-776-3449). $9.95/month for 5 hours, then $2.95/hour.
The simplest online service, easy for beginners; rivaled only by CompuServe in number and variety of services.

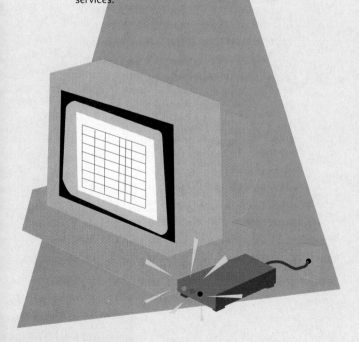

services (described next) are also used. E-mail not only speeds communications, it can also reduce telephone, postage, and secretarial costs.

ONLINE INFORMATION SERVICES. An *online information service* provides access to all kinds of databases and electronic meeting places to subscribers equipped with telephone-linked microcomputers. Says one writer:

> *Online services are those interactive news and information retrieval sources that can make your computer behave more like a telephone; or a TV set; or a newspaper; or a video arcade, a stock brokerage firm, a bank, a travel agency, a weather bureau, a department store, a grocery store, a florist, a set of encyclopedias, a library, a bulletin board and more.*[17]

There are scores of online services, but perhaps the most prominent are those listed at left. *(See ■ Panel A.6.)* To use these services, you need a microcomputer with hard disk, printer, and modem, plus communications software. Communications software is often sold with (is bundled with) modems. Popular information services such as Prodigy, CompuServe, and America Online provide subscribers with their own software programs for going online.

Before you can use an online information service, you need to open an account with it, using a credit card. Billing policies resemble those used by cable-TV and telephone companies. As with cable TV, you may be charged a fee for basic service, with additional fees for specialized services. In addition, the online service may charge you for the time spent while on the line. Finally, you will also be charged by your telephone company for your time on the line, just as when making a regular phone call. However, most information services offer local access numbers. Thus, unless you live in a rural area, you will not be paying long-distance phone charges. All told, the typical user may pay $10–$20 a month to use an online service, although it's possible to run a bill of $100 or more. To keep costs down, many users go online only during off-hours (evenings and weekends), when the charges intended for business users are reduced.

As one of the hundreds of thousands of subscribers connected to an online service, you can have access to *e-mail, computer games* (both single-player and multi-player), *travel services, shopping services,* and *research.* The only restriction on the amount of research you can do online is the limit on whatever credit card you are charging your time to. Depending on the online service, you can avail yourself of several encyclopedias. Many online services store unabridged text from newspapers and magazines. CompuServe's Magazine Database Plus carries full-text articles from more than 90 general-interest publications (business, science, sports, and so on). With Prodigy you can have access to book and movie/video news, contests, health reports, parenting advice, car-rental information, microwave cooking instructions, and on and on.

ELECTRONIC BULLETIN BOARD SYSTEMS. An *electronic bulletin board system (BBS)* is a centralized information source and message-switching system for a particular computer-linked interest group. There are more than 57,000 BBSs, according to one estimate.[18] Many BBSs are free, some charge a nominal fee, and others may charge up to $10 an hour. The BBS is often an inexpensive way of learning to go online. If a BBS is local, as so many are, you pay only the cost of a local phone call. Bulletin boards that require a membership fee (charged to a credit card) generally give you a trial period to explore the BBS free of charge. BBSs are basically of two types: big ones operated by giant corporations and small ones operated by individuals:

- **Large commercial BBSs:** All the major online services operate bulletin boards. However, BBSs are only *one* of several services offered by commercial online services. And, of course, you are charged by the organization for using this particular service.

- **Small BBSs:** Small BBSs may be free or for-profit, but they are generally run by individuals, often out of their homes. BBS system operators are called *sysops.* Many bulletin boards are locally oriented or are devoted to a single hobby or theme. The best way to find BBSs in your area is to check with local computer publications (which may be free) or computer stores. BBSs are also listed in the magazines *Computer Shopper, Boardwatch,* and *Online Access,* available at many newsstands.

The primary difference between a BBS and an online service is the single focus. "Typically, BBSs are targeted at a particular single-issue topic," says one expert, "and online services are kind of like department stores that have a thousand different topics that are being talked about."[19]

After turning on the computer with the communications software, you simply dial up the bulletin board by pressing the numbers on your keyboard. You are then usually greeted by a welcome screen from the BBS that tells you what to do—what rules to follow and how to get help, if you need it.

As you move around the BBS, you will probably find a library of materials, such as computer games, that you can copy for your own use. You will also find places where other users have posted messages or where you can "chat" (type your messages and read theirs) with people who have similar interests. There seem to be no limits to the topics of electronic talk forums ("conferences" or "chat rooms") on bulletin boards. The participants range from bird watchers to socialists to Francophiles to Trekkies.

THE INTERNET. The computer, modem, and telephone line that explore online services and BBSs can also be used to connect with the global network of computers known as the Internet. The *Internet* is an international network connecting approximately 36,000 smaller networks. An estimated 24 million people in the United States and Canada alone are already on the Internet—fully 11% of the North American population over age

16. A third of Internet users are women.[20]

Some principal services of the Internet are as follows:

- **E-mail:** Internet electronic mail is essentially like the e-mail in an office except that you can exchange messages all over the world. E-mail messages on the Internet can be transmitted from one user to another usually in a matter of seconds.

  Although Internet addresses may seem strange at first, they are not complicated. The Internet address for the President of the United States, for example, is *president@whitehouse.gov*. The first part is the user's name—in this case, *president*. (Yours might be your nickname, initials and last name, or some combination.) The second part is the computer network you use, which follows the @ sign—in this case, *@whitehouse*. The third part, following a period, is the network's "domain"—in this case, *gov* for "government." Other domains are *com* (commercial organizations), *edu* (education), *mil* (military), *net* (network resources), and *org* (private organizations).

- **Information gathering:** "Try as you may," says one writer, "you cannot imagine how much data is available on the Internet."[21] Besides hundreds of online databases from various universities and other research institutions and online library catalogs, here is a sampling:

  The Library of Congress card catalog. The daily White House press releases. Weather maps and forecasts. Schedules of professional sports teams. Weekly Nielsen television ratings. Recipe archives. The Central Intelligence Agency world map. A ZIP Code guide. The National Family Database. Project Gutenberg (offering the complete text of many works of literature). The Alcoholism Research Data Base. Guitar chords. U.S. government addresses and phone (and fax) numbers. The Simpsons archive.[22]

- **Discussion and news groups:** One of the Internet's most interesting features are the news groups, or bulletin board discussion groups. For example, *Usenet* is a loose confederation of 5000 *newsgroups* or discussion groups on every conceivable subject. Users can post messages for others to read, then check back later to see what responses have appeared.

  Examples of topics offered by Usenet news groups are *misc.jobs.offered*, *rec.arts.startrek.info*, and *soc.culture.african.american*. The category called *alt* news groups offers more free-form topics, such as *alt.rock-n-roll.metal* or *alt.internet.services*.

- **World Wide Web:** The *World Wide Web (WWW, or simply "the Web")* is the Internet's most graphical and usable service. It resembles a huge encyclopedia filled with thousands of topics or sites (called "pages"), which have been created by computer users and businesses around the world. Each site has cross-reference links to other sites. Sites may theoretically be in *multimedia* form—meaning they can appear in text, graphical, sound, animation, or video form—although at present there are lots of pictures and text but little live, moving content. However, this is in the process of changing.

  In order to find your way through the dense data fields of the Web, you need a software program called a *browser*. Browsers allow you to use a mouse to click-and-jump through the various sites. Two popular Web browsers are Netscape and Mosaic.

  There are three principal ways of getting connected to the Internet:

- **School or work:** The people with the easiest access to Internet are those involved with universities and colleges, government agencies, and some commercial businesses. College students often get a free account through their institution. However, students and faculty living off-campus may not be able to use the connections of campus computers.

- **Commercial online services and bulletin boards:** The large commercial online services—such as America Online, CompuServe, and Prodigy—offer access to the Internet. So do some electronic bulletin board systems.

- ***Commercial access providers:*** The commercial online serices may be the easiest path to the Internet, but they may charge more than independent access providers. These are companies that will provide public access to the Internet for a fee, from a few dollars an hour to thousands of dollars a year. The cheapest kind of access is the dial-up connection. Here the independent access provider charges a monthly and/or hourly fee for dialing into an intermediary source that then connects to the Internet.

One thing to find out when you're looking into Internet connections is whether you will be getting e-mail only or full access. E-mail gives you virtually instantaneous worldwide communication. However, full access will allow you to acquire information, software, games, pictures, and other riches.

A network information center called InterNIC has been set up to serve as a clearinghouse for Internet information. To find out more, call (800) 444-4345, or e-mail *info@internic.net*. For public access sites, ask about the PDIAL list.

notes

CHAPTER 1—TRANSITION

1. Passell, P. (1992, August 19). Twins study shows school is sound investment. *New York Times,* p. A14.

2. Reich, R., interviewed in Belton, B. (1994, September 2). Reich: College education a buffer against recession. *USA Today,* p. 3B.

3. Shilling, A. G. (1991, December 10). Good news: more productivity; bad news: high unemployment. *Wall Street Journal,* p. A14.

4. Wessel, D. (1994, September 26). For college graduates, a heartening word. *Wall Street Journal,* p. A1.

5. U.S. Bureau of the Census. Cited in: Healy, M. (1994, July 22). Time (in school) is money. *USA Today,* p. 1D.

6. Katz, J. (Ed.) (1968). *No time for youth: Growth and constraint in college students.* San Francisco: Jossey-Bass.

7. Kalat, J. W. (1990). *Psychology* (2nd ed.). Belmont, CA: Wadsworth, p. 440.

8. Levitz, R., & Noel, L. (1989). Connecting students to institutions: Keys to retention and success. Pp. 65 – 81 in Upcraft, M. L., & Gardener, J. N., & Associates (Eds.). *The freshman year experience: Helping students survive and succeed in college.* San Francisco: Jossey-Bass.

9. Levitz, R., & Noel, L. (1989). Connecting students to institutions: Keys to retention and success. Pp. 65–81 in: Upcraft & Gardener, 1989.

10. Adapted from Friday, R. A. (1988). *Create your college success: Activities and exercises for students.* Belmont, CA: Wadsworth, pp. 116–19.

11. Anonymous. (1990, January). Der Mensch wird immer dümmer. *Der Spiegel,* pp. 98–103.

CHAPTER 2—SUCCEEDING

1. Anonymous. (1995, April). What's your biggest regret in life? *Health,* p. 14.

2. Person, E. S. Quoted in: Anonymous (1990, September). Motivation. *Self,* p. 215.

3. Upcraft, M. L., & Gardner, J. N. (1989). A comprehensive approach to enhancing freshman success. Pp. 1–12 in Upcraft, M. L., & Gardener, J. N., & Associates (Eds.). *The freshman year experience: Helping students survive and succeed in college.* San Francisco: Jossey-Bass.

4. Carter, C. (1990). *Majoring in the rest of your life: Career secrets for college students.* New York: Noonday Press, pp. 61–62.

5. Rotter, J. B. (1966). Generalized expectancies for internal versus external control of reinforcement. *Psychological Monographs, 80*(Whole No. 603).

6. Findley, M. J., & Cooper, H. M. (1983). Locus of control and academic achievement: A literature review. *Journal of Personality & Social Psychology, 44,* 419–27.

7. Lefcourt, H. M. (1982). *Locus of control: Current trends in theory and research.* Hillsdale, NJ: Erlbaum.

8. McGinnis, A. Quoted in: Maushard, M. (1990, October 22). How to get happy: What makes optimists tick. *San Francisco Chronicle,* p. B5. Reprinted from *Baltimore Evening Sun.*

9. McGinnis, A. L. (1990). *The power of optimism.* San Francisco: Harper & Row.

10. Szent-Györgyi, A. Quoted in: von Oech, R. (1983). *A whack on the side of the head.* Menlo Park, CA: Creative Think, p. 7.

11. von Oech, 1983, p. 21.

12. Hyatt, C., & Gottlieb, L. (1987). *When smart people fail.* New York: Simon and Schuster, p. 20.

13. Garfield, C. Quoted in: Rozak, M. (1989, August). The mid-life fitness peak. *Psychology Today,* pp. 32–33.

14. Coburn, K. L. Quoted in: Kutner, L. (1992, September 3). For college freshmen, the first breath of freedom can hold a difficult and frightening lesson. *New York Times,* p. B4.

15. Kutner, 1992.

CHAPTER 3—RESOURCES

1. Kramer, G. L., & Spencer, R. W. Academic advising. P. 97 in Upcraft, M. L., Gardner, J. N., & Associates (Eds.). (1990). *The freshman year experience: Helping students survive and succeed in college.* San Francisco: Jossey-Bass.

2. Crockett, D. S. Academic advising. Pp. 244–63 in Noel, L., Levitiz, R., & Saluri, D., & Associates (Eds.). (1985). *Increasing student retention.* San Francisco: Jossey-Bass.

3. Hudson Institute, Workforce 2000, U.S. Bureau of Labor Statistics, in Anonymous (1988, July). Jobs for women in the nineties, *Ms,* p. 77.

4. Naisbitt, J., & Aburdene, P. (1990). *Megatrends 2000.* New York: Morrow, p. 19.

5. Freedberg, L. (1993, November 12). Women outnumber men at college. *San Francisco Chronicle,* pp. A1, A9.

6. Adelman, C., U.S. Department of Education. *Women at thirtysomething.* Cited in: Stipp, D. (1992, September 11). The gender gap. *Wall Street Journal.*

7. Cage, M. C. (1993, March 10). Openly gay students face harassment and physical assaults on some campuses. *Chronicle of Higher Education,* pp. A22–A24.

8. Freedberg, L. (1992, June 28). The new face of higher education. *This World, San Francisco Chronicle,* p. 9.

9. Beck, B. (1991, November 11). School day for seniors. *Newsweek,* pp. 60–65.

10. Simpson, J. C. (1987, April 3). Campus barrier? Black college students are viewed as victims of a subtle racism. *Wall Street Journal.*

11. Evans, G. (1986, April 30). Black students who attend white colleges face contradictions in their campus life. *Chronicle of Higher Education,* pp. 17–49.

12. Barringer, F. (1991, June 12). Immigration brings new diversity Asian population in the U.S. *New York Times,* pp. A1, D25.

13. Marriott, M. (1992, February 26). Indians turning to tribal colleges for opportunity and cultural values. *New York Times,* p. A13.

14. Kotkin, J. (1993, February 24). Enrolling foreign students will strengthen America's place in the global economy. *Chronicle of Higher Education,* pp. B1–B2.

15. Hall, H. (1988, December). Trying on old age. *Psychology Today,* p. 67.

16. Belkin, L. (1992, June 4). In lessons on empathy, doctors become patients. *New York Times,* pp. A1, A13.

17. Jaschik, S. (1993, February 3). Backed by 1990 law, people with disabilities press demands on colleges. *Chronicle of Higher Education,* p. A26.

18. Shapiro, J. P. (1993). *No pity: People with disabilities forging a new civil rights movement.* New York: Times Books.

1. Myers, D. G. (1992). *The pursuit of happiness: Who is happy—and why.* New York: William Morrow, p. 116.

2. Myers, 1992, p. 116.

3. Myers, 1992, pp. 136–37, quoting Csikszentmihalyi, M. The future of flow. In Csikszentmihalyi, M., & Csikszentmihalyi, I. S. (Eds.). *Psychological studies of flow in consciousness.* Cambridge: Cambridge University Press, 1988.

4. Nielsen Media Services survey of 1990–91 television season. Cited in: Cronin, A. (1992, July 26). This is your life, generally speaking: A statistical portrait of the 'typical' American. *New York Times,* sec. 4, p. 5.

5. Goleman, D. (1990, October 18). TV: More evidence of a 'plug-in drug.' *San Francisco Chronicle,* p. B3; reprinted from *New York Times.*

6. Myers, 1992, p. 136.

7. Myers, 1992.

8. Lakein, A. (1973). *How to get control of your time and your life.* New York: Peter H. Wyden.

9. Zimbardo, P. G. (1977). *Shyness: What it is, what to do about it.* Reading, MA: Addison-Wesley, p. 14.

10. Beneke, W. M., & Harris, M. B. (1972). Teaching self-control of study behavior. *Behavior Research & Therapy, 10,* 35–41.

11. Kessinger, T. G. Quoted in: Marriott, M. (1991, April 12). In high-tech dorms, a call for power. *New York Times,* pp. A1, A8.

12. Rimer, S. (1991, October 27). Television becomes basic furniture in college students' ivory towers. *New York Times,* sec. 1, p. 14.

13. Moffatt, M. (1989). *Coming of age in New Jersey.* Rutgers, NJ: Rutgers University Press.

14. Marriott, 1991.

15. Ellis, D. (1991). *Becoming a master student* (6th ed.). Rapid City, SD: College Survival, Inc., p. 53.

1. Haber, R. N. (1979). Twenty years of haunting eidetic imagery: Where's the ghost? *Behavioral & Brain Sciences, 2,* 583–629.

2. Lapp, D. C. (1992, December). (Nearly) total recall. *Stanford Magazine,* pp. 48–51.

3. Lapp, 1992, p. 48.

4. Crovitz, H. F., & Schiffman, H. (1974). Frequency of episodic memories as a function of their age. *Bulletin of the Psychonomic Society, 4,* 517–18.

5. Ebbinghaus, H. (1913). *Memory.* New York: Teachers College. (Original work published 1885.)

6. Survey by National Institute for Development and Administration, University of Texas. Cited in: Lapp, 1992.

7. Pauk, W. (1989). *How to study in college* (4th ed.). Boston: Houghton Mifflin, p. 92.

8. Pauk, 1989, p. 92.

9. Guild & Garger, 1986. Cited in: Ducharme, A., & Watford, L., Explanation of assessment areas (handout).

10. Ducharme & Watford.

11. Lapp, 1992, p. 49.

12. Krueger, W. C. F. (1929). The effect of overlearning on retention. *Journal of Experimental Psychology, 12,* 71–78.

13. Weiten, W., Lloyd, M. A., & Lashley, R. L. (1990). *Psychology applied to modern life: Adjustment in the 90s* (3rd ed.). Pacific Grove, CA: Brooks/Cole.

14. Bromage, B. K., & Mayer, R. E. (1986). Quantitative and qualitative effects of repetition on learning from technical text. *Journal of Educational Psychology, 78*(4), 271–78.

15. Zechmeister, E. B., & Nyberg, S. E. (1982). *Human memory: An introduction to research and theory.* Pacific Grove, CA: Brooks/Cole.

16. Kalat, J. W. (1990). *Introduction to psychology* (2nd ed.). Belmont, CA: Wadsworth, p. 295.

17. Underwood, B. J. (1957). Interference and forgetting. *Psychological Review, 64,* 49–60.

18. Fowler, M. J., Sullivan, M. J., & Ekstrand, B. R. (1973). Sleep and memory. *Science, 179,* 302–304.

19. Thorndyke, P. W., & Hayes-Roth, B. (1979). The use of schemata in the acquisition and transfer of knowledge. *Cognitive Psychology, 11,* 83–106.

20. Craik, F. I. M., & Lockhart, R. S. (1972). Levels of processing: A framework for memory research. *Journal of Verbal Learning & Verbal Behavior, 11,* 671–84.

21. Raugh, M. R., & Atkinson, R. C. (1975). A mnemonic method for learning a second-language vocabulary. *Journal of Educational Psychology, 67,* 1–16.

22. Intons-Peterson, M. J., & Fournier, J. (1986). External and internal memory aids: When and how often do we use them? *Journal of Experimental Psychology: General, 116,* 267–80.

23. Bower, G. H. (1970). Organizational factors in memory. *Cognitive Psychology, 1,* 18–46.

24. Bower, G. H., & Clark, M. C. (1969). Narrative stories as mediators of serial learning. *Psychonomic Science, 14,* 181–82.

25. Weiten, W., Lloyd, M. A., & Lashley, R. L. (1990). *Psychology applied to modern life: Adjustment in the 90s* (3rd ed.). Pacific Grove, CA: Brooks/Cole, p. 24. Adapted from Bower & Clark, 1969.

26. Paivio, A. (1986). *Mental representations: A dual coding approach.* New York: Oxford University Press.

27. McDaniel, M. A., & Einstein, G. O. (1986). Bizarre imagery as an effective memory aid: The importance of distinctiveness. *Journal of Experimental Psychology: Learning, Memory & Cognition, 12,* 54–65.

28. Crovitz, H. F. (1971). The capacity of memory loci in artificial memory. *Psychonomic Science, 24,* 187–88.

CHAPTER 6—LECTURES

1. Lindgren, H. C. (1969). *The psychology of college success: A dynamic approach.* New York: Wiley.

2. Weiten, W., Lloyd, M. A., & Lashley, R. L. (1990). *Psychology applied to modern life: Adjustment in the 90s* (3rd ed.). Pacific Grove, CA: Brooks/Cole, p. 22.

3. Bromage, B. K., & Mayer, R. E. (1986). Quantitative and qualitative effects of repetition on learning from technical text. *Journal of Educational Psychology, 78*(4), 271–78.

4. Pauk, W. (1989). *How to study in college.* Boston: Houghton-Mifflin, p. 122.

5. Lucas, S. E. (1989). *The art of public speaking.* New York: Random House.

CHAPTER 7—READING

1. Robinson, F. P. (1970). *Effective study* (4th ed.). New York: Harper & Row.

2. Pauk, W. (1989). *How to study in college* (4th ed.). Boston: Houghton Mifflin, p. 181.

3. Pauk, 1989, 171.

4. Pauk, 1989, pp. 171–84.

5. Ray, M., & Myers, R. (1986). *Creativity in business.* Garden City, NY: Doubleday, p. 42.

6. Donahue, P. A. (1989). Helping adolescents with shyness: Applying the Japanese Morita therapy in shyness counseling. *International Journal for the Advancement of Counseling, 12,* 323–32.

7. Zastrow, C. (1988). What really causes psychotherapy change? *Journal of Independent Social Work, 2,* 5–16.

8. Braiker, H. B. (1989, December). The power of self-talk. *Psychology Today,* p. 24.

1. Walter, T., & Siebert, A. (1990). *Student success* (5th ed.). Fort Worth, TX: Holt, Rinehart and Winston, pp. 96–97.

2. Walter & Siebert, 1990.

3. Starke, M. C. (1993). *Strategies for college success* (2nd ed.). Englewood Cliffs, NJ: Prentice Hall, p. 82.

4. Bok, S. Cited in: Venant, E. (1992, January 7). A nation of cheaters. *San Francisco Chronicle*, p. D3; reprinted from *Los Angeles Times*.

5. Dobrzeniecki, A. Quoted in: Butler, D. (1991, March 2). 73 MIT students guilty of cheating. *Boston Globe*, p. 25.

6. Mason, C. Quoted in: Venant, 1992, p. D4.

7. Josephson, M. Quoted in: Venant, 1992, p. D3.

8. Himmelfarb, S. (1992, June 1). Graduates feel anxious, not just about jobs [letter]. *New York Times*, p. A14.

9. Woodell, M. L. (1991, November 24). Fraud? Imagine you're in the spotlight. *New York Times*, sec. 3, p. 11.

10. Tetzeli, R. (1991, July 1). Business students cheat most. *Fortune*, pp. 14–15.

CHAPTER 9—COMMUNICATION

1. Walter, T., & Siebert, A. (1990). *Student success: How to succeed in college and still have time for your friends.* Fort Worth, TX: Holt, Rinehart and Winston, pp. 108–109.

2. Osborn, A. (1953). *Applied imagination.* New York: Scribner's.

3. Ray, M., & Myers, R. (1986). *Creativity in business.* Garden City, NY: Doubleday, p. 42.

4. Ray & Myers, 1986, p. 92.

5. Walter & Siebert, 1990, p. 103.

6. Randi, J. (1992, April 13). Help stamp our absurd beliefs. *Time*, p. 80.

7. Ruchlis, H., & Oddo, S. (1990). *Clear thinking: A practical introduction.* Buffalo, NY: Prometheus, p. 109.

8. Ruchlis & Oddo, 1990, p. 110.

9. Kahane, H. (1988). *Logic and contemporary rhetoric: The use of reason in everyday life* (5th ed.). Belmont, CA: Wadsworth.

10. Rasool, J., Banks, C., & McCarthy, M.-J. (1993). *Critical thinking: Reading and writing in a diverse world.* Belmont, CA: Wadsworth, p. 132.

11. Rasool, Banks, & McCarthy, 1993, p. 132.

12. Alessandra, T., & Hunsaker, P. (1993). *Communicating at work.* New York: Fireside, p. 169.

13. Wohlmuth, E. (1983). *The overnight guide to public speaking.* Philadelphia: Running Press, p. 119.

14. Wohlmuth, 1983, p. 118.

15. Theibert, P. (1993, August 2). Speechwriters of the world, get lost! *Wall Street Journal*, p. A16.

16. Wohlmuth, 1983, p. 31.

17. Walters, L. (1993). *Secrets of successful speakers: How you can motivate, captivate, and persuade.* New York: McGraw-Hill, p. 203.

18. Alessandra & Hunsaker, 1993, p. 179.

19. Alessandra & Hunsaker, 1993, p. 169.

20. Walters, 1993, p. 32.

21. Malouf, D. Cited in: Walters, 1993, p. 33.

22. Walters, 1993, p. 36.

23. Walters, 1993, p. 37.

24. Wohlmuth, 1983, p. 133.

25. Robinson, J. R. (1991, November 6). [Letter to editor.] U.S. students memorize, but don't understand. *New York Times*, p. A14.

26. Elder, J. (1991, January 6). A learned response. *New York Times*, sec. 4A, p. 23.

CHAPTER 10—MONEY

1. Tobias, A. (1980). *Getting by on $100,000 a year (and other sad tales)*. New York: Washington Square Press.

2. Malveaux, J. (1994, December 18). Who's middle class? *San Francisco Examiner*, p. B-2.

3. Quoted in: Reeves, R. (1986, October 31). No time to be young. *San Francisco Chronicle*, p. 75.

4. Quoted in: Mundis, J. (1986, January 5). A way back from deep debt. *New York Times Magazine*, pp. 22–23.

5. Sheehy, G. Quoted in: Tobias, A. (1978). *The only investment guide you'll ever need*. New York: Harcourt Brace Jovanovich, p. 131.

6. Phillips, M. (1974). *The seven laws of money*. Menlo Park, Calif., and New York: Word Wheel and Random House, p. 41.

7. Phillips, 1974, p. 32.

8. Mundis, J. (1988). *How to get out of debt, stay out of debt and live prosperously*. New York: Bantam Books, p. 63.

9. Higher Education Research Institute, University of California at Los Angeles, survey sponsored by American Council on Education. Reported in: Associated Press (1992, January 13). College freshmen feeling pinch. *San Francisco Chronicle*, p. A3.

10. Kelly, D. (1991, February 19). Students leave in deeper debt. *USA Today*, p. 6D.

11. Rigdon, J. E. (1991, January 3). Student loans weigh down graduates. *Wall Street Journal*, p. B1.

12. Seligman, K. (1992, March 29). More and more college students on '7-year plan'. *San Francisco Examiner*, p. A-1.

13. Anonymous. (1995, April 18). The rich get richer faster [editorial]. *New York Times*, p. A16.

14. *Washington Monthly* (1993, March). Cited in: Ouellete, L. (1993, September/October). Class bias on campus. *Utne Reader*, pp. 19–24.

15. Kelly, 1991.

16. Astin, A. W., Dey, E. L., Korn, W. S. et al. (1991). *The American freshman: National norms for fall 1991*. Los Angeles: Higher Education Research Institute, Graduate School of Education, University of California, Los Angeles.

17. Gottesman, G. (1991). *College survival*. New York: Prentice Hall Press, pp. 13–14.

18. Gottesman, 1991, pp. 196–97.

19. Melia, M. K. (1992, May). Carry-out cash. *American Demographics*, p. 6.

20. Anonymous (1991, February 9). Credit cards become big part of life. *New York Times*, p. 16.

21. Brookes, A. (1994, November 5). Lesson for teen-agers: Facts of credit-card life. *New York Times*, p. 31.

22. Foren, J. (1991, December 1). College students piling on credit card debt. *San Francisco Examiner*, p. E-9.

23. Kutner, L. (1993, August 19). College students with big credit card bills may be learning an economics lesson the hard way. *New York Times*, p. B4.

24. Warner, J. (1992, July 20). It's chic to be cheap: A penny-pincher's primer. *Business Week*, pp. 94–95.

25. Kiplinger's Changing Times (1988). *Success with your money*. Washington, DC: Kiplinger Changing Times, p. 132.

26. Nemko, M. (1992, June 28). A grown-up's guide to financial aid. *This World, San Francisco Chronicle*, pp. 11–12.

27. Manegold, C. S. (1994, September 19). U.S. has high hopes for a revamped student loan program. *New York Times*, p. A10.

CHAPTER 11—HEALTH

1. Anonymous. (1987, October). The perils of burnout. *Newsweek on Campus*.

2. Lazarus, R. S. (1981, July). Little hassles can be hazardous to health. *Psychology Today*, p. 61.

3. Selye, H. (1974). *Stress without distress.* New York: Lippincott, pp. 28–29.

4. Holmes, T. H., & Rahe, R. H. (1967). The social readjustmentrating scale. *Journal of Psychosomatic Research, 11,* 213–18.

5. Selye, 1974, p. 27.

6. Lazarus, R. S., & Forlman, S. (1982). Coping and adaptation. In W. D. Gentry (Ed.). *Handbook of behavioral medicine.* New York: Guilford Press.

7. Hinkle, L. E., Jr. (1987). Stress and disease: The concept after 50 years. *Social Science & Medicine, 25,* 561–66.

8. Kiecolt-Glazer, J., & Glaser, R. (1988). Major life changes, chronic stress, and immunity. *Advances in Biochemical Psychopharmacology, 44,* 217–24.

9. Kiecolt-Glazer, J. et al. (1987) Stress, health, and immunity: Tracking the mind/body connection. Presentation at American Psychological Association meeting, New York, August 1987.

10. Kannel, W. B. (1990). CHD risk factors: A Framingham study update. *Hospital Practice, 25,* 119.

11. Eliot, R., & Breo, D. (1984). *Is it worth dying for?* New York: Bantam Books.

12. McCulloch, A., & O'Brien, L. (1986). The organizational determinants of worker burnout. *Children & Youth Services Review, 8,* 175–90.

13. Girdano, D. A., & Everly, G. S., Jr. (1986). *Controlling stress and tension.* Englewood Cliffs, NJ: Prentice-Hall.

14. Matthews, A. (1993, March 7). The campus crime wave. *New York Times Magazine,* pp. 38–42, 47.

15. Anonymous. (1987, August). Dear diary. *American Health.*

16. Mee, C. L., Jr. (Ed.). (1987). *Managing stress from morning to night.* Alexandria, VA: Time-Life Books.

17. Zajonc, R. B. (1985). Emotion and facial efference: A theory reclaimed. *Science, 228,* 15–21.

18. Adelmann, P. K., & Zajonc, R. B. (1989). Facial efference and the experience of emotion. *Annual Review of Psychology, 40,* 249–80.

19. Zajonc, R. Cited in: Goleman, D. (1989, June 29). Put on a happy face—it really works. *San Francisco Chronicle,* p. C10. Reprinted from *New York Times.*

20. Donahue, P. A. (1989). Helping adolescents with shyness: Applying the Japanese Morita therapy in shyness counselling. *International Journal for the Advancement of Counselling, 12,* 323–32.

21. Zastrow, C. (1988). What really causes psychotherapy change? *Journal of Independent Social Work, 2,* 5–16.

22. Braiker, H. B. (1989, December). The power of self-talk. *Psychology Today,* p. 24.

23. Cousins, N. (1979). *Anatomy of an illness.* New York: Norton.

24. Dillon, K. M., Minchoff, B., & Baker, K. H. (1985–86). Positive emotional states and enhancement of the immune system. *International Journal of Psychiatry in Medicine, 15,* 13–18.

25. Long, P. (1987, October). Laugh and be well? *Psychology Today,* pp. 28–29.

26. Siegel, B. (1986). *Love, medicine, and miracles.* New York: Harper & Row.

27. Reifman, A., & Dunkel-Schetter, C. (1990). Stress, structural social support, and well-being in university students. *Journal of American College Health, 38,* 271–77.

28. Leerhsen, C., et al. (1990, February 5). Unite and conquer. *Newsweek,* pp. 50–55.

29. Snyder, M. (1988). Relaxation. In J. J. Fitzpatrick, R. L. Taunton, & J. Q. Benoliel (Eds.). *Annual review of nursing research, 8,* 111–28. New York: Springer.

30. Benson, H. (1989). Editorial: Hypnosis and the relaxation response. *Gastroenterology, 96,* 1610.

31. Levenson, H. S., & Bick, E. C. (1977). Psychopharmacology of caffeine. Pp. 451–63 in: M. E. Jarvik (Ed.). *Psychopharmacology in the practice of medicine.* New York: Appleton-Century-Crofts.

32. Weidner, G., & Itvan, J. (1985). Dietary sources of caffeine [letter]. *New England Journal of Medicine, 313,* 1421.

33. Gilbert, R. M. (1984). Caffeine consumption. *Progress in Clinical Biological Research, 158,* 185–213.

34. Schwartz, J. (1994, October 5). Caffeine lust finally labeled an addiction. *San Francisco Chronicle,* pp. A1, A7; reprinted from *Washington Post.*

35. Ray, O., & Ksir, C. (1990). *Drugs, society, and human behavior* (5th ed.). St. Louis, MO: Times Mirror/Mosby.

36. Gilliland, K., & Andress, D. (1981). Ad lib caffeine consumption, symptoms of caffeinism, and academic performance. *American Journal of Psychiatry, 138,* 512–14.

37. Williams, B., & Knight, S. (1994). *Healthy for life: Wellness and the art of living.* Pacific Grove, CA: Brooks/Cole.

38. Clements, G. L., & Dailey, J. W. (1988). Psychotropic effects of caffeine. *American Family Physician, 37,* 162–72.

39. Kenny, M., & Darragh, A. (1985). Central effects of caffeine in man. Pp. 278–88 in: S. D. Iversen (Ed.). *Psychopharmacology: Recent advances and future prospects.* Oxford: Oxford University Press.

40. Gilliland & Andress, 1981.

41. Bruce, M. S., & Lader, M. (1989). Caffeine abstention in the management of anxiety disorders. *Psychological Medicine, 19,* 211–14.

42. Mathew, R. J., & Wilson, W. H. (1990). Behavioral and cerebrovascular effects of caffeine in patients with anxiety disorders. *Acta Psychiatrica Scandinavica, 81,* 17–22.

43. Ray & Ksir, 1990.

44. van Dusseldorp, M., & Katan, M. B. (1990). Headache caused by caffeine withdrawal among moderate coffee drinkers switched from ordinary to decaffeinated coffee: A 12 week double blind trial. *British Medical Journal, 300,* 1558–59.

45. Ray & Ksir, 1990.

46. van Dusseldorp & Katan, 1990.

47. Johnston, L. D., O'Malley, P. M., & Bachman, J. G. (1990). *Illicit drug use, smoking, and drinking by America's high school students, college students, and young adults: 1975–1989.* Rockville, MD: National Institute on Drug Abuse.

48. Kilbourne, J. (1988). Cigarette ads target women, young people. *Alcoholism & Addiction, 9,* 22–23.

49. Marsh, A. (1984). Smoking: habit or choice? *Population Trends, 37,* 19–20.

50. Kadunce, D. P., Burr, R., Gress, R. et al. (1991). Cigarette smoking: Risk factor for premature facial wrinkling. *Annals of Internal Medicine, 114,* 840–44.

51. Glina, S., Reichelt, C., Leao, P. et al. (1988). Impact of cigarette smoking on papaverine-induced erection. *Journal of Urology, 140,* 523–24.

52. Hagen, R., & D'Agostino, J. (1982). Smoking may be hazard to male sexual response. *Brain-Mind Bulletin, 7,* 3.

53. Office on Smoking and Health. (1989). *Reducing the health consequences of smoking: 25 years of progress. A report of the Surgeon General.* DHHS Pub. No. (CDC)89-8411. Washington, DC: U.S. Department of Health and Human Services.

54. Willett, W. C., Green, A., Stampfer, M. J. et al. (1987). Relative and absolute excess risks of coronary heart disease among women who smoke cigarettes. *New England Journal of Medicine, 317,* 1303–1309.

55. La Vecchia, C., Franceschi, S., Decarli, A. et al. (1987). Risk factors for myocardial infarction in young women. *American Journal of Epidemiology, 125,* 832–43.

56. Abbott, R. D., Yin, Y., Reed, D. M. et al. (1986). Risk of stroke in male cigarette smokers. *New England Journal of Medicine, 315,* 717–20.

57. Darnton, J. (1994, September 21). Report ties smoking to epidemic of death. *New York Times,* p. A16.

58. Centers for Disease Control and Prevention. Cited in: Levy, D. (1994, December 23). 46 million smoke; 70% want to quit. *USA Today,* p. 1A.

59. Glover, E. D., Laflin, M., Flannery, D. et al. (1989). Smokeless tobacco use among American college students. *Journal of American College Health, 38,* 81–85.

60. Winn, D, M. (1988). Smokeless tobacco and cancer: The epidemiologic evidence. *Ca: A Cancer Journal for Clinicians, 38,* 236–43.

61. U.S. Public Health Service. (1986). *The health consequences of involuntary smoking: A report of the Surgeon General.* DHHS Pub. No. (CDC)87-8398. Washington, DC: U.S. Government Printing Office.

62. Goodkind, M. (1989, Spring). The cigarette habit. *Stanford Medicine,* p. 13.

63. Okene, J. K. (1989). Promoting cessation. *Journal of the American Medical Women's Association, 44*(2), 60–63.

64. Haron, D. (1994, June 23). Campus drinking problem becomes severe [letter]. *New York Times,* p. A14.

65. Hanson, D. J. (1994, September 28). Parents: Don't panic about campus boozers [letter]. *New York Times,* p. A11.

66. Wechsler, H. et al. (1994, December 7). Health and behavioral consequences of binge drinking in college. *Journal of the American Medical Association.*

67. Adler, J., & Rosenberg, D. (1994, December 19). The endless binge. *Newsweek,* pp. 72–73.

68. Center on Addiction and Substance Abuse, Columbia University (1994). *Rethinking rites of passage.* Cited in: Adler & Rosenberg, 1994.

69. Associated Press (1992, September 20). Study finds more drinking at small colleges than large ones. *New York Times,* sec. 1, p. 20.

70. Bedell, T. (1991, February). Saintly suds. *Men's Health,* pp. 58–61.

71. Miller, A., & Springen, K. (1990, March 5). This safe suds is for you. *Newsweek,* p. 42.

72. Centers for Disease Control. (1990). Alcohol-related mortality and mortality and years of potential life lost—United States, 1987. *Morbidity & Mortality Weekly Report, 39*(11), 173–77.

73. Kinney, J., & Leaton, G. (1987). *Loosening the grip: A handbook of alcohol information* (3rd ed.). St. Louis: Times Mirror/Mosby College Publishing, p. 25.

74. Mello, N. K. (1987). Alcohol abuse and alcoholism: 1978–1987. Pp. 1515–20 in: H. Y. Meltzer (Ed.). *Psychopharmacology: The third generation of progress.* New York: Raven Press.

75. Wilsnack, S. C., Klassen, A. D., & Wilsnack, R. W. (1984). Drinking and reproductive dysfunction among women in a 1981 national survey. *Alcoholism: Clinical & Experimental Research, 8,* 451–58.

76. Plant, M. A. (1990). Alcohol, sex and AIDS. *Alcohol & Alcoholism, 25,* 293–301.

77. U.S. Department of Health and Human Services (1987). *Alcohol and health.* Rockville, MD: U.S. Department of Health and Human Services.

78. Schuster, C., director National Institute of Drug Abuse. Cited in: Medical Tribune News Service (1991, January 25). High school seniors report less drug use. *San Francisco Chronicle,* p. A12.

79. National Institute of Drug Abuse (1988). *National Household Survey on Drug Abuse: Main findings 1988.* DHHS Pub. No. (ADM)90-1682. Washington, DC: U.S. Department of Health and Human Services.

80. Adler & Rosenberg, 1994.

81. Shedler, J., & Block, J. (1990. May). Adolescent drug use and psychological health. *American Psychologist,* pp. 612–624.

82. Perlman, D. (1990, May 14). Furor over report on teenage drug use. *San Francisco Chronicle,* p. A10.

83. Johnson, B. A. (1990). Psychopharmacological effects of cannabis. *British Journal of Hospital Medicine, 43,* 114–16.

84. Jones, R. T. (1980). Human effects: An overview. Pp. 54–80 in: R. C. Peterson (Ed.). *Marijuana research findings: 1980.* Rockville, MD: National Institute on Drug Abuse.

85. Maisto, S. A., Galizio, M., & Connors, G. J. (1991). *Drug use and misuse.* Fort Worth, TX: Holt, Rinehart and Winston.

86. McGlothin, W. H., & West, L. J. (1968). The marihuana problem: An overview. *American Journal of Psychiatry, 125,* 370–78.

87. Flynn, J. C. (1991). *Cocaine: An in-depth look at the facts, science, history and future of the world's most addictive drug.* New York: Carol Publishing Group, p. 14.

88. Chychula, N. M., & Okore, C. (1990). The cocaine epidemic: A comprehensive review of use, abuse and dependence. *Nurse Practitioner, 15*(7), 31–39.

89. Goleman, D. (1992, March 31). As addiction medicine gains, experts debate what it should cover. *New York Times,* p. B6.

90. Walters, L. S. (1990, June 18). Teen gambling is the latest addiction of choice. *San Francisco Chronicle,* p. B5; reprinted from *Christian Science Monitor.*

91. Associated Press. (1989, June 23). 1 in 20 college students are compulsive gamblers— survey. *Reno Gazette-Journal,* p. 6D.

92. Goleman, D. (1991, July 17). Reining in a compulsion to spend. *New York Times,* pp. B1, B8.

93. Wolf, N. (1991). *The beauty myth: How images of beauty are used against women.* New York: William Morrow, p. 184.

94. Britton, A. G. (1988). Thin is out, fit is in. *American Health, 7,* 66–71.

95. Hutchinson, M. (1985). *Transforming body image: Learning to love the body you have.* Freedom, CA: Crossing Press.

96. Rodin, J. (1992, January/February). Body mania. *Psychology Today,* pp. 56–60.

97. Gallup survey, December 1990. Cited in: Sietsema, T. (1991, January 2). Fat's back. *San Francisco Chronicle,* Food Section, pp. 1, 5.

98. Brody, J. E. (1991, June 27). Study links yo-yo dieting to an increased death rate. *New York Times,* p. A9.

99. Gallup poll. Cited in: Brownell, K. (1988, March). The yo-yo trap. *American Health,* 78–84.

100. Brownell, K. D. (1989, June). When and how to diet. *Psychology Today,* 40–46.

101. Anonymous (1991). The easy road to fitness. *University of California, Berkeley Wellness Letter, 7,* 6.

102. Tucker, L. A., Cole, G. E., & Friedman, G. M. (1986). Physical fitness: A buffer against stress. *Perceptual & Motor Skills, 63,* 955–61.

103. Sime, W. E. (1984). Psychological benefits of exercise. *Advances, 1,* 15–29.

104. Roth, D. L., & Holmes, D. S. (1987). Influence of aerobic exercise training and relaxation training on physical and psychological health following stressful life events. *Psychosomatic Medicine, 49,* 355–65.

105. Rippe, J. M. Quoted in: Cardozo, C. (1990, September). The new feel-great prescription: Even a few minutes of exercise can enhance creativity, self-esteem, and chase away the blues. *Self,* p. 124.

106. Greist, J. H., Eischens, R. R. et al. (1978). Running out of depression. *The Physician & Sportsmedicine, 6*(12), 49–56.

107. Monahan, T. (1986). Exercise and depression: Swapping sweat for serenity? *The Physician & Sportsmedicine, 14*(9), 192–97.

108. Morgan, W. P., & O'Connor, P. J. (1987). Exercise and mental health. In: Dishman, R. K. (Ed.). *Exercise adherence.* Champaign, IL: Human Kinetics Publishers.

109. Farmer, M. E., Locke, B. Z., Moscicki, E. K. et al. (1988). Physical activity and depressive symptoms: The NHANES I epidemiologic follow-up study. *American Journal of Epidemiology, 128,* 1340–51.

110. Thayer, R. E. (1988, October). Energy walks. *Psychology Today,* 12–13.

111. Thayer, R. E. (1987). Energy, tiredness, and tension effects of a sugar snack versus moderate exercise. *Journal of Personality & Social Psychology, 52*(1), 119–25.

112. Mott, P. (1990, October 7). Mental gymnastics. *Los Angeles Times,* pp. E1, E18–E19.

113. Gondola, J. C. Cited in: Cardozo, 1990, p. 124.

114. Martin, J. E., Dubbert, P. M., & Cushman, W. C. (1990). Controlled trial of aerobic exercise in hypertension. *Circulation, 81,* 1560–67.

115. Kelemen, M. H., Effron, M. B., Valenti, S. A. et al. (1990). Exercise training combined with antihypertensive drug therapy. *Journal of the American Medical Association, 263,* 2766–71.

116. Somers, V. Cited in: Associated Press. (1991, June 11). Study finds exercise alone can reduce blood pressure. *New York Times,* p. A6.

117. Hansen, H. S. et al. Cited in: Medicine Tribune News Service. (1991, September 25). Exercise lowers children's blood pressure. *San Francisco Chronicle,* p. D6.

118. Paffenbarger, R. S., Hyde, R. T., Wing, W. L. et al. (1986). Physical activity, all-cause mortality, and longevity among college alumni. *New England Journal of Medicine, 314,* 605–613.

119. Lee, I.-M., Paffenbarger, J. Jr., & Hsieh, C. (1991). Physical activity and risk of developing colorectal cancer among college alumni. *Journal of the National Cancer Institute, 83,* 1324–29.

120. Kirkpatrick, M. K., Edwards, R. N., & Finch, N. (1991). Assessment and prevention of osteoporosis through use of a client self-reporting tool. *Nurse Practitioner, 16*(7), 16–26.

121. Ornstein, R., & Sobel, D. (1989). *Healthy pleasures.* Reading, MA: Addison-Wesley, p. 103.

122. Clark, N. (1990). *Sports nutrition guidebook.* Champaign, IL: Leisure Press.

123. Applegate, L. (1991). *Power foods: High-performance nutrition for high-performance people.* Emmaus, PA: Rodale.

124. Applegate, L. (1991). Fast-track snacks. *Men's Health, 6,* 40–41.

125. Dinges, D. F., & Broughton, R. J. (Eds.) (1989). *Sleep and alertness: Chronobiological, behavioral, and medical aspects of napping.* New York: Raven Press.

126. Dolnick, E. (1992, February/March). Snap out of it. *Health,* pp. 86–90.

127. Nordheimer, J. (1991, September 8). It's Sunday afternoon, and in counterpoint to Friday highs, blues settle in. *New York Times,* p. 15.

128. Locitzer, K. (1989, July/August). Are you out of sync with each other? *Psychology Today,* p. 66.

129. Carlinsky, D. (1990, March 14). Not everyone needs eight-hour slumber. *San Francisco Chronicle,* pp. B3–B4.

130. Kates, W. (1990, March 30). America is not getting enough sleep. *San Francisco Chronicle,* p. B3.

131. Mass, J. Cited in: Kates, 1990, p. B3.

132. Johnson, L. C. (1982). Sleep deprivation and performance. In W. B. Webb (Ed.). *Biological rhythms, sleep and performance.* New York: Wiley.

CHAPTER 12—RELATIONSHIPS

1. Ishii-Kuntz, M. (1990). Social interaction and psychological well-being: Comparison across stages of adulthood. *International Journal of Aging & Human Development, 30*(1), 15–36.

2. Claes, M. E. (1992). Friendship and personal adjustment during adolescence. *Journal of Adolescence, 15*(1), 39–55.

3. Stein, J. (Ed.) (1973). *The Random House dictionary of the English language.* New York: Random House.

4. Schaefer, M. T., & Olson, D. H. (1981). Assessing intimacy: The pair inventory. *Journal of Marital & Family Therapy, 7,* 47–60.

5. Rice, F. P. (1989). *Human sexuality.* Dubuque, IA: Wm. C. Brown.

6. Shea, J. A., & Adams, G. R. (1984). Correlates of male and female romantic attachments: A path analysis study. *Journal of Youth & Adolescence, 13,* 27–44.

7. Rubin, L. (1973). *Liking and loving.* New York: Holt, Rinehart & Winston.

8. Hatfield, E., & Sprecher, S. (1986). *Mirror, mirror . . . The importance of looks in everyday life.* Albany: State University of New York Press.

9. Dutton, D., & Aron, A. (1974). Some evidence for heightened sexual attraction under conditions of high anxiety. *Journal of Personality & Social Psychology, 30,* 510–17.

10. Hatfield, E., & Walster, G. W. (1978). *A new look at love.* Reading, MA: Addison-Wesley.

11. Rindfuss, R. Cited in: Larson, J. (1991, November). Cohabitation is a premarital step. *American Demographics,* 20–21.

12. Viorst, J. (1979). Just because I'm married, does it mean I'm going steady? Pp. 283–89 in: B. J. Wishart & L. C. Reichman (Eds.). *Modern sociological issues.* New York: Macmillan.

13. Saxton, L. (1977). *The individual, marriage, and the family* (3rd ed.). Belmont, CA: Wadsworth.

14. Phillips, D. (1980). *How to fall out of love.* New York: Fawcett.

15. Weiten, W., Lloyd, M. A., & Lashley, R. L. (1991). *Psychology applied to modern life: Adjustment in the 90s* (3rd ed.). Pacific Grove: CA: Brooks/Cole.

16. Weiten, Lloyd, & Lashley, 1991, p. 179.

17. Burns, D. D. (1989). *The feeling good handbook.* New York: Plume.

18. Burns, 1989, p. 371.

19. Beck, A. (1989). *Love is never enough.* New York: HarperPerennial.

20. Burns, 1989, p. 379.

21. Crooks, R., & Baur, K. (1990). *Our sexuality* (4th ed.). Redwood City, CA: Benjamin/Cummings, p. 268.

22. Alberti, R. E., & Emmons, M. L. (1970). *Your perfect right: A guide to assertive behavior.* San Luis Obispo, CA: Impact.

23. Alberti, R. E., & Emmons, M. L. (1975). *Stand up, speak out, talk back!* New York: Pocket.

24. Jakubowski-Spector, P. (1973). Facilitating the growth of women through assertive training. *Counseling Psychologist, 4,* 75–86.

25. Weiten, Lloyd, & Lashley, 1989.

26. Horner, M. J. Toward an understanding of achievement related conflicts in women. *Journal of Social Issues, 28,* 157–76.

27. Freundl, P. C. (1981, August). Influence of sex and status variables on perceptions of assertiveness. Paper presented at meeting of the American Psychological Association, Los Angeles.

28. Smye, M. D., & Wine, J. D. (1980). A comparison of female and male adolescents' social behaviors and cognitions: A challenge to the assertiveness literature. *Sex Roles, 6,* 213–30.

29. Weiten, Lloyd, & Lashley, 1991.

30. U.S. Supreme Court, *Meritor Savings Bank v. Vinson.* Cited in: Goldstein, L. (1991, November). Hands off at work. *Self,* pp. 110–13.

31. U.S. Merit Systems Protection Board. Cited in: Deutschman, A. (1991, November 4). Dealing with sexual harassment. *Fortune,* pp. 145–48.

32. Anonymous. (1991, October 12). Proving harassment is tough in court, lawyers say. *San Francisco Chronicle,* p. C10; reprinted from *New York Times.*

33. Karl, T. Cited in: O'Toole, K. (1991, November-December). How to handle harassment. *Stanford Observer,* p. 8.

34. U.S. Merit Systems Protection Board, 1991.

35. Anonymous. (1989, April). Offering resistance: How most people respond to rape. *Psychology Today,* p. 13.

36. Stanford Rape Education Project. Cited in: Anonymous. (1991, January-February). Men, women interpret sexual cues differently. *Stanford Observer,* p. 15.

37. National Victim Center. Cited in: Anonymous. (1992, May 4). Unsettling report on epidemic of rape. *Time,* p. 15.

38. Cells, W. 3d. (1991, January 2). Growing talk of date rape separates sex from assault. *New York Times,* pp. A1, B7.

39. Cells, 1991, p. B7.

40. Stanford Rape Education Project, 1991.

41. Coffe, J. (1993, January/February). To escape rape. *American Health*, p. 18.

42. Schroepfer, L. (1992, November). When the victim is a woman. *American Health*, p. 20.

43. Gross, J. (1991, May 28). Even the victim can be slow to recognize rape. *New York Times*, p. A6.

44. Centers for Disease Control. (1992). The second 100,000 cases of acquired immunodeficiency syndrome—United States, June 1981 - December 1991. *Morbidity & Mortality Weekly Report, 41*, 28–29.

45. Brundage, J. F. (1991). Epidemiology of HIV infection and AIDS in the United States. *Dermatologic Clinics, 9*, 443–52.

46. Peaceman, A. M., & Gonik, B. (1991). Sexually transmitted viral disease in women. *Postgraduate Medicine, 89*, 133–40.

47. Blattner, W. A. (1991). HIV epidemiology: past, present, and future. *Faseb Journal, 5*, 2340–48.

48. Giesecke, J., Scalia-Tomba, G., Hakansson, C. et al. (1990). Incubation time of AIDS: Progression of disease in a cohort of HIV-infected homo- and bisexual men with known dates of infection. *Scandinavian Journal of Infectious Diseases, 22*, 407–411.

49. Snell, J. J., Supran, E. M., Esparza, J. et al. (1990). World Health Organization quality assessment programme on HIV testing. *Aids, 4*, 803–806.

50. Navarro, M. (1995, January 20). Women in Puerto Rico find marriage offers no haven from AIDS. *New York Times*, p. A8.

51. Padian, N. S., Shiboski, S. C., & Jewell, N. P. (1991). Female-to-male transmission of human immunodeficiency virus. *Journal of the American Medical Association, 266*, 1664–67.

52. Staver, S. (1990, June 1). Women found contracting HIV via unprotected sex. *American Medical News*, pp. 4–5.

53. Kerr, D. L. (1991). Women with AIDS and HIV infection. *Journal of School Health, 61*, 139–40.

54. Centers for Disease Control. (1991). The HIV/AIDS epidemic: The first 10 years. *Morbidity & Mortality Weekly Report, 40*, 357.

55. Kimmel, M., & Levine, M. (1991, May 10). AIDS is a disease of men involved in risky behavior. *San Francisco Chronicle*, p. A25.

56. Addiction Research Foundations. Reported in: Reuters. (1991, July 10). Needle swap credited for Canada's drop in AIDS. *San Francisco Chronicle*, p. A9.

57. Coates, R. A., Rankin, J. G., Lamothe, F. et al. (1992). Needle sharing behaviour among injection users (IDUs) in treatment in Montreal and Toronto, 1988–1989. *Canadian Journal of Public Health, 83*, 38–41.

58. Fisher, J. D. Cited in: Adler, J., Wright, L., McCormick, J. et al. (1991, December 9). Safer sex. *Newsweek*, pp. 52–56.

59. Montefiore, S. S. (1992, October). Love, lies and fear in the plague years . . . *Psychology Today*, pp. 30–35.

60. Adler et al., 1991.

61. Cochran, S. D., & Mays, V. M. (1993). Sex, lies, and HIV [letter]. *New England Journal of Medicine, 322*, 774–75.

62. Cochran, S. Quoted in: Roberts, M. (1988, December). Dating, dishonesty and AIDS. *Psychology Today*, p. 60.

63. Hatcher, R., Guest, F., Stewart, F. et al. (1990). *Contraceptive technology: 1990–1992.* (15th ed.). New York: Irvington.

64. Forrest, J. D. (1987). Has she or hasn't she? U.S. women's experience with contraception. *Family Planning Perspectives, 19*, 133.

65. Workman, B. (1991, May 2). Sex at Stanford not always safe, poll finds. *San Francisco Chronicle*, p. A20.

CHAPTER 13—THE FUTURE

1. Leider, D. (1988, July/August). Purposeful work. *Utne Reader*, p. 52; excerpted from *On Purpose: A Journal About New Lifestyles & Workstyles*, Winter 1986.

2. Dominguez, J., & Robin, V. (1992). *Your money or your life*. Bergenfield, NJ: Penguin.

3. Needleman, J. (1991). *Money and the meaning of life*. New York: Doubleday.

4. Needleman, J. Quoted in: Carman, J. (1990, June 26). Talking about money on PBS. *San Francisco Chronicle*, p. E1.

5. Gallup Organization October 1989 survey for National Occupational Information Coordinating Committee. Reported in: Associated Press (1990, January 12). Working at the wrong job. *San Francisco Chronicle*, p. C1.

6. Falvey, J. (1986). *After college: The business of getting jobs*. Charlotte, VT: Williamson.

7. Yate, M. J. Quoted in: McIntosh, C. (1991, May). Giving good answers to tough questions. *McCall's*, pp. 38, 40.

8. Falvey, 1986.

9. McGregor, J., doctoral dissertation, Florida State University, Tallahassee. Reported in: Associated Press. (1992, July 21). TV gives kids false view of working, study says. *San Francisco Chronicle*, p. D5.

10. Lieberman Research Inc. 1990 mail poll of 2320 people for *Sports Illustrated*. Reported in: USA Snapshots. (1991, November 8). I wish I was a . . . *USA Today*, p. 1D.

11. Falvey, 1986.

12. Shertzer, B. (1985). *Career planning* (3rd ed.). Boston: Houghton Mifflin.

13. Deci, E. L., & Flaste, R. (1995). *Why we do what we do: The dynamics of personal autonomy*. New York: Grosset/Putnam.

14. Holland, J. (1975). *Vocational preference inventory*. Palo Alto, CA: Consulting Psychologists Press.

15. Bolles, R. N. Quoted in: Rubin, S. (1994, February 24). How to open your job 'parachute' after college. *San Francisco Chronicle*, p. E9.

16. Bolles, R. N. (1994). *What color is your parachute?* Berkeley, CA: Ten Speed Press.

17. Bolles, R. N. (1990). *The 1990 quick job-hunting (and career-changing) map: How to create a picture of your ideal job or next career*. Berkeley, CA: Ten Speed Press.

18. Bolles, R. N. Cited in: Minton, T. (January 25, 1991). Job-hunting requires eyes and ears of friends. *San Francisco Chronicle*, p. D5.

19. Falvey, 1986.

20. Pender, K. (1994, May 16). Jobseekers urged to pack lots of 'keywords' into resumes. *San Francisco Chronicle*, pp. B1, B4.

21. Howe, K. (1992, September 19). Firm turns hiring into a science. *San Francisco Chronicle*, pp. B1, B2.

22. Bulkeley, W. M. (1992, June 23). Employers use software to track resumes. *Wall Street Journal*, p. B6.

23. Kennedy, J. L., & Morrow, T. J. (1994). *Electronic resume revolution: Create a winning resume for the new world of job seeking*. New York: Wiley.

24. Palladino, B. (1992, Winter). Job hunting online. *Online Access*, pp. 20–23.

25. Anonymous. (1992, October). Online information. *PC Today*, p. 41.

26. Strauss, J. (1993, October 17). Online database helps job seekers. *San Francisco Sunday Examiner & Chronicle*, Help wanted section, p. 29.

27. Murray, K. (1994, January 2). Plug in. Log on. Find a job. *New York Times*, sec. 3, p. 23.

28. Mannix, M. (1992, October 26). Writing a computer-friendly resume. *U.S. News & World Report*, pp. 90–93.

29. Bulkeley, W. M. (1992, June 16). Job-hunters turn to software for an edge. *Wall Street Journal*, p. B13.

30. Anonymous. (1992, June). Pounding the pavement. *PC Novice*, p. 10.

31. Anonymous. (1993, September 13). Personal: Individual software ships ResumeMaker with career planning. *EDGE: Work-Group Computing Report*, p. 3.

32. Mossberg, W. S. (1994, May 5). Four programs to ease PC users into a job search. *Wall Street Journal*, p. B1.

33. Kennedy, J. L., & Morrow, T. J. (1994). *Electronic job search revolution: Win with the new technology that's reshaping today's job market.* New York: Wiley.

34. Bennett, H., & McFadden, C. (1993, October 17). How to stand out in a crowd. *San Francisco Sunday Examiner & Chronicle,* help wanted section, p. 29.

35. Bolles. Quoted in: Rubin, 1994.

36. Gardner, J. W. 1991 commencement address, Stanford University, June 16, 1991. Quoted in: Gardner, J. W. (1991, May–June). You are what you commit to achieve. *Stanford Observer,* pp. 10–11.

SPECIAL SECTION

1. Stewart, T. A. (1994, April 4). The information age in charts. *Fortune,* pp. 75–79.

2. Anonymous. (1991, November). Typewriters and word processors. *Consumer Reports,* pp. 763–67.

3. McGee, C. cited in Meers, T. (1993, September). College computing 101, *PC Novice,* pp. 18–22.

4. Pope, K. (1993, December 1). Once very hot, mail-order PCs are cooling off. *Wall Street Journal,* p. B1.

5. Tynan, D., & Wood, C. (1994, June). Most likely to succeed . . . or fail. *PC World,* pp. 119–38.

6. Gottesman, G., & friends. (1991). *College Survival.* New York: Arco Books/Prentice Hall, p. 89.

7. Williams, R. (1993, April 10). On the hunt for a used computer. *The Globe & Mail* (Toronto), p. B13.

8. Larson, J. (1992, October). Buying a portable computer: There's something for everyone. *PC Novice,* pp. 14–19.

9. Freedman, F. (1993). *The Computer Glossary,* 6th ed. New York: AMACOM, p. 406.

10. Mossberg, W. S. (1993, January 21). Organizer program takes a leaf from date books. *Wall Street Journal,* p. B1.

11. Kirkpatrick, D. (1993, December 27). Groupware goes boom. *Fortune,* p. 100.

12. White, R. (1994, January). In search of the ultimate notebook. *PC/Computing,* pp. 184–209.

13. Arnst, C. (1993, June 28). The tiny shall inherit the market. *Business Week,* pp. 50–51.

14. Robinson, P. (1994, February). Subnotebooks have surfaced as the portable of choice. *San Jose Mercury News,* p. 2E.

15. Jerome, M. (1994, January). Killer color notebooks. *PC/Computing,* pp. 142–145.

16. Watson, A., quoted in Editors of *PC World.* (1992, November 23). Mobile computing [special pullout section sponsored by Intel]. *Newsweek,* p. N26.

17. Branigan, M. (1992, January). The cost of using an online service. *PC Novice,* pp. 65–71.

18. *Boardwatch,* cited in Schmidt, R. (1994, October). How to set up a bulletin board system. *PC Today,* pp. 48–50.

19. Toplanski, M., quoted in Larson, J. (1993, March). Telecommunications and your computer. *PC Novice,* pp. 14–19.

20. Nielsen Media Research, cited in Sandberg, J. (1995, October 30). Internet's popularity in North America appears to be soaring. *Wall Street Journal,* p. B5.

21. Tetzeli, R. (1994, March 7). The Internet and your business. *Fortune,* pp. 86–96.

22. Landis, D. (1993, October 7). Exploring the online universe. *USA Today,* p. 4D.

sources & credits

CHAP. 2: **Pers Expl #2.3** adapted from Nowicki-Strickland Scale and results from Nowicki, S. Jr. & Strickland, B. R. (1973, February). A locus of control scale for children. *Journal of Consulting & Clinical Psychology, 40*(1), 148 - 54. Copyright © 1973 by the American Psychological Association. Adapted by permission. **Pages 17, 19 - 20** adapted from suggestion by Donald W. Green, Genesee Community College.

CHAP. 3: **Panel 3.1** courtesy Genesee Community College. **Panel 3.3** adapted from San Jose State University Police Department (1989). *Safety and security at San Jose State.* San Jose, CA: San Jose State University, Police Department, Investigations/ Crime Prevention Unit.

CHAP. 5: **Pers Expl #5.1** adapted from Weintraub, P. (1992, March). Total recall. *American Health,* pp. 77 - 78. American Health © 1992 by Pamela Weintraub. **Panel 5.1** from Weiten, W. (1989). *Psychology: Themes and variations.* Pacific Grove, CA: Brooks/Cole, p. 254. Used with permission. Based on material from D. van Guilford, Van Nostrand, 1939. **Pers Expl #5.2** adapted from "Modality Inventory" by Ducharme, A., & Watford, L., Middle Grades Department, Valdosta State University, Valdosta, GA 31698. Reprinted with the kind permission of Dr. Adele Ducharme and Dr. Luck Watford. **Panel 5.2** from Lapp, D. (1992, December). Nearly total recall. *Stanford Magazine,* p. 50. By permission of Danielle Lapp. **Pages 104 - 5,** material beginning "A

Rustler . . .; from Weiten, W., Lloyd, M. A., & Lashley, R. L. (1990). *Psychology applied to modern life: Adjustment in the 90s* (3rd ed.). Pacific Grove, CA: Brooks/Cole, p. 24. Adapted from Bower, G. H., & Clark, M. C. (1969). Narrative stories as mediators of social learning. *Psychonomic Science, 14,* 181 - 82. Copyright © 1969 by the Psychonomic Society. Adapted by permission of the Psychonomic Society.

CHAP. 6: **Panel 6.1** adapted from Lindgren, H. C. (1969). *The psychology of college success: A dynamic approach.* New York: Wiley. **Pers Expl #6.1** adapted from "Modality Inventory" by Ducharme, A., & Watford, L., Middle Grades Department, Valdosta State University, Valdosta, GA 31698. Reprinted with the kind permission of Dr. Adele Ducharme and Dr. Luck Watford. **Panel 6.6** adapted from work developed by John Dahlberg; reprinted by permission of Genesee Community College.

CHAP. 7: **Pers Expl #7.1** adapted from Cortina, J., Elder, J., & Gonnet, K. (1992). *Comprehending college textbooks: Steps to understanding and remembering what you read* (2nd ed.). New York: McGraw-Hill, pp. 3 - 4. Adapted with permission of McGraw-Hill. **Panel 7.1** reproduced from Weeks, J. R. (1992). *Population: An introduction to concepts and issues* (5th ed.). Belmont, CA: Wadsworth. **Panel 7.2,** page reproduced from Biagi, S. (1994). *Media/Impact: An introduction to mass media,* updated second edition. Belmont, CA: Wadsworth, p. 180.

CHAP. 9: **Pers Expl #9.1** Adapted from Adams, J. L. (1974). *Conceptual blockbusting.* Stanford, CA: Stanford Alumni Association (The Portable Stanford), p. 106. **Pages 202 - 4,** section headed "Critical Thinking: What It Is, How to Use It," adapted from Williams, B. K., & Knight, S. M. (1994). *Healthy for life: Wellness and the art of living* (Pacific Grove, CA: Brooks/Cole), pp. 14.33 - 14.45. Used with permission.

CHAP. 10: **Panel 10.1,** Bureau of Labor Statistics, in chart from Anonymous (1995, April 16). The low end goes lower. *New York Times,* sec. 4, p. 3. Copyright © 1995 by the New York Times Company. Reprinted by permission.

CHAP. 11: Portions of chapter adapted from Williams, B. K., & Knight, S. M. (1994). *Healthy for life: Wellness and the art of living* (Pacific Grove, CA: Brooks/Cole), especially Units 2, 4, 5, 6, 7. Used with permission. **Pers Expl #11.1** from Mullen, Cathleen, & Costello, Gerald. (1981). *Health awareness through self-discovery.* Edina, MN: Burgess International Group. **Panel 11.2** from Benson, H. (1989). Editorial: Hypnosis and the relaxation response. *Gastroenterology, 96,* 1610. **Panel 11.3** based on data from Wechsler, H., & McFadden, M. (1979). Drinking among college students in New England. *Journal of Studies in Alcohol, 40,* 969 - 96; Wechsler, H., & Isaac, N. (1991). *Alcohol and the college freshman: "Binge" drinking and associated problems.* Washington, DC: AAA Foundation for Traffic Safety; Wechsler, H., & Isaac, N. (1992). "Binge" drinkers at Massachusetts colleges: Prevalance, drinking style, time trends, and associated problems. *Journal of the American Medical Association, 267,* 2929 - 31. **Pers Expl #11.2,** Michigan Alcoholism Screening Test, adapted from Selzer, M. L. (1971). The M-A-S-T. *American Journal of Psychiatry, 127,* 1653. Copyright 1971, the American Psychiatric Association. Reprinted by permission. **Panel 11.5** adapted from Anonymous. (1994, December 7). Snapshot: Drugs in college. *New York Times,* p. B8; based on Wechsler, H. (1994, December 7). Health and behavioral consequences of binge drinking in college. *Journal of the American Medical Association.* Copyright © 1994 by The New York Times Company. Reprinted by permission. **Panel 11.6** adapted from Dr. Stephen Franzoi, Marquette University. Graphic © 1991 San Francisco Chronicle in: Goleman, D. (1991, October 31). *San Francisco Chronicle,* pp. D3, D5; © San Francisco Chronicle. reprinted by permission. **Pers Expl #11.3,** table reprinted with permission from National Academy of Sciences (1989). *Diet and health: Implications for reducing chronic disease risk.* Washington, DC: National Academy Press. © 1989 by the National Academy of Sciences. Courtesy of the National Academy Press, Washington, DC. **Panel 11.8** excerpted from Anonymous. (1991, February). The easy road to fitness. *University of California at Berkeley Wellness Letter,* p. 6. Reprinted by permission. © Health Letter Associates, 1991. **Panel 11.9** U.S. Department of Agriculture. **Pers Expl #11.4** reprinted from American Cancer Society (1989). *Eating smart,* 85-250M, Rev. 3/93. No. 2942. Courtesy of the American Cancer Society, Inc., and its Minnesota Division, 800-ACS-2345.

CHAP. 12: Portions of chapter adapted from Williams, B. K., & Knight, S. M. (1994). *Healthy for life: Wellness and the art of living* (Pacific Grove, CA: Brooks/Cole), especially Units 8, 9, 11. Used by permission. **Pers Expl #12.1** from Sternberg, R. J., & Soriano, L. J. (1984). Styles of conflict resolution. *Journal of Personality & Social Psychology, 47,* 115 - 26; Weiten, W., Lloyd, M. A., & Lashley, R. L. (1991). *Psychology applied to modern life: Adjustment in the 90s* (3rd ed.). Pacific Grove: CA: Brooks/Cole; Williams, B. K., & Knight, S. M. (1994). *Healthy for life: Wellness and the art of living* (Pacific Grove, CA: Brooks/Cole), pp. 8.36 - 8.39. **Pers Expl #12.2** from Lazarus, A. A. (1971). Assertiveness questionnaire, in *Behavior theory and beyond.* New York: McGraw-Hill. Reproduced with permission of McGraw-Hill. **Panel 12.1** adapted from: Commission on the Status of Women. (1991). *How to create a workplace free of sexual harassment*. San Francisco: Commission on the Status of Women; Karl, T., cited in: O'Toole, K. (1991, November-December). How to handle harassment. *Stanford Observer*, p. 8; Goldstein, L. (1991, November). Hands off at work. *Self*, pp. 110-12. **Pers Expl #12.3** adapted from: Anderson, D. M., & Christenson, G. M. (1991). Ethnic breakdown of AIDS related knowledge and attitudes from the National Adolescent Student Health Survey. *Journal of Health Education, 22*, 30-34; Timoshok, L., Sweet, D. M., & Zich, J. (1987). A three city comparison of the public's knowledge and attitudes about AIDS. *Psychology & Health, 1*(1), 43-60; Weiten, W., Lloyd, M. A., & Lashley, R. L. (1991). *Psychology applied to modern life: Adjustment in the 90s* (3rd ed.). Pacific Grove, CA: Brooks/Cole, p. 408. **Panel 12.4** data from Centers for Disease Control and Prevention. **Panel 12.5** from Williams, B. K., & Knight, S. M. (1994). *Healthy for life: Wellness and the art of living*. Pacific Grove, CA: Brooks/Cole, pp. 9.8-9.9. Used with permission. Based on data from Centers for Disease Control (1990). *Contraceptive options: Increasing your awareness*. Washington, DC: NAACOG. Hatcher, R., Guest, F., Stewart, F. et al. (1990). *Contraceptive technology, 1990-1992*. New York: Irvington. Leads from the MMWR (1988). Condoms for prevention of sexually transmitted diseases. *Journal of the American Medical Association, 259*, 1925-27. Harlap, S., Kost, K., & Forrest, D. (1991). *Preventing pregnancy, protecting health: A new look at birth control choices in the United States*. New York: Alan Guttmacher Institute. Anonymous (1991, December). Deconstructing the condom. *Self*, pp. 122-23. Consumers Union (1989, March). Can you rely on condoms? *Consumer Reports*, pp. 135-41. Consumers Union (1995, May). How reliable are condoms? *Consumer Reports*, pp. 320-25. **Panel 12.6** artwork reproduced with the permission of The Alan Guttmacher Institute from Kathryn Kost, Jacqueline Darroch Forrest, and Susan Harlap. (1991, March/April). Comparing the health risks and benefits of contraceptive choices. *Family Planning Perspectives, 23(2)*, 54-61, table 1.

CHAP. 13: Portions of chapter adapted from Williams, B. K., & Knight, S. M. (1994). *Healthy for life: Wellness and the art of living* (Pacific Grove, CA: Brooks/Cole), especially pp. 2.32, 16.31. Used with permission. Parts of chapter also adapted from Williams, B. K., Sawyer, S. C., & Hutchinson, S. E. (1995). *Using information technology: A practical introduction to computers & communications*. Burr Ridge, IL: Irwin, pp. 589-92. Used with permission of Richard D. Irwin, a Times Mirror Higher Education Group, Inc., company. **Pers Expl #13.1** adapted and reproduced by special permission of the Publisher, Psychological Assessment Resources Inc., Odessa, FL 33556, from the *Self-Directed Search Assessment Booklet* by John L. Holland, Ph.D. Copyright 1970, 1977, 1985, 1990, 1994 by PAR, Inc. Further reproduction is prohibited without permission from PAR, Inc. The Self-Directed Search materials are available for purchase through PAR, Inc. by calling 1-800-331-8378. **Panel 13.2** from Falvey, J. (1986). *After college: The business of getting jobs*. Charlotte, VT: Williamson Publishing, p. 37. **Panel 13.3** adapted from Williams, B. K., Sawyer, S. C., & Hutchinson, S. E. (1995). *Using information technology: A practical introduction to computers & communications*. Burr Ridge, IL: Irwin, pp. 591-92. Used with permission of Richard D. Irwin, a Times Mirror Higher Education Group, Inc., company. **Panel 13.5** from Pender, K. (1994, May 16). Resume dos and don'ts. *San Francisco Chronicle*, p. B4. © San Francisco Chronicle. Reprinted by permission.

SPECIAL SECTION: Special section adapted from Williams, B. K., Sawyer, S. C., & Hutchinson, S. E. (1995). *Using information technology: A practical introduction to computers & communications*. Burr Ridge, IL: Irwin. Used with permission of Richard D. Irwin, a Times Mirror Higher Education Group, Inc., company. **Panel A.2** from Williams, Richard. (1993, April 10). On the hunt for a used computer. *The Globe & Mail* (Toronto), p. B13. **Panel A.5** adapted from the Editors of *PC World Magazine* (1992, November 13). Mobile computing, special pullout section sponsored by Intel. Newsweek, p. N26.

glossary/ index

a row one or more times in a two-week period. 251–52

Birth control, 302–5

Bisexuality
AIDS, 295
sexual history, 298

Blood alcohol concentration (BAC) is a measure of the amount of alcohol in the blood. 254–55

Blue books, 153

Body clock, 272

Boldface (dark type), 130, 133
key terms, 139
studying for tests, 152

Books in Print, 192

Bookstore, 49
blue books 153

Boredom, 119
with readings, 126

Brain storming means jotting down all the ideas that come to mind in response to the directions in the question. 164
resumes, 327
term papers, 183–85

Budget. *See* Money plan

Bulimia, 265

Burnout, 244

Business office is the campus office where students go to pay college fees or tuition. 47

Calorie, 264

Campus bulletin is a periodical which informs students of campus activities and events. 34

Campus calendar is a publication listing the deadlines and dates for various programs during the academic year. 33
time management, 73

Campus center. *See* Student union

Campus tour, 33

Car insurance, 234

Card catalog contains information about each library book typed on a 3-by-5 inch card and stored in a wooden file drawer. 190–91

Career
career changes, 310
competencies needed, 311–12
counseling, 312–17
importance of choosing, 309
relationship to majors, 311

Career counseling center is the campus office that helps students with decisions about career goals and majors. 48
choosing a major, 36

job placement center, 312–13, 317
"Career video" exercise, 314–15

Cashier's office is the campus office where students go to pay college fees and tuition. 47

Catalog. *See* College catalog

CD–ROM catalogs look like music compact disks (CDs), except that they are used to store text and images. CD–ROM stands for Compact Disk—Read Only Memory. 190

Change
handling, 20–22
self–image and, 30

Chapter summary, 133

Charge cards are those that require that the bill be paid off every month. 232

Charts, 146–47

Cheating is using unauthorized help to complete a test, practice exercise, or project. 172
penalties, 174
reasons for, 172–73

Child care facilities, 48

Circular reasoning argument rephrases the statement to be proven true. It then uses the new, similar statement as supposed proof that the original statement is in fact true. 208

Class attendance, 110–12

Class participation in lectures, 120, 122–23

Classroom game, 119–23

Codependency, 261

College catalog is a book containing requirements for graduation, requirements for degree programs, and course descriptions. 33, 35–36
academic calendar, 73
advising period, 40
courses for major, 70
time management, 73
where to obtain, 49

College newspaper is a student–run news publication that is published on some campuses. 34

Communication, 279–84
good and bad communication, 282

Community services, 48

Companionate love or friendship love, has feelings of friendly affection and deep attachment. 278

Comparison charts are useful for

studying several concepts and the relationships between them. 146–47

Complex carbohydrates are foods such as whole grains, barley, whole–wheat pasta, vegetables, and fruit. 270–71

Computers
buying, 230–31
CD–ROMs, 190
indexes online, 194–95
as job–search tool, 318, 325
learning to use, 43–44
in library, 186
networks, 193, 195
online catalogs, 192
online job listings, 324
outlining program, 187
portable, 197
reference services, 194
reorganizing writing, 203
resume database services, 325
resumes, 322–25
rewriting class notes, 117, 118
word processing, 179, 180

Concept maps are visual diagrams of concepts. 146–47

Conceptual blocks, 183

Condom is a thin sheath made of latex rubber or lamb intestine. 300
birth control, 302
latex, 299, 300–301

Conflict in relationships, 279–82

Contraception or birth control, is the prevention of fertilization or implantation. 302

Cooperative education programs allow you to improve your marketability upon graduation by giving you work experience in your major. 237

Coping strategies, 245–48

Copyright page (on the back of the title page) gives the date the book was published. 130

Counseling center, 45
emotionally upsetting tasks, 85

Course list is a list of the courses being taught in the current school term. 34

Cramming is defined as preparing hastily for an examination. 95
3Rs method, 137
forgetting, 114
short-term memory and, 129
time management, 90
versus memorizing, 117

Creative thinking consists of imaginative ways of looking at known ideas. 182–83

physical activity and, 267

Creativity, 25–26

Credit cards are those that allow the charges to be paid off in installments plus interest, provided you make a minimum payment every month. 232–33

Crisis is an especially strong source of stress. 241–42

Critical thinking means skeptical thinking or clear thinking. It is actively seeking to understand, analyze, and evaluate information in order to solve specific problems. 206–8

Culture, 54–57

Cumulative knowledge, 144

Curriculum worksheet is a list of courses required for the major and the semesters in which it is recommended the students take them. 39

Date rape is rape by a person with whom the victim has had a date. 290

Deadlines, 182

Debit card enables you to pay for purchases by withdrawing funds electronically directly from your savings or checking account. 232

Deductive argument is defined as follows: If its premises are true, then its conclusions are true also. 207

Degree program is a list of courses a student must take to obtain a college degree in a specific field. 39

Demonstrated financial need means that you have proven you need financial aid according to a certain formula. 235

Dependence refers to the reliance on or need for a substance. 258

Dependencies, 260–61

Dependent love is love that develops in response to previously unmet psychological needs. 278

Depressants slow down the central nervous system, making you feel relaxed, even anesthetized. 249

Depression, 267

Depth-of-processing principle states that how shallowly or deeply you hold a thought depends on how much you think about it

and how many associations you form with it. 103

Diagrams, 146–47

Diet, 268–71

Disabilities. *See* Physical disability

Discipline, personal, 312

Distractions, 81–89

while writing, 199

Distress is the effect when stress occurs owing to a negative event. 242

Distressor is the result when the source of stress is a negative event. 242

Distributed practice is when the student distributes study time over several days. It is more effective for retaining information. 101

Diversity means variety—in race, gender, ethnicity, age, physical abilities, and sexual orientation. 51–58

Dormitory is a facility providing rooms, or suites of rooms, for groups of students. 49

Drinking. *See* Alcohol consumption

Dropping out of college, reasons for, 8–9

Drugs, illegal

AIDS and, 294

amphetamines, 259

cocaine use, 256–58

crack cocaine, 258

experimentation, 256, 258

hallucinogens, 259

heroin, 259

marijuana, 256–58

psychedelics, 259

"speed," 259

stress and, 245

Drugs, legal

alcohol, 251–56

barbiturates, 259

caffeine, 249–50

codeine, 259

depressants, 259

passive smoking, 251

soft drinks, 250

stress, 245

tobacco, 250–51

Valium, 259

Eating disorders, 265

Eidetic imagery, 93

Electronic communication systems, 51–52

Electronic study guide is a floppy disk that students can use on their personal computer (IBM-style or Apple Macintosh) to

rehearse practice questions and check their answers. 152

Employment office. *See* Job placement office

Encyclopedias, 195

Energy and physical activity, 267

Energy balance is the state in which the calories expended are the same as the calories consumed. 264

English as a second language, 128

Erotic love is sexual love. 278

Essays

guiding words, 164–65

long–answer, 162, 163–69

organizing paragraphs, 167–69

outlines, 166

short–answer, 162

time management, 170

Ethics, 170–75

lying on resumes, 320

unloading, 157

Eustressor is stress caused by a positive event. 242

Examination approach, six-step, 157–58

Exams. *See* Tests

Exercise. *See* Fitness

Expulsion means you are kicked out of school permanently; you are not allowed to return. 174

Extra edge, 88–89

Extracurricular activities, 48–51

life goals, 70, 71

Failure, nature of, 26

Fakery is when a person makes up or fabricates something. 172

Faking it, 68

Fallacies are patterns of incorrect reasoning. 207

False cause is a type of fallacy in which the conclusion does not follow logically from the supposed reasons stated earlier. 207

Fatigue, 119

Fears about higher education experience, 20–22

Fertilization or conception, occurs when the male reproductive cell, the sperm, meets the female reproductive cell, the egg or ovum. 302

Fill-in-the-blank questions require you to fill in an answer from memory to choose from options offered in a list. 161

Finances, personal. *See* Money

Financial aid refers to any kind of

Job search
  contacts, 318–19
  cover letter, 326
  informational interview, 319
  internships, 319
  interview, 326
  online databases, 324
Journal, how to keep, 14
Jumping to conclusions is a type of
  fallacy. It happens when a conclusion has been reached when
  not all the facts are available. 207
Junk food, 271

Keywords are important terms or
  names that you are expected to
  understand and be able to
  define. 139
  keyword zone, 197
  in library to find specific informa-
    tion, 190
  on resumes, 232
  on tests, 157
Kinesthetic learners learn best
  when they touch and are physically involved in what they are
  studying. 99–100
  diagrams, charts, and maps, 146

Learning center is a special center
  where students go to learn a
  specific subject or skill. 43
  important to newcomers, 36
  reading skills, 128
Learning environment
  differences from high school, 4
  four main approaches, 6–7
Learning lab. *See* Learning center
Learning objectives are topics the
  student is expected to learn,
  which are listed at the beginning of each chapter. 133
Learning skills
  compared to high school, 41
  coping with information explo-
    sion, 13
Learning styles are the ways in
  which people acquire knowledge. 97–100
  determining your own. 98–99
  types, 97–100, 109
Lectures, 100, 107–24
  class participation, 120, 122
  homework before, 112–13, 122,
    123
  learning styles, 100
  note-reviewing skills, 116–18
  note-taking system, 113–14, 123
Legal services, 48
Library, 36, 43

card catalog, 186, 190–92
doing research, 186, 188–98
indexes and guides, 193–95
Library of Congress subject headings, 191
online catalog, 186, 192
parts of, 189
reference librarians, 189
reference materials, 192–95
specialized libraries, 195
as study places, 85, 86
visiting, 199
Life energy, 309
Listening
  active, 119–22
  skills, 282, 283
Literature, flashcards for, 145
Loan is money you have to pay
  back, either as money or in
  some form of work. 236
Locus of control refers to one's
  beliefs about the relationship
  between one's behavior and the
  occurrence of rewards and punishment. 22–26
Loneliness, 241
Long–answer essay generally
  requires three or more paragraphs to answer. 162, 163–69
  strategies, 163–69
Long–term memory entails remembering something for days,
  weeks, or years. 95, 113–14
  reading, 128–29
Love, types of, 278–79
Lying is simply misrepresentation of
  the facts. It can occur by omission or by commission. 172
  reasons for, 172–73
  on resumes, 320

Major is a student's field of specialization. 39
  career counseling center, 33
  courses needed, 39
  dropping out and, 8
  life goals and, 68
  relationship to career, 311
Maps, 146–47
Massed practice is putting all your
  studying into one long period
  of time, 101. *See also* Cramming
Matching questions require you to
  associate items from one list to
  items from a second list. 161
Mathematics
  flashcards, 145
  math anxiety, 142
Media center, 43
Medical services. *See* Health service

Meditation is concerned with directing a person's attention to a
  single, unchanging or repetitive
  stimulus. It is a way of quelling
  the "mind chatter." 248, 249
"Melting pot," 51
Memory is defined as a mental
  process that entails three main
  operations: recording, storage,
  and recall. 93
  5R Steps, 113–14
  improving skills, 100–105
  long-term, 95, 113–14
  memory aids, 103–5
  memory tips, 105
  practice, 101
  types of, 95
  visual memory aids, 105
Mental imagery is also known as
  guided imagery and visualization. It is a procedure in which
  you essentially daydream an
  image or desired change, anticipating that your body will
  respond as if the image were
  real. 248
Mentor, academic advisor as, 40
Merit–based financial aid is based
  on some sort of superior academic, music, sports, or other abilities. 235
**Method of loci ("method of
  places")** is a memory technique
  that involves memorizing a
  series of places and then using a
  different vivid image to associate each place with an idea or a
  word you want to remember.
  105
Mindsets, 206–7
Minor is a minor field of specialization chosen by a student. 39
Mixed–modality learners are able to
  function in any of three learning styles or "modalities"—auditory, visual, and kinesthetic. 100
Mnemonic devices are tactics for
  making things memorable by
  making them distinctive. 103–5
Money, 215–38
  banks and ATMs, 232
  budget, 224–28
  cash flow, 222
  controlling spending, 230–31
  credit cards, 232–33
  diagnostic report, 223
  emotions about, 217
  expense record, 224, 229
  how to handle, 230–34
  money management, 230–34